THE HOPKINS TOUCH

DAVID L. ROLL

THE HOPKINS TOUCH

Harry Hopkins and the Forging
of the Alliance to Defeat Hitler

OXFORD
UNIVERSITY PRESS

OXFORD

UNIVERSITY PRESS

Oxford University Press is a department of the University of Oxford.
It furthers the University's objective of excellence in research,
scholarship, and education by publishing worldwide.

Oxford   New York

Auckland   Cape Town   Dar es Salaam   Hong Kong   Karachi
Kuala Lumpur   Madrid   Melbourne   Mexico City   Nairobi
New Delhi   Shanghai   Taipei   Toronto

With offices in

Argentina   Austria   Brazil   Chile   Czech Republic   France   Greece
Guatemala   Hungary   Italy   Japan   Poland   Portugal   Singapore
South Korea   Switzerland   Thailand   Turkey   Ukraine   Vietnam

Oxford is a registered trademark of Oxford University Press
in the UK and certain other countries.

Published in the United States of America by
Oxford University Press
198 Madison Avenue, New York, NY 10016

Library of Congress Cataloging-in-Publication Data
Roll, David L., 1940–
The Hopkins touch : Harry Hopkins and the forging of the alliance to defeat Hitler / David L. Roll.
p.   cm.
Includes bibliographical references and index.
ISBN 978-0-19-989195-5 (alk. paper)
1. Hopkins, Harry L. (Harry Lloyd), 1890–1946.
2. World War, 1939–1945—Diplomatic history.
3. World War, 1939–1945—United States.
4. United States—Foreign relations—1933–1945.
5. Roosevelt, Franklin D. (Franklin Delano), 1882–1945—Friends and associates.
6. Statesmen—United States—Biography. I. Title.
D753.R64   2013
940.53'2—dc23   2012012254

1 3 5 7 9 8 6 4 2

Printed in the United States of America
on acid-free paper

For Nancy
Together wing to wing
—Robert Frost

CONTENTS

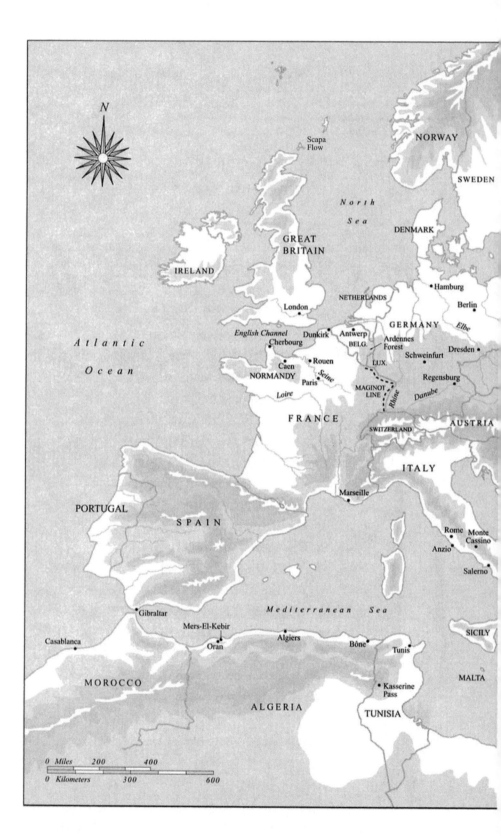

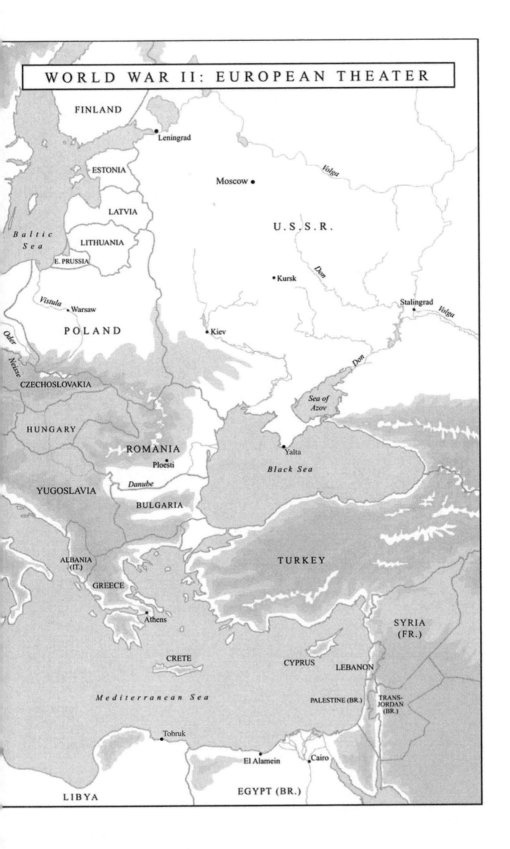

WORLD WAR II: EUROPEAN THEATER

FINLAND

Leningrad

ESTONIA

Volga

Moscow

LATVIA

U.S.S.R.

Baltic
Sea

LITHUANIA

E. PRUSSIA

Kursk

Don

Stalingrad

Volga

Vistula

Warsaw

POLAND

Kiev

Oder

Neisse

CZECHOSLOVAKIA

Don

Sea of
Azov

HUNGARY

ROMANIA

Yalta

Ploesti

Black Sea

Danube

YUGOSLAVIA

BULGARIA

ALBANIA
(IT.)

TURKEY

GREECE

Athens

SYRIA
(FR.)

CRETE

CYPRUS

LEBANON

Mediterranean Sea

PALESTINE (BR.)

TRANS-
JORDAN
(BR.)

Tobruk

El Alamein

Cairo

LIBYA

EGYPT (BR.)

THE HOPKINS TOUCH

Moving In

It was Friday, May 10, 1940, the day the German Wehrmacht overran the Low Countries and its Panzer divisions massed in the Ardennes woods for a lightning drive to the French coast, the day Winston Churchill became prime minister of Great Britain.

After dinner Harry Hopkins, secretary of commerce, was upstairs in the White House with President Franklin Roosevelt. As always when the two were together, the conversation ranged back and forth from the latest gossip to ribald stories to a relaxed but serious discussion of the newest developments in Europe. Hopkins and Roosevelt had known one another for a decade—Hopkins was one of the key figures of the New Deal—but it was only in the past couple of years that he had become the president's most valuable advisor and closest companion. They had vastly different backgrounds: Hopkins was the Iowa-born son of an itinerant harness maker; FDR was about as patrician as the country knew. But they shared a combination of idealism and razor-sharp political instincts. Both were committed to improving the lives of the poor while preferring the society of the rich and wellborn. Their inconsistencies were complementary; their paradoxes fit like pieces in a puzzle.

Commenting on Hopkins's value as an advisor to Roosevelt, Lord Moran, Churchill's personal physician, said that Hopkins knew the president's moods "like a wife watching the domestic climate." "He will sit patiently for hours blinking like a cat," continued Moran, "waiting for the right moment to put his point; and if it never comes he is content to leave it to another time."[1] Marquis Childs, a prominent columnist, wrote that Hopkins's gift lay "in understanding, sensing, divining, often guessing—and usually guessing right—what is in Franklin Roosevelt's mind."[2]

Whatever the complexities underlying their relationship, and this book will explore many of them, Roosevelt and Hopkins plainly enjoyed one another's company. The president relished Hopkins's sardonic sense of humor, irreverence, and blunt manner of speaking. He appreciated what Lord Moran and Childs—and they weren't alone—had noted about Hopkins: his sense of timing, his remarkable instinct for knowing when to press forward on a matter of substance, when to tell a joke, and when to simply listen. He had the right touch.

Knowing that his stature and effectiveness in government derived from his proximity to power, Hopkins coveted and jealously guarded his intimacy with Roosevelt. But his affection for the man was genuine; his friendship was authentic. Some of his happiest moments were telling stories and engaging in trivial banter during the late-afternoon "children's hour," when the president gathered members of his inner circle and mixed his famously dreadful martinis (it was rumored he used substandard gin, despite having a stock of better quality).[3] Hopkins's affection for FDR had deep roots, the president and his family having comforted grief-stricken Harry and looked after his young daughter, Diana, following the death of his second wife (Diana's mother). Hopkins felt as if he had been taken into the Roosevelt family. He would be ever grateful for these acts of kindness.

The president knew that Hopkins, age forty-nine, felt miserable that balmy evening in May. After an operation at the Mayo Clinic in December 1937, during which two-thirds of his stomach was removed (the doctors claimed it was cancer), Hopkins suffered from acute malnutrition and anemia. He had returned to Mayo for treatment in 1939 and spent the past few months recovering at home. Instead of sending him back to his rented house in Georgetown, where the widower lived with his daughter, Roosevelt insisted that Hopkins spend the night at the White House.

Hopkins borrowed a pair of pajamas and slept in a canopied, four-poster bed in the spacious second-floor room overlooking the South Lawn that had once served as Abraham Lincoln's office. A plaque on the wall, then as now, reads, "In this room Abraham Lincoln signed the Emancipation Proclamation." Shortly thereafter Hopkins subleased his house and moved Diana to a room above the two-room Lincoln suite near the sky parlor on the third floor. Without any particular title or portfolio, and at one point serving for several months without a government salary, Hopkins set up a card table in the Lincoln suite and conducted business for the president from there.

Hopkins and Diana would live in the White House with the Roosevelts for most of the next three and a half years. Eleanor Roosevelt followed through on her promise to him that she would provide Diana with a home in the White House, doing "everything that you would normally do with a child as a mother . . . everything except the arms around the body," recalled Diana years later.[4] In the summer of 1942, in the president's Oval Study on the second floor, Harry married again, this time to Louise Gill Macy, the former Paris fashion editor of *Harper's Bazaar*, and the couple, plus Diana and their poodle, Suzy, would continue to live in the White House until late 1943.

During those years, as the nation was drawn into the maelstrom of World War II, sickly, pauper-thin Harry Hopkins would devote himself to helping the president win the war. He would shortly form a lasting friendship with Winston Churchill and even earn the respect of Joseph Stalin, each of whom, like Roosevelt, grew to be profoundly impressed by Hopkins. Churchill wrote, "Harry Hopkins always went to the root of the matter. I have been present at several great conferences, where twenty or more of the most executive personages were gathered together. When the discussion flagged and all seem baffled, it was on these occasions he would rap out the deadly question, 'Surely, Mr. President, here is the point we have got to settle. Are we going to face it or not?' Faced it always was, and being faced, was conquered."[5]

This book tells the story of Hopkins's role—improbable and yet crucial—in helping to create and preserve the Anglo-American-Soviet coalition that ultimately won World War II. Hopkins has not lacked for attention over the years, beginning with Robert Sherwood's Pulitzer Prize–winning *Roosevelt and Hopkins: An Intimate History*, a thousand-page memoir cum history that has, deservedly, set the standard since it was published in 1948. Sherwood, a tall (6'8"), erudite member of the Algonquin crowd who won three other Pulitzer Prizes as a playwright and screenwriter, worked with Hopkins as a speechwriter for Roosevelt and was close to both of them, although each had died before Sherwood began his book (Roosevelt of a cerebral hemorrhage in April 1945, Hopkins of cirrhosis of the liver in January 1946). Other biographies and histories involving Hopkins have necessarily owed a great deal to Sherwood, as does this work. His portrait of the president and his most important advisor is vivid, detailed, and deeply human. It is a work born in affection and a sense of obligation that sought to portray the chemistry of these two men, one the titanic figure of his age and greater than life, the other his gaunt, chain-smoking shadow.

Acknowledging its debt to Sherwood and all previous accounts, this volume offers a fresh look at Harry Hopkins, his accomplishments and shortcomings. Much has happened since 1948, bringing new perspectives, shifts in attitudes, and revisions upon revisions from all sides relative to the Anglo-American-Soviet coalition during World War II. A host of diaries, letters, and documents have surfaced that were simply not available to Sherwood and other biographers and historians. For example, letters written by and about Hopkins that were not discovered until 2011 reveal new aspects of Hopkins's relationship with the Roosevelts, including previously undocumented fissures. An extensive collection of papers, diaries, and photos was donated by the late Robert Hopkins and made available by Georgetown University for the first time in 2011. (Robert Hopkins, one of Hopkins's three sons from his first marriage, was present with his father at the wartime summit conferences at Casablanca, Tehran, and Yalta.) J. Edgar Hoover's fascinating FBI surveillance file on Hopkins and his third wife was released in the 1990s. Notebooks from KGB archives were published in 2009 that flatly disprove widely publicized allegations that Hopkins was a Soviet agent. Diana Hopkins, the last living witness of her father's life with the Roosevelts in the White House, has spoken more publicly and, to my enormous benefit, agreed to a wide-ranging interview in 2011. She and Merloyd Ludington Lawrence, Hopkins's niece by marriage, also provided me complete access to their scrapbooks and private photo collections. These materials add insight and texture to the years covered in this book and are reason enough for a new look at the man who, along with Roosevelt, gave his life to forging and preserving the coalition.

From these documents and all that has emerged since 1948, Hopkins's role in the wartime alliance—one of the great feats of history—becomes even more vivid than the magnificent portrait drawn by Sherwood. More is known about how Hopkins managed the alliance and the great figures of the age—not only Roosevelt, Churchill, and Stalin, but also George Marshall, Dwight Eisenhower, Vyacheslav Molotov, and Harry Truman. New evidence from documents and diaries can now be pieced together with the old, as has been done in this book, to show how, against the advice of all U.S. military advisors, Hopkins worked behind the scenes with Roosevelt and Churchill to engineer what turned out to be the most consequential Allied strategic decision of World War II: the decision to invade French North Africa rather than launch a frontal assault on fortress Europe.

It was the chemistry between Hopkins and Roosevelt, however, that proved so fateful to the nation and the world. If not for their relationship, Hopkins would never have met leaders like Churchill and Stalin, much less have had any influence over the wartime coalition. Their relationship worked mainly because Hopkins, a linear thinker, could translate and then convert the president's vision into concrete action. Each was afflicted with a serious physical disability; each feared dependency even though the moment forced them into codependency. Roosevelt depended on Hopkins because Hopkins understood better than anyone what the president had in mind and how best to get it done. Hopkins relied on Roosevelt to provide him with access to information and the levers of government, which in turn satisfied his ambition: having the power to influence important people and events. As a consequence, during the war years Hopkins would become the only person in the U.S. government other than the president to thoroughly understand the interrelationships of war, diplomacy, politics, economics, and logistics. He was the only civilian allowed into the secret White House Map Room. Hopkins therefore appreciated the overriding importance of preserving the coalition at all costs through negotiation, strategic and tactical compromise, and the value of personal diplomacy, what one British journalist, quoting Shakespeare's *Henry V*, called "a little touch of Harry."[6] That "touch" was not little, nor was it light: it played a weighty role in the outcome of the greatest event of the twentieth century and one of the greatest in human history.

1

Ambitious Reformer

In 1939, a year before he moved into the White House, Harry Hopkins traveled to Grinnell, Iowa, the small town where he lived for much of his boyhood and the home of Grinnell College, from which he graduated in 1912, having majored in political science and history. He had just joined Roosevelt's cabinet as secretary of commerce and was both nationally acclaimed and widely criticized as the man who dispensed billions of dollars of federal relief to unemployed Americans during the Great Depression. Hopkins had been invited to address the student body in the chapel of his alma mater. Looking up from his prepared remarks, glasses perched on his nose, he grinned and said, "I am really in no mood to make a speech. . . . The talk I had in mind is rapidly leaving me."

At this, the students perked up, sensing that they were about to be amused. Hopkins didn't disappoint them. In less than thirty seconds, they erupted in laughter and applause as he ad-libbed a story about his pathetic performance as a right fielder on Grinnell's baseball team during its last and worst season. Then he leaned forward and said, "When I hear people talking about what a College is for—its curriculum—I know the plural of that too, I know that one of the best things in College is to have fun. You have plenty of time later in life to get banged around or to get solemn about it, but here you have great fun, and I think that is good, of and by itself."

There were other moments in this speech when Hopkins, sounding as though he intended to run for president in 1940, waxed solemn, proclaiming passionately that the "country cannot continue to exist as a democracy" with ten to twelve million unemployed and that a "way must be found and a way will be found" to abolish poverty in America.[1] But after he finished the speech and was strolling across the campus, his thoughts returned to the carefree joy of those years at Grinnell and how he had gotten "banged around" in the quarter century since leaving Iowa for the East Coast.

Hopkins's light side, his penchant for poking fun at pomposity and his love of gambling, came from his father, David Aldona Hopkins, who liked to be called Al. Al Hopkins was born in Bangor, Maine, the son of a Civil War veteran, but grew up in Sioux City, Iowa. At eighteen he embarked on the first of his many risky and ultimately unsuccessful ventures, joining an expedition into the Black Hills of the Dakota Territory in search of gold. After returning to Sioux City without an ounce, Al and his widowed mother moved to Vermillion, a tiny hamlet near the Nebraska-Iowa border, where he began working in a harness shop. It was there that Al began courting Anna Pickett, a schoolteacher who would become Harry's mother and from whom Harry would inherit his blend of intensity of purpose and passion for social justice.

Anna was born in Lowville, Ontario, where her kinfolk, strong Methodists, had lived since her great-grandfather, a circuit-riding saddlebag preacher, arrived there from Connecticut to spread the gospel. When Anna was ten, her family moved to Vermillion, where her father, a carpenter who took his religion very seriously, had staked a claim for 160 acres of land. Anna, quietly intelligent and pious, was fascinated by the gregarious, gladhanding Al Hopkins, who had a reputation as an adventurer. She was not a beauty, but Al was attracted to her because she satisfied his need for stability and he admired her steely moral convictions, qualities that he lacked.

The oddly matched couple were married by a Methodist minister on May 1, 1881. The following spring the Missouri River flooded out most of Vermillion, forcing Al and Anna to leave. Thus began an odyssey to the west across the harsh plains of Nebraska, where the couple briefly settled in a series of small towns, Anna delivering four children and Al finding dead-end jobs in harness shops and not earning enough to keep the bill collectors at bay. After their fourth child died in infancy, the Hopkinses moved back east to Sioux City on the banks of the Missouri River. Harry was born in this small Iowa town—the place where Al had begun his wanderlust years—on August 17, 1890.[2]

They didn't stay long. For a decade, as the nation's economy suffered the consequences of the Panic of 1893, the family moved into and out of a succession of towns in Nebraska and Iowa, finally ending up in Chicago in 1900, where Al landed a job as a traveling salesman. It was in Chicago that ten-year-old Harry contracted a serious case of typhoid, the harbinger of a lifetime of poor health.[3] By this time, Anna had had it with the constant moving around. Al could continue to travel, but the family needed a real home. She was determined that their oldest child, Adah, who was then a young woman of eighteen, would earn a college degree, and she wanted the younger children to attend good schools and have an opportunity to go to college. With Al's acquiescence, Anna decided that she and the children—Al would follow later—would move to Grinnell. How and from whom she learned about Grinnell is not known. Nonetheless the choice made perfect sense.

The town of Grinnell, located about fifty miles east of Des Moines, was founded in the 1850s as a temperance community by Josiah Bushnell Grinnell, a Congregational minister from Vermont who had been driven out of a church in Washington, D.C., for preaching the evils of slavery and advocating abolition with an excess of passion. He purchased a tract of land in Iowa that became the town of Grinnell and persuaded Iowa College, then located in Davenport, to move its tiny library and scant assets there. Modeled after small New England colleges like Amherst and Williams, which offered a classical education, Grinnell also admitted women and banned fraternities. Almost from its inception, Grinnell College and the community surrounding it were committed to the social gospel movement. Infused with Methodism, the movement called for the application of Christian teachings to the social ills arising out of the dehumanizing effects of industrialization: child labor, urban slums, political corruption, corporate exploitation of workers, and the concentration of wealth in the hands of a few. This movement and Methodism were precursors to the progressive movement, which was championed by Theodore Roosevelt and Woodrow Wilson during the opening decades of the twentieth century.[4] To Anna, Grinnell was the place where her commitment to the principles of Christianity and social justice and an excellent education for her children all came together. And as Harry, her fifth child, would tell his audience in Grinnell's chapel in 1939, it was the place where his social conscience was born.

In 1901 the Hopkins family rented a small house not far from the campus. Adah enrolled in the freshman class at the college that fall, and Harry, age eleven, entered the Cooper School across the street from their home. Al continued working as a traveling salesman, dropping by from time to time and somehow scraping together enough money from his salary and occasional gambling winnings to support his family. Anna's brother, John Pickett, who had established a successful harness and leather goods business in Manilla, Iowa, helped defray the college tuition costs of the Hopkins children.[5]

From all accounts, Harry's teenage years in Grinnell were blissful, full of sports, friends, girls, and pranks. Known first as "Skinny," then "Hoppy," tall, underweight Harry loved to defy authority, engineering the election of a popular but academically average student as junior class president over the protests of the school authorities, who always rigged class elections to favor the best students. He befriended the awkward son of the college president who was being unmercifully teased, and he broke up a high school girls' party when he "kidnapped" one of the girls who was known as a snob.[6] Throughout his life, Harry would side with the underdog and expose the pompous.

At home Harry's mother was a domineering, controlling influence. During those years when the children were in school and Al was traveling, Anna became an even more zealous churchgoer. She gathered her children for

Bible reading and hymn singing around a household pump organ and made sure that they attended the Methodist church daily and twice on Sundays. She devoted her spare time to the Methodist Home Missionary Society of Iowa, eventually becoming its president. "She was a strait-laced believer in the poor and the hungry and that kind of thing," recalled her granddaughter Diana Hopkins many years later.[7]

In almost comic contrast, Al Hopkins's passion was ten-pin bowling, a sport at which he was fiercely competitive and on which he gambled compulsively as he traveled throughout the Midwest hawking harnesses. Al was free to place bets, swear, and swap stories with his bowling pals, but when he was home he had to conform to Anna's standards of decorum. Harry recalled the time when his father returned after a bowling match and coaxed him to go down to the cellar out of Anna's hearing to brag about the contest and impress him with the $500 roll of bills he had won. "I wasn't supposed to tell my mother there was that amount of money in the house; she would have made Dad give it away to the church missions."[8] In 1910 Al received a cash settlement as a result of an accident he had in Chicago and invested the money in a harness shop near the Grinnell campus. At age fifty-four he finally stopped traveling. But as the number of automobiles and trucks exploded in the first two decades of the twentieth century, the demand for harnesses plummeted. Al was forced to add newspapers, magazines, and candy to his inventory, and he sold cigarettes without a license to the college students. For the rest of his life he would be affectionately called "Dad" by customers, friends, and family.[9]

Harry always admired his mother, taking from her a bedrock belief, based on the teachings of Christianity, that service to others was the highest form of human activity. But he loved his father's gambling heart and his worry-free spirit of adventure, as well as the adulation he received in the local newspapers when he won a bowling tournament. The "Do unto others" Christianity of his mother and the unfulfilled dreams of his father would kindle in Harry a determination to succeed.

Following in the wake of his older sister's dazzling college record, Harry's ambitions were only dimly perceptible when he entered the freshman class of Grinnell College in 1908. He had watched Adah's progress at Grinnell with great admiration. She delivered a prize-winning oration on child labor in her junior year and was chosen Outstanding Senior in 1905, before launching a career in social work in Philadelphia and later New York City.[10] Academically Harry was a very slow starter. During his first two years, he racked up a number of Ds and failed an English course. His classmate Florence Kerr, who became a lifelong friend and a New Dealer, said that she "used to wonder if he'd ever graduate, because he was always turning up missing with required credits."[11] In his junior and senior years, however, he was drawn in by two members of Grinnell's impressive faculty, and his academic performance began to improve. His favorite teacher was Jesse Macy, Grinnell's most famous professor at the time, who Robert Sherwood, the author of *Roosevelt and Hopkins*, described as "the originator of the first college course in political science."[12] Macy taught that government could be understood and improved through application of the scientific method and that everyone had a duty to work for a just society. In his senior year, Harry received an A in Macy's course.

The other professor who inspired Harry was Dr. Edward Steiner. Born in Czechoslovakia, Steiner was a Jew who had converted to Christianity and a leading proponent of the social gospel. He occupied Grinnell's chair of Applied Christianity ("creating the kingdom of God on earth through justice and social reform"). In the first semester of his senior year, Harry was captivated by Steiner's course, "The Development of Social Consciousness in the Old Testament," on the ethical and religious development of the Jews and the poets and prophets of Israel. Steiner, who had been a friend of Leo Tolstoy, was famous for beginning the course by saying, "Jesus was a bastard." Harry excelled in this class, receiving another one of his rare As.[13]

Outside the classroom, Harry's drive was visible from the first days of his freshman year, although it was veiled by his seemingly carefree attitude and propensity for pranks. Starting as a member of the social committee of the freshman class, he rose to become the permanent president of the senior class, the only elected position he ever held. He took advantage of almost every extracurricular activity Grinnell had to offer: editing the yearbook, serving on the College Council, winning the leading role in the senior play, and organizing the Woodrow Wilson Club to promote Wilson's presidential bid.[14] On Grinnell's championship basketball team, Harry played with a competitive ferocity inherited from his father that made him a big man on campus. Long before Clint Eastwood's movie, he was known as "Dirty Harry" because of the number of personal fouls he incurred. In Grinnell's most memorable game in those years, Dirty Harry's six points and gritty defensive play helped the little college defeat heavily favored Kansas University, the reigning champion of the Missouri Valley Conference, by a score of 17–16 in Grinnell's bandbox gym.[15]

In the spring of his senior year, Harry talked about going into the newspaper business in Bozeman, Montana, with his friend and classmate Chester Davis, a future agriculture and war food administrator in the Roosevelt administration. He was also considering social work, following the path of his sister, but, according to Florence Kerr, Professor Steiner discouraged that choice, advising Harry that he didn't have the requisite compassion. When Harry mentioned the possibility of social work to Louis Hartson, his young psychology professor, Hartson invited Harry to join him that summer to work at a camp for poor New York City boys that was located a short ferry ride across the Hudson River in Bound Brook, New Jersey. The camp was operated by the Christadora Settlement House (Greek for "gift of Christ"), located on the Lower East Side. Harry knew about the House because Adah had worked there for Christina Isobel MacColl, its founder. When Hartson suggested to him that he would have an opportunity to work in the city after the summer was over, Harry accepted the job on the spot. He was terribly excited, having had a taste of New York once before, on a trip with his mother, and also because Adah was there, as was his brother Lewis, who was attending medical school.[16]

June 1912 was a time of great promise for Harry Hopkins and for America. Spurred by social gospel Christianity, the progressive movement was remaking the United States. It was, wrote the historian Richard Hofstadter, "the age of reform." Women's suffrage, settlement houses, anti-vice campaigns, Prohibition, and educational reform were the order of the day. Political democracy and the economic rights of individuals could be restored, it was thought, by enacting laws and regulations to curb corporate power, attack social ills, and uplift the poor. Progress was possible, argued theologians like Walter Rauschenbusch, "because evil resided in the world, not in man." Through science and the force of reason, government and its experts could address and solve society's ills, including the abolition of wars for all time.[17] Speaking at Grinnell's commencement exercises, William Allen White, the influential Kansas newspaper editor, told the graduates that they had "two objectives in life: to promote social justice; and to develop in the masses such an enthusiasm for this social justice that they will be willing to follow the proper leaders at a personal sacrifice." White called Christ "the greatest social reformer and the greatest democrat of all time."[18]

A few days after graduating, as he traveled east with Hartson, stopping in Chicago, Hopkins had his first glimpse of Theodore Roosevelt, the ebullient former president who had inaugurated the Progressive Age. Posing as Elihu Root's secretary—Root having been secretary of war under McKinley and Teddy Roosevelt and the winner of the 1912 Nobel Peace Prize—Hopkins wangled his way into the Republican National Convention at Chicago Stadium. There he saw Roosevelt bolt the GOP to form the Bull Moose Party, shouting in his high-pitched voice that the renomination of William Howard Taft by the Republicans would be "naked theft."

Hopkins and Hartson did not have to be at the camp until early July, so they spent a few days in Washington because Hopkins wanted to see the White House. They then went up to Baltimore to attend the Democratic convention in the Fifth Regimental Armory. There Hopkins heard his father's political hero, William Jennings Bryan of Nebraska, rail against the Tammany Hall bosses and saw him break the deadlock by throwing his support to Woodrow Wilson. He cheered with hope as Wilson, who would ride the high tide of the progressive movement, received the nomination.

According to Sherwood, the two months Hopkins spent as a camp counselor at Bound Brook were "his real birth as a crusader for reform." He had witnessed his father and families in the neighborhood back in Grinnell struggling to pay bills, but never before had he seen malnourished immigrant boys from the city slums, who arrived at the camp in rags. They were completely lacking in the discipline, self-respect, and values that he was accustomed to in the Midwest. Most of the boys were from the Lower East

Side. He later recalled, "[Until then] I'd never seen a Jewish boy in my life." For the first time, his eyes were opened to the real consequences of poverty and how it damaged the spirit of the children of immigrants forced to grow up in the degradation of city slums.[19]

In the fall, Christina MacColl offered Hopkins a job as head of activities for boys at Christadora House, which he readily accepted. Like most employees, he lived at the House, which was located at 147 Avenue B on the Lower East Side, the neighborhood with the largest concentration of immigrants (four thousand per block) in the United States. Christadora, one of the many houses in the settlement movement then prevalent in large American and British cities, sought to uplift the lives of immigrants and other poor people in the neighborhood, especially children and young adults, by providing education, training, and social and recreational programs. Christadora purported not to try to change the religion of those who participated in its programs, but there is no denying that a strain of evangelical Protestantism permeated the House and that there was rejoicing when a Catholic or Jew converted.[20]

Like most settlement houses, Christadora was a large, elegant manor house with fine furniture, china, drapes, and fresh flowers—a sanctuary in the midst of the grime and soot of the teeming slums. It was a graceful place, designed to be both attractive to poor immigrants in the neighborhood and suitable for the young middle-and upper-class Protestant college graduates who worked there, almost all of whom were young women recruited from East Coast institutions like Smith and Wellesley. Hopkins was one of the very few men who lived and worked at Christadora.[21]

Described by one of his coworkers as "very eager and young . . . and full of the desire to help," Hopkins organized and ran the boys' clubs and all of their recreational activities.[22] As a "friendly visitor," he climbed the stairs of dumbbell-shaped tenements to visit the boys and their families in their dark, airless apartments and investigated requests for assistance. He was appalled and enraged by what he saw. Regarding his boys as "keen, ambitious," he gradually began to understand that the urban poor, especially the children, were trapped by society's ills through no fault of their own, and he began to develop his own ideas about how to provide effective relief without compromising their dignity.[23]

In January 1913 Hopkins met twenty-six-year-old Ethel Gross, most likely at a women's suffrage meeting at Christadora House.[24] They were instantly attracted to one another. Ethel was drawn to Hopkins because he was boyish, charming, and light-hearted, yet at the same time ambitious and energetic. Everything about him was utterly American. On his part, Hopkins was entranced by Ethel's natural dark-haired beauty and, as he wrote in his first love letter to her, by the fact "that [they had] lived absolutely different lives up til now."[25] Although they had vastly different backgrounds, Ethel, then a cosmopolitan working woman, shared Hopkins's commitment to social reform. Within a month they had fallen deeply in love, and Hopkins was already talking of marriage, writing, "I love you if I ever love anybody in my life."[26] Like his mother and sister, Ethel was a strong-minded woman with a keen social conscience. She would play a key role in his rise to become the most prominent social reformer in America.

Ethel Gross was born into a Jewish middle-class family in a small town in Hungary. Her father died of tuberculosis when she was five, and Ethel's mother, with five children ranging in age from three to sixteen, sold everything they owned and booked steerage for America. They settled in a tenement six blocks from where Christadora House would open a few years later. Shortly after they arrived, one of the children died, leaving Ethel with two brothers, Benjamin and Edward, and an older sister, Francesca. Ethel enrolled in public school but dropped out after the eighth grade because of ill health, recalling later that she was always ashamed and afraid in school because of her foreignness. Fortunately she caught the eye of Christina MacColl, Christadora's charismatic founder and headmistress. MacColl became Ethel's mentor, restoring her to health, employing her to run recreational programs for young children at Christadora, and encouraging her to master shorthand and the new typewriting machine.

During her teenage years, Ethel earned money as a counselor to the children at Christadora and as MacColl's personal secretary.[27] In 1908, on MacColl's recommendation, she became the private secretary to Katherine Mackay, the wife of the founder and CEO of the U.S. Telegraph & Cable Company, the leading high-tech company of that era. Mackay, a wealthy socialite and committed social activist, had just established a new women's suffrage organization whose membership consisted of women from New York's "Four Hundred," the most socially prominent families. (The number was said to represent the capacity of Mrs. William Backhouse Astor Jr.'s ballroom in the 1880s.) Thus Ethel, an immigrant from the ghetto of the Lower East Side, was introduced to the manners and Protestant values of the richest and most progressive movers and shakers in New York.

While working for Mrs. Mackay and learning to adapt to her world, Ethel suffered a terrible emotional trauma. In 1910 or 1911 she discovered her mother's body in the shabby tenement apartment where she lived. Her mother, who had sought a better life in America to raise her children but never adjusted to what she regarded as a foreign country, had committed suicide by gassing herself in the kitchen oven. Ethel did her best to sublimate her horror and guilt. She did not speak of her mother for the next fifty years.[28]

The tragedy seemed to fuel Ethel's drive to assimilate into progressive New York society. Her work required her to shuttle between Mrs. Mackay's swank offices in Manhattan and her Long Island mansion. She organized rallies, attended dinner parties with the liberal elite, and learned the strategies and tactics of women's political action, marching in the streets with the suffragettes in their stark white dresses and plumed hats. She also accompanied Mackay on two first-class voyages to Europe. On the second of those trips, in the autumn of 1912, media attention was riveted on Mrs. Mackay because she was carrying on a scandalous public affair with a prominent New York doctor. Ethel became uncomfortable and disaffected. During a trip back to New York to visit her sister over the Christmas holidays, she decided she could not return to Paris to work for Mackay and asked her mentor MacColl for a job. MacColl promptly hired Ethel to work as her secretary and to supervise the children's drama programs at Christadora.[29]

Ethel and Hopkins carried on their courtship in secret during the first several months of 1913. Mindful of the social pressures against mixed marriages and the rampant anti-Semitism of the time, both were reluctant to reveal their romance, let alone their marriage plans, to their families, and in particular to their joint mentor, MacColl, for fear that they would strongly disapprove and try to talk them out of marriage. Writing to Ethel, who was living with her sister in Harlem, not at Christadora, Hopkins predicted the reactions of their respective families:

> But girl, there is going to be an awful row when your family learns how you have fallen from grace. . . . Oh! but my father! Ye Gods—it is lucky that he hasn't any money for he certainly would leave me out. I love to think how it would rock the very foundations of our dining room. The poor old dears are badly in need of something to talk of and they are going to get enough to last for at least a week.[30]

In turn, Ethel wrote to Hopkins, quoting a letter from her sister in which she says that she "does not believe in inter marriages because that born prejudice against the jew might be slumbering sometimes but it is never dead no matter how broad-minded they are."[31] In a another letter to "My Dearest," she wrote:

> I'm not at all worried about my end of it, about the attitude of my friends and my family. Whatever the first shock will be—it won't last and when they see how happy we're going to be and how fine and big—and altogether how ideal you are—they will say it is what they always wanted for me.[32]

Undoubtedly the thrill of the clandestine romance and the sense that they were a pathbreaking couple, united as equals in challenging social taboos, added to the emotional intensity of the relationship. Setting aside their anxieties, Hopkins and Ethel were married in October 1913 at the Ethical Culture Society, a socially sanctioned institution for interfaith marriages. Ethel had long since abandoned her Jewish faith. Hopkins had turned away from Methodism and would never again join a formal church, instead believing, as Ethel later said, that "service to others was the most important way to manifest religion."[33]

In the spring of 1913, twenty-two-year-old Hopkins began working for the Association for Improving the Condition of the Poor (AICP), the oldest (founded in 1843), largest, and most influential social welfare agency in New York. Its director was John Kingsbury, a prominent social worker and humanitarian reformer who had served as an advisor to Theodore Roosevelt on social welfare issues in the Bull Moose Party platform in 1912.[34] Kingsbury quickly recognized Hopkins's gift for cutting to the heart of tough problems and his promise as a reformer. He adopted Hopkins as his protégé, and they became lifelong friends, although in later years Hopkins would give Kingsbury every reason to end the friendship. Kingsbury was to play a critical role in shaping Hopkins's thinking and advancing his career in social work.

Within a few months, Hopkins was put in charge of AICP's Employment Bureau and was asked to study and write a report on the causes of rising unemployment in the city and what could be done about it. Under Kingsbury's guidance, he produced a report that presaged the philosophy he would put into practice twenty years later: that most of the jobless preferred an honest day's work to charity (what was then called "the dole") and that they were unemployed not because of moral shortcomings (e.g., laziness) but because of social or economic conditions beyond their control. The solution in hard times, he argued, involved public works projects, regulation to prevent factory closures, unemployment insurance, and workmen's compensation. Given prevailing attitudes—which despite the rise of progressivism remained conservative and suspicious of the foreign-born—these ideas bordered on the radical.

Before long Hopkins had a chance to test one of his new ideas. In 1915, facing an economic downturn and alarmingly high unemployment in New York, he and William Matthews, the head of AICP's Welfare Division, organized the first work-relief program in New York, a program in which more than 230 previously unemployed men were paid a living wage by AICP to work on improvements to the Bronx Zoo. It was a modest program, but it served as a prototype for future public works programs. In his memoirs, Matthews wrote that the Bronx Zoo project was "the beginning of work relief in the United States, a method of relief which sixteen years later was to become a major form of aid for the casualties of the Great Depression."[35]

Meanwhile Hopkins and Ethel had settled into an apartment in the city. Ethel supplemented their income by working part time as a secretary for the Women's Political Union, a suffrage organization founded by Harriot Stanton Blatch, the daughter of Elizabeth Cady Stanton, an early leader of the women's rights movement. Given Ethel's connections with political activists in women's suffrage organizations and Hopkins's burgeoning friendship with John Kingsbury and other social workers, the couple was quickly embraced by New York's young left-wing political and social set. Hopkins registered to vote for a Socialist candidate for mayor, a fact he at first denied and then tried to explain away at his confirmation hearings for secretary of commerce in 1939 by resorting to the "I was a young idealist" defense.

When the United States became involved in World War I in 1917, Hopkins was refused induction into the armed services because of defective vision in one of his eyes. Wanting to contribute to the war effort as a patriotic duty—though he opposed the decision to declare war—Hopkins accepted an offer from the American Red Cross to help families of servicemen who were suffering the loss of their breadwinners. At the behest of President Wilson, the Red Cross, which was normally concerned with disaster and humanitarian relief in the United States, created a new department to provide assistance to those families and was actively recruiting experienced social workers. Hopkins was initially assigned to the Gulf Division, based in New Orleans.

He ended up staying with the Red Cross until well after the war was over, eventually rising to become head of the entire Southern Division (covering nine states). Under his leadership, an organizational structure was established that provided support and services to 200,000 families of soldiers and sailors.[36] But it was Hopkins's personal involvement in disaster relief that brought him publicity and national attention as a can-do administrator in that star-crossed part of the nation that would suffer Hurricane Katrina, the BP oil spill, and massive floods in the next century. On August 6, 1918, Lake Charles, in southwestern Louisiana, was struck by a hurricane and subsequent flooding, destroying 2,600 homes and causing millions in property damage. The day after, Hopkins wired Ethel, who was spending the summer with their two-year-old son, David, on Long Island, "Conditions in Lake

Charles bad one. Thousands homeless. Am in charge of all relief work."[37] Hopkins was at his best in this kind of unexpected emergency, just as he would be in leading assistance efforts during the deadly influenza epidemic later in 1918 and the disastrous earthquake in Vera Cruz, Mexico, in January 1920.

The letters and telegrams between Ethel and Hopkins during the summer and fall of 1918 when Ethel was staying with David and her brothers on Long Island provide clues to the beginning of tensions in their marriage. As Hopkins became absorbed in providing relief to the Lake Charles victims, his communications became shorter, less frequent and sometimes testy; and they also reveal a relentless campaign by Hopkins to postpone Ethel's return to New Orleans into October, ostensibly because of the heat and out of a concern for her and baby David's comfort. Ethel, who yearned to be a partner in Hopkins's relief work, sensed that his reasons for delaying her return were a pretext, that he thought her presence would get in the way of his job or that perhaps he was involved in an affair with another woman. Her letters express disappointment at being excluded from his important work and ask veiled questions about his female co-workers that disclose her understandable anxieties and evident mistrust.[38]

For the most part this correspondence ended when Ethel and David moved to New Orleans near the end of 1918. In 1920 the family moved to Atlanta when Hopkins took over leadership of the Southern Division. Hopkins's performance during his four and a half years with the Red Cross enabled him to attain a national reputation in the field of social work and disaster assistance. However, he craved more power, more recognition. He needed to get out of the Deep South. With the encouragement of Ethel and Kingsbury, who was heading a public health organization in New York, he became more and more interested in health and its relationship to poverty. From his training in social work and his experience with the Red Cross in the South, he knew that one of the most effective ways to alleviate poverty was to prevent or control infectious diseases, especially tuberculosis, which was so prevalent then among the poor. So, with public health and an even higher profile in mind, Hopkins and his family (Ethel had delivered a second son, Robert) returned to New York, where Hopkins was named executive director of what would become known as the New York Tuberculosis and Health Association. Over the next seven years he brought several other disease prevention services under the umbrella of that organization and sought to expand its jurisdiction to cover improvements in sanitation, pasteurization of milk, and health education. By 1930 his organization, financed through philanthropy and sales of Christmas Seals, was responsible for serving more than 3 million people in Manhattan, the Bronx, and Staten Island and was credited with playing a major role in disease prevention and poverty reduction. Hopkins was among the most well-known social workers in America. He had helped to found the National Association of Social Workers, an organization that set professional standards for social workers, and in the mid-1920s he was elected its president. Three years later he spoke at the National Conference of Social Work about the relationship between social justice and public health.[39]

It was during these years that Hopkins's talents as a coalition builder began to emerge. Instead of establishing top-down lines of authority, he preferred to balance competing interests and seek compromise and cooperation to achieve the larger good. He was contemptuous of process and bureaucracy, and he encouraged free and open exchanges of ideas during staff meetings, which one colleague described as "just like old time prayer meetings."[40] Hopkins motivated his employees with his intensity, his lack of formality (everyone called him "Harry"), and his charm, always giving them the sense that they were at the forefront of social change, finding new ways to improve health and curb poverty. "He was intense," recalled one of his coworkers, "seeming to be in a perpetual nervous ferment—a chain smoker and black coffee drinker." Employees were captivated by his utter lack of regard for his personal appearance; his suits were frayed, and he often arrived at "the office looking as though he had spent the previous night sleeping in a hayloft."[41]

Up until 1926, Hopkins had been "banged around" a bit by life—suffering bouts of pneumonia, the loss of an infant daughter to whooping cough, and fissures in his marriage due to absorption in his work and Ethel's suspicions, perhaps justified, about his fidelity—but nothing that had shattered him. For the most part, his life and that of his family seemed idyllic. A third son, Stephen, was born in 1925, and the family, at Ethel's insistence, moved to the suburbs, first to Mount Vernon to be close to John and Mabel Kingsbury, and then farther out to Scarborough-on-Hudson, with a summer cottage in Byrdcliff, an artists' colony above Woodstock in the Catskills.[42] Hopkins developed a keen but improbable interest in fungi, tramping through the woods with Kingsbury in search of specimens and learning, as a *New Yorker* profile put it, "the difference between mushrooms and toadstools."[43] He was reading poetry, acquiring a lifelong interest in the works and lives of the English romantic poets, especially John Keats.

But beneath the surface, the marriage was beginning to lose its stitches. Ethel, with her professional background in women's rights and proven capability in the workplace, wanted to continue in her role as Hopkins's partner and advisor in the world of New York social work. Equally important, while still harboring childhood fears resulting from her foreign background and having suffered the loss of both parents, she needed lots of loving reassurance and intimacy. But Hopkins was working ever longer hours in the city and was almost never home. He no longer regarded her as his career guidance counselor and was often emotionally unavailable. For his part, he saw himself as the hardworking breadwinner and Ethel as much too clingy.[44]

In addition there were money problems. Hopkins was earning $10,000 a year, far more than most Americans made, yet he could not manage to live within his means, a circumstance that had persisted since his days living in hotels and eating in expensive restaurants in New Orleans. He simply didn't care about money; his currency was power. He entertained his friends at the finest speakeasies and restaurants, stayed at five-star hotels, booked first-class travel, bought rare books with abandon, and bet on "horses, cards and the time of day."[45] It is entirely possible that he had inherited his father's "champagne appetite," a phrase coined by Hopkins's brother to explain why the Hopkins family barely got by while Al gambled on bowling matches, attended business conventions, and traveled about the country.[46] Frequently short of money, Hopkins borrowed from Ethel's brothers. Whether they made disparaging hints about his spending habits is not known. It is likely, however, that the mere fact of borrowing within the family exposed fault lines in the relationship between him and Ethel.

The most serious stress on the marriage, however, didn't involve money. Sometime in 1926 Hopkins met and fell in love with Barbara Duncan, who was working as a secretary at the Tuberculosis and Health Association. Duncan, ten years younger than Hopkins, was an upper-middle-class Protestant from Port Huron, Michigan, who had attended the University of Michigan for two years and trained as a nurse at New York's Bellevue Hospital. Barbara was much less demanding than Ethel, content to remain on the sidelines and accepting of Hopkins's long hours on the job and frenetic habits. With soft, rounded features, she was pleasantly attractive and had a sunny, nonthreatening, and accommodating disposition. Although Ethel did not know of the affair for some time, Hopkins used the excuse of his work to secretly spend as much time as he could with Barbara.[47] During the next two years, his relationship with Ethel completely unraveled. Riven with guilt, he sought to blame the rising tensions on Ethel's excessive worrying rather than his own infidelity. In November 1927 he convinced Ethel that a trial separation might help, and he persuaded her to take a boat trip down the Mississippi to see friends. In a newsy letter to her during the trip, he concluded, "I am alright—this is the best move we have made in years and is sure to help—*And don't worry about it.*" A week later Ethel wrote back, bitterly challenging him for inventing "the little legend about my nerves" and threatening to leave him and "start on a mad career of pleasure."[48]

In 1928 Hopkins, who saw his marriage and family life slipping away, began seeing an eminent psychoanalyst, Dr. Frankwood Williams. Williams concluded that Hopkins had feelings of inadequacy because, as the fifth child, his mother had neglected him. He encouraged Hopkins to resurrect his marriage and end his relationship with Barbara.[49] As the summer approached, Hopkins and Barbara agreed to stop seeing each other, and he embarked on a trip of several weeks to Europe with Kingsbury to attend the first International Conference of Social Workers in Paris. On the voyage over, Hopkins discussed his marriage with Kingsbury, whose notes of the conversation indicate that Hopkins had fallen away from Ethel because of her "domineering" personality, her neediness, and his dislike of her "Jewish relatives and customs." Hopkins told Kingsbury that he married Ethel because he pitied the "poor struggling Jewish girl" and wanted to "shock the good Methodists back in Iowa," meaning his parents. To his best friend he swore that there was no other woman, although it is unlikely that Kingsbury believed him.[50]

Hopkins's version of the marriage was built on evasion, rationalization, and outright lies. Clearly he felt profoundly guilty about the fact that the marriage was not working and that he had fallen in love with another woman. He continued his evasiveness, trying his best not to cause more pain to Ethel. Stopping in London on his way back to the States, he wrote a curiously warm and affecting letter to her about the "Keats Walk" in Hampstead Heath: "It was [as] tho I could reach out and touch him—quite like a dream. . . . I fairly walk on air and wanted you to know."[51] In the next breath, he told Ethel he would be home on August 15. He actually returned to New York a few days earlier so he could go up to Saranac Lake to see Barbara, who was in a sanatorium with a mild case of tuberculosis.[52]

At some point, probably in the winter of 1928–29, Hopkins faced up to the fact that the marriage was over and admitted to Ethel that he was in love with Barbara. He moved out of the family home. His personal finances were in disarray. In April 1929 he returned several household bills to Ethel with a note saying, "I simply cannot pay them," and then confessed, "As a matter of fact, I am financially bankrupt." To add to this despair, he wrote in a postscript that his father would likely "die before another week."[53]

The optimism that would inspire hope to the unemployed during the coming Great Depression and later to the British people when they fought alone against the Nazis was not in evidence in Hopkins's life at this time. Instead there was despair, shame, and feelings of inadequacy as his marriage ended, his friendship with Kingsbury was ruptured, and his sister Adah refused to speak to him. That summer Hopkins's father, having spent his last days owning a bowling alley in Spokane, Washington, died of stomach cancer; his mother went to her grave three years later. Hopkins must have been recalling these painful memories when he spoke about getting "banged around" in his 1939 chapel speech to the Grinnell student body.

Hopkins and Ethel permanently separated in 1929, a month before the crash of the stock market. Their seventeen-year marriage ended with a decree of divorce on May 11, 1931, which required Hopkins to pay half of his salary to Ethel for alimony and child support. A month later, Hopkins, age forty, married Barbara.[54]

Asks for Nothing Except to Serve

Though it was devastating to most Americans, the onset of the Great Depression enabled Harry Hopkins to escape the shame of his marital breakup and resurrect his personal and professional life. The "global economic hurricane of the 1930s," as the historian David Kennedy has called it,[1] which grew out of the end of one world war and would not be spent until the start of the next, provided him with opportunities to provide relief to millions of Americans and a pathway to power, influence, and fame in the nation's capital. For Hopkins, it began, as it would end fourteen years later, with Franklin Roosevelt.

In 1931 Roosevelt, in his second term as governor of New York, was faced with economic chaos and widespread misery. There were at least 750,000 unemployed people in New York alone, many facing homelessness and malnutrition. Looking back on that perilous time when the state unemployment rate was nearing 25 percent and continuing to climb, Hopkins wrote, "Almost every time the clock ticked a man lost his job."[2]

In his historic "What Is the State?" speech delivered to an emergency session of the New York State Legislature on August 28, 1931, Governor Roosevelt laid out a philosophy of American government, declaring for the first time that the state has a "social duty" to care for those who cannot care for themselves—meaning, among others, the unemployed.[3] To implement this lofty declaration, Roosevelt established the Temporary Emergency Relief Administration (TERA), a new agency charged with the responsibility of providing emergency relief to the growing ranks of the unemployed, and he persuaded the state legislature to appropriate $23 million in initial funding. New York thus became the first state to set up a taxpayer-supported agency to provide relief to the victims of the Depression. Roosevelt appointed Jesse Isadore Straus, president of Macy's, to chair the three-person board that would oversee TERA. The first choice of Straus and the other board members to become the administrator of TERA was William Hodson, head of the New York City Welfare Council. Hodson either would not or could not take the new post, so Hodson asked Hopkins, with whom he had worked on the Welfare Council, if he was interested in the job. Without a moment's hesitation Hopkins replied, "I would love it."[4]

The timing was perfect. Hopkins was just settling down with Barbara and trying to stabilize his life. He had been volunteering what free time he had to the Emergency Work Bureau, putting thousands of unemployed men back to work on city park projects in Manhattan and the Bronx. As the economic crisis deepened, Hopkins, who always thrived on crises, found this work challenging, exciting, and immensely rewarding. On October 8, 1931, the day after he was granted a leave of absence by the Tuberculosis and Health Association and approved by Straus and his board, Hopkins began his new job as head of TERA.

Utilizing what would become a familiar combination of direct relief to the poor (chits for food, shelter, and health care) and programs to create jobs (e.g., infrastructure projects), under Hopkins's leadership TERA furnished direct aid to 1.2 million New Yorkers (10 percent of the population) and was credited with creating upward of 80,000 jobs. As the U.S. economy reached its lowest ebb in 1932, Hopkins and Governor Roosevelt spoke by telephone and met with one another quite often on TERA matters, but the relationship was strictly professional. Eleanor Roosevelt, who had a background in social work, often contacted Hopkins about those she thought should be receiving TERA assistance, but again no special friendship developed.[5]

Roosevelt's "What Is the State?" speech and his creation of TERA catapulted him to the top ranks as a prospective Democratic nominee for the presidency in the campaign of 1932. In a radio address on April 7, 1932, FDR electrified listeners by promising to support "the forgotten man at the bottom of the economic pyramid."[6] He thus drew a sharp contrast between his philosophy of government and that of the incumbent, Herbert Hoover, who resisted federal relief programs and tried to downplay the significance of the economic crisis and its impact. Roosevelt appeared to be the front-runner as the date for the convention approached in the summer of 1932, but his chances of securing the necessary two-thirds vote of the delegates were by no means certain. By launching a corruption investigation, he had alienated the bosses at Tammany Hall, who threw their support to Al Smith, the 1928 Democratic nominee, and therefore he could not control the New York delegation, the largest at the convention. John Nance "Cactus Jack" Garner, speaker of the House, had the solid backing of his home state Texas delegation and had a good shot at taking California, where he had won the primary.

Hopkins, of course, was a very strong supporter of Roosevelt's nomination and bid for the presidency in 1932, although he was not a policy advisor, nor did he appear to play any active part in the campaign. Writing to his brother Lewis, Hopkins said he "had no confidence" in Hoover's plan to make loans to the states for unemployment relief and that he was supporting Roosevelt because he "is not afraid of a new idea," "not identified with big business," "fearless," and "a very able executive."[7] Hopkins attended the Democratic National Convention in Chicago and watched in suspense as Roosevelt fell one hundred votes short of the nomination after the first ballot. As dawn broke over Lake Michigan and two more rounds of balloting took place in the vast convention hall, Roosevelt gained votes at the expense of Garner, still the leading challenger, but he did not have the requisite two-thirds. Just before the next ballot, Garner, sensing his chances of a place on the ticket slipping away and desperate for the Democrats to win the presidency after sixteen years, released his delegates and threw his support to Roosevelt. On the fourth ballot, Roosevelt clinched the nomination.

The following morning, Roosevelt shattered tradition. Instead of waiting at his home for official notification, as all previous nominees had done, he chartered a Ford Trimotor airplane and flew all day to Chicago to accept in person the nomination and to address both the delegates and the nation via radio. To the millions of desperate and unemployed Americans who listened to him that evening, Roosevelt proclaimed with infectious confidence, optimism, and hope:

> I pledge you, I pledge myself, to a new deal for the American
> people. Let us all here assembled constitute ourselves prophets
> of a new order of competence and of courage. This is more than a
> political campaign. It is a call to arms. Give me your help, not to win
> votes alone, but to win this crusade to restore America to its own
> people.[8]

The New Deal was born. With the help of Harry Hopkins and a growing number of other Roosevelt believers, the words would soon begin with capital letters and enter into the American lexicon.

The campaign for the presidency began in earnest in early September, when Roosevelt embarked on a whistle-stop journey across the continent to the West, where he laid out his philosophy of government in a series of speeches and put the lie to the whispering campaign that a partially paralyzed man did not have the strength to be president. As the campaign gained traction, Roosevelt began attracting larger and larger crowds to his speeches and rallies. Independent voters were moving into his camp. Change was in the air. At his final rally in Madison Square Garden on the Saturday before Election Day, Roosevelt essentially declared victory:

> From the time that my airplane touched ground in Chicago up to the
> present, I have consistently set forth the doctrine of the present-day

Democracy. It is the program of a party dedicated to the conviction that every one of our people is entitled to the opportunity to earn a living, and to develop himself to the fullest measure consistent with the rights of his fellow men. . . . Tonight we set the seal upon that program. After Tuesday, we go forward to the great task of accomplishment.[9]

The following Tuesday, Roosevelt won by a landslide, beating Hoover by 7 million votes and carrying forty-two of the forty-eight states. Congressional Democrats were swept into office, giving the House and Senate overwhelming majorities. In Roosevelt's words, "the great task of accomplishment" lay just ahead. Harry Hopkins was offstage, waiting for the opportunity to serve.

On Saturday, March 4, 1933, moments after he was sworn in as president, Roosevelt faced the crowd of 150,000 spread over forty acres before the inaugural stand on the east side of the Capitol. The sun broke briefly through the overcast skies. "This is a day of national consecration," he began. He would need divine guidance because he and his new administration were taking office in the midst of the greatest crisis the nation had faced since the Civil War. Fifteen million Americans had lost their jobs. The banking system had collapsed. People were starving. Although Americans for the most part suffered in silence, there were those who stoked fears of violent revolution. Chicago's mayor, Anton Cermak, warned a House committee that "the federal government had a basic choice: relief or troops."[10] Of course, the most quoted phrase in Roosevelt's first inaugural speech was "The only thing we have to fear is fear itself." But there were other words that gave hope to millions. Promising to reform Wall Street and the banks, which were widely blamed for causing the Depression, Roosevelt intoned, "The money changers have fled from their high seats in the temple of our civilization. We may now restore that temple to the ancient truths." With calculating but breathtaking boldness, the new president announced, "I shall ask the Congress for the one remaining instrument to meet the present crisis—broad Executive power to wage a war against the emergency, as great as the power that would be given to me if we were in fact invaded by a foreign foe."[11] It was, said Hopkins later, "the best speech he ever made."[12]

━━━━━━━━

Just days after Roosevelt was inaugurated, Hopkins and William Hodson arrived at Union Station in Washington with an ambitious plan to create a new federal agency to provide direct relief to the nation's poor and unemployed and to administer a vast new jobs program. No one had invited them, "they just came," recalled Frances Perkins, the newly confirmed secretary of labor. Hopkins and Hodson had arranged to meet with Perkins, a fellow New Yorker whom they had known when she was the industrial relations commissioner during Governor Roosevelt's administration. Perkins, a politically adept, excessively earnest Mount Holyoke graduate, who was often photographed wearing a three-cornered felt hat with a veil, was a lifelong fighter for the working class and underprivileged. In a "hole under the stairs" at the jammed Women's University Club just off Dupont Circle, Hopkins and Hodson presented Perkins with their joint federal-state relief and jobs plan.[13] Backed by their years of experience, Hopkins and Hodson argued, "It's got to be done quickly or the country won't hold."[14] Perkins, "impressed by the exactness of their knowledge and the practicability of their plan," advocated adoption of the plan to Roosevelt.[15] Roosevelt quickly agreed, and the essence of the emergency program, together with an initial appropriation of $500 million, was enacted into law sixty days later, on May 12, 1933.

According to Perkins, Hopkins and Hodson proposed that the job of heading the new agency should go to one of them and they didn't care which.[16] It is likely, however, that Hopkins cared a great deal about who got the job. Before the inauguration, he had written a personal letter to President-elect Roosevelt, advocating essentially the same federal-state program that he and Hodson had presented to Perkins, and he had testified before the Senate on the program.[17] Letters have been found suggesting that Hopkins was actively lobbying to head the new emergency jobs program.[18]

In mid-May Roosevelt called Hopkins to offer him the top job but said it would probably be temporary. On May 19 Hopkins accepted, and the next day, a Saturday, he was confirmed without comment by the Senate. On Monday, May 22, 1933—the seventy-ninth day of Roosevelt's first Hundred

Days—Hopkins arrived at the White House for a five-minute meeting with the president. FDR briefed him, urging him to get adequate relief into the hands of the unemployed immediately and "never to ask whether a person needing relief is a Republican, Democrat, Socialist or anything else."[19]

Within an hour Hopkins found a desk and a telephone in a suite of offices on the tenth floor of the shabby Walker-Johnson Building on New York Avenue, next to the Corcoran Gallery. One visitor said the place smelled like "a combination of hospital, locker room and stable," the hospital odor due to insecticides used to kill the cockroaches.[20] Hopkins immediately wired the forty-eight state governors to form state relief organizations. By nightfall he had dispensed more than $5 million to seven states.[21] The next day, under the headline "Money Flies," the *Washington Post* reported, "The half-billion dollars for direct relief of states won't last a month if Harry L. Hopkins, new relief administrator, maintains the pace he set yesterday."[22]

Hopkins and his brand-new agency faced daunting challenges. The unemployment rate was 25 percent. Fueled by coffee, chain-smoking Lucky Strikes, and working crushingly long hours, he met the challenge head-on. He quickly assembled top aides from his vast network of contacts in the world of social work, instructing them not to "waste any time drawing" organizational charts.[23] When an advisor promised that a proposed new project would work out in "the long run," Hopkins snapped, "People don't *eat* in the long run; they eat every day."[24]

Hopkins and his staff quickly became masters at getting the relief money out the door to the states by bending the rules, taking administrative shortcuts, and ruffling more than a few political feathers. As to some $250 million in discretionary funds that Hopkins was authorized to dispense on the basis of need, the historian David Kennedy asserts that those funds "flowed disproportionately to certain 'swing' states, outside the already secure solid South, in an effort to win votes and cultivate political loyalty."[25] Hopkins was heard to say, "I'm not going to last six months here, so I'll do as I please," and his staffers happily, and wearily, followed his lead.[26]

But the number of Americans needing relief continued to increase, and, most discouraging to Hopkins and the president, the work-relief programs run mostly by the states were not putting enough people back to work. In the fall of 1933, eyeing the approach of a brutal winter for the millions of unemployed, Hopkins drew up a plan, approved by the president in an executive order, to create a temporary *federal* jobs agency that would provide paying jobs to the unemployed, mainly on public works and infrastructure projects. The agency would be funded in large part by money controlled by Harold Ickes, the cantankerous secretary of the interior, initiating a turf war between Hopkins and Ickes that would become white hot in the coming years.[27]

Appointed by the president as head of the new temporary jobs agency, Hopkins produced astounding results. By November 23, 800,000 Americans were working on quick-starting construction and infrastructure projects. By mid-January 1934, more than 4 million citizens had been put back to work. Reporting to Roosevelt, Hopkins said, "Well they're all at work but for God's sake don't ask me what they're doing."[28] In February Hopkins was on the cover of *Time* magazine; the article within credited him with doing "a thoroughly professional job" despite political interference and charges of waste and corruption.[29] With an eye to the midterm elections in 1934, however, and an ear to the mounting criticism by Republicans and conservative Democrats of the $1 billion spent on the temporary jobs program, Roosevelt instructed Hopkins to wind it down by the end of March 1934. Although privately disappointed, Hopkins obeyed orders, and the program was terminated. The administration was hoping the economy would improve on its own without a public works stimulus program.[30]

Despite the crushing workload, long hours, and almost a 50 percent cut in salary, Hopkins managed to maintain a reasonably stable family life. Barbara and baby Diana, who had been born in 1932, moved down to Washington in the summer of 1933, and by the end of the year the family had settled into the new Art Deco Kennedy-Warren apartments on Connecticut Avenue. Since half of his $8,000 annual salary was supposed to go to Ethel, friends of Hopkins in New York quietly persuaded philanthropies to donate $5,000 a year to Hopkins until 1936, when his government salary was increased to $12,000. Hopkins also made time to penetrate the Roosevelt inner circle, befriending Louis Howe, the president's mentor and closest advisor, meeting frequently with Eleanor Roosevelt, and accepting invitations to attend cruises and weekends at Springwood, the Roosevelts' home in Hyde Park, and Campobello, their summer retreat in Canada.[31]

Reporters took a liking to Hopkins because his sarcasm and cynical wit made good copy. Reacting to criticism of his work relief program by Governor Eugene Talmadge of Georgia, Hopkins wisecracked, "He doesn't contribute a dime but he's always yapping." Later, when Talmadge complained about salaries paid to those on work relief, Hopkins shot back, "Some people just can't stand seeing others make a decent living."[32] When a reporter remarked that Governor Alf Landon of Kansas, a Republican who would run against Roosevelt in 1936, had balanced the state budget, Hopkins responded: "Oh yeah—and he is taking it out of the hides of his people!"[33] Ernie Pyle, the folksy, widely syndicated newspaper columnist, was enchanted by the way Hopkins looked and acted, profiling him to his readers:

And you, Mr. Hopkins, I like you because you look like common people. . . . You sit there so easy swinging back and forth in your swivel chair, in your blue suit and blue shirt, and your neck is sort of skinny, like poor people's necks, and you act honest, too.

And you answer the reporters' questions as tho you were talking to them personally, instead of being a big official. . . .

And that old office of yours, Mr. Hopkins, good Lord, it's terrible. It's so little in the first place and the walls are faded and water pipes run up the walls and your desk doesn't even shine. But I guess you don't care. Maybe it wouldn't look right for you to have a nice office anyway, when you're dealing in misery all the time. One nice thing about your office being so little, tho, the reporters all have to pack close up around your desk, and they can see and hear you and it's sort of like talking to you in your home. . . .

The reporters tell me, Mr. Hopkins, that you're about the fastest thinker of any of the big men who hold press conferences.[34]

Hopkins and the president could not yet be characterized as friends, but they were slowly moving toward a closer relationship, the president relying more and more on Hopkins's judgment and the two men beginning to share what Frances Perkins described as a "temperamental sympathy" with one another, "which made their relationship extremely easy as well as faithful and productive."[35] Because he had so much respect for Hopkins and his ability to deliver the results he wanted, FDR gave him a number of special domestic assignments, including appointment to a cabinet-level committee to devise a social security system. Regarded as the most active member of the committee, Hopkins converted many of the ideas into practical programs that would be incorporated into the Social Security Act of 1935.[36]

In the late spring of 1934, Roosevelt, sensing that Hopkins needed a break from "the steady grind," asked him to travel to Europe, ostensibly to "look over the housing and social-service schemes in England, Germany, Austria and Italy," but also, as Hopkins confided to a friend, to assess the personnel in the U.S. embassies of those countries and provide him with a confidential report.[37] This was the first in a series of trips to Europe in which the president would entrust Hopkins to function as his eyes and ears. FDR was well aware of the ominous political situation in Europe, and he knew he would need to have loyal and reliable representatives in the key capitals to carry out his policies and instructions. Although Roosevelt's foreign policy principles were well hidden at the time, his instincts mirrored the muscular views of his cousin Theodore, who believed that in the real world war between nations was inevitable. Distancing himself from the precepts of Wilsonian internationalism, FDR regarded the League of Nations as "merely a beautiful dream" and scoffed at the "soft mush about everlasting peace which so many statesmen are handing out to a gullible public."[38]

Adolf Hitler, whom Roosevelt had privately called a "madman" two months after he became German chancellor in February 1933,[39] was plotting to consolidate complete control of the government and the military. In mid-June 1934 Hitler held the first of many meetings with Benito Mussolini, the fascist dictator of Italy. Three weeks later, German and Italian troops massed along Austria's borders after members of Hitler's SS (short for *Schutzstaffel*, the Nazi party's so-called protective squadron), clad in Austrian army uniforms, assassinated Chancellor Dollfuss of Austria and seized the radio station in Vienna, thus setting the stage for the *Anschluss*, the union of Germany and Austria that Hitler had pledged in the first paragraph of *Mein Kampf*. On June 30, 1934, Hitler's black-shirted SS bodyguard murdered Ernst Röhm, Hitler's chief rival, who was angling to take control of all military forces, and roughly two hundred of Röhm's rowdy Brown Shirts in what became known as the "night of the long knives" or the "blood purge." A month later President Hindenburg of Germany died at the age of eighty-seven. Pursuant to a secret pact with the German defense minister, who controlled the German armed services, Hitler succeeded as head of state and commander in chief of the armed forces. The title of president having been abolished, Hitler became known thereafter as the führer and Reich chancellor.[40]

These momentous events were taking place as Hopkins and Barbara toured Europe that summer of 1934. In Berlin Hopkins tried to arrange an interview with Hitler, but the führer declined due to the press of business, which allowed Hopkins later falsely to brag that he had "refused to shake hands with a murderer." Hopkins did manage to arrange an interview with Mussolini in Rome, although Il Duce preferred to talk about his "contempt . . . of Hitler's murders and his stupidity" instead of housing and social services. Hopkins's notes of the conversation describe Mussolini as a dominating character with "the face of a strong man and a personality of great power."[41]

After Hopkins and Barbara returned from Europe in late August, he lunched with the president, and then the couple spent the Labor Day weekend at the Roosevelts' rambling estate above the Hudson River, ninety miles north of New York. There is no record of the conversations between Hopkins and the president, but Hopkins must have conveyed his impressions of events in Nazi Germany and fascist Italy, and there is evidence that he told Mrs. Roosevelt that some of the U.S. diplomats he encountered lacked an understanding of the countries to which they were assigned, thus reinforcing FDR's suspicions about the reliability of reports he had been receiving from embassy personnel.[42]

As the midterm elections approached in the fall of 1934, Roosevelt talked with Hopkins about launching a new and bigger jobs program, declaring, "We will not tolerate a large army of unemployed," but he deflected concrete plans until after the elections.[43] On November 6 the administration defied conventional wisdom as the Democrats gained seats and established overwhelming majorities in both houses. It was an emphatic endorsement of Roosevelt, the New Deal, and the relief and jobs programs run by Hopkins. Hopkins was overjoyed. Driving to the Laurel, Maryland, racetrack with close aides one warm November afternoon, he fairly shouted, "Boys, this is our hour. We've got to get everything we want—a works program, social security, wages and hours, everything—now or never. Get your minds to work on developing a complete ticket to provide security for all the folks of this country up and down and across the board."[44] Back from the races, Hopkins and his staff, with input from Ickes, formulated a plan for a new jobs program. When he had a workable draft, Hopkins headed to Warm Springs, Georgia, just before Thanksgiving to pitch his plan to the president.

On Friday, January 4, 1935, Roosevelt, wearing a frock coat and on the arm of his son James, made an unprecedented trip to the Capitol to address a joint session of Congress in what would be known thereafter as the annual State of the Union speech. It was short and to the point. FDR recommended the abolition of existing relief agencies and the adoption of a "single new and greatly enlarged" national plan to provide jobs on public works and other projects to 3.5 million Americans. His voice rising with moral urgency, the president proclaimed, "We must preserve not only the bodies of the unemployed from destitution but also their self-respect, their self-reliance and courage and determination."[45] Congress acted swiftly, on April 8, 1935, passing an emergency jobs bill and appropriating $4.8 billion to be spent on work relief.[46]

Now the question was who would run the new jobs program and how it would be organized. The contenders for the top spot were fierce rivals: Ickes, who controlled the public works machinery in the Department of Interior, and Hopkins, who knew how to deliver jobs quickly. Roosevelt opted for speed. "Harry gets things done. I am going to give this job to Harry," Roosevelt told Donald Richberg, his aide and the executive director of the National Recovery Administration.[47] To keep Ickes from resigning, Roosevelt created a byzantine organizational structure, one that gave Ickes the illusion of control but in fact ceded Hopkins most of the authority.

(To downplay Hopkins's role, FDR referred to him publicly as a "bookkeeper.")
On May 6, 1935, the president created, by executive order, the Works
Progress Administration, known thereafter as the WPA, "responsible to
the President for the execution of the work relief program as a whole." He
named Hopkins its director.[48]

The WPA became the centerpiece of the New Deal, and Hopkins would
remain its director for the next three and a half years. Under his leadership, in its first year the WPA put almost 3 million people to work; over its
eight-year existence it was credited with employing 8.5 million citizens and
pumping more than $10 billion into the economy. The WPA constructed
roads, schools, hospitals, libraries, airports, and sewer systems and initiated programs such as hot lunches for children, day care for the children of
working women, and literacy classes for immigrants.[49]

As leader of the WPA, Hopkins became a highly visible public figure, his
sharp nose, pointed chin, thinning hair, and large, penetrating eyes recognizable to most Americans. Though he attracted considerable praise and adulation because of the success of the WPA and the billions it controlled, he was
also a lightning rod for criticism, particularly as the election season heated up
in 1936. With some justification, Republicans charged that Hopkins was operating a huge patronage scam for the Democratic Party and its entrenched
big-city bosses, although his largesse also benefited some progressive Republicans, such as New York mayor Fiorello La Guardia. Southerners were
enraged that the WPA sponsored mixed-race programs. Ignoring the charges
of political favoritism and other criticism, Hopkins responded, "I haven't a
thing to apologize for about our so-called mistakes. If we have made mistakes we have made them in the interests of the people that were broke."[50] As
Marquis Childs wrote, Hopkins "was rarely tactful or tactical. Only half trying, you could get out of him a fine, angry contempt for all [his enemies]."[51]

Because Hopkins "had a tongue like a skinning knife,"[52] and the WPA
was a target for Republicans and conservative Democrats, FDR campaign
strategists, principally Jim Farley, sought to muzzle him during Roosevelt's
reelection run against Landon in the fall of 1936. Nevertheless Hopkins
was permitted to make a western speaking tour, during which even Repub-
lican-leaning newspapers gave him favorable front-page publicity.[53] In his

speech in Los Angeles, one of his best, Hopkins said he was "sick and tired" of critics calling people on WPA relief roles "chiselers and cheats." They are, said Hopkins, "just like the rest of us." They "don't drink any more than the rest of us, they don't lie any more, they're no lazier than the rest of us— they're pretty much a cross section of the American people."[54] Later Jim Farley wrote Hopkins and told him he had heard on good authority "that [he] made a very good speech in Los Angeles."[55]

On election night, Hopkins and Barbara were in the Iridium Room of the Hotel St. Regis in New York as the returns were coming in. The room was packed with Republicans, and when it became clear around midnight that Roosevelt would again win by a landslide, losing only Maine and Vermont, *Herald Tribune* columnist Dorothy Thompson, wearing an Alf Landon sunflower, asked Hopkins to propose a toast to the president. Hopkins said, "Here? Are you crazy? We'd probably be lynched."[56] The next day, on the train back to Washington, Hopkins told a reporter, "I tell you I'm the happiest man in the world. I was supposed to be the millstone around the President's neck. Am I rejoicing? Am I!"[57]

Not long after Roosevelt's second inaugural speech, in which he said, "I see one-third of a nation ill-housed, ill-clad, ill-nourished,"[58] Barbara was diagnosed with breast cancer. For several weeks, while she was being treated in New York and Hopkins was busy supervising relief efforts following the great Ohio and Mississippi River floods, the couple lived in the St. Regis Hotel. Hopkins therefore was out of town when the president conceived and announced his proposal to alter the makeup of the Supreme Court by increasing the number of justices. FDR was displeased with rulings that had struck down his New Deal programs. His ill-fated "court-packing plan" was a thinly disguised effort to place more liberal justices on the high court.

Barbara's cancer did not respond to treatment and began to spread. The doctors told her it was incurable. In the summer of 1937, Hopkins, Barbara, and young Diana spent a last vacation together at Saratoga Springs. In September they moved from their apartment into a small house on N Street in Georgetown, and in early October Barbara was admitted to Garfield Hospital. Shortly before dawn on October 7, 1937, with her husband at her bedside, Barbara Hopkins died at age thirty-seven. Hopkins was devastated. Immediately after her death, Frances Watson, the wife of Roosevelt's close friend and military aide Colonel Edwin "Pa" Watson, drove Hopkins to St. Matthews Cathedral and sat with him while he prayed and wept. According to Aubrey Williams, his close friend and aide, in his despair Hopkins regarded Barbara's death as retribution for his own sins.[59]

Less than a month later, while staying at Hyde Park with the Roosevelts, an anguished Hopkins handwrote a fourteen-page letter to his five-year-old daughter about her mother that was found among the possessions of Hopkins's government driver and not publicly available until 2011.

> My dear Diana. . . .
>
> This morning I found you at breakfast—you told me you had dreamed a happy dream "that mother was coming back."—My darling, she will not come back—tho I think she will live ever happily in your mind as she will in mine. She loved you so dearly and you will remember her as the most beautiful of mothers—with her dark hair and flashing eyes and lovely, bright clothes. I think you will remember her best this summer at Saratoga taking you to the races—and the weeks you spent with her on the beach in New Jersey where you swam and played so many happy hours together. . . .
>
> We had such a happy summer, Barbara, you and I—I think the happiest time we ever had together—which is saying much for our days together were ever dream days. But this summer your mother and I loved each other more than ever—and your gorgeous little self made it quite complete.[60]

While caring for Barbara, Hopkins began to suspect that something was terribly wrong with his digestive system. Having been treated for a duodenal ulcer in 1935, he was having difficulty eating, and he reflected on the fact that his father had died of stomach cancer. In December he checked into the Mayo Clinic in Rochester, Minnesota. The diagnosis was grim: stomach cancer, technically called adenocarcinoma. On December 20, 1937, a large part of his stomach was removed and the plumbing reconnected. The surgeons said the operation was successful, but Hopkins would suffer the aftereffects of this operation for the rest of his life.

After he was discharged from Mayo in January 1938, he traveled to New Orleans to recuperate at the home of his wealthy horse-owning pal, John Hertz, the founder of Yellow Cab and Hertz-U Drive, and then to Joseph P. Kennedy's winter estate on the ocean at Palm Beach.[61] As chairman of the Securities Exchange Commission and Federal Maritime Commission, Joe Kennedy had gotten to know Hopkins, and according to Amanda Smith, editor of the Joseph Kennedy letters, the two were "on cordial terms," although they later parted ways over aid to Great Britain.[62] Since Kennedy and his entire family would be busy that winter getting ready to leave for London, where Kennedy would serve as ambassador to the Court of St. James, he invited Hopkins to stay at his Florida home for as long as he liked.

Hopkins gradually emerged from his grief and depression over the death of Barbara and his own feelings of hopelessness. His spirits were lifted when FDR invited him to Warm Springs in March 1938, where he and Aubrey Williams, the future head of the National Youth Administration, presented a bold plan, inspired by the British economist John Maynard Keynes, to increase government spending as a way to lift the nation out of what was called "the depression within the depression"—a precipitous decline in the economy in late 1937. This worrisome second depression was most likely caused by a tightening of reserve requirements by the Federal Reserve, increased taxes to pay for the new social security program, and Roosevelt's decision to decrease government spending in order to reduce the deficit. On his own initiative, Hopkins convinced Roosevelt that he could revive the economy by reversing course and engaging in Keynesian deficit spending. On the train back to Washington, the president told Hopkins he would ask Congress to increase spending and for the Federal Reserve to loosen credit.[63] "This genuine conversion," said Rexford Tugwell, a Columbia University economist who was part of Roosevelt's original Brain Trust, "can be credited to Harry Hopkins as much as to anyone."[64]

As it turned out, FDR was at best only half converted. He asked for and received an emergency appropriation of $3 billion, but it was too little and too late to effect recovery. At the same time he befuddled the business community and diminished any beneficial effect that deficit spending might have had by advocating both a balanced budget and greatly enhanced antitrust enforcement.[65] In the end, although these and other actions by Roosevelt throughout the 1930s provided a measure of security to many vulnerable American citizens, the only action that ended the Great Depression, including the depression within the depression, was the onset of World War II.

Later that spring, 1938, Hopkins's notes reveal an extraordinary conversation with the president. Speaking of his own "personal disinclination" and the opposition of Mrs. Roosevelt to his running for a third term in 1940, FDR ticked off the liabilities of the possible Democratic candidates for president and eliminated each as incapable of getting the nomination, except Jim Farley. According to these notes, Roosevelt said that if Hopkins could recover his health by 1940, he could head off Farley, secure the nomination, and get elected. Roosevelt also indicated that he would help position Hopkins politically by appointing him secretary of commerce, where he could get out of the WPA hot seat and build support among the business community. Hopkins's notes say Roosevelt gave him "assurances and hopes."[66] While Hopkins may have thought Roosevelt gave him the green light to pursue the nomination in 1940, Ray Moley and others who knew Roosevelt well were certain that the president was not serious, that this kind of "encouragement was merely a friendly way he had of dawdling with intimates."[67]

Preferring to take the president seriously, Hopkins began to actively promote speculation about his presidential prospects. In late May 1938, as part of Roosevelt's carefully orchestrated but largely unsuccessful campaign to "purge" conservative Democrats from Congress, Hopkins told a Des Moines Register reporter that if he could vote in the Iowa primary he would not vote for Senator Guy Gillette, a moderate Democrat who had earned FDR's enmity by voting against his court-packing plan and a few of his other New Deal bills. This purely partisan public statement, Hopkins's first as WPA director, turned out to be a serious misstep, not only because it undercut his attempt to portray himself as a nonpartisan relief administrator but also because the candidate he backed, Congressman Otha Wearin, a fellow graduate of Grinnell, was defeated. The press viewed his unsuccessful intervention in the Iowa primary as a harbinger of his limited political influence and vote-getting ability. A year later some members of Congress cited his attempt to influence the election in Iowa as justification for passing the Hatch Act, which, to this day, forbids all federal employees from participating in politics.[68]

Hopkins's presidential ambitions received another setback later in 1938, when press reports appeared in hundreds of newspapers recounting the following remarks allegedly made by him to a racetrack friend that: "We shall tax and tax, spend and spend, and elect and elect." The statement was denied by Hopkins and those with him at the track that day, but the story, whether true or not, took on a life of its own and diminished his standing even within his own party.[69]

Once Hopkins entered the political arena, public perception of him shifted; instead of a highly efficient and generally idealistic bureaucrat, he was now seen as a manipulative, partisan zealot. In addition, given that Hopkins was considered by Republicans and conservative Democrats as an increasingly obvious but unannounced candidate, they worked even harder to tarnish his image. Nevertheless, with the enthusiastic support of Averell Harriman, chairman of Union Pacific Railroad and head of the Business Advisory Council, FDR made good on his pledge to bring Hopkins into his cabinet.[70] At a press conference on December 23, 1938, asked whether he would accept the post of secretary of commerce if it were offered, Hopkins replied, "Don't kid me boys. This is the Christmas season and I'm accepting anything." That day Hopkins resigned as director of the WPA, and on December 24 Roosevelt announced that Harry Hopkins would join his cabinet as his commerce secretary.[71]

Despite his fading political fortunes, Hopkins pressed forward in early 1939. He hired journalists to feed favorable information about him to the press. Accompanied by Harriman, Hopkins gave his first major speech as confirmed secretary of commerce in Des Moines, Iowa, a dumbed-down, ghost-written talk laden with obvious political overtones that Jim Farley sarcastically dubbed "Hopkins' Acceptance Speech."[72] While in Iowa, he rented a farm near Grinnell with a view to establishing a voting residence, talked about renewing his membership in the Methodist Church, and gave his chapel speech at the college.[73] All of these transparent efforts to revive his sagging political ambitions failed. In addition his tenuous health was declining once again. As a consequence, any remaining illusion (or delusion) that he had a shot at the presidency was snuffed out forever.

Hopkins, however, remained proud of this period in his life. Sherwood wrote that "one of the last requests" Hopkins made to him before he died was that, "if anything should be written about him, there should be no attempt to disguise the fact that he once had ambitions for the highest office and that he worked and schemed to further them."[74]

In the meantime, the political situation in Europe had been getting more dire. Fulfilling the pledge he'd made fifteen years before, Hitler annexed Austria in March 1938. Then, as a consequence of the Munich Pact in September 1938, while the rest of the world stood by and watched, the Germans secured the Sudeten area of Czechoslovakia without firing a shot. As information flowed into the White House, it became apparent to Roosevelt that England and France had sacrificed the Czechs at Munich because they could not come close to matching German air power. Joseph Davies, former U.S. ambassador to the Soviet Union and a friend of both Hopkins and Roosevelt, was beginning to worry aloud that by appeasing Hitler, the British and the French, particularly the British, who Stalin regarded as increasingly hostile toward Russia, would drive the USSR toward an alliance with Germany.[75] Davies's instincts were correct. Stalin had no confidence that Britain and France would ever say no to Hitler. To secure his western borders, Stalin might be forced to ally with the Germans.

Hopkins and Roosevelt (who understood German) listened to Hitler's Nuremberg speech in the president's specially fitted railroad car on September 12, 1938, shortly before the Munich capitulation. William Shirer, the CBS correspondent who had been following Hitler's rise in Berlin, wrote in his *Berlin Diary*, "I have never heard Adolf so full of hate, his audience quite so on the borders of bedlam. What poison in his voice."[76] Deeply concerned about these developments and thinking about the prospect of supplying war planes to England and France to offset Germany's air superiority, Roosevelt asked Hopkins to embark on a secret mission to the West Coast to assess American capacity to build military aircraft and how best to increase production. This was the beginning of Hopkins's education in national security, armaments, and military logistics, subjects he would master in a few short years. The West Coast mission had to be kept secret because isolationist sentiment was at a fever pitch and the WPA was precluded by law from being involved in military matters.[77] Little is known about exactly what Hopkins told Roosevelt after his trip, but it is clear that the president concluded from Hopkins's assessment that U.S. aircraft manufacturing capacity could and must be vastly increased.

At a top-secret meeting in the White House on November 14, 1938, attended by Hopkins, General George Marshall, and other key military leaders, Roosevelt said he had decided that the United States needed to greatly expand its capacity to produce warplanes in order to deter further aggression and that he was prepared to ask Congress for authorization to do so.[78] Just after Christmas, Hopkins invited Marshall, then deputy chief of staff, to meet with him alone in his cavernous office at the Commerce Department to talk in depth about defense preparedness.[79] Why Hopkins picked that time and whether Roosevelt had asked him to set up the meeting is not documented. It is entirely possible that Roosevelt was thinking about appointing Marshall chief of staff (to succeed General Malin Craig) and wanted Hopkins to size him up and make a recommendation. It is likewise plausible that Roosevelt had asked Hopkins to sound out Marshall on options for funding the construction of aircraft and munitions manufacturing plants so that the United States could supply Great Britain and France with weapons to fight the looming German menace. The latter instruction would be consistent with FDR's decision to send Hopkins on the West Coast inspection trip, as well as with Hopkins's presence at the secret White House meeting on November 14, a meeting at which he met Marshall for the first time.

Marshall was an intimidating presence. He had a stiffly formal manner, avoided small talk, and seemed devoid of humor. About the only thing he had in common with Hopkins was that both were chain smokers. Nevertheless Hopkins was greatly impressed. In response to his questions, Marshall delivered a logical and concise explanation of what needed to be done to rebuild the nation's military capability to meet the threats posed not only by Germany and Italy in Europe but by Japan's aggression in the Far East. (After annexing Manchuria in 1931, Japanese troops moved south into the Chinese heartland, and a full-scale war had erupted in July 1937.) A few months later, on Sunday, April 23, 1939, Roosevelt met with Marshall in the stamp-cluttered—stamp collecting being one of FDR's passions— Oval Study on the second floor of the White House and informed Marshall that he would succeed Craig as chief of staff. It was one of the president's most significant decisions. Marshall later said he always believed Hopkins was responsible for his appointment.[80]

In the opening months of 1939, as Hitler publicly pledged "the annihilation of the Jewish race in Europe" and tore up the Munich Pact,[81] Hopkins's health began to deteriorate again. He was experiencing bouts of vomiting and diarrhea and, even more troubling, swelling in the hands and feet, poor vision, and general weakness. Roosevelt's personal physician, Dr. Ross McIntire, put Hopkins on a strict low-fat diet. Hopkins tried to rest and recuperate at Bernard Baruch's sprawling plantation, Hobcaw, in South Carolina, although Baruch was constantly peppering him with predictions of the coming war in Europe and Asia and the woeful state of U.S. preparedness.[82] Baruch, a wealthy Wall Street speculator and Democratic Party financier, was an expert on military mobilization issues, having served as head of the War Industries Board during World War I.

After tests and X-rays to rule out the recurrence of cancer, Hopkins spent a quiet week at Warm Springs with the president and his assistant, Missy LeHand, followed by a few days with wealthy friends in Versailles, Kentucky, where he found time to visit Keeneland Race Track and see the great racehorse Man o' War. After returning to Washington, he had to rent formal wear, including striped pants, to attend a dinner at the British Embassy for King George VI and Queen Elizabeth, who were visiting the Roosevelts in June 1939. Just before dinner Mrs. Roosevelt introduced six-year-old Diana Hopkins to the queen as the monarch emerged from her room in the White House, leaving Diana with a vivid memory of meeting the "fairy queen."[83]

As a retreat for the summer months, Hopkins leased Delabrooke, a prerevolutionary estate on the Patuxent River in Maryland, fifty miles southeast of Washington. Writing about his visit to Delabrooke with his brother Stephen during the summer of 1939—the last summer before the outbreak of World War II—Hopkins's son Robert described his father:

> We were both amazed at how sick he was. When we first arrived he was quite active. . . . Then he began having trouble with his legs. The muscles in his calves seemed to tighten up. Soon he didn't have the strength to step into the rowboat. He spent more and more time in bed. . . . Still, he maintained his sense of humour. On more than one occasion I can remember him saying: "Well, it's time for me to have my spinach"—whereupon he would whip out a hypodermic and give himself a shot in the leg.[84]

Hopkins's health did not improve; in fact it worsened. He was not absorbing nutrients. He was literally starving. Prompted by David Niles, Hopkins's friend and political advisor in the Commerce Department, he returned to the Mayo Clinic on August 22, the day before the Nazi-Soviet nonaggression pact was announced. As Joe Davies had predicted several weeks before in a letter to FDR, "the Old Bear [Russia] will get tired of being cuffed around [by the appeasement of England and France] and make peace on his own terms possibly with Germany."[85] Once this fateful pact was signed, the stage was set for the invasion of Poland by the Germans from the west and the Soviets from the east. Monitoring developments in Berlin and Moscow from the White House, the president found time that day to write Hopkins an affectionate, albeit belated birthday note. "Your birthday has come and gone and although I had it very much on my mind to send you a ribald radio [off-color telegram], things began to pop in Europe and I let the day pass by. . . . I am delighted that you are at Mayo's. It was the only wise thing to do."[86]

The invasion of Poland commenced on September 1, 1939, with German tanks and troops pouring into Polish Silesia and Stuka dive-bombers screaming down on Warsaw. In accordance with a secret protocol accompanying the ironically entitled nonaggression pact, Stalin ordered the Red Army to invade the eastern half of Poland in mid-September. The British and French leaders, having given their word that they would no longer appease Hitler—that their nations would go to war if he invaded Poland—had little choice but to declare war on Germany. "It has come at last," said Roosevelt when he was told at 3 a.m. on September 1 that the Germans were already deep in Polish territory. "God help us all."[87] World War II had begun.

Hopkins was already depressed when he got the news at the Mayo Clinic. The doctors couldn't agree on what was wrong with him and had not been able to find a remedy. He was losing hope and thought he would die. Fortunately, however, Aubrey Williams paid a visit and persuaded him, with help from Roosevelt, to permit another doctor at Mayo, Andrew Rivers, to take over the case. Dr. Rivers prescribed a cocktail of blood transfusions, intravenous feedings, and injections of vitamin and iron. The combination seemed to work. By mid-September Hopkins was allowed to return to Washington.[88]

Hopkins spent the fall of 1939 and the early months of 1940 in his Georgetown house with Diana and their cocker spaniel, Buffer (so named by Barbara in honor of Hopkins whom she regarded as an excellent buffer), struggling to regain his strength and vitality and planning defense projects while the Commerce Department was run by the undersecretary, Edward Noble, a former board chairman of Life Savers Corporation.[89] But he would never fully recover. For the remainder of his life, Hopkins would suffer recurrent bouts of diarrhea, weight loss, and weakness. All his doctors agreed that he had an inability to absorb nutrients, but they disagreed over the cause. Many believed that the stomach surgery in 1937 had resulted in a "mechanical problem" whereby his stomach contents were "dumped" too rapidly into the small intestine to properly mix with digestive juices. One doctor at the Mayo Clinic was convinced that Hopkins's symptoms were due to nontropical sprue, an inherited intestinal disorder in which the body cannot tolerate gluten.[90]

While Hopkins remained at home that spring of 1940, an eerie quiet prevailed in Europe. Poland had been crushed. The Soviet Union had absorbed the Baltic states and reached a settlement with Finland after the so-called

Winter War, which had exposed serious weaknesses in the Red Army (e.g., inadequate preparation and training for winter fighting, poor interarmy coordination, and failure to appreciate the value of radio communications). Although Great Britain and France were at war with Germany, there was no fighting. It was called the Phony War or the *Sitzkrieg*.

Roosevelt knew it would not be long before hostilities in Western Europe would begin. He had sent Undersecretary of State Sumner Welles, an old friend and fellow Grotonian, to meet Hitler in March 1940, a few weeks before German troops occupied Denmark and landed along the Norwegian coast from Oslo to Narvik. Through Welles, Hitler delivered an apocalyptic-sounding warning to the president: "I believe that German might is such as to ensure the triumph of Germany, but if not, we will all go down together."[91] Roosevelt also knew that with the Democratic convention only a few months away, and with an invasion of France and Belgium a virtual certainty, he would break tradition and allow his name to be placed in nomination for an unprecedented third term.[92] In seeking to do what no other incumbent president had done, he would be risking his political legacy. He could have retired to Hyde Park, but with war in the offing he envisioned an opportunity to achieve greatness as a wartime president, a singular success that would overcome the failure of his New Deal to quell the Great Depression.

These matters weighed on the president that evening in May when he asked Hopkins to stay the night. The Democratic convention would begin on July 15. The Phony War had ended, and Hitler had begun his lightning invasion of Western Europe. Roosevelt needed both a loyal confidant and a friend with whom he could relax. He also needed to bring within his innermost circle a person who could help him secure the nomination because without it, he would be a lame duck president with diminished powers for the remainder of 1940.

Why Harry Hopkins? He was the perfect confidant. Referring to the president, Hopkins used to say, "He knows I keep my mouth shut."[93] On keeping secrets, Hopkins's mother remarked, "I can't ever make Harry out. He never tells me anything about what he's *really* thinking."[94] He was also great fun to be around. Roosevelt "needed a little touch of frivolity and sparkling, occasionally aimless, conversation in his life," wrote James Roosevelt of his father, and Hopkins had just the touch.[95]

But it was more than that. The president respected Hopkins's judgment and admired his understanding of human nature. Like FDR himself, Hopkins was calculating and shrewd in sizing up people and their motives. He understood power—how it motivates and corrupts. Making use of that faculty, "Harry could disarm you," recalled Franklin Roosevelt Jr. "He could make you his friend in the first five minutes of a conversation."[96] He had a marvelous ability to draw people out, and his judgments, passed along to the president, were valued. Hopkins also shared Roosevelt's sensitivity to the feelings of others, sparing them pain when appropriate and inspiring confidence as needed. When the president's son James was having marital problems, his father enlisted Hopkins to talk to him about this most delicate and private matter.[97]

Hopkins filled a void in Roosevelt's life. The president was often lonely and isolated. Eleanor Roosevelt functioned as a partner, but there was no intimacy or real companionship; his sons and daughter were adults, leading their own lives; his political mentor, Louis Howe, was dead; Tommy Corcoran, once his good friend, a brilliant New Deal lawyer who loyally fought for his court-packing scheme but was not, in Corcoran's view, suitably rewarded, was on the verge of leaving the administration; and Missy LeHand, who some regarded as his second wife, would soon depart. Hopkins was Roosevelt's remaining close pal. He was a window into the world that Roosevelt, bound to his wheelchair and his office, could not inhabit: night clubs, race tracks, the theater, beautiful women. "Hopkins was a man's man and he loved the flesh pot," observed Williams.[98] During poker games and fishing trips or just lounging in the Oval Study, Roosevelt loved to hear Hopkins's stories about his exploits. When Hopkins explained how Agriculture Secretary Henry Wallace was going to reduce pork production—thus raising pork prices for farmers—by requiring all male hogs to wear roller skates on their hind legs, the president roared with laughter at his barnyard humor.[99]

There were selected moments, however, when Hopkins chose to play the heavy with FDR. As Paul Appleby, a Grinnell classmate who worked for the

Department of Agriculture in the 1930s, observed with awe, Hopkins "was one who fought with the President and fought without gloves. He fought roughly and hard and he argued hard."[100] Roosevelt admired those flashes of passion; given his own prodigious political abilities, he had special appreciation for Hopkins's skills as a hard-nosed bureaucratic infighter. "Hopkins was adept at 'throwing sand in the gears' of any potential competitor for influence over FDR," said the future Supreme Court associate justice William O. Douglas.[101]

Perhaps the most revealing comment by Roosevelt about why he invited Hopkins to live in the White House was made to the Republican presidential contender Wendell Willkie, who felt an intense dislike, if not contempt, for Hopkins, believing he was not worthy of the president's trust. Willkie asked FDR, "Why do you keep Hopkins so close to you?" Roosevelt replied:

> I can understand that you wonder why I need that half-man around
> me. But—some day you may well be sitting here where I am now
> as President of the United States. And when you are, you'll be looking
> at that door over there and knowing that practically everybody who
> walks through it wants something out of you. You'll learn what a
> lonely job this is, and you'll discover the need for somebody like
> Harry Hopkins, who asks for nothing except to serve you.[102]

In cruelly diminishing Hopkins as only a "half-man," Roosevelt downplayed Hopkins's influence on him and at the same time revealed a defensive shield that he wrapped around his own disability, suggesting to Willkie that he was much more than half, perhaps even whole. In his darker moments, however, alone in bed on the second floor of the White House, the president had to have despaired of his condition. Left unstated was the fact that he was drawn to Hopkins because they shared disabilities that both handicapped and empowered them. And each respected the other because they understood the courage it took to function under enormous pressure each day.

Roosevelt was probably correct in telling Willkie that Hopkins wanted "nothing except to serve," although, as Sherwood observed, in earlier New

Deal years Hopkins had used his access to the president to advance "his own interests and those of the agencies with which he was personally concerned." Others, such as Corcoran, Kennedy, and even Harriman, in each of whom FDR had placed a measure of trust, had their own agendas. But by the spring of 1940, wrote Sherwood, "a special bond had developed between Roosevelt and Hopkins, due to the fact that both men had fought with death at close range, both were living on borrowed time."[103]

With Hopkins at his side, Franklin Roosevelt would win the presidency for the third time, and together they would nudge the nation toward war. Hopkins would become arguably the most powerful presidential aide in the history of the American republic. Once FDR conferred the power, Hopkins asked for nothing more.

He Suddenly Came Out with It—The Whole Program

When he awoke that first morning in the White House, May 11, 1940, Harry Hopkins doubtless groped for his package of Lucky Strikes, as he did every morning, lighting the first of dozens he would smoke that day. He didn't realize it, but he was about to become a permanent houseguest, joining the odd ménage of individuals encircling Franklin and Eleanor Roosevelt, most of whom functioned as both intimate companions and employees.

Physical intimacy between Franklin and Eleanor had ended more than twenty years before, when Eleanor discovered a packet of love letters from Lucy Mercer to Franklin. The marriage survived, Franklin having pledged never to see Lucy again, but Eleanor had gradually established her own identity while maintaining a kind of working partnership with her husband. Referring to the relationship between Franklin and Eleanor, Hopkins told his friend Florence Kerr, "Watch them. Watch them, because they do all their communication with each other in public."[1]

The president's closest female companion living in the White House was glamorous, capable Marguerite "Missy" LeHand, "as close to being a wife as he ever had—or could have," observed Ray Moley, a member of Roosevelt's original Brain Trust and writer of most of his first inaugural address.[2] With large gray-blue eyes and prematurely graying hair, LeHand was lively and charming, injecting "an essential femininity" into the lives of both FDR and Hopkins.[3] She had worked as personal secretary for Franklin Roosevelt since 1921, shortly after he contracted polio. She lived in a cozy room under the eaves on the third floor, just above the president's bedroom. Hopkins, who had known and flirted with the forty-one-year-old LeHand for years, was rumored to have fallen in love with her after Barbara died. But even if there was truth to these rumors, she never fell for him. As Doris Kearns Goodwin put it in *No Ordinary Time*, "Missy was in love with her boss and regarded herself as his second wife."[4]

On the second floor, three doors down the long central hall from Hopkins's room, the object of LeHand's affection, fifty-eight-year-old Franklin Roosevelt, awoke about eight o'clock in a small bedroom next to the Oval Study. If Hopkins's first gesture was to reach for his cigarettes, Roosevelt's would have been to press a buzzer to summon his valet, Irvin "Mack" McDuffie, a former barber Roosevelt had met in Warm Springs, Georgia, in 1927. After McDuffie helped him to the bathroom, he would drape a navy-blue cape with a red "F.D.R." monogram over Roosevelt's thick neck and heavily muscled shoulders. The president would eat a breakfast of scrambled eggs in bed while reading through a pile of newspapers and dispatches.[5]

Two doors farther down the hall, in a bedroom in the southwest corner, Eleanor Roosevelt, already dressed and at her desk, would likely be discussing her schedule with short, stocky Malvina "Tommy" Thompson, her constant companion and secretary, who had rooms elsewhere in the White House. In a few months forty-seven-year-old Lorena "Hick" Hickok, a boisterous former Associated Press reporter with whom Mrs. Roosevelt had had a passionate relationship during the early 1930s and who had worked for Hopkins as a roving WPA field investigator, would move into a small room across from the First Lady. She lived there for four years while working as executive secretary of the Women's Division of the Democratic National Committee. Hick had been an invaluable asset to Hopkins when she worked for him in 1933–34, reporting from the field about the fear and hunger of the unemployed and putting a human face on the devastating impact of the Depression. Bonded by compassion, irreverence, and a love of gambling (she preferred poker), Hopkins and Hick remained good friends over the years and were delighted to find themselves living under the same roof.

Having been told the night before that Hopkins would stay over, Eleanor looked forward that morning to stopping by his room for a chat. By 1940 the two were extremely close, sharing a belief that those who needed it deserved government help and that the New Deal could provide that help. As she later recalled to her son Elliott, the First Lady expected that Hopkins would remain her loyal friend after he moved into the White House. "It was strange, but when I came back from New York that first night of the German invasion [May 10, 1940], I felt a great sense of foreboding, a fear that the war would get in the way of all the domestic progress we were making. But when I saw Harry back in the White House, I felt better, for I knew that he had never been interested in military affairs and that he'd stick with me no matter what happened."[6]

It would take weeks for her fully to appreciate what was happening to her relationship with Hopkins, but after that morning in May, as the German armed forces swept across Western Europe, Hopkins would become an expert in military and foreign affairs and would focus all of his energies and talents on helping the president prepare for and then manage the war. Understandably Mrs. Roosevelt would feel rejected, suspecting that Hopkins had used their friendship to become her husband's closest advisor and confidant. She would join the growing ranks of those who felt that Hopkins was a manipulative opportunist rather than a committed New Deal reformer.[7] As we've seen, she had taken a motherly interest in Diana, Hopkins's young daughter. She arranged birthday parties and sleepovers for Diana at the White House while her father was hospitalized or otherwise bedridden, and expressed concern about Diana's lonely existence with her preoccupied father.[8] She even volunteered to be her guardian should anything happen to Hopkins.[9] Within a day or two after he moved into the White House, Diana's things were brought over and she too became a permanent guest, living in a bedroom on the third floor near LeHand. In light of all she had done for Hopkins and Diana, it must have been especially painful for Mrs. Roosevelt when he seemed to distance himself from her and almost disappear into the exclusive embrace of her husband.[10]

Downstairs the White House housekeeper, Henrietta Nesbitt, would have been supervising the preparation of breakfast for the household. Nesbitt, a plain, stern woman who used to sell homemade baked goods from her kitchen in Hyde Park, was regarded as the worst cook in White House history. One morning the president was heard shouting, "My God! Doesn't Mrs. Nesbitt know that there are breakfast foods besides oatmeal? It's been served to me morning in and morning out for months and months now and I'm sick and tired of it!"[11] But despite Roosevelt's outbursts, snide comments, and knowing glances at LeHand when Nesbitt's chipped beef on toast or overcooked broccoli was placed before him, he could not summon the will to fire her, and Mrs. Roosevelt, who was indifferent to food, kept Nesbitt on for the duration of their years in the White House.[12] For his part, Hopkins had little reason to complain, eschewing breakfast for gallons of coffee and cigarettes in the morning and occasionally skipping out in the evenings with a date or a pal to one of Washington's posh restaurants—subject always to the tolerance of his weak digestive system and his sporadic adherence to the bland diets prescribed by his doctors.

There were other guests who stayed in the Roosevelt White House for months (Crown Princess Martha of Norway and her children), weeks (Winston Churchill), or just a night or two (the actress Helen Gahagan Douglas, wife of the actor Melvyn Douglas and a future congresswoman). And then there were the advisors, assistants, and companions who slept somewhere else but spent almost every waking hour inside: Pa Watson, FDR's "loveable" appointments secretary and military aide, as well as the hapless object of Hopkins's jokes and pranks, who lived in the Kennedy-Warren with his wife, Frances, and niece;[13] Admiral Ross "Doc" McIntire, Roosevelt's personal physician, an ear, nose, and throat specialist who would later be criticized, even excoriated, for failing to address FDR's high blood pressure and heart condition; Steve Early, the president's hot-tempered but candid and skillful press secretary; and Grace Tully, who would eventually become the president's primary secretary after LeHand suffered a stroke in 1941. Into this small society that was the Roosevelt White House came "Harry the Hop," as Roosevelt liked to call him. Hopkins would distance himself from Eleanor and the circle that served her but gain the lasting trust and affection of the larger group that surrounded the president. Roosevelt allowed no one to penetrate, as Sherwood so aptly put it, his "heavily forested interior,"[14] but Hopkins came as close as anyone to gaining admittance.

From his catbird seat inside the White House, Hopkins witnessed the whirlwind of events in May and June 1940 that inched the United States closer to war as France and the Low Countries collapsed in the face of the German blitzkrieg and England stood alone against the Nazi onslaught. On May 15, 1940, five days after Hopkins had become a permanent guest, Churchill sent his first cable as prime minister to Roosevelt, urgently requesting the United States to send forty or fifty older destroyers and several hundred late-model airplanes, antiaircraft guns, and ammunition: "The scene has darkened swiftly. The small countries are simply smashed up, one by one, like matchwood. We expect to be attacked ourselves in the near future. If necessary we shall continue the war alone. . . . But I trust you realise, Mr. President, that the voice and force of the United States may count for nothing if they are withheld too long."[15]

Roosevelt, who had been repeatedly told by Joe Kennedy and others that Churchill, who was "always sucking on a whiskey bottle," was trying to drag the United States into the war in order to save the British Empire, did not have a favorable impression of the prime minister.[16] Indeed he had harbored a personal dislike for Churchill from the time he first encountered his brusque arrogance in London during World War I. "He acted like a stinker at a dinner I attended, lording it over all of us," FDR told Kennedy in 1939.[17] When Roosevelt was informed that Churchill had been elevated to prime minister on May 10, he reportedly said to his cabinet that he "supposed Churchill was the best man that England had, even if he was drunk half of the time."[18]

Notwithstanding his personal feelings toward Churchill, FDR understood that the security of the United States was directly linked to Great Britain's survival. The day after receiving Churchill's request, he addressed a joint session of Congress and asked for a supplemental defense appropriation of $1.2 billion; at the end of the month, he asked for another $1.9 billion.[19] In cables to Churchill, he agreed to provide—cash and carry—the airplanes, guns, ammunition, and other matériel to Britain but demurred on the request for destroyers, believing that congressional approval would be required and that the isolationists in the Senate would block that approval. During the summer, however, as British chances of survival improved, the cabinet (including Hopkins as secretary of commerce), the Century Group (a bipartisan group of Eastern establishment individuals), and persuasive legal arguments by Dean Acheson set forth in an August 15 letter published by the *New York Times*, convinced Roosevelt that he could work out a deal to provide the destroyers to the British in exchange for naval and air bases on British territory in the Americas—and without going through Congress. With Hopkins's assistance, an agreement with the British was reached. On September 3 FDR announced the deal, whereby the United States would provide fifty vintage destroyers (most dated from World War I) in exchange for ninety-nine-year leases of eight British bases in Bermuda, Newfoundland, and the Caribbean.[20]

At the end of May, following the surrender of the Belgian army, the embattled British held off seven German divisions and successfully evacuated 338,000 troops from Dunkirk across the Channel to England, leaving behind all of their arms, ammunition, equipment, and vehicles. During those days, Hopkins was helping to form the National Defense Advisory Commission, the seven-member parent organization that would control and set priorities for war production and the mobilization of civilian manpower. The commissioners, handpicked and with no designated chairman, reported directly to the chief executive, which meant that Roosevelt, through Hopkins, maintained complete control over the national defense program.[21]

Hopkins was also deeply engaged in laying the groundwork for a top-secret program, approved by FDR, that would lead to the Manhattan Project and the development of the atomic bomb. Knowing that Hopkins was the best way to get access to Roosevelt, Vannevar Bush, former dean of engineering at MIT and president of the Carnegie Institute in Washington, met with Hopkins to discuss a plan for mobilizing key American scientists to design new weapons to offset, if not overcome, the threat posed by German technology. Hopkins was "immediately impressed" and arranged for a meeting at which Bush presented his proposal to FDR. The president, having already established the Advisory Committee on Uranium to study the relationship of uranium fission to national defense, approved the proposal on Hopkins's recommendation. Hopkins then drafted a letter, signed by Roosevelt on June 15, that created the National Defense Research Council, placed the uranium committee under its jurisdiction, and put Vannevar Bush in charge.[22]

As the dates for the 1940 nominating conventions approached, Roosevelt's calculated silence about his intention to run for a third term paralyzed his potential rivals and confounded the pundits. Those who knew the president well believed he was orchestrating a draft and that he had enlisted Hopkins to organize a pro-Roosevelt movement that would gain momentum and then spontaneously peak on the eve of the Democratic convention. Harold Ickes, a shrewd observer of Roosevelt and Hopkins, as we've seen, confided to his diary, "The President's refusal to take anyone, with the possible exception of Harry Hopkins, into his confidence annoyed me. I have thought for some time that he was overplaying his role of indifference and was displaying too much coyness. It is all very well for him to try to create the impression generally that he had nothing to do with the third-term movement and was indifferent to it, but I know that this has not been his state of mind."[23]

Neither Roosevelt nor Hopkins left any written tracks revealing FDR's active complicity in the third-term movement, but Sherwood recalled that he was urged by Hopkins in April 1940 to "persuade the greatest possible number of [his] friends" to write letters urging the president to run.[24] Moreover while continuing to remain silent about his intentions, Roosevelt pulled off a political masterstroke that greatly enhanced his electability and at the same time weakened the Republicans. On June 19, 1940, less than a week before the Republican convention was to convene in Philadelphia,

FDR announced that he was bringing in Henry Stimson to head the War Department and William Franklin "Frank" Knox to run the Navy Department. Stimson, the esteemed foreign policy spokesman for the Republicans, had been President Hoover's secretary of state and President Taft's secretary of war. Knox, a former Teddy Roosevelt Roughrider who had been Alf Landon's Republican running mate in 1936, was the publisher of the conservative *Chicago Daily News*. Thus in one dramatic announcement and without having to say anything about his own plans to run, Roosevelt undercut isolationist opposition to his candidacy, created a bipartisan war cabinet, and cast a pall over the Republican convention.[25]

The next day, June 20, Roosevelt and Hopkins entrained to Hyde Park for a four-day respite. There they received the news that France had capitulated and accepted Hitler's terms in the same historic railroad carriage in Compiègne where Germany had signed the Armistice in 1918.[26] According to the terms of the surrender, the Germans would occupy all of the French Atlantic coastline and a large swath of the French interior to a line south of the Loire River. Hitler permitted the rest of France to be ruled by a vassal government headed by Marshal Philippe Pétain, the hero of Verdun in World War I, which was based in the spa town of Vichy. At some point during their four-day holiday, Roosevelt and Hopkins read the text of Churchill's stirring speech to the British people, acknowledging the fact that France had left the field and that Britain now stood alone: "Let us brace ourselves to our duty and so bear ourselves that if the British Empire and its Commonwealth should last for a thousand years, men will still say: 'This was their finest hour.'"[27]

Although there is no direct evidence confirming discussions between Hopkins and FDR at Hyde Park about the third term, the subject must have come up. Less than a week later Hopkins was in Chicago, the site of the Democratic convention, to discuss arrangements with Mayor Edward Kelly. According to Sherwood, "Hopkins was now moving to take charge of the third term nomination himself."[28] With the survival of Western civilization at stake and anti-interventionist sentiment running high—Congress had just banned sales of military equipment to any foreign power unless deemed "nonessential" to national defense[29]—it was virtually certain that Roosevelt had decided he would run for a third term and that he had conveyed his intention, at least implicitly, to Hopkins. Roosevelt was well aware that Hopkins had a number of detractors in the Democratic Party. But he chose him to organize the draft on site because he had cultivated a large network of influential politicians throughout the United States. During his years dispensing work relief funds during the Depression, Hopkins had done favors for many of the powerful big-city bosses, not only Ed Kelly of Chicago but also Frank Hague of Jersey City, Tom Pendergast of Kansas City, Ed Flynn of the Bronx, and the mayors of San Francisco, Pittsburgh, and St. Louis. In addition, through his work for the WPA, he had befriended several Democratic state governors as well as a number of New Deal congressmen and senators.

By the time Frances Perkins, Harold Ickes and other New Dealers arrived in Chicago for the start of the convention in mid-July, Hopkins was already ensconced in suite 308/309 at the Blackstone Hotel and had a direct line to the White House installed in the bathroom.[30] He had with him petitions signed by congressmen and labor unions urging the president to run and a letter handwritten by Roosevelt on yellow lined paper asking Speaker of the House Will Bankhead, the temporary chairman of the convention, to convey the following message to the delegates:

> When you speak to the Convention on Monday evening will you say something for me which I believe ought to be made utterly clear?
>
> You and my other close friends have known and understood that I have not today and have never had any wish or purpose to remain in the office of the President, or indeed anywhere in public office after next January.
>
> You know and all my friends know that this is a simple and sincere fact. I want you to repeat this simple and sincere fact to the Convention.[31]

This was, of course, a monumentally disingenuous statement. "Friends" who believed the president had no "wish or purpose" to serve another four years were virtually nonexistent.

On the eve of the Democratic convention, the survival of Great Britain was in grave danger. Hitler issued Directive No. 16, later known as "Operation Sea Lion," to his forces arrayed along the Channel facing England, instructing them to prepare for the invasion.[32] Churchill, in a radio address to the nation, sought to strengthen the resolve of the English people, declaring, "We await the impending assault. We shall seek no terms, we shall tolerate no parley."[33]

The Democratic National Convention opened on Monday, July 15, 1940, and for the next thirty-six hours confusion reigned. Some delegates resented Hopkins for trying to control the process and were appalled at his abrasive and imperious attitude.[34] Listening to the proceedings on the radio at Val-Kill, her cottage in Hyde Park, Eleanor Roosevelt remarked, "Harry seems to be making all his usual mistakes. He doesn't seem to know how to make people happy."[35] On Tuesday evening the substance of the president's handwritten statement was read to the delegates. At first they sat for what seemed like fifteen seconds in shocked silence. Then, from loudspeakers all over the hall, a powerful baritone boomed, "We want Roosevelt! We want Roosevelt!" The chant was picked up on cue by Mayor Kelly's supporters, spread quickly across the convention floor, and flowed up into the grandstands. The owner of the baritone voice was Thomas Garry, the mayor's leather-lunged superintendent of sewers, who was speaking into a microphone from a tiny room in the basement of Chicago Stadium. By midnight the next day, Roosevelt, who had received 946 votes on the first round of balloting to Bill Farley's 72, was renominated by acclamation.[36]

If the convention had ended at this point, an exhausted and bruised Hopkins could have taken some solace in the success of the "Draft Roosevelt" movement. However, Roosevelt quickly presented him and the delegates with an even more difficult challenge. In a sharp departure from the accepted practice of the time, Roosevelt insisted on choosing his own running mate rather than letting the convention delegates dictate the choice. His choice was Henry Wallace, his formerly Republican agriculture secretary, a seed corn scientist and boomerang-throwing religious mystic who was popular in the farm belt, where isolationism was strong. Because Wallace was not regarded as a loyal Democrat, party regulars came close to defying Roosevelt and staging a revolt. Hopkins tried to change Roosevelt's mind, urging him to select Supreme Court Associate Justice William O. Douglas.[37] Roosevelt remained adamant, however, and even dictated a statement to be delivered to the delegates, saying he would not accept the nomination if the convention rejected Wallace.[38] Hopkins got the message and, with the help of Senator James "Jimmy" Byrnes of South Carolina and Assistant Secretary of Agriculture Paul Appleby, frantically worked the delegates to vote for Wallace.

However, were it not for Eleanor Roosevelt, Wallace might not have prevailed and the president might have declined to accept the nomination. At the urging of Frances Perkins and with the enthusiastic approval of Jim Farley, chairman of both the convention and the Democratic Party, Mrs. Roosevelt left Val-Kill on a chartered plane to Chicago, arriving in the early evening on Thursday, before the voting on Wallace began. When she appeared on the platform before the convention, the audience stood and roared its approval. She began:

> This is no ordinary time. No time for weighing anything except
> what we can best do for the country as a whole. No man who is a
> candidate or who is president can carry this situation alone. This is
> only carried by a united people who love their country and who will
> live for it to the fullest of their ability, with the highest ideals, with
> a determination that their party shall be absolutely devoted to the
> good of the nation as a whole.[39]

According to the *New York Daily News*, Mrs. Roosevelt's remarks did "more to soothe the convention bruises than all the efforts of astute Senators." When the roll was called, tempers had cooled and Wallace prevailed, garnering 627 of the convention's 1,100 votes.[40]

<hr />

After the Chicago convention, Hopkins concluded that it was time to resign as secretary of commerce and leave the administration. He had alienated many party regulars and, with the help of his numerous critics, he could see that he was becoming a political liability to the president. He was no longer regarded as a champion of the poor and unemployed, and his illness had prevented him from accomplishing anything noteworthy in the Commerce Department. On August 22 he submitted his formal letter of resignation, which the president accepted "only in its official sense," declaring, "Our friendship will and must go on as always." In a touching handwritten note, Hopkins spoke from the heart to the president about his days in the administration:

> I think of the things that have made my years with you the happiest time of my life. The first exciting days—the exultation of being part of government—our first formal dinner in the White House when I met [Supreme Court Associate Justice] Cardozo and another [when Attorney General] Bob Jackson tried to sell me some old underwear. . . . Then there were those old cigarettes in my pocket—it seems to me in all decency you should forget that one.
>
> And one day you went to church with me when the going wasn't so good—and life seemed ever so dark. . . .
>
> And there was always New Year's Eve—and the warm glow of Auld Lang Syne—with champagne. That's about the only time we get champagne around your house. . . .
>
> And one day two nice people came to visit you—he was a king— and I hope will be for a long time and she was a Scotch girl who got to be a Queen. And after dinner that night you and Missy and I talked it all over til 2 a.m. . . .
>
> All these things I think of—and Mac and Steve and Tommy and Ben and Felix and Sam and Missy—I know they are important because I remember them—and they are good.
>
> This letter is simply to say that I have had an awfully good time— and to thank you very much. And by the way—my weather bureau tells me that it will be fair tomorrow.[41]

Having gone off the government payroll and with no visible means of financial support, Hopkins moved out of the White House and rented a one-bedroom apartment at the Essex House, overlooking Central Park in New York, which is where Diana "gained first-hand experience of Harry's fortissimo snoring."[42] To a close friend from his days in the WPA who asked what it was like to be a "has-been," Hopkins replied, "Maybe it's all over now, but the son of a harness maker did make the cabinet of Franklin D. Roosevelt. That's the thing they can't take away from me. And it's also a pretty good answer to those who say democracy doesn't work."[43]

Sherwood wrote, not very convincingly, that Hopkins made this move to New York because he was planning to work at the presidential library that was being built in Hyde Park and "to do some writing on the side."[44] The much more likely explanation is that Roosevelt had asked him to work behind the scenes on the fall campaign, away from Washington and the White House. It is also likely that the Roosevelts arranged through friends and supporters for Hopkins to receive financial assistance so that he could pay for his expensive apartment and his lavish lifestyle while at the same time provide some support to Ethel and his three boys as well as his daughter, who that fall was attending boarding school in Deerfield, Massachusetts.[45]

Hopkins soon emerged as a key campaign operative, functioning as an organizer and one of Roosevelt's principal speechwriters. On a Sunday in late August he was at a party on Long Island with Sherwood, whom he had known since 1938. In his typical confrontational way, Hopkins cornered Sherwood and asked, "What are you warmongers up to?" He was referring to Sherwood's membership in William Allen White's pro-interventionist committee and suggesting that White's group was undermining FDR's re-election campaign. (White, who spoke at Hopkins's graduation, was both an influential journalist and a prominent progressive.) Sherwood launched into an impassioned argument about the dangers of isolationism and the reasons why Great Britain and other nations fighting fascism should be supported by the United States. Hopkins, impressed by Sherwood's command of the issues, grinned and said, "All right then—why do you waste your breath shouting at *me*? Why don't you get out and say these things to the people?"[46]

In early October Hopkins invited Sherwood to his Essex House apartment. As Sherwood later wrote, Hopkins looked at him "sharply" and said that the president was giving a speech on Columbus Day about Hitler, whose defeat he thought the most important issue facing the world. "What do you think the President ought to say?" he asked. At first, as Sherwood recalled, he was "flabbergasted." They talked for a while and then Hopkins abruptly said, "Come on—Let's go and see Sam Rosenman," who lived in a cluttered apartment a few blocks away on Central Park West.[47] From that point on, through the end of the Roosevelt administration, Sherwood, Rosenman, and Hopkins would be FDR's wordsmiths, the trio who worked closely with Roosevelt and wrote many of his greatest speeches.

As Hopkins became immersed in the campaign and pulled together the speechwriting team, the threats to American peace and security increased dramatically. The first serious attacks on England began in early July 1940, the precursor to an invasion of the British Isles by the Germans. The Battle of Britain, as the air war over Great Britain was called, had begun. At first the bombing runs by the Luftwaffe concentrated on coastal defenses, airfields, and other purely military targets. Then, in late August, the Germans bombed the cities of Birmingham, Liverpool, and Bristol. A few bombs fell on London, but it wasn't until after Churchill retaliated by ordering bombing raids on Berlin that Hitler decided to concentrate on central London and the civilian populations of other cities. In a speech at the Sportpalast in Berlin, Hitler promised the audience that the invasion of England would take place, saying, "Don't worry, we're coming." His voice rising, he thundered, "If they attack our cities, we will wipe out theirs."[48]

On September 7, 1940, the Blitz began. It would last until the following April and include not only London but other cities throughout England and Scotland. Forty-three thousand civilians were killed during the Blitz. Millions of Americans listened to nightly radio broadcasts from London by Edward R. Murrow and others covering the attacks and devoured newspaper reports and photographs. Americans overwhelmingly supported aid to Great Britain, but even more overwhelmingly they did not want their country to send troops to die fighting the Germans in another European war.

On the other side of the world Japan was on the march, and the odds had increased that the United States would be faced with a two-front war. In its quest to continue building an empire in East Asia following its victory over Romanov Russia in 1905, Japan occupied Manchuria in 1931–32 and launched a brutal invasion of eastern China in 1937. However, after three years of war, the Japanese army failed to quell Chinese resistance in the vast interior of the country and a stalemate ensued. In July 1940 the civilian government of Japan was brought down by a military-dominated regime that vowed to finish the war in China and end dependence on foreign imports of oil, rice, rubber, tin, iron, and steel, especially oil from the United States.[49]

The new government in Tokyo was emboldened by events in Europe and sought to weaken the hold of the British, French, and Dutch empires on their resource-rich colonies in Southeast Asia. Exerting pressure on the British, who were preoccupied with the Germans, and on the weak Vichy government in France, the Japanese forced closures of the British-controlled Burma Road into China and the French Indochina border with China, thus cutting supplies to Chiang Kai-shek's government forces inside China. Since the United States continued to support the Nationalist government of China and it appeared that the Japanese were going to make further moves on European colonies in Southeast Asia, the Roosevelt administration imposed what it thought were "slap on the wrist" restrictions on the sale of high-octane aviation gasoline and certain premium grades of iron and steel scrap to Japan. These restrictions motivated the new Japanese government to step up its efforts to replace U.S. imports. On September 23, 1940, the Vichy government allowed the Japanese army to occupy the northern part of French Indochina, thus aiding Japan's strategy to replace imports from the United States. A few days later Roosevelt banned all exports of iron and steel to Japan and announced a $100 million loan to China.[50] In addition to sanctions on imports, he believed that basing the U.S. fleet in Pearl Harbor would act as a deterrent to Japanese aggression in the Far East. The commander of the fleet, Admiral James Richardson, strongly disagreed and traveled to Washington to urge that the fleet be returned to the West Coast, where his ships "could be better prepared for war."

In meetings with Roosevelt in the White House more than a year before the Pearl Harbor attack, Richardson told the president that his command was not prepared for war and that its presence in Hawaii would not deter Japanese actions. FDR responded, "Despite what you believe, I know that the presence of the fleet in the Hawaiian area has had, and is now having, a restraining influence on the actions of Japan."[51]

On September 27, 1940, Japan announced that it had signed the Tripartite Pact, in which it recognized the leadership of Germany and Italy (the Berlin-Rome Axis) in the establishment of a new order in Europe and those two nations recognized Japan's hegemony in Greater East Asia. Thereafter the three nations were often referred to as the Axis powers. Under the Pact, a complete surprise to the United States, the three powers agreed to "assist one another with all political, economic and military means" if one of the parties should be attacked by a third party who was not then at war, a provision obviously aimed at the United States.[52] By threatening a two-front war, the agreement was designed to deter the United States from entering the European war to aid the beleaguered British or from taking action in Asia to halt Japanese aggression.

"I'm fighting mad," Roosevelt told Ickes on October 17, 1940.[53] He was referring to speeches by his Republican opponent, Wendell Willkie, portraying him as a warmonger. Willkie was telling audiences, "You may expect war by April, 1941, if he [Roosevelt] is elected."[54] Gallup polls were showing that FDR's commanding lead was slipping. Italian, German, and Irish voters, mainstays of Roosevelt and the Democrats, were starting to defect.[55] "This fellow Willkie is about to beat the Boss," fretted Hopkins.[56] The president's appearance at a War Department ceremony to select the first number under the Selective Service Act, in which 800,000 men would be drafted into the army, increased Hopkins's distress.[57] So, on October 18, the White House announced that the president would make a series of speeches in the final days of the campaign to correct Republican misstatements (they consciously avoided using Willkie's name).

Hopkins and his speechwriting team of Sherwood and Rosenman were on the train with Roosevelt for the final push. Riding slowly through New

England, Hopkins handed FDR a telegram from Ed Flynn, chair of the Democratic Party, pleading with the president to assure the voters that he had no intention of going to war. As Sherwood wrote, the president pushed back, saying, "It's in the Democratic platform and I've repeated it a hundred times." Sherwood responded, "I know it, Mr. President, but they don't seem to have heard you the first time."[58] This gave birth to the words inserted into Roosevelt's Boston Garden speech five days before the election, words that would dog him until the Pearl Harbor attack: "And while I am talking to you mothers and fathers, I give you one more assurance. I have said this before, but I shall say it again and again and again: Your boys are not going to be sent into any foreign wars."[59]

On election night, November 5, 1940, Hopkins was in Hyde Park at Springwood (often called "the Big House"), which was crowded with family and guests, the president having staked out a place at the cluttered dining-room table within hearing distance of a radio and news tickers. Hopkins, Sherwood, and a few others were in Hopkins's bedroom upstairs, listening to a cheap radio and tallying the results as they came in. At first Willkie was holding leads in large Democratic strongholds and Hopkins "seemed really worried," recalled Sherwood.[60] However, by nine o'clock the big industrial states were going for Roosevelt, and by midnight it became clear that Roosevelt had won an unprecedented third term by a large margin. With a huge voter turnout (62.5 percent of the electorate), the final returns showed that Roosevelt had captured 55 percent of the popular vote and in the Electoral College was given 449 votes to Willkie's 82. The Democrats picked up six seats in the House and lost three in the Senate (although they still had a 2–1 majority).[61]

Among the many congratulatory messages was one Roosevelt received from Churchill as the bombs rained on London:

I did not think it right for me as a Foreigner to express my opinion upon American politics while the election was on, but now I feel you will not mind my saying that I prayed for your success. Things are afoot which will be remembered for as long as the English language is spoken in any quarter of the globe. In expressing the comfort I feel that the people of the United States have once again cast these great burdens upon you, I must avow my faith that the lights by which we steer will bring us all safely to anchor.[62]

In the days after the election, Hopkins traveled to Grinnell to attend the funeral of Rome Hopkins, his ne'er-do-well brother who couldn't hold a job and had been constantly borrowing money from him and others. Hopkins spent Thanksgiving weekend with Averell and Marie Harriman and an assortment of actors, literati, and polo and croquet players at Arden, their forty-bedroom, twenty-thousand-acre estate on the edge of the Catskills,[63] while Roosevelt, in Washington and Hyde Park, was inundated by news of Great Britain's deepening plight. Nightly bombing raids over its cities continued to increase in number and ferocity. Civilian casualties skyrocketed. More than five hundred British merchant ships, the lifeline to the island, were sent to the bottom of the Atlantic by German U-boats, surface vessels, and aircraft.[64] What's more, the British Treasury was almost empty, having been drained by the "cash up front" requirements of the U.S. Neutrality Act. Great Britain's financial predicament was brought to a head when Lord Lothian, its ambassador to the United States, upon landing at LaGuardia Field on November 23 on a flight from London, told newsmen, most undiplomatically, "Well boys, Britain's broke; it's your money we want."[65]

This flippant comment angered the president. He thought Lothian was trying to pressure him into asking Congress to drop the cash-and-carry provisions of the Neutrality Act, which, as he had reluctantly concluded, was the only way he could legally continue to provide supplies to Great Britain. As always, Roosevelt did not like to be pressured. He was not ready to risk a confrontation with the isolationists and anti-interventionists on Capitol Hill. Instead he stepped out of the Washington pressure cooker, as he often did during his years as president. Gathering his pals Harry the Hop, Pa Watson, and Doc McIntire and his newest pal, Fala, a Scottish terrier puppy given to him by his cousin Margaret "Daisy" Suckley, FDR departed the capital on December 3 for two weeks in the Caribbean aboard the heavy cruiser *Tuscaloosa*. Publicly the cruise was to inspect base sites, but the real purpose was restorative—sunshine, fishing, occasional visitors (e.g., the Duke of Windsor), Cuban cigars (from Guantánamo), and poker and movies at night.[66] "I didn't know for quite a while what he was thinking about, if anything," recalled Hopkins. "But then I began to get the idea he was refueling, the way he so often does when he seems to be resting and carefree."[67]

On December 9 a Navy seaplane splashed down alongside the *Tuscaloosa* and delivered to the president a four-thousand-word letter by Churchill, "one of the most important of my life," Churchill later said. The letter began with a masterful review of the entire war situation. As the prime minister had known since late September from decoded German General Staff messages,[68] the danger of a German invasion of England "had very greatly receded," but he warned of a "long, gradually maturing danger, less sudden and less spectacular, but equally deadly." The "mortal danger," wrote Churchill, emanated from the increasing destruction of supply ships by German sea and air attacks, which would cripple Britain's ability to continue the fight. To meet this danger, he requested "the gift, loan or supply of a large number of American vessels of war, above all destroyers," along with an extension of U.S. "sea control of the American side of the Atlantic." Churchill tried to assure Roosevelt that such a "decisive act of constructive non-belligerency" would not cause the Germans to declare war on America: "[Hitler] does not want to be drawn into a war with the United States until he has gravely undermined the power of Great Britain. His maxim is 'one at a time.'" Regarding "the question of finance," Churchill concluded:

> The moment approaches when we shall no longer be able to pay
> cash for shipping and other supplies. While we will do our utmost,
> and shrink from no proper sacrifice to make payments across
> the Exchange, I believe you will agree that it would be wrong in
> principle and mutually disadvantageous in effect if at the height of
> the struggle Great Britain were to be divested of all saleable assets,
> so that after victory was won with our blood, civilization saved, and
> the time gained for the United States to be fully armed against all
> eventualities, we should stand stripped to the bone.[69]

Hopkins told the prime minister later that the president "read and re-read" the letter, sitting alone on the deck in a place protected from the wind. With his flair for the dramatic, Churchill wrote that Roosevelt was "plunged in intense thought, and brooded silently."[70] On the evening of December 11, two days after receiving the letter, FDR shared with Hopkins the basic concept of what would become known as lend-lease. "He suddenly came out with it—the whole program," said Hopkins. "He didn't seem to have any clear idea of how it could be done legally. But there wasn't any doubt in his mind that he'd find a way to do it."[71] The "it" was a simple idea: America would lend war matériel to the British with the understanding that they wouldn't have to pay for anything until after the war.

Hopkins's accounts of the origins of lend-lease, conveyed later to Sherwood and Churchill, downplayed his own role and gave all of the credit to Roosevelt for coming up with the basic concept. Warren Kimball, a highly respected historian, suggests that Hopkins's account "seems implausible" and that the two of them, given their close working relationship, must have devised the proposal together.[72]

The next day, December 11, Roosevelt learned that Lord Lothian, the British ambassador who had so recently kindled his anger, had died suddenly, his last public words promising victory over the Germans but *only* if the Americans provided aid to the British *now*. Since Roosevelt had recently accepted with relief and hidden pleasure the resignation of Joe Kennedy, the U.S. ambassador to the Court of St. James, who for some time was predicting defeat of the British and advocating peace negotiations with the Germans, this meant that each country lacked an ambassador to the other.[73] Thus as FDR was weighing the risks of lending war matériel to Britain and protecting its ships on the high seas, he also must have begun thinking about how to get a reliable assessment of Churchill: his political standing, his commitment to fight to the end, and his ability to lift the morale of the British people. Lothian was dead; Kennedy was unreliable and dangerous. Roosevelt needed eyes and ears in London. It was therefore perfectly plausible, as Forrest Davis and Ernest Lindley write, that while still on the *Tuscaloosa* cruise Roosevelt considered sending Hopkins to London to make the assessment, but then changed his mind.[74]

———

Back in the White House, Hopkins worked with Roosevelt to shape the rationale and find the words to convince the public and Congress to support the idea of leasing or lending to Great Britain that portion of America's productive capacity that would best serve its own security interests.[75] At the president's press conference on December 17, all of the evidence indicates it was Roosevelt, not Hopkins, who actually constructed the "neighborly analogy" and came up with the simple words that foreshadowed victory for congressional approval of lend-lease,[76] albeit after months of bitter debate. Explaining to the White House press corps that armaments and other war materials produced in the United States would be much more useful to its defense if they were used by Great Britain instead of being "kept in storage here," the President then said:

> Now, what I am trying to do is eliminate the dollar sign. That is something brand new in the thoughts of everybody in this room, I think—get rid of the silly, foolish, old dollar sign.
>
> Well, let me give you an illustration. Suppose my neighbor's home catches fire, and I have a length of garden hose four or five hundred feet away. If he can take my garden hose and connect it up with his hydrant, I may help him put out his fire. Now what do I do? I don't say to him, "Neighbor, my garden hose cost me fifteen dollars; you have to pay me fifteen dollars for it." No! I don't want fifteen dollars. I want my garden hose after the fire is over.[77]

Beginning on Christmas day and continuing until the evening of December 29, Hopkins, Sherwood, and Rosenman labored on draft after draft of a fireside chat in which Roosevelt would seek to persuade the public that in order to avoid sending American boys to fight in Europe or Asia, "we must become the great arsenal of democracy."[78] The "arsenal of democracy" speech, as it became known, moved public opinion. By early January of 1941, a Gallup poll showed 68 percent of Americans favored lend-lease.[79]

Sherwood and others credited Hopkins with providing FDR with the words "arsenal of democracy," and it may be true that he was the one who plucked them from some article or speech. However, the phrase had been previously coined by Jean Monnet, a wealthy French banker whose family were cognac merchants, and passed on to Supreme Court Associate Justice Felix Frankfurter and Assistant Secretary of War John J. McCloy.[80]

During the week after Christmas, Hopkins brought up the subject of traveling to London to assess Churchill, which Roosevelt had likely briefly considered on the *Tuscaloosa*. Sensing high adventure and a new challenge, Hopkins desperately wanted to go. Roosevelt again demurred, claiming he needed Hopkins in Washington to work on the State of the Union speech and his third inaugural address and to help him with the lend-lease battle looming in Congress. Hopkins resorted to the back door, enlisting the support of Frankfurter and LeHand. Still Roosevelt resisted, concerned that Hopkins might not get on with Churchill.[81]

The year 1940 ended with Hopkins moving back into his room in the White House and working on the president's State of the Union message. He was paid no salary. He had no title. Nightly radio broadcasts were reporting that thousands of fires ignited by Luftwaffe bombs continued to burn in London. The bells in the steeple of Christopher Wren's St. Bride's Church, built after the Great Fire of 1666, had melted. The medieval Guildhall was destroyed.[82] From the roof of the Air Ministry, Arthur Harris, at the time deputy chief of the Air Staff, could see the dome of St. Paul's above the flames. "They are sowing the wind," he said.[83] On New Year's Eve Churchill wrote from No. 10 Downing Street, "Remember, Mr. President, we do not know what you have in mind, or exactly what the United States is going to do, and we are fighting for our lives."[84]

4

The Right Man

On Friday morning, January 3, 1941, Hopkins was in his frayed bathrobe working in his room at the White House on what would become known as the Four Freedoms speech, the historic State of the Union message in which FDR lifted the hopes of millions in America and around the globe by envisioning "a world founded upon the four essential freedoms": freedom of speech, freedom to worship, freedom from want, and freedom from fear.[1] According to Sherwood, Steve Early called Hopkins that morning from the West Wing to congratulate him.

"On what?" responded Hopkins.

"Your trip!" said Early.

"What trip?"

"Your trip to England," said Early. "The President just announced it at his press conference."[2]

Meeting with the press downstairs, the president told the reporters crowded around his desk that he "was asking Harry Hopkins to go over [to England] as [his] personal representative," and he would leave "very soon."

FDR added, with emphasis, that Hopkins wouldn't have a title, nor would he have a special mission or powers. In fact, however, Hopkins was given at least two specific assignments. First, he was to assess whether the British people and their government, with aid from the United States, could withstand the attacks from air and sea and eventually prevail over the Germans. Second, without committing the nation to anything specific, especially while the lend-lease legislation was pending in Congress, Hopkins was to convey to Churchill the sense that America would support Great Britain as it fought the Nazis. The president told the reporters that Hopkins would not be on the government payroll, although he joked, "I suppose they will pay his expenses—probably on a per diem, not very large." Downplaying the importance of Hopkins's mission, Roosevelt said, "He's just going over to say 'How do you do?' to a lot of my friends" and would be talking "to Churchill like an Iowa farmer." Asked by a reporter whether Hopkins would be named the new ambassador to Great Britain, Roosevelt said, "You know Harry isn't strong enough [well enough] for that job."[3]

Hopkins's ambitious friend, Averell Harriman, pleaded with Hopkins to take him along. "Let me carry your bag, Harry. I've met Churchill several times and I know London intimately."[4] Hopkins put him off, telling him that the president wanted him to travel alone, although he suggested that FDR "might have something" for him after he returned from London.[5]

It is doubtful that Hopkins was actually surprised by the president's announcement; however, it makes for a good story. Within the next twenty-four hours he had a series of face-to-face prep meetings that likely had been scheduled before the president's press conference. On the afternoon of January 3, he met with Secretary of State Cordell Hull for forty-five minutes and then had a "long talk" with Jean Monnet. Monnet, astute and well-connected, had fled France and was temporarily assigned to the British Purchasing Commission. He told Hopkins not to waste time on the various ministers in the British government. "Churchill *is* the British War Cabinet and no one else matters," he advised. Hopkins, revealing his social worker bias against Churchill's conservative domestic policies and zealous advocacy of British imperialism, listened to Monnet and then replied,

"I suppose Churchill is convinced he is the greatest man in the world!" Felix Frankfurter, who had arranged the meeting with Monnet, admonished Hopkins. "Harry—if you're going to London with that chip on your shoulder, like a damned little small-town chauvinist, you may as well cancel your passage right now."[6]

On Saturday Hopkins met with Nevile Butler, acting head of the British Embassy in Washington, telling him that the president wanted him to obtain from Churchill and others during his visit "pretty precise" estimates of the types and numbers of ships, aircraft, munitions, and other war matériel actually needed by the British. "The president's chief desire," said Hopkins, was to convey to the British that as a matter of self interest the United States intends to provide all of the armaments needed to "enable Great Britain to beat Hitler."[7] Hopkins was making sure that Butler clearly understood what the president wanted him to achieve during the trip so that Butler could alert Churchill in advance by cable, which he promptly did.

To make sure that Churchill made the best impression on Hopkins, Frankfurter spoke to his friend Richard Casey, Australia's ambassador to the United States, and asked him to let Churchill know that Hopkins was coming to London as Roosevelt's alter ego and he should be treated with the greatest candor, respect, and goodwill, as if he were Roosevelt himself. Frankfurter told Casey that Hopkins was under the impression that Churchill did not regard Roosevelt as a great statesman and that therefore the prime minister would be well advised to disabuse Hopkins of this impression and to repeatedly indicate that he had the highest esteem for the president.[8]

That evening Hopkins had a long talk with the president about his forthcoming trip. On Sunday, having packed for a two-week trip, Hopkins boarded the train to New York. There he met Joe Kennedy in his suite at the Waldorf to pump him for information about Churchill and the other British officials he would be seeing. In addition he tried his best to convince Kennedy to support the lend-lease legislation that would shortly be considered by Congress. (In his altogether confusing testimony before Congress on January 31, Kennedy essentially opposed H.R. 1776, the lend-lease bill.)[9] Kennedy did not have a high opinion of Hopkins, commenting in his diary,

"I don't think Hopkins is any regular man," which in the parlance of the day essentially meant that he thought Hopkins was not the right man to meet with Churchill.[10]

Early Monday morning, January 6, Hopkins was surrounded by reporters as he waited on the wooden dock in New York with his daughter (who had come down from boarding school) and two of his sons (David and Stephen) to board the Pan American "Yankee Clipper" at the LaGuardia marine terminal on Bowery Bay. The trip had been arranged by Juan Trippe, the legendary CEO of Pan Am, who personally drove Hopkins to the terminal. The Clipper was a long-range flying boat, one of the largest aircraft of the day.

Three days later, after hopping from Bermuda to the Azores and then changing to a British Overseas Airways plane in Lisbon, Hopkins arrived at Poole Bay on England's south coast, seventy miles from London, so exhausted and ill that he could not unbuckle his seatbelt and disembark along with the other passengers. Brendan Bracken, the parliamentary private secretary to the prime minister and one of Churchill's closest friends, had been sent to meet the plane and was alarmed when he saw Hopkins, looking pale and skeletal, feverish dark eyes glittering, as he lay back in his seat in a state of collapse.

It took some time, but Hopkins rallied, and he and the greeting party boarded the special train of Pullmans, complete with white-gloved conductors, that Churchill had arranged to transport the very special American visitor to London. As the train rolled through the coastal towns of Poole, Bournemouth, and Southampton, Hopkins could see the bomb damage along the tracks. Leaving the coast, the train picked up speed, angling to the northeast through rural Hampshire. Peering through the window at the darkening countryside and slowly gathering energy, Hopkins asked Bracken, "Are you going to let Hitler take these fields from you?" Bracken of course replied, "No," but it was the opening of a conversation in which Hopkins probed the depth of Britain's commitment to defeat the Germans and at the same time revealed his own.[11] Bracken, who had met Hopkins several years earlier "on the Long Island croquet-playing circuit,"[12] was impressed by his honesty, quick wit, and blunt manner of speaking. By the time the train pulled into Waterloo Station at 7 p.m., having passed over a patch of tracks that had recently been bombed by hundreds of incendiaries, Bracken was "sold" on Harry Hopkins.[13]

Hopkins was met at the station by Herschel Johnson, chargé d'affaires at the American Embassy, whose driver carefully drove them through the blackout to Claridge's Hotel, the elegant red-brick establishment in Mayfair. Hopkins wanted to learn as much as he could from Johnson and others before facing Churchill, so he begged off the prime minister's dinner invitation, claiming he was too tired from the long trip. To the muffled sound of antiaircraft guns banging away in Hyde Park, he dined with Johnson in the latter's room at Claridge's. According to Sherwood, by the end of dinner Johnson was "heartened by the sincerity and intensity of Harry Hopkins' determination to gain firsthand knowledge of Britain's needs and of finding a way to fill them." Unlike others who had come from America, skeptical of whether "the British really needed the things they were asking for," Hopkins "wanted to find out if they were asking for *enough* to see them through. . . . He made [Johnson] feel that the first real assurance of hope had at last come—and he acted on the British like a galvanic needle."[14] After dinner General Raymond Eliot Lee, the embassy's military attaché, was invited to join the two of them in Johnson's room. Lee, a cultured man with close ties to the British intelligence establishment, wore Savile Row suits instead of his uniform because, as a neutral observer, he was not permitted to appear in uniform in London. Only five days earlier Lee had condescendingly characterized Hopkins in his journal as an "obscure social worker" who was "not a success" as head of WPA and "of no consequence" as secretary of commerce. Yet in a journal entry following a conversation with Hopkins that lasted until 12:45 a.m., Lee wrote approvingly, "Hopkins is quiet, unassuming, and very much to the point." In their conversation Hopkins agreed with Lee that lend-lease should be sold not as "a 'Help Britain' Proposition" but as the best and quickest way to defeat Hitler, a matter of paramount importance to the security of the United States.[15]

Hopkins's first appointments the next morning, Friday, January 10, were in his rooms at Claridge's: a briefing on the grim military situation by Admiral Robert Lee Ghormley, U.S. naval attaché, and General Lee. He was then driven to the Foreign Office for courtesy visits with Foreign Secretary Anthony Eden (Hopkins's first impression: "suave, impeccable, unimportant") and the permanent undersecretary, Sir Alexander Cadogan ("seems simple and nice"), followed by a more substantive meeting with Lord Halifax, the newly appointed British ambassador to the United States, who would leave the following week for America aboard a British battleship. In his first longhand report to Roosevelt, written that night on Claridge's stationery, Hopkins observed, "[Though Halifax is] a hopeless Tory—that isn't too important now if we can but get on with our business of licking Hitler. I would not like to see him have much to say about a later peace—I should like to have Eden say less."[16]

At around one o'clock on Friday afternoon, Hopkins arrived at the front door of No. 10 Downing Street, the prime minister's residence, where he was met by Brendan Bracken, who showed him around the "old and delightful" house. Because workmen were repairing windows on the main and upper floors that had been blown out by bombs, Bracken led Hopkins to a small dining room in the basement and left him with a glass of sherry to await the prime minister. As Hopkins wrote that night to Roosevelt, "A rotund—smiling—red faced, gentleman appeared—extended a fat but none the less convincing hand and wished me welcome to England . . . with a clear eye and a mushy voice." These were Hopkins's first impressions of Winston Churchill. The two sat down to a simple lunch of soup, cold beef, green salad, and cheese, accompanied by light wine and port. They talked for three hours.

Churchill held forth on the war situation as only he could, ranging from the sweep of events in North Africa, Spain, Greece, and Suez to the details of Britain's coastal defenses designed to repel an invasion by the Germans, an invasion that he doubted Hitler would attempt. Foreshadowing the profound differences that would divide the British and Americans on military strategy, Churchill told Hopkins that with the help of America, British air power will doom "Germany with all her armies" and "that this war will never see great [land] forces massed against one another."[17]

According to Churchill's recollection several years later, Hopkins assured him that the president was determined that they win this war together. "Make no mistake about it. He has sent me here to tell you that at all costs and by all means he will carry you through, no matter what happens to him."[18] It is difficult to believe that Roosevelt would have expressly authorized Hopkins to make such an unconditional commitment, although it is entirely possible that Hopkins felt FDR had given him discretion to make assertions like this in order to provide Churchill with the means to head off those who wanted to negotiate an armistice with Hitler. There is no reference to these statements in Hopkins's report to the president later that evening. Perhaps these are the words that Churchill thought he heard or wanted to hear.

It is virtually certain, however, that after Hopkins explained the purpose of his mission, Churchill assured him that he would make "every detail of information and opinion available" so that Hopkins would know the "exact state of England's need and the urgent necessity of the exact material assistance Britain requires to win the war."[19] This conclusion is based not only on Hopkins's contemporaneous report to the president but also on subsequent events, when British government officials opened their files and provided Hopkins with detailed lists of what would be needed to defeat Hitler. At some point during the long luncheon with the prime minister, Hopkins casually mentioned that "there was a feeling in some quarters" that Churchill did not like Americans and in particular Roosevelt. According to Hopkins, that triggered a "fairly restrained attack" by Churchill on Joe Kennedy, who he believed was responsible for generating this false impression.[20] Hopkins also told Churchill that the president was anxious to meet with him but not until April, after lend-lease was enacted.[21] Churchill said he too was "very anxious to meet with the President face to face."[22]

Hopkins was late for a press conference at the U.S. Embassy, but when he finally arrived he charmed the British journalists with deadpan humor. Asked at the outset what he had done that day, Hopkins put on a serious face and responded, "I got up this morning about eight o'clock and took a look out the window for the weather. Then I went into the bathroom and turned on my bath and when the tub was full I got into it." He went on like this as the room erupted in laughter. He revealed nothing of substance, saying only that "he was here on urgent business of the greatest importance to both our countries."[23] But he had the working press exactly where he wanted them.

By the end of his first day in London, it was clear that Churchill and Hopkins had impressed one another and the groundwork had been laid for a critically important relationship. Reflecting on his first meeting with Hopkins, Churchill wrote in his memoirs:

> Thus I met Harry Hopkins, that extraordinary man, who played, and was to play, a sometimes decisive part in the whole movement of the war. His was a soul that flamed out of a frail and failing body. He was a crumbling lighthouse from which there shone the beams that led great fleets to harbour. He had also a gift of sardonic humour. I always enjoyed his company especially when things went ill. He could also be very disagreeable and say hard and sour things.[24]

Back at Claridge's, Hopkins, that crumbling lighthouse, remarked to General Lee that he had almost never had "such an enjoyable time as [he] had with Mr. Churchill." Then, according to Lee, Hopkins lit a cigarette and added, "But God, what a force that man has!"[25] A few days later, referring to that first meeting, Hopkins reiterated his admiring awe of Churchill to Oliver Lyttleton (later Viscount Lord Chandos), a businessman and member of the cabinet: "Jesus Christ! What a man!"[26]

Hopkins spent his second evening in London with Edward R. Murrow, CBS's famous and hugely influential chief radio correspondent in Europe who had been broadcasting nightly from London throughout the Blitz. Murrow was eager to get breaking news from Hopkins that he could then broadcast to the world. Instead Hopkins interviewed Murrow, probing for facts and informed impressions about British morale, the personalities of Churchill and other politicians, and economic conditions. When Murrow finally got a chance to ask Hopkins to describe his mission, Hopkins responded, "I suppose you could say that I've come to try to find a way to be a catalytic agent between two prima donnas. I want to get an understanding of Churchill and the men he sees after midnight." The other "prima donna," of course, was his boss, Franklin Roosevelt.[27]

That weekend Hopkins, the left-leaning son of a small-town shopkeeper and a churchgoing mother devoted to social justice, would join

Churchill and other members of the British aristocracy at Ditchley, a late seventeenth-century mansion near Woodstock, north of Oxford, one of England's great country houses. Notwithstanding the staggering demands of the war, Churchill and his cabinet usually adhered to the custom of the British upper class, leaving London most weekends by automobile for the countryside. Normally Churchill would go to Chequers, the prime minister's country residence in Buckinghamshire, but on this weekend there was a full moon. The possibility of a German bomber attack when that well-known house was illuminated by a bright moon caused his security detail to insist that Churchill stay at another location. There was no rest for Churchill at Ditchley, however. The owner, Ronald Tree, a grandson of Chicago's Marshall Field, had set aside three rooms on the ground floor that housed the prime minister's communications equipment, maps, and staff. Churchill brought the battlefront from London to Ditchley. He would do the same at Chequers.[28]

On Saturday evening, January 11, after "the ladies had left the table," Hopkins and the English gentlemen settled in the elegant candlelit dining room with their tobacco and brandy. Having been briefed on how best to handle Hopkins, Churchill launched into what Oliver Lyttleton called a "majestic monologue" in an effort to convince Hopkins that the English and Americans shared "similar views and aspirations." Speaking of British war aims, Churchill concluded:

> We seek no treasure, we seek no territorial gains, we seek only the
> right of man to be free. . . . As the humble labourer returns from his
> work when the day is done, and sees the smoke curling upwards
> from his cottage home in the serene evening sky, we wish him to
> know that no [banging] of the secret police upon his door will
> disturb his leisure or interrupt his rest. We seek government with the
> consent of the people, man's freedom to say what he will.

Addressing Hopkins, Churchill asked, "What will the president say to all this?" According to Lyttleton, who was there, Hopkins, with a keen ear for artifice, responded in his flat Midwestern accent, "Well, Mr. Prime Minister,

I don't think the President will give a dam' for all that. . . . You see, we're only interested in seeing that that Goddam sonofabitch, Hitler, gets licked."[29] Jock Colville, one of Churchill's secretaries who was also present, recalled Hopkins using similar but less colorful words. (Refusing to hear about "war aims," the president "was intent only on one end: the destruction of Hitler.")[30]

Based on everything he had been told about Hopkins and Roosevelt, Churchill was clearly trying to draw them in as brothers in arms by cleverly linking the postwar goals of the British people to the New Deal, connecting England's "humble labourer" to the "forgotten man" of the Depression. Yet Hopkins delinked this in his response and cut to the heart of the immediate and most important problem at hand: the defeat of Hitler. By all accounts, including Churchill's own, Hopkins broke through to Churchill, gaining his respect and advancing his friendship. From that point forward, Churchill would often say, "Harry Hopkins always went to the root of the matter."[31] Like Roosevelt, who was the master of the art, Hopkins possessed an unusual ability to compartmentalize and then prioritize. At Ditchley, and later when he set aside principles and red tape to rush aid to Stalin and the Russians, Hopkins focused above all on winning the war. In doing so, as one Churchill biographer said, "Hopkins quickly acquired a personal position in the Churchill court."[32]

Following a brief audience with the king and queen at Buckingham Palace, Hopkins traveled with Churchill and several others on the prime minister's private train to deliver Lord and Lady Halifax to Scapa Flow, a natural anchorage surrounded by the Orkney Islands in northern Scotland, home to the British fleet. There a new battleship, *King George V*, was waiting to take Lord Halifax and his wife to America. The battleship would also take on a special cargo consisting of several British officers, as well as the Americans General Lee and Admiral Ghormley, who would be going to Washington to engage in the secret planning of Anglo-American military strategy. On the final leg of the trip by rail into Scotland—the same day hearings began in the House of Representatives on the lend-lease bill—Hopkins shared a compartment with General Lee, who wrote in his journal that Hopkins, with "sallow skin and [a] rather crooked chin . . . listens most of the time and gives the impression of being shrewd if not sagacious . . . but now and then he breaks into forthright conversation which . . . seems quite frank."[33] Whether or not Hopkins sensed Lee's somewhat patronizing reservations, he entrusted the general with a sealed handwritten letter on small squares of Claridge's stationery and asked him to deliver it personally to President Roosevelt. In part the letter stated:

> The people here are amazing from Churchill down and if courage alone can win—the result will be inevitable. But they need our help desperately and I am sure you will permit nothing to stand in the way. Some of the ministers and underlings are a bit trying but no more than some I have seen.
>
> *Churchill* is the gov't in every sense of the word—he controls the grand strategy and often the details—labor trusts him—the army, navy, air force are behind him to a man. The politicians and upper crust pretend to like him. I cannot emphasize too strongly that he is the one and only person over here with whom you need to have a full meeting of the minds.
>
> Churchill wants to see you—the sooner the better—but I have told him of your problem until the [lend-lease] bill is passed. I am convinced this meeting between you and Churchill is essential—and soon—for the battering continues and Hitler does not wait for Congress. . . .
>
> I cannot believe that it is true that Churchill dislikes either you or America—it just doesn't make sense. . . .
>
> This island needs our help now Mr. President with everything we can give them.[34]

At Thurso, a town on the northern Scottish coast, the party boarded a minesweeper. Hopkins had brought with him two cartons of Camels, and he had purchased in London what he thought were enough warm clothes.[35] He borrowed a hat from Churchill and fur-lined boots and a sweater from Lieutenant General Hastings "Pug" Ismay. Nevertheless he was still horribly cold and generally miserable. In rough seas amid a raging blizzard, he lost his footing as he tried to jump from the minesweeper onto the heaving deck of a destroyer. Churchill, already aboard the destroyer and smoking a fat cigar, leaned over the rail and watched as Hopkins was hauled over by the scruff of his neck by a British sailor.[36] The destroyer steamed out to the home fleet riding at anchor at Scapa. Without incident, the party boarded the *King George V* for a farewell lunch in honor of Lord and Lady Halifax. Hopkins was perhaps not fully aware of it at the time, but Churchill was glad to be rid of Halifax since he had been an advocate of a negotiated peace with Hitler and a political rival.[37]

That evening, having been conveyed to the flagship *Nelson* in the admiral's barge, Hopkins and Churchill were guests of honor of Admiral Sir John Tovey, commander in chief of the fleet, who within a year would watch from the bridge as the German battleship *Bismarck* was pounded by shells from the big guns on the *Rodney* and the *George V*. Churchill's personal physician, Lord Moran, prevailed on Hopkins to stay in bed for the next two days to rest and recuperate from the bone-chilling cold while the prime minister, former first lord of the Admiralty and a lover of the Royal Navy, inspected the ships in the fleet.[38]

On the trip back to London, Churchill took full advantage of Hopkins's presence, introducing him to cheering crowds along the way as "the personal representative of the President of the United States."[39] At a dinner at the Station Hotel in Glasgow hosted by Tom Johnston, secretary of state for Scotland, Churchill called on Hopkins to say a few words. Looking thin, frail, and unkempt in his wrinkled suit and shirt, Hopkins remained seated for several seconds. He then slowly rose and turned toward the prime minister:

I suppose you wish to know what I am going to say to President Roosevelt upon my return. Well, I am going to quote you one verse from that Book of Books in the truth of which Mr. Johnston's mother and my own Scottish mother were brought up: "Whither thou goest, I will go; and where thou lodgest, I will lodge; thy people shall be my people, and thy God my God" [—He paused and added very quietly—] even to the end.[40]

By all accounts, Churchill was brought to tears. Capturing the prime minister's reaction, Lord Moran wrote, "He knew what it meant. Even to us the words seemed like a rope thrown to a drowning man."[41]

While eloquent, moving, and spoken from the heart, Hopkins's brief remarks in Glasgow, which implied that America would shortly join the British in the war, were beyond his authority and likely provided fodder for isolationists, anti-interventionists, and others in the United States who were opposing lend-lease and doing everything in their power to keep the nation out of another European war. The rallying point for the opposition was the America First Committee, founded at Yale; the brains behind it were thought to include former President Hoover; and its public spokesman and star attraction was Colonel Charles A. Lindbergh, a world famous hero for having made the first transatlantic flight from New York to Paris in 1927. On Capitol Hill the opposition to lend-lease was led by Representative Hamilton Stuyvesant Fish, FDR's Dutchess County neighbor who the Germans regarded as their ally; Senators Burton Wheeler of Montana and Hiram Johnson of California, early supporters of the New Deal who broke with Roosevelt over his court-packing scheme; and Gerald Nye of North Dakota, outspoken leader of the antiwar movement.

Hopkins's words from the Book of Ruth, which spread throughout England within a few days despite wartime censorship, gave false hope. It would be almost a year before America entered the war. Nonetheless, Hopkins had to throw the British people a lifeline; he had to convince Churchill and his government that with America's help the British would survive and defeat Germany. He may have doubted that the British could beat Germany without the United States entering the war but he knew his words would buy time for the United States to rearm and would discourage efforts in some British quarters to negotiate peace with Hitler, a deal that could have the disastrous result of neutralizing the British fleet or even turning it over to the Germans. As Hopkins was well aware, Churchill was not only beset by British pro-appeasement groups, ranging from the Communists on the far Left to theater luminaries such as George Bernard Shaw and right-wing fascists; he also had to contend with persuasive politicians within his own cabinet, notably Rab Butler, undersecretary in the Foreign Office, one of the most aggressive advocates for appeasement in the government.

Hopkins may have fudged the truth and raised false hopes but Churchill was also engaged in a delicate dance of diplomacy and hidden meanings. While quieting calls by his own countrymen for a negotiated peace, Churchill had to persuade Hopkins and his government that the British had the wherewithal to fight on alone so that the "arsenal of democracy" would continue to supply them with war matériel. At the same time, desperate to get America into the war as soon as possible, Churchill had to convey the sense that the British were in great danger of losing, with the possibility that the fleet would be captured. For this reason he never told Hopkins that he already knew from British Enigma decryptions and signals intelligence that Hitler had called off Operation Sea Lion, the German invasion of England.[42]

Hopkins and Churchill returned to London on Saturday, January 18, in a snowstorm. Although he had originally planned to stay in England for only two weeks, Hopkins asked Roosevelt for permission to stay longer in order to complete his mission. Secretary of State Hull suggested to Roosevelt that Hopkins extend his visit until the new ambassador to Great Britain, John G. "Gil" Winant, the former Republican governor of New Hampshire, was confirmed by the Senate and ready to leave for England. Roosevelt cabled Hopkins with the news that he should extend his stay, adding, "Do get some sleep."[43] Hopkins's visit ended up lasting for almost five weeks, which gave him plenty of time to deepen his relationship with Churchill and all of his cabinet ministers, undersecretaries, and military leaders, including Chief of the Imperial General Staff Sir John Dill, First Sea Lord Admiral Dudley Pound, and Chief of the Air Staff Sir Charles Portal. The extra time also enabled him to establish close contacts with heads of state of various governments in exile (e.g., the Netherlands, Norway, Poland) and to compile detailed lists of munitions and war matériel that Great Britain needed to sustain the fight.

It is likely that it was more than the completion of his important mission that motivated Hopkins to extend his stay. Though under siege, London in 1941 was the most exciting city in the Western world. It was *the* place to be—freewheeling, dangerous, cosmopolitan, uninhibited. "Sex hung in the air like a fog," wrote United Press reporter Harrison Salisbury, who would go on to win a Pulitzer Prize for his reporting in Moscow.[44] "The normal barriers to having an affair with somebody were thrown to the winds," said William Paley, head of CBS.[45] Hopkins, single but twice married, with an affinity for attractive women, "the fleshpots," and the high life, had to have been intoxicated by the hedonism that permeated the city. There are suggestions that he was "lured by the well-known charms" of Fred Cripps's wife, Violet (he was the brother of the Labour politician Sir Stafford Cripps, British ambassador to the Soviet Union) and was enchanted by the "delicious-looking" Pamela Digby Churchill, age twenty, then married to Churchill's son Randolph.[46] Later known for her affairs with powerful men, Pamela eventually married Hopkins's friend Averell Harriman when he was seventy-nine, became an American citizen, and served as the U.S. ambassador to France under President Bill Clinton. Whether or not Hopkins actually had affairs or intimate encounters—and there is no evidence that he did—there is no doubt that he was seduced by the city and that he thoroughly enjoyed himself when there.

One of the most colorful and controversial characters that Hopkins met in London was Lord Beaverbrook, minister of aircraft production in Churchill's cabinet and a ruthlessly acquisitive press baron. Although the two would later become close friends, they took an instant dislike to one another during their first meeting. Nevertheless Beaverbrook organized a dinner at Claridge's in Hopkins's honor that was attended by dozens of publishers, editors, and reporters of the leading newspapers in London and throughout the United Kingdom. According to an account of the dinner written by Percy Cudlipp of the London Daily Herald, one of the editors who was there, after the tables were cleared and the doors to the dining room had been closed, Beaverbrook stood and invited Hopkins to speak, telling him that he would be talking to "the masters of the Government," by which he meant "the leaders of the British Press."

Hopkins rose, looking lean, shy and untidy, grasping the back of his chair, and he continued to look shy throughout his speech. . . .

Hopkins told us how the President and those around him were convinced that America's world duty could be successfully performed only in partnership with Britain. He told us of the anxiety and admiration with which every phase of Britain's lonely struggle was watched from the White House, and of his own emotions as he travelled through our blitzed land. His speech left us with the feeling that although America was not yet in the war, she was marching beside us, and that should we stumble she would see that we did not fall. Above all, he convinced us that the President and the men about him blazed with faith in the future of Democracy.

After Hopkins "addressed [the group] as a whole," he went on a "slow journey around the table" and spoke to each journalist individually. "We went away content," wrote Cudlipp:

None of us British journalists who had been listening to the man from the White House was in any illusion about the peril which accompanied our island. But we were happy men all; our confidence and our courage had been stimulated by a contact which Shakespeare, in "Henry V," had a phrase: "A little touch of Harry in the night."[47]

FBI agents, already in London being tutored on homeland security by MI5 and Scotland Yard, were stationed in the adjoining coffee room at Claridge's that evening to secretly monitor the reaction to Hopkins's comments at the Beaverbrook dinner. A few days later J. Edgar Hoover, director of the FBI, reported to Roosevelt through Pa Watson, "In no instance was any unfavorable comment made and the entire gist of . . . conversations relative to Mr. Hopkins was positive and commendatory."[48] Given FDR's enthusiastic embrace of intelligence operations, and in particular his support of Hoover's FBI, it is likely that the president would have had no objection to FBI surveillance of Hopkins while he was in London. However, it is a stretch to surmise, as does the intelligence historian David Stafford, that

Roosevelt was "delighted" to know that "G-men in London were checking up on his personal emissary."[49]

                ▬▬▬▬▬▬▬▬▬▬

While he was in England, Hopkins spent three weekends at Chequers with Churchill and his family. "I think he suffered desperately from the cold at Chequers," recalled Churchill's daughter Mary (Lady Soames), who found Hopkins to be "a most curious, fascinating character." She continued, "It's a great big Elizabethan house and we all found it fairly cold. But I think Harry Hopkins must have thought it was the North Pole and, poor man, we discovered . . . he used to take refuge in the downstairs bathroom where all the hot pipes ran through. He found it very convenient to sit there in his overcoat reading all the official papers."[50] Pamela Churchill recalled Hopkins being oblivious to his health. "He would have a Scotch," but he "never seemed to eat anything," she observed. She went on to describe Hopkins as "small, shrunken, sick. . . . This large overcoat over this small man and always kind of a dead cigarette out of the side of his mouth, looking sort of like a very sad dog." But, she added, "then his face would light up and he would start talking about the war, and his purposes for being there and FDR and the whole man would change. . . . He became very determined . . . very strong. . . . If you heard him talk, you would listen with great respect."[51]

Hopkins formed an especially strong bond with Clementine, Churchill's wife, who he found to be the "most charming and entertaining of all the people he met." Mary wrote of the relationship, "My mother, who was quite a critical person, and wasn't at all prone to naturally take to people at first sight, was captivated by him. She realized how frail he was and took pains when he came to visit to make sure he had what he needed."[52] Both Churchill and Clementine came to adore Hopkins's "offbeat raffishness," "his mordant humor," and his "distinct touch in pricking the prime minister sharply but not offensively."[53]

On January 23, 1941, Charles Lindbergh testified against lend-lease in Congress, preferring, he told the House Foreign Affairs Committee, to "see a negotiated peace" between Great Britain and Nazi Germany.[54] At the same time Hopkins was meeting in London with British experts on finance, production, and shipping, sending numerous cables to Roosevelt and Secretary of State Hull, specifying the types and quantities of war matériel that the

British needed. Hopkins reduced Britain's most urgent needs to a list of items the U.S. military called "Hopkins' 14 Points."[55] At the top of the list: "10 destroyers a month beginning April 1st." Next was "the urgent need of more merchant shipping at once. British cannot wait until new ships are built."[56]

Churchill took advantage of Hopkins's extended stay to take him to Dover, where they inspected the heavy gun batteries and peered across the English Channel toward Occupied France, just twenty miles away. Hopkins heard one of the workmen mutter as Churchill walked by, clenching a wet cigar stub in his teeth, "There goes the bloody British Empire."[57] A week later they toured the bomb-damaged Portsmouth docks, where Churchill gave the "thumbs-up" to cheering workers.[58] That evening, January 31, after Hopkins and the prime minister had returned to Chequers, Hopkins produced a box of American phonograph records in the Great Hall for after-dinner entertainment. To tunes wafting across the dimly lit hall, Churchill walked about in silence, occasionally swaying to the rhythm and executing what witnesses noted were surprisingly delicate dance steps. In a letter describing the evening, Eric Seal, one of Churchill's aides, wrote, "He gets on like a house afire with Hopkins. . . . It is quite extraordinary how Hopkins [has] endeared himself to everyone here he has met."[59]

As the time for Hopkins's departure approached, Churchill arranged for him to have lunch with the king and queen at Buckingham Palace which, given Hopkins's unabashed delight in the company of the rich and well-born, was the high point of his visit. Hopkins had already had a brief formal audience with the king (during which, to his embarrassment, he had forgotten to deliver FDR's sealed letter to the king; it was delivered by messenger the next day).[60] However, this luncheon was more of a social occasion—chatty and unusually informal, partly due to the fact that an air raid alert caused the party to move to a shelter in the palace basement. In a memo to himself recounting the visit, Hopkins wrote, "If ever two people realized that Britain is fighting for its life it is these two. They realize fully that this conflict is different from the other conflicts in Britain's history and that if Hitler wins they and the British people will be enslaved for years to come."[61]

At a luncheon at the Foreign Office on Saturday, February 8, his last day in England, Hopkins declined Anthony Eden's request that the United

States join Great Britain in informing Japan that they would declare war if Japan attacked the Dutch East Indies or British territories. Eden had replaced Halifax as foreign secretary. "I am pretty sure what the President would do if Hong Kong were attacked," Hopkins told him, "but I cannot tell you about it."[62]

Hopkins spent his final afternoon and evening at Chequers, saying his goodbyes to the Churchill family and working with the prime minister on a radio address that he would be giving on the need for U.S. aid. Since the speech would be aimed at American as well as British citizens, Hopkins helped Churchill through the delicate task of drafting language that would convince Americans that the British were strong enough to fight on alone without the need for U.S. troops, but not so strong as to be able to survive without being supplied with enormous quantities of armaments and other war matériel by the United States. Both Hopkins and Churchill were delighted to learn that day that the House of Representatives had passed lend-lease by a vote of 260–165. Now it would be up to the Senate.

That night a special train took Hopkins from Chequers to Bournemouth, where he was scheduled to fly to New York via Lisbon. He bore with him massive bundles of top-secret documents, including technical materials relating to new weaponry and intelligence-gathering devices. Lieutenant Anthony McComas, a British security officer, assumed responsibility for the safekeeping of these documents and would accompany Hopkins to the United States. Foul weather delayed takeoff, so Hopkins was able to hear Churchill's speech Sunday night in the lounge of the Branksome Tower Hotel.[63] Addressing himself directly to the American people, Churchill assured them, "We shall not fail or falter; we shall not weaken or tire. Neither the sudden shock of battle, nor the long-drawn trials of vigilance and exertion will wear us down. Give us the tools and we will finish the job."[64] Notwithstanding his powerful rhetoric, Churchill knew there was little chance that the British could finish the job alone. The United States would have to enter the war.

Early the next morning, Hopkins entrusted Brendan Bracken—who had accompanied him on his departure just as he had greeted his arrival—with a farewell note, written in longhand, to be delivered to Churchill:

My dear Mr. Prime Minister—

I shall never forget these days with you—your supreme confidence and will to victory. Britain I have ever liked—I like it the more.

As I leave for America tonight I wish you great and good luck—confusion to your enemies—victory for Britain.

Ever so cordially,

Harry Hopkins[65]

After the long flight from Lisbon and down the coast of West Africa, across the Atlantic to Brazil, and then north over the Caribbean, the Pan Am Clipper splashed down amid whitecaps in Bowery Bay, Queens. Because of the wind, the flying boat had to be towed to the landing float at the LaGuardia marine terminal. As Hopkins emerged from the cabin, Gil Winant, the newly confirmed ambassador to the Court of St. James, who was waiting along with Averell Harriman to greet him, shouted, "Are they going to hold out?" Seeing the gaggle of reporters on the dock, Hopkins called out, "Of course they are."[66]

Out of earshot of the press, Hopkins was less optimistic. Meeting with Winant and Harriman at the Hotel Roosevelt in Midtown Manhattan, he told them he was convinced that the British—"about as tough a crowd as there is"[67]—would keep on fighting, but their needs were far greater than anyone in America realized. He also told them that the British had unrealistic expectations about Roosevelt's abilities and intentions. The British public believed that the president could quickly secure passage of lend-lease and that he would cause America to enter the war within a few months.

Hopkins had other concerns that he kept to himself. Had he overstated America's willingness and capacity to support the British? Did he give Churchill and his ministers the impression that it was only a matter of weeks or months before the United States would declare war on Germany and Italy? In an effort to please his British hosts, did he make statements that could be used by the opponents of lend-lease to defeat the legislation? Hopkins could well have been haunted by what happened to Colonel

Edward House, President Wilson's closest and most trusted advisor, who upon his return from armistice negotiations with the British and French in Paris after World War I was accused by Wilson of wrecking the American plan for peace. The breach ended House's public career.

Despite these worries, Hopkins had reason to be satisfied with what he had accomplished. The first and by far the most important was that he had established a relationship of trust with Churchill and the beginnings of a genuine friendship that would last until the end of his life. In the final days of Hopkins's visit, Churchill cabled FDR, "It has been a great pleasure to me to make friends with Hopkins who has been a great comfort and encouragement to everyone he has met. One can easily see why he is so close to you."[68] Reflecting on Hopkins's first trip to England, Pamela Churchill observed, "Perhaps no one, who was not there then, could fully appreciate the impact he made, especially on the great war leader who would become his friend."[69] Complimenting both Roosevelt and Hopkins, she said, "The President knew his man and he sent the right man to the right place at the right time."[70]

Hopkins had perhaps overstepped his authority, and he surely fueled Britain's unrealistic expectations. But as one with scant experience in foreign relations and military affairs, he proved intuitively gifted in the art of personal diplomacy. Scarcely six months earlier, at the Democratic convention, where he was on familiar ground and knew all of the key players, he had made "all his usual mistakes" and seemed unable to make them "happy," observed Eleanor Roosevelt. In Great Britain, faced with a host of new and unfamiliar people and problems, he had pleased virtually everyone. The pattern would repeat itself, as we shall see. Hopkins "had this marvelous ability to grow into any new situation," recalled Franklin Roosevelt Jr., "to totally dominate the details of any new situation."[71] He drew strength from confronting the new; his energy flagged when he trod old and familiar ground.

Hopkins was indeed the right man. Now both Roosevelt and Churchill, to the extent these two shrewd and worldly politicians trusted anyone, trusted Harry Hopkins. Like the king in *Henry V*, Hopkins had walked from "tent to tent" on the eve of battle. With "sweet majesty" and a "liberal eye" he thawed fear and mistrust, finding a way to bring these two great men together. "A little touch of Harry."[72]

First Glimpse of Dawn?

Hopkins arrived back in Washington as the Senate began floor debate on the lend-lease legislation. Democratic Senator Burton Wheeler, the bill's most implacable opponent, infuriated Roosevelt by calling lend-lease another "New Deal AAA foreign policy—plow under every fourth American boy." Senator Hiram Johnson, a Republican from California, simply intoned, "This bill is war."[1] Robert Hutchins, president of the University of Chicago and one of the most prominent academic leaders in the country—he had been made dean of Yale Law School at the age of twenty-eight—warned, "The American people are about to commit suicide."[2]

The opponents had the rhetoric. Roosevelt had the votes. On Saturday night, March 8, 1941, the Senate, exhausted by the lengthy and rancorous debate, passed lend-lease by a vote of 60–31. The House accepted the Senate amendments, thus obviating the need for a joint conference, and passed the amended bill by a huge bipartisan margin, 317–71, on March 11. Hopkins left a telephone message for Churchill at Chequers. When he got the news, Churchill immediately cabled Hopkins, "The strain has been serious so I thank God for your news."[3]

Entitled "An Act to Promote the Defense of the United States," the lend-lease law authorized the president to "sell, transfer title to, exchange, lease, lend, or otherwise dispose of" any munitions or defense-related item to "any country whose defense the President deems vital to the defense of the United States."[4] Critics were right when they said Roosevelt was given a blank check; his discretion was virtually unlimited. He immediately sought and quickly obtained from Congress an initial appropriation of $7 billion, candidly telling Americans to be prepared to make sacrifices in their daily lives, including longer work hours, lower profits, and higher taxes.[5] From London, Churchill touted lend-lease as "a new Magna Charta."[6]

Hopkins kept a low profile while the lend-lease legislation was being debated, but he was working behind the scenes with the president to make sure he would control administration of the program once it became law. Secretary of War Stimson proposed that the new program be administered by an executive secretary who would report to a four-person, cabinet-level committee with supervisory authority. He recommended General James Burns, a respected career officer who headed the army ordnance department, for the post. With Hopkins at his side, Roosevelt turned the perfectly reasonable Stimson proposal into one of his typical bureaucratic contrivances that guaranteed complete White House control. The four-person, cabinet-level committee would be an advisory committee, ordered Roosevelt, and he would "ask Harry Hopkins to act as Secretary of this Committee . . . because of his intimate acquaintance with the needs of Britain and his understanding of governmental relations here."[7] Thus, to the profound disgust of Hopkins's countless rivals and critics, notably House Minority Leader John Taber, lend-lease would be run out of Hopkins's bedroom in the southeastern corner of the White House.

Pundits were writing that Hopkins had returned from London "a completely changed man," "more serious" and with a "fuller sense of urgency."[8] It was perhaps accurate to observe that Hopkins seemed more driven than he had been during the previous several months working on the campaign. However, in truth he approached the present emergency with the same sense of urgency, the same zeal, and the same disdain for delay and red tape that he had exhibited when providing relief and jobs during his New Deal, New Orleans, and New York days. Instead of supplying relief to the poor and jobs to the unemployed, he was now responsible for supplying Great Britain and eventually Russia with the fruits of America's industrial strength in what Sherwood characterized as the greatest emergency "that had ever befallen the human race."[9] Hopkins was in his element. He had been facing down emergencies his entire working life. As Stimson confessed in his diary, "It is a Godsend that Harry Hopkins is at the White House."[10]

Hopkins quickly assembled a staff, recruiting the brilliant Isidore Lubin from the Labor Department to be his closest aide and arranging for a command center to be set up in the white marble confines of the new Federal Reserve Building on the Mall. Henry Morgenthau, the treasury secretary, derisively called the staff "Hopkins' bedroom boys."[11] Knowing that his friend Averell Harriman was eager to assist and was familiar with many of the principals in Churchill's government, Hopkins convinced Roosevelt to send the fifty-year-old railroad tycoon to London to coordinate all matters concerning lend-lease and other aid to Great Britain. Over a lunch in the Oval Study prepared by Florence Nesbitt, consisting of spinach soup, toast, and "three large fat pancakes," which Harriman pronounced a "most unhealthy meal," the president breezily instructed Harriman to "go over to London and recommend everything we can do, short of war, to keep the British Isles afloat."[12]

Leaving his staff behind, Hopkins accompanied the president and a party of his pals, including Attorney General Robert Jackson—who would later become a Supreme Court associate justice and the lead prosecutor at the Nuremberg trials—on the last of FDR's leisurely fishing cruises. In rough seas aboard the presidential yacht *Potomac* near Great Isaac, a small island in the Bahamas, Roosevelt put Hopkins back on the government payroll for the first time since August 1940, when Hopkins had resigned from his $12,000 job as secretary of commerce. Handing him a letter dated March 27, 1941, the president appointed Hopkins "to advise and assist [him] in carrying out the responsibilities placed upon [him]" by lend-lease at an annual salary of $10,000.[13] It is notable that there was no mention of the cabinet-level advisory committee; that temporary contrivance had already been set aside by Roosevelt's implicit assumption of supervisory authority over Hopkins's work.

One evening during that last peacetime fishing trip, when the *Potomac* was berthed at Ft. Lauderdale because of high winds, Hopkins, Jackson, and Steve Early arrived at dinnertime dressed in evening clothes and told Roosevelt they were going to Miami for a night on the town. According to Jackson, the president "lit into Hopkins like an angry father with a wayward son. He reminded Harry that he had been ill . . . that he brought him on the trip to get some rest and . . . told him bluntly that if he went to Miami and stayed out . . . that he would not take him on another trip." It was a rare outburst by FDR, although it is not certain whether he was actually concerned about Hopkins's health or upset because he couldn't go with them. "Sheepishly the dinner coats came off and we spent a quiet evening, retiring early," wrote Jackson.[14]

At a press conference after returning to Washington, Roosevelt, keenly aware that Hopkins remained highly controversial, attempted to downplay his new role as the individual responsible for organizing lend-lease. Hopkins would merely function "as a bookkeeper, recording the expenditures and remaining balances of the Lend-Lease funds," Roosevelt told the press. This statement failed to fool those who remembered that just a few years earlier Roosevelt had announced that Hopkins, as the new head of the WPA, would function only as a bookkeeper. Indeed the statement led to a new outbreak of virulent attacks on Hopkins, some of them very personal, by Congress, the press, isolationists, and New Deal critics.[15] Congressman Taber called Hopkins's role in organizing lend-lease "the worst blow the President has struck at national defense."[16]

Operating from his rooms in the Lincoln suite, his bed littered with papers, notebooks, and ashtrays, Hopkins set out to gain the confidence and trust of key players on both sides of the Atlantic so that they would use him and his organization as the channel of communication to resolve their differences. He advised Churchill that the U.S. Army and Navy would oppose many of the British requests and that he would therefore need to have military experts carefully scrub them to make sure they were absolutely necessary.

At home he cultivated the military chiefs, particularly General George Marshall, telling them that the British would be asking for more than "actual necessities."[17] By subtly playing them off against each other, he ensured that his organization functioned as a two-way transoceanic pipeline through which requests from the British and supplies from America would flow and that he would referee the disputes. He used key staff appointments to mollify the principal bureaucracies in the United States that fought with one another and with him over the nature and quantity of supplies to be allocated. He curried favor with the War Department, which feared that the nation's defenses would be weakened by sending supplies to England, by appointing General Burns, an ordnance expert, as his deputy. Knowing that Secretary Morgenthau would object to Burns on the theory that he would favor the army's needs over Britain's, Hopkins recruited two of Morgenthau's trusted aides, Oscar Cox and Philip Young, from the Treasury Department to work for him.

Though these moves served to quiet some of the criticism that swirled around him, Hopkins soon managed to alienate his liberal friends because he was overtly, though quite understandably, courting big business in an effort to increase the production of war matériel. Ties between Hopkins and leaders of organized labor began to fray: "He would have thrown the whole labor movement overboard at this stage if it would help Lend-Lease," said Isidore Lubin. Eleanor Roosevelt complained that Hopkins had "lost his sense of values."[18] Having totally committed himself to saving Great Britain and defeating the Nazi menace, Hopkins astonished Sherwood when he remarked with considerable irritation, "I'm getting sick and tired of having to listen to complaints from those goddamn New Dealers!"[19]

While Hopkins was organizing the administration of lend-lease, top-secret war-planning talks in Washington between American and British military staff officers, called the American-British Conversations (ABC), were winding down. Hopkins knew the British military chiefs were meeting with their U.S. counterparts in the capital because he was introduced to many of them on January 15, the day they had all departed for America from Scapa Flow aboard the *King George V* along with Lord Halifax. At first Roosevelt tried to downplay the significance of the ABC talks, insisting that they be "non political" and that only "methods of cooperation" should be discussed. However, by the time the talks concluded—after fourteen sessions—on March 29 with the issuance of a report called ABC-1, the British and Americans had agreed on a vitally important strategic issue: that Germany was *the* principal enemy, no matter what the Japanese did in the Pacific, and would remain so until it was defeated. If the United States was drawn into a two-front war, the Anglo-American strategy would be to concentrate forces on Germany first, maintain interests in the Mediterranean, and stay on the defensive in the Pacific theater until victory was won in the west. For the Americans, the premise underlying this decision was that Nazi Germany rather than imperial Japan presented the greater threat to their security. Both the British and the Americans reasoned that once Germany and its influence in Europe collapsed, Japan would be forced to give up its gains in European-controlled countries in Southeast Asia.

The priorities and plans emanating from ABC-1 provided Hopkins with critical guidance in his administration of lend-lease. As the American and British staff officers continued to debate and refine strategy, tactics, and logistics in Washington and London, Hopkins was necessarily consulted and his advice was increasingly sought. Lend-lease involved a constant tug of war with the procurement officers in the War and Navy Departments and with the demands of the British armed forces.[20] Hopkins was in the middle of it all.

As the spring of 1941 wore on, a sense of doom pervaded Washington and London. Almost everywhere the British were forced onto the defensive. The Luftwaffe dominated the central Mediterranean, thus allowing the Afrika Korps under General Erwin Rommel to mount a counterattack across the Libyan desert toward Egypt. Britain's Atlantic lifeline continued to weaken as Hitler extended his combat zone farther west in the North Atlantic and his U-boat wolf packs inflicted staggering losses on merchant shipping from the United States (142 ships, totaling 818,000 tons, were sunk during the three-month period ending May 1). Shipyards and port facilities in England were being constantly pounded by massive air attacks. The Battle of the Atlantic was being lost, and the war as a whole was slipping away. The survival of civilization seemed in jeopardy.

Hopkins was frustrated. He had done a masterful job of quickly organizing and staffing the lend-lease program, but even his legendary ability to cut through red tape could not hasten the movement of American industry to a wartime footing. By mid-May 1941 only $17 million in lend-lease supplies had actually been shipped.[21] Following lunch with Hopkins on May 14, Morgenthau wrote in his diary, "I think that both the President and Hopkins are groping as to what to do. They feel that something has to be done but don't know just what. Hopkins said that the President has never said so in so many words, but he thinks the President is loath to get us into this war, and he would rather follow public opinion than to lead it."[22]

In contrast to the president, Hopkins had come to the view that America *had* to enter the war within the next few months because Britain would be defeated or completely isolated by the time lend-lease could become effective.[23] Sensitive to Roosevelt's reluctance, Hopkins played a key part in nudging him toward leading rather than following public opinion. On Sunday, May 25, while Rosenman and Sherwood were working on a major speech for Roosevelt (the so-called Pan-American Day speech, which had been delayed due to FDR's "flu bug"), Hopkins went out on a limb, telling them that he thought the president would wish to conclude his speech with an announcement that he was proclaiming a state of "unlimited national emergency." (Since 1939 there had been a state of "limited emergency.")[24] Such a proclamation would greatly increase the president's executive powers and, as Assistant Secretary of State Adolf Berle said, "scare the daylights out of everyone."[25]

The "unlimited national emergency" announcement was included in the draft that the president began to read aloud to the speechwriters in the Oval Study after dinner. When he came to the newly inserted phrase, he stopped and stared at Sherwood, then demanded, "What's *this*? Hasn't someone been taking liberties?" Hopkins was conveniently absent at this point, having trundled down the hall to take some medicine. With considerable trepidation, Sherwood responded, "Harry had told us that the President wanted something along these general lines." Roosevelt didn't say another word. The proclamation remained in the speech, which was delivered in the East Room on the evening of May 27 to a huge international audience. It had been a risk, but Hopkins succeeded in pushing the president to move public opinion toward acceptance of a more aggressive posture toward the German menace. Late that evening FDR's bed was littered with telegrams. "They're ninety-five percent favorable," the president told his speechwriters. "And I figured I'd be lucky to get an even break on this speech."[26]

The next day a *New York Times* editorial began, "President Roosevelt struck a mighty blow last night for freedom." It went on to say that "the course" to which he "pledged the country, and the action taken, will have the endorsement of the vast majority of our people."[27] Yet later in the day, at his press conference, Roosevelt, apparently still not sure how mighty the blow should be, retreated from the aggressive stance into which he had been nudged the night before. He told the press corps that the "unlimited emergency" proclamation didn't really have any teeth because it could be made effective only through "a series of executive orders" that he "had no plans for issuing . . . at the present time."[28] He also declared that he had no plans for asking for repeal of the Neutrality Act or for instituting convoy operations to supply the British. Even Hopkins, who knew Roosevelt's mind better than anyone, was at a loss to explain why the president was so reluctant to follow through.[29]

When news arrived in Washington of the sinking of the American merchant ship *Robin Moor*—a Hog Islander–class ship, so called because it was unprepossessing but sturdy—by a German U-boat, Hopkins tried once again to nudge Roosevelt, this time on a course that could lead to a shooting war. In a memo to the president he recommended that the Navy be authorized to provide "security" patrols for all U.S.-flagged ships, "leaving it to the judgment of the Navy as to what measures of security are required to achieve that objective."[30] Roosevelt, however, issued no such instruction and instead merely condemned the sinking as "the act of an international outlaw."[31] Perhaps Morgenthau was right. Roosevelt was simply "loath" to get into the war.

While Roosevelt was exhibiting extreme caution about doing anything that could incite the noninterventionists or trigger further attacks by the Germans, Hopkins watched helplessly as the president endured and then appeared to ruthlessly set aside what must have been one of the most devastating emotional losses of his life. It began at a dinner on the evening of June 4 hosted by Harry Sommerville, manager of the Willard Hotel, for FDR and his White House staff. Hopkins, Missy LeHand, Pa Watson, and several others were there. The First Lady was in Hyde Park. The dinner was an annual affair. In years past it took place at the Willard, but this time the event was held at the White House to make it easier for the president to attend. After dinner and a sing-along of Roosevelt's favorite songs around the piano, the president retired for the evening. A few minutes after he left, LeHand stood up, screamed, and then collapsed on the floor, unconscious. She was ultimately diagnosed as having suffered a mild stroke, but at the time Doc McIntire concluded that her collapse was due to overwork, stress, and sleeplessness (she had been taking opiates for insomnia).[32]

Both Hopkins and the president visited LeHand's room on the third floor the following morning and over the course of the next several days. Her condition worsened. Two weeks later she suffered a massive second stroke that paralyzed her right arm and leg and destroyed her ability to speak coherently. As the nation teetered on the brink of war, her complete breakdown was mourned by Hopkins and everyone else who resided in the White House, but it was a personal catastrophe for Roosevelt. "Missy was somehow involved with everything FDR did for fun," recalled Lillian Parks, a White House maid. "She made every day exciting for FDR." Speaking for all of the servants, Parks said, "Missy was the substitute wife and we honored her for it."[33] In a profile of LeHand that appeared in the *Saturday Evening Post* long before her stroke, Doris Fleeson wrote, "No invitation is accepted by Missy if it means leaving the President alone. . . . Missy is attuned to his moods, knows how to keep him company, both with conversation and with silence."[34]

Like LeHand, Hopkins was attuned to FDR's moods. He knew how much she meant to the president and how deeply he would miss her. He had lived with Roosevelt's ingrained reticence, his uncanny ability to mask his true emotions and to hide his grief. To outsiders, however, Roosevelt's reaction to LeHand's condition seemed cold, emotionless. The journalist Eliot Janeway observed, "Roosevelt had absolutely no moral reaction to Missy's tragedy. It seemed only that he resented her for getting sick and leaving him in the lurch."[35] Hopkins knew the truth but he also knew that the president was above all driven by an unshakeable sense of responsibility. He was the president, and the American people depended on him, particularly during these days of great danger to the country. Ruthlessly, callously, his personal feelings were sublimated.

Ironically, a few days before LeHand's stroke, FDR had arranged for Lucy Mercer, the love of his life, whom he had sworn never to see again, to visit him at the White House, her first recorded visit. At that time she was married to the elderly Winthrop Rutherfurd, who had suffered a stroke and was confined to a wheelchair. Logged in at the White House under the name "Mrs. Paul Johnson," she arrived on the afternoon of June 5, the day after LeHand's first stroke. Eleanor was still in Hyde Park. Lucy and Franklin met in the Oval Study on the second floor for an hour and twenty minutes. The White House log indicates that as soon as she left, Roosevelt was taken up to LeHand's room to visit with her for the third time that day.[36] The timing was a coincidence, of course, but it was as if Mercer had taken LeHand's place. Hopkins may not have known of this particular visit by Mercer, but he very likely knew that the president had been seeing her outside the White House and in the coming months and years he would become aware of her several visits to the White House when Mrs. Roosevelt was away. Years later, referring to the affair, Hopkins confided to a close friend that the president was "so severely handicapped . . . that any pleasure he could have, he was more than entitled to."[37]

At 9:30 on Saturday evening, June 21, 1941, a Navy ambulance pulled up to the White House portico. Having just suffered her second stroke, LeHand was wheeled out on a stretcher.[38] Roosevelt and Hopkins were upstairs, digesting the first sketchy reports of cataclysmic events halfway around the world that would completely change the course of the war. At 8:15 p.m. (EST) on June 21 (0315 hours on Sunday morning, June 22, Moscow time), Hitler had unleashed Operation Barbarossa, an attack against the USSR, his former ally (or perhaps more accurately, the cosigner of a nonaggression pact). Along an 1,800-mile front, stretching from the Baltic in the north to the Black Sea in the south, 3 million German troops poured across the lightly defended borders and marched eastward.[39]

Hopkins had spent that Saturday afternoon at the races. Listening to the reports of the massive invasion, a true clash of civilizations, his first thought, according to Sherwood, was relief. "The President's policy of support for Britain has really paid off! Hitler has turned to the left."[40] Whether or not that was his first thought, he quickly had to have had more sobering second thoughts. Great Britain was hanging by a thread. Hitler was not stupid. Why would he suddenly turn his back on the British Isles and commit virtually all of his military forces to an invasion of the vast reaches of Russia? Late that evening the answers began to dawn on Hopkins. Hitler's decision had a certain logic. His generals, like those in Britain and America, believed that the Red Army would be defeated within a few months. A quick defeat would undermine Britain's hopes for survival and allow Hitler to turn his full fury on the British without a threat to his rear. Perhaps Britain would even sue for peace. At the same time, the German attack on a Communist dictatorship would reenergize the large bloc of anti-Communists and isolationists in Congress and throughout America who believed that Bolshevism should be wiped out because it posed a greater threat than Nazism. Roosevelt was already reluctant to get too far out ahead of American opinion. Hitler's attack would make him even more cautious.

Hitler was not, however, thinking about American public opinion and its effect on Roosevelt. From his new underground headquarters, the Wolfsschanze (Wolf's Lair), in the forests of East Prussia, he committed his reasoning to paper about twelve hours before the attack began. In a long letter to his Axis partner Mussolini, Hitler confirmed much of the logic underlying his decision to invade the Soviet Union that would occur to Hopkins. But as to the possible effect of his decision on America, Hitler had a different idea that was both strategically brilliant and diabolical. In his letter to Il Duce, Hitler said that the quick elimination of Russian military power would mean that Japan would not have to worry about Russian expansion in East Asia, thus freeing Japan to pose a "much stronger threat to American activities" through "intervention."[41] By attacking the USSR, Hitler would free Japan to attack the United States.

It was well after midnight in England when Churchill heard the first reports of the German attack on the USSR. Following dinner at Chequers
with U.S. Ambassador John Winant and others, Churchill was strolling
on the lawn with Jock Colville, his private secretary. Colville asked how
Churchill could now side with the Russians in light of his public statements
throughout his political career decrying the "wickedness" of Communism.
According to Colville's diary, the prime minister replied that he "had [now]
only one single purpose—the destruction of Hitler—and his life was much
simplified thereby; if Hitler invaded Hell he would at least make a favorable reference to the Devil [in the House of Commons]!"[42] Addressing the
nation on BBC radio the next day, Churchill described Hitler as a "blood-
thirsty guttersnipe" but made no reference to Hell or the Devil. "No one
has been a more consistent opponent of Communism than I have," he said,
"[but] any man or state who fights on against Nazidom will have our aid. . . .
That is our policy and that is our declaration. It follows, therefore, that we
shall give whatever help we can to Russia and the Russian people."[43]

The attack on his country should not have been a surprise to Marshal
Stalin. He had been warned repeatedly of Hitler's plans to launch an all-out
attack on the USSR in the late spring of 1941. On March 20 Assistant Sec-
retary of State Sumner Welles delivered a top-secret document to Stalin's
ambassador to the United States that provided a detailed description of
Operation Barbarossa, including the approximate date it would begin.[44]
In April a personal message from Churchill was delivered to Stalin warning him of the impending attack.[45] Richard Sorge, a Soviet spy, informed
Moscow in April that preparations for the invasion were complete.[46] Yet
Stalin and his government ignored these and many other warnings and
signs, refusing to believe that Hitler would "have the madness . . . to undertake a war in the East . . . before finishing off the war in the West."[47] They
also ignored the warnings because of their own form of madness: a para-
noid suspicion of the West. They thought the Western democracies were
trying to save Britain by deliberately fomenting a war between Germany
and the Soviets that would end up destroying Communism.

Consequently when General Georgi Zhukov telephoned Stalin at 3:30
on the morning of June 22 to tell him of the attack, Stalin was not even in

his Kremlin apartment; he was sleeping peacefully at his weekend dacha in the Moscow suburb of Kuntsevo. Jarred awake by the news, he rushed back to the Kremlin, but his initial orders—to counterattack along the entire 1,800-mile front—were irrational and incapable of being followed. He seemed distraught, disoriented. Inexplicably he returned to his green-painted dacha, where he remained incommunicado for a week. Historians have speculated that Stalin may have suffered a nervous or mental breakdown.[48] He might have been depressed, or he may have calculated that the Politburo, the USSR's governing council, whose members were terrified of showing any signs of disloyalty, would eventually come to him.

On June 30 a Politburo delegation duly arrived at Stalin's dacha and revived his spirits by almost begging him to head a new State Committee of Defense (the Stavka) that would give him absolute authority to direct the war and rule the USSR. The next day Stalin returned to the Kremlin and accepted the appointment. On July 3 at 6 a.m. he addressed the frightened and clueless Russian people by radio for the first time. In his thick Georgian accent, he began with the reassuring words, "Comrades, brothers and sisters." After laying out the grim facts and admitting, "Our country is in serious danger," Stalin told his people they were not alone. "In this great war we shall have true allies in the peoples of Europe and America." He went on to say that Britain and the United States had signified "readiness to render aid."[49] Though there is no way Stalin could have known this at the time, his words were prophetic. Within three weeks Harry Hopkins would begin a mission to Moscow to offer aid to Russia.

In Washington leading politicians, anticipating an administration move to provide aid to Stalin and the Communists, voiced their objections. Democratic Senator Bennett Champ Clark of Missouri, said, "Stalin is as bloody-handed as Hitler. I don't think we should help either one."[50] The other senator from Missouri, Harry Truman, declared, "If we see Germany is winning we ought to help Russia, and if Russia is winning we ought to help Germany, and that way let them kill as many as possible."[51] Former president Hoover added, "Now we find ourselves promising aid to Stalin and his militant conspiracy against the whole democratic ideals of the world. . . . If we go further and join the war and we win, then we have won for Stalin the grip of Communism on Russia, and more opportunity for it to extend in the world."[52]

Secretary of War Stimson, Secretary of the Navy Knox, and all of the military experts were advising Roosevelt and Hopkins that there was no point in providing aid to the Soviet Union because the Red Army would be defeated within a "minimum of one month and a possible maximum of three months."[53] At first Hopkins supported this view, whereas Roosevelt was skeptical, believing the opinions of the military were heavily influenced by strong anti-Communist prejudice.[54] Roosevelt's skepticism was fueled by Joe Davies, who had served as his ambassador to the Soviet Union from November 1936 until June 1938. Known in Washington circles as "Paper Collar Joe," Davies had remained good friends with FDR since serving with him in the Wilson administration, Roosevelt as assistant secretary of the Navy and Davies as chairman of the Federal Trade Commission. In the 1920s Davies had accumulated an unusual amount of wealth as a Washington lawyer, beginning with his successful representation of the Dodge automobile family in a huge court case against the Internal Revenue Service and continuing into the 1930s, when he represented several foreign governments and married the cereal heiress Marjorie Merriweather Post, at one time the richest woman in America.[55] As ambassador to the USSR, Davies impressed Roosevelt as a shrewd and objective observer of Stalin and the Soviet economy, with an ability to predict events much more accurately than the so-called Soviet experts in the State Department.[56] Davies had also impressed Hopkins. In January 1939 Davies correctly warned Hopkins from Brussels that British appeasement of Hitler would lead to a crisis in the Polish corridor.[57] He had also accurately predicted that British and French appeasement would drive Stalin into a nonaggression pact with Hitler.

Thus a few days after the German invasion, when Davies publicly predicted that "the extent of the resistance of the Red Army would amaze and surprise the world,"[58] Hopkins's faith in the military experts was shaken and Roosevelt's skepticism was confirmed. At a lunch with Acting Secretary of State Sumner Welles (Hull was ill) in early July, Davies sent a message through Welles to Hopkins and Roosevelt, urging that the United States, like the British, should immediately promise "all-out" aid to the USSR "as allies" in order to forestall any temptation Stalin might have to enter into a peace agreement with Hitler.[59] On July 8, following the Oval Office swearing-in of his old friend Jimmy Byrnes as Supreme Court associate justice, Davies accompanied Hopkins upstairs to the Lincoln suite to "talk about the Russian situation." (The swearing-in was held in the west wing Oval Office, not the second floor Oval Study. FDR often used the Oval Office for more formal meetings and ceremonies.) Pointing to a large map of Europe on Hopkins's bedroom wall, Davies showed him the locations of numerous "military manufacturing plants" behind the Ural Mountains and argued that even if White Russia (the eastern part of present-day Belarus), Moscow, and Ukraine were overrun by the Germans, Stalin could continue the fight beyond the Urals, provided he had full assurance of U.S. aid and support. "Word ought to be gotten to Stalin direct [from the president] that our attitude is 'all out' to beat Hitler and that our historic policy of friendliness to Russia still exists," Davies emphasized.[60]

On the same day, Davies delivered a memorandum to Hopkins that underscored the urgency of aiding the Soviets and provided sound advice on how to handle Stalin, advice that in the months ahead Hopkins would come to value and apply. "Stalin is oriental, coldly realistic and getting along in years. It is not impossible that he might even 'fall' for Hitler's peace as the lesser of two evils. . . . It is, therefore, of vital importance that Stalin be impressed with the fact that he is not 'pulling the chestnuts out of the fire' for the allies who have no use for him."[61]

Largely because of Davies, Hopkins was coming around to Roosevelt's view: the Soviets might be able to hold out, and they should be given some assurance of aid. On July 10 Hopkins and Roosevelt met with Soviet Ambassador Constantine Oumansky in the White House. Roosevelt pledged that the United States would do its best to fill urgent orders for military and industrial equipment, provided they were immediately placed and to the extent consistent with the need to also supply the British. The next day Hopkins assured Oumansky that tough-minded Adolf Berle and other "incorrigible anti-Soviet types," presumably meaning officials such as Loy Henderson and Elbridge Durbrow in the State Department's European Division, would be removed from responsibilities for U.S.-Soviet relations, and that FDR was drawing people like Joe Davies close to him.[62] Although none of these officials lost their positions, Hopkins, through his control of aid to the Soviets, would effectively diminish their influence.

After dinner on Friday, July 11, Hopkins and Roosevelt talked long into the night about the problem of supplying Russia; the threat to the Atlantic lifeline; whether to support the British in their defense of the Middle East; the desirability of a face-to-face meeting with Churchill as soon as possible; and issues relating to implementation of lend-lease in Washington and London. Tearing a small map of the Atlantic Ocean from a *National Geographic* magazine, the president penciled a thick north to south line in the North Atlantic about two hundred miles east of Iceland that hooked around the southern coast of Iceland and headed straight south through the Azores. The huge area of the North Atlantic between the east coast of North America and FDR's line would be policed by U.S. Navy warships, thus freeing British convoys to escort supply ships north to Russia in what would become known as the "Murmansk run." Roosevelt handed the map to Hopkins and told him to start packing. He was to fly to London on Sunday for discussions with Churchill and others about the adjustments that would need to be made in shipping, convoy protection, and lend-lease in order to provide war matériel to the Soviet Union. He was ordered, however, not to talk about the United States entering the war. He was also instructed to arrange the time and place of a shipboard meeting between the president and Churchill.[63]

Hopkins was reasonably clear on how he was to handle discussions relating to the map. But what was he supposed to tell Churchill about the purpose of the meeting with the president? Nowhere in the few contemporaneous notes of the discussions between Roosevelt and Hopkins was the purpose revealed. Nor does Sherwood in his recounting of Roosevelt's instructions touch on the purpose. The only extant explanation is cryptic and vague, a private memorandum written later by the president in which he said that because he was "faced by a practical problem of extreme difficulty"—presumably the existential threat to the United States if the USSR and then Britain were to fall—he desired to meet with Churchill secretly to "talk over the problem of the defeat of Germany."[64] That is likely as much detail as he had in his own mind, or was willing to reveal, when he sent Hopkins off once again to meet with Churchill.

Hopkins knew he would have a difficult time dealing with Churchill, who would surely view America's entry into the war against Germany as the main objective of the meeting at sea, a subject Hopkins was forbidden to discuss. But he was not troubled by the president's failure to spell out an agenda for the meeting. Hopkins relished the trust FDR placed in him, instinctively appreciating the competing considerations that weighed on the president's mind.

As always when he was about to embark on a foreign mission for the president, Hopkins was energized by the challenge and elated to be on his own. As he prepared to depart for England, he was still not convinced that the Red Army could hold out, but he understood why Roosevelt had to provide assurances that aid would be provided to the USSR. Without such assurances, conditioned as they were on preexisting obligations to supply Great Britain, Stalin might cut another deal with Hitler. While Davies confidently recorded in his diary that Hitler's invasion of Russia was the "first glimpse of dawn in a black night,"[65] Hopkins wasn't so sure. He preferred to conduct his own on-site investigation and judge for himself.

6

Vodka Has Authority

On Sunday morning, July 13, 1941, Hopkins climbed aboard a B-17 bomber, called a "Flying Fortress," for the first leg of his trip to meet again with Churchill in London. The Flying Fortress, a rugged, Boeing-built four-engine heavy bomber, was state of the art for the U.S. Army Air Corps. Delayed in Gander, Newfoundland, by foul weather, Hopkins spent the next day trout fishing with Colonel Elliott Roosevelt, the president's third oldest son, who was stationed there. "In one day," recalled Elliott in his memoir, "Harry seemed to shed ten years of age."[1] Hopkins flew the final leg of the trip in the noisy belly of a twin-tail B-24 "Liberator" bomber. The B-24's fuselage was shorter than the B-17's, but it had a longer wing-span, greater range, and a higher top speed. Hopkins's Liberator, along with nineteen other B-24s, was being ferried across the North Atlantic courtesy of lend-lease. He landed on July 16 in Prestwick, Scotland, weak and nause-ated, and was met by Averell Harriman, who accompanied him on the long train ride south to London.[2]

On the warm, sunny afternoon of July 17 Hopkins and Churchill met again, this time as congenial friends, on a broad terrace behind No. 10 Downing Street that looked out over a walled lawn and afforded a full view of St. James Park. At the outset Hopkins told Churchill that the president wanted to meet him during the second week of August in "some lonely bay or other." Churchill immediately agreed (subject to cabinet approval), and, as he wrote later, "Placentia Bay in Newfoundland, was chosen, the date of August 9 was fixed, and our latest battleship, *The Prince of Wales*, was placed under orders accordingly."[3] Hopkins also discussed with the prime minister the map torn from the pages of the *National Geographic* that the president had handed him the night before his departure, showing the much larger area of the Atlantic that would be policed by American warships. Churchill was pleased, of course, but wanted to nail down a precise definition of "policing."[4]

Later that same afternoon, Churchill, wishing to convey the impression of openness and trust, invited Hopkins to attend a meeting of the British war cabinet, confiding to him that he was the first foreigner to have been invited to do so. As we have seen, Roosevelt had instructed Hopkins not to "talk about [going to] war."[5] However, the minutes of the meeting reveal that he told the cabinet members that although the American people were not eager to enter the war, if and when the president decided it was time to join the fight against Germany, a majority of both political parties would support him.[6] As Warren Kimball, editor of the complete correspondence between Churchill and Roosevelt, has written, Hopkins's attendance at the war cabinet meeting was a bit of a charade. After he was escorted out of the room, having been told that the cabinet was turning to domestic matters of no interest to him, Churchill's men proceeded to "discuss the delicate issue of U.S. policy regarding Japan."[7]

For the next several days, Hopkins met with a series of top government and military officials to resolve lend-lease and related supply issues and to confer on war strategy. In addition he claimed that he made an effort to resolve tensions in the working relationship between Harriman and Ambassador Winant, giving Harriman "explicit instructions not to touch anything which is in any way political," and asking Churchill to "deal with

Winant . . . in all matters which have any political aspect whatever."[8] If Hopkins actually delivered these admonitions, they would have been almost impossible to follow, because lend-lease, which was Harriman's responsibility, and U.S. policy toward Great Britain, which was Winant's domain, often were inseparable. The friction between them was both inevitable and understandable. Moreover because of his close friendship with Harriman, there is reason to doubt whether Hopkins made a sincere effort to resolve these turf wars.

Bearing gifts of cheese (a luxury in wartime England) and Cuban cigars, Hopkins spent the weekend of July 19 at Chequers, where he was reunited with Clementine, who was delighted to see him again. As before, she was charmed by Hopkins and lavished motherly concern over his health, always making sure that he was warm and well-fed—although she could not prevent him from staying up half the night with Churchill, drinking and smoking. As Quentin Reynolds, the hard-drinking American war correspondent for *Collier's* magazine and a good friend of Hopkins, recalled, "Around 11 o'clock in the evening she would start trying to persuade him to go to bed, saying 'You have a long day tomorrow and you can have a nice talk with Winston in the morning. I've fixed your bed and put a hot water bottle in it.'"[9]

That weekend Hopkins met Ivan Maisky, the Soviet ambassador to Great Britain. By this time—only a month after Operation Barbarossa was launched—Field Marshal Fedor von Bock's Army Group Center, despite stiffening resistance by the Red Army, had already captured Smolensk, Russia's oldest city, on the main axis toward Moscow, and Army Group North was threatening to encircle the northern city of Leningrad (now St. Petersburg). Losses on both sides were staggering. Maisky had driven out to Chequers to deliver a written plea from Stalin for the British to establish a "second front" in northern France that would divert German divisions away from the eastern front in Russia. Churchill regarded Stalin's request as completely unrealistic and told Maisky, with some impatience, that any attempt by the British to invade France with their inferior forces would only result in a "bloody repulse."[10] Churchill introduced Maisky to Hopkins and left them alone in the drawing room, Hopkins standing with his back to the fire even though it was summertime.[11] Maisky, who later described Hopkins as "tall, very thin . . . with a long face and lively eyes," came away from that first meeting with the impression that Hopkins was more committed than Churchill to aiding the Russians.[12] Indeed, concluding that Hopkins was dead serious about helping the Soviet Union, Maisky arranged through Winant to meet Hopkins for lunch at the U.S. Embassy in London on Tuesday, July 22. According to Maisky, at the luncheon Hopkins said that, as a "non-belligerent," the United States was not in a position to open a "second front" but that it could help "as regards supplies." He asked Maisky what they "required." The Soviet ambassador replied that he was unable to provide specific information about what was needed, and he proposed that Hopkins go to Moscow himself and obtain information about war requirements from those in the know.[13] Historians and journalists alike have cast doubt on Maisky's claim that he was the first to propose that Hopkins travel to Moscow.[14] But whether it was Maisky, Churchill, Winant, or Hopkins himself who first conceived the idea, the record is clear that on Friday, July 25, Hopkins cabled Roosevelt to say, "I am wondering whether you would think it important and useful for me to go to Moscow." Hopkins's argument for going was not so much to obtain details of supplies needed by the Red Army, as suggested by Maisky, but to convince Stalin, through a "personal envoy" from the president of the United States, that the Russians should keep on fighting the Germans "even though they be defeated in this immediate battle [because] we mean business on a long term supply job."[15]

At about the time Hopkins's request to travel to Moscow arrived at the White House, Roosevelt was meeting in the Oval Study with the Japanese ambassador, Admiral Nomura Kichisaburo. Taking advantage of the West's preoccupation with the Germans, Japanese warships and troop transports had moved aggressively south into Indochina (now Vietnam and Cambodia). Under an agreement with Vichy France, the Japanese acquired rights to airfields by which they could threaten supply routes to China, the Dutch East Indies, and points south. The Japanese government claimed that it was only protecting its rice supply against moves by "de Gaullist French agents" and "Chinese agitators" to create unrest in the region. Roosevelt knew this was a pretext, but he offered Nomura a deal. He would "do everything in his power" to broker an international agreement that would protect Japan's rice supply in Indochina if Japan would withdraw its forces from the region.[16] The ambassador was not encouraging, so Roosevelt decided not to wait for an official response to his offer. The next day, July 26, the president issued an executive order that set the stage for an economic war on Japan. The order froze all Japanese assets in the United States and provided that future trade with Japan, including sales of crude oil and petroleum products, could be conducted only pursuant to licenses granted by the U.S. government for each shipment.[17] Since Japan's economy and military power depended on U.S. oil, the Japanese knew that Roosevelt now had his hands firmly around Japan's neck and he could start squeezing whenever it suited his purposes. However, to the dismay of hawks in the administration, the president chose not to squeeze, saying he was "inclined to grant the licenses for shipment as the applications [were] presented."[18]

A few hours after releasing his executive order, Roosevelt cabled an affirmative response to Hopkins's request to travel to Moscow. The cable arrived at Chequers, where Hopkins was spending the weekend, having worked most of Saturday—"dog-tired" and suffering "a touch of the grippe"—with Quentin Reynolds on a radio speech to the British public that Hopkins would deliver on Sunday night.[19] The president's cable, which Hopkins read early Sunday morning, began, "Welles and I highly approve Moscow trip and assume you would go within a few days." Referring to his meeting with the Japanese ambassador on Saturday, the president optimistically instructed Hopkins, "Tell Former Naval Person [Churchill] our concurrent action in regard to Japan is, I think, bearing fruit. I hear their Government much upset and no conclusive future policy has been determined."[20] Though the cable was inelegantly phrased, the president wanted the prime minister to know that his decision to publicly set the stage for an oil embargo without actually cutting off supplies might cause the Japanese government to reconsider its policy of aggression in Southeast Asia. Roosevelt was hoping that his actions would satisfy Churchill's pleas that he adopt strong measures to deter Japan without at the same time provoking war.

With cable in hand, Hopkins padded down the hall to Churchill's bedroom in his bathrobe and slippers, probably pausing to scratch Nelson, the Churchills' ill-natured cat, behind the ears. (Hopkins was an inveterate animal lover.) Churchill read the cable in bed and then issued orders for a special train to take Hopkins to Invergordon, Scotland, Sunday night following his broadcast and for a flying boat to transport him around the North Cape to Archangel, Russia, on Monday. Churchill wanted Hopkins to make the trip as soon as possible so that he would be back in time to accompany him on the *Prince of Wales* for the historic meeting with Roosevelt in Placentia Bay.

The remainder of that Sunday was a blur of activity. In addition to preparing for his important radio broadcast that evening and socializing with the weekend guests at Chequers—among them, his friend Dorothy Thompson, the famous American newspaper columnist, and her husband, the Pulitzer Prize winner Sinclair Lewis—Hopkins asked Ambassador Winant to take care of getting him a visa from the Soviet Embassy and to find someone to pack clothes that he had left at Claridge's and get them to Euston Station in London. (It would be weeks before Hopkins's hotel bill was paid.) Also, with the help of General Marshall, Hopkins commandeered two U.S. military experts in London to accompany him to Moscow: Colonel Joseph McNarney, a logistics wizard, later to serve as commander in chief of U.S. forces in occupied Germany, and Army Air Force Lieutenant John Alison, a fighter pilot who knew the capabilities of U.S. military aircraft and could comprehend technical details about Soviet airpower.[21] Alison would soon distinguish himself as an ace in Burma and China, shooting down seven Japanese aircraft in his P-40 Warhawk and playing a key role in protecting India against invasion.

Hopkins's BBC broadcast on Sunday evening, July 27, in which he pledged, "The President is at one with your Prime Minister in his determination to break the ruthless power of that sinful psychopath in Berlin," predictably lifted the spirits of the English people and likely outraged anti-interventionists in America.[22] After the speech, Hopkins and Churchill strolled alone on the lawn at Chequers. Though close to ten in the evening, it was still light. Churchill told Hopkins of the efforts Britain would make to help the Soviets in their desperate fight and stressed the critical role they would be playing in killing German troops on the eastern front. Hopkins asked what he should say about this to Stalin. "Tell him that Britain has one ambition today, but one desire—to crush Hitler. Tell him that he can depend on us. . . . Good-by—God bless you, Harry."[23]

Minutes later Hopkins was being driven through the gathering dusk by Harriman and his daughter Kathleen to Euston Station. As the train was pulling out of the dimly lit train shed, Winant rushed onto the platform and thrust passports and visas for Hopkins and his two military advisors through the window into Hopkins's compartment. In his breast pocket Hopkins was carrying a message from Roosevelt that was to be hand-delivered to Stalin. The body of the message, drafted by the State Department, said that the purpose of Hopkins's visit was to clarify the USSR's "most urgent requirements" and suggested that "the immediate concern of both governments should be to concentrate on the matériel which can reach Russia within the next three months." The concluding paragraphs, which appear to have been dictated by Roosevelt, asked Marshal Stalin, "Treat Mr. Hopkins with the identical confidence you would feel if you were talking directly to me" and expressed "the great admiration all of us in the United States feel for the superb bravery displayed by the Russian people in defense of their liberty."[24]

Twenty-eight-year-old Royal Air Force Flight Lieutenant David McKinley and the crew of his American-made PBY Catalina flying boat had been picnicking Sunday afternoon at Loch Lomond, one of the most storied lakes in Scotland. At about 4:00 a reconnaissance plane circled overhead and flashed signals, directing McKinley and his crew to return to their base at Oban. There McKinley was ordered to fly to Invergordon on the east coast of Scotland, where he was to pick up three unnamed VIPs and fly them nonstop more than two thousand miles north to Archangel, a Russian city on the White Sea. McKinley was an experienced pilot, having flown long-range missions over the North Atlantic, but he had never flown north of the Arctic Circle around the North Cape of Norway to Archangel.

McKinley met Hopkins and his two military advisors when they arrived at Invergordon on Monday, July 28, but the airfield was socked in by bad weather. During the delay Hopkins was taken for a drive over the moors (the heather "unspeakably lovely," he wrote), had tea at "Mrs. Simpson's shop," and attended a cocktail party. As he was headed for dinner, a message arrived that his flight was ready to depart, so he and his party rushed back to the airfield.[25]

Because of the length of the flight, extra fuel had to be pumped into the Catalina's tanks. That, plus the weight of the three new passengers, meant that the flight crew had to be reduced from six to five. As the passengers boarded the flying boat, they found that even with the reduced crew size the fuselage was crowded and uncomfortable and that there would be al-most nowhere to stretch out and sleep during the twenty-one-hour flight. Adding to the discomfort, recalled McKinley, many of the bulky flight suits provided for the three VIPs, designed to keep them warm in the Arctic cold, "were illfitting," which "detracted from their usefulness."[26]

Late on the afternoon of July 28, the Catalina roared through the choppy seas on takeoff. Just as the fuel-heavy boat was lifting off the water, the an-chor hatch blew off. McKinley landed the craft and circled around while the hatch was being secured. As he recalled in his flight memo, this incident raised an "element of doubt" among "one or two of the passengers" about the whether the flight should proceed in light of the "load conditions." Assuring the passengers that there "was no cause for alarm," McKinley powered up the twin Pratt & Whitney radial air-cooled engines. The Catalina took off without incident and headed north, well west of the coast of Norway, where squadrons of German Messerschmitt fighter planes were based.[27]

Hopkins spent most of his time during the long flight crammed into the Plexiglas tail blister, which was equipped with a machine gun. Progress was slow because the PBY could manage only 135 mph when fully loaded and its maximum speed at seven thousand feet was 175 mph.[28] He pitched in on cooking detail since the crew was one man short, and he tried to sleep on a canvas cot but could not doze for long because of the cold in the unheated cabin, the throbbing engines, and the perpetual daylight in the northern latitudes. During the last several hours of the flight, the Catalina rounded the North Cape and, over fog and sea ice, ran down the shore of the White Sea. With assistance from an Archangel radio signal, they touched down near the Archangel harbor and taxied to shore.[29] According to Hopkins, "Archangel looked like a peaceful American seaside city," with "beaches crowded with bathers" and a temperature of "about eighty degrees." In his flight journal McKinley wrote, "Mr. Hopkins was looking very tired ... an early indication of [his] determination to totally disregard personal comfort."

Hopkins and his party were greeted by a large delegation consisting of Soviet Army, Navy, and Air Force officers, representatives of the U.S. and British embassies, local commissars, and the ubiquitous NKVD (People's Commissariat of Internal Affairs), secret police who would tail Hopkins throughout his stay in Russia. He was told that he could not proceed on to Moscow that night because planes were not permitted to land there after dark. Thinking that would mean he could get some sleep, Hopkins was delighted. However, a Soviet admiral immediately prevailed on him and his two military advisors to be his dinner guests aboard his yacht anchored in the Dvina River, and Hopkins felt he it would be impolite and impolitic to turn down the invitation. As Hopkins later wrote, "Dinner on the Admiral's yacht was monumental. It lasted almost four hours. There was an Iowa flavor to it what with the fresh vegetables, the butter, cream, greens." He went on describing the meal, as if he were writing for *Gourmet* or *Travel* magazine. "There was the inescapable cold fish, caviar and vodka. Vodka has authority. It is nothing for the amateur to trifle with. Drink it as an American or an Englishman takes whiskey neat and it will tear you apart. The thing to do is to spread a chunk of bread (and good bread it was) with caviar, and while you are swallowing that bolt your vodka. Don't play with the stuff. Eat while you're drinking it—something that will act as a shock absorber for it."[30]

The dinner ended at 1 a.m. After two hours of fitful sleep, Hopkins was driven to the Archangel airfield for his flight to Moscow. He was pleased to see that he would be making the six-hundred-mile trip in an American-made Douglas Aircraft transport with a comfortable interior. During the four-hour trip almost due south, he was fascinated by the vast forest that spread below him, uninterrupted for hundreds of miles in all directions. He began to appreciate the challenges that faced the advancing German armies, particularly the mechanized divisions, and for the first time he could visualize how the Red Army could constantly outflank the Germans and interdict their lengthening supply lines in the rear.

On the morning of July 30, as Hopkins's plane approached Moscow, flying "low over the Volga, solid with barges,"[31] Bock's Army Group Center, after repelling determined Soviet counterattacks, halted its drive toward Moscow at Smolensk, on the banks of the Dnieper River, having marched 412 miles east into Russia's interior. The Germans were slightly ahead of Napoleon's progress in 1812, but they were still 250 miles from Moscow.[32] The Russians prepared to make a stand at Smolensk, just as they had when they slowed Napoleon's march on Moscow. They would be aided this time by a key strategic error by Hitler: his decision to divert General Heinz Guderian's panzer divisions south toward Kiev and the Crimea, to focus on encircling and besieging Leningrad, and to place Army Group Center on the defensive for a much needed respite before resuming its assault on Moscow in September. Hitler's reasoning was that capturing the coal and oil reserves in the south and Leningrad in the north was vitally important and that despite almost a two-month pause, Army Group Center could still take Moscow before the onset of winter. Bock, Guderian, and many senior Wehrmacht officers believed Hitler should have ordered Army Group Center to continue its march toward Moscow in August, but Hitler held fast, making one of his most fateful mistakes.[33]

In Berlin Reich Marshal Hermann Goering was working up a directive to Reinhard Heydrich, head of the security arm of the SS. The directive, dated July 31, 1941, ordered Heydrich to "carry out all preparations" for a "total solution of the Jewish question" in Russia and the territories conquered by the Nazis and to submit a memo describing "the measures already taken for the intended *final solution* of the Jewish question."[34] Hopkins certainly understood the gravity of his mission to Moscow; however, he had no idea that the Nazis were preparing to murder, on an industrial scale, every Jew in occupied Europe.

Descending over Moscow, its hundreds of churches gleaming in the sunlight, Hopkins could see scattered bomb damage resulting from Hitler's order, issued only a week before, to reduce Moscow to rubble from the air.

"The enormous airport we landed on had been hit but it was still entirely useable," he wrote. Once again a huge reception committee greeted him as he stepped onto the tarmac. "I shook hands as I have never shaken hands before."[35] American Ambassador Laurence Steinhardt rescued Hopkins and his two military aides from the crowd and whisked them off to Spaso House, the U.S. Embassy, where Hopkins, appearing completely exhausted, was persuaded to go to bed at once. Built in 1914 for a wealthy merchant and manufacturer, Spaso House was located in a square about a mile west of the Kremlin near the Arbat. Although a few nearby buildings had been demolished by the Luftwaffe, Spaso House was largely unscathed, sustaining only a few broken windows.

Hopkins bounced up after a couple of hours of rest, eager to find out as much as he could from Steinhardt before meeting with Stalin. During their long conversation, Steinhardt was guardedly optimistic that the Red Army could hold out. However, he pointed out that he based his conditional optimism on both Russian history—the parallel to 1812 was widespread by this point—and culture, without benefit of any hard facts or real news as to what was actually happening on the battlefields. Embassy personnel were virtual prisoners, subjected to daily rations of official propaganda and prevented from interviewing knowledgeable government and military officials.[36]

In the late afternoon Hopkins, Steinhardt, and their interpreter were driven in an embassy automobile through the gates of the Kremlin to an unassuming three-story yellow house. At 6:30, the scheduled time, they were shown into Marshal Stalin's study, described by Hopkins as "spacious . . . perhaps fifty feet by thirty . . . almost as austere as the man himself."[37] A death mask of Lenin under glass adorned one wall and a painting of Stalin was hung on another. Bookshelves and military maps, the "finest" Hopkins had ever seen, covered the other open wall spaces. Stalin's plain desk was almost bare except for "five or six telephones and a battery of press buttons" to summon aides.[38] Stalin rose from his desk and strode toward them, hand outstretched in greeting. He was much shorter than Hopkins expected but heavy-boned, with a powerful frame and a broad chest. He was "built like a football coach's dream of a tackle," wrote Hopkins.[39] Stalin wore a plain gray tunic without medals or insignia that revealed a slight paunch. His baggy gray trousers were stuffed into highly polished knee-high leather boots. As they shook hands, Hopkins could see that Stalin's sallow face was pockmarked from the ravages of smallpox and that his teeth below his thick black mustache were stained yellow, a result of tar, nicotine, and a poor diet. Hopkins accepted Stalin's offer of a Russian cigarette, and he, in turn, offered a Camel, having been told it was the marshal's favorite brand.

After lighting up and sitting down across from one another, flanked by their interpreters, Hopkins opened the interview, assuring Stalin of President Roosevelt's conviction "that the most important thing in the world today is to defeat Hitler and Hitlerism," and that the president, backed by the U.S. government, was determined "to extend all possible aid to the Soviet Union at the earliest possible time." Looking straight into Hopkins's eyes, as though Hopkins "understood every word [of Russian] that he uttered,"[40] Stalin said that in order for international society to exist, nations must observe a "minimum moral standard." He stressed that since the Nazi leaders ignored treaty obligations and broke their sworn promises, they knew "no such minimum moral standard," and therefore the USSR and the United States were in agreement that Germany was an "anti-social force in the world" that must be destroyed.[41]

In retrospect, given Stalin's criminal background and his instrumental role in the intentional starvation of millions of his own people, the Gulag, the purges, the nonaggression pact with the Nazis, the Katyn massacre, and countless other moral outrages, his hypocrisy was breathtaking. Hopkins, of course, knew only of the nonaggression pact, which led to the destruction of Poland, and was only dimly aware of many of Stalin's other monstrous acts. Nevertheless in his demeanor and words Hopkins conveyed both absolute support for Stalin's newfound moral standards and obsequious admiration for the man he referred to reverentially as "this austere, rugged, determined figure."[42] There was a logic to the obsequiousness. He was pulling out all stops to earn some measure of trust from the famously suspicious Soviet leader.

Hopkins brought out a notepad so he could get down to business. He began by asking Stalin what the Soviets needed that the United States "could deliver immediately" and what their requirements were "on the basis of a long war."[43] Without hesitation or the "waste of word, gesture or mannerism," Stalin laid it all out, "like an intelligent machine."[44] Immediately they needed x number of light anti-aircraft guns, medium caliber; y number of heavy anti-aircraft artillery; so many .50 caliber machine guns; one million .30 caliber rifles; and so on. For a long-range war, they needed high-octane aviation gasoline, aluminum, and other items on a list already presented to the U.S. government. "Give us anti-aircraft guns and aluminum and we can fight for three or four years," Stalin said emphatically but without raising his voice.[45]

During the remainder of the two-hour meeting, Hopkins and Stalin discussed the best routes to ship supplies from the United States to the Soviet Union (Archangel was the "most practicable"), what types of aircraft the Soviets needed (short-range bombers), and what planes the United States was prepared to supply immediately (Curtiss P-40 Tomahawk fighters, which turned out to be inferior to Soviet production fighters in speed, rate of climb, and armaments but better in range, endurance, and maneuverability). Near the end of this first meeting, Hopkins told Stalin that his stay in Moscow "must be brief" and asked him whether he would be available to carry on further conversations personally or preferred that Hopkins meet with others in the Soviet government. Stalin replied, "You are our guest; you have but to command."[46]

Later that evening Hopkins, General McNarney, and Major Ivan Yeaton, the U.S. Embassy's military attaché, met with Red Army General Anatoli Yakovlev in the Kremlin to discuss technical aspects of items on Stalin's list of war matériel. When Hopkins asked whether the Soviets needed anything in addition to the items on Stalin's list, Yakovlev declined to add anything. Incredulous, Hopkins asked about the need for tanks and anti-tank guns. Yakovlev replied, "I am not empowered to say whether we do or do not need tanks or anti-tank guns."[47] Thus, Hopkins quickly learned that Stalin's subordinates were afraid to deviate from a prescribed agenda and that the marshal was the person he needed to deal with on all matters of substance. Stalin was the only one in the Soviet government who could make commitments.

Hopkins had glimpsed the limitations of the totalitarian state. With absolute power concentrated in a single human being and underlings fearing to act on their own, efficiency and speed in setting up systems to supply the Soviets in the coming months would inevitably suffer. As a doer, a man who knew how to delegate authority and get things done, Hopkins must have had misgivings about the Stalinist regime. Yet there is no evidence that he questioned the system and its reliance on terror and coercion. He was concerned about dealing with events as they presented themselves, not with why and how the Communist experiment in Russia had evolved into a dictatorship. If Hopkins had thought more about *why*, he might have seen that while Stalin paid lip service to Western concepts of moral integrity and cooperation with brothers in arms when he needed military assistance, his priority would always be the accumulation of power and the territorial security (meaning dominance over Eastern Europe) that would preserve his power and that of his regime. As it was, Hopkins was focused entirely on helping the Russians defeat the German armies. Principle and consistency would fall victim to this singular objective.

When they stepped out into the warm night, Hopkins was impressed by the complete blackout in Moscow, which was much more comprehensive than in London. An air-raid siren sounded, and, as the anti-aircraft guns began booming, they drove to the bomb shelter in the Moscow subway that had been assigned to Hopkins. According to Steinhardt, the shelter was equipped with caviar, vodka, champagne, chocolates, and cigarettes: "[Hopkins] laughed heartily when I told him that no bomb shelter had ever been placed at *my* disposal and I owed this night's protection to his presence."[48]

In his memoirs Major Yeaton recalled that he had breakfast alone with Hopkins in the downstairs embassy mess hall the day after the first meeting with Stalin. Yeaton warned Hopkins of the pitfalls that lay ahead in dealing with Stalin, saying he and his henchmen in the Kremlin could not be trusted. He strongly urged Hopkins to require the Soviets to provide verifiable information (e.g., locations of munitions plants, troop dispositions, aircraft production) that would enable U.S. military experts to make an informed judgment of the USSR's odds of survival in exchange for America's commitment to provide military and economic assistance. Apparently Yeaton somewhat heatedly questioned Stalin's integrity, and Hopkins abruptly ended the conversation, saying, "I don't care to discuss the subject further." Ambassador Steinhart, who overheard the conversation, recalled that Yeaton and Hopkins "pound[ed] the breakfast table until the dishes danced in argument." From that time forward, Yeaton was convinced that Hopkins "was an enemy of our country" and was not shy in expressing his view.[49]

Later that morning, August 31, Steinhardt took Hopkins sightseeing and shopping with Margaret Bourke-White, the *Life* magazine photographer on assignment to Russia who was staying at Spaso House with her husband, the American novelist Erskine Caldwell (author of the 1932 best seller *Tobacco Road*). With guidance from Bourke-White, Hopkins picked out Russian peasant dresses for his daughter and Betsey Cushing Roosevelt, the wife of Jimmy Roosevelt, one of FDR's sons. At a shop specializing in antique silver, Steinhardt bought Hopkins a teapot engraved with a likeness of the Kremlin.[50] That afternoon Hopkins met Soviet Foreign Minister Vyacheslav Molotov for the first time. It was Molotov whom Stalin had dispatched to Berlin in 1939 to enter into the nonaggression pact with his Nazi counterpart, Joachim Ribbentrop, that led to the joint German-Soviet conquest of Poland and the beginning of World War II. Unlike Stalin, who occasionally evidenced a sense of humor and would respond with bark-like laughter, or at least a smile, to Hopkins's sardonic remarks, Hopkins could not penetrate Molotov's expressionless demeanor. It would take longer than a sixty-minute meeting for him to connect on an emotional level with this bland diplomat. The main topic of their conversation was the possibility that Japan would make an aggressive move on Siberia while the Soviet Union was fighting the Germans far to the west on a thousand-mile front. Molotov suggested that Roosevelt should issue a "warning" to Japan that if it made such a move the United States would "come to the assistance of the Soviet Union." Like a seasoned diplomat, Hopkins responded that while the U.S. government "ha[d] no desire to be provocative in its relations with Japan," he would pass Molotov's suggestion on to the president.[51]

At 6:30 p.m. Hopkins was ushered into Stalin's study for his second and final meeting with the marshal. This time Hopkins was alone. In an effort to establish a relationship of trust and intimacy, he did not even bring his own interpreter, and he wisely left Steinhardt, whom Stalin would soon denounce as a "defeatist and rumormonger . . . chiefly interested in his personal safety,"[52] at Spaso House. Maxim Litvinov, former Soviet foreign minister and, before that, a gunrunner for Lenin and Stalin, acted as interpreter for both Hopkins and Stalin. Litvinov, a Jew and a favorite of the West, had been brutally shunted aside when Stalin ordered, "Purge the Ministry of Jews"[53] and replaced him with Molotov during the talks with the Nazis that led to the nonaggression pact in 1939; he had not been seen since (some thought he had been shot). Before disappearing, Litvinov, married to an Englishwoman, had been, wrote William Shirer, "the archapostle of collective security, of strengthening the power of the League of Nations, of seeking Russian security against Nazi Germany by a military alliance with Great Britain and France."[54] He had obviously been liberated from what Sherwood called "the vast silences" because of his presumed appeal to Hopkins. However, Hopkins sensed that, as with General Yakovlev, Litvinov was deathly afraid of Stalin, functioning only as an interpreter and offering not a single substantive comment. To Hopkins, Litvinov seemed "like a morning coat that had been laid away in mothballs."[55]

At Hopkins's request, Stalin began by providing an "appreciation and analysis" of the war between the USSR and Germany that Hopkins said he would report to the president.[56] It was a virtuoso performance, by Hopkins's account, and in the end it convinced him and FDR that the Soviets could hold out, that the pessimistic predictions of U.S. military leaders were wrong and Joe Davies was right. As Hopkins cabled the next day to Roosevelt, Welles, and Hull, "I feel ever so confident about this front. The morale of the population is good. There is unbounded determination to win."[57]

Stalin's lengthy overview of the war was also an exercise in deception because it was based on omissions, half-truths, and outright misrepresentations. He told Hopkins that when he had been confronted with "a surprise attack" by the Germans, he had taken "all precautions possible to mobilize his army" and that there had been no mass surrenders.[58] In fact, as we have seen, Stalin had been repeatedly warned of the invasion. His soldiers were unprepared and dangerously exposed when the Germans attacked on June 22. In the first seven days of fighting, 290,000 Red Army troops were caught by the Wehrmacht in a giant pincer movement around Minsk and forced to surrender. On the first morning almost 1,200 Soviet aircraft were drawn up wing to wing and destroyed on the ground. By the end of the first week almost all of the Red Army's new armored corps had been annihilated.[59]

Stalin was not about to enlighten Hopkins as to these discouraging facts. A master at spin control, he emphasized the positive: the overwhelming manpower that he could continue to pour into the meat grinder (a decisive truth); superior heavy tanks (Guderian regarded the Russian T-34 as "the best battle tank in any army up to 1943"); higher quality fighters and bombers (certainly not across the board, but the Russians had a very effective tank-buster and an excellent twin-engine dive-bomber); better-trained pilots (based on a few anecdotes by captured fliers); projected parity with the Germans in plane production (Stalin said that by January 1942 Russia would be producing 2,500 bombers and fighters per month, about the same as Germany); and, most important, rain and mud in September and October, followed by a long, brutal winter.[60] He failed to mention, however, that Soviet casualties had been ten times that of the Germans in the first six weeks of battle and that almost half of Russia's total population, as well as her industrial and agricultural production, had fallen into enemy hands. Nor did he disclose that another 100,000 prisoners had been taken at Smolensk, along with 2,000 tanks and 1,900 guns, and that Moscow itself was in grave jeopardy.[61]

Hopkins was impressed by Stalin's "extraordinary grasp of detail" and "his capacity for clear and simple statement."[62] He was equally impressed by Stalin's commanding personality and presence and, despite his inability to confirm anything he was told, generally accepted the marshal's optimistic overview. Even when Stalin proposed that America send troops to the Russian front under U.S. command, Hopkins did not pick up the scent of desperation. Stalin succeeded in persuading him that the Red Army and the Russian people, with aid from the United States and Britain, would stall the German attack. And Hopkins determined that it was unlikely Stalin would ever again negotiate a separate peace with Hitler. This was a fight to the death.

Near the end of the almost four-hour meeting, Hopkins pointed out that America and Great Britain could not commit to supply heavy munitions to the Soviets in the quantities needed for the long term "unless and until a conference had been held between our three Governments." Stalin replied that he would "welcome such a conference," provided it was held in Moscow.[63] As the meeting was breaking up, Bourke-White was brought in to photograph Stalin and Hopkins. She wrote, "As I crawled on my hands and knees from one low camera angle to another, Stalin thought it was funny," she said. "[But] when the smile ended, it was as though a veil had been drawn over his features. . . . This was the strongest most determined face I had ever seen."[64]

By the time Hopkins departed Moscow at about noon on August 1 for the return flight to Archangel on the Douglas transport plane, he had dictated from his extensive notes an extraordinary three-part memorandum that set forth in detail all of the information that he had acquired during his two days with Stalin and the others. Parts I and II, sent to FDR, Stimson, Knox, and Hull, summarized Stalin's overview of the war, the supplies he said were needed, and the three-party conference proposed by Hopkins. By September these parts of Hopkins's top-secret memo were in the hands of Stalin and the NKVD, allegedly transmitted by Lauchlin Currie, a Canadian-born U.S. economist who at the time was working for Hopkins in Washington as a lend-lease administrator.[65] Part III, for the president's eyes only, reported Stalin's confession that it would be "very difficult" for Britain and the USSR alone to win the war and his request that the United States declare war on Germany, "the one thing that could defeat Hitler."[66]

Hopkins "looked very tired and ill" when he and his two advisors boarded the Catalina anchored in the harbor off Archangel late in the afternoon. During the flight from Moscow, he discovered that he had accidentally left behind the satchel containing his extensive dispensary of dietary supplements and medicines. Deprived of his lifeline, he was not looking forward to the twenty-four-hour flight ahead of him.

Flight Lieutenant McKinley and his crew were delighted to have been released from their enforced confinement on a houseboat during the time Hopkins was in Moscow. They were anxious to deliver their precious cargo to the *Prince of Wales* at Scapa Flow, but they also knew they were in for a long, rough flight because of severe headwinds. McKinley was very concerned about Hopkins's weak condition and lack of medicines. When he asked Hopkins whether he would like to rest for a few hours before taking off, Hopkins stressed the urgency of his rendezvous with the *Prince of Wales* and then said, "Whatever the next 24 hours will bring, it cannot be as trying as the last three days."[67]

Loaded with a cargo of Russian platinum and the three VIPs, the Catalina took off in a gathering storm and flew up the coast of the White Sea. While Hopkins fell into a deep sleep—"the best sleep I'd had since leaving Chequers"[68]—the Catalina was fired upon by one or more destroyers, probably Russian, off the Murman Coast east of the Kola Inlet. McKinley wrote in his flight memo that it was "evident" that Hopkins was "critically ill and only fit to lie down and take what rest was possible." After a flight lasting more than twenty-four hours and several aborted attempts to land at Scapa Flow in heavy seas, the Catalina finally splashed down, at which time "a struggle was commenced between wind, tide and marine craft." A British naval launch maneuvered alongside the port blister of the pitching aircraft, and, as McKinley recalled, "Mr. Hopkins had to make a hazardous leap from the aircraft to the launch followed by his luggage which was literally hurled across the several yards of open water separating us from the launch."[69] Hopkins laughed all this off and waved goodbye to McKinley, who would write later of Hopkins's "unbelievable courage" and "unparalleled devotion to duty."[70]

In a state of near collapse, Hopkins was taken to the *Prince of Wales*. After dinner with Admiral Sir John Tovey and Ambassador Winant, who had come from London, Hopkins was given blood transfusions and sedated by the ship's doctors. He slept for the next eighteen hours.[71] In two days the great battleship, with Hopkins, Churchill, and his entourage aboard, would cross the North Atlantic to meet President Roosevelt in Placentia Bay.

The trip to Moscow brought Hopkins close to death, but it was a spectacular success. His laser-like focus on what the Soviets needed in order to defeat Hitler had clearly impressed Stalin and the other Soviet leaders he met. The fact that he approached the meetings not as a negotiator exploiting weakness but as one asking "How can we help?" earned him Stalin's apparently sincere lifelong respect and a degree of trust accorded almost no other outsider. Stalin later told Charles Bohlen, who would later serve as U.S. ambassador to the USSR, that Hopkins was the first American he had met who had spoken "'po dushe'—from the soul."[72] Quentin Reynolds overheard Molotov and his deputy, Andrei Vyshinski, referring to Hopkins with reverence and awe.[73]

Just as Hopkins touched Stalin, the Soviet dictator had an equally profound impact on Hopkins. Seeing Stalin in action, Hopkins was convinced that the Soviet Union had at its helm an immensely competent leader. More important, he was persuaded that the Red Army, if properly supplied, could halt the German advances and eventually take the offensive. Finally, based on the murderous look in his eyes and the force of his words, Hopkins believed that Stalin's "cold, implacable hatred" for Hitler was visceral, although he remained concerned that unanticipated battlefield reverses or Politburo pressures might drive Stalin to cut an armistice deal with the Germans.[74]

Though Hopkins would often refer to Stalin thereafter as "Uncle Joe"— indeed Hopkins was probably the first to give him that nickname—he was by no means naïve about the Soviet dictator or his regime, as some would later claim. Sensing Stalin's faintly contemptuous treatment of Molotov and Litvinov and seeing the fear in Yakovlev's eyes, Hopkins understood that the marshal was no one's lovable uncle. There was an aura of power and menace about him that set him apart from any of the formidable leaders Hopkins had thus far confronted.

Yet on some level Hopkins was able to connect emotionally with Stalin just as he had with Roosevelt and Churchill. How did he do it? No one will know with any degree of certainty. However, it is reasonable to surmise, based on Stalin's "from the soul" comment and Hopkins's own writings, that it was Hopkins's candor and lack of pretense more than anything else that got through to the Russian leader. As Roosevelt had said to Willkie, Stalin could see that Hopkins sought nothing in return, that he was there only to serve. His all-business demeanor and terse replies resonated with Stalin. Moreover, Stalin had been conditioned to like the man, having heard stories about his prowess with women and his brave front during the dangerous flight from Britain. Finally, one must always keep in mind the highly important fact that Hopkins was an extension of the president of the United States, the only man who had the power to save the USSR. Stalin respected power.

The most significant aspect of Hopkins's trip, however, was its influence on Roosevelt. In his cables from Moscow and during his meetings with FDR upon his return, Hopkins convinced the president that aid to the USSR, with no strings attached, far outweighed the risks that the Soviet Union would be defeated or negotiate peace with Hitler. As Roosevelt indicated to his son Elliott, Churchill at the time had "zero" faith in Russia's ability to stay in the war. "'Harry Hopkins has more. He's able to convince me.'"[75]

At Last We Have Gotten Together

Hopkins was positioned beneath the massive fourteen-inch guns of the *Prince of Wales* as the prime minister and his party boarded on August 4, 1941, for the voyage to meet the U.S. president in Placentia Bay. Greeting Hopkins with affection, Churchill said, "Ah, my friend. How are you? And how did you find Stalin?" "I must tell you about it," replied Hopkins, and they went below together.[1] Late that evening Churchill wired Roosevelt jauntily, "Harry returned dead beat from Russia but is lively again. We shall get him in fine trim on the voyage. We are just off. It is just 27 years ago that the Huns began the last war. We must all make a good job of it this time. Twice ought to be enough."[2]

As always when he traveled, Churchill ignored wartime privations. The ship's mess was stocked with Scottish beef and ninety freshly killed grouse, along with the prime minister's favorite brandy (Hine), champagne (Pol Roger), and cigars (Romeo y Julietas). Hopkins contributed caviar he had brought from Moscow. Churchill said that it was very good, "even though it meant fighting with [on the side of] the Russians to get it."[3] The two spent six days together playing backgammon—at a shilling a game—walking about the deck, watching films (the first evening, *Pimpernel Smith*, a remake of the original *Scarlet Pimpernel*, starring Leslie Howard as an English intellectual trying to smuggle people out of Nazi-occupied rather than revolutionary Paris), and reading (*Flying Colours* by C. S. Forester, whose first Hornblower novel was published in 1937 and was immediately a bestseller; Churchill himself pronounced the fictional Captain Hornblower "admirable"). Hopkins caught up on his correspondence, including arrangements to pay his Claridge's bill, which he had neglected due to his hasty departure from England to meet Stalin. Churchill, focusing on his chief objective—drawing Roosevelt into the war—peppered Hopkins with questions about FDR's likes, dislikes, and "real" opinions. So eager was Churchill to make a good impression on FDR that Hopkins said later, "You'd have thought Winston was being carried up into the heavens to meet God!"[4]

In Washington Roosevelt was exuberant about getting out of the White House for his rendezvous at sea with Churchill. However, at a cabinet meeting just before leaving, he directed an outburst of vitriol at the War Department for "dragging its feet" on aid to Russia. "I am sick and tired of hearing they [the Soviets] are going to get this and going to get that; the only answer I want to hear is that it is under way."[5] The president was probably reacting to Hopkins's memos from Moscow, expressing the Red Army's desperate need for war matériel. That evening, putting aside his anger, Roosevelt dined alone with Lucy Mercer Rutherfurd, who had been admitted again to the White House as "Mrs. Johnson."[6] Two days later he left by train for New London, Connecticut, where he boarded the presidential yacht *Potomac* for what the press had been told was a fishing vacation. While the *Potomac* was observed passing through the Cape Cod Canal with a man on deck disguised as the president (rimless glasses, cigarette holder), Roosevelt was actually aboard the heavy cruiser *Augusta*, heading for Placentia Bay off the coast of Newfoundland along with his military chiefs. Although Roosevelt delighted in planning the hoax and loved the unfolding drama of what he thought would be a top-secret meeting in the North Atlantic with Churchill, the Germans weren't fooled. In Lisbon their agents learned of the meeting (but not the details), and it was announced in a German radio broadcast.[7]

On Saturday morning, August 9, Placentia Bay was shrouded in heavy white mist as the *Augusta*, its sister ship *Tuscaloosa*, the old battleship *Arkansas* (it had been launched in early 1911), and several U.S. destroyers awaited the arrival of the prime minister and his party. When the *Prince of Wales*, battle-scarred from its duel with the *Bismarck*, loomed into view, its band struck up the Sousa march "Stars and Stripes Forever," and the *Augusta*'s band responded with "God Save the Queen." Camouflaged with black stripes painted over her original gray, the enormous 35,000-ton British battleship, studded with turreted big guns and three dozen "pom-pom" antiaircraft guns, and its destroyer escorts steamed through the lane of American warships, crews in dress whites lining the rails. The sun burned through the mist, revealing warplanes circling overhead in a bright blue sky and a harbor crowded with vessels at anchor.[8]

Hopkins was immediately transported via barge from the *Prince of Wales* to the *Augusta* to prepare the president for the meetings with Churchill. Concerned about Hopkins's loss of weight and unhealthy appearance as he approached on the quarterdeck, FDR inquired, "How are you Harry? Are you all right? You look a little tired."[9] Hopkins assured him that he was fine. The two old friends chatted privately for a few minutes, Hopkins listening to what the president had in mind for the initial meetings ("get acquainted" sessions, with no agenda) and providing the president with a sense of how best to handle Churchill, given his current mood. After settling a dispute over the presence of two journalists on the *Prince of Wales* and arranging to send American cigarettes, candy, and food over to the British seamen, Hopkins dictated a note to be delivered by Roosevelt's naval aide, Captain John R. Beardall, to Churchill: "I have just talked to the President and he is very anxious after dinner tonight [scheduled to be held aboard the *Augusta*], to invite in the balance of the staff and wants to ask you to talk very informally to them about your general appreciation of the war. . . . I imagine there will be twenty five people altogether. The President, of course, does not want anything formal about it."[10]

At about eleven in the morning, Hopkins watched as Churchill, wearing the plain blue uniform of warden of the Cinque Ports, boarded the *Augusta* and walked toward Roosevelt, who was standing, with the aid of his steel braces, under an awning just below the bridge on the arm of his son Elliott. Roosevelt was wearing a light tan Palm Beach suit. With a barely perceptible bow, the prime minister presented the president with a letter from King George VI. Roosevelt extended his hand, saying, "At last we have gotten together." "We have," responded Churchill and they shook hands.[11]

Hopkins, Roosevelt, and Churchill—just the three of them—were served lunch below, while the American and British military chiefs dined separately. Nervous about this first encounter, Hopkins saw his role as being a facilitator, almost a marriage broker, keeping the conversation between president and prime minister light and informal and avoiding subjects he knew might irritate one or the other (such as the pace of lend-lease shipments). Characterizing the conversation as Hopkins later recounted it to him, Sherwood wrote, "They were two men in the same line of business. . . . They established an easy intimacy, a joking informality and a moratorium on pomposity and cant—and also a degree of frankness which, if not quite complete, was remarkably close to it."[12] To cousin Daisy, a genteel spinster whose quiet company FDR enjoyed, Roosevelt wrote of his first encounter with Churchill, "I like him—& lunching alone [although Hopkins was there] broke the ice both ways."[13] To the relief of Hopkins, by the end of the lunch they were "calling each other 'Franklin' and 'Winston.'"[14]

At 6:45 that evening the prime minister and his party returned to the *Augusta* as guests of the president. At dinner Hopkins presented an overview of his trip to Moscow, the point of which was to persuade the skeptical military chiefs (on both sides) that the Red Army could survive the German onslaught, but only if the Americans and British were deadly serious about expediting the delivery of armaments and supplies. After the table was cleared and senior officers who were not at the dinner were invited in, Churchill treated the assemblage—there had to have been well over twenty-five present—to an "appreciation of the war," similar to the after-dinner talk Hopkins had heard him give at Ditchley in January, and with similar effect. "The listener had the vivid impression that he was living at a time of great human struggle, or to change the image, stood upon some battlefield at a turning point in history," wrote Oliver Lyttleton.[15] This time, however, with the benefit of Hopkins's advice, Churchill shaped his remarks to conform to Roosevelt's political constraints, stressing the need for material aid and protection of supply lines but avoiding an explicit plea for immediate American entry into the war. He emphasized heavy bombing, blockades, mechanized mobility, and attacks on the periphery of the Axis empire, suggesting that victory could be achieved without clashes of massed armies on the plains of Europe. To deter further aggression by Japan and the frightening possibility of a second war in the Far East, Churchill argued that Britain and the United States should issue very stern warnings in parallel, including threats of force. His overall and yet underlying message was subtle but unmistakable: America's primary role would be to produce armaments, but eventually it would, as a matter of survival, have to come into the war.[16] As Elliott Roosevelt wrote later, his father was accustomed to dominating every gathering. "But not tonight. Tonight Father listened."[17] FDR wrote Daisy that the evening, "Was very grand . . . a very good party & the 'opposite numbers' are getting to know each other."[18]

The emotional apex of the conference—Roosevelt called it the "keynote" of his meeting with Churchill—was a religious service the following morning, Sunday, on the *Prince of Wales* that was attended by all of the conferees and hundreds of sailors. Carefully choreographed by Churchill to be "fully choral and fully photographic" and aided by Hopkins's knowledge of Roosevelt's favorite hymns, the president and prime minister were seated on the fantail in bright sunlight, facing a pulpit theatrically draped with the Union Jack and the Stars and Stripes.[19] Their military chiefs and top civilian advisors stood just behind them. Hopkins was one of the few wearing an overcoat. American and English chaplains conducted the service, led the recitation of the General Confession and the Lord's Prayer, and offered prayers, previously vetted by Churchill, to the king, the president, and the millions suffering from Nazi aggression. The lesson, read as usual by the ship's captain, was from the first chapter of the Book of Joshua, God's marching orders to the great Old Testament warrior: "Be strong and of good courage." Sharing hymn books, the "close-packed ranks of British and American sailors" sang "O God Our Help in Ages Past" and "Onward, Christian Soldiers."[20] Churchill wept openly. Two lines in the closing hymn,

"Eternal Father, Strong to Save," were prophetic: "O hear us when we cry to Thee, For those in peril on the sea."[21] In four months the *Prince of Wales* would be sunk by Japanese dive and torpedo bombers off the coast of Malaya, and half of the British officers and men attending the service would be dead.[22]

"Every word stirred the heart," Churchill wrote later. "It was a great hour to live."[23] To Elliott, FDR said, "If nothing else had happened while we were here, that would have cemented us. 'Onward, Christian Soldiers.' We *are*, and we *will* go on, with God's help."[24]

Emotion faced reality in the remaining two days of the conference, as Churchill encountered Roosevelt's visceral aversion to making clear-cut decisions and his reluctance to be cornered. Churchill and his advisors thought they had extracted a commitment from the president to deliver a statement to Japan's government, along with a similar note from the British, that further aggression by the Japanese in the Far East "might lead to war." The British felt strongly that such a threat would pressure Japan to back down. FDR, although privately harboring doubts, gave Churchill an assurance he would carry through with this threat, but in fact he did not. The message he actually handed to Ambassador Nomura back in Washington on August 17 contained watered-down State Department diplomat-speak but no threat of war.[25]

After listening to Roosevelt explain the current mood of Congress, Churchill knew he could not achieve his primary objective of persuading him to ask for a declaration of war against Germany. However, with Hopkins's assurance of support, the prime minister succeeded in pushing the president another step closer to hostilities.[26] Based on the map torn from the *National Geographic*, FDR expressly agreed that the United States would provide *armed escorts* for British convoys as far as the line he had drawn that curved two hundred miles to the east of Iceland, thus putting real teeth into the concept of policing that had been left up in the air. This commitment, which Roosevelt promptly implemented, was a bold step that raised the stakes in the Atlantic war. He also agreed to ask Congress for another $5 billion in lend-lease aid.[27] Some historians have written that Roosevelt privately assured Churchill that America would "wage but not declare war" and would try to force an "incident" with a German U-boat that would justify a declaration of war.[28] Whether or not true, it is clear that Churchill came away from the conference believing Roosevelt had given him this commitment. But to Churchill's great distress, Roosevelt would soon tell the American press that no private deals were made at the conference and that the United States was no closer to entering the war.[29]

As an alternative to specific pledges and decisions that might not play well on the home front, Roosevelt had stressed since his first session with Churchill the need for a joint declaration of general principles on which the two governments "base[d] their hopes for a better future for the world."[30] This declaration, called the Atlantic Charter, which Roosevelt wanted to release to the press at the conclusion of the conference, was an expression of lofty intentions but was vague and noncommittal, hardly what Churchill had in mind. However, he agreed to the concept because Roosevelt was insistent and he felt it would at least proclaim to the world that the bonds between the two nations had grown much closer at the conference. For the most part, the British public, hoping that the United States would enter the war, regarded the provisions of the Atlantic Charter as little more than a press release—although they would have far-reaching implications. In America the Charter was criticized by isolationists and anti-Communists for failing to mention freedom of religion, and as the historian Max Hastings wrote, it "aroused little popular enthusiasm."[31]

Among other principles, the Charter proclaimed the rights of people to choose their own form of government, an assurance of freedom from fear and want after the Nazi tyranny had been destroyed, a call for disarmament, and the establishment of a postwar international organization for general security (a precursor to the United Nations). Roosevelt had initially balked at the idea of a permanent peacekeeping organization, mindful of Woodrow Wilson's failure to bring the United States into the League of Nations after World War I. Sumner Welles and Hopkins, however, persuaded him. Welles pointed out that even if the victorious nations undertook to police the postwar world, the smaller nations would need an assembly to voice their complaints; Hopkins argued that the American people would support a strong organization to enforce peace and that it would be pointless to include a call for disarmament in the Charter without at the same time having an enforcement mechanism.[32]

On the last day of the conference, August 12, the entire Atlantic Charter almost foundered over Point 4, the free trade provision. It was at this juncture that Hopkins, who had stayed in the shadows at the conference, stepped forward, saying it was "inconceivable that the issues of the joint declaration should be held up by a matter of this kind."[33] The British operated under a system whereby countries within their commonwealth could give each other preferential treatment in trading with one another (called "the imperial preference"), whereas the United States, despite a long history of protectionism, had maintained a free-trade stance during the past nine years under Secretary of State Cordell Hull. The Americans were insisting on language in the Charter that would eliminate the imperial preference, and Churchill was claiming he could not agree without seeking approval by the dominion prime ministers, which would significantly delay issuance of the Charter and therefore dilute its impact. Judging pragmatically that a possible reduction in trade barriers was not as important as the release of the Atlantic Charter to the world press at the conclusion of the conference, Hopkins undermined the State Department and suggested language that essentially preserved the imperial preference. Welles, representing the State Department (Hull was not there), was furious. Roosevelt, however, sided with Hopkins.[34]

Final revisions to the Atlantic Charter were agreed to early on the afternoon of August 12, and it was released to the world in mimeographed form two days later. (To avoid presenting it to the Senate for approval as a treaty, it was not inscribed, signed, and sealed by the president; however, it was approved by Churchill's war cabinet.) It was a remarkable document for the president to endorse since it advocated the "destruction of Nazi tyranny" despite the fact that the United States was still formally neutral. Consequently the Charter was regarded by many as sounding the death knell of American isolationism and a commitment by the United States to wage war and make world peace together with Great Britain. By agreeing "to respect" the right of self-government, which some interpreted as a guarantee, it also presaged the dissolution of the British Empire, although that was certainly not Churchill's intention. Read in context, the self-determination provisions seemed to be aimed at preventing the eventual victors (the United States, Great Britain, and hopefully the Soviet Union) from establishing postwar boundaries for the nations overrun by the Axis powers without the support and participation of the people affected.

As the conference was ending, word came from Washington that the draft-extension bill had passed the House by a single vote (203–202). Had the bill not passed, all of those previously drafted into the Army by the Selective Service Act of 1940 would have been released from their twelve-month commitment and could have gone home; the Army would have melted away just a few months before the Pearl Harbor attack.[35] Although the vote was good news, the one-vote margin was disheartening, especially to the British, and drove home the depth of FDR's political challenges. It had a "decidedly chilling effect" on everyone at the conference, recalled Hopkins.[36]

With handshakes all around, Churchill saw the presidential party off the *Prince of Wales* at about 3:30 p.m. on August 12. Cradling in his arms the ship's cat, Blackie, who had tried to follow them, Churchill saluted them as their launch headed over to the *Augusta*. Ninety minutes later, in what Roosevelt described as "a very moving scene," the *Prince of Wales* passed out of the harbor, with all crews at quarters, its band playing "Auld Lang Syne." At 5:10 the *Augusta* "stood out of the harbor with [her] escort, homeward bound."[37]

Hopkins had reason to be satisfied. His coaching of Roosevelt and Churchill on how to deal with one another had worked beautifully. He had used wit, whispered asides, and his characteristic caustic and irreverent humor to ease tensions and increase rapport between the two strong-willed leaders and their respective countrymen. Anticipating a flare-up over lend-lease, he would cool tempers and provoke laughter by suggesting that instead of garden hoses the British should ship their statues to America to repay in kind.[38] His humor often challenged pretense but was oddly endearing. In a few months he would send Churchill a birthday letter: "Dear Winston, happy birthday. How old are you anyway?"[39]

Hopkins functioned as a mediator. When he sensed that disagreements could be bridged, he urged compromise. If views seemed to be hardening, he met privately with one or the other leader, and sometimes both, to find a middle ground. In no small part because of him, the president and the prime minister came away from the conference with mutual feelings of warmth, affection, and respect. "But," as Sherwood shrewdly observed, "neither of them ever forgot for one instant what he was and represented or what the other was and represented."[40]

Hopkins's greatest influence involved shaping policy. He counseled Churchill on how to push Roosevelt into taking further steps toward war. He emerged from the shadows when matters threatened to dismember or delay the Atlantic Charter, convincing Roosevelt that the American people would favor a world peacekeeping organization and persuading him to compromise on the free trade provision.

As the *Augusta* headed toward the Maine coast, where the president would hold a press conference, Hopkins was completely exhausted but pleased with what he had accomplished during the month he had been away from the United States. He had traveled thousands of miles by air and sea to bring Roosevelt and Churchill together and to lay the foundation for bringing Stalin into what would be the winning coalition.

Back in Washington, Hopkins proudly showed friends the hat Churchill had given him in London with the cherished "W.S.C." embossed in the liner. To reciprocate, Hopkins sent Churchill a flip-top portable radio so he could listen to BBC broadcasts at Chequers.[41]

Roosevelt, meanwhile, was biding his time, perhaps waiting for a provocative incident, while assuring the press that Churchill had not succeeded in moving the United States any "closer to war." Churchill cabled Hopkins, reporting "a wave of depression through the Cabinet and other informed circles here about the President's many assurances about no commitments and no closer to war, etc. If 1942 opens with Russia knocked out and Britain left alone again, all kinds of dangers may arise. . . . You will know best whether anything more can be done. Should be grateful if you give me any kind of hope."[42] By this time Churchill understood that Hopkins had an uncanny sense of knowing when and how to approach Roosevelt about "whether anything more can be done." Within a day or two Hopkins found the right moment to show Churchill's cable to FDR and suggested that if the British concluded America would not enter the war, the appeasers in Britain might persuade Churchill's government to consider cutting a "peace in our time" deal with Hitler. Roosevelt listened but did not react.

The "incident" that Churchill hoped would finally rouse the U.S. president took place on September 4, 1941. In an area of the North Atlantic not far from Iceland, where Roosevelt ordered armed escorts to accompany British convoys, the same area Hitler had declared a German war zone, the flush-deck destroyer *Greer*, having been alerted by a British patrol plane, began closely tracking via sonar the location of a German U-boat. (By September 1941 the QC series sonar had been installed as standard equipment on all U.S. destroyers.) The *Greer* radioed location coordinates to the British plane, which proceeded to drop several depth charges on top of and around the submerged submarine. The German submarine commander most likely thought that the destroyer, which had been tracking him and pinging his hull for hours, actually dropped the depth charges. He therefore fired torpedoes at the *Greer* in self-defense. The *Greer* then dropped at least eleven depth charges around the U-boat before breaking off the engagement. Neither the U-boat nor the *Greer* sustained damages or casualties. The German commander may not have known whether the tracking destroyer was American or British.

Viewing the encounter objectively, it was the *Greer*, not the U-boat, that was the aggressor. However, Roosevelt was not interested in objectivity. The next day, meeting with Hopkins and Hull at lunch, the president decided to give a fireside chat wherein he would use the incident to move public opinion as well as Congress closer to a state of open hostilities with the Germans. Because the normally cautious Hull seemed unusually outraged that day, Roosevelt asked the State Department to prepare the first draft of the speech, which would be worked over by Hopkins and fellow speechwriter Sam Rosenman.[43]

The fireside chat had to be delayed. Over the weekend of September 6–7, Sara Delano Roosevelt, the president's mother, died at Hyde Park of a blood clot that lodged in her lung. His mother's death had a profound effect on Roosevelt. Even Hopkins, who knew him as well as anyone, "could not presume to guess at the quality of sorrow caused him," wrote Sherwood.[44] Sara Delano was difficult to deal with, and Franklin often clashed with her, but her devotion to him ran far deeper than anyone else's, and he loved being the singular object of her joy in living. Eleanor was at his side and "consoled him," said their son James, showing him "more affection during those days than at any other time that [he could] recall."[45]

Hopkins was reluctant, but he felt he had no choice except to phone Roosevelt at Hyde Park several hours after Sara passed away. The draft of the fireside chat prepared by Hull and the State Department was completely unacceptable—once again it lapsed into diplomatic babble, failing to be explicit as to precisely what action would be taken as a result of the *Greer* incident and why. Hopkins needed Roosevelt's approval to rewrite it. Roosevelt agreed it needed to be redone and asked Hopkins and Rosenman to meet his train in New York City after the funeral so they could work over the new draft together while returning to Washington.[46] For the next few days, reported the *New York Times*, Roosevelt "shut himself off from the world more completely than at any time" since he had become president.[47] He wore a black mourning band on his left sleeve and would wear it everywhere for the next year. He broke down only once, after opening a box of letters he wrote to his mother when he was a boy that she had carefully wrapped in tissue paper.[48]

On the evening of September 11, the president delivered his fireside chat, which the administration claimed afterward was heard by the second-largest American audience on record. (The largest was probably the "arsenal of democracy" speech.)[49] He began with a deceptive account of the *Greer* incident, telling the American people that the German U-boat "deliberately fired a torpedo at the *Greer*" but omitting the fact that the destroyer had provoked the attack. He then sought to move American opinion another step closer to war with phrases crafted by Hopkins, Rosenman, and of course himself: "We have sought no shooting war with Hitler. We do not seek it now. . . . But when you see a rattlesnake poised to strike, you do not wait until he has struck before you crush him. These Nazi submarines and raiders are the rattlesnakes of the Atlantic. . . . [If they enter waters] which we deem necessary for our defense . . . they do so at their own peril."[50] In other words, for the first time, American naval vessels and planes were authorized to shoot, bomb, and sink German submarines and surface vessels to protect merchant shipping. Hopkins had wanted the president to go even further—to order his forces to hunt and sink all German ships in the American-proclaimed zone of defense—but Roosevelt felt he had gone far enough.[51] The next day newspapers blared that the war in the North Atlantic had become "a shooting war," and a several days later headlines characterized the new rules of engagement as "shoot on sight."[52]

Roosevelt and Hopkins expected the rattlesnake speech to trigger a wave of adverse press from the isolationist opposition. However, on the same night as FDR's fireside chat, Charles Lindbergh, the most prominent spokesman for isolationism, delivered a nakedly anti-Semitic speech at an America First rally in Hopkins's home state of Iowa that was broadcast nationally. Jews constituted "the greatest danger to this country," he proclaimed, because of "their large ownership and influence in our motion pictures, our press, our radio and our government," all of which were agitating for war.[53] The uproar in the press over his address drowned out criticism of Roosevelt's provocative new policy and resulted in a significant setback to the isolationist cause.[54]

As he no doubt knew it would, Roosevelt's policy resulted in the kind of incidents on the high seas that inexorably moved public opinion closer to war. In October the U.S. destroyer *Kearney* was hit but not sunk by a U-boat torpedo that killed eleven and wounded several others. Later that month the destroyer *Reuben James* was sunk off the west coast of Iceland, losing 115 officers and crew. In a speech given on Navy Day, October 27, Roosevelt elevated the rhetoric and his voice: "The shooting has started . . . and history has recorded who fired the first shot. . . . America has been attacked!"[55] He claimed to possess secret Nazi documents, including maps, showing plans to "abolish all existing religions" and to take over Central and South America, including "our great life line—the Panama Canal." There is now considerable evidence that these documents, which Roosevelt refused to produce, were forgeries prepared by British agents and designed to draw the United States into the war.[56]

The loss of life in the North Atlantic and Roosevelt's Navy Day speech probably led to attainment of the majority in Congress that was needed to amend the Neutrality Acts, which had been passed throughout the 1930s. Since early October Roosevelt had been pleading with Congress to revise the Acts so that merchant ships could be armed and war matériel could be delivered to ports in Great Britain and Russia. (The Acts barred U.S. merchant vessels from calling at ports of nations engaged in war.) On November 7 the amendments were passed by slender majorities in both the House (212–194) and the Senate (50–37).[57] On the same day Roosevelt exercised his authority under the lend-lease legislation and ordered that the USSR should be covered along with Britain.[58]

During the conference in Placentia Bay, Roosevelt and Churchill had agreed that there should be a three-power supply meeting in Moscow in late September. On the last day of the shipboard conference, Hopkins had helped Churchill persuade Lord Beaverbrook, the thin-skinned British minister of supply, to be the British delegate to the Moscow meeting.[59] It was assumed that Hopkins would be the U.S. delegate, but after he returned to Washington he realized that he was not strong enough for another grueling trip to the Soviet Union, so he suggested Averell Harriman. Roosevelt approved.[60] A "Hopkins creation from beginning the end," as one historian has put it, the purpose of the Beaverbrook-Harriman mission to Moscow was to determine precisely what supplies were needed by the Soviets in the next twelve months and, perhaps more important, how to get the supplies safely into their hands.[61] From his room in the White House, Hopkins assembled a team to accompany the mission, including the controversial Colonel Philip Faymonville, to serve as its executive secretary. Faymonville, a West Pointer, was uniquely qualified because he had served in Russia for years, knew the language, and had the confidence of Soviet authorities. However, because he was so pro-Russian, the War Department was suspicious and suspected him of being a Communist. There were also rumors that he was homosexual.[62] When the Army balked at his appointment to the mission, Hopkins held firm, saying, "You might as well get his papers ready because he's going over."[63] On September 14 Harriman, Faymonville, and the rest of the American delegation left Washington for London and from there traveled by ship and air to Moscow.

By the time the Beaverbrook-Harriman team arrived in Moscow, factories were being dismantled and moved farther east as Field Marshal von Bock's Army Group Center resumed its advance, called Operation Typhoon, toward the capital. More than half a million Soviet troops had surrendered near Kiev on September 16, and the Red Army suffered 350,000 casualties in the losing defense of that city. Leningrad had been cut off, and its residents were facing starvation.[64] Churchill was genuinely concerned that if the supply mission attempted to extract concessions from Stalin or did anything to arouse suspicions as to their motives, the Soviets would negotiate a separate peace with the Nazis. Reflecting this concern, Beaverbrook said as he departed, "We are going to Moscow not to bargain but to give."[65]

After three days of talks with Stalin and Molotov, an agreement was signed committing the British and the Americans to supplying seventy items of armaments and goods in specified quantities by June 30, 1942, at a cost of $1 billion.[66] The Anglo-American group did not conduct due diligence on the need for any of the items, how they would be used, or how they would be financed. (The USSR would not be covered by lend-lease until November 7.)[67] After the agreement was signed, Maxim Litvinov, the former foreign minister who was acting as interpreter, jumped up, saying, "Now we shall win the war!"[68] As the Beaverbrook-Harriman team was preparing to depart Moscow, Hopkins cabled the announcement that Colonel Faymonville had been appointed head of lend-lease in Russia and would be staying on in Moscow. The War and State Departments objected, the embassy staff in Moscow protested, and even Harriman was "shocked."[69] But Hopkins stuck to his guns. Faymonville was his man in Moscow.

Two weeks after the supply mission left, snow began to fall on Moscow with increasing intensity, developing into a five-day blizzard.[70] Into the teeth of the early onset of the Russian winter, Bock's armies attacked Moscow from the north, west, and south, occupying points in the closing days of November only fifteen miles from the city. However, they were approaching the limits of their strength as Red Army soldiers, no longer retreating in panic, fought and died where they stood. On December 1 Bock launched his final, all-out strike at Moscow along the entire three-sided front. In Stalin's office the telephone rang. According to General Alexander Golovanov,

Stalin picked up the receiver and held it away from his ear so Golovanov could hear. An officer on the staff of General Zhukov, the commanding general in the field, requested authority to move Zhukov's headquarters east of Moscow because they thought they were about to be overrun.

Speaking into the receiver, Stalin told the staff officer to "ask them whether they have any spades."

"What sort of spades, Comrade Stalin? Entrenching tools or some other kind?"

"It doesn't matter what sort."

"Yes there are spades, Comrade Stalin. What should they do with them?"

Stalin calmly replied, "Tell your comrades to take their spades and dig themselves some graves. The Stavka's [General Headquarters] not leaving Moscow. I'm not leaving Moscow."[71]

On December 5 the Red Army launched a counterattack in temperatures ranging from zero to forty below zero over the ensuing days.[72] The Germans never entered Moscow.

After Harriman left Washington in September 1941 to join Beaverbrook for their mission to Moscow, Hopkins's strength and stamina still had not bounced back following his exhausting summer. His day-to-day responsibilities, however, continued to increase. In an effort to spur lagging war production and the shipment of supplies to Russia and Britain, the president interposed another one of his incomprehensible bureaucratic creations between the White House and existing agencies. And to make sure ultimate control stayed in the White House, he assigned Hopkins a spot on the board of the new agency.[73]

As his responsibilities grew and his health deteriorated, Hopkins persuaded Roosevelt to appoint his friend Edward Stettinius to take over the actual administration of the rapidly expanding lend-lease program. Stettinius, the silver-maned former chairman of United States Steel, described being summoned to the White House, where he found Hopkins in bed surrounded by papers, some stuffed under his pillow. "Ed," said Hopkins, "the President wants you to take over administration of the Lend-Lease program. He thinks there is nothing more important now for the country than getting this Lend-Lease show moving at top speed." Stettinius accepted the request and said he would do his best. "Does the President want to talk it over with me first?" Hopkins replied in the negative, saying "So far as the President is concerned, you're elected, Ed."[74]

The pressures on the president and the ailing Hopkins that autumn were enormous and unrelenting, but the two of them found time to relax and dream of a peaceful future together. FDR often talked about building a fishing camp on Channel Key in Florida, and Hopkins wrote to a friend about the feasibility of acquiring the island. Exchanging sketches and notes about their plans, they continued to chat about the fishing camp into the first week of December.[75]

Oil—that is, the shortage of oil—would precipitate the Japanese attack on December 7. As noted, in the summer of 1941, before leaving for Placentia Bay, Roosevelt had ordered a freeze on Japanese assets, which required the Japanese to seek and obtain licenses to export and pay for each shipment of goods from the United States, including oil. Although this move was most distressing to the Japanese because they were dependent on the United States for most of their crude oil and refined petroleum products, the president's intention was to keep the oil flowing by continuing to grant licenses. He had a noose around Japan's neck, but he chose not to tighten it. He was not ready to cut off its oil lifeline for fear that such a move would be regarded as tantamount to an act of war.[76] While Roosevelt, Hopkins, and Welles were attending the shipboard conference off Newfoundland and Hull was on vacation at the Greenbrier in West Virginia, the authority to grant licenses to export and pay for oil and other goods was in the hands of a three-person interagency committee dominated by Assistant Secretary of State Dean Acheson, who one historian described as the "quintessential opportunist of U.S. foreign policy in 1941."[77] Acheson favored a "bullet-proof freeze" on oil shipments to Japan, claiming it would not provoke war because "no rational Japanese could believe that an attack on us could result in anything but disaster for his country." With breathtaking confidence in his own judgment, and ignoring the objections of others in the State Department, Acheson refused to grant licenses to Japan to pay for goods in dollars, effectively ending Japan's ability to ship oil and all other goods from the United States. His actions cut off *all* American trade with Japan. When Roosevelt returned, he decided not to overturn the "state of affairs" initiated by Acheson, apparently because he feared he would be regarded as an appeaser.[78]

Once Roosevelt perpetuated Acheson's trade embargo, the planners in Japan's imperial military headquarters knew that oil to fuel their fleet, as well as rubber, rice, and other vital reserves, would soon run out. By the end of the year at the latest, Japan would need to capture new supply sources in the oil-rich Dutch East Indies, which the United States would surely oppose. And to protect its long exposed flank as it moved south, the Japanese Navy would have to deliver a knockout blow to U.S. naval and air power in the Pacific. Without oil, Japan could not survive a long war.[79] The blow would be delivered at Pearl Harbor.

Throughout the summer and autumn the First Carrier Division of the Japanese Navy secretly practiced low-level torpedo bombing in Kagoshima Bay, which bore a resemblance to Pearl Harbor.[80] The plans for the Pearl Harbor attack were being developed by Admiral Yamamoto Isoroku, an innovative thinker with what the historian Gordon Prange has called "a gambler's heart."[81] In September the prime minister, Prince Konoye Fumimaro, who had been urging a personal meeting with the president to reach a peace agreement, was almost assassinated by pro-war fanatics wielding ceremonial knives. Weakened by the attempt to overthrow him and losing power and influence to militarist elements, Prince Konoye's government fell on October 16.[82] That day, meeting with Hopkins and his top military advisors, FDR expressed concern that the new government would be "much more anti-American" than the old.[83] Sure enough, two days later General Tojo Hideki, leader of the militarists and the minister of war, became Japan's prime minister.[84]

Anticipating a move southward by the Japanese, the United States began reinforcing its air forces in the Philippines and constructing a chain of airfields from Hawaii toward Australia and the Philippines. These moves provided hard evidence to support Tojo's arguments for war as soon as possible.[85]

In Washington Ambassador Nomura, who begged to be relieved after Tojo took over the government, was ordered to stay on and continue to offer elaborate proposals for settling the looming crisis, proposals that

Tojo knew would be rejected by the United States. The Japanese offered to reverse their aggressive designs on Indochina and to begin to withdraw troops only if peace with China was achieved without interference by the United States (in other words, on Japan's terms) and only if the United States restored trade in oil and other resources. The United States could not possibly agree to this because it would amount to an abandonment of China and its Nationalist government. For its part, the Roosevelt administration, as the price for lifting trade sanctions, continued to insist that Japan withdraw its troops from China and Indochina and reconsider its commitment to the Tripartite Pact (by which Japan would declare war if the United States joined in the European war against Germany). In the final days Secretary of State Hull also proposed that in any settlement with China, the United States and Japan would agree to recognize no Chinese government other than that of the Nationalists led by Chiang Kai-shek. There was not the slightest chance that Tojo would accept these proposals.

Nomura pleaded with Tojo for more time to negotiate, but he refused, saying a settlement agreement with the United States must be signed by November 29. "After that, things are automatically going to happen."[86] At a cabinet meeting on November 7, Hull warned that Japan might attack at any time.[87] Roosevelt ordered him to keep the negotiations going and to "do nothing to precipitate a crisis."[88]

On November 22 Admiral Yamamoto ordered the First Carrier Division at Hitokappu Bay in the Kuriles, north of Japan's main islands, to "move out . . . on 26 November and proceed without being detected to the evening rendezvous point . . . set for 3 December. X-day will be December 8 [Japanese time]."[89] At a large rally in Tokyo on November 30, Prime Minister Tojo incited the crowd, claiming that the United States and Britain, in order to "satisfy their greed," were preventing development of the "East Asia Co-Prosperity Sphere." "We must purge this . . . practice from East Asia with a vengeance," he said.[90] It was this speech that caused Roosevelt to cut short a belated Thanksgiving in Warm Springs and return to Washington the next day.[91]

Throughout the fall of 1941 Hopkins had been focused on production and supply matters, but he was kept apprised of the ongoing negotiations with the Japanese through Roosevelt, Hull, and Welles. During a five-day working session at Hyde Park with the president in early November, Hopkins experienced difficulty in walking, saying, "My pedal extremities refused to work anymore."[92] On November 5 he checked into the Naval Hospital, which at that time was located at 24th and E Streets, not far from the White House. While receiving blood transfusions and nutrients, he continued to direct from his hospital room what had become known as the "Hopkins Shop," a loose, informal circle of advisors centered on lend-lease but with tentacles reaching into the military, American corporations, various cabinet departments, government agencies involved in production and shipping, and contacts in London and Moscow. Meeting with production officials in late November, Ed Stettinius, a charter member of the Hopkins Shop and an admirer of the man who ran it, said, "Harry is better—lots better. He'll be able to leave the hospital soon. And he will be back with us before long.[93]

As the crisis with Japan was entering its final stages, Hopkins was released from the hospital. On December 3 he returned to his rooms in the White House and was once again at Roosevelt's side. The same day special Japanese envoy Kurusu Saburo, dining with the financier and FDR political advisor Bernard Baruch at the Mayflower Hotel, repeated a Hail Mary proposal he had made to Cordell Hull—that Harry Hopkins be sent to Japan as Roosevelt's emissary to broker a peace settlement.[94] Kurusu, a professional diplomat who was married to an American and spoke fluent English, was carrying out the penultimate act of an elaborate deception. He must have known that peace was no longer possible, although he almost certainly did not know his government was about to launch a surprise attack on Pearl Harbor.

8

We Are All in the Same Boat Now

"This son of man has just sent his final message to the son of God."[1] Roosevelt was making a weak joke, his voice suffused with sarcasm. He had just dispatched a last-ditch personal appeal to Emperor Hirohito for "peace throughout the whole Pacific area."[2] It was about nine in the evening on Saturday, December 6, 1941. Hopkins and Roosevelt were together in the Oval Study, the president having excused himself from a small dinner downstairs. Earlier that day reports had reached the White House that three Japanese convoys, including forty-six troop transports, a battleship, and a number of cruisers and destroyers, had rounded Cambodia Point and were entering the Gulf of Siam, headed west for either the Kra Isthmus on the Malay peninsula (north of Singapore) or Thailand (then Siam), or possibly south toward the oil fields of the Dutch East Indies.[3] FDR knew it was too late to make peace. However, with a view to making it part of the official record, he decided personally to write a message to the emperor, appealing to their "sacred duty" as leaders, and pleading to His Majesty "to give thought in this definite emergency to ways of dispelling the dark clouds."[4]

Minutes later, as Hopkins paced the floor, Commander Lester Schulz entered the study and handed a typewritten document to the president. It contained the first thirteen parts of a fourteen-part message from Tokyo to the Japanese Embassy in Washington that had been decoded by the cryptologists in the Army Intelligence Service. They had broken the Japanese diplomatic code and had been reading messages from Tokyo to embassies for more than a year. (The decrypts were code-named "Magic.")[5] For the most part, the document restated the Japanese position, characterizing their moves into Southeast Asia as peaceful and blaming the United States and its Western allies for increasing tensions in the region. In a tone of defiance, the final pages made it clear that "because of American attitudes," there was no chance of reaching a diplomatic settlement between the two nations.[6]

After reading every page, Roosevelt handed the sheaf of papers to Hopkins. When Hopkins was finished reading, the president, seated at his desk, declared, "This means war." In saying this, the president most likely was not suggesting that an imminent attack on U.S. naval forces or bases in the Pacific was about to take place. Rather in light of the tone and content of the decrypted Japanese document and his knowledge that Japanese troop transports at that moment were headed toward British or possibly Dutch possessions in Southeast Asia, FDR was expecting an outbreak of war that would inevitably involve the United States. Hopkins agreed, saying in substance that it was too bad the United States couldn't preempt the coming attack by striking the first blow. "No, we can't do that," replied Roosevelt. "We are a democracy and a peaceful people." Raising his voice, he continued, as if to formalize what he was about to say, "But we have a good record."[7]

By ten o'clock the next morning, December 7, the fourteenth and final part of the message, which had been deliberately delayed for twelve hours before being sent from Tokyo to its embassy in Washington, had been decrypted and delivered to Roosevelt. Couched in diplomatic rhetoric and again casting all blame on America and Great Britain for obstructing "Japan's efforts toward the establishment of peace through the creation of a New Order in Asia," the last words from the Tojo government ordered the termination of all negotiations with the United States.[8] Nomura and Kurusu, the chief diplomats in the embassy on Massachusetts Avenue, were instructed personally to deliver all fourteen parts of the message to Secretary of State Hull at precisely one o'clock that afternoon, which would be 7:30 a.m. in Hawaii. (In 1941 Hawaii was 5.5 hours behind the time on the U.S. East Coast.)

Two hundred twenty miles north of Oahu, Vice Admiral Nagumo Chūichi, commander of the First Air Fleet, turned his six carriers into the wind, increased their speed to twenty-four knots, and began to launch the first wave of his fighters, bombers, and torpedo-planes. A wedge-shaped battle formation of 350 planes gathered above the carriers and began heading toward their targets: dozens of U.S. warships arrayed in rows in Pearl Harbor and hundreds of fighter planes packed wing to wing on tarmacs at Hickam and Wheeler Fields and Kaneohe Air Station. It was 6:20 a.m. Hawaii time, 11:50 a.m. in Washington.[9]

A few minutes after noon, Eleanor Roosevelt's invitees for luncheon in the Blue Room—"thirty friends, relatives and New Deal functionaries, some from the Army Medical Corps"—began to arrive, ambling through the gates of the White House off Pennsylvania Avenue. One of the guests was heard to say, "Mrs. Roosevelt's secretary is cleaning up the edges of her social list." No one stopped them to ask for identification. It was bright and sunny, a brisk forty-three degrees.[10]

Upstairs in the Oval Study, the president, dressed in a turtleneck sweater and nursing a cold, had just concluded a meeting with Dr. Hu Shih, the Chinese ambassador, during which he monopolized the conversation by reading aloud—and providing a running commentary on—the letter he had sent to Emperor Hirohito the night before. Tearing open the envelope of select stamp specimens delivered every Saturday by the State Department, Roosevelt asked an usher to invite Hopkins to join him for lunch. He had begged off the luncheon downstairs.[11] The two had sandwiches and soup on trays prepared by Henrietta Nesbitt, engaging as always in chitchat, banter, and gossip. When FDR's tray was removed from the rack on his homemade wheelchair and Hopkins's tray was rolled away, the president turned to his stamp collection, munching an apple. Hopkins, in sweater and slacks, "lounged on a couch."[12]

At 1:47 p.m. the White House telephone operator rang the Oval Study and said that Frank Knox, secretary of the Navy, insisted on speaking with the president. "Put him on," said FDR. "Mr. President," Knox said, his voice cracking with emotion, "it looks as if the Japanese have bombed Pearl Harbor." "No," was the president's instinctive response.[13] Putting down the phone, he told Hopkins that a radio report had just been received from Honolulu, saying that Pearl Harbor was being attacked by air and that it was "no drill." Hopkins thought the report was wrong. As he noted in a memorandum that he wrote about events that day, "I expressed the belief that there must be some mistake and that surely Japan would not attack in Honolulu."[14] Like virtually all civilian and military Washington insiders, Hopkins expected an attack in Malaysia, the East Indies, or possibly the Philippines. Roosevelt retorted that the report was probably correct— that this was just the kind of thing the Japanese would do if they could.[15] Given the repeated war warnings that had been sent from Washington to the nine Navy and Army chiefs responsible for defending Pearl Harbor and other military assets throughout the Pacific during the preceding two weeks, Roosevelt and Hopkins assumed that the fleet and air forces at Pearl Harbor were prepared for the attack and that they were engaged in a furious counterattack. At this early moment no one in Washington knew how completely surprised and unprepared they were.

For a few minutes Roosevelt and Hopkins discussed the implications of the attack. According to Hopkins's notes, Roosevelt remarked that if the report was accurate, and he "thought it was," the decision to go to war had been taken "entirely out of his own hands, because the Japanese had made it for him."[16] Roosevelt's first action was to telephone Cordell Hull and inform him of the attack, for he knew Nomura and Kurusu were scheduled to be at the State Department by one o'clock. Hull told him that the Japanese envoys had asked for a postponement and were only then arriving. The president instructed Hull to say nothing about the Pearl Harbor report, accept delivery of the fourteen-part document, "and bow them out."

A few minutes later Grace Tully, FDR's secretary, put through a call from Admiral Harold "Betty" Stark, chief of naval operations. Stark confirmed the accuracy of the initial radio report. He informed the president that the attack had inflicted very severe damage on the fleet and that loss of life was considerable.[17] Roosevelt accepted the devastating news calmly, almost with a sense of relief, and without recriminations about the evident lack of preparedness. "His reaction to any great event was always to be calm," observed Eleanor Roosevelt. "If it was something bad, he just became almost like an iceberg, and there was never the slightest emotion that was allowed to show."[18]

Hopkins was with the president for most of the rest of the day and late into the evening. At 3 p.m. Roosevelt convened his war council—Hull, Stimson, Knox, Marshall, and Stark. While they were hearing Hull's report of his meeting with Nomura and Kurusu (Hull referred to them as "bastards" and "pissants") and discussing diplomatic messages, war mobilization orders, and military deployments, a call came from Gil Winant, the U.S. ambassador to Great Britain, who was spending the weekend with Churchill.[19] Winant, Churchill, and guests had been dining at Chequers when Sawyers, Churchill's valet, brought in the portable flip-top radio that Hopkins had given Churchill so that they could listen to the 9 p.m. BBC news broadcast (3 p.m. Washington time). Averell Harriman, one of the guests, heard the announcer say, "The Japanese have raided Pearl Harbor," but others thought he had said "Pearl River," the river leading to Canton and for years the major trading route between the West and China. Minutes later the Admiralty called, however, and confirmed that Pearl Harbor had indeed been attacked.[20]

When Winant got Roosevelt on the telephone, he told him that he was with a friend who wanted to speak with him. He handed the phone to Churchill. "Mr. President, what's this about Japan?" "It's quite true," FDR responded. "They have attacked us at Pearl Harbor. We are all in the same boat now." Roosevelt added that he would be going to Congress the next day to ask for a declaration of war. The prime minister said he would do the same in the House of Commons. "This certainly simplifies things," said Churchill. "God be with you."[21]

Churchill, who had "seemed tired and depressed" earlier in the evening, snapped out of his lethargy.[22] As he wrote later, "To have the United States at our side was to me the greatest joy." After midnight he dictated a cable to Hopkins: "Thinking of you much at this historic moment—WINSTON,

AVERELL." Then, "being saturated and satiated with emotion and sensation," he "went to bed and slept the sleep of the saved and thankful."[23]

As the war council meeting in Washington was drawing to a close at half past four in the afternoon, Hopkins advised Roosevelt to convene two meetings later that evening—one of the entire cabinet and another with key congressional leaders.[24] While Hopkins excused himself to help organize these meetings and attend to the preparation and issuance of presidential orders, FDR called Grace Tully to the Oval Study at about 5 p.m. Taking a deep drag on his cigarette, he said, "Sit down, Grace. I'm going before Congress tomorrow. I'd like to dictate my message. It will be short."[25]

The first draft of Roosevelt's "date which will live in infamy" message to Congress was ready when Hopkins, Tully, the president, and his son Jimmy gathered in the Oval Study for a light dinner of scrambled eggs, cold cuts, and an apricot Bavarian cream pie.[26] The phone was ringing constantly as increasingly disheartening news of the Pearl Harbor attack was being reported to the president. The death toll was climbing and the amount of damage seemed unthinkable. Hopkins and the president went over the speech, Hopkins making suggestions and the president inserting a few corrections.

Outside, silent crowds gathered along the White House fence, faces looking up anxiously toward the brightly lit windows on the second floor. Guards brandishing machine guns surrounded the White House. Automobiles moved slowly along Pennsylvania Avenue.

At 8:30 the entire cabinet entered the Oval Study and "formed a ring completely around the President," wrote Hopkins who was seated next to FDR at his desk.[27] Recalling the cabinet meeting convened by Abraham Lincoln that led to the outbreak of the Civil War, a meeting held around a scuffed walnut table in the very same room, Roosevelt began, "This is the most serious meeting of the Cabinet that has taken place since 1861."[28] He recounted the damage caused by the attack, revealing for the first time the depth of his disappointment and even anger that both the Navy and the Army Air Force had been caught so completely unprepared. "Find out, for God's sake," he twice asked Knox, "why the ships were tied up in rows."[29] FDR read the message that he planned to deliver to Congress the next day. Hull argued that he should explain in detail the background leading up to the attack, but Roosevelt "stuck to his guns," preferring a short message, less than five hundred words.[30]

After about an hour Vice President Wallace and eight congressional leaders joined the cabinet meeting. Roosevelt brought them up to date on the extent of the damage. "It looks as if out of eight battleships, three have been sunk, possibly a fourth," he informed them. "I have no word on Navy casualties which will undoubtedly be heavy."[31] The Senators and House members "sat in dead silence," wrote Stimson.[32] Finally, Texas Senator Tom Connally, chairman of the Foreign Relations Committee, spoke up: "How did it happen that our warships were caught like tame ducks in Pearl Harbor?.... They were all asleep!... Where were our patrols?"[33]

The meeting with the leadership disbanded around eleven, it having been agreed that the president would address a joint session of Congress on the morrow. FDR and Hopkins were still wound up, so the president asked Bill Donovan (who had been summoned earlier from a football game in New York) and Ed Murrow (who was waiting downstairs with his wife, having had dinner with Mrs. Roosevelt) to join them in the Oval Study for beer and sandwiches. Roosevelt grilled Donovan, his Columbia Law School classmate who would become head of clandestine intelligence (the OSS) and was then coordinator of information, on whether the Germans were behind the surprise attack on Pearl Harbor. From Murrow, the CBS correspondent who had just returned from London, the president wanted to know how he thought the attack would affect American opinion. Without asking Murrow to keep his comments off the record, Roosevelt let his hair down, confessing his despair at how the Japanese had caught his armed forces off guard. "Our planes were destroyed on the ground, by God, on the ground!" he said, striking his fist on his desk. Murrow anguished over whether to report what the president told him, but in the end he kept his remarks confidential until after the war.[34]

By this time, after midnight, the president signaled that he was ready to retire. Hopkins invited Murrow down the hall to continue their discussion about the day's events while he got ready for bed. Sitting on the end of the bed, his wasting body hidden beneath too-large pajamas, he told Murrow that the Japanese attack was a godsend because it meant the country would enter the war united. Thinking of what lay ahead, he said in a barely audible whisper, "Oh God—if I only had the strength."[35]

On Monday morning Hopkins helped the president finalize his message to Congress. During the night and early morning, the overall scale of Yamamoto's grand strategy became apparent as reports of additional coordinated attacks by the Japanese in the Philippines, Malaya, Hong Kong, Guam, Wake Island, and Midway Island came pouring in. These needed to be added to Roosevelt's speech.[36]

At half past twelve, having arrived at the Capitol in an open car, grim-faced Franklin Roosevelt, steadied by steel braces, stood before the joint session of Congress and delivered his powerful twenty-five-sentence "infamy" speech. Letting the facts "speak for themselves," he catalogued Japan's aggression in the Pacific. Thunderous applause followed his final two sentences, the first written by Hopkins, the last by FDR: "With confidence in our armed forces—and with the unbounding determination of our people—we will gain the inevitable triumph—so help us God. I ask that the Congress declare that since the unprovoked and dastardly attack by Japan on Sunday, December 7, 1941, a state of war has existed between the United States and the Japanese Empire."[37]

In less than an hour Congress voted to declare war against Japan—unanimously in the Senate and with a single dissenter in the House, Jeannette Rankin of Montana, a pacifist who had also voted against war in 1917. Earlier that day, in London, Churchill's cabinet had authorized a declaration of war against Japan based on the landings in Malaya and the bombings of Singapore and Hong Kong. In his address to the House of Commons, Churchill struggled to identify a nexus with Nazi Germany, claiming, "Hitler's madness has infected the Japanese mind."[38]

For the president, a critical question hung in the air: What about Germany? Because of the sneak attack, Congress and the American public were united in going to war against Japan. However, Roosevelt, his military chiefs, and his foreign policy advisors had always believed that Germany was by far the greater threat to national security. Should Roosevelt risk dissent and push for a declaration of war against Germany?

He chose to wait. A cable sent from Berlin to Tokyo on November 29 that had been decrypted by Magic assured Japan that if it became involved in war against the United States, "Germany would of course join in the war immediately."[39] Thus the president had reason to believe Hitler would make the first move, though he couldn't be sure. Read literally, the Tripartite Pact did not obligate Hitler to declare war against America because Japan rather than the United States was the aggressor.

The führer certainly did not act immediately. When he learned of the Pearl Harbor attack on the evening of December 7, he was at the Wolfsschanze in East Prussia, ordering his troops to execute a tactical retreat as the resurgent Red Army launched its counterattack in the snows outside of Moscow. (His troops, however, were already retreating.) The Japanese attack at Pearl Harbor came as a complete surprise—Hitler's spies and diplomats had given him no forewarning. The next day he rushed back to Berlin by train.[40]

With no word from Germany, the suspense grew in Washington. Roosevelt and Hopkins and other speechwriters began shaping a fireside chat that Roosevelt wanted to deliver to the American people on Tuesday evening, December 9. The objective was to persuade the people and hence Congress that if Germany did not declare war on the United States within the next few days, then Congress *must* vote to declare war on Germany without lengthy debate because, it would be argued, conflict with Germany was indissolubly linked with the war against Japan. A related objective was to provoke Hitler into making the first move by hurling a few more threats and insults his way. The fireside chat was a success, although, like the "rattlesnake" speech, the president engaged in deception to make it so. To a radio audience of 60 million, he linked Japan's aggression with that of Germany, claiming, without any evidence, that the two nations "conducted their military and naval operations according to a joint plan." He also claimed, falsely, that Hitler was responsible for Pearl Harbor: "For weeks Germany has been telling Japan that if Japan did not attack the United States, Japan would not share in dividing the spoils when peace came." In a final provocation he said that the "sources of international brutality"—meaning the Nazis—"must be absolutely and finally broken."[41]

Hitler finally made his move on December 11, a decision characterized as "Hitler's greatest miscalculation" by the American military historian Rick Atkinson and as "the single most decisive act of the Second World War" by the British historian Martin Gilbert.[42] In a speech to the Reichstag assembled in the Kroll Opera House in the early afternoon, Hitler responded to FDR's fireside chat, directing a tirade against "that man who, while [German] soldiers are fighting in snow and ice . . . likes to make his chats from the fire-side, the man who is the main culprit of this war." Comparing his own success in achieving economic recovery from the Great Depression with Roosevelt's failure, Hitler said that Roosevelt, incited by American Jewry, had "turned to war as a solution of his difficulties." "The German Government," he concluded, "considers herself . . . in a state of war with the United States of America."[43] Italy immediately followed suit. By 3:05 on the afternoon of December 11, Congress voted unanimously to "recognize a state of war" between the United States and Germany and Italy (Congresswoman Rankin abstained).[44] Noting that the nation was now at war with all three of the Axis powers, Roosevelt joked grimly at the subdued signing ceremony, "I've always heard things came in threes."[45]

The president was relieved, although he had not expected to have a two-front war on his hands so soon. Hopkins too was relieved that Hitler had blinked and made the first move. In a transatlantic telephone conversation with Beaverbrook and Harriman at 5 p.m. on December 11, Hopkins said, "If Hitler thought he could start a war and [outproduce and outfight us] he is going to be greatly mistaken. . . . Things are going to turn out far better for you over there in the long run. . . . They made another mistake, by God."[46]

By the time Hitler declared war on the United States, reports of losses suffered at Pearl Harbor and other targets in the Pacific at the hands of the Japanese Navy had been tallied. Approximately 2,400 Americans perished; at least 1,100 were wounded. Five of the eight battleships at Pearl Harbor were sunk or damaged beyond repair, and it was estimated that it would take months before the remaining three could put to sea. Several cruisers, destroyers, and other vessels had been severely damaged or destroyed, although all three aircraft carriers in the Pacific Fleet escaped damage because they were not in the harbor during the attack.[47] More than 340 planes at Pearl were beyond repair, and eighteen precious B-17s and fifty-six fighters were destroyed on the ground at Clark Field in the Philippines.[48] The premier British battleship *Prince of Wales* and the heavy cruiser *Repulse* were sunk by Japanese planes with heavy loss of lives.

The losses were regarded as crippling by the Anglo-American military. The loss of life shocked the civilian leadership. To Joseph Stalin, however, such losses were trifling. Since June 22, when the Germans invaded, two to three *million* Soviet men and women mobilized for war had been killed or taken prisoner; on the front facing Moscow, 956,000 Red Army troops had been killed or captured.[49] By the end of the war an estimated *27 million* Soviet citizens, military and civilian, would die in combat or as a direct result of the brutal conflict.

Stalin learned of the Pearl Harbor attack late on the evening of December 7 while he was directing the crucial counteroffensive being waged in waist-deep snows in front of Moscow. He was pleased, of course, because he knew he would have an ally of enormous power that could threaten the Germans from the west, but the news did not cause him to send any message of condolence or support to Roosevelt. Given the immediate peril to the Russian capital, the Japanese attacks in the Pacific did not even make the front pages of the Moscow newspapers.[50]

By coincidence, on the morning of December 7 Maxim Litvinov, who was back in Stalin's good graces as his new ambassador to the United States, arrived in Washington after a long journey from Moscow. He and his very social English-born wife, Ivy Low, were having lunch that afternoon with Hopkins's pal Joe Davies at Tregaron, Davies's estate in northwest Washington on the edge of Rock Creek, when they learned of the Pearl Harbor attack. That night the lights burned late in the ornate Soviet Embassy on Sixteenth Street (the former Pullman mansion) as Litvinov began developing a strategy to pressure the United States to open a second front against the Germans in Western Europe. As noted earlier, Hopkins had met Litvinov briefly in Moscow, but through dinners and social occasions arranged by Davies, the two of them would quickly establish a close personal and confidential relationship.[51]

In London Churchill was worried that America's outrage over the sneak attack by the Japanese would cause Roosevelt and his advisors to abandon the "Germany first" strategy that had been agreed on in March 1941 and to instead concentrate on Japan. To head off this possibility, which he was convinced would be a monumental mistake, he cabled the president on December 9: "Now that we are as you say 'in the same boat' would it not be wise for us to have another conference? We could review the whole war plan in the light of reality and new facts, as well as production and distribution." Churchill proposed coming to Washington "by warship . . . with necessary staffs." "Delighted to have you here at the White House," the president responded.[52] The forthcoming White House conference with Churchill would be code-named Arcadia. Including side trips by Churchill to Canada and Florida, it would last for more than three weeks.

A few days later the prime minister and his entourage departed Greenock on River Clyde aboard the battleship *Duke of York*. On the stormy eight-day voyage in U-boat-infested seas, Churchill prepared strategy memos covering his five key points: "Germany first"; getting supplies to Russia; invading North Africa in 1942; closing the ring around Europe; and fighting naval but not land battles in the Pacific.[53] He need not have been worried about Roosevelt's adherence to "Germany first." At a critical conference convened by Roosevelt on the day before Churchill arrived, which included Hopkins, Stimson, Knox, Marshall, and the other military chiefs, the president agreed that Germany was still the prime enemy and her defeat the key to victory.[54]

Sweeping in "like a breath of fresh air, giving Washington new vigor," as *Time* magazine put it, the prime minister and his aides, bearing red leather dispatch cases, arrived at the White House on the evening of Monday, December 22.[55] Greeted by Eleanor Roosevelt and Alonzo Fields, the chief butler, as they emerged from the elevator on the second floor, Churchill explored the available rooms and decided to take up residence in the Rose suite, directly across the hall from Hopkins. The Monroe Room, next door to Hopkins, was transformed into a map room, where large maps of every theater of the war were hung, colored pins marking troop, ship, and air deployments. In the coming days Churchill and Roosevelt would spend many hours together surrounded by those maps, the clouds of smoke from Churchill's cigars mingling with that from the president's cigarettes.[56]

After cocktails mixed by FDR (which Churchill could not abide) and dinner that evening, Hopkins listened with deepening concern as the prime minister presented his arguments for an Anglo-American operation to invade French North Africa in 1942 (code-named Gymnast).[57] Since General Marshall and other U.S. military experts who favored a mass frontal offensive in Western Europe aimed at the heart of Germany were not present, the president had no protection from Churchill's powerful rhetoric and nearly irresistible blandishments—a situation that Hopkins and others would guard against in the future. There is no record of exactly what FDR said, and perhaps Churchill heard what he wanted to hear. In any case, the prime minister happily reported to his war cabinet, "The President . . . favoured the idea of a plan to move into North Africa . . . with or without invitation."[58] Thus in the very first hours of the Arcadia conference, the U.S. commander in chief had seemingly agreed, without any War or Navy Department input, to a major strategic war initiative.

Churchill was on a roll. The next morning he summoned Alonzo Fields to his bedroom. "Now Fields," he said to the butler, "we want to leave as friends, right? So I need you to listen. One, I don't like talking outside my quarters; two, I hate whistling in the corridors; and three, I must have a tumbler of sherry in my room before breakfast, a couple of glasses of scotch and soda before lunch and French champagne and 90 year old brandy before I go to sleep at night."[59]

That afternoon, after his customary nap, the prime minister went to work on the White House press corps. Standing atop a chair so that he could be seen in the crowded room, he replied to a question about how long it would take to win the war: "If we manage it well it will take only half as long as if we manage it badly." The reporters erupted in laughter. They loved the chubby bulldog in polka-dot bowtie and striped trousers with the impossibly long cigar clenched in his teeth.[60]

Nine-year-old Diana Hopkins wasn't sure what to make of the prime minister. One morning she was summoned to his room and found him in bed "smoking a cigar and sipping (possibly) a brandy." Due to "the combination of a stutter and an English accent," not to mention his lisp, she had trouble understanding what he wanted, but finally she understood him to say, "Come and give me a little kiss." As she later recalled, she "delivered the requested kiss and fled the room in high embarrassment."[61]

────────

When the military leaders arrived on the scene and the plenary sessions began, Churchill had a more difficult time getting his way. It began when Churchill was confronted with the stolid logic of Army Chief of Staff George Marshall and ended during a private meeting set up by Hopkins. At an early session Marshall had told the top American and British officers that based on failures he observed in the command structure during World War I and at Pearl Harbor (when the Army didn't know what the Navy was doing and vice versa), "the most important consideration [was] the question of unity of command." Continuing in his quiet but forceful way, Marshall said that he was "convinced that there must be one man in command of the entire theater—air, ground and ships": "We cannot manage by cooperation. . . . If we make a plan for unified command now, it will solve nine-tenths of our troubles."[62]

Churchill was not so sure. He was concerned that as the Americans surpassed the British in numbers of troops and quantities of arms, theater commanders would more likely be American, not British. In a meeting with Roosevelt, Hopkins, Lord Beaverbrook, and others, Churchill argued that one-man theater command was not advisable, especially in huge areas in the Pacific where "the troops [were] separated by a thousand miles."[63] Beaverbrook passed a note to Hopkins. "You should work on Churchill," he had written. "He is being advised. He is open-minded & needs discussion."[64] At his next opportunity Hopkins took Churchill aside and advised him not to "be in a hurry to turn down the proposal [for unity of command]." He then set up a private meeting between Churchill and Marshall at which Marshall presented his case for unity of command and suggested that the commander for the Southwest Pacific be General Archibald Percival Wavell, then commander of British imperial forces in India. Churchill was persuaded. "It was evident that we must meet the American view," he later wrote.[65]

Once the principle of unity of command was agreed upon, the next question was to whom the theater commanders should report. The answer fell into place rather quickly and without acrimony. Marshall and the foul-tempered Admiral Ernest King, who was about to replace Admiral Stark as chief of naval operations, persuaded Roosevelt to adopt what was originally a British suggestion: the creation of a joint Anglo-American committee to implement strategic decisions. This committee was officially named the Combined Chiefs of Staff (CCS) and comprised the U.S. and British chiefs of staff of the Army, Navy, and Air Forces. At Roosevelt's insistence, the CCS would sit in Washington, which made sense because the United States would soon be contributing most of the armaments and manpower, and its capital was situated between the European and Pacific theaters. Reluctantly the prime minister agreed.[66]

"This is a strange Christmas eve," observed Churchill.[67] The world was at war. But in America, and in Washington in particular, it was quiet and peaceful. Christmas traditions were being observed at the White House, though blackout curtains had been installed in the windows, manned sentry boxes appeared along the perimeter, and gas masks were issued, including one for the president, which he hung on his wheelchair. Outside the White House 15,000 Washingtonians gathered on the surrounding streets in unusually balmy weather to watch the twentieth lighting of the National Community Christmas Tree.[68] Inside, although the Roosevelt offspring were absent, the president's mother was gone forever, and Missy LeHand was in Warm Springs, stockings had been hung and stuffed with gifts, one by the fireplace in Hopkins's room for Diana and another for Fala, FDR's Scottish terrier.[69] On the South Portico, after lighting the national tree, the president introduced Churchill, who spoke eloquently but briefly about the "sense of unity and fraternal association" he felt with the people of the United States. Concluding, he said, "Let the children have their night of fun and laughter. Let the gifts of father Christmas delight their play."[70]

When the presidential party moved inside to the Red Parlor for tea and cakes, Churchill engaged Roosevelt in a discussion about the need for reinforcements to defend Singapore, bastion of the British Empire. According to notes of that meeting, Roosevelt proposed to turn over to the British those American troops who were already on their way to the Philippines to reinforce General Douglas MacArthur, who had fled Manila and was retreating to the mountains, jungles, and swamps on the Bataan peninsula.[71] Reading the notes of the meeting that were delivered to him on Christmas morning, Marshall's iron self-control gave way to volcanic fury. He believed that Churchill had maneuvered Roosevelt into making a military decision that favored the British cause against the interests of the United States.[72] Marshall informed Henry Stimson, secretary of war, who was equally furious. As Stimson wrote in his diary, his "anger grew" after he went home for lunch and he "finally called up Hopkins."[73]

In the West Hall of the White House, Diana Hopkins and the children of Norway's Crown Princess Martha were ripping open presents. Churchill had given Diana a huge stuffed, dog, "a cuddly treasure," she later recalled.[74] Tall and willowy Princess Martha had become one of the president's favorites. She had been living in the White House with her children since the fall of 1940. As a present FDR had arranged a holiday trip by her husband, Prince Olav, to the White House from London, where he was living in exile with his father, King Haakon VII. Roosevelt, Churchill, Eleanor Roosevelt, and the Norwegian royal couple were watching the children and opening their own presents. Fala was running about amid the wrappings.[75]

Hopkins took the call from Stimson, who said that if what Marshall told him about the diversion of American troops was true, "the President would have to take my resignation."[76] Hopkins was obviously "surprised and shocked" at Stimson's resignation threat and said he would check with the president and get back to him. Hopkins located Roosevelt and asked him in the presence of Churchill about the diversion of reinforcements intended for MacArthur. Roosevelt denied making such a commitment, and Churchill graciously backed him up.[77] Stimson didn't believe Roosevelt and told Hopkins so.[78] Hopkins calmed Stimson by telling him that he had personally warned Roosevelt to be more careful in his discussions with Churchill. That evening Hopkins, Stimson, and Marshall met privately with the president. According to Stimson, FDR "flung out the remark that a paper had been going round which was nonsense and entirely misrepresented a conference between him and Churchill." Nothing more was said about the incident. In his diary Stimson wrote, "This has been a strange and distressful Christmas."[79]

Early on the morning of December 27, working in bed, Hopkins dictated his comments on a compromise draft of the most important document to emerge from the Arcadia conference. It was originally entitled the Declaration of Associated Powers, but it was Roosevelt who came up with the name that would enter the history books: Declaration by United Nations. From the outset of the conference, Roosevelt and Churchill had agreed that a coalition or alliance of the nations fighting the Axis powers needed to be formed, memorialized in written form, and announced to the world. The document was to express both the commitments the Allies would make to the military effort and the values for which they were fighting. In his comments on the latest draft, Hopkins advised that the Soviet Union and China should be lifted out of the alphabetical listing of more than twenty signatories and placed at the beginning along with the United States and Great Britain. This was a forerunner of the "four policemen" concept that Roosevelt advocated later.[80] Hopkins recommended that a new sentence be added to the Declaration, clearly stating that war aims include preservation of "human freedom, justice and security . . . for all people in the world." He also counseled FDR to "make every effort to get religious freedom" into the document because its exclusion from the Atlantic Charter had triggered criticism from anti-Communists and religious organizations in the United States.[81] Hopkins knew that the Soviets would object to the inclusion of religious freedom and urged Roosevelt to discuss this issue with Ambassador Litvinov at lunch later that day.

At that lunch, with Churchill in attendance and Hopkins at his elbow, Roosevelt persuaded Litvinov that religious freedom meant freedom to not practice any religion, or even for a citizen to peacefully oppose religion, which was consistent with the Soviet Constitution. He also told Litvinov of the criticism heaped upon him when religious freedom was left out of the Atlantic Charter and begged the Soviets to help him out of his predicament "even though he knew that they might not like it."[82] Overcoming his fear of irritating or offending Stalin, Litvinov sent a wire asking the marshal for permission to make this change; Stalin promptly agreed.

Sometime before New Year's Day the words *United Nations* popped into Roosevelt's head as a substitute for the dull-sounding *Associated Powers*. For the rest of his life Hopkins dined out on his tale of how Roosevelt communicated his inspiration to Churchill. According to Hopkins, FDR was so excited that he had himself wheeled into Churchill's bedroom and shouted, "I've got it! United Nations," just as the prime minister was emerging from his morning bath, "stark naked and gleaming pink." The president apologized and began to back out of the room. "Think nothing of it," said Churchill. "The Prime Minister of Great Britain has nothing to conceal from the President of the United States." It is a great story but probably not true. Churchill later told Sherwood that he never received the president without at least a towel wrapped around him and that he "could not possibly have made the statement attributed to him."[83]

At dinner on New Year's Day Eleanor Roosevelt asked that the Declaration by United Nations be read aloud. While Hopkins was upstairs retrieving the final version, Churchill recited from memory a few eerily apt lines from Lord Byron's "Childe Harold's Pilgrimage":

Here, where the sword United Nations drew,
Our countrymen were warring on that day
And this is much—and all—which will not pass away.[84]

Hopkins returned and Churchill read the Declaration aloud. The signatories would pledge to defend lofty ideals—"life, liberty, independence and religious freedom"—and to "preserve human justice." Each would agree to devote full resources to the war, cooperate with one another, and not make a separate peace with their enemies.[85]

After dinner the Declaration was spread out on the president's desk, the one made from the oak planking of HMS *Resolute*. President Roosevelt was the first to sign. Turning to Hopkins, he asked whether he should sign as commander in chief. "President ought to do," responded Hopkins.[86] Churchill signed next, for Great Britain and Northern Ireland but not for the nations of the British Commonwealth, who, at Roosevelt's insistence (backed by Hopkins), would sign separately. Then, in the order proposed by Hopkins, Litvinov signed for the Soviet Union and T. V. Soong, the new Chinese ambassador, signed for China.[87] The next day Assistant Secretary of State Adolph Berle had the job of corralling signatures in person or by cable from representatives of the remaining twenty-two signatories, including that of India.[88] At 1:30 p.m. on January 3, 1942, Steve Early distributed copies of the Declaration by United Nations to Washington reporters. The document was released to the world a half hour later.[89]

Buoyed by the signing of the Declaration and with Churchill in Pompano Beach, Florida, for a brief vacation, Roosevelt delivered his State of the Union message to a joint session of Congress on January 6, 1942. "The militarists of Berlin and Tokyo started this war. But the massed, angered forces of humanity will finish it," he began. He then unveiled a breathtaking set of production goals for 1942: 60,000 planes; 45,000 tanks; 20,000 anti-aircraft guns; 6 million tons of merchant shipping. "These figures will give the Japanese and the Nazis a little idea of just what they accomplished at Pearl Harbor," he said as Congress and those in the gallery stood and cheered.[90] The night before the speech, Hopkins, who thought he knew more than almost anyone in the government about America's productive capability, wondered where in the world the astonishing numbers inserted into FDR's speech had come from. With a dismissive wave of his hand, the president said, "Oh, the production people can do it if they really try."[91] In fact the numbers most likely came from Lord Beaverbrook, the British minister of supply, who suggested that Roosevelt should simply multiply the projected Canadian production figures for planes and tanks by fifteen.[92]

While Roosevelt was on the Hill delivering his State of the Union message, Hopkins was Litvinov's luncheon guest at the Soviet Embassy. Hopkins thought Litvinov was one of the "most informed and intelligent" diplomats he had met, but he also knew that he lacked confidence because "one false move" and Stalin would recall him at once.[93] Over caviar and vodka, the Soviet ambassador, still smarting from a shouting match he had had with Churchill over his refusal to agree to a last-minute word change in the Declaration that would have allowed General Charles de Gaulle's Free French to sign, took the opening steps in what would be a long campaign by the Soviets to drive a wedge between the Americans and the British. As leader of the Free French, that is, those French citizens who chose to fight and not collaborate with or peacefully submit to the Germans, the haughty and unyielding de Gaulle was a polarizing figure, garnering the admiration and support of Churchill for standing up to the Nazis and the enmity of Roosevelt for liberating two tiny islands off Newfoundland that had been controlled by the collaborationist Vichy government in France, a government that FDR's administration remained friendly with in order to assure neutralization of the French fleet. Litvinov exploited the division. In remarks that no doubt emanated from the Kremlin, he told Hopkins that Churchill would "not be very useful after the war was over" and that Roosevelt "would be the dominating person at the peace table."[94]

On the last day of the Arcadia conference, Wednesday, January 14, 1942, a serious rift with the British that had been building for days came to the forefront. It will be recalled that early in the conference, Churchill had been persuaded to agree to the principle of unity of command and to the CCS, a command structure headed by the joint military chiefs that would be based in Washington. Fearing a loss of British control over the war effort, Churchill found another way to restore his influence. With his endorsement, a British-inspired proposal eventually surfaced whereby a new civilian authority would be created to allocate the production and distribution of all armaments and munitions. The new authority, called the Munitions Assignment Board, would operate independently of the CCS and would have two branches, one headed by Beaverbrook in London, reporting to Churchill, and the other headed by Hopkins, reporting to Roosevelt. Hence both Churchill and Roosevelt would control decisions over the allocation of war matériel among the theaters of the war and among the allied forces fighting in them. Given his powers of persuasion, the prime minister would maintain substantial influence over key strategic decisions.

Since it had taken days to shape the proposed Munitions Assignment Board and to obtain the agreement of Roosevelt, Churchill, and their civilian aides, it was not until the last day of the conference that General Marshall's input was sought by the president. As Marshall was shown into the Oval Study, Hopkins was seated in front of the president's desk, showing the strain of the past three weeks and appearing to be on the verge of physical collapse. Just a few days before, Churchill's physician, Lord Moran, had written that Hopkins's "lips [were] blanched as if he had been bleeding internally, his skin yellow like stretched parchment and his eyelids contracted to a slit so that you [could] just see his eyes moving about restlessly, as if he was in pain."[95]

Marshall's opposition to the agreed Munitions Assignment Board was immediate and heated. It was presented by Roosevelt and Hopkins as a compromise proposal, but Marshall believed it gave Churchill and the British everything they wanted: control over both American production and war strategy. He minced no words. Stressing that allocation of war matériel was an integral part of military strategy and thus must be subordinate to and controlled by the CCS, Marshall said he would resign as chief of staff if the agreement to create the Munitions Assignment Board was put into effect. Roosevelt was shaken. Marshall was not the kind of man to make idle threats, and he could not afford to lose him. Hoping as always to avoid making a clear-cut decision, the president turned to Hopkins. To Marshall's surprise (as he recalled later), Hopkins rose up in his chair and "supported [him] vociferously." In addition, Hopkins told FDR, if Marshall's position was not adopted, then he "could not assume any responsibility" for the allocation of munitions.

A few minutes later the final plenary session of Arcadia began. Backed forcefully by Marshall and Hopkins, Roosevelt stunned Churchill, Beaverbrook, and the British chiefs by announcing that the Munitions Assignment Board would have to be subordinate to the CCS. The British protested, at times with so much rancor that it appeared the conference might end in a deadlock. Finally Churchill essentially gave in but proposed a face-saving way to defuse the acrimony: let's try it "for a month," he suggested. Roosevelt was delighted. "We will call it a preliminary agreement and try it out that way."

In fact the "preliminary agreement" lasted for the duration of the war. Under it, Hopkins was responsible for the Washington part of munitions distribution and allocation, making him the dominant player, given that the United States produced most of the war matériel.[96]

On the final evening of the Arcadia conference, Hopkins, Churchill, and the president had dinner together in the White House. Henrietta Nesbitt outdid herself and prepared English lamb pie in honor of the prime minister. According to Hopkins's memorandum, during dinner Roosevelt and Churchill initialed several agreements "relative to shipping, raw materials and the allocation board." They reviewed "the work of the last three weeks," and Churchill expressed "confidence that great steps had been taken towards unification of the prosecution of the war."[97]

At 9:45 p.m. Roosevelt and Hopkins drove with Churchill to the railroad siding at Sixth Street, where Churchill was to board his train to Norfolk and fly from there on a Boeing flying boat to England. To one of Churchill's aides Hopkins slipped an envelope containing a letter he had written to Clementine Churchill, which read in part, "You would have been quite proud of your husband on this trip. First, because he was ever so good natured. I didn't see him take anybody's head off and he eats and drinks with his customary vigor, and still dislikes the same people. If he had half as good a time here as the President did in having him about the White House he surely will carry pleasant memories of the past three weeks."[98]

The president said goodbye to Churchill in the car. "Trust me to the bitter end" were FDR's parting words.[99]

———

Day by day, from Pearl Harbor through the end of Arcadia, Hopkins worked to strengthen the ties that would bind the Anglo-American-Soviet coalition. He understood that holding the coalition together was critical to victory. By supporting Marshall on the supremacy of the combined chiefs of staff and the principle of unity of command, over the opposition of Churchill and even to the point of openly disagreeing with the president, he played a critical part in establishing one of the most successful collaborations in military history.[100] As the individual who emerged from Arcadia with dominant influence over the allocation of war matériel, Hopkins was perfectly, and perhaps uniquely, positioned to use that influence to keep the Soviets in the coalition and discourage any attempt to broker a separate peace with Hitler. Moreover it was Hopkins who recommended that the USSR (along with China) join the United States and Great Britain as the first signatories of the United Nations Declaration, thus presaging the postwar role of the Soviet Union as one of the four policemen of the world.

As 1942 dawned, Hopkins was at the center of the war effort. He was the one and only individual with close personal relationships with the big three: Roosevelt, Churchill, and Stalin. The generals and admirals sitting on the CCS, notably General Marshall, were indebted to him for preserving its independence. And he stood atop the bureaucracy that would distribute the armaments soon to flow from the arsenal of democracy.

Hopkins seemed to have the right touch—a talent for reading moment and mood in the company of a wide variety of personalities. With a combination of humor, flattery, irreverence, and self-deprecation, he dissolved tensions and convinced those with opposing views that their interests intersected. He calmed the tempers of Stimson, Marshall, and King and usually found common ground. One of his favorite expressions was "We must have a meeting of minds."[101] On hard cases he had a way of establishing bonds of intimacy by needling, aiming well-timed jibes, or relentless kidding. He was entertaining, always ready with a vivid story, a person who was fun to be around. Yet he listened sympathetically and was a gifted conversationalist. He had the genius of friendship.

Hopkins's friendships with Churchill and Roosevelt were critically important to the success of the Arcadia conference. In private sessions with Churchill, he bridged countless disagreements and misunderstandings, sometimes significant, often petty. Given his relationship with the president, Hopkins was the only person who could counsel him about the dangers of loose talk with Churchill. "Hopkins did a lot to keep the President on the beam," wrote Admiral King, who had a reputation for judging men harshly but shared Hopkins's love of gambling and carousing. "I've seldom seen a man whose head was screwed on so tight."[102]

The day after Arcadia ended, Hopkins wrote his friend Jean Monnet, the man generally credited with creating the European Union. "There are great and heroic days ahead. I think we have laid the groundwork for final victory."[103]

Some Sort of a Front This Summer

Exhausted and barely able to walk, Hopkins checked into the Navy Hospital on January 16, 1942, two days after Churchill left Washington in the hopeful afterglow of Arcadia. Over the next two weeks he received blood transfusions and intramuscular injections of liver extract.[1] When he was finally released, Roosevelt cabled Churchill, "Harry is much better but I am trying to confine him to barracks until he learns to take care of himself."[2]

The war news was profoundly disheartening. On Christmas Day 1941 the British garrison at Hong Kong surrendered to the Japanese. After Manila was evacuated a few days later, American and Filipino troops under the command of General Douglas MacArthur retreated to the Bataan Peninsula and the island of Corregidor, where many thousands would surrender and die. Supposedly impregnable, Singapore, the Gibraltar of the East, swiftly fell on February 15, 1942, thus opening the way for Japanese invasions of Burma, the Dutch East Indies, and possibly even India and Australia.

In North Africa the freshly supplied Afrika Korps, led by General Rommel, already known as the Wűstenfuchs, or the Desert Fox, for his tactical genius in the field, was getting ready to roll eastward to take Cairo, thereby threatening the Suez Canal, Turkey, and the entire Middle East. In Moscow Stalin ordered his skeptical generals simultaneously to mount a major offensive in the south toward Kharkov, relieve the besieged city of Leningrad in the north, and renew the Red Army's counterattack on German forces outside the capital. All of these grandiose moves met with failure, the Soviets having seriously underestimated German strength and grossly overestimated their own resources.[3] Waiting for the spring thaw, Hitler's armies were poised to drive southeast into the Caucasus, with its rich oilfields on the Caspian Sea. An unthinkable catastrophe—the linkage of the German armies with the Japanese Navy and Air Force somewhere in the Middle East, perhaps in the Persian Gulf—was becoming a truly frightening possibility.[4] Along the East Coast of the United States, a naval slaughter was taking place, committed by a small number of German U-boats that surfaced at night in U.S. territorial waters and picked off hundreds of tankers silhouetted by the glare of lights from coastal cities and towns from Portland, Maine, to Miami. After three months of carnage, the military finally succeeded in overriding civilian objections to a blackout. In the meantime, however, the lifeline of supplies to Russia, Britain, and the Middle East was virtually cut off.[5]

The disastrous winter of 1942 reminded Hopkins and FDR's other speechwriters of the daunting odds George Washington and his frozen troops faced at Valley Forge. During the president's fireside chat on February 23, the day after Washington's birthday, Valley Forge was used to evoke the significance of the dark war news and at the same time to boost morale and stiffen the resolve of the American people. Quoting Tom Paine—"on a drumhead, by the light of a campfire"—Roosevelt spoke of the "times that try men's souls," ending with Paine's famous admonition: "Tyranny, like hell, is not easily conquered." Invoking the strength and courage of Washington, who "held to his course," the president assured his listeners that he too would persevere and lead them to victory.[6] Whether the Valley Forge analogy originated with Hopkins, another speechwriter, or Roosevelt himself is not known. What is known is that 61 million adults listened to the speech and it was quickly regarded, as the *New York Times* put it the next day, as "one of the greatest of Roosevelt's career."[7] However, a bit of his thunder was stolen by a single Japanese submarine that surfaced off the California coast while he was speaking, the first attack by a foreign power on mainland America since the War of 1812. The sub lobbed a few shells toward an oil refinery; they exploded harmlessly on ranch property near Santa Barbara.[8]

While Hopkins languished in the hospital, Captain John McCrea, the president's newly appointed naval aide, was assigned the task of creating a White House map room similar to Churchill's traveling map room that he had brought with him for the Arcadia conference, a move that would provide Hopkins with access to the strategic and diplomatic nerve center of World War II. Fortuitously, McCrea had been introduced to Naval Reserve Lieutenant Robert Montgomery, the movie star, who had spent several weeks in London as an observer in the Admiralty map room. (Not long before, Montgomery had appeared with Carole Lombard in Alfred Hitchcock's *Mr. and Mrs. Smith*.) With Montgomery's help, McCrea staked out a large room on the ground floor of the White House, between the oval diplomatic reception room and Doc McIntyre's office, a few steps across the hall from an elevator frequently used by the president. By the time Hopkins was released from the hospital, the new map room had become the repository of all communications to and from Churchill, Stalin, Chiang Kai-shek, and other civilian and military leaders. The walls were draped with large charts of the Atlantic, Pacific, and other war theaters, showing locations of troop deployments, convoys, capital ships, and naval task forces. Montgomery added a Hollywood flourish: a small cigar to show the movements of Churchill, a cigarette holder for Roosevelt, and a briar pipe for Stalin. Other than a select group of military personnel, Hopkins was the only civilian who had access to everything in the White House map room, staffed around the clock by a two-man team. Hopkins could gain admittance at any hour and peruse the latest cable traffic.[9]

The cables from the White House to Downing Street in early March were regarded as bombshells by the British and represented the opening salvos in hard-fought and often contentious arguments that would take months to settle. On March 7 Roosevelt and Marshall advised Churchill that because of the need to allocate some of their precious few trained troops and landing craft to address the "grave" situation in the Pacific, "Gymnast"—the name given by Churchill to the proposed Anglo-American invasion of North Africa in 1942—"[cannot] be undertaken" and that "any American contribution to land operations on the continent of Europe in 1942 [will] be materially reduced." Two days later Roosevelt, conveying to Churchill his "purely personal view," advocated the "temporary shelving of Gymnast" and said he was "becoming more and more interested in the establishment" of a "new front" in Western Europe *this summer*" (emphasis added).[10] Thus FDR appeared to have rejected the British plan for invading North Africa and was pushing for a cross-Channel invasion of France within the next five months—an assault that would surely result in very heavy casualties inflicted on what would have to be a mostly British invasion force. (The Americans could contribute only two divisions.) Hopkins must have been aware of Roosevelt's cables and the reasoning behind them, though there is no evidence that he had a hand in drafting them.

The suggestion of an early invasion of the continent must have appalled Churchill, whose strategic doctrine was shaped by World War I, when hundreds of thousands of young men were cut down by machine-gun fire, artillery, and poison gas during four years of ghastly trench warfare in the fields of France. British war planners proposed to avoid a frontal attack in Western Europe by bringing Germany to the point of collapse through aerial bombing, blockade, engagement at the periphery of the Axis Empire, and the hope of internal dissension. By contrast, Marshall and his new head of War Plans, General Dwight Eisenhower, always believed that the quickest and most effective way to defeat Germany was an invasion in force of Western Europe, preceded by the establishment of air superiority and massive bombing staged from England. In late January Eisenhower had confided to his diary, "We've got to go to Europe and fight. . . . We've got to begin slugging with air at West Europe, to be followed by a land attack as soon as possible." However, as Eisenhower, Marshall, and the president knew, the proposed assault in force on the continent could *not* be launched in the summer of

1942, or at any time later that year, because of the shortage of landing craft, shipping, and trained American troops.[11] Therefore, in an effort to support the convictions of his chief military planners, the president was proposing that a limited, almost sacrificial cross-Channel invasion should take place in the summer of 1942 in order to forestall a British-inspired diversion elsewhere in North Africa or the Middle East—one that Marshall and Eisenhower were convinced would occupy Anglo-American forces for at least a year and delay a full-scale invasion of the continent, the main objective, beyond 1943.

Hopkins understood that FDR had an even deeper motive for proposing an invasion in 1942, a motive Hopkins shared. Both were concerned that a stalemate on the eastern front might cause Stalin and Hitler to negotiate an armistice and peace treaty that would guarantee Russian borders. It was, they knew, vitally important to keep the Soviets in the war, killing Germans by the bushel every day, and the best way to do this was by promising a second front that would draw German divisions from the eastern front to the west while at the same time keeping a river of lend-lease aid flowing to Archangel and Iran (for shipment north by rail into the USSR). A superb analyst but by no means a trained military strategist, Hopkins believed the president should be guided by three objectives: to keep Stalin in the war by opening a second front in 1942; to preserve the alliance with the British through cooperation; and to fight Germans on the ground in 1942. In a memo to Roosevelt dated March 14, 1942, Hopkins advised, "I doubt if any single thing is as important as getting some sort of a front this summer against Germany. This will have to be worked out very carefully between you and Marshall, in the first instance, and you and Churchill, in the second. I don't think there is any time to be lost because if we are going to do it plans need to be made at once."[12] Note that Hopkins referred to "some sort of a front," suggesting it could be somewhere other than France. For Roosevelt's eyes only, he was implicitly taking Gymnast, the North Africa invasion, off the shelf and putting it right back on the table. As events unfolded, this March 14 memo likely had a significant impact on the president's thinking.

At Hopkins's urging, on March 25 Roosevelt convened a luncheon meeting around the cabinet table in the White House to enable Marshall to present the latest version of the War Department's plan for the invasion of Western Europe. Before Marshall could get started, Roosevelt "toyed awhile" with the idea of a North Africa invasion, which Stimson characterized in his diary as "the wildest kind of dispersion debauch."[13] Marshall eventually found an opening and outlined his main plan, which called for a cross-Channel invasion by forty-eight divisions to take place in the spring of 1943. He also summarized the plan for a much more limited "sacrifice" operation (code-named "Sledgehammer") designed to establish a bridgehead in Normandy at Cherbourg that would take place in September 1942—but only if Soviet resistance in the east was about to collapse or the German situation in the west became "critically weakened," events that seemed increasingly unlikely.[14]

The fact, if not the likelihood, that these two events might never take place meant that the War Department was essentially at odds with the preference of both Roosevelt and Hopkins for the establishment—without condition—of "some sort of a front" against Germany in 1942. Nevertheless while Hopkins apparently remained silent, FDR, who was impressed by Marshall's answers to his questions, tentatively approved Marshall's plan, although it was clear that he did not yet "own" it.[15] When the president suggested that it be submitted to the CCS for their consideration, Hopkins spoke up strongly to object, saying that "it would simply be pulled to pieces and emasculated." Instead Hopkins recommended that "someone"—meaning Marshall—should take the invasion plan to London first and sell it directly to Churchill, Chief of the Imperial General Staff Alan Brooke, and the other British chiefs. Roosevelt agreed and then ordered that the plan be put into final shape over the weekend.[16]

A few days later, at a White House meeting to review and approve the final version of the War Department plan, Hopkins made a point of getting Admiral King, chief of naval operations, to commit to the plan in the presence of Roosevelt and Marshall because he believed that King, with his hands full in the Pacific, might be wavering on his support for the "Germany first" policy. (In fact King never doubted its wisdom.) Roosevelt loved to tell stories about King's toughness, saying "he shaved with a blow torch" and "cut his toenails with a torpedo net cutter."[17] Turning to King, Hopkins asked, "Do you see any reason why this cannot be carried out?" The crusty admiral replied, "No. I do not."[18] With that, the plan, designated the Marshall Memorandum, was approved by the president, and it was decided that Hopkins and Marshall would fly to London to present it to Churchill and his cohorts. Later that day, April 1, Roosevelt wrote Churchill, "I have come to certain conclusions that are so vital that I want you to know the whole picture and to ask your approval. The whole of it is so dependent on complete co-operation by the U.K. and U.S. that Harry and Marshall will leave in a few days to present to you first of all the salient points." Two days later FDR sent a personal letter beginning, "Dear Winston":

> What Harry and Geo. Marshall will tell you about has my heart and *mind* in it. Your people and mine demand the establishment of a second front to draw off pressure from the Russians [who] . . . are today killing more Germans and destroying more equipment than you and I put together. Even if full success is not attained, the *big* objective [relief of the pressure on the Russians] will be. . . . Make Harry go to bed early, and let him obey Dr. Fulton, U.S.N., whom I'm sending with him as super-nurse with full authority.[19]

That evening Hopkins and Roosevelt dined alone.[20] They must have discussed the approach that Hopkins should take in the critical meetings with Churchill, Brooke, and the others in London. Did Roosevelt agree with Hopkins that it was essential to get American boots on the ground against the Germans in the coming summer? Should Hopkins hint at the possibility of reviving Gymnast? Although there is no record of what they discussed that evening, certain statements by Hopkins in London suggest that he was given discretion to push for the opening of a front somewhere, not necessarily Western Europe, at the earliest possible date.

On Saturday morning, April 4, Hopkins, Marshall, Dr. Fulton, and a handful of aides departed Baltimore in a Pan Am Clipper. Hopkins had already wired Churchill, "Will be seeing you soon so please start the fire."[21] He enjoyed needling the prime minister about the lack of central heating at

Chequers. In contrast to his previous wartime transatlantic flights, this trip to England was luxurious and restful. He and his colleagues had the entire Clipper and its comfortable sleeping berths to themselves. Due to engine trouble, they enjoyed a three-day layover in Bermuda, beginning on Easter Sunday, during which Hopkins arranged through an Army aide for two crates of vegetables to be loaded aboard as gifts for Churchill and Brooke.[22]

After checking in at Claridge's, Hopkins and Marshall met at No. 10 Downing Street with the prime minister on Wednesday afternoon, April 8, and presented the "broad outlines" of Marshall's plan for a massive invasion of Western Europe in the spring of 1943 and a far more limited assault in the fall of 1942 that would be launched, but only if certain emergency conditions prevailed. According to Hopkins's notes of the meeting, Churchill seemed to be "well aware" of the plan and "indicated that he had told the Chiefs of Staff that, in spite of all the difficulties, he Churchill was prepared to go along."[23] In fact three days earlier Churchill and the British chiefs had been fully briefed on the contents of the Marshall Memorandum by Brigadier Vivian "Dumbie" Dykes, a British officer attached to the CCS in Washington as a senior secretary, who somehow had "glanced at" the document and relayed a summary to the war cabinet in London. Therefore Churchill and his military chiefs had plenty of time to formulate a response to Marshall's plan.[24]

The British were in a difficult spot. Their military experts, led by the aloof and condescending Field Marshal Sir Alan Brooke, a stiff-necked Ulsterman, were convinced that a cross-Channel invasion would be premature and could not succeed until German war production and fighting capability had been significantly weakened by bombing, losses inflicted by the Red Army on the eastern front, and peripheral operations by the British and Americans in the Mediterranean, the Middle East, and perhaps Norway. At the same time they desperately needed a buildup of American troops in Britain to forestall an invasion by the Germans should the Soviets collapse or strike a peace agreement with the Nazis. Moreover they feared that if they gave Marshall reason to believe that they flatly opposed a cross-Channel invasion, the Americans would abandon their "Germany first" strategy and concentrate all of their efforts on the Pacific. Indeed only a few days earlier, Eisenhower had sent a memorandum to Marshall recommending that "the United States should turn its back on the Atlantic area and go full out against Japan" if the British refused to endorse a cross-Channel invasion at the earliest possible date consistent "with a fair chance of success."[25]

Consequently the British strategy was to agree in principle with the plan for a cross-Channel invasion and advocate a buildup of troops in England, but also continue to suggest reasonable-sounding conditions that would have to be met before an invasion would actually take place. Even at their first meeting, Hopkins suspected that Churchill and his colleagues were not entirely on board. "Marshall was more optimistic about the interview than I was," he noted. That evening at dinner Brooke's remarks indicated "that he had a great many misgivings about our proposal."[26]

During the next two days Marshall and his aides discussed the details of his plan with the British chiefs while Hopkins reviewed the plan and its implications, first with Churchill and then separately with various members of his war cabinet. Field Marshal Brooke, speaking for all of the British military experts, expressed very strong doubts about the chances of success of Sledgehammer, the plan for an invasion in September 1942 in the event of a Russian collapse in the east or a significant weakening of Germany. Indeed the bulk of the discussion focused not on the main event—the large-scale invasion of France in April 1943—but on the many reasons why a 1942 emergency invasion might fail, ranging from an inadequate number of troops to lack of shipping and landing craft.[27] On Saturday morning at Chequers, Hopkins cabled Roosevelt to assure him that the discussions with Churchill and the British chiefs of staff were moving along, but he did not disclose his doubts about whether the British were really on board. Poking fun at wartime censorship, he added, "Although I am not allowed to talk about the weather, I can tell you that my heavy underwear is itching like the devil." There was no need to tend to the fireplaces at Chequers that weekend; spring was breaking out in Buckinghamshire. "It is only when you see the country in the spring," wrote Hopkins, "that you begin to understand why the English have written the best goddamn poetry in the world."[28]

Ignoring Dr. Fulton's orders, Hopkins was still awake at 3 a.m. on Sunday, sipping brandy with Churchill, when a cable arrived from the president that he asked Hopkins to deliver to Churchill immediately. The cable concerned an effort to provide a measure of self-government to India in exchange for the support of the Indian people in defending the country against a possible Japanese invasion. A compromise deal had been worked out by representatives of Churchill (Sir Stafford Cripps) and Roosevelt (Colonel Louis Johnson) with India's political leaders in New Delhi, but Churchill, unwilling to cede any independence to India during wartime, had withdrawn his support. Roosevelt's cable was an effort to get him to reconsider. Churchill was so outraged at this intrusion into imperial affairs that he told Hopkins he was tempted to resign as prime minister. Hopkins, who had recent experiences with people in high places threatening to resign, spent the remaining hours of the night calming him, assuring him, falsely, that Louis Johnson was acting without Roosevelt's approval. It was almost sunrise when Hopkins finally reached the president by telephone and said that nothing further could be done because Churchill's representative had left India two days before and explanations had already been issued to Indian and British authorities in Delhi.[29] Realizing that he had subjected Hopkins to an exhausting all-night tirade from the prime minister, the president cabled Marshall, "Please put Hopkins to bed and keep him there under 24-hour guard by Army or Marine Corps. Ask the King for additional assistance if required on this job."[30]

Later that Sunday Churchill asked Hopkins and Marshall to join him outside while one of the gardeners prised open the two crates of vegetables that Hopkins had shipped on the Clipper. Anticipating exotic delicacies, Churchill started laughing when the cover of the first crate was opened. Inside were Brussels sprouts, a staple of the British diet and the only vegetable in plentiful supply.[31]

On Sunday evening Churchill cabled Roosevelt that he and his chiefs of staff "are in entire agreement in principle" with everything proposed in the Marshall Memorandum. He said the "whole matter" would be discussed at a meeting on April 14 to which "Harry and Marshall" were invited. Churchill concluded: "I have no doubt that that I shall be able to send you our complete agreement."[32]

With all of the explanatory meetings, staff discussions, dinners, and social get-togethers behind them, Hopkins, Marshall, and the British Defence

Committee met at No. 10 Downing Street at 10 p.m. on Tuesday, April 14, to hear the official response of the British government to the Marshall Memorandum. Churchill opened the meeting, stating that he "had no hesitation in cordially adopting the plan," which he characterized as a "momentous proposal." He put forth "one broad reservation," however, and that had to do with the "ominous possibility" that the Japanese might gain control of India and link up with the Germans in the Middle East. He warned that India and the Middle East had to be successfully defended even if that meant diversion of resources from "the main object proposed by General Marshall."[33] Field Marshall Brooke, who had earlier expressed serious reservations about a cross-Channel invasion in 1942, saying it could be "only on a small scale" and would have only limited military value,[34] said the British chiefs of staff were in "entire agreement" with Marshall's proposals for an invasion of France in 1943. However, like Churchill, Brooke brought up the specter of a linkage between the Germans and the Japanese in the Middle East, which would threaten oil supplies, and said the Americans might have to take resources away from the invasion plans to prevent Japan from taking control of the western Indian Ocean.[35] This emphasis on the threat from the Japanese struck Hopkins as ironic and suggested that the British might not be as firmly committed to Marshall's plan as they said they were. Only a few months previously they had expressed fear that because of the Pearl Harbor attack the Americans would concentrate all of their attention on the Japanese in the Pacific and fail adequately to protect the British Isles. Now they were warning that the buildup in Britain for a cross-Channel invasion might expose the Allies to grave danger coming from the Japanese in the Far East.

Hopkins stopped doodling on Downing Street stationery and spoke up. He reminded the British that public opinion in America favored an all-out effort against Japan and that it would only intensify when General Jonathan Wainwright was forced to surrender on Corregidor, as seemed likely.[36] (Leaving Wainwright in command, MacArthur, by order of the president, left Corregidor on the night of March 11 with his senior staff, his wife, and his four-year-old son, fleeing by PT boat and B-17 to Australia.) Hopkins went on to say that despite prevailing public opinion, the president and his military advisors were committed to the "Germany first" policy for strategic reasons. However, if American boys did not get into the fight soon, the divergence between the president and public opinion could endanger the entire war effort. "The United States wished to fight," emphasized Hopkins. "They wished to fight in the most useful place, and in the place where they could attain superiority, in an enterprise with the British." Everyone in the room should understand, he stressed, that the decision they were making that evening must be honored and was not subject to change.[37]

The words Hopkins chose, as recorded in the minutes, are highly revealing. Consistent with his advice to FDR in his March 14 memo, Hopkins was telling the British that the most important thing for the United States—the root of the matter—was to get American troops fighting Germans alongside the British as soon as possible "in the most useful place, and in the place where they could attain superiority." He didn't say France. He said "the most useful place"—a place where they would be superior in numbers and a place where the British were willing to fight. Hopkins therefore cracked open the door to a revival of Gymnast. His implication was clear: if American boys did not fight the Germans somewhere and very soon, public opinion would force the United States to shift its focus to the Pacific.

Without mention of Gymnast or any other alternative to a cross-Channel invasion, Churchill closed the meeting, confirming that while details still needed to be worked out, "there was complete unanimity on the framework" of the Marshall Memorandum and that the British government was firmly committed to "this great enterprise."[38] Churchill thus clearly signaled the British government's approval of the plan for a cross-Channel invasion in its entirety; he did not distinguish between the main assault planned for April 1943 and Sledgehammer, the much smaller, conditional invasion set for September 1942.

In fact Churchill, like Brooke, had deep reservations about Sledgehammer, preferring that Anglo-American troops fight the Germans in 1942 in North Africa or Norway.[39] As to the main assault on the continent planned for 1943, Lieutenant-General Sir Hastings "Pug" Ismay, Churchill's chief of staff whose nickname was based on his appearance, although it also applied to his canine-like loyalty to his boss, believed the prime minister was firmly opposed unless conditions made it "a cast-iron certainty."[40] Churchill's physician, Lord Moran, who was well acquainted with the prime minister's views on strategy, said Churchill must have "decided that the time ha[d] not come to take the field as an out-and-out opponent of a Second Front in France."[41] In his memoirs, published after the war, Ismay, who participated in the meeting on April 14, wrote, "We should have come clean, much cleaner than we did."[42] Whether or not Churchill's failure to "come clean" was deliberately deceptive, Marshall came away from the meeting with the impression that Churchill and his military chiefs were much more firmly committed to all aspects of his plan, including Sledgehammer, than they in fact were.

As for Hopkins, he was of the view that it was more important to get American ground troops into the fight alongside the British sometime in 1942 than it was to achieve agreement on Marshall's cross-Channel invasion plan. And he realized that even under Marshall's plan American troops would cross the Channel to fight the Germans in 1942 *only* if certain improbable conditions were met. Because Marshall's plan did not expressly promise a second front in 1942, Hopkins was beginning to have second thoughts. Putting himself in Roosevelt's shoes, he was concerned that American public opinion, including that of members of Congress, would not tolerate a year's delay. He was also worried about what the president would be able to tell the Soviets about the prospects for actually opening a second front in 1942. His worry was compounded because he knew that FDR had already asked Stalin to send Foreign Minister Molotov to Washington in a few weeks to be told in person about the invasion plans.[43] Would the president be able to assure Molotov and hence Stalin that the United States would open a second front on the European continent in 1942? Hopkins had serious doubts. Gymnast had its shortcomings—it was a sideshow to Europe—but it might be the only alternative. To be sure, it wasn't what Stalin had in mind, but it offered "some sort of a front," and it might be feasible to pull it off before the end of 1942.

As Hopkins was preparing to return to America, he received a veiled hint from the president that Gymnast might in fact be practicable. In an April 18 cable to Hopkins, Roosevelt said that a major impediment to the invasion of North Africa in 1942, the anticipated resistance of large numbers of French troops stationed there to Allied landings, might no longer exist because fervently pro-Nazi Pierre Laval was probably going to get "control" of the French government in Vichy. This would mean that French armed forces in North Africa might refuse to follow orders from Vichy to resist an American-led invasion.[44] To cover his tracks and avoid being accused of undermining Marshall, Roosevelt said in his cable that he was not suggesting the "revival" of Gymnast. But Hopkins understood what was going on in the president's mind. Taking a calculated risk, he telephoned Churchill and, according to Sherwood, told him "it was possible that some sort of Allied expedition to North Africa might be launched immediately."[45] Hopkins therefore opened the door a bit wider for the prime minister, who would shortly seize on the opening. Gymnast was back in play.

On the night of April 18 Hopkins, Marshall, and their aides departed via Pan Am Clipper from Stranraer, near Port Patrick on the west coast of Scotland, and were in New York City by noon the next day. That evening Hopkins boarded the president's train returning from Hyde Park at Claremont Station, "looking unusually well, in better flesh and better color than when he left Washington," observed William Hassett, a hard-drinking former reporter from Vermont who served as FDR's correspondence secretary.[46]

Looking good and feeling great, Hopkins was happy to back in the States and anxious to see "Louie"—that is, Louise Macy—again. In January, when he was in the hospital, he had received a letter from Eleanor "Barry" Lowman, a former *Harper's Bazaar* model and editor married to a CBS executive whom he had probably dated when she was single, asking if he would help a good friend of hers, Louise Macy, get a job. In her letter Lowman described her friend as "good looking, smart without being 'chi chi' and as healthy and strong as ten horses."[47] Hopkins had probably already heard about Macy, who had carried on a well-publicized affair with John Hay "Jock" Whitney, the wealthy New Yorker and producer of *Gone With the Wind*. Hopkins responded to Lowman the next day, saying "he was doing his usual tour in the hospital" but that he would be glad to see Louise in New York when he was "up and about."[48]

It wasn't until February or March that Hopkins was able to get to New York City to meet Louise Macy. Over breakfast at the St. Regis, he learned something of her life story and found that they ran in the same crowd, having many friends in common. Born in Southern California, Macy was very close to her two sisters because her parents had died when the children were quite young. She had boarded at the Madeira School outside Washington, attended Smith College for two years, and then, after a disastrous marriage to an alcoholic that lasted only six months, became a fashion writer, working for Hattie Carnegie in New York. During the two years before France fell to the Germans, Louie, as Hopkins always called her, was the popular and successful Paris editor of *Harper's Bazaar*. She managed to escape Europe and return to New York, where she and Pauline Fairfax Potter started a fashion house called Macy-Potter, which was a critical success but a financial bust. By that time she and Jock Whitney had parted ways. (He would marry Betsey Cushing, the ex-wife of FDR's son Jimmy.) Her other beaux included James Forrestal, who would become Navy secretary and the first secretary of defense, and the New York writer Robert Benchley, who was married and known to her family as "Uncle Bobby."[49] Louie was thirty-six years old. Named one of the ten best-dressed women in New York, she was taking courses at Memorial Hospital to become a nurse's aide.[50]

Macy was described by Liz Gibbons, a former model and close friend, as "ebullient, apple-cheeked . . . a dynamo of energy and an endless font of laughs, most directed at herself."[51] Hopkins was enchanted. Macy found him to be immensely appealing. As Doris Kearns Goodwin has written, "There was still a great physical attractiveness in Hopkins," his vital energy and sharp wit overshadowing his sallow complexion, wispy hair, and bony frame.[52] Since Barbara had died, he had been linked romantically with a number of glamorous women, including Betsey Cushing, the Hollywood stars Carole Lombard (who married Clark Gable in 1939 and was killed in a plane crash in January 1942) and Paulette Goddard, and a number of others. In October 1938 the socialite and marginally talented actress Dorothy Hale caused a tabloid sensation by jumping to her death from the sixteenth story of the Hampshire House on Central Park South, reportedly despondent after being jilted by Harry Hopkins.[53]

Hopkins told Macy he would scout around and see if he could find the right job for her. When he returned from his trip to England, he arranged to meet her for dinner in Manhattan and offered her a job with one of the agencies in Washington. She declined, preferring to complete her nurse's aide course work. But during the dinner a strong chemistry developed, and by the end of the evening they both knew that they would continue to see one another. In the coming weeks she would spend a weekend with him at the White House and "two at Hyde Park, at the invitation of Eleanor Roosevelt."[54]

Meanwhile the need to draw German divisions away from the eastern front and the growing public and congressional sentiment for the opening of a second front in 1942 weighed heavily on the president. On May 6, 1942, in a fateful "eyes only" strategy memo to Stimson, Marshall, King, Hopkins, and Henry "Hap" Arnold (head of the U.S. Army Air Force), Roosevelt, as commander in chief, said he had decided that the "necessities" of the war situation called for the initiation of "active operations" by Anglo-American infantry against the Germans in 1942.[55] Hopkins likely had a hand in drafting the memo, but even if the president wrote all of it himself, Hopkins's earlier advice emphasizing the singular importance of launching "some sort of a front" in 1942 and his concern about the shortcomings of Marshall's plan must have influenced the evolution of FDR's thinking.

Whether or not he foresaw its implications, Roosevelt's decision to put American troops on the ground in 1942 conferred upon the British a veto over Sledgehammer—the limited cross-Channel invasion planned for 1942—because the Americans, with only two trained divisions, could not even consider conducting that operation without at least seven more divisions, all of which would have to be British. Thus once it was decided that Americans must fight the Germans in 1942, the British, with most of the troops, could decide where it would take place. Churchill and his military chiefs didn't realize it yet, but they had been put in the driver's seat.[56]

Three weeks later Churchill began to come clean and took the first of many small steps toward dictating the place where the fight would take place. In a May 28 telegram to Roosevelt he said he was sending Lord Louis

"Dickie" Mountbatten, head of British commandos, to Washington to "explain the difficulties of [a cross-Channel invasion] in 1942." Near the end of the message, Churchill seized on the alternative that Hopkins had suggested as he was departing Scotland for the United States, saying to the president, "We must never let GYMNAST pass from our minds." In a second telegram to Roosevelt sent that day, Churchill reported that he had just finished meeting with Foreign Minister Molotov, who had stopped in London on his way to Washington. He said he told Molotov that a cross-Channel invasion in 1942, even if successful, would not "draw off large numbers of enemy land forces from the Eastern Front."[57] In effect Churchill was sending a message to Roosevelt and his military chiefs, just as he had to Molotov, that the British had profound doubts about the success and effectiveness of Sledgehammer.

Vyacheslav Molotov, the Soviet foreign minister, arrived at the White House on Friday afternoon, May 29. Like Stalin, whose last name had been changed to the Russian equivalent of *steel*, Molotov was a pseudonym meaning *hammer*. In private Roosevelt would refer to him as "Stone Ass" because of his rigid self-control, wooden demeanor, and complete lack of spontaneity.[58] A protégé and loyal supporter of Stalin since the early 1920s, Molotov was personally involved in orchestrating the famine in Ukraine that had led to the deaths of between 7 million and 11 million peasants, and he was one of the few "old Bolsheviks" that survived the Great Purges of the 1930s. Replacing Litvinov in 1939, Molotov negotiated the Nazi-Soviet nonaggression pact that allowed the Soviets to annex Estonia, Latvia, Bessarabia, and part of Poland.[59]

By the time Molotov touched down in Washington in a four-engine Soviet bomber, the spring offensive by the Germans was well under way. The Red Army was engaged in savage battles, particularly on the Kerch peninsula and at Kharkov, as the Wehrmacht drove south toward the Caucasus and the oil fields; 170,000 Red Army soldiers were taken prisoner on the Kerch and some 250,000 would be lost at Kharkov. The military historian Chris Bellamy said these battles "were probably the most stupendously costly operations the Russians ever engaged in."[60] The situation on the eastern front was desperate. Even so, during Molotov's meetings with Churchill in London, the prime minister had offered almost no hope for immediate relief. As he was driven to the White House, Molotov was expecting much more encouraging news, if not a commitment for an early invasion, from the U.S. president.

The old Bolshevik would spend the night in the Rose Suite across the hall from Hopkins, the same bedroom that Churchill had stayed in. While Molotov was getting acquainted with Roosevelt and Hull in the Oval Study, a White House valet unpacked his bags and discovered among his clothing a sausage, a loaf of black bread, and a loaded pistol. Eleanor Roosevelt later wrote of the incident, "The Secret Servicemen did not like visitors with pistols but on this occasion nothing was said. Mr. Molotov evidently thought he might have to defend himself and also he might be hungry."[61]

There is some evidence that in order to ingratiate himself with Molotov, Roosevelt dispatched Hopkins to Molotov's room that evening to let him know, confidentially and off the record, that while the president was strongly in favor of a second front in Europe in 1942, his generals were not convinced of "its real necessity."[62] Whether or not this actually happened, in the meetings on the following day with Marshall, King, Roosevelt, and Hopkins, Molotov made a very strong case that if the cross-Channel invasion was delayed beyond 1942, "Hitler might be the undisputed master of Europe" and the Soviet Union would accordingly be defeated. He made it clear that if an invasion by the United States and Great Britain could draw off forty German divisions, the war would be decided favorably in 1942. He then asked for a "straight answer": Were the Americans prepared to initiate a second front in Europe in 1942? According to the minutes of the meeting, the president turned to Marshall and asked "whether developments were clear enough so that we could say to Mr. Stalin that we were developing a Second Front." Marshall replied, "Yes, Mr. President." Then, without asking for Marshall's endorsement, Roosevelt "authorized Mr. Molotov to inform Mr. Stalin that we expect the formation of a Second Front *this year* [emphasis added]."[63] Marshall was appalled; he knew FDR's statement was misleading if not disingenuous, but he could not contradict his president in the presence of Molotov.

A few days later Molotov proposed language for a public statement to be simultaneously issued in Washington, London, and Moscow. The operative sentence read, "In the course of the conversations [between Roosevelt and Molotov in Washington] full understanding was reached with regard to the urgent tasks of creating a Second Front in Europe in 1942."[64] When Marshall saw this sentence in draft form, he immediately objected because in context it strongly suggested that the United States intended to commence its main assault on Europe in 1942. Marshall knew that was not possible. There would not be enough trained troops and landing craft, and besides, the British would never agree since they would have to provide the bulk of the men. Marshall still favored Sledgehammer in 1942, a limited sacrifice invasion of the Cotentin peninsula, mainly because it would prevent a diversion to North Africa and allow time to build up troops and armaments for an invasion of France in 1943.[65]

To avoid trouble down the road with the Soviets, Marshall tried to enlist Hopkins to persuade the president to delete the reference in the public statement to "1942." In his written notes, Hopkins says he "called this particularly to the President's attention," but that Roosevelt "wished" to leave it in the public statement.[66] Given Hopkins's previous statement for Roosevelt's eyes only about the importance of opening a front somewhere in 1942, it is not likely that he pressed FDR on the point.

On his way back to Moscow, Molotov stopped in London to see Churchill again. Churchill agreed to sign on to the public statement that a "full understanding was reached regarding the urgent tasks of creating a Second Front in 1942." However, in an aide-mémoire he objected to the reference to 1942, stating forthrightly that because of the shortage of landing craft, the British could "give no promise" for a landing in August or September 1942.[67] (After September weather in the English Channel precluded an amphibious invasion.)

At least Churchill had come clean, albeit belatedly. But what about Roosevelt and Hopkins? What kind of a game were they playing? They knew that the main invasion of *Festung Europa* (Fortress Europe) would not take place in 1942. And they knew that the British would likely oppose Sledgehammer. Yet Roosevelt, with Hopkins at his side, signed on to a public statement strongly suggesting that the second front—a main assault on Western Europe—would be launched in 1942. Even if Molotov and Stalin were not actually misled, and Molotov later claimed he was not, Roosevelt had handed Stalin a huge diplomatic and propaganda weapon that he would deploy later when his Western brothers in arms began to backtrack on what the marshal would regard as their solemn promise.[68]

Why Roosevelt would do this will never be known for certain. Perhaps he suspected that Stalin was on the verge of cutting a deal with Hitler, or that the Red Army was about to collapse and that an assurance of an immediate invasion in the west was the only hope. Maybe he did it in order to satisfy the growing public clamor for getting into the fight, what Marshall later referred to as the need in a democracy to keep the public "entertained."[69] Or perhaps he thought he could later put a spin on the public statement by saying that it actually referred to the opening of a second front in North Africa, not Western Europe. It is a stretch, but it is at least plausible that Roosevelt and Hopkins had convinced themselves that they could always claim that the words of the public statement were literally true. After all, there was in fact a "full understanding" between the United States and the British of the "urgent tasks" involved in "creating a Second Front" in Western Europe in 1942. But they had to have known that Stalin would seize on the operative phrase "Second Front in 1942"; that he would claim, with considerable justification, that the Americans gave their word that they would invade the continent before the end of that year; and that he would be able to say that they had reneged.

The Hopkins Touch

During the first week of June 1942, Hopkins anxiously pored over the cables coming into the White House map room. The Battle of Midway was being fought in the Central Pacific, and the U.S. Navy seemed to be getting the upper hand, indeed decisively so. "Our reports this morning are quite good," he wrote to Churchill on June 6. "Whether the beating [the Japanese] have taken is going to force them to withdraw we do not know, but it rather appears so."[1] In fact by that time Vice Admiral Nagumo, the hero of Pearl Harbor, had received orders from Admiral Yamamoto to withdraw what was left of his task force, which had failed to achieve its objective: the capture and occupation of Midway Island. In a game-changing defeat at the hands of U.S. Navy dive bombers, four of the six first-line Japanese aircraft carriers had been sunk and countless aircraft and experienced pilots were lost. Together with the standoff a month earlier in the Battle of the Coral Sea, when the Japanese attempt to capture Port Moresby in the Southwest Pacific was checked, the Midway victory altered the balance of power in the Pacific and had vitally important strategic consequences.[2]

As Hopkins glibly observed, "The Japs simply cannot stand the attrition."[3] From this point forward they would be on the defensive in the Pacific. Unable to dominate the Indian Ocean, the Japanese would not be able to launch an invasion of India. The link-up of the Japanese Navy and German forces in the Persian Gulf could no longer be regarded as a plausible threat. Without that threat, it would seem that the buildup of troops and resources in England for a cross-Channel attack could be accelerated.

Admiral Louis Mountbatten, a great-grandson of Queen Victoria, known as a daring but careless naval commander with an enthusiasm for gadgetry, arrived in Washington as the far-reaching implications of the Midway victory on grand strategy were being digested. He had been sent by Churchill to explain to Roosevelt and his military planners the "difficulties" of launching a successful invasion of Western Europe in 1942. While Mountbatten did meet with the joint chiefs to discuss landing craft shortages, air cover, and various other challenges, General Marshall and Admiral King were outraged to learn, after the fact, that they had not been invited to join Mountbatten at a private dinner meeting with the president, the only occasion on which he was permitted to directly confront FDR with all of the "bogies about the hazards of a cross-Channel operation."[4] Indeed the only person other than Roosevelt and Mountbatten who attended that crucial session was Hopkins. According to Mountbatten's report of the meeting, which lasted well into the evening, the president stressed "the great need" for American soldiers to fight "as soon as possible" and asked Mountbatten to remind Churchill that he had previously agreed to a "sacrifice landing" in France in the summer of 1942 (Sledgehammer) if things were "going very badly for the Russians." Roosevelt was taken aback when Mountbatten pointed out that there were "some 25 German divisions already in France" and that therefore an Anglo-British landing in 1942 would not draw off any German troops from the eastern front. What would be the point of a sacrifice landing if it did not provide any relief to the Russians?

Without his military advisors, the president was not in a position to question Mountbatten's assertions. Instead he countered by proposing that, as an alternative to continuing to build up American troops in England, "six American divisions should be sent straight to fight in North Africa," and he made a point of telling Mountbatten that he was mindful of the prime minister's "remark in a recent telegram: 'Do not lose sight of GYMNAST.'"[5] Again, as Marshall and King had feared, Roosevelt turned to North Africa. There is no record of what Hopkins said at this meeting, but given his previous advice it seems likely that he had a role in prompting the president's suggestion. Since March Hopkins had been advising that the most important "single thing" was to fight the Germans in 1942. If France was not a viable option, then French North Africa was the next best alternative.

Churchill was delighted to hear from Mountbatten that the president had not lost sight of Gymnast, especially since Rommel's Afrika Korps had pushed the British Eighth Army almost to the Egyptian border and was threatening Tobruk, a vital supply port in Libya. Sensing an opportunity to exploit a potential split between Roosevelt and Marshall over Sledgehammer versus North Africa, the prime minister cabled Roosevelt, "In view of the impossibility of dealing by correspondence with all the many difficult points outstanding, I feel it is my duty to come see you." (Through Hopkins, Churchill already knew that Roosevelt was on the verge of inviting him to make a "quick trip" over to discuss "matters of high policy.")[6]

Seated at the wheel of his hand-controlled Ford convertible, Roosevelt greeted Churchill as he climbed out of a small plane at an airfield not far from Hyde Park on Friday, June 19.[7] The prime minister's Boeing Clipper had landed the day before on the Potomac River in Washington bearing a small party consisting of Churchill, Chief of the Imperial General Staff Alan Brooke, Admiral Pug Ismay (Churchill's personal chief of staff), and a few others who remained in Washington while Churchill spent the weekend in Hyde Park alone with the president and Hopkins.[8] Churchill, Roosevelt, and Hopkins talked for hours in the small first-floor study in the Big House. Grace Tully had been told not to put any calls through or allow any visitors to interrupt them.[9] One of the first orders of business was settled quickly and casually. In the presence of Hopkins, the president and the prime minister orally agreed that the United States would assume complete responsibility for designing and building the atomic bomb, the so-called Tube Alloys project; that their two nations would pool information on atomic fission; and, in Churchill's words, they would "work together on equal terms and share the results, if any, equally."[10] Given the fact that this massive endeavor (eventually called the Manhattan Project) was to be entirely funded by the United States and controlled by its military, Roosevelt must have suspected that he might not be able to honor his agreement to share equally.[11]

Then, referring to a memorandum that he handed Roosevelt and Hopkins, Churchill presented the case for why Sledgehammer should *not* be attempted. Pointing to the shortage of landing craft and the inadequate number of trained troops, Churchill argued that any landing would end in disaster, subject the French populace to brutal reprisals at the hands of the Nazis, and, in any case, would not help the Russians by drawing German troops away from the eastern front. "No responsible British military authority," he said, "has so far been able to able to make a plan [for a cross-Channel attack in 1942] which has any chance of success. . . . Have the American Staffs a plan? If so, what is it?" Without waiting for responses, he posed the fundamental question, one that he knew Roosevelt and Hopkins had to answer in the negative: "Can we afford to stand idle in the Atlantic theatre during the whole of 1942?" Without pausing, he answered his own question with another. "Ought we not be preparing . . . some other operation . . . to take some of the weight off Russia? It is in this setting," he argued, "that the operation GYMNAST should be studied."[12]

Churchill's arguments were powerful and persuasive. Yet the president and Hopkins were keenly aware that Marshall, Eisenhower, and virtually all of FDR's military advisors were dead set against Gymnast, which they were convinced would constitute a major diversion of troops and resources, resulting in a postponement, almost certainly beyond 1943, of an invasion of France. Given these sharply opposing views, the president decided that he, Churchill, and Hopkins should cut short their weekend at Hyde Park and return to Washington.[13]

―――――――――

Shortly after lunch on Sunday, June 21, Churchill and Field Marshal Brooke were in the Oval Study chatting with the president, who was seated at his desk. Marshall entered the room brandishing a pink-tinted telegram that he handed to Roosevelt. The message reported the news that

Tobruk had fallen and that Rommel's Afrika Korps had captured 25,000 British soldiers (the actual number was later revised upward to 33,000). Roosevelt read it quickly and passed it to Churchill. Remembering the shock years later, Churchill wrote, "This was one of the heaviest blows I can recall during the war."[14] Roosevelt broke the silence. "What can we do to help?" he asked. Brooke later wrote, "I remember vividly being impressed by the tact and real heartfelt sympathy that lay behind these words. There was not one word too much or too little."[15] Gathering himself, Churchill said, "Give us as many Sherman tanks as you can spare."[16] By the end of the day three hundred tanks and one hundred self-propelled guns were rerouted for shipment to North Africa. It was a defining moment in the Anglo-American special relationship.[17] No one who was there ever forgot Roosevelt's question, whose simplicity and timing were foundational.

Notwithstanding the devastating news, the pros and cons of Sledgehammer and Gymnast were vigorously debated throughout the rest of that Sunday and late into the evening. Churchill argued, forcefully as ever, that an invasion of French North Africa would lead to the collapse of Italy, the opening of the Mediterranean to Anglo-American shipping, a supply route to Russia through the Suez and Iran, and a testing ground for green American troops. On his part, Marshall contended that the only way to divert German troops from the eastern front and relieve the Soviets was by an invasion of Western Europe. Landings in North Africa, he argued, would indefinitely postpone a cross-Channel invasion and result in a series of indecisive operations on Europe's southern flank.

A mushy compromise was reached. Notes indicate that the parties agreed to continue to prepare for Sledgehammer and at the same time plan for Gymnast. If the chances of success of a 1942 cross-Channel invasion were deemed "improbable," Gymnast would go forward, wrote Pug Ismay, because "it [was] essential that the United States and Great Britain . . . act offensively in 1942."[18] Marshall came away with the understanding that the parties would wait until September 1 to make a final decision, although the notes on that issue are by no means clear.[19]

At some point during the long hot day, Hopkins, who was present during most of the debate, reached out to Alan Brooke, who had not previously met FDR or any of the other Americans present. Hopkins had already sensed that the British chief of staff—Marshall's counterpart—had mettle. Peering through his large, round horn-rimmed glasses, Brooke was a forbidding character, often responding to an argument by snapping his pencil and saying, "I flatly disagree." According to Brooke's diary, Hopkins approached him and said, "Would you like to come round to my room for a few moments' talk? I could give you some of the background which influenced the President in the statements he has just made and the opinions he has expressed." Brooke continued:

> I went with him expecting to be taken to his office. Instead we went to his bedroom where we sat on the edge of his bed looking at his shaving brush and tooth brush, whilst he let me into some of the President's inner thoughts! I mention this meeting as it was so typical of this strange man with no official position, not even an office in the White House, and yet one of the most influential men with the President. A man who played a great and nebulous part in the war as the President's right hand man. A great part that did him all the more credit when his miserable health is taken into account.[20]

Hopkins was glad to get out of Washington the next day. On the train to New York he marked up a speech he was to give that evening, but his mind was on Louise Macy. She met him at Madison Square Garden, where, along with a handful of others, he was to speak at the Russian War Relief rally to a live audience numbering in the thousands and to millions of radio listeners. Sharing the podium with Ambassador Maxim Litvinov, Hopkins spoke of his trip to Moscow and the indomitable fighting spirit of the Russian people. He promised a "second front," which brought the crowd to its feet, and then said, "Yes, and if necessary, a third and a fourth front. The American people are bound to the people of the Soviet Union."[21] Hopkins knew that as long as he was vague about when and where these fronts would be established he could not be accused of misstating the truth and his hyperbole could be forgiven. Nevertheless in light of the inconclusive debates going on in Washington, he must have had some misgivings.

After the rally Hopkins and Macy went to El Morocco, the popular Manhattan nightclub, and they talked until he had to leave to catch the 12:50 a.m. train to Washington. Recalling that evening and the following day, Hopkins told a writer for the *New Yorker*, "I had never dreamed of getting married again. I got to my room the next morning and thought: you're in love with her, you talked like a sixteen-year-old last night." Hopkins wasted no time. He called Macy from the White House and persuaded her to take the train to Washington that afternoon, June 23. "I wanted to get it settled before dinner," he said. In the Harrimans' suite at the Mayflower, where Macy had gone to change for dinner, Hopkins proposed marriage and she accepted. Making light of the moment, Hopkins later told a friend, "Marie Harriman came in just as I was about to kiss her."[22]

That evening Hopkins, Macy, and Churchill dined together at the British Embassy at an event hosted by Lord Halifax, the British ambassador. When told of the engagement, Churchill was surprised and delighted. After dinner he invited Macy to join him on a nighttime walk in the gardens of the embassy because he wanted to see the fireflies. By one account, he told her that night that Hopkins "was the finest man he knew."[23] Returning later to the White House— after Churchill departed on a special train with Marshall, Brooke, and others that would take them to army maneuvers in South Carolina—Hopkins walked into FDR's study and told him he was engaged to Macy and that they planned to marry near the end of July. Roosevelt laughed and said, "That's wonderful." He suggested that the wedding ceremony be held in the White House and that the couple live in Hopkins's two-room suite on the second floor.[24]

On the night of June 25 Hopkins was alone with Churchill on the drive from Washington to Baltimore, where Churchill and his party would board the flying boat for the return trip to England. Hopkins took the occasion to assure the prime minister that his marriage would not affect his "personal and working relationship with the President."[25] He also imparted his heartfelt best wishes because he knew his friend would be facing a vote of no confidence in the House of Commons as a result of the fall of Tobruk.[26] Churchill's government was being bitterly criticized not only for the Tobruk debacle but for a string of battlefield defeats, equipment shortcomings, and poor military leadership. Like Roosevelt, Churchill was a politician who had to face powerful opponents, an increasingly anxious public, and the ballot box. The vote of no confidence was soundly defeated in the House of Commons but not until after Churchill's enemies had their say.

Hopkins himself must have had qualms about whether his marriage might weaken his role as chief intermediary between Churchill and Roosevelt. Why else would he feel the need to assure Churchill that it would not change? Churchill may have been facing a vote of no confidence, but Hopkins too had to have been concerned about how his stature might change once he would no longer be available to the president—physically and emotionally—all of the time. After all, Hopkins had seen how Roosevelt could ruthlessly distance himself from former intimates, such as Missy LeHand after her strokes and Thomas "Tommy the Cork" Corcoran after he decided to marry. Corcoran, a brilliant lawyer, had lobbied tirelessly and effectively for FDR's New Deal legislation and fronted for the president on his court-packing scheme, but after he gave up bachelorhood and married, Roosevelt excluded him from his inner circle.

As rumors of Hopkins's impending marriage began to appear in newspapers, he also sought to reassure General Marshall that nothing would change and that he would continue to work night and day, doing everything he possibly could to help win the war. Ever concerned about Hopkins's health and his prodigious work habits, Marshall sent a letter to the future Mrs. Hopkins. "To be very frank," he began, "I am intensely interested in Harry's health and happiness, and therefore in your impending marriage." Her fiancé, he wrote, "is of great importance to our National interests . . . and he is one of the most imprudent people regarding his health that I have ever known. . . . I express the hope that you will find it possible to curb his indiscretions and see that he takes the necessary rest."[27]

Eleanor Roosevelt confirmed the rumors of the Hopkins-Macy engagement at a press conference in the White House on Saturday afternoon, July 4. With each of them at her side, she announced that the couple would be married at a ceremony in the White House on July 30 and that they would reside in the White House so Hopkins could be "close to his job."[28]

Field Marshal Sir John Dill, Churchill's personal representative on the combined chiefs of staff, had established an unusually close friendship with

General Marshall. On July 8, 1942, he was witness to one of Marshall's few displays of rage. Dill had just handed him a message from Churchill to FDR, saying the British war cabinet had decided *not* to proceed with Sledgehammer—to which of course the British had pledged three weeks earlier to aggressively prepare until September 1, when a go/no go decision would be made. (At least that was Marshall's understanding.) As a substitute, Churchill and his war cabinet had reverted to Gymnast. Shrewdly appealing to Roosevelt's vanity, Churchill's note continued, "This [Gymnast] has all along been in harmony with your ideas. In fact it is your commanding idea. Here is the true second front of 1942. . . . Here is the safest and most fruitful stroke that can be delivered this autumn."[29]

Marshall was beside himself. Since April he had spent countless hours arguing, cajoling, negotiating, and finally reaching agreements with the British, only to have them back away by misstating conditions and employing slippery language, notably saying they agreed "in principle" or were committed to the "framework" of his cross-Channel plans. Feigning "unanimity" when in fact they flatly disagreed, the British kept urging diversionary operations that would not help the Soviets. It was now apparent, he angrily concluded, that they never had any intention of participating in an invasion of Europe in 1943, or perhaps even in 1944. Knowing full well the effect this would have on Dill, Marshall told him that the only way to have a decisive effect on the global war in 1942 was for the United States to reverse grand strategy and focus on the Pacific: defeat Japan first, and then turn to Germany.[30] Dill hoped Marshall's faith in "Germany first" would be restored when he cooled down. He was wrong. By July 10 the other joint chiefs (King and Arnold) had signed on to a memo to the president prepared by Marshall and endorsed by Stimson and Knox that proposed an ultimatum to the British: if they would not commit themselves irrevocably to a "concentrated effort against Germany," the United States would "turn to the Pacific and strike decisively against Japan."[31] (Marshall probably could not have appreciated it at the time, but the victory at Midway a few weeks earlier ended the ability of the Japanese to mount a sustained offensive, turned the war in the Pacific to a war of attrition, and in effect confirmed the wisdom of the "Germany first" strategy.)

Marshall's "showdown" memorandum was delivered to FDR on Saturday morning, July 11, at Hyde Park, where he and Hopkins were staying for the weekend and into the following week. Roosevelt realized at once that he had a very big problem on his hands, one that would test to the limit his considerable political and interpersonal skills. Every single one of his top hand-picked military advisors, as well as the civilian leadership of the War and Navy Departments that he had appointed, were advocating a fundamental shift in war strategy that he believed would lead to disaster. In his judgment, a turn to the Pacific could lead to the collapse of the Red Army, enslavement of the entire European continent by Hitler, and the invasion of Great Britain, not to mention the prolongation of the war and consequent vastly increased casualties. He had always believed that the defeat of Germany would quickly lead to the surrender of Japan, but not vice versa.

Was Marshall bluffing? Historians have debated the question over the years without arriving at a definitive answer. Whether or not it was a bluff, Roosevelt and assuredly Hopkins were viscerally opposed to threatening to abandon their ally to Hitler's Wehrmacht in order to force it to accept a strategy that all of the British military leaders believed was premature and thus could not succeed. Roosevelt and Hopkins understood Marshall's anger at the slippery and ambiguous language used by the British, but as politicians they appreciated its necessity. In the end they believed that preservation of allied unity was critical and that disagreements had to be resolved through negotiation and compromise. This principle was inherent in Hopkins's March 14, 1942, memo to the president ("I doubt if any single thing is as important").

The long weekend at Hyde Park was crammed with distractions. Louise Macy arrived on Saturday morning, "to the happiness of Harry Hopkins, who languishes with love," wrote William Hassett in his diary.[32] Queen Wilhelmina of the Netherlands and her entourage of princesses and ladies in waiting needed to be entertained, and Roosevelt was closeted with Wendell Willkie, head of the Republican Party, on that rainy Saturday afternoon to discuss an around-the-world trip that Willkie wished to take as the president's personal representative to spread goodwill and instill confidence in the allied fight for freedom. Although defeated by FDR in 1940, Willkie had supported the president on lend-lease and other policies and was a committed internationalist. Roosevelt enthusiastically approved Willkie's trip and indeed admired him for it.[33]

During times when they could break away, FDR and Hopkins met alone in the president's first-floor study to discuss what to do about Marshall's proposed ultimatum. By Monday afternoon a decision had been reached and a message to Marshall had been drafted, probably by Hopkins. Feeling "very desolate," wrote Hassett, Hopkins put Louise on the train for New York City on Monday evening and stayed up half the night drinking with Captain McCrea.[34]

The following morning Roosevelt telegraphed Marshall the final draft of his decision, saying he disapproved of the Pacific proposal and that he had "definitely decided to send you, King and Harry to London immediately." The reasoning underlying the decision to reject Marshall's Pacific proposal was cogently articulated. First, said the president, a turn to the Pacific plays into the hands of the Germans, who will be free to concentrate on defeating the Soviet Union; second, fighting in a number of small Pacific islands "will not affect the world situation this year or next"; and third, the Pacific proposal would "not help Russia or the Near East." Not too subtly, and unusually for him, the telegram was signed, "Roosevelt C-in-C."[35]

On Wednesday morning, having returned to Washington, the president and Hopkins met with Marshall and Stimson in the White House. FDR tried to lessen the tension by listening with apparent sympathy as Marshall vented his frustrations, referring in particular to Churchill's history of "half-baked" schemes for avoiding concentration of force on the enemy's vital center. Roosevelt suggested that his own preference was a cross-Channel invasion of France but that he was firmly opposed to using the Pacific alternative as a threat to force the British to bend to the will of the Americans. Addressing Stimson, the president said that if he and Marshall were really serious about turning to the Pacific, it would be like "taking up your dishes and going away," meaning akin to a fit of childish petulance. Roosevelt was well aware that such a power play by the United States would weaken and perhaps lead to the fall of Churchill's government at a time when the prime minister was facing severe criticism because of the debacle at Tobruk. He believed that keeping Churchill in power was vital to the national security of the United States.[36]

That evening, July 15, Hopkins and Roosevelt dined alone and talked long into the evening about the instructions that would guide the mission of Marshall, King, and Hopkins, who would be leaving the next day to meet with Churchill and his military chiefs in London. As reflected in Hopkins's notes and in the three-page written memorandum finalized the next day, the instruction "of highest importance" was that a definite and irrevocable agreement be reached with the British, committing U.S. ground troops to fight German ground forces *in 1942*. Signing again as "C-in-C," the president, with a tip of his hat to Marshall, urged the group to press the British "with the utmost vigor" for a cross-Channel invasion. But if they could not be persuaded, then the parties must "determine upon another place for U.S. Troops to fight in 1942." The instructions made it clear that "another place" did not mean the Pacific. "Defeat of Germany means the defeat of Japan, probably without firing a shot or losing a life," read the memo in what turned out to be a monumental example of wishful thinking. Expressing a hope that "total agreement" could be reached within a week after arrival, the president's instructions closed by emphasizing "three cardinal principles—speed of decision on plans, unity of plans, attack combined with defense but not defense alone."[37] Hopkins appreciated FDR's one-week deadline, as well as his emphasis on "speed of decision," because he had to get back in time for his July 30 wedding.

Aided by Hopkins, Roosevelt's instructions effectively doomed all of the efforts by Marshall and Eisenhower to fashion a coherent global strategy that, from a purely military perspective, they were convinced represented the best and quickest way to help the USSR and defeat Germany. By taking away the threat of a Pacific alternative, insisting on British concurrence with invasion plans, and requiring that American troops fight Germans in 1942, the president surely knew, before Marshall, King, and Hopkins had even departed for London, that the only plan for 1942 that the British would agree to would involve landings somewhere in French North Africa. At the same time, the president must have known, because he had been told repeatedly by Marshall and others, that a diversion into North Africa in 1942 would probably mean there would be no cross-Channel invasion of France until 1944 at the earliest, and in any case it would not help the USSR. Marshall and Eisenhower believed that once a million American soldiers landed in North Africa, they and the trillions of tons of matériel needed to support them would be sucked into the Mediterranean area for at least two years, which would eviscerate the buildup of troops, landing craft, and equipment needed for a cross-Channel assault in 1943.

If it would delay a cross-Channel assault until 1944 and not help the Soviets why did Roosevelt and Hopkins regard it as "of the highest importance that U.S. ground troops be brought into action" against Germany in 1942?[38] Why not follow the advice of their chief military advisors by building up an adequate quantity of troops, landing craft, and other resources during the remainder of 1942, and then launch a massive and decisive cross-Channel knockout blow in the spring of 1943?

The answer: morale and politics. The president could not afford to ask the people of the United States to continue to sacrifice on the home front for another full year without getting their boys into action against the Nazis. In rallies across the country the public was clamoring for a "second front now!"[39] In addition the midterm elections in early November, nowhere mentioned in any of the documents preserved by Roosevelt and Hopkins, were looming. They knew perfectly well that the elections would in part constitute a referendum on the president's handling of the war, and they were concerned about the decline since 1936 of the Democratic majority in Congress. Substantial losses at the polls could strengthen the hand of Jim Farley, FDR's emerging rival in the Democratic Party, increase the odds that the Republicans could take the presidency in 1944, and jeopardize the New Deal legacy, programs to which Roosevelt had devoted his presidency and Hopkins his entire life force.

The TWA Boeing Stratocruiser carrying Hopkins, Marshall, King, and their aides (including Hopkins's doctor) landed at Prestwick in southern Scotland early on Saturday morning, July 18. A special train, sent by Churchill, was waiting to take them to Chequers for the weekend. Marshall insisted that they decline Churchill's invitation to stay the night at Chequers and instead proceed nonstop to London, so that he could consult with Eisenhower and his staff officers and meet informally with their British counterparts before the formal conference was to begin with Churchill on Monday.

The American party checked into Claridge's, taking sixteen rooms on the fourth floor that were quickly converted into a small military headquarters with a communications center, scrambler telephones, and sentries at every door. Shortly after their arrival, Churchill telephoned Hopkins and vented his fury at Marshall's snub, claiming that the American chief of staff was attempting to subvert his constitutional authority as prime minister and minister of defense by meeting with British officers against his express wishes. "The Prime Minister threw the British Constitution at me with some vehemence," reported Hopkins to Roosevelt. Then he joked, "As you know, it is an unwritten document so no serious damage was done. Winston is his old self and full of battle."[40]

Unable to dissipate Churchill's wrath and concerned about the upcoming talks, Hopkins drove to Chequers on Sunday to spend the day. There is no written record of what the two of them talked about that day, except Hopkins's brief report to the president that by Sunday evening everything "was cleared up" and that Churchill was "in the best of spirits."[41] However, piecing this day together with later events, it is likely that Hopkins had soothed Churchill by giving him, in strict confidence, a sense of the president's instructions to his negotiating team and reminding him that Roosevelt had not lost sight of Gymnast. Indeed all Hopkins had to do was signal Churchill that the Pacific alternative had been taken off the table and Churchill would know that he and his military chiefs could safely oppose all of Marshall's plans for a 1942 or 1943 cross-Channel invasion.

Meanwhile, in London, Marshall, Eisenhower, and their staffs, with help from enthusiastic younger members of Mountbatten's Combined Operations Group, worked all night Saturday and most of Sunday putting together a revised Sledgehammer plan. Instead of an emergency or sacrifice landing in 1942, the new plan contemplated the seizure of Cherbourg and a permanent lodgment of Anglo-American troops on the Cotentin peninsula in Normandy, beginning with an invasion in September 1942 and lasting until the spring of 1943, when the main cross-Channel invasion would take place. This was more ambitious than the original plan, but it was designed to meet one of Churchill's principal objections: that the original plan did not assure a permanent lodgment of ground forces.[42]

Marshall, of course, realized that he had been hamstrung by the instructions prepared by Roosevelt and Hopkins and, because of his prior dealings with Churchill, Brooke, and the rest of the British, knew as well that it would be virtually impossible to persuade them to commit to a 1942 cross-Channel operation for which they would provide most of the troops. Nevertheless, with Hopkins's ostensible support, he intended to pull out all stops trying. For the next two days Marshall summoned all of his rhetorical skills in an effort to persuade Brooke and Churchill of the merits of his revised Sledgehammer plan. They wouldn't budge. Nothing Marshall said, recalled Hopkins, "appeared to make the slightest impression on General Brooke's settled convictions.... He kept looking into the distance."[43] With his "tongue shooting out and round his lips," the fast-talking and self-assured Brooke argued that because of the lack of air superiority and his conviction that the Germans could quickly concentrate overwhelming forces on the Cotentin peninsula, the invasion force would never survive the winter.[44] As Brooke wrote in his diary, Marshall "failed to realize that such an action could only lead to the loss of some 6 divisions without achieving any results!"[45]

On Tuesday night, July 21, at 11 p.m., Brooke was summoned to No. 10 Downing Street. Upon arrival he found that Hopkins and British Foreign Secretary Anthony Eden were behind closed doors with Churchill. In his diary later that night, Brooke wrote, "I was not allowed to join them for fear that Marshall and King should hear of it and feel that I had been briefed by Hopkins against them according to President's wishes!!"[46] Based on this contemporaneous entry, it appears that Hopkins needed to be able to deny that he had met with Brooke that night; that Brooke was informed by Churchill (not by Hopkins) that Roosevelt was not committed to Marshall's Sledgehammer plan for 1942; and that Hopkins was the covert bearer of this critical piece of information. Once Churchill and then Brooke clearly understood that neither the president nor Hopkins was foursquare behind Marshall, they knew they could remain firm in their opposition to Sledgehammer and that Gymnast would soon emerge as the only alternative.

The next afternoon, in a major showdown with Churchill, Marshall made one last attempt at selling Sledgehammer, arguing—sometimes heatedly—that without it they were "faced with a defensive attitude in the European theatre."[47] Churchill, agreeing with the opinions of Brooke and his other chiefs of staff, remained firmly opposed. The parties had come to a complete stalemate. Eisenhower, who had invested so much of himself in the cross-Channel planning, recorded the moment in his diary, with more than a hint of melodramatic overstatement that he later regretted, as "the blackest day in history."[48]

At about that point, Hopkins passed a note on Downing Street stationery to someone at the table, "probably Marshall" (wrote Sherwood), that simply said, "I feel damned depressed." The note was carefully saved and has been quoted and reproduced on numerous occasions as evidence of Hopkins's stalwart support of Marshall and extreme disappointment at his failure to persuade the British to agree to Sledgehammer.[49] It is unlikely, however, that he could have genuinely felt "depressed" because it was he who had encouraged British intransigence—the purported source of his depression—by helping Roosevelt write the negotiating instructions that severely circumscribed Marshall and by very likely conveying the gist of those instructions to Churchill either at Chequers the previous Sunday or on Tuesday night, July 21. Indeed an entry in the diary of British Major-General John Kennedy on the very day of the "I feel damned depressed" note provides strong evidence that Brooke was fully aware of the Roosevelt-Hopkins negotiating instructions. According to Kennedy, Brooke told him on July 22 that Roosevelt "had given instructions to Marshall to the effect that the American Army must get into action somewhere against the Germans and that he was to go and make plans accordingly."[50] Brooke therefore knew that his opposition to Sledgehammer would result in the Americans turning to North Africa. And Hopkins was the most likely source of the leak.

Hopkins wrote the note not because he was actually depressed but because he knew Marshall and his aides would be experiencing something akin to depression—as Eisenhower's diary notation reveals clearly was the case—and he feared that word of "this disagreement should get noised abroad."[51] Although the note was disingenuous—and had a political motivation—Hopkins was trying to make them feel he was on their side. In this light, the note is the quintessential example of the Hopkins touch: quick, deft, sympathetic, and faintly disingenuous. Without revealing his full intentions, Hopkins was telling the recipient what he most wanted to hear and at the same time he expressed the truth of the moment. Of course Hopkins may have written and preserved the note in an effort to provide cover for his backdoor disclosures of the president's negotiating instructions. In the last few months of his life, Hopkins told Sidney Hyman, who was assembling his papers for a possible book, "Beware of documents—they lie. People want to read well in history. They're editing themselves in advance of historians."[52] Nonetheless the note carries its own weight.

Advised of the stalemate, Roosevelt cabled his team that he was not surprised that the British refused to agree to Sledgehammer. He therefore ordered them to reach a consensus on some other place where American troops could fight the Germans on the ground in 1942, suggesting that French North Africa was his first choice.[53] Marshall and his staff spent the next day putting together a new, cleverly written plan, one that purported to comply with the commander in chief's orders yet at the same time, depending on the Russian situation, would preserve a go/no go decision on what was always and would remain Marshall's prime objective: a massive cross-Channel invasion in 1943. Part 1 of the plan required that preparations would continue for the invasion of France in 1943. Part 2 called for landings in North Africa in 1942, *provided* the parties understood that the 1943 invasion of France would be "impracticable" and that they would "definitely" assume a strategic "defensive" posture in Europe. Part 3 stipulated that a final decision to either proceed with a cross-Channel invasion in 1943 or invade North Africa in 1942 would be put off until September 15 and would depend on "the situation on the Russian front."[54]

Marshall hoped that the proviso in part 2 might cause Brooke and perhaps others to reconsider, given that acceptance would mean an admission that there would be no significant Anglo-American ground action in Europe until 1944 at the earliest, as well as implicit permission for the Americans to concentrate more on the Pacific. Up until then the British had always argued that there was nothing inconsistent about launching Gymnast in 1942 and a massive cross-Channel invasion in 1943. They were also fearful of any sign of a U.S. departure from the "Germany first" policy.

The British, however, accepted Marshall's plan with alacrity and no doubt considerable relief. Notwithstanding its provisos and delayed-decision date, they regarded the plan as little more than an abandonment of Sledgehammer and the substitution of Gymnast—exactly what they had been advocating from the beginning. By the end of the day—Friday, July 24—Brooke, Churchill, and the British war cabinet had approved the plan, designated CCS 94. In his diary Brooke wrote, "We have got just what we wanted out of U.S. Chiefs."[55] But Hopkins was not yet on board. He was concerned about part 3 of CCS 94, which allowed for a postponement of the final go/no go decision until September 15. Beginning with his memo in March and through all of his discussions with Roosevelt, he was convinced that the most important "single thing" was to get American troops into the fight in 1942; this provision could jeopardize that goal.

That evening Hopkins kept his reservations to himself, except perhaps when he was able to draw Churchill aside for a few private moments in the midst of the elaborate entertainment. Along with other important guests, Hopkins was taken by launch from Whitehall to a large dinner party hosted by the Lords of the Admiralty in honor of Admiral King in the painted hall of the Old Royal Naval College at Greenwich, the baroque masterpiece designed by Christopher Wren.[56] According to a letter written by Churchill's private secretary, Sir John "Jock" Martin, after an "excellent dinner" the party adjourned to the "young officers' gun-room," where Churchill, Hopkins, and a large crowd of admirals and Wrens (members of the Women's Royal Naval Service) gathered around a piano, played by the First Lord of the Admiralty, and "sang at the top of their voices (not excluding the P.M.)." The "most cheerful party," ended the evening with "Auld Lang Syne and the two national anthems."[57]

"The thing I fear," wrote Hopkins the next morning in a cable to Roosevelt, "is that if a firm decision is not made now to go for Gymnast and a reasonably early date fixed, delay and procrastination may take place." He "very strongly" urged the president to set a date for the North Africa invasion "not later than October 30th, 1942," because of the dangerous "situation in Russia."[58] Because Hopkins had been told that the North Africa landings would draw few if any German troops away from the eastern front, his stated rationale for selecting this precise date does not ring true. Indeed it is difficult to explain this deadline other than on the basis of domestic politics. October 30 was four days before the midterm elections. With the help of his friend Pug Ismay, Hopkins dispatched this cable to Roosevelt through the British Foreign Office to the British Embassy in Washington with instructions to deliver it to the president. In doing so, Hopkins deliberately circumvented Marshall and King.[59]

Roosevelt responded quickly in a cable addressed to Hopkins, Marshall, and King, saying it was his "opinion" (he didn't say "order") that the Gymnast landings should take place no later than October 30. He instructed them to tell Churchill he was "delighted" that a final decision had been made and that his orders were "full speed ahead."[60] In a separate message to Hopkins, FDR said, "Give Winston my best and tell him that not even he can stop that wedding."[61]

A few minutes later Roosevelt, at his office in the White House, read these messages to Generals McNarney and Arnold. McNarney immediately cabled Marshall that his effort to postpone a final decision until September 15 had been countermanded by the president. Marshall must have been extremely upset, if not humiliated, by this news. Adding to Marshall's distress, McNarney also told him that FDR had breezily observed during their meeting that even though the United States had now decided to proceed with the North Africa invasion in 1942, he, the president, "could see no reason" why it would prevent the main cross-Channel attack in 1943.[62] Marshall, backed by Eisenhower and his military planners, had told the president and Hopkins time and again that a decision to invade North Africa in the fall of 1942 would mean there could be no cross-Channel invasion of France in 1943; part 2 of his plan, memorialized as CCS 94, indicated exactly that.

On Saturday evening, the Americans' last full day in England, Hopkins, Marshall, and King dined at Chequers with Churchill, Brooke, and several others. After dinner they were shown Cromwell's death mask and

Queen Elizabeth's ring.[63] (They must have reacted, as most did, to the peculiar growth on Cromwell's lower lip and his crooked nose.) The three Americans and their aides then left by train for Prestwick and the flight to the United States. Hopkins was particularly anxious to get back, having received a telegram from Louise reminding him, "You better keep that date."[64]

Two days later Churchill cabled Roosevelt to say how pleased he was that they had "reached agreement on action," while at the same time cementing "relations of cordial intimacy and comradeship . . . between [their] high officers." He singled out Hopkins for the critical role he played, a role perhaps far more significant than disclosed by the written record. "I doubt that success would have been achieved without Harry's invaluable aid."[65] Roosevelt responded a few hours later: "The three musketeers [Hopkins, Marshall, King] arrived safely this afternoon and the wedding is still scheduled. . . . I cannot help feeling that the past week represented a turning point of the whole war and that we are now on our way shoulder to shoulder."[66]

As far as Roosevelt, Churchill, and Hopkins were concerned, a final decision to invade North Africa on or before October 30, 1942, had been made. Marshall, however, had not given up. He continued to believe that landings in North Africa, optimistically renamed "Torch," would be a diversion that would not help the Soviet Union and would only delay the defeat of Germany. The proper strategy, he believed to his core, was concentration of force on northwestern France and a rapid thrust to the heart of Germany. He would have his day.

It was a euphoric homecoming for Hopkins. At noon on Thursday, July 30, he and Louise Macy were married in the president's Oval Study on the second floor of the White House, the only wedding ever performed there and the first White House wedding since Woodrow Wilson married Edith Bolling Galt in December 1915. "Nervous Harry Hopkins" entered the room on schedule, "his hair freshly trimmed, his blue business suit unwrinkled for the occasion," reported *Time*. He was accompanied by the Reverend Russell Clinchy, the same pastor who had married Hopkins and Barbara Duncan and who had presided at Barbara's funeral and her burial at Rock Creek Cemetery. Hopkins's best man was the president, who was wheeled in wearing a white linen suit and white shoes. Awaiting the bride, the other guests who assembled in the study included Eleanor Roosevelt and Hopkins's nine-year-old daughter, Diana; Hopkins's three sons, David, Robert, and Stephen (David and Robert in military uniforms, Stephen a senior at the Hill School); Louise's sisters Gert and Min; and General Marshall and Admiral King.

Outside in the hallway a Marine Corps string ensemble played the "Wedding March" from *Lohengrin*. Dressed in a "simple deep-blue frock, with a matching halo hat," Louise entered the study on the arm of her brother-in-law, Navy Lieutenant Nicholas Ludington. According to William Hassett, "Harry trembled like an aspen leaf throughout the service, but managed to fish the wedding ring out of his pants pocket at the proper time, albeit with trembling fingers." After the service, which lasted for little more than ten minutes, the ensemble played "I Married an Angel" from the current Broadway musical of that name, and "the immediate relatives remained" for a modest luncheon of jellied salmon, hot chicken sandwiches, jellied vegetable rings, and a "mountainous wedding cake." Champagne was served and the president "made a little speech." At about 3 p.m., "just before a daylight air-raid drill took place," Louise and Harry left for a ten-day honeymoon at a small farm in Connecticut.[67]

Marshall and King excused themselves from the wedding luncheon to attend a meeting of the joint chiefs of staff, the first to be presided over by Admiral William Leahy, who had been appointed by FDR to serve as his representative in that group. Leahy was in for a rude surprise. At the outset of the meeting, he quite understandably said it was his "impression" that a final decision had been made to proceed with Torch, the invasion of French North Africa, and that all preparations should move forward as rapidly as possible. He was shocked when Marshall, backed by King, said no final decision had been made. Pointing to part 2 of CCS 94, Marshall said that until both the president and the prime minister explicitly abandoned the proposed 1943 cross-Channel invasion of France in favor of North Africa in 1942, there could be no final decision. He also pointed to the fact that the president had expressed his "opinion" that Torch be launched by

October 30, but his opinion was by no means a final decision and certainly did not constitute an order.

Leahy must have wondered how the president and his chief of staff could disagree over whether a decision of such fundamental importance was or was not made. As soon as he informed Roosevelt of Marshall's position, concurred in by King, the president ordered his military chiefs to the Oval Study to set them straight once and for all. At 8:30 p.m. on July 30, only a few hours after Hopkins had departed for his honeymoon, Roosevelt said he had "definitely" decided that Torch was the "principal objective" and would be undertaken at the earliest possible date, "preferably within two months." There would be "no Sledgehammer against France." Moreover, against all advice from his military and logistics experts, he still envisioned a massive cross-Channel invasion of France in 1943.[68]

Thus ended what the military historian John Keegan has called "the hardest-fought strategic debate in the war."[69] In direct opposition to the recommendations of his chief of staff, chief of naval operations, and secretaries of war and navy, Roosevelt, aided by Hopkins, had sided with the British and made by far the most important U.S. military decision of World War II. In light of the lack of battle experience of American troops and their officers, the decision turned out to be militarily wise. Given public opinion and the upcoming elections, the decision was politically correct. Yet it would result in American troops and resources being drawn into the Mediterranean for the next three years and the postponement of the main assault on Fortress Europe until June 1944.

Hopkins had been deeply involved in the decision-making process on both sides of the Atlantic. His early emphasis on the singular importance of fighting Germans on the ground in 1942, a stance that put the British in the driver's seat as to where the fight would take place, must have had an influence on the president even if it only strengthened an instinct that he already embraced. The other key judgment, the one that led directly to the ultimate decision to invade North Africa, was the rejection of Marshall's Pacific ultimatum, an unequivocal directive that emerged from meetings of Roosevelt and Hopkins alone at Hyde Park and deprived Marshall of his leverage against the British. Given Roosevelt's pre-existing views on the importance of Germany First, it is probable that the president knew his mind and that Hopkins merely reinforced his resolve.

Hopkins played his most influential role on the other side of the Atlantic, where the evidence suggests that he disclosed the substance of Roosevelt's negotiating instructions to Churchill and signaled to him that if he and his military chiefs continued their opposition to Sledgehammer, the Americans would not turn to the Pacific but would ultimately have to settle on North Africa. Though he resorted to arguably devious back-door dealings, Hopkins was always committed, as was Roosevelt, to the preservation of the Anglo-American coalition and to keeping Churchill's government in power. The prime minister was both sincere and correct in praising "Harry" for his "invaluable aid."

On substance, George Marshall, the biggest loser in this "hardest-fought" strategic debate, was not at all influenced by Hopkins, nor did he seem to harbor any resentment toward him. Marshall may have suspected that Hopkins had a hand in undermining him, but there is no evidence that he confronted Hopkins or that their relationship suffered. Long after the war Marshall spoke warmly of Hopkins, saying, "He was always the strong advocate, it seemed to me, of almost everything I proposed."[70] Up until the final decision—in fact for a week thereafter—Marshall persisted in opposing Torch and arguing for a cross-Channel invasion in 1943.[71] Yet with the exception of one known disagreement, discussed in the next chapter, Hopkins continued to enjoy a warm, cordial relationship with this steely general known for his straight talk, selflessness, and "granitic constancy."[72] Marshall must have suspected that Hopkins was not always supportive. He could have leaked derogatory information about him through colleagues. However, there is no evidence that he ever criticized Hopkins or directed one of his rare outbursts of anger at him. The closest Marshall came was a comment tinged with sarcasm about the final decision to invade North Africa, aimed more at Roosevelt than Hopkins: "I did not realize how in a democracy the public has to be kept entertained."[73]

11

Lighting the Torch

When Hopkins told nine-year-old Diana that he was going to marry Louise Macy, all the little girl knew about her future stepmother was that she "was very pretty and pleasant—and had a dog." However, it didn't take long before Diana started calling her "Mummy." Louise "cinched the deal," recalled Diana, by presenting her with a "Brownie box camera" and taking her to "Best & Co. in New York to buy a pair of spectator pumps."[1]

Having looked after Diana "with great kindness and good sense" for three years, Eleanor Roosevelt had doubts about the wisdom of Louise moving into the Lincoln suite "bag and baggage" with Diana's father.[2] "I'm worried about Harry's marriage & Diana's adjustment if they live in the White House," she confided to her old friend Lorena Hickok, who by then had been residing in the White House for more than a year (White House ushers referred to her as the "enduring guest").[3] Eleanor hoped that they would eventually move out and get a place of their own, but for the time being she had little choice but to defer to the wishes of her husband. "Franklin said finally that the most important thing in the world at that time was the conduct of the war and that it was absolutely necessary that Harry be in the house," wrote the First Lady. "That settled that."[4]

For the past few years the temperature of the relationship between Harry and Eleanor continued to cool as he became her husband's closest confidant and was almost wholly absorbed by the demands of the war. Hopkins's fascination with his fashionable new wife and her wealthy socialite friends in Manhattan, Oyster Bay, and Santa Barbara caused Eleanor to feel that he had "lost some of his values." In a bitter tone, she wrote her friend Esther Lape that she had once thought Hopkins's "affection" was for her, but that she now believed he was "only interested in getting to Franklin."[5]

Things between the First Lady and Hopkins approached a breaking point the weekend before he left for London in mid-July 1942. Pressured by A. Philip Randolph, the civil rights leader, to intercede on behalf of an African American sharecropper who was about to be executed for murder in Virginia following a flawed trial before an all-white jury, Eleanor decided to appeal to her husband, who was up in Hyde Park with Hopkins, dealing with Marshall's "Pacific first" ultimatum. To get Franklin on the telephone so she could persuade him to stop the execution, Eleanor called Hopkins from the White House several times. Knowing FDR did not want to speak to her—he had already sent a letter to the Virginia governor suggesting clemency and felt he had done what he could—Hopkins kept telling her the president was unavailable. Finally, as her anger mounted, he passed the phone to the president, who told her that he could do nothing further since it was not a federal crime. The sharecropper was electrocuted the next day, July 13, 1942. Mrs. Roosevelt took out her frustrations and anger on Hopkins. She believed he had abandoned the noble principles he championed during the Great Depression.[6]

After a brief honeymoon in Connecticut, Hopkins and Louise moved into the freshly painted Lincoln suite on August 11, 1942, the smaller room serving as Louise's bedroom and the larger with the big green canopied bed functioning as a combination bedchamber for Hopkins and a living room with fireplace, sofa, and chairs for the two of them. According to Diana, they slept in separate rooms because her father "snored something fierce!" In the absence of closets, Hopkins kept his clothes in a large wardrobe behind his desk. Wedding presents were stacked atop the bookcases, and their Capehart radio-phonograph sat on a table along the wall beneath a map of the world. Louise brought her maid, Margaret "Margy" Jones, and her poodle, Suzy, from New York and hired a French governess ("Mademoiselle"), who for a time lived in a room next to Diana on the third floor. "It has a queer atmosphere of its own," Louise remarked with evident affection.[7] Diana remembers Louise as a "feminine, fluffy type of person," who was warm and affectionate. "I was dying for a mommy," she recalled. In the fall of 1942 Louise enrolled Diana as a day student at the Potomac School. "Every morning I'd walk across Lafayette Park to catch a trolley to school."[8]

On weekday mornings Louise, looking chic in her hospital uniform, would leave early and walk down Pennsylvania Avenue toward Georgetown to her job as captain of nurse's aides at Columbia Hospital, while Hopkins, when he was not traveling, would discuss the day's activities with the president in his bedroom or the Oval Study. When she returned in the late afternoon, the two would often have cocktails in the big Lincoln room with friends or with Anna Boettiger, the president's daughter, who had moved into the White House after her husband began serving as an army officer. If FDR was available, they would move down the hall to join him and his guests for his ritual "children's hour," causing Mrs. Roosevelt to remark, "They really are quite high sometimes before they sit down to dinner."[9]

As the midterm elections approached in the weeks following the wedding, Hopkins became the object of highly publicized and politically motivated attacks. Anonymous letters were sent to Senators Prentiss Brown of Michigan and Millard Tydings of Maryland, claiming that the conversion of a private yacht for wartime use by the Coast Guard had been delayed so that Hopkins could enjoy a honeymoon cruise on the plush vessel with his new bride. Newspapers picked up the story and rumors ran rampant. The FBI opened an investigation and found, after interviewing the owner of the yacht (Roy Fruehauf, the Detroit truck manufacturer) and several others, that there was no substance to the allegations. The small farm in Connecticut where Hopkins and Louise actually spent their honeymoon was a long way from navigable waters.

Another rumor was that Hopkins and his new wife accepted an emerald necklace worth a half million dollars from Lord Beaverbrook as a wedding present in appreciation for the vast amount of lend-lease aid Hopkins had funneled to Great Britain. The rumor, vigorously denied by Hopkins, gained traction in newspapers throughout the nation, including a column by Hopkins's former Georgetown neighbor, Drew Pearson.[10] A congressional investigation was threatened, but nothing came of it. Years later Diana recalled that although her stepmother never received an emerald necklace from Beaverbrook, he did give her a diamond tiara that had been in his family for years—a magnificent piece made from old diamonds that Napoleon allegedly had made for his wife Josephine and that Louise kept in a "very old red-leather case."[11]

While Hopkins and Louise were on their honeymoon, Churchill, with considerable anxiety and trepidation, was preparing to travel to Moscow to inform Stalin that the Americans and British would *not* open a second front in Europe in 1942, but instead would land in North Africa. His mission, Churchill later said, "was like carrying a lump of ice to the North Pole."[12] To convey the impression of solidarity, Churchill secured Roosevelt's approval to take Averell Harriman with him, telling the president, "I feel that things would be easier if we all [U.S. and U.K.] seemed to be together. I have a somewhat raw job."[13]

When Churchill and Harriman entered the large plain room in the Kremlin on August 12, Stalin was much better prepared than they were. Through highly placed spies in the U.S. and U.K. governments, including in particular a source close to the British Imperial General Staff, Stalin had already been fully briefed on the details of the meetings in London that had taken place during the week of July 21, including the fact that the British war cabinet rejected Marshall's plan for a limited cross-Channel invasion in 1942. The British military historian Max Hastings suggests that Hopkins himself inadvertently leaked details about the London talks to a Soviet NKVD agent, although he did not identify his source.[14]

Stalin remained in command throughout the three days of meetings. He not only possessed detailed information about Anglo-American military plans and disagreements, but he also knew he had maximum leverage to extract supply commitments because his allies feared that if they didn't meet his demands he might make a separate peace with Hitler and stop killing Germans. Keeping his guests off balance, Stalin began by mocking if not insulting Churchill, saying such things as "You can't win wars if you aren't willing to take risks" and "You must not be so afraid of the Germans."[15] He sought to drive wedges between the Americans and the British, pulling Harriman aside to tell him that he had "little respect for the British military effort but much hope in that of the U.S." On the second day he shifted ground. To explain the plan to attack North Africa, the prime minister had drawn an outline of a crocodile, pointing out that its long curved abdomen was analogous to Europe's Mediterranean coastline. Handing the drawing to Stalin, Churchill stated that Operation Torch was aimed at the "soft underbelly" of the Axis; the attack on the snout—western France—would come later. With no perceptible hint of sarcasm, Stalin, the former seminarian, dictator of an atheistic state, lifted the prime minister's spirits by saying of Torch, "May God prosper this undertaking."[16]

Churchill departed Moscow "definitely encouraged." Referring to Stalin and his colleagues, he said in a fit of overstatement, "Now they know the worst, and having made their protest are entirely friendly."[17] Likewise, in his report to FDR, Harriman was optimistic, expressing confidence in the Red Army's ability to withstand the summer offensive and passing along Stalin's desire to meet with Roosevelt in person sometime during the coming winter.[18]

For his part, Stalin came away from the meetings with Churchill and Harriman tethered to one reality: the Soviet Union would continue to be engaged in an apocalyptic bloodbath. The Germans were driving deep into the Caucasus, and Field Marshal Friedrich Paulus was poised for a final thrust across the Don toward Stalingrad. While the Red Army was losing soldiers at the rate of several thousand per day, Stalin was convinced that the British and Americans would remain reluctant to take risks and shed blood in order to relieve them. Churchill was deluding himself if he really thought the Soviets had become "entirely friendly."

In Washington and at Hyde Park, where he celebrated his fifty-second birthday, Hopkins was enjoying married life and pleased to have Harriman substitute for him on the trip to Moscow, a trip he had not been keen to make. But he was about to be put back into the pressure cooker. As Stalin had predicted when he teased Churchill, the Western allies continued to be risk-averse, wary of failure in confronting the Wehrmacht. This time, however, it was General Marshall and the American chiefs of staff, not the British, who were hedging their bets. Marshall's initial plan for Torch proposed that the landings in French North Africa be delayed until November (after the midterm elections) in order to provide more time for training exercises in the United States. Moreover to protect supply lines and lessen the risk of a successful counterattack by the Germans, possibly aided by French fighters, the plan envisioned a major landing on the Atlantic coast near the city of Casablanca in Morocco and only one landing on the Mediterranean, inside Gibraltar, at Oran. The plan ruled out any landing at Algiers or points farther east on the North African coast.[19]

When Churchill heard of Marshall's plan, he immediately cabled Roosevelt, saying, "We are all profoundly disconcerted. . . . It seems to me that the whole pith of the operation will be lost if we do not take Algiers as well as Oran on the first day." The prime minister was concerned that a failure to land at Algiers would enable German troops to occupy both that city and Tunis and frustrate what he regarded as "the main objects of the campaign": the enlistment of "French cooperation" and an eventual "attack upon Italy." (Note that Churchill was already laying the groundwork for what turned out to be a protracted campaign in Italy.)[20]

At a luncheon meeting in the White House on Friday, August 28, Roosevelt and Hopkins listened without interruption while Marshall defended his plan. Roosevelt stressed the importance of having exclusively American troops make the initial landings in order to minimize if not eliminate French opposition. The United States had maintained diplomatic relations with Vichy France, whereas the British had severed theirs, hence French troops in North Africa would be less likely to take up arms against Americans. FDR also urged Marshall to launch the attacks at the earliest possible date.[21] It was perhaps at this meeting that Roosevelt reportedly said to Marshall, his hands clasped in prayer, "Please, make it before election day."[22]

That afternoon Roosevelt, Hopkins, and a few aides departed by automobile for the newly appropriated rustic retreat in the Catoctin Mountains in northern Maryland. Roosevelt called it "Shangri-La," the name of the Asian monastery in James Hilton's popular 1933 novel *Lost Horizon*, which Frank Capra had made into a movie in 1937. (President Eisenhower renamed it "Camp David" after his grandson.) The site, a former Marine training station, consisted of several pine cabins situated above a tumbling mountain stream.[23] The following day, seated on the screen porch of the president's four-bedroom cabin overlooking the valley, Hopkins prepared a message in longhand to Churchill that Roosevelt then edited. In essence the message proposed two wholly American landings, one at Casablanca and the other at Oran; that these landings would take place preferably by October 14 but no later than October 30; and that British forces should land at Algiers and other points eastward at the end of the first week in November. With Marshall's reluctant approval, this message was cabled to Churchill on August 30.

Churchill pushed back. He maintained that in order to beat the Germans to the punch, Algiers must be "occupied simultaneously with Casablanca and Oran" and that Marshall's insistence on landings in the Atlantic surf near Casablanca was likely to result in a delay in achieving the objectives of the overall operation until mid-November. The president, with Hopkins's support and Marshall's eventual concurrence, gave in. On September 2 he cabled Churchill proposing that 10,000 American troops land at Algiers, "followed within the hour by British troops to make the landing secure." This would be coupled with an assurance to the French that British troops would not remain in French territory but would shortly "march into Axis held Tripoli from the rear." He also indicated that the Americans were prepared to land 58,000 troops near Casablanca and 45,000 at Oran. Eisenhower, who had already been named commander in chief of the Allied Expeditionary Force, would command the entire operation.

Churchill promptly agreed to the proposed "military layout." Roosevelt replied, "Hurrah!" Churchill shot back, "Okay full blast."[24] Torch was finally lit.

━━━━━━━━

As war production was ramped up in the spring and summer of 1942, the American economy was on the verge of overheating after a decade of stagnation. The threat of runaway inflation was real. The price of milk had jumped from 34 cents per gallon in 1941 to 62 cents. To "keep the cost of living from spiraling upward," the president had already imposed a series of price and allocation controls by executive order.[25] However, Congress, led by Republican Senators Robert Taft of Ohio and Kenneth Wherry of Nebraska, had curtailed his ability to hold down farm prices, which meant that he could not really control the cost of living, given that food costs were such a large part of everyone's daily expenses. During the last weekend of August—the same weekend they worked on the message to Churchill about the Torch landings—Roosevelt and Hopkins wrestled with the tricky issue of inflation control out on the screen porch at Shangri-La. Either the president could exercise his emergency war powers and issue an order imposing lower ceilings on farm prices, or he could ask Congress to enact legislation. He could also request Congress to increase taxes, which would dampen demand and curb upward pressure on prices.[26]

With midterm elections looming, members of Congress were understandably reluctant to alienate farmers or to increase income taxes. Rosenman, Sherwood, and others advised the president to promptly issue an executive order to hold down farm prices rather than risk delay and the possibility that Congress might not act. Hopkins, worried that the president's detractors could accuse him of being dictatorial, recommended that FDR issue an ultimatum to Congress: "You act before October 1st or I will."[27] Hopkins reasoned that from a political standpoint the president should not arrogate to himself an essentially legislative function without first demonstrating to the public that Congress would not act on an issue vital to the war effort.

Hopkins's advice prevailed. In a message to Congress delivered at noon on September 7 and a fireside chat broadcast that evening to the nation from the new FDR Library at Hyde Park, Roosevelt asked Congress to give him authority to set maximum prices on farm commodities and on all other as yet uncontrolled items. If Congress did not act by October 1, he warned, "It will leave me with an inescapable responsibility to the people of this country to see to it that the war effort is no longer imperiled by the threat of economic chaos. . . . I shall accept the responsibility, and I will act." With regard to taxes, Roosevelt made a breathtaking request—particularly in view of the upcoming midterm elections. Characterizing a tax increase as "one of our most powerful weapons in our fight to stabilize living costs," as well as a measure to finance the war and redistribute wealth, he proposed a confiscatory tax increase that would effectively limit every individual to a maximum net income of $25,000. (At the time, the average annual salary of an American worker was $1,299 and the minimum wage was $.43 per hour.) He also proposed a wartime excess profits tax on corporations.[28]

While Congress deliberated, Roosevelt and the First Lady left on a two-week transcontinental tour of war factories, Army camps, and Navy yards. Roosevelt liked to pretend that the trip was both a secret and nonpolitical, but in fact it gained wide publicity, providing assurance to the public that under his leadership, labor and management were united in the war effort. Hopkins stayed behind in Washington "to act as a messenger," as he said in a letter to Lord Beaverbrook.[29] Before the president departed, Hopkins, experienced infighter that he was, drafted an order for the president's signature designed to guarantee that he would remain in control of all war-related matters while the president was gone. The order, which was signed by Roosevelt and delivered to Admiral Leahy, the president's chief of staff and his representative on the Combined Chiefs of Staff, said, "I am anxious to get the cables to me from the Prime Minister and other heads of government in various countries, and my replies to them, coordinated through Harry because so much of them refer to civil things." According to George Elsey, a young naval officer assigned to the map room, "This rationale [for taking Leahy out of the loop] was pure nonsense."[30] Elsey was probably right. Virtually all cable traffic from Churchill and other leaders dealt not with "civil things" but with the war. Hopkins was simply making sure that he, not Leahy, would remain in control of all significant war-related communications as well as civil matters while Roosevelt was gone.

In addition to keeping Roosevelt posted on the inflation-control legislation while he was out of Washington, Hopkins began formulating a series of initiatives to improve U.S. relations with the Soviet Union. First and perhaps most important, he urged Roosevelt to meet with Stalin personally to convince him that the United States had no hostile or ulterior purpose—other than the total defeat of Hitler—in its conduct of the war. In discussions with Joe Davies in September and October 1942, Hopkins was told that the Soviet leadership was deeply suspicious of Churchill, believing he had persuaded the Americans to delay the opening of a second front in order to bleed Russia dry so the British would have a stronger hand in carving up Europe at the end of the war.[31] Hopkins's decision to advocate a face-to-face meeting with Stalin marked the beginning of an effort to separate U.S. policy toward the USSR from that of Great Britain. Second, in an effort to expedite aid to the Soviet Union, Hopkins decided to ask the president to create a Soviet Protocol Committee, with Hopkins as chairman. One of its main objectives would be to consolidate oversight and put an end to the insistence by Admiral William Standley, U.S. ambassador to the USSR, and others that lend-lease aid not be extended without airtight agreements allowing access by U.S. personnel to verify appropriate use. Hopkins's view was that the job of the Americans was to get the supplies to the Soviet Union as quickly as possible, no questions asked, and he made sure that his man in Moscow, Philip Faymonville, had the authority to get the job done without interference by Standley and his supporters in the State Department.[32]

Finally, Hopkins orchestrated a plan to mollify the Soviets, who would be extremely upset when they learned that Allied supply convoys around the North Cape would have to be suspended in order to release enough ships for the Torch landings. Hopkins's proposal, which he recommended to Roosevelt without first obtaining approval from the joint chiefs, was to offer to deploy British and American air forces in the Caucasus in order to "encourage Russian resistance" to the furious attacks by the Germans as they drove toward Stalingrad and the Caucasus.[33] Correctly predicting that the Wehrmacht would "not break through the Caucasus this winter," Hopkins asked the president to make "a firm commitment" to put a token air force in the Caucasus by the winter of 1942–43 and "a real force on ready to make the fight" by the following spring.[34] Roosevelt approved the proposal and forwarded it to Stalin. However, it was never put into effect because of the dramatic improvement in the odds that the Red Army would win the battle of Stalingrad during the closing weeks of 1942.

On October 2, the day after Roosevelt returned from his two-week trip, revitalized by his contact with American workers and the immensity of the war effort, Congress passed the Economic Stabilization Act, which conferred power on the executive branch to cap prices on all farm commodities. The following day FDR created the Office of Economic Stabilization and, with Hopkins's help, persuaded Jimmy Byrnes to resign from the Supreme Court and serve as its director. Actually it didn't take much persuading. As a former senator from South Carolina, Byrnes was more at home as a political operator than as a member of the Supreme Court, which he regarded as a "marble mausoleum." With responsibility for controlling "prices, rents, wages, salaries, profits, rationing, subsidies and all related matters," Byrnes—later a secretary of state and governor of South Carolina—would have extraordinary power to control America's war mobilization machinery.[35] By one account, Roosevelt told Byrnes when he appointed him to the job, "For all practical purposes you will be assistant president."[36]

Byrnes was an ambitious conservative southern Democrat and protégé of the bigoted "Pitchfork Ben" Tillman, the former senator and governor of South Carolina. But he was nonetheless a devoted follower of FDR, having guided passage of much of the New Deal legislation on the Senate floor and supported Roosevelt on his court-packing plan. Possessing charm and a probing intellect, Byrnes had often clashed with Hopkins during the New Deal years and was well aware of Hopkins's ability to undercut potential rivals. Thus he was on guard when Hopkins stopped by shortly after he moved into his office in the newly built east wing of the White House. Suspecting Hopkins might try to interfere with his access to the president or otherwise circumscribe his authority, Byrnes cocked his head to one side and said, "There's just one suggestion I want to make to you, Harry, and that is to keep the hell out of my business." Reporting this remark to Sherwood, Hopkins said, "[Byrnes] smiled very pleasantly when he said it, but by God he meant it, and I'm going to keep the hell out." (Wrote Sherwood much later, "It is improbable that Hopkins was entirely faithful in living up to this resolve.")[37]

It wasn't until mid-October that Congress finally acted on the other part of Roosevelt's inflation-control plan: major tax increases. While the lawmakers did not accept the president's proposal to impose a 100 percent tax on personal net income in excess of $25,000, they increased the maximum marginal tax rate on individuals to 88 percent, reduced personal exemptions, tripled the number of people subject to income taxes, and imposed a special Victory Tax of 5 percent on anyone earning more than $624 per year.[38] With little more than two weeks before the midterm elections, those in Congress who voted for the tax increase acted with courage and at the same time handed the president another legislative victory.

Leaving Louise behind in Washington due to her hospital work, Hopkins spent election day, November 3, at the Big House in Hyde Park with the president.[39] Like the cold rain falling from gray skies outside, the outlook for Democrats was not good. In addition to the tax increase, the administration had just announced that coffee rationing would be reduced to a single cup per day. The Sunday papers reported that another aircraft carrier, the USS *Hornet*, had been sunk off Guadalcanal in the Pacific, leaving the Navy with only three active carriers. Republicans were pounding away at the lack of progress in the war. Voter turnout would be low.

As it turned out, there was a significant shift to the right, but the Democratic losses could have been much greater than they were. The Republicans scored a net gain of ten seats in the Senate, but the Democrats still held a commanding nineteen-seat majority. In the House the Republicans cut more deeply into the Democratic majority with a net gain of forty-seven seats, leaving the Democrats with a slim margin of thirteen seats. Republicans picked up nine governorships, including Tom Dewey in New York, who would challenge Roosevelt for the presidency in 1944 (and Truman in 1948). Within both parties many liberals were defeated, while conservative incumbents tended to hold onto their seats.[40]

Had the elections been held a week later, the Democrats might have done much better because the war news by then had brightened considerably. Shortly after the close of polls on election day, it had become clear that the German thrust southeast to the oilfields in the Caucasus had stalled and that the Wehrmacht was not about to run the Red Army out of Stalingrad. On November 4, still at Hyde Park, Roosevelt received word from Churchill of the great British victory over Rommel's German and Italian troops at El Alamein in Egypt. Taking 30,000 prisoners and inflicting upward of 15,000 casualties, General Bernard Montgomery and his forces drove the Afrika Korps out of Egypt into neighboring Libya. In his message to the president about the victory, Churchill wrote, "I feel sure you will regard this as a good prelude to Torch."[41]

From the standpoint of American public opinion, however, the Torch landings in French North Africa were the best news of all. On the day the landings were scheduled, Saturday, November 7, Roosevelt, Hopkins, Louise, Grace Tully, and a few others were at Shangri-La. Tully recalled that Roosevelt was "on edge" throughout the day, but she didn't know why, nor did any of the other guests except Hopkins. All that afternoon calls had been coming in, and the tension in the living room of the small cabin continued to grow. Shortly after dinner a call came in from the War Department, and Tully handed the phone to Roosevelt. "The Boss's hand shook as he took the telephone from me," she later wrote. "He listened intently, said nothing as he heard the full message, then burst out: 'Thank God! Thank God! That sounds grand. Congratulations.'" Putting down the receiver, he turned to the others: "We have landed in North Africa. Casualties are below expectations. We are striking back."[42]

Both Roosevelt and Hopkins were visibly relieved. Notwithstanding initial opposition by Marshall, Eisenhower, Brooke, and most other military advisors, the enormously complex three-part seaborne landings achieved almost complete strategic and tactical surprise. From the outset, the overriding worry was that the landings in French North Africa would be aggressively resisted by French troops, the French fleet, and the citizens themselves. In an effort to prevent armed conflict with the French in Morocco and Algeria, Roosevelt issued appeals to the French people and to Marshal Philippe Pétain, leader of Vichy France, whose government nominally ruled southern France and French North Africa, although it was entirely beholden to Hitler. Pétain, unwilling to provoke Hitler, rejected Roosevelt's appeal, declaring, "We are attacked; we shall defend ourselves," and ordering all French armed forces in North Africa to repel the American and British invasion.[43] During the first few days following the landings, American troops ran into fierce opposition from French forces around Casablanca and in the Oran harbor, which they attempted to take by direct assault. French troops and artillery inflicted 1,400 casualties on American soldiers, who regarded themselves as liberators of the French from the Nazi yoke, not invaders of French territory.[44]

In Algiers, where the predominantly British troops landed, there was no resistance at all, but it was in that city that the infamous "Darlan deal" was worked out, a deal that ended all French armed opposition.[45] Admiral Jean-François Darlan, a former head of government in Vichy France, the ranking French officer in North Africa, and a despised collaborator with the Nazis, happened to be in Algiers visiting his polio-stricken son when the landings took place. From November 9 to 12 Consul General Robert Daniel Murphy, a career State Department diplomat, aided by the explosive temper of Major General Mark Clark (Eisenhower's deputy), hammered out an agreement with the opportunistic Darlan. Pursuant to the deal, Darlan ordered all French troops to cease fire and lay down their arms in exchange for his appointment as high commissioner in North Africa and immunity from prosecution for collaborating with the Nazis.[46]

Eisenhower, the theater commander, accepted full responsibility for the Darlan deal, although it was widely criticized as a pact with the devil. In truth, his first choice to end the resistance of French forces in North Africa was General Henri Giraud, who had fought against the Germans in 1940 until he was captured. After two years in a German prison camp, Giraud escaped and was transported by submarine to Gibraltar, where, from Eisenhower's headquarters in a cave beneath the Rock, he broadcast an order on November 9 to the French forces that they "cease fighting against the Allies" and that he would assume "the leadership of French North Africa." To the extreme mortification of Eisenhower and his advisors, Giraud's order was ignored by the pro-Vichy commanders.[47] Three days later French forces decided to accept Darlan as their leader and to obey his order to cease fire. By that time the Germans had reacted to the landings in North Africa by occupying Vichy and the rest of France and rapidly pouring troops into Tunisia. Pétain was effectively under house arrest. With their country now entirely under the yoke of the Nazis, the French forces in North Africa believed Darlan when he told them he had been secretly authorized by Pétain to order a cease fire.[48]

Endorsed by Eisenhower, Darlan as high commissioner became the political leader of North Africa. General Giraud agreed to serve under Darlan as his military chief. Meanwhile in London, Charles de Gaulle, who had been anointed by the British as leader in exile of the Free French ("Fighting France") and claimed he was willing to support Giraud as leader of French forces in North Africa, was outraged when he heard of the Darlan appointment, as was Foreign Secretary Anthony Eden. Roosevelt intensely disliked and distrusted de Gaulle and ordered that he not be informed of the Torch landings in advance. On the other hand, he had no objection to the Darlan appointment, provided it was treated as a temporary expediency. Unlike Churchill's government, the Roosevelt administration had maintained diplomatic relations with the Vichy government and did not share with the British their intense hatred of Pétain's regime.

The Darlan deal put Eisenhower in a difficult position. He was roasted by politicians and newspapers in Washington and London for empowering a Nazi collaborator, skewered by de Gaulle, and ridiculed by the Nazis for his hypocrisy. The British cabinet expressed "doubts and anxieties" about the deal.[49] On Saturday, November 14, while Hopkins and his wife were in Hyde Park with Roosevelt to celebrate Diana's tenth birthday, the president received a lengthy cable from Eisenhower, defending the Darlan deal on grounds of military necessity and expediency.[50] Roosevelt was so impressed with its reasoning and sincerity that he read it aloud to Hopkins.

Roosevelt stood foursquare behind his commander. At the urging of Hopkins, Rosenman, and Sherwood, the president issued a public statement, supporting "the present temporary arrangement in North and West Africa," which he said saved American, British, and French lives and "the vital factor of time."[51] He also asked Hopkins to prepare a response to Eisenhower's cable to express the president's "complete support of this and any other action [Eisenhower was] required to take in carrying out [his] duties." The draft message pointedly reminded Eisenhower, however, that the U.S. government did "not trust Darlan"; that a "collaborator of Hitler" should not remain in power "any longer than [was] absolutely necessary"; and that Darlan's "movements should be watched carefully and his communications supervised."[52] For some reason, Roosevelt decided not to send this message to Eisenhower, preferring instead to communicate his three reservations concerning Darlan to Eisenhower via Marshall.[53]

As events unfolded, Eisenhower did not have to monitor Darlan's movements for more than a few weeks. On Christmas Eve day, Darlan was assassinated in Algiers by a young French student whose politics were characterized as "Gaullist-Royalist."[54] The assassin was convinced that he had liberated France and would be rescued by a "high and powerful outside source," but within two days he was tried and executed by a firing squad. All trial and related records were permanently sealed by Henri Giraud, who succeeded Darlan as high commissioner of North Africa.[55]

General Mark Clark described the murder of Darlan as "an act of providence" and "like the lancing of a troublesome boil."[56] But conspiracy theories were spun and suspicions were raised as to who was really behind this most convenient development. The historian David Reynolds argues that the British, who strongly supported de Gaulle as the true leader of the Free French, were behind the murder, citing among other things the fact that Sir Stewart Menzies, head of the British Secret Intelligence Service, was in Algiers on Christmas Eve when Darlan was murdered.[57] Others who stood to gain by Darlan's death included de Gaulle, whose followers had been frozen out of the temporary government and whose deputy was in Algiers at the time of the assassination, conferring with Eisenhower about plans to replace Darlan; Giraud, who had always believed he should be the de facto ruler of North Africa; and, of course, Roosevelt, Eisenhower, Marshall, and a host of other U.S. government and military leaders who were convinced that the Darlan deal was a huge embarrassment that inflicted enormous damage on American prestige and credibility. As Hopkins wrote in the draft that Roosevelt sent to Marshall (to be communicated to Eisenhower), Darlan should not be permitted remain in power "any longer than absolutely necessary."[58]

Responsibility for the Darlan assassination remains one of the most intriguing unsolved crimes of World War II. In his memoirs, de Gaulle suggested obliquely, and without citing any evidence, that the United States was responsible, but the truth will probably never be known.[59]

Although there is no evidence that he or anyone else in the Roosevelt administration had anything to do with the Darlan assassination, Hopkins was deeply involved throughout the fall of 1942 in advising the president on limiting the damage caused by the Darlan deal. Hopkins perhaps didn't realize it at the time, but he was getting an education in foreign policy and European politics, one that would prepare him to play a key role in bringing Giraud and de Gaulle together at the Casablanca conference in January 1943.

In fact Roosevelt was providing Hopkins with a broad education in foreign affairs so he could serve as his chief foreign relations advisor in the coming months. Secretary of State Hull and his State Department, particularly Robert Murphy, were under ferocious attack by the American press for their role in promoting the Darlan deal and their pro-Vichy stance.[60] Murphy had been the initiator of a controversial agreement with the Vichy government that became known as the Murphy-Weygand Accord, by which American goods could be shipped to French North Africa despite the British blockade. For these reasons and also because the president preferred to bypass Hull and function as his own secretary of state, Hopkins would fill in for Hull at Casablanca and other wartime conferences.

To recognize Hopkins's "increased responsibilities," Roosevelt raised his salary to $15,000, the same amount paid to Hull and the other cabinet members.[61] A few days later, on Thanksgiving Day, Hopkins was tasked with the job of meeting Madame Chiang Kai-shek's plane and serving as her companion while she received treatment at Presbyterian Hospital in New York City for an old injury to her spine.[62] During their time together, Madame Chiang, the Wellesley-educated wife of the leader of the Chinese government, argued forcefully that General Claire Chennault should replace General Joseph "Vinegar Joe" Stilwell as the top American commander in China because of Chennault's plan to "accomplish the downfall of Japan" within six months to a year through nothing more than an aggressive air offensive.[63] Hopkins, no military strategist, was persuaded that this outlandish plan would succeed, and he advised Roosevelt, as he had done on previous occasions, that he should recall Stilwell. Marshall was extremely upset when he learned that Hopkins was meddling in military strategy and command decisions, resulting in what the historian Kenneth Davis said was the only "serious" disagreement "between Marshall and Hopkins in the whole of the war."[64] With Stimson's help, Marshall convinced Roosevelt that Hopkins was wrong and that Stilwell should not be relieved.

During the days leading up to Christmas 1942, Hopkins's judgment was once again questioned. By the end of November government rationing of food, clothing, housing, and travel had cut deeply into the lives of every American. The new single-cup coffee rationing had just gone into effect, and an article in the *American Magazine* ghost-written for Hopkins predicted even harsher government restrictions.[65] In the face of these privations, newspapers throughout the country gleefully reported that Hopkins and his new wife had accepted another expensive wedding gift. This time it was a lavish pre-Christmas dinner dance for sixty guests at Washington's Carleton Hotel hosted by Hopkins's friend, the millionaire Bernard Baruch. From caviar to petit fours, the elaborate menu was reprinted in full. The guest list included many members of the Roosevelt administration, although the president himself did not attend.[66]

Politicians and pundits used this mini-scandal to attack Hopkins, but because he was so closely associated with Roosevelt they were implicitly criticizing the president. Hopkins worried that he had become a political liability. Roosevelt, however, laughed off the Baruch dinner and continued to tutor Hopkins on foreign affairs. At a private dinner on December 18 at the home of Felix Frankfurter on Dumbarton Street in Georgetown, Hopkins demonstrated some of what he had learned, holding forth with the same kind of pragmatic, occasionally principled, and often inconsistent approaches to foreign relations practiced by his teacher. Responding to Frankfurter's ruminations about postwar relations with Great Britain, Hopkins expressed a Rooseveltian faith in democracy and the power of the people. In the presence of Lord Halifax, Vice President Wallace, and other guests (the president did not attend), Hopkins predicted that FDR's anti-colonial policy would eventually succeed, Britain's empire would begin to crumble, and Churchill's government would not survive the war.

But in the next breath Hopkins backed away from democratic principles and endorsed the hard-headed realpolitik practiced in equal measure by his mentor. Postwar relations with Russia and China, he said, should be governed by mutual self-interest rather than ideals and moral scruples. Commenting on both Stalin and Chiang Kai-shek, Hopkins said they "used words not to portray their thoughts or to tell the truth but merely to get the desired effect." He didn't say so at the Frankfurter dinner, but it was also realpolitik, certainly not ideology, that dictated U.S. relations with Vichy France, Admiral Darlan (until his death), and Chiang Kai-shek's corrupt government in China.[67]

As 1942 drew to a close, Hopkins had reason for optimism. His health had stabilized. His relationship with lighthearted, free-spirited Louise—"She was not what you would call an intellectual," recalled Diana—brought him a profound sense of contentment.[68] He remained Roosevelt's closest companion and most trusted advisor despite the criticisms and negative publicity he had attracted since his marriage.

On the war front, Hopkins was likewise optimistic. The Germans had been stopped far short of the oilfields in the Caucasus. The Red Army counterattack at Stalingrad had succeeded in surrounding General Paulus's entire Sixth Army. In the Pacific the power of the Japanese fleet had been broken, and the Japanese were being annihilated on Guadalcanal. The North Africa landings were successful, and the odor of the Darlan deal was dissipating in the wake of his assassination. The only disappointment was that Eisenhower and his commanders in North Africa felt compelled by weather to postpone indefinitely their drive eastward into Tunisia.

From Stagg Stadium at the University of Chicago came the classified news that the first nuclear chain reaction had been achieved by the Italian physicist Enrico Fermi and his team, which meant that the United States had a realistic chance of winning what those in the know thought was a race against the Germans to be the first to build the atomic bomb. (In fact the Germans had already scuttled their project to build such a bomb.)[69] Given his involvement in the Tube Alloys project from the beginning and his intimate relationship with the president, it is certain that Hopkins knew of this historic achievement. As with Roosevelt, this news lifted Hopkins's spirits, though he did not know whether the experiment could be converted into a bomb, nor did he dream of its power to incinerate cities and obstruct, or arguably preserve, world peace for generations.

Like others in the Roosevelt administration, Hopkins was braced for setbacks and a long slog, but almost all signs were pointing in the direction of ultimate victory. Referring to the North Africa landings, Churchill famously pronounced, "Now this is not the end. It is not even the beginning of the end. But it is, perhaps, the end of the beginning."[70] A few days later Roosevelt suggested in a speech that the nation had reached the other side of the "turning point" in the war.[71]

As Hopkins rose from the dinner table to join Louise, the Roosevelts, and other guests in the White House screening room on New Year's Eve 1942, he was more hopeful about the future than he had been in years. That evening the group viewed *Casablanca* with Humphrey Bogart and Ingrid Bergman, a story of doomed love, first in Paris and then in Morocco.[72] Beyond the love story, the film is a political allegory, its writers advocating principle over realpolitik. Bogart's Rick, as Roosevelt, gambles on which side to back (Vichy versus Free French), and eventually his conscience compels him to close his casino and join the Free French. Captain Renault, played by Claude Rains, has a change of heart, redeeming himself by shooting a Nazi villain and then dropping a bottle of "Vichy water" into a wastebasket as he goes off with Rick to fight with the Free French in Brazzaville.[73] The millions of Americans whose hearts were captured by the Academy Award–winning movie in late 1942 and 1943 must have been persuaded that their government, like Rick and Captain Renault, was also taking the moral high ground.

Hopkins, Roosevelt, and perhaps a few others in the White House audience that night, however, knew that the film was misleading. Far from tilting toward de Gaulle's Free French, the Roosevelt administration never took steps to sever its ties with Vichy. (Instead relations were terminated by Vichy at German insistence after the landings in November 1942.) And it did not officially recognize de Gaulle until October 1944. In fact the administration was permitting Darlan's successor, General Giraud, to continue to rely on Vichy officials to run his North African government and to terrorize and imprison citizens who opposed him.

If it did not obscure these inconvenient facts, the emotional power of the film certainly blurred them. For this reason, Roosevelt and Hopkins had to have been pleased with the movie and its impact. Indeed, by selecting *Casablanca* to be shown at the White House, a form of endorsement, it is conceivable that the president, with his deft political instincts and his genius for melding opposing ideas, sought both to reinforce the high-minded political message of the film and at the same time convince the American public that the powerful movie was an endorsement of his administration's policies. But even if these Machiavellian motives were not present, the screening on New Year's Eve certainly enabled Roosevelt and Hopkins to savor a private joke. In ten days they would leave Washington for a secret wartime meeting with Churchill. Destination: Casablanca.

12

The View from Marrakech

"He acted like a sixteen-year-old," recalled Hopkins.[1] He was referring to the president's boyish delight as the two of them sat side by side in the "Dixie Clipper," a Boeing 314 flying boat that was about to lift off from the Pan Am base in Miami. It was a few minutes after six in the morning on Monday, January 11, 1943. They would fly south to Brazil and then east across the Atlantic to meet Churchill in Morocco. Roosevelt would be the first president to leave the United States in wartime, the first since Lincoln to visit troops in the field, and the first to fly while in office. Because plane crashes during those years were not infrequent and numerous prominent politicians and military leaders had perished because of them, aides to FDR warned against the dangerous and arduous trip. "There's only one son of a bitch around here who is crazy enough to promote such a thing," grumbled Pa Watson, "and his name is Hopkins."[2]

The president's ostensible motive for the trip was to inspect American troops and to confer with Churchill as to where the Anglo-American forces should be deployed after they drove the Germans out of North Africa. But, as Hopkins observed, the wheelchair-bound president's overriding desire was to get out of the White House and enjoy the thrill of an adventure.[3]

The journey was a closely held secret, which added to Roosevelt's excitement. Thirty hours earlier, Roosevelt and Hopkins (code-named Don Quixote and Sancho Panza) had departed Washington at midnight from a railroad spur hidden beneath the Bureau of Printing and Engraving on the newly renovated presidential rail coach, a rolling armor-plated fortress named the *Ferdinand Magellan*. To fool rail workers and anyone else who might observe the massive train emerge from the tunnel, the engineer was instructed by the Secret Service to head north into Maryland as if they were going to Hyde Park. At Fort Meade the train turned around on a siding and rolled south at thirty-five miles per hour.[4]

After the "Dixie Clipper" reached altitude—only 9,000 feet because, as Hopkins recalled, Doc McIntire was "quite disturbed about the President, who appeared to be very pale at times"—Hopkins moved to a table where, in his own distinctive handwriting, he summarized the genesis of the Casablanca conference. According to his notes, it was assumed that the Germans would soon be forced out of North Africa and that there was no "agreed-upon plan as to what to do next." The Americans and the British "had to strike somewhere," and the question was whether it should be "across the Channel"— wishful thinking on Hopkins's part—or "at Sardinia, Sicily or thru Turkey." Acting on Hopkins's recommendation that Stalin be involved in resolving this key strategic issue, Roosevelt had invited the marshal to meet with him and Churchill. However, Stalin twice refused, citing the urgent need to stay in the USSR to direct military operations and to be near his troops at the front. "The next best thing," wrote Hopkins, "was a meeting between Churchill, Roosevelt and their respective staffs." Since the president wanted to meet in North Africa so he could inspect the troops, they decided to hold the conference "at a safe place outside of Casablanca" that the U.S. Army had found.[5]

In contrast to Hopkins's succinct summary, Roosevelt's cables on the lead-up to the Casablanca conference read as if he were planning a luxury vacation. In one of the missives, he confessed, like many vacation-goers, that it would do him "an enormous amount of good to get out of the political atmosphere of Washington for a few weeks." In a cable, he told Churchill that a meeting in Iceland or Alaska would be "impossible" for him in the winter, that the conference could not be in Algiers—"I don't like mosquitoes"—and that he preferred "a comfortable oasis to the raft at Tilsit." This last was an allusion to a July 1807 meeting on a raft in the Niemen River in East Prussia, where Emperor Napoleon and Czar Alexander I had signed the Treaty of Tilsit and redrawn the map of Europe. Roosevelt added a double meaning to "oasis" by writing later that "an oasis is never wholly dry," thus assuring Churchill that there would be an abundance of alcohol when the two got together for several days in the winter sunshine near Casablanca.

To underscore his relaxed attitude toward the upcoming conference, the president stressed to Churchill that he would be bringing a "very small staff," which would include "Harry and Averell but no State Department representative." With Hopkins and Harriman at his side, Roosevelt felt no need for additional foreign affairs experts, especially Cordell Hull, his earnest secretary of state (Washington insiders called him "Parson Hull"), whose past affinity for maintaining relations with the Vichy government and prejudice against de Gaulle might cause problems at Casablanca. Since FDR would not be bringing Hull to the conference, he pointedly requested Churchill not to invite Hull's counterpart, Anthony Eden, saying, "I think you and I need no foreign affairs people with us—for our work will be essentially military."[6] As Roosevelt must have known, however, a fair amount of his "work" at Casablanca with Churchill would not involve military strategy but an attempt to negotiate a political deal involving the merger of the Free French forces led by de Gaulle and the French troops in North Africa under the command of General Giraud.

Flying the final leg of the trip in a four-engine Douglas C-54 (dubbed "the Sacred Cow") from an airfield at the town of Bathurst, near the mouth of the Gambia River in West Africa, Roosevelt and Hopkins landed at Casablanca in the late afternoon on Thursday, January 14. The rest of the "very small staff," consisting of General Marshall, the other military chiefs, and a few aides, had arrived three days earlier.[7] The British, on the other hand, fielded a much larger delegation. Because of heavy seas, they switched from flying boats and were packed into several B-24 Liberator bombers for the rough flight from England to Casablanca. A few miles offshore in the

Atlantic, the *Bulolo*, a six-thousand-ton command-and-communications ship, lay at anchor, fully staffed. Crammed with files and reports that today could be downloaded from satellite to laptop, it was ready to quickly produce facts, figures, studies, and briefing papers for Churchill (code-named "Air Commodore Franklin") and his team on the ground.[8] The British were ready to make the case for continuing the Mediterranean campaign; they knew Marshall regarded operations there as diversionary and that once again he would push hard for early landings in France.

The site of the conference was the ancient Phoenician hilltop town of Anfa, located about six miles west of Casablanca (today it is a neighborhood of the city) and overlooking the sea. As if a Roman camp were being reconstructed, an area about a mile square, containing the Anfa Hotel and eighteen villas, had been staked out and surrounded by barbed wire. The plenary sessions of the conference would be held in the hotel, a white Art Deco building whose twin stacks, four decks, and shaded galleries made it look like a Mississippi steamboat beached in the desert.[9]

Roosevelt and Hopkins might have been reminded of the movie *Casablanca* as they entered the Anfa compound in Vichy North Africa. These lines from the film, as they pertain to the mysteries of French politics and the stalled campaign in Tunisia seem particularly apt:

CAPTAIN RENAULT: What in heaven's name brought you to Casablanca?
RICK: My health. I came to Casablanca for the waters.
RENAULT: The waters? What waters? We're in the desert.
RICK: I was misinformed.

Within minutes after Roosevelt and Hopkins were installed in Villa dar es Saada, Hopkins walked next door to Villa Mirador, where Churchill was staying, and brought him back to their villa for "a drink before dinner" with the president. Roosevelt asked Hopkins to invite the American and British military chiefs who were having cocktails in the hotel to join them for dinner. "Much good talk of war—and families—and the French," wrote Hopkins of the evening. "I went to bed at twelve but I understand the Pres. and Churchill sat up till two."[10]

During the next four days the American and British military chiefs continued to meet and debate overall and theater war strategy in the sunny banquet room off the main corridor of the Anfa Hotel. Whatever behind-the-scenes disagreements they had among themselves, Churchill and his British team were united at the conference table. Following defeat of the Germans in North Africa, the British argued, Anglo-American forces should continue to fight in the Mediterranean theater, with the goal of forcing the Italians to surrender, encouraging partisans in the Balkans, and bringing Turkey into the war. The Americans, on the other hand, were divided. Marshall unsurprisingly continued to maintain that after victory over the Germans and Italians in Tunisia, Allied forces should be moved to Great Britain to prepare for the invasion of Western Europe. Admiral King pressed for greater emphasis in the Pacific. And General "Hap" (short for Happy) Arnold, an aviation pioneer who had been taught to fly by the Wright brothers and had unlimited confidence in air power, hoped to capture bases in Italy from which his air forces could stage massive bombing raids against the German homeland and the oilfields in Romania. The split came out into the open at a meeting on January 15, when, according to Brooke's diary, "the President expressed views favouring operations in the Mediterranean."

After dinner that evening, Hopkins and Harriman visited Brooke, who wrote of Hopkins, "[He was] in rather a bitter mood which I had not yet seen him in."[11] It was becoming clear to Hopkins that with the Allied forces tied down in North Africa and the president's preference for continued operations in the Mediterranean, there would never be enough troops and ships to mount a successful cross-Channel invasion of France by late September 1943, after which the Channel became impassable. Marshall had of course predicted this would happen during the meetings in London the previous July, when the decision to launch Torch was made. Hopkins, however, had held out hope that there could still be an invasion of Western Europe in 1943. He had pinned his hopes in part on Eisenhower's bold gamble to seize Tunisia and drive most of the Germans and Italians out by the end of 1942. In fact a slender spearhead of British and American infantry and armor had been rushed east and almost reached Tunis before it was stopped and forced to retreat by a remarkably swift German buildup and devastating counterattacks. At that point Eisenhower was compelled to call off the offensive, and rain, mud, and lack of supplies led to a winter stalemate of indefinite duration.[12] Now it appeared that Marshall was right all along and that the Allies would have to break their promise to Stalin again.[13] It was apparent to Hopkins that there would be no second front in Europe until 1944.

Hopkins's education in the ways of war was soon to take a more personal turn. A week before Christmas 1942, Hopkins's son, Robert, a twenty-one-year-old Army combat photographer, was assigned to cover the 13th Armored Regiment as it advanced up the Medjerda Valley toward Tunis. Unable to fend off a well-executed German counterattack, the inexperienced regiment was ordered to withdraw at night while Robert was asleep in the mud and rain. In the morning he awoke to find himself alone, behind German lines. With the help of knife-wielding Moroccan fighters called *Goums*, he eventually located his unit, whereupon he was approached by an Army colonel and ordered, without explanation, to hitchhike his way back to Algiers.[14]

Several days later, just before lunch on January 18, Corporal Hopkins, sporting a British battle jacket since he had lost part of his uniform during a nighttime bombing raid, was escorted by an Army captain through heavily guarded checkpoints and dropped off at the front door of Villa dar es Saada. As he walked inside carrying his photographic equipment and musette bag—a small haversack—he was "astonished" to see his father, whom he had last seen at the wedding in the Oval Study. "A roar of laughter drew [Robert's] attention to another figure in the room." It was the president. Without telling Hopkins, Roosevelt had arranged for Robert to be assigned to the conference as an official photographer.[15]

To Robert, a slender, sensitive boy who had dropped out of the University of North Carolina to work on newsreels at *The March of Time* in New York before enlisting, the opportunity to spend time with his father seemed heaven-sent. Robert was just seven when Hopkins fell in love with Barbara Duncan and left his family. Since then Robert and his two brothers, David and Stephen, had only rarely visited Hopkins, and they usually had to share their father with his important friends and busy schedule. In the summer of 1937 Hopkins had invited Robert and Stephen to join him at the home of one of his wealthy friends, Herbert Bayard Swope, in Saratoga Springs. Robert (age sixteen) and Stephen (twelve) spent two days riding their bicycles from their home in Northfield, Massachusetts, to the Swope estate. Arriving after dark, they found a note saying Hopkins and Barbara had left for Washington.[16] Robert expected his father to attend his graduation from the Mt. Hermon Academy in June 1940. Instead he received a note of apology and regret on White House stationery, one of the few letters written to him by his father.[17] Trying to make up for their years of separation, father and son found moments to be together every day while the conference lasted, usually at a morning meal and sometimes late at night.[18]

Robert was not the only family member present in the Anfa compound. Churchill had ordered his son Randolph brought back from the Libyan desert, where he was part of an elite special forces unit operating behind German lines.[19] Elliott "Bunny" Roosevelt, an officer in the Air Force, was there as well, as was Franklin Jr., who was serving on a destroyer in the Atlantic. "These meetings meant a great deal to Franklin and also to the boys," wrote Eleanor Roosevelt, "and Franklin always came home full of stories of what they had said and done."[20]

A few hours after Robert's arrival, the American and British military chiefs gathered in the living room of the president's villa to present their report on future war strategy to Churchill, Roosevelt, and Hopkins (the only civilian in the room). By this time Marshall had accepted what was now staring them all in the face: the Anglo-American troops in Tunisia would be bogged down for several weeks, if not months. This, together with the blizzard of facts and documents generated by platoons of British planners, meant that he would never be able to persuade the British to join the Americans in trying to assemble an adequate number of trained troops, ships, and landing craft to launch a cross-Channel assault on France in 1943. Therefore, on the afternoon of January 18, the Combined Chiefs of Staff presented a compromise plan that was quickly approved by Roosevelt and Churchill.

The grand war strategy plan seemed to concede something for everyone, although it actually authorized only one new major operation: the Torch armies would invade Sicily following the defeat of the Germans and Italians in North Africa. To preserve the illusion that a second front might still take place in 1943, the plan provided that the British and American Allies would continue to build up troops and landing craft in England for a possible "thrust across the Channel," although, as a practical matter, the commitment to invade Sicily precluded any such thrust in 1943. In a concession to Admiral King, the plan called for almost a doubling of the war effort in the Pacific in order to permit offensive operations in eastern New Guinea, Rabaul, and the Marshall Islands and an invasion of Burma in December 1943 (to open the Burma road to China).[21] According to his notes, Hopkins told Churchill that the final version of the war strategy plan was "a pretty feeble effort for two great countries in 1943," which probably reflected his true feeling.[22] Nevertheless he graciously complimented Sir John Dill, who had brokered the compromise language, saying, "[It is] a *very* good paper and a damn good plan—so I am feeling much better."[23]

In his autobiography, General Albert Wedemeyer, who attended the Casablanca conference as one of Marshall's principal planning officers, accused Hopkins of being one of the "drugstore strategists" responsible for influencing Roosevelt to favor the Mediterranean strategy instead of heeding the advice of Marshall and King.[24] In fact Hopkins rarely injected himself into matters of war strategy during this conference. On one occasion he counseled Churchill in private to refrain from pressing for a commitment to invade Italy in 1944. However, he did this not to influence grand strategy but to avoid a new round of bitter arguments that would only prolong the conference.[25] At a later meeting of the principals, after the basic war strategy had been agreed upon, Hopkins made the surprising recommendation that supply convoys to Russia be suspended in their entirety during the buildup for the invasion of Sicily—purely as a matter of military necessity. While Marshall wholeheartedly supported the recommendation, it was overruled by Roosevelt, who feared a violent objection by Stalin.[26]

Leaving the Anfa compound behind, Hopkins and Robert spent a glorious day with the president as he journeyed eighty-five miles northwest to Rabat in an olive-drab Daimler to inspect the troops. Along the way, Robert filmed the soldiers of the 2nd Armored Division as Roosevelt slowly drove by; he "was amused to see their jaws drop open when they realized it was the president of the United States inspecting them."[27] Later Robert photographed his father, the president, Lieutenant General Clark (three stars), and General George S. Patton (two stars) eating a "lunch of boiled ham and sweet potatoes at an Army field kitchen," surrounded by soldiers of the 9th Infantry Division.[28]

The following morning, January 22, alone at breakfast with Robert, Hopkins said, "Tell me about the war." Although his firsthand experience was limited to a small slice of the Tunisian front, Robert said it was not going to be a cakewalk. The Germans and Italians had full control of the air. He told of seeing a Stuka dive bomber pivot in midair, descend rapidly to an altitude of 300 feet, and drop a bomb next to his half-track. One soldier next to Robert was killed outright; the other had his leg blown off. The American Sherman tanks (called "Purple Heart boxes") were no match for the more heavily armored German Tigers. "When they hit our tanks," Robert recalled, "the rivets would shear off, killing or maiming the tank crew." Robert spoke of watching the army chaplains remove dog tags from dead soldiers and photographing burned-out tank hulks. He recounted an incident one night when friendly fire "knocked out our own tanks," killing and wounding the crews. Most discouraging, Robert opined that the German infantry "were better equipped and more skillful."[29]

From his son, Hopkins was getting an education in what had already dawned on Marshall, Eisenhower, and those battling the Wehrmacht in the mud and rain of Tunisia. Fighting and winning against the battle-hardened German veterans, masters of maneuver, fields of fire, and counterattack, would take time and a buildup of command and combat experience. The soldiers and commanders in the U.S. Army were fine men, but they were not yet a good army.

Afterward, still shaken by what his son had told him, Hopkins ambled over to Churchill's villa, finding him "in bed in his customary pink robe, and having, of all things, a bottle of wine for breakfast." Seeing Hopkins's amused look, the prime minister explained that "he had a profound distaste on the one hand for skimmed milk, and no deep rooted prejudice about wine," so he had resolved the "conflict in favor of the latter." Churchill told

Hopkins that at age sixty-eight he had "no intention of giving up alcoholic drink, mild or strong, now or later."[30] Perhaps Churchill was fortifying himself for the dinner that evening with the sultan of Morocco, when Muslim custom would forbid the serving of alcohol. In a note to Roosevelt about the forthcoming dinner, Churchill lamented, "Dry, alas!; with the Sultan. After dinner, recovery from the effects of the above."[31] Later, at the dinner itself, as the minutes ticked slowly by, Churchill, already in a glum mood due to the absence of drink, scowled when he heard Roosevelt brightly telling the sultan and his party about the postwar era, when the yoke of colonialism would be thrown off and "oppressed peoples of the world would be liberated."[32] According to Hopkins's notes, Churchill cooked up an early escape by arranging to have a British Marine rush into the dining room with an urgent dispatch that demanded immediate attention.[33]

Although he had only a peripheral role in war strategy at the Casablanca conference, Hopkins waded into the murky waters of French politics. He and Roosevelt had come to the conference with a proposal (drafted by Jean Monnet) that the tricky problem of French leadership and control of French troops in North Africa be resolved through a joint power-sharing arrangement.[34] It was vitally important to the war effort and the eventual liberation of France to have the French fighting the Germans alongside the Anglo-American forces. Under the Roosevelt-Hopkins proposal as it evolved during the conference, General Giraud, who was temporarily in charge of civilian and military affairs in French North Africa but who was regarded by Roosevelt as a "dud of a leader,"[35] would share power with General de Gaulle, the symbol of French resistance who controlled Free French forces scattered around the world. The idea that de Gaulle would share French leadership with Giraud appealed in particular to Churchill. De Gaulle was arrogant and difficult to deal with, but Churchill could not help admiring him because he had cast his lot with the British in 1940 instead of allying himself and his followers with the Vichy government. A joint power-sharing arrangement would not only elevate de Gaulle's stature; it would also enable the British government to shift the considerable expenses of supporting him and the Free French to the North African government. (The Free French had received some £70 million from the British.)

Roosevelt and Churchill decided that they would try to broker an agreement by inviting Giraud and de Gaulle to meet with them in the Anfa compound under their auspices. Convincing Giraud to attend was relatively easy since he was already in North Africa. On January 19 Roosevelt and Hopkins met with him for the first time in the president's villa. "I gained a very favorable impression of Giraud," wrote Hopkins. "I know he is a Royalist, and is probably a right winger in all his economic views, but I have a feeling he is willing to fight . . . and that he was going to do whatever the President wanted in Africa."[36]

Roosevelt and Hopkins had produced "the bride" in the person of Giraud. It was Churchill's task to persuade de Gaulle, "the bridegroom," to fly from London to Casablanca, and he was having a most difficult time getting him to the altar.[37] De Gaulle felt insulted because he had not been notified in advance of the Torch landings, and he was angry at Roosevelt for reneging on an invitation to visit Washington after Darlan was assassinated. "De Gaulle is on his high horse," reported Churchill to Roosevelt. "Refuses to come down here. Refuses pointblank."[38] Roosevelt had not come all this way to be rebuffed by de Gaulle. In a note to Cordell Hull, the president characterized him as "a snooty" and "temperamental lady" who shows no "intention of getting into bed with Giraud."[39] Seeking to press Churchill to put more heat on de Gaulle, the president asked whether the leader of the Free French received any compensation, and if so, who paid it. Churchill replied that de Gaulle was taking a tidy sum out of funds supplied by the British government to his Free French movement. Then, according to FDR's letter to his cousin Daisy Suckley, "W.S.C. beamed— good idea—no come—no pay!"[40]

The next day de Gaulle landed at Fedala Airport near Casablanca and was driven in secret to the Anfa compound. During the following two days, little progress was made toward French unity as de Gaulle met separately with Giraud, Harold MacMillan (Churchill's personal representative in Algiers), and Churchill, and with Roosevelt and Hopkins together. According to Robert Hopkins, de Gaulle was suspicious of Hopkins and preferred to meet with the president alone. He "didn't understand how the President of the United States could have a confidant like my father," recalled Robert.[41]

Early Sunday morning, January 24, the last day of the conference, Hopkins was informed at breakfast that de Gaulle was willing to "cooperate" with Giraud but would never work under him. Giraud felt the same way. However, they would be willing to take turns as chairman of a single French governing committee or to have their organizations establish a liaison and function along parallel lines. Hopkins saw an opening. He asked Robert Murphy and MacMillan, experienced diplomats, to start working on a joint statement to be signed by de Gaulle and Giraud.[42] Hopkins sought out Roosevelt, telling him he believed "Giraud and de Gaulle want[ed] to work together" and urging him to be "conciliatory" toward de Gaulle. "If there is any beating [on de Gaulle] to be done," advised Hopkins, "let Churchill do it because the whole Free French movement is financed by them." Hopkins told the president, "We [will] get an agreement on a joint statement issued by de Gaulle and Giraud—and a picture of the two of them."[43]

There wasn't much time. The conference was about to end. Photographers and press correspondents had been told there would be a concluding press conference at noon in the garden outside the president's villa. Acting on Hopkins's advice, Churchill began "beating" on de Gaulle in Villa Mirador around 11 a.m., telling the French general that he would turn British public and world opinion against him and he would be denounced in the House of Commons if he persisted in opposing a joint power-sharing deal with Giraud. While Churchill and de Gaulle were still going at it, Giraud arrived at the president's villa at 11:30. Hopkins was present along with the president's son and Robert Murphy. Calling de Gaulle a "self-seeker" and "a bad general," Giraud at first resisted FDR's efforts to get him to "sit down with de Gaulle" and "work out a joint plan." Then, as Hopkins later wrote, Giraud softened and agreed to "play ball with de Gaulle." Giraud left the president's villa just as de Gaulle and his small staff arrived. "I liked him," wrote Hopkins of de Gaulle, but the leader of the Free French told Roosevelt and Hopkins there would be "*no* joint communiqué" and that Giraud must serve "under him." The president "in pretty powerful terms . . . made an urgent plea to de Gaulle to come to terms with Giraud to win the war and liberate France." De Gaulle gave way: "Leave me be. There will be a communiqué even if it is not yours."

At about that moment, a secret service agent notified Hopkins that Giraud was just outside saying goodbye to Churchill. Hopkins rushed out and followed Giraud down the street as Churchill entered the president's villa. It was almost noon. Hopkins believed that if he could get all four of them—Roosevelt, Churchill, Giraud, and de Gaulle—"into a room together we could get an agreement."[44] Hopkins coaxed Giraud into the living room of the president's villa. "The President was surprised at seeing Giraud but took it in his stride," wrote Hopkins. "De Gaulle was a little bewildered. Churchill grunted."

The "President went to work on them with Churchill backing him up vigorously." When de Gaulle once again became obstreperous, the prime minister waved his finger in his face and said in his poor French: "Mon Général, il ne faut pas obstacler la guerre!" (literally, "General, don't block the war!"). Confronted with Roosevelt's charm and Churchill's passionate outburst, de Gaulle agreed that he and Giraud would sit down and draw up a joint statement later.

The garden was filling up with photographers and newsmen. Roosevelt turned to de Gaulle. "Will you agree to be photographed beside me and the British Prime Minister, along with General Giraud?"

"Of course," replied de Gaulle, "for I have the highest regard for this great solider."

The president pressed further. "Will you go so far as to shake hands with General Giraud's hand in our presence and in front of the cameras?"

"I shall do that for you," responded de Gaulle in English.

"Come on," said Roosevelt with a wide grin. "Pictures!"[45]

The correspondents and photographers, including Robert Hopkins, murmured with astonishment when the folding glass doors to the terrace were thrown open to the garden fragrant with mimosa and begonia. Roosevelt was carried to his chair while the other three emerged into the bright sunlight (Churchill kept his hat on) and sat in chairs arranged in a semicircle on the lawn. Hopkins leaned against an orange tree, observing the proceedings along with dozens of generals and admirals. The president began with a few sketchy comments about the conference. In French he asked de Gaulle and Giraud to stand and shake hands to demonstrate their commitment to the liberation of France. The two proud uniformed French-men stood stiffly at a distance from one another, quickly shook hands, and sat down. Their reluctance was unmistakable. Sammy Schulman, one of the civilian photographers sitting cross-legged on the grass, called out, "I didn't get it, Mr. President." The president, still beaming, asked them to stand and shake hands again, which they did.[46]

Robert Hopkins photographed and took movies of the handshake. Within a few days, photos of the historic moment, dubbed "the shotgun marriage," appeared in newspapers around the world. It was a public rela-tions triumph. But it was more than that. True to their word, de Gaulle and Giraud issued a joint communiqué, vaguely declaring that the "liberation of France . . . [would] be attained by a union in war of all Frenchmen."[47] With the help of Jean Monnet, this led to a merger of their rival organizations into the Committee of French National Liberation on June 3, 1943.[48]

Hopkins's efforts to get Giraud and de Gaulle to work together, culmi-nating in his last-minute decision to persuade the departing Giraud to re-turn to the president's villa, significantly altered the outcome of the Casa-blanca conference. During the meeting with Giraud beginning at 11:30 that day, when Roosevelt had apparently given up hope that an agreement with de Gaulle could be reached, the president initialed a document that recognized Giraud as the individual with the "right and duty of preserving all French interests."[49] Hopkins was unaware that FDR had done this. In-deed during the previous evening Hopkins had advised the president not to sign such a document. It is probable that Roosevelt hastily initialed this document, which was thrust before him by Giraud along with another doc-ument involving exchange rates and military equipment, because the press conference was about to begin and he had to have something to announce. If it were not for Hopkins's quick action moments later, the world would have been told that General Giraud was in charge of all French military and civilian affairs; de Gaulle would have stalked off in high dudgeon. The merger of French forces in North Africa and the Free French forces would have been indefinitely delayed. And the British, who had not been consult-ed, would have been outraged since they were committed to the support of de Gaulle's Free French. Fortunately the document that Roosevelt initialed never saw the light of day. Churchill subsequently amended the text to confer equal standing on de Gaulle, and Roosevelt approved.[50] The potential rift with de Gaulle and his Free French forces was averted.

After the handshake, de Gaulle and Giraud departed through the banana trees and Roosevelt launched into the meat of the press conference. Glancing down at his notes, the president briefly summarized the substance of the conference, characterizing the meetings as "unprecedented in history" because they ranged over the "whole global picture." It didn't take him long, however, to get to his main point. Recalling for the audience the fact that General Ulysses Grant was often called "Unconditional Surrender Grant," FDR announced that he and Churchill had agreed that "peace can come to the world" only through the "unconditional surrender by Germany, Italy and Japan."[51] The reporters frantically scribbled his words in their notebooks. This was news.

Roosevelt's objective was to assure the world that, unlike World War I and the Armistice, there would be no deals, no "escape clauses," that could later lead to the emergence of another Hitler. As Sherwood wrote, "The ghost of Woodrow Wilson was again at [Roosevelt's] shoulder." The president "wanted to ensure that when the war was won it would stay won."[52] On the other hand, by publicly announcing a policy of unconditional surrender, Roosevelt had handed the Nazis and the Japanese a powerful propaganda weapon that they could use to incite their troops and citizens to fight even harder. Churchill, who would claim later that he was caught by surprise by Roosevelt's announcement, rose from his chair and said, "I agree with everything the president has said." Underscoring the president's point, the prime minister concluded his remarks by saying the war would be pursued until the Allies had "procured the unconditional surrender of the criminal forces who plunged the world into storm and ruin."[53]

The wisdom of the unconditional surrender policy would be debated for years. However, it was by no means a last-minute improvisation. It had been discussed by Roosevelt and Churchill on January 18, and the British war cabinet unanimously approved it on January 21.[54] The president had been considering the concept for months and had raised it with his military chiefs during a meeting in the White House on January 7.[55] Hopkins himself was well aware of the policy prior to the press conference. On January 23 he assured the grand vizier of Morocco that the war would be pursued until the Axis powers "agree to unconditional surrender."[56]

Roosevelt was mindful of the argument that the policy might prolong the war. However, he believed that the potential danger was outweighed by the need to allay the Russians' suspicions that the Americans and British might negotiate a separate armistice with Germany. Roosevelt saw the policy as another way to convince Stalin of his goodwill, a "political and psychological substitute for a second front."[57] Turning the page on balance-of-power thinking, FDR was looking ahead to a postwar world, when the Europeans and Japanese would have to shed their empires and he would be able to work with Stalin to maintain global peace.

In the closing hours of the conference, Churchill convinced Roosevelt to journey by car with Hopkins and their respective sons to Marrakech, the jewel of Morocco. "I must be with you when you see the sunset on the snows of the Atlas Mountains," said the prime minister to the president.[58] With fighters circling overhead and Patton's infantry guarding the roadway, the party traveled south for four hours, stopping for a picnic lunch of "boiled eggs, mincemeat tarts," and "plenty of wine and scotch." By late afternoon they had arrived at their destination, a fifteen-bedroom stucco villa called La Saadia on the outskirts of Marrakech that had been built by the American industrialist Moses Taylor in 1927 but was currently occupied by Kenneth Pendar, the American vice consul. (Hopkins and Pendar quickly found common ground; Louise Macy had rented Pendar's apartment in Paris before the war.) Atop the villa was a six-story observation tower with a winding staircase. It was the view of the snow-capped mountains from this tower that Churchill wanted Roosevelt to see.[59]

While Hopkins, Robert, and Randolph Churchill visited the ancient trading market inside the red walls of the city, two men carried the president up the sixty stairs of the observation tower, "his legs dangling like the limbs of a ventriloquist's dummy," wrote Lord Moran.[60] There the president and the prime minister sat quietly for a half hour as the setting sun cast pink light on the mountains and they listened to the calls to evening prayer wafting up from the minarets in Marrakech. "It's the most lovely spot in the whole world," said Churchill.[61]

The party gathered that evening for a lobster and filet mignon dinner. Describing the conviviality, Hopkins wrote, "Company aglow—much banter—Churchill at his best."[62] Dressed in his dark blue zippered siren suit and monogrammed black velvet slippers, Churchill held forth. Playing to the president when the subject of de Gaulle came up, he provoked gales of laughter when he remarked, "Oh, let's don't speak of him. We call him Jeanne d'Arc and we're looking for some bishops to burn him."[63]

Following several toasts and a group sing-along (both FDR and the prime minister loved to sing), at midnight Roosevelt and Churchill moved to two cleared tables in an adjoining salon to review and edit draft cables to Premier Stalin and Generalissimo Chiang Kai-shek, reporting on the results of the Casablanca conference. The cable to Chiang, prepared by Hopkins, was brief, citing "the vital importance of aiding China" and noting that General Arnold, commander of the Army Air Force and a veteran airman, was on his way to Chungking to deliver in person the plans for Anglo-American operations in Burma and the Southwest Pacific.[64]

The more lengthy eight-point cable to Stalin, drafted by Hopkins and Harriman, revealed in general terms the crucial decision of the Casablanca conference "to launch large-scale amphibious operations in the Mediterranean at the earliest possible moment." Seeking to justify the wisdom and strategic significance of this decision, the cable maintained that the Mediterranean operations would compel the enemy to "divert both land and air forces" away from the eastern front. The cable began and ended on an optimistic note; however, buried in the middle of point 5 was the news that the Americans and British would continue their buildup in the United Kingdom "to prepare themselves to re-enter the Continent of Europe [meaning France] as soon as practicable."[65]

Hopkins and everyone else working in the salon knew that that this would be a bitter pill for Stalin. "Nothing in the world will be accepted by Stalin as an alternative to our placing 50 or 60 divisions in France by the spring of this year," said Churchill. "I think he will be disappointed and furious," he correctly predicted.[66] Nevertheless, after much discussion and minor edits, Churchill and Roosevelt agreed on the text of the cable to Stalin, as well as the one to Chiang, and both were finalized and dispatched. Hopkins wrote that the cables were on their way when he retired at 2 a.m., leaving a 7 a.m. wakeup call for the morning flight.[67] Apparently the prime minister and the president stayed up for at least another hour. Finishing a nightcap, FDR said, "Now, Winston, don't you get up in the morning to see me off. I'll be wheeled into your room to kiss you goodbye."[68]

In the morning Hopkins was at the airfield to see Robert off on the flight back to Algiers with Harriman. Robert planned to sign up for assault training for the invasion of Sicily.[69] After Robert's plane took off, the president's Daimler rolled onto the tarmac and Hopkins could see that Churchill was with Roosevelt, having decided at the last minute to join him to say bon voyage. "He was wearing his ever flaming bathrobe," wrote Hopkins of Churchill's quilted dressing gown embellished with red dragons, plus "bedroom slippers and the inevitable cigar."[70] (Kenneth Pendar described it as "the weirdest outfit [he had] ever seen.")[71] After the president was pushed up a ramp in his wheelchair into the Sacred Cow, Hopkins and Churchill "took one last walk together." Wrote Hopkins, "[The prime minister] is pleased by the conference—expressed great confidence in victory—but warned of the hard road ahead."[72] As the Sacred Cow bearing Roosevelt and Hopkins lifted off, Churchill turned to Pendar, and said, "If anything happened to that man," referring to Roosevelt, "I couldn't stand it. He is the truest friend; he has the farthest vision; he is the greatest man I've ever known."[73] While the plane "skirted" the Atlas Mountains—Doc McIntire "did not want the President to fly so high," wrote Hopkins, without elaboration[74]—and headed south over the desert to Bathurst on the Gambia River, Churchill returned to La Saadia, looking forward to a day of painting. He was delighted at himself for having gotten up so early. "You can get in an extra cigar," he quipped.[75]

Aboard the American cruiser *Memphis*, anchored in the Gambia in West Africa, Hopkins slept, loafed, and read for two days. The president, despite a "bad cough" and a low-grade fever, insisted on traveling up the river in a British seagoing tug and then flying to Monrovia, Liberia, where he inspected U.S. troops (African Americans) and lunched with President

Edwin Barclay.[76] This visit by a sitting American president to an African head of state was another "first."

The trip back to the States in the Boeing Clipper was leisurely, with stops in Brazil and Trinidad. On the final leg to Miami, Hopkins helped Roosevelt celebrate his sixty-first birthday. A famous photo shows Hopkins sitting across from the president at a table for four in the roomy cabin as FDR delightedly cuts into a large white birthday cake.

Hopkins and Roosevelt returned to Washington on January 31, for the Soviets a day of far greater significance than December 7 or June 6. On that day, a Sunday, German Field Marshal Paulus was captured in his bunker in the basement of the central department store at Stalingrad after 162 days of the most ferocious and grueling fighting in the history of modern warfare. More than 170,000 men under Paulus's command had already been killed in the epic battle for Stalingrad. The 91,000 frost-bitten survivors who had been surrounded and cut off by the Red Army for more than two months were marched off into captivity, deliberate starvation, and almost certain death. Only 9,626 would ever return to Germany, some not until 1955.[77]

The Soviet losses at Stalingrad were almost beyond comprehension. Of the men and women fighting for the Motherland, 479,000 were killed or captured and 651,000 were wounded or taken sick. Casualties therefore totaled 1.13 million.[78] The USSR lost far more soldiers in this *single* battle than those lost in the entire war by the United States (292,000 deaths in battle) or Great Britain and her colonies (344,000 war deaths).[79]

Stalin therefore had ample reason to scoff when he read the cable from Roosevelt and Churchill claiming the decisions they made at the Casablanca conference "may well bring Germany to her knees in 1943."[80] In his judgment the Red Army, without any help from the West, had brought Germany to her knees at Stalingrad. Belittling the efforts of his Western allies, especially the British, Stalin fumed to General Zhukov, his top commander, "Hundreds of thousands of Soviet people are giving their lives in the struggle against fascism, and Churchill is haggling with us about two dozen Hurricanes [British fighter planes]. And anyway those Hurricanes are crap—our pilots think nothing of them."[81]

The president and the prime minister were sincere when they cabled Stalin from Marrakech that their "main desire" was to "divert strong German land and air forces from the Russian front and to send to Russia the maximum flow of supplies."[82] And the decisions made at Casablanca eventually did result in drawing some German forces away from the eastern front and increasing the flow of lend-lease supplies to the USSR through Iran. Nevertheless it was the sinew of the Red Army and the Soviet people, with only modest assistance from the West, that confronted and then defeated the main strength of the German armed forces on land and in the air. Led by Stalin and his generals, the Soviet Union was primarily responsible for breaking the back and the morale of the German war machine.

Stalin would have wholeheartedly agreed with Hopkins's characterization of the military decisions made at the Casablanca conference: "It seemed to me a pretty feeble effort for two great countries in 1943." In retrospect, however, Hopkins's comment seems unfair, especially as it related to the United States. In January 1943 the American military and industrial buildup, that had not begun in earnest until Pearl Harbor, was still getting under way. The U.S. Army, which was smaller even than Poland's in 1939, was largely untested. It would never attain a size and strength comparable to that of the Soviets during the war years. In truth, the military decisions made at Casablanca—notably the decision to invade Sicily—were aligned with the capabilities of the Anglo-American forces at the time. Nevertheless, as a consequence of Stalin's stupendous victory at Stalingrad and the disingenuous statements made by Roosevelt and Churchill to him about launching a cross-Channel invasion of France in 1942, Stalin had gained very substantial leverage over his Western allies. He would use it for the rest of the war and into the postwar period, constantly demanding more and reminding the Americans and British of their "feeble" efforts to assist while millions of Soviet soldiers and civilians were slaughtered in the East.[83]

Fault Lines

S talin did not hesitate to take advantage of the power shift resulting from the Red Army victory at Stalingrad. In the weeks following the Casablanca conference, he put Roosevelt and Churchill on the defensive, sending a series of blunt messages reminding them of their earlier promises to launch a cross-Channel invasion of France "as early as 1942 or this spring at the latest" and complaining that the two-month winter pause of Anglo-American forces in Tunisia had enabled the Germans to transfer as many as thirty-six fresh divisions to fight the Red Army on the eastern front.[1]

As Stalin turned the screws, relations with the Soviet leader started to fray. Churchill and Roosevelt had little to offer except vague promises to invade France "at the earliest practicable date" and a wildly optimistic if not disingenuous assertion, drafted by Churchill and amended by FDR, that they were "pushing preparations to the limit of [their] resources" for a "cross channel operation" in August or September of 1943.[2] On February 13, 1943, when Allied troops were again on the move in Tunisia and it was thought that the Germans and Italians would be cleared out of North Africa by the end of March, Churchill cabled Hopkins, urging that the planned invasion of Sicily, set for July, should be moved up to June to relieve pressure on the Soviets. "I think it is an awful thing," he wrote, "that in April, May and June, not a single American or British soldier will be killing a single German or Italian soldier while the Russians are chasing 185 divisions around."[3] A stunning rout in central Tunisia rendered Churchill's request inoperative. During the five days of the Battle of Kasserine Pass, February 14–19, the U.S. II Corps was severely mauled, suffering 6,600 casualties against German losses of fewer than a thousand.[4] From a military point of view, it was a tactical setback, not a strategic debacle, but it was nevertheless a humiliating defeat "for the proud and cocky Americans," wrote Harry Butcher, a former CBS executive who was Eisenhower's naval aide and confidant.[5] As General Harold Alexander wired Churchill on February 27, it meant that "victory in North Africa is not (repeat not) just around the corner."[6]

On top of this setback, relations with the Soviets spiraled further downward after Ambassador Standley held a press conference in Moscow on March 8, during which he accused Soviet authorities of failing to acknowledge—and concealing from their people—the true extent of lend-lease aid provided by the United States. No doubt Stalin had provoked Standley's impolitic remarks by giving a speech two weeks before in which he portrayed the Red Army as fighting alone against Germany (largely true) and made no mention of having received any aid from the United States. Recalling Standley's press conference, the *Collier's Weekly* editor Quentin Reynolds wrote, "[The] Ambassador dropped a bomb that was heard all over the world."[7]

In fact because of the slow ramp-up of American industry to a war footing and the need to suspend convoys and divert shipping for the Torch landings in summer and fall of 1942, U.S. supplies of lend-lease aid to the USSR did not begin to reach impressive levels until mid-1943, although more than three thousand American-made tanks were sent to the Soviet Union in 1942. During the first few weeks of 1943, only three convoys managed to reach Murmansk. "We've lost millions of people, and they want us to crawl on our knees because they send us Spam," complained one Soviet observer.[8]

Hopkins was deeply concerned. He was reading reports from the American minister in Sweden that Hitler was offering a peace deal to the Soviet Union via Japan on very favorable terms, including, among other things, restoring the 1939 borders with Poland established in the Nazi-Soviet nonaggression pact, the so-called Curzon Line on the River Bug.[9] If consummated, the deal would free up all of the 185 German-led divisions in the USSR to move west and invade England. Something had to be done to forestall this frightening prospect.

Once again Hopkins called on his friend Joe Davies, former ambassador to the Soviet Union, for advice. During a telephone conversation and soon after that a White House meeting with Hopkins, Davies provided his interpretation of the reasons for the decline in U.S.-Soviet relations, focusing not so much on Standley's press conference as on the refusal of the United States to join the British in recognizing Soviet postwar entitlement to Polish territory (up to the Curzon Line), the delay in opening a second front in Europe, and the suspension of convoys to Murmansk. Although Davies was aware of the German peace feeler, he did not believe Stalin would seriously entertain it. The only way to improve relations with the Soviets quickly, he advised, was for the United States to recognize their territorial claims in Poland and all three of the Baltic states.[10] While Hopkins tended to agree with this approach, Roosevelt did not want to deal with Soviet territorial issues until the postwar peace conference.

In separate but coordinated meetings on March 14, both Hopkins and Roosevelt tried to persuade Davies to go to Moscow to "repair" relations with the Soviets, either as a permanent ambassador or as a temporary special envoy. Davies, begging off because of his precarious health, urged Hopkins to go in his place, arguing that he "could be more effective than anyone else." Hopkins declined, and the president backed him up. "I can't spare Hopkins. I need him here."[11] Davies was about to check into the Lahey Clinic in Boston to have, in his words, his "gut normalized."[12] He told the president and Hopkins that he would follow the advice of his doctors as to whether or not he should go to Moscow. Hopkins, who had demonstrated little regard for the health warnings of doctors, told Davies that whatever the doctors decided, Davies "must go anyhow" because relations with the

Soviets "were critical": "[It is] vital that their confidence in us or our attitude toward them should not be impaired." Reminding Davies that "Roosevelt had been trying for months to get Stalin to meet with him," Hopkins flattered the former ambassador by suggesting that he was the only person who could convince Stalin to meet one-on-one with the president.[13]

Two days later, March 16, Stalin turned up the heat. In a cable to Roosevelt, the Soviet leader concluded with some foreboding, "I must give a most emphatic warning, in the interest of our common cause, of the grave danger with which further delay in opening a second front in France is fraught."[14] Was Stalin about to cut a deal with Hitler? Was the Red Army on the verge of collapse? Hopkins, for one, didn't think so. Based on his conversations with Davies, he believed this was Stalin's opening shot in negotiations aimed at securing territorial buffers to protect the Soviet Union against future aggression. That evening he met with Ambassador Litvinov and asked him straight out what Stalin wanted. According to Hopkins's notes, Litvinov said Russia (that is, Stalin) wanted "the Baltic States," a boundary in Finland where "the Russian armies were at the end of the Finnish War," and "'her territorial rights' on the Polish frontier" (meaning the Curzon Line).[15] Stalin was not contemplating a peace deal with the Nazis; he was aiming to maximize his leverage at the postwar peace conference.

Ironically while Hopkins and Roosevelt were trying to persuade Davies to travel to Moscow for the purpose of repairing U.S.-Soviet relations, British Foreign Minister Anthony Eden was in Washington proposing to go on the same mission. Churchill had sent him to talk to Roosevelt and Hopkins about acting as a "friendly broker" to reestablish good relations between the United States and the Soviet Union.[16] When Davies returned from the Lahey Clinic and learned why Eden was in town, he told the president that the "shoe [was] on the wrong foot." Because of "generations" of hostility between Russia and Britain and the fact that Stalin and Churchill "just naturally clashed," noted Davies, the United States, not Great Britain, should be the "good broker." According to Davies, the "one remedy" was for the president to meet personally with Stalin. The president agreed. "You must arrange such a meeting, if possible," he told the former ambassador.[17] Either because he felt he could not refuse the president or because his "gut" had "normalized," or both, Davies relented. He would go to Moscow.

During the next few weeks Hopkins prepared him for his trip, the "primary purpose" of which "was to secure the meeting between Stalin and the president." Davies was to take with him a list of questions drafted by Hopkins that he should ask Stalin concerning his postwar plans and a sealed envelope containing an invitation from Roosevelt for a private shipboard meeting on either side of the Bering Straits sometime in the summer of 1943. Churchill was not to be included.[18]

In the days before his departure, Davies's advice proved prescient, as Soviet relations with the British became much worse than those with the United States. In April German radio announced the discovery of the corpses of thousands of Polish officers in the Katyn Forest near Smolensk. Josef Goebbels, Nazi propaganda minister, claimed the dead officers were POWs who had been executed by the Soviets in 1940 and thrown into shallow graves.[19] Churchill and the exiled Polish government in London believed the German claims were true—as they were—whereas Davies, Roosevelt, and Hopkins tended to side with the Soviet Union's denials. (Indeed when the Poles exiled in London publicly denounced the Soviets for the massacre, Hopkins responded that they were troublemakers, interested only in preventing their large estates from falling into Russian hands.) The Soviets, claiming that the Germans were guilty of the atrocity, severed relations with the London Poles and announced the establishment of a puppet Polish government in Moscow. Churchill warned Stalin that Britain would not recognize the Moscow Poles. This open wound would not even partially heal until 1990, when Mikhail Gorbachev officially acknowledged that Stalin's government was responsible for ordering the murders of the cream of the Polish officer corps and then of concealing the crime, and apologized to the Polish people.[20]

On May 5, the day Davies departed for Moscow, Churchill and his party were at Gourock, Scotland, boarding the *Queen Mary* for the United States. Churchill would have been very displeased had he known Davies was flying to Moscow to arrange a meeting between Roosevelt and Stalin, one from which he would be excluded. The prime minister was on his way to what would be called the Trident conference, the third wartime conference involving Churchill and Roosevelt and the Combined Chiefs of Staff, to be held in Washington. Prompted by Churchill, the purpose of the conference was to ensure that there would be no delay in commencing the invasion of Sicily and to address the key question, Where do we go from here?[21]

As far as Churchill was concerned, the answer was obvious: Italy. On the passage across the Atlantic, he told his military chiefs that after the conquest of Sicily, "the greatest step [they] could take in 1943 . . . would be the elimination of Italy."[22] On the assumption that Sicily would fall by the end of August, Churchill argued that the Anglo-American forces already there should press on to invade Italy instead of being transported to Great Britain to prepare for a cross-Channel invasion. "We cannot afford to have idle armies while the Russians are bearing such a disproportionate weight," he wrote in the notes he would use for his opening argument at Trident.[23]

Wearing a tan raincoat and the gray felt Scott & Co. hat with the "W.S.C." initials that Churchill had given him in 1941, Hopkins was waiting on the docks at Staten Island for the arrival of the prime minister. It was Tuesday morning, May 11. Through the fog and mist that hung low in the harbor he could make out the triple stacks and enormous profile of the famous liner, her bright peacetime paints covered over by coats of gray. Although her upper decks comfortably housed Churchill and his party of almost one hundred, below decks the *Queen Mary* had been converted into a prison ship, bearing a heavily guarded cargo of five thousand German and Italian POWs captured in North Africa and bound for Canada.

Hopkins greeted Churchill warmly as he stepped out of the lead launch onto the dock. Instead of the dull, blue woolen siren suit that he had worn during most of the voyage, the prime minister was decked out in the uniform of the Royal Yacht Squadron, a double row of brass buttons with three anchors and the letters "RYS" adorning his navy blue reefer jacket. The two old friends smoked and chatted amiably while suitcases and crates were loaded into the baggage car of the *Ferdinand Magellan,* the armored presidential train that would take them to the B&O ferry terminal at Tottenville and then on to Washington.[24]

Once again Churchill was ensconced in the Rose Suite across the hall from Hopkins, although during this stay he would be more careful than before about wandering into the Lincoln rooms without warning due to the presence of Louise.[25] Washington hotels during wartime were booked solid, but somehow the conference organizers scrounged rooms for the rest of the British delegation at various hotels, private homes, the British Embassy, and military barracks.

On the eve of the Trident conference, the war news was improving. The most heartening reports were streaming in from North Africa. On May 8 the U.S. Army occupied Bizerte in Tunisia, Africa's northernmost city, and the British took Tunis. A quarter million German and Italian soldiers were captured, although Rommel, on sick leave in the Austrian Alps, escaped. From Casablanca to Cairo, the North African littoral and much of the Mediterranean were in the control of U.S. and British ground, naval, and air forces. As a result, the Suez Canal was about to be reopened, the Middle East oil fields were nowhere near as vulnerable, and the entire southern flank of Europe—the belly of Churchill's crocodile—lay exposed to attack.

Nevertheless the Axis powers controlled vast territories: all of continental Europe and the entire eastern littoral of Asia. Even though the tide had turned against the Wehrmacht at Stalingrad, Hitler still commanded three hundred divisions, and his satellites, Hungary and Romania, had many more. The Red Army was still hundreds of miles from Germany's eastern border. In the Pacific the Japanese had been driven from Guadalcanal and Papua, and Admiral Yamamoto, the architect of the Pearl Harbor attack, had been killed when the Mitsubishi G4M "Betty" Bomber in which he was flying was attacked and downed by P-38 fighter planes. Still the Japanese occupied Burma and much of China, and their homeland was protected by an arc of fortified islands, from the Kuriles in the north to the central Solomons in the south.

The Trident conference officially began at 2:30 p.m. on Wednesday, May 12, in the Oval Study.[26] Unlike at the Casablanca conference, this time the American joint chiefs came fully prepared, with binders full of briefing papers, and were backed by a delegation as large as that of the British. Moreover this time they were unified, agreeing almost to a man that the move after Sicily should be the cross-Channel landings in western France and expressing "antipathy to an invasion of the Italian mainland."[27] Their principal concern was Roosevelt himself. "The man from London [Churchill] . . . will have his way with our Chief and the careful and deliberate plans of our staff will be overridden," wrote Secretary of War Stimson in his diary. "I feel very troubled about it."[28]

Hopkins, the only civilian in the room, listened carefully as "the man from London" answered his own question of what should come next by eloquently urging an attack on Italy to knock her out of the war. At first Roosevelt seemed to hang tough, responding that "he had always shrunk from the thought of putting large armies in Italy," a diversion that "could result in attrition" of the Allied forces. Then, to the dismay of Marshall, FDR strayed from the script agreed on with his military chiefs before the talks began. After arguing for a definite and final decision to launch an all-out, massive cross-Channel invasion in the spring of 1944, one that would allow them to sweep across France and strike at the heart of Germany, the president equivocated, suggesting that they might consider landing a much smaller invasion force that would establish a temporary bridgehead in France.[29] This was exactly what Marshall feared, for it gave the British an opening to convince Roosevelt that Italy was a better prospect than a half-hearted stab at France.

Except for a weekend break, the CCS and their aides continued the debate over the next several days, away from the presence of Roosevelt and Churchill (and Hopkins), in the Federal Reserve Building on Constitution Avenue. Even though the president had opened a crack in American unity—suggesting rather than declaring his preference—Marshall and his military commanders stuck to their preconference plan, arguing forcefully for a definite commitment to launch a major cross-Channel invasion in the spring of 1944. Alan Brooke, speaking rapidly in his squeaky voice and with an impressive command of facts and strategy, countered just as forcefully that such an attempt would not succeed beyond establishing a bridgehead in France, whereas an invasion of Italy stood a good chance of "breaking the Axis and bringing the war with Germany to a successful conclusion in 1944."[30]

They were at loggerheads. Finally, at 4:30 on Wednesday afternoon, May 19, Marshall proposed that everyone leave the room except for the principals, the eight chiefs of staff. They were scheduled to meet Roosevelt and Churchill at the White House in two hours. They had to reach a decision; they could not risk throwing this critical matter of war strategy into the laps of these two politicians.

The room was cleared. Ninety minutes later the combined chiefs emerged with a written agreement. Not surprisingly it was a compromise, "a bridge across which we could meet," wrote Brooke in his diary.[31] A cross-Channel invasion of France would be launched with a "target date of May 1, 1944 to secure a lodgement on the Continent from which further offensive operations can be carried out." It would be called Operation Overlord. Seven of the twenty-nine divisions needed for Operation Overlord would be transferred from the Mediterranean to staging areas in Britain after the conclusion of the campaign in Sicily. With respect to Italy, General Eisenhower, the commander in chief, North Africa, was "instructed to mount such operations . . . as are best calculated to eliminate Italy from the war and to contain the maximum number of German forces."[32]

At the 6 p.m. meeting at the White House, Brooke summarized the compromise agreement, which was received without comment by the president and the prime minister. Hopkins was present and also said nothing.[33] However, Churchill was not at all happy about the agreement because it did not explicitly commit the Allies to invade Italy. Later, working himself into a rant, he angrily complained to Lord Moran, "[Roosevelt] is not in favor of landing in Italy. I only crossed the Atlantic for this purpose. I cannot let the matter rest where it is."[34]

In fact he did not let the matter rest. During the evening of May 24 and well into the next morning, the prime minister tried to amend the wording of the agreement to provide a definite commitment to invade Italy.[35] For the first time at the Trident conference, Hopkins stepped fully into the debate over war strategy and the wording of the delicate compromise, warning Churchill, "If you wish to carry your point you will have to stay here another week, [and] even then there is no certainty."[36] Churchill backed down, writing later that Hopkins exercised a "mollifying and dominating" influence.[37] As Brooke gratefully wrote in his diary the next day, "Luckily Harry Hopkins succeeded in getting him to withdraw it at the last moment." Brooke even made a special point of thanking "Hopkins for all his help."[38]

Such praise coming from Brooke, who with his undisguised disdain for most Americans and his belief, according to Lord Moran, that he and no one else could keep "Winston on the rails in the conduct of the war," was rare indeed.[39] Once again Hopkins's combination of timing and tone, his sense of when to speak and what to say, headed off what could have been a costly rift in Churchill's relationship with Roosevelt and the American military chiefs. As it was, Churchill's last-minute attempt to alter the agreement rekindled the suspicions of the Americans that he would *never* agree to cross-Channel landings in France, that he would continue to advocate diversionary operations in Italy, the Aegean, and the Balkans.

During the first weekend of the Trident conference, Roosevelt and Marshall orchestrated elaborate plans to spirit their English guests out of Washington for a couple of days of bonding, conviviality, and relaxation. Marshall and the combined chiefs flew in two Army transports to southeast Virginia, where they toured the Yorktown battlefield (to much laughter, Pug Ismay claimed he could not recall "the name of that chap who did so badly here") and on to Colonial Williamsburg (restored with Rockefeller money), staying at the Williamsburg Inn and dining at the Raleigh Tavern.[40] The president and his party of Churchill, Hopkins, Lord Beaverbrook (who served as Churchill's Lord Privy Seal, a kind of minister without portfolio, from 1943 to 1945), Mrs. Roosevelt, and the Roosevelt's daughter Anna, traveled north by automobile to Shangri-La. As they approached Frederick, Maryland, Churchill, sitting in the front seat, asked if he could see the home of Barbara Frietchie, the inspiration for John Greenleaf Whittier's poem about the brave woman who displayed the Union flag as the Confederate Army marched by. Accounts differ, but at this point it was either Hopkins or Roosevelt who quoted the first two lines of the poem: "Shoot if you must this old gray head, But spare your country's flag, she said."[41] When it became apparent that these were the only two lines that could be recalled, Churchill astonished everyone in the car when he "gabbled the whole poem," reciting all sixty lines.[42] The prime minister continued to amaze Hopkins and his car mates. Passing a sign for Gettysburg, Churchill said, "Why, this may have been the very road by which Longstreet moved up."[43] He then launched into a comprehensive review of the Gettysburg battle, followed by highlights of the careers of Stonewall Jackson and Robert E. Lee.

Most accounts of the weekend at Shangri-La emphasize the quiet hours that Roosevelt and Churchill spent together, casting for trout at creek-side or working on the president's stamp collection. However, there was one jarring incident, and it was triggered by Hopkins. Before the weekend began, Lord Beaverbrook had infuriated Churchill by backing Marshall's position that the next move should be cross-Channel landings in France rather than an invasion of Italy. When the president invited Beaverbrook to join Churchill and the others at Shangri-La, he diplomatically tried to decline, knowing that Churchill would not welcome his company. Hopkins telephoned Beaverbrook, indignantly informing him that "the President of the United States [was] not in the habit" of having his invitations refused.[44] Beaverbrook acceded reluctantly. At some point during the weekend, probably right after Beaverbrook argued for an invasion of western France instead of Italy in the presence of Roosevelt, Churchill erupted, telling Beaverbrook that he had no business injecting himself into war strategy and accusing him of disloyalty to his country. Beaverbrook stormed out in anger and returned to Washington, where for the next month he continued to undermine Churchill by lobbying Hopkins and others for a second front in France and against an invasion of Italy.[45]

It is entirely possible, if not likely, that Hopkins insisted that Beaverbrook come to Shangri-La because he knew that "the Beaver," as he was called, would argue passionately for a second front in France and he wanted him there both to help persuade Roosevelt and to offset Churchill's opposing arguments. Churchill's outburst and Beaverbrook's abrupt departure injected some awkward and unpleasant moments into an otherwise bucolic weekend but Hopkins's purposes were probably served. He also knew that Churchill and Beaverbrook had maintained an uncommonly intimate yet tumultuous friendship for years and that they would soon get past this latest blowup. Beaverbrook would remain, in Hopkins's words, "one of the men who saw Churchill after midnight."

────────

Meanwhile Joe Davies had arrived in Moscow with the objective of arranging a face-to-face meeting between Stalin and Roosevelt. Shortly after 9 p.m. on May 20, 1943, Davies was in the Kremlin, presenting the personal invitation from the president to Stalin that he carried with him. As the translator read the letter, "Stalin didn't flicker an eyelash," wrote Davies. "He looked taciturn and grim." When the translator read the part indicating that Churchill would be excluded from the proposed meeting with FDR and presumably Hopkins, Stalin interrupted. "Why?" Davies suggested that Roosevelt and Churchill did not "always see eye to eye" and that Roosevelt's ideas concerning the postwar world, particularly regarding "colonial and backward peoples . . . differed from those of the Prime Minister." Davies hastened to point out to Stalin that Roosevelt and Churchill "were always loyal" to one another and that there had to be "unity" among the three of them, but it was nevertheless essential that Stalin meet with Roosevelt alone so that they would "understand each other." Stalin countered, "I am not so sure. . . . Understanding alone is not enough. There must be reciprocity and respect." Davies responded, "If you knew the President as I know him, you would know that is exactly what you would get and, in fact, you are getting now."[46]

An hour later, after Davies apologized for postponing the cross-Channel invasion in 1942 and assured Stalin that the Curzon Line issue would be resolved to his satisfaction, Stalin said, "You may tell your President I will be glad to meet with him." He suggested July 15 in Fairbanks, Alaska, subject to possible delay because of "military developments."[47] Davies was ebullient. He thought he had accomplished his mission.

As Davies was flying back to Washington to trumpet the success of his mission to Roosevelt and Hopkins, Stalin was reading a decrypted cable dated May 29 from one of his espionage agents in the United States that rekindled all of his long-held suspicions about his so-called allies that Davies had sought to dispel.[48] Based on information from a confidential source known as "source 19," who had attended a meeting a few days before with Roosevelt and Churchill at the Trident conference, Stalin learned for the first time that, in deference to the views of Churchill, the Americans and British agreed once again to put off the second front. This despite promises in February that cross-Channel landings would be launched in August or September 1943.

During the 1990s it was claimed in sensation-seeking news stories and at least one well-reasoned scholarly article that Hopkins himself was source 19, the individual who either wittingly or negligently leaked the key decision made at Trident to a Soviet spy.[49] However, in the spring of 2009 Alexander Vassiliev, a former KGB agent who was given unprecedented access to KGB archives, donated his notebooks to the Library of Congress. The notebooks clearly identify source 19 as Laurence Duggan, a Department of State official and nephew of Sumner Welles, who either fell or jumped from the sixteenth floor of a building in Manhattan in late1948, ten days after being questioned by the FBI about his contacts with Soviet intelligence.[50]

Regardless of the identity of source 19, Stalin was incensed, if not entirely surprised, when he learned of the postponement of the second front until 1944. This latest news confirmed his suspicions that the Americans and British, particularly the British, were trying to bleed Russia white, standing on the sidelines while the motherland drained her treasury and pumped millions of her citizens into the meat grinder. Within a few days Stalin would be officially advised by Ambassador Standley of the postponement.[51] The Soviet leader would deliver an ice-cold reply, accusing FDR and Churchill of breaking their promises and telling them that the postponement left "a disheartening negative impression" on the Soviet people and its army.[52]

Hopkins was really worried. Stalin's cable indicated that Roosevelt's plan for a one-on-one meeting was almost certainly dead in the water. Reports were circulating again that German and Soviet officials were meeting in Sweden. Stalin recalled his ambassadors from London and Washington. Moreover Churchill was likely to find out, probably through Beaverbrook, that Roosevelt had gone behind his back and tried to get Stalin to meet with him secretly in Alaska. The three-party coalition that Hopkins had been nurturing since his visits to London and Moscow in 1941 was in danger of flying apart. "Things were bad and had been breaking fast," Hopkins told Davies shortly after the former ambassador returned from his trip to Moscow. At Davies's estate on Rock Creek, Hopkins explained that Churchill and his military chiefs again drove the decision to postpone the cross-Channel invasion and asked how Stalin and the Soviets would react once they knew the full story. "It would shake their confidence in Roosevelt and the United States as being only the fifth wheel in the wagon being steered by the British," responded Davies. "It would shake the unity of the Big 3 to its foundation." Hopkins agreed. "Yes, it's not good. What makes it most dangerous [is that] the Russians are pretty 'cocky' over Stalingrad and don't need the West to beat Hitler."[53]

The two of them turned to a discussion of the delicate problem of how to tell Churchill about Roosevelt's plan to meet with Stalin alone before he found out from other sources. Hopkins's "solution" was to send Harriman, who was "very pro-Churchill," to "break the news to him before Beaverbrook saw him." (Harriman was in London.) Davies agreed, adding, "If anyone could do it, Averell ought to be able to."[54]

As Sherwood recalled, Hopkins "laughed as he wished Harriman the best of luck in his mission."[55] By all accounts, Harriman's late night/early morning session with Churchill was rough. Churchill expressed deep disappointment at being excluded and explained how his prestige at home would suffer. The next day he cabled Roosevelt, "Averell told me last night of your wish for a meeting with U.J. ["Uncle Joe" Stalin] in Alaska a deux." He begged the president to reconsider.[56]

Roosevelt's reply was remarkable but not out of character. He began with an outright lie, maintaining that it was not his but Stalin's idea that they meet alone. In the same sentence he said that the proposed encounter with Stalin would be "preliminary," thereby suggesting, falsely, that they intended to include Churchill after an initial get-acquainted session.[57] Then, as a palliative, Roosevelt invited Churchill to meet with him in August in Quebec. Hopkins's part in drafting this cable is unknown. However, since he was Roosevelt's most intimate advisor, particularly on matters involving Churchill, it is likely that he either drafted the cable or advised the president on the wisdom of sending it. No doubt the two of them conspired to lie because they were embarrassed to tell the truth to their friend and ally. With the Red Army victorious at Stalingrad and the American arsenal producing at full capacity, the Soviet Union and the United States would emerge from the war as the world's foremost powers. Excluding Churchill from the meeting with Stalin would be seen by enemy propagandists and the world at large as symbolic of the fact that Great Britain and its empire, virtually bankrupt, were in decline. Although Churchill was almost always transparent—his daughter chose the word "limpid"[58]—Roosevelt and Hopkins could not bear to be direct, knowing how exclusion would hurt Churchill's standing at home and around the globe. "You know I am a juggler," Roosevelt famously told Treasury Secretary Morgenthau. "I am perfectly willing to mislead and tell untruths if it will win the war."[59]

Predictably the meeting "a deux" with the Soviet leader never took place. Stalin was disgusted by the decision to postpone the landings in France until 1944 at the earliest. Through lies and charm, Roosevelt managed to patch things up with Churchill, but the prime minister knew that the balance of power was shifting and that he would no longer be treated as an equal partner.

On July 6, 1943, Hopkins received a memo from Oscar Cox, one of his top aides and a close associate since their days together at the WPA. According to the memo, Cox and two other prominent American Jews, Ben Cohen and Felix Frankfurter, had met the evening before with Jan Karski, a member of the Polish underground. Disguised as a guard, Karski had penetrated a Nazi death camp (Bełżec) where Jews were being exterminated. Twice he had been smuggled into the Warsaw ghetto so he could witness firsthand the awful fate of Polish Jews. These stories, wrote Cox to Hopkins, "will make your hair stand on end."[60]

For more than a year Hopkins had been aware of Nazi atrocities, including reports that Hitler was carrying through on his threat to "annihilate the Jewish race."[61] As early as June 1942 he had prepared a memorandum to the president concerning German and Japanese atrocities and proposed the creation of a United Nations Commission on Atrocities, the objective of which would be to serve as a warning that war crimes would be prosecuted and hence to deter additional atrocities.[62] Beyond this memo, however, almost nothing has been written about what, if anything, Hopkins did in the face of the mounting evidence that Jews were being singled out for extermination and that European Jewry was threatened with extinction. Given his relationship with Roosevelt, and through him his ability to influence the policies of Churchill and possibly even Stalin, Hopkins might have advocated relaxation of immigration policies, encouraged rescue efforts, argued for bombing railways to the death camps, or sought to publicize the plight of the Jews. Like Roosevelt and so many others, he also could have remained largely silent. In most respects it appears that Hopkins chose the latter course, lingering in the shadows of this issue.

Hopkins's Commission on Atrocities memo, however, took on a life of its own, eventually evolving into a declaration that attracted more press attention than any of the earlier stories about the extermination of the Jews. As amended by Roosevelt, the Hopkins memo was handed to Churchill when he was in Washington in June 1942.[63] In London, where the British government—and various governments-in-exile located there—were under greater public pressure than in the United States to take some action that might deter the destruction of the European Jews, the Hopkins memo became the basis for a proposed War Crimes Commission that was tentatively approved in July by Churchill and the British war cabinet.

U.S. Ambassador Gil Winant, who assisted the British in turning the Hopkins memo into the framework for a War Crimes Commission and passionately believed the Nazi atrocities provided a moral basis for war, sent the Commission proposal to Roosevelt for his approval via air courier on August 6, 1942. Weeks went by with no response, not even an acknowledgment that it had been received. Finally, Hopkins responded on September 21, telling Winant that his request to Roosevelt had been "mislaid" for a time but that it was being handled by the State Department.

At this point Hopkins, having been none too helpful in securing approval of his own War Crimes Commission proposal, dropped out of the loop, and Winant began his education in dealing with both the State Department's intransigence and the president's hesitance in facing matters involving the Holocaust. After another two weeks, the War Crimes Commission was approved, although the word *atrocities* was stricken and the president insisted that only "ringleaders" be punished. (Arguably this modification handed those who managed the actual killing apparatus a defense that they were only following orders.)[64]

In Great Britain the people, the politicians, and the governments-in-exile were clamoring for something stronger than the watered-down version of the War Crimes Commission originally proposed in the Hopkins memo. Foreign Minister Eden, responding to this pressure, prepared a draft declaration, the objective of which was to strengthen the deterrent effect of the Commission and make it clear to the free world that the Nazis were killing men, women, and children simply because they were Jews. On December 7, 1942, Winant forwarded the draft to Secretary of State Hull, requesting that he let the British know the views of the United States later that week.[65]

The next day Rabbi Stephen Wise, head of the American Jewish Congress, and four other Jewish leaders met with Roosevelt in the first-floor Oval Office. They wanted to make sure the president was aware of the enormity of the crimes being committed in Europe and to plead with him to focus world attention on what was happening. At the end of the meeting they handed Roosevelt a twenty-page report summarizing the evidence, entitled "Blue Print for Extermination." Apparently Hopkins was not present, although he undoubtedly was told of the meeting. Rabbi Wise's session with the president had its intended effect. Within a few days the State Department, which initially was inclined to oppose issuance of the Eden declaration as "too strong and definite," reversed course, probably because of a call from FDR or one of his aides following the meeting with Wise.[66]

On December 17, 1942, the United Nations Declaration on War Crimes was broadcast to the world, the three Allied governments proclaiming that Hitler's intention to "exterminate the Jewish people in Europe" was being carried into effect and promising to punish the perpetrators. Originally the declaration said there was "no room for doubt" that exterminations of Jews were taking place. However, the State Department insisted that this language be dropped. Instead the declaration as issued said merely that the Allied governments had "received numerous reports" that the exterminations were

taking place. Clearly there were those in the State Department who continued to question the authenticity of the reports of mass murder.[67]

Although weakened by State Department changes, the Declaration on
War Crimes was front-page news in the United States. For the first time
the American public was told of widespread reports that Jews throughout
occupied Europe were being exterminated by the Nazis. The memo written
by Hopkins in June had been transformed, mainly at the insistence of the
British, from a modest call for a postwar investigation of war crimes into a
public indictment of Hitler and his regime for murdering European Jewry.
But notwithstanding the publicity, there was no outpouring of national
outrage, no calls for immediate action to save the Jews. The president did
not add his voice to the Declaration. Instead, until the spring of 1944 he
maintained, as Michael Beschloss writes, "a terrible silence."[68] He chose not
to expend his political capital on changing immigration policies or initiating rescue schemes.

What about Hopkins? More than even the president, he was almost
completely silent after referring the British plan for a War Crimes Commission to the State Department in the fall of 1942. He must have had plenty
of chances to recommend action or speak out. For example, in March 1943
he participated in a meeting with Eden during which the issue of getting
"60 or 70 thousand Jews . . . threatened with extermination" out of Bulgaria was discussed. As Hopkins's memo of the meeting recounts, Eden said
that it would be "extremely difficult" for the British to undertake such a
rescue. Even if they offered to try to transport the Bulgarian Jews to Palestine, it would encourage "the Jews of the world" to pressure the British "to
make similar offers in Poland and Germany."[69] There is no indication that
Hopkins responded to this cynical reasoning. Indeed there is no record of
Hopkins's views concerning the question of rescuing Jews in Bulgaria or
any other European country.

Given his close associations with Jewish immigrants from Eastern
Europe when he was a social worker in New York City, his marriage into
Ethel Gross's family, and his many Jewish coworkers and friends, Hopkins, more than most American gentiles, must have empathized with the
plight of European Jewry. Yet the record is bereft of any evidence that he

became involved, or sought to become involved, in specific efforts to rescue them from extermination. He was scheduled to meet with Jan Karski in July 1943 to hear an eyewitness account of the Holocaust and to discuss ways the United States might help. However, the meeting was inexplicably canceled.[70]

The only evidence that Hopkins broke silence came from John J. McCloy, assistant secretary of war. In 1983, when he was eighty-eight but still "alert and vigorous," McCloy told a *Washington Post* reporter during lengthy, on-the-record interviews that Hopkins had *opposed* a plan advocated by Jewish spokespersons to bomb the rail lines leading into Auschwitz in order to save Hungarian Jews from extermination. McCloy explained that his own role on the issue of whether or not to bomb Auschwitz began with a request by Hopkins to meet with him and possibly Sam Rosenman. According to McCloy, Hopkins told him that "the Boss [Roosevelt] was not disposed to" the bombing of Auschwitz. That, plus the opposition allegedly expressed by General Hap Arnold, was "the end of that," McCloy told the reporter. Auschwitz was never bombed.[71]

The controversial question of whether to bomb rail lines leading into Auschwitz or Auschwitz itself was debated in June and July 1944. During those months, as will be seen, Hopkins did very little work, spending virtually all of that time convalescing in West Virginia and the last three weeks of July recovering at home. It is unlikely, therefore, that McCloy's memory of a meeting with Hopkins to discuss the bombing of Auschwitz was accurate. On the other hand, Hopkins could have participated in a telephone conversation with McCloy; or the discussions referred to by McCloy could have taken place in or after late August when Hopkins returned to work or conceivably before January when Hopkins left Washington for the Mayo Clinic.

In all probability, the primary explanation for Hopkins's near silence is that, in Churchill's words, "he always went to the root of the matter." The key to ending the mass murder of Jews, he would have reasoned, was winning the war as quickly as possible. Hopkins was wholly dedicated to "the defeat, ruin and slaughter of Hitler, to the exclusion of all other purposes, loyalties or aims," wrote Churchill.[72] Rightly or wrongly—and there are those who argue persuasively that he was profoundly misguided—Hopkins was convinced that interim rescue efforts would divert resources from the main goal, with the result that the war would be prolonged and more Jewish lives would be lost than saved.[73]

A second and related explanation is that along with the president Hopkins understood the political obstacles as well as the strength of prevailing American anti-Semitism that stood in the way of effective rescue efforts. Congress was not inclined to suspend immigration laws and admit large numbers of Jewish refugees. Church leaders were not speaking out. Even American Jews were divided on what actions should be taken.

Although Hopkins never met Jan Karski, Roosevelt finally granted him an hour-long audience in the Oval Study on July 28, 1943. Responding to Karski's appeal for immediate measures to stop the genocide, the president said simply, "Tell your nation we shall win the war."[74] Had Hopkins sat in on this meeting, his response would have been the same. The obvious problem with this response is that by the time the war was won there might be no Jews left to save.

14

The Alliance Shifts

For Hopkins and Louise, living in the White House in the summer of 1943 was not without its complications. After Louise moved in, the social dynamics, always unstable, became ever more volatile. Because she was glamorous, gregarious, and funny, the president was instantly attracted to her and loved her company. Initially she was flattered by his attention, and Hopkins viewed her relationship with FDR as furthering his own ambition to remain the president's closest advisor. Yet at the same time, he and Louise were newly in love, understandably anxious to chart their own lives as a married couple, and beginning to chafe at always needing to be at the beck and call of the housebound president. "Can you imagine," Louise confided to her sister Gert, "never having breakfast with your own husband?"[1]

Despite carping from Louise, Hopkins did his best to preserve his intimate relationship with Roosevelt. However, the president sensed that he was not as accessible. A narrow but unmistakable fissure was opened. In love with Louise, Hopkins seemed to be no longer "the half man" whose company FDR could completely dominate. It wasn't fair to Hopkins, but Roosevelt felt betrayed, just as he did when Tommy Corcoran married Peggy Dowd and Missy LeHand briefly fell in love with William Bullitt (former ambassador to the USSR and France). It was then that Roosevelt spent more and more time with the beautiful and effervescent Princess Martha at Pooks Hill, her estate in Maryland, borrowing Louise at a moment's notice to serve as a chaperone and to watch over the children while FDR and Martha had tea. "This was one hell of a situation for Mummy to get into," observed Diana, "but she did it with as much good grace as she had."[2]

As to the relationship between Eleanor Roosevelt and Louise, accounts vary. According to Diana, they "were not the best of pals, but they got along as two women will, forced into a situation living in the same house." They "were just totally different personalities": politics and idealism dominated Eleanor's life, but Louise didn't have a "political cell in her body."[3] Yet having cared for Diana for the past four years and for FDR since he was stricken with polio in 1921, Eleanor must have must felt some resentment when Louise, whom she regarded as a lightweight socialite, swept into the White House with her poodle and her New York maid and almost immediately won the affections of both Diana and her own husband. Anna Boettiger, the Roosevelts' daughter, thought Louise was presumptuous. "Louise would arrange dinner parties and seat the table," she recalled. "My mother would be home and this would annoy the pants off her."[4] On at least one occasion Louise reportedly changed Eleanor's seating plan at a White House dinner, "and that," said Eleanor's friend Trude Pratt Lash, "you did not do."[5] Anna also believed Eleanor was jealous of Louise. Her mother was a "jealous person," she recalled, "jealous even of me." It wasn't romantic rivalry, but rather a feeling that Louise and the many other women that FDR was attracted to were trying to "usurp" her "position with Father."[6]

Louise (and Hopkins too) must have sensed that other women in Roosevelt's domestic circle regarded her as a rival and gossiped about her behind her back. Cousin Daisy, FDR's Hudson Valley neighbor who was particularly close to him, wrote in her diary about Louise's struggles to fit in: "She is pretty, and I think has all good intentions, but she's 'not very bright,' as the P. [president] put it one day, and her conversation is never illuminating, at least when I have heard it."[7] Louise aggravated the situation, especially at cocktail time. "With a couple of drinks in her," Sam Rosenman recalled, Louise "would talk about Eleanor in a way that caused me to wish that she would lower her voice."[8] In his unpublished biography of Hopkins, James Halsted wrote that Louise would tell friends that "FDR could be very boring in telling the same funny story several times."[9] (Halsted, a physician, had been Anna Roosevelt's third husband, before marrying Diana Hopkins.) The anti-Roosevelt press and gossip columnists picked up on the simmering tensions, making up stories about "interfamily clashes" and referring to the White House as "that 2-family flat."[10] By midsummer of 1943 Louise had convinced Hopkins that it was time to move out. She wanted a home where they could build a married life together, a private place where she could entertain guests of her choosing and serve meals not prepared under the supervision of Mrs. Nesbitt.

It was not an easy decision for Hopkins. He knew that the president, with a breezy wave of his hand, would give his blessing but deep down would be displeased. Bound to his wheelchair, Roosevelt would feel abandoned by the lively, engaging couple who lived just down the hall. Nevertheless at some point during the summer, possibly during their fishing excursion to Lake Huron, Hopkins broke the news to the president.[11] Eleanor was relieved, writing to her friend Joe Lash, "Harry and Louise are going to move to their own house, though P[resident] doesn't like their going."[12] Louise located a modest three-story townhouse among much grander houses on tony N Street in Georgetown at the corner of 34th (cater-cornered from the house where Jack and Jackie Kennedy would live when he was senator); they signed a lease on July 19, providing for November occupancy.[13] To his former brother-in-law, Donald Duncan, captain of the carrier *Essex*, Hopkins wrote, "[The move] will suit me no end."[14] When a Republican congressman from Ohio got wind of the move, he falsely complained that Hopkins exercised undue influence to obtain a new refrigerator for the house, a luxury not available to ordinary citizens during wartime.[15]

It is perhaps true, as Doris Kearns Goodwin surmised, that after Hopkins told FDR he and Louise were moving, a "frost descended on their relationship."[16] Joe Davies also sensed a cooling off, noting in his diary around that time that "the 'Boss' was a little out of patience with Harry," although

Davies thought it had to do not with the move but with Hopkins taking Churchill's side on some issues.[17] According to Churchill, who was with Hopkins at Hyde Park in August, Hopkins feared "he had lost the favour of the President."[18]

Deep beneath the surface, the tectonic plates of their relationship may have shifted, but only slightly. In the coming months, especially when they were outside Washington, Hopkins would remain entrenched as Roosevelt's closest confidant and companion. He had yet to reach the apogee of his influence not only with him but with Churchill and even with Stalin.

The *Ferdinand Magellan* crossed the international border into Canada at Rouses Point at half past noon on August 17, 1943.[19] The president and his party, consisting of Hopkins, Steve Early, Grace Tully, Doc McIntire, a small number of aides, and Fala, were rolling toward Quebec City for another wartime strategy conference with Churchill and the Combined Chiefs of Staff.[20] This conference, code-named Quadrant, would be the fourth held in North America. Roosevelt and Churchill had planned to meet in September, but battlefield successes and political challenges made it necessary to meet earlier. Following landings on July 10, the British and American invasion forces in Sicily had advanced more quickly than anticipated and were about to encircle the entire island. Indeed on the evening of August 17, the U.S. 3rd Army under General Patton took Messina, which effectively ended the Sicilian campaign. Meanwhile, in Rome Mussolini was unexpectedly deposed and arrested on July 25, opening up the prospect of a complete capitulation by Italy, including the surrender of all of its armed forces and its fleet. The Americans and the British needed to decide what forces to commit to the Italian mainland without jeopardizing Overlord and whether, through political maneuvering, they could remove Italy from the war.

As the train approached Quebec City in the late afternoon, the president and his entourage gathered around Hopkins in the president's car. It was Hopkins's fifty-third birthday. He celebrated by treating the president and his party to a round of "Old Fashion[ed]s."[21] Hopkins was feeling good. An unusually favorable profile of him in the *New Yorker* had just been published, causing him to proudly quip that it portrayed him as "a mixture of a

Baptist preacher and a race track tout."[22] He was in the afterglow of a successful weekend of hot dogs and swimming at Hyde Park with FDR and the prime minister, whom the president had invited for off-the-record talks before they gathered for the official conference in Quebec. During the weekend Hopkins had strongly advised Roosevelt not to weaken his commitment to Overlord and helped persuade Churchill that since American troops would far outnumber the British in Overlord, an American, namely George Marshall, should be "Supreme Commander for the cross Channel operations."[23]

Accompanied by the governor-general of Canada, the president, Hopkins, and two other aides were driven from the train station to the Citadel, the governor-general's summer residence, where Churchill had been staying since he arrived in Quebec City a few days earlier.[24] The Citadel is a majestic eighteenth-century military stronghold situated on the crest of Cape Diamond overlooking the St. Lawrence River and the Plains of Abraham, where the British defeated the French in 1759 and won Canada. All of the other British and American military chiefs and civilian aides were staying at the nearby Château Frontenac Hotel, another magnificent edifice, where they occupied all sixteen floors down to the lobby.

A temporary White House map room had been set up next to the president's bedroom in the Citadel. Churchill, who loved maps and had installed his own competing map room down the hall, would burst unannounced into the White House map room at all hours of the night. He was particularly fascinated by the maps and photos depicting the naval shelling and landings by American troops in the Aleutians that had been designed to dislodge the Japanese. His fascination turned to amusement when he learned that the soldiers were greeted not by the guns of the Japanese but by barking dogs.[25] For the rest of the conference Churchill would begin conversations with the Americans with the greeting, "How are we today—*woof, woof, woof*!!" wrote George Elsey, the young Harvard-educated map room watch officer. At first they laughed with Churchill, but after a while his sarcasm "began to grate" on the Americans, especially FDR, who found it "intensely annoying."[26]

Hopkins's main objective at Quadrant was to nail down Churchill's commitment to launch Overlord in May 1944. He was certain he would have the unwavering support of Marshall and Secretary of War Stimson, and he was confident, based on discussions earlier at Hyde Park, that he would be carrying out Roosevelt's wishes. Hopkins had been forewarned by Stimson, who had met with Churchill in July, that the prime minister was still obsessed about the risks of Overlord, referring ominously to the prospect "of having the Channel full of corpses of defeated Allies."[27] According to Stimson, while Churchill and his government had "rendered lip service" to Overlord, "their hearts [were] not in it."[28] Instead they would push for a full-scale invasion of Italy, followed by operations in Greece and the Balkans.

Consequently at the first meeting of the CCS with Roosevelt and Churchill, held at the Citadel on August 19, Hopkins was ready to challenge Churchill and his military chiefs. He didn't have to wait long. In the first few minutes of the session, Churchill observed that if the number of German divisions in northern France proved to be greater than anticipated, the entire Overlord plan should be "subject to revision" (meaning deferred, if not abandoned). Hopkins jumped in, suggesting that the prime minister should not take such a "rigid view" based simply on the number of divisions and pointing out the difficulty of predicting in advance the actual fighting strength of their adversary. Hopkins even had the temerity to say that the plans drawn up by the British generals were too "inelastic." Churchill responded that "there should be elasticity in deciding" whether Overlord should even be mounted. Then, in the next breath—at least according to the official record—he abruptly reversed course and backed down, saying he "strongly favored Overlord for 1944" and offering suggestions for strengthening the initial assault.[29]

Hopkins was not at all convinced Churchill was sincere. The next day he sought out Lord Moran. As Moran recalled in his diary, Hopkins remarked, "Winston is no longer against Marshall's plan for landing on the coast of France. At least, so he says." Then Hopkins "grinned" and added, "But he might change his mind again, as he did last year. I don't believe he is really converted." In his diary Moran noted that Hopkins was bitter and his tone strident, and he speculated that Hopkins felt Churchill's "drawn-out struggle to postpone a second front in France, ha[d], in fact, prolonged the war; that if he had been reasonable earlier [they] might now be in sight of peace."[30] No doubt Hopkins was exasperated by Churchill's penchant for resisting an absolute commitment to Overlord, but whether he actually blamed Churchill for prolonging the war is open to question. Indeed Hopkins and his fellow Americans had reason to be grateful for Churchill's resistance to a cross-Channel invasion in 1942. Most military experts agree that it would have met with failure. As the events in North Africa demonstrated, American troops and their commanders needed to be blooded in combat before confronting the full fury of the Wehrmacht on the beaches and in the hedgerows of Normandy.

There were moments at Quadrant when Hopkins felt frustrated with Churchill, but he almost always treated him with affection, warmth, and wit, as if they had been close friends since boyhood. At the conference table one afternoon Churchill took a sip of ice water and remarked to Hopkins, "This water tastes funny." "Of course it does," responded Hopkins. "It's got no whiskey in it. Fancy you a judge of water."[31]

Often heated, the talks went on for another four days, but in the end the Americans seem to have prevailed. Operation Overlord, the cross-Channel invasion of France, would be launched on May 1, 1944, and would have priority over all other U.S.-British ground and air efforts in Europe and the Mediterranean. In addition, to the lasting disappointment of Brooke, chief of the Imperial General Staff, it would be commanded by an American, presumably Marshall. Having received reports from Sicily that Italy was on the verge of surrender, General Eisenhower was authorized to launch a limited invasion of southern Italy with the understanding that seven divisions and a a large number of precious landing craft would be transferred from the Mediterranean to Britain by November 1, 1943, to take part in Overlord.[32] To coincide with Overlord, landings in *southern* France were proposed by the Americans and reluctantly agreed upon by the British, although Churchill would fight "implacably" against this decision in future months.[33]

Churchill's instinctive aversion to landings in France, particularly the heavily fortified beaches in western France, was shaped by memories of World War I, when tens of thousands of his countrymen were slaughtered in the fields of France, and his awareness from that war that offensive action was at least twice as costly in casualties as defensive warfare. "He recoiled in horror from any suggestion of a direct approach," recalled one British general.[34] "Bodies floating in the Channel haunted him," said Marshall.[35] In mid-August 1942 half of the six thousand Canadian and British troops who assaulted the fortified port of Dieppe on the French coast, in what was characterized as a "reconnaissance in force," were dead or in German prison camps. Churchill also had on his conscience the disastrous amphibious landings at Gallipoli in 1915, which led to his forced resignation from the government.

Although Churchill had agreed to go forward with Overlord, in his heart he remained convinced that a Mediterranean strategy would lead to a quicker and less costly victory. He believed that an Allied invasion of Italy in force was strategically preferable to landings in France because it would result in the quick surrender of Italy, followed by the movement of substantial German forces from the Balkans and the eastern front into Italy (which would relieve some of the pressure on the Red Army); provide air bases for the bombing of the oil fields in Romania and Germany; and open the way for an Allied capture of Vienna and an advance into the Balkans. German officers would overthrow Hitler and the Wehrmacht would surrender, he reasoned, without the need for a frontal attack with massed armies on the German homeland. This kind of optimistic thinking was entirely in character. Over his long career, Churchill had always been able to convince himself that the military strategy he favored would result in a momentous victory.

One morning in the Rose salon of the Château Frontenac the combined chiefs were about to end a particularly rancorous closed session when Admiral Louis Mountbatten—the architect of the Dieppe debacle and later the last viceroy of India—insisted on demonstrating to the American chiefs his outlandish plan, enthusiastically backed by Churchill, for building huge self-propelled floating aircraft bases made out of ice and wood pulp. To illustrate the indestructibility of the ice-pulp mixture, known as Pykete after its inventor, Geoffrey Pyke, Mountbatten "pulled a revolver out of his pocket" and fired at an ordinary block of ice, which instantly shattered. He then fired a round at his indestructible mixture, which ricocheted "like an angry bee" around the room and between the legs of the chiefs.[36] In a room outside the salon, one of the junior officers who had been excluded from the closed session shouted, "Good heavens, they've started shooting now."[37]

While the Americans apparently prevailed on most issues at Quadrant, there was one vital issue—involving an agreement to share information on atomic fission and development of the atomic bomb—where Churchill came away with what he thought was a win. And Hopkins helped him broker the deal.

Roosevelt and Churchill had briefly discussed Tube Alloys, the code name for the atomic bomb project, at Hyde Park in June 1942. In the presence of Hopkins, they agreed orally that although the United States would actually build the bomb, the two nations would pool all research and information on atomic fission and share results. The prime minister had every reason to expect that Roosevelt's government would abide by the agreement, since British scientists, acknowledged leaders in nuclear physics, had already provided critically important information to the Americans that convinced them that a bomb was feasible (the so-called "Maud Report"). However, once the Manhattan Project was established under the autocratic and security-conscious Brigadier General Leslie Groves, new policies were adopted that severely restricted information flowing to British scientists, particularly secrets concerning the atomic bomb manufacturing process.[38] Churchill was upset. He was worried that the restrictive policies might slow down the development of the atomic bomb and enable the Germans or even the Soviets to win the atomic race. (In fact the Russians made little progress during the war, and, as noted earlier, the Germans abandoned their project in 1942.) Churchill was also concerned that Great Britain would emerge from the war without nuclear weapons and without the potential commercial advantages attendant on the possession of nuclear technology.

Rather than confronting Roosevelt himself, Churchill turned to Hopkins for help in persuading the president and his government to abide by the agreement to share. In a series of cables sent during the first half of 1943, the prime minister pleaded with Hopkins to intercede with the War Department, the president, and his science advisors to restore the flow of information to

British scientists.[39] Hopkins began making inquiries on Churchill's behalf. Meanwhile the president was being lobbied by Vannevar Bush, director of the Office of Scientific Research and Development, James Conant, chairman of the National Defense Research Committee, and Henry Stimson that the British should not be provided with any further information about the atomic bomb. In a White House meeting on June 24, Bush told FDR, "Our program is not suffering for lack of interchange . . . and the British had practically quit their efforts."[40] Caught between his casually made oral agreement with Churchill and the views of the War Department and his own science advisors, the president asked Hopkins what he should do. On July 20, 1943, Hopkins sided with Churchill, writing, "Dear Mr. President: I think you made a firm commitment to Churchill in regard to this when he was here [in 1942] and there is nothing to do but go through with it." Later the same day Roosevelt told Bush to "renew . . . the full exchange of information with the British government regarding Tube Alloys."[41]

Churchill was pleased, but he wanted it in writing, and a draft agreement was prepared by his office.[42] At Quadrant on August 19, either just before or during the evening after the meeting at which Churchill flip-flopped and said he "strongly favored Overlord for 1944," the president and the prime minister signed and dated a four-page sharing agreement typed on Citadel stationery. Entitled "Articles of Agreement Governing Collaboration . . . in the Matter of Tube Alloys," the preamble provided for the pooling of "British and American brains and resources" in order "to bring the Tube Alloys project to fruition at the earliest moment."[43] The record shows that Hopkins was present for part but perhaps not all of the time during which the agreement was finalized and signed.[44]

It may have been only a coincidence, but the timing of the nuclear sharing agreement suggests that Roosevelt and Hopkins offered it either to incentivize Churchill to support Overlord—as he did at the meeting on August 19—or as a reward for having done so. Churchill was on record as having stated that a sharing agreement was "so important" that a failure to agree "might affect seriously British-American relationships."[45] Given its importance to Churchill, Roosevelt's readiness to sign the agreement at the outset of the Quadrant meetings may well have played a part in bringing

Churchill to the point of saying he strongly favored Overlord, even though, as Hopkins noted, he "might change his mind again."[46]

While the Americans and British wrestled at Quadrant over plans for Overlord, the invasion of Italy, and operations in the Pacific, sketchy reports were coming in concerning a titanic land battle in Russia. Those gathered in Quebec couldn't have appreciated its significance at the time, but the Red Army inflicted a decisive defeat on the Wehrmacht in what became known as the Battle of the Kursk Salient (or the Bulge), a battle that enabled the Soviets to recapture western Russia and eventually invade the German homeland.

Kursk was the largest single battle in the history of warfare. Ranging over an area the size of the United Kingdom, 2 million men and thousands of tanks and aircraft fought for fifty days. The German losses were appalling: half a million men killed, wounded, missing, or taken prisoner. Soviet casualties were even greater. Stalingrad may have been the turning point, but most German officers on the eastern front believed that after Kursk Germany simply could not win the war militarily. In the midst of the Kursk struggle, Hitler learned that Anglo-American troops had invaded Sicily and would no doubt move into southern Italy, and he ordered the withdrawal of II SS Panzer Corps from the Kursk salient and sent it to Italy.[47] Stalin would never admit it, but Churchill's Mediterranean strategy—at least the part that involved Italy—was starting to pay dividends.

Hopkins was particularly sensitive to the fact that the Soviet Union would be the decisive factor in defeating the Axis powers and thus would occupy a dominant position in postwar Europe. Two days before the Quadrant conference, Hopkins, as chair of the President's Soviet Protocol Committee, prepared a "very high level" strategic estimate (for U.S. eyes only) arguing that the Soviet Union "must be given every assistance and every effort must be made to obtain her friendship." To draw the Soviets into a closer and more trusting relationship, the paper recommended that the United States should distance itself from the United Kingdom (and implicitly from Churchill's imperialistic policies). In addition it suggested that Ambassador Standley be replaced by a civilian ambassador to the USSR, someone "who advocates the policy of the 'good neighbor and sincere friend.'"[48]

■ Scrappy and tenacious, Harry Hopkins, sometimes called "Dirty Harry," starred on Grinnell's basketball teams. In 1912 he was elected permanent class president, the only elective office he ever held.

Courtesy of June Hopkins.

■ "Very eager and young . . . and full of the desire to help," Hopkins began his career as a social worker at Christadora House, a settlement house on the Lower East Side of Manhattan that sought to improve the lives of impoverished immigrants in the neighborhood.

Courtesy of Robert Hopkins Papers at Georgetown University Library Special Collections Research Center.

■ Ethel Gross, a Hungarian-born cosmopolitan woman involved in the women's suffrage movement, met Hopkins at Christadora House on Manhattan's Lower East Side, where Hopkins ran clubs and recreational programs for the poor boys living in the surrounding tenements. The two social reformers were married in 1913.
Courtesy of June Hopkins.

■ During World War I and its aftermath, Hopkins led Red Cross units in the Deep South, working with the U.S. Army to provide relief to servicemen's families and assistance to victims of floods, earthquakes, and the flu epidemic. Courtesy of Robert Hopkins Papers at Georgetown University Library Special Collections Research Center.

Hopkins in his early thirties with two of his three sons: David (left), born 1914, and Robert, born 1921. A third son, Stephen, was born in 1925. Courtesy of Robert Hopkins Papers at Georgetown University Library Special Collections Research Center.

Hopkins and Barbara Duncan, his second wife, returning to New York after a trip to Europe in the summer of 1934. Hopkins fell in love with Barbara in 1926, when she was working as a secretary at the New York Tuberculosis and Health Association, which he headed. Courtesy of Franklin D. Roosevelt Library.

Hopkins speaking at a WPA State Administrators luncheon, Mayflower Hotel, Washington, D.C., June 1935. Florence Kerr (at left, holding a glass of water) was a classmate of Hopkins's at Grinnell who he recruited to supervise women's projects at the WPA; Eleanor Roosevelt (to the right of Hopkins) was Hopkins's close friend and supporter during his New Deal days; and Ellen Woodward (far right) was assistant administrator of the Women's Division of the WPA. This group worked to make sure unemployed women received their fair share of WPA jobs. Courtesy of June Hopkins.

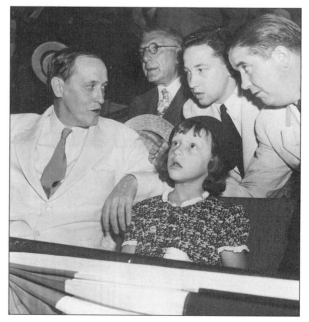

Hopkins at the 1940 Democratic National Convention in Chicago with his daughter, Diana, age seven. From left to right behind them: John Hertz, founder of the Hertz car rental empire and a close friend of Hopkins; David, Hopkins's twenty-eight-year-old son; and Edwin Lahey, *Chicago Daily News*. Using very sharp elbows, Hopkins managed the third-term "draft" of Roosevelt to become the party's nominee. Courtesy of Franklin D. Roosevelt Library.

■ Prime Minister Winston Churchill greeting Hopkins outside No. 10 Downing Street on January 10, 1941, when Hopkins arrived as President Roosevelt's personal representative to assess Churchill and convey the sense that America would support the British as they fought alone against Germany. Of that meeting Churchill wrote, "Thus I met Harry Hopkins, that extraordinary man, who played, and was to play, a sometimes decisive part in the whole movement of the war." Courtesy of Burling Library Archives, Grinnell College.

■ By mid-January 1941 Hopkins had already established an easy friendship with Churchill when they boarded a destroyer in the bitter cold and gale winds that would take them to Scapa Flow in the north of Scotland, home to the British fleet. Churchill, aware of FDR's interest in naval warfare, wanted Hopkins to see Britain's newest battleship, *King George V*. Courtesy of Diana Hopkins Halsted.

Hopkins, Clementine Churchill, Winston Churchill, and the mayor of Southampton cheerfully inspecting bomb damage, January 31, 1941. Clementine took a motherly interest in Hopkins because, whether inside or outside, he was always suffering from the cold, damp British winter. Courtesy of Diana Hopkins Halsted.

Hopkins and Joseph Stalin posing in the Kremlin for *Life* magazine's photographer Margaret Bourke-White following Hopkins's courageous flight to the Soviet Union in late July 1941. As Hitler's armies drove toward Moscow, Hopkins assured Stalin that Roosevelt was determined to extend all possible aid to the Soviet Union. Courtesy of Time & Life Pictures, licensed by Getty Images.

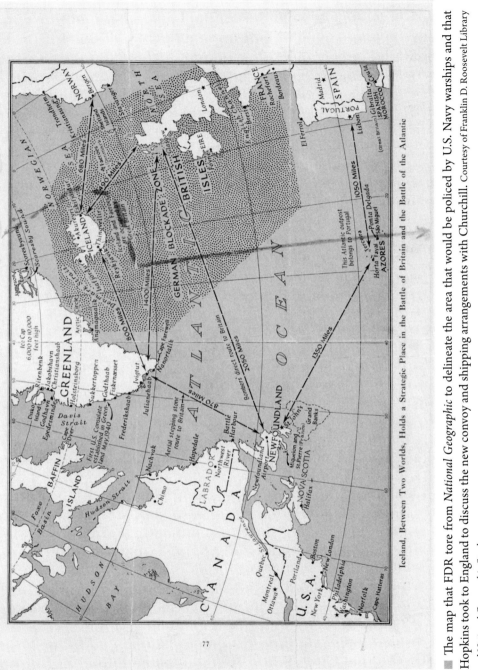

Iceland, Between Two Worlds, Holds a Strategic Place in the Battle of Britain and the Battle of the Atlantic

■ The map that FDR tore from *National Geographic* to delineate the area that would be policed by U.S. Navy warships and that Hopkins took to England to discuss the new convoy and shipping arrangements with Churchill. Courtesy of Franklin D. Roosevelt Library and National Geographic Stock.

Under the fourteen-inch guns of the British battleship *Prince of Wales* in August 1941, Churchill, Hopkins, and British officers discuss the forthcoming meetings with President Roosevelt off the coast of Newfoundland in what became known as the Atlantic Conference. Courtesy of Franklin D. Roosevelt Library.

Hopkins standing behind Roosevelt during the carefully orchestrated religious services aboard the *Prince of Wales* on Sunday morning, August 10, 1941. It was the emotional apex of the Atlantic Conference, Roosevelt's first wartime meeting with Churchill. Courtesy of Franklin D. Roosevelt Library.

Churchill showing off his blue zippered siren suit outside the White House during his Christmas 1941 visit several days after the United States entered the war. Hopkins's daughter, Diana, is holding the leash of Roosevelt's beloved Scottish terrier, Fala, At this conference, codenamed Arcadia, Hopkins (at left) helped Roosevelt and Churchill line up the coalition of nations that would fight the Axis powers. Photograph by Thomas D. McAvoy. Courtesy of Time & Life Pictures, licensed by Getty Images.

Hopkins conferring with Roosevelt in the Oval Study, June 1942. Courtesy of Franklin D. Roosevelt Library.

With the president as best man, Hopkins marries Louise Macy, former Paris editor of *Harper's Bazaar*, on the second floor of the White House. The couple would live in the two-room Lincoln suite until late 1943. Courtesy of Diana Hopkins Halsted.

■ At the Casablanca conference, Roosevelt's sons Elliott (left) and Franklin Jr. (center) relax over lunch with Hopkins (second from left) and an unidentified U.S. officer in January 1943. Roosevelt is still wearing a black armband honoring the death of his mother, Sara Delano. Courtesy of Robert Hopkins Papers at Georgetown University Library Special Collections Research Center.

■ Robert Hopkins, a U.S. Army combat photographer, chatting with his father outside the president's villa in Casablanca. Hopkins arranged for his son to be recalled from the front in Tunisia to serve as an official photographer at the conference. Courtesy of Robert Hopkins Papers at Georgetown University Library Special Collections Research Center.

After visiting American troops in Rabat, Morocco, Hopkins, General Mark Clark (second from left), Roosevelt, and General George Patton (right) discuss the North Africa campaign during a lunch in the field. Courtesy of Franklin D. Roosevelt Library.

Roosevelt celebrating his sixty-first birthday in the roomy cabin of his Boeing Clipper with Admiral Leahy (left), Hopkins, and Captain Howard Cone, the Clipper commander (right). They were on the final leg of their return from the Casablanca conference. Courtesy of Franklin D. Roosevelt Library.

■ At the Tehran conference outside the Soviet Embassy, December 1943, left to right: General George Marshall shaking hands with Britain's ambassador to the Soviet Union, Archibald Clark Kerr, Hopkins, V. N. Pavlov (Stalin's interpreter), Joseph Stalin, and Vyacheslav Molotov (with mustache). It was at this conference that Roosevelt leaned over and said, "Dear Harry, what would we do without you?" Courtesy of Franklin D. Roosevelt Library.

Stephen Peter Hopkins
Age 18

"Your son, my lord, has paid a soldier's debt:
He only liv'd but till he was a man;
The which no sooner had his prowess confirm'd
In the unshrinking station where he fought,
But like a man he died."

Shakespeare.

To Harry Hopkins from Winston S. Churchill
13 February, 1944.

Winston Churchill

■ Churchill sent this parchment scroll to Hopkins a few days after Hopkins learned that his youngest son, Stephen, a private in the Marine Corps, was killed in action at Kwajalein Island in the Pacific. Courtesy of Robert Hopkins Papers at Georgetown University Library Special Collections Research Center.

In their own home, 3340 N Street, Georgetown, 1944. Suzy (the poodle), Diana, Louise, and Hopkins. Photograph by Louise Dahl-Wolfe. Posthumous digital reproduction from original negative. Courtesy of Louise Dahl-Wolfe Archive, Center for Creative Photography. © Arizona Board of Regents.

Roosevelt in lend-lease jeep greeting Hopkins, with Molotov standing to the left of Hopkins, upon arrival at Saki airfield for the Yalta conference, January 1945. Courtesy of Robert Hopkins Papers at Georgetown Library Special Collections Research Center.

At the conference table, Yalta, January 1945. Right to left: Roosevelt, Hopkins, Edward Stettinius, secretary of state, and Admiral William Leahy. Far left: Stalin.
Courtesy of SSPL collection, Daily Herald Archive, licensed by Getty Images.

Ill and exhausted on the night the Yalta conference ended, Hopkins lies in bed aboard an old wooden rail carriage that once belonged to the Romanovs. Courtesy of Robert Hopkins Papers at Georgetown Library Special Collections Research Center.

▓ Aboard the cruiser *Quincy* that would take the presidential party back to the United States from the Yalta conference, Hopkins confers with the president and Ed Stettinius, secretary of state. This is one of the last, if not the last, photograph of Hopkins and Roosevelt together. Too sick to continue the voyage home, Hopkins disembarked at Algiers on February 18, 1945, leaving Roosevelt to continue without him. The two would never see one another again. Courtesy of Robert Hopkins Papers at Georgetown Library Special Collections Research Center.

▓ Louise "Louie" Hopkins charmed the Soviet officers as she and Hopkins toured Berlin on their way back from Moscow in June 1945. They "smelled the odor of death," wrote Chip Bohlen, and "inspected the bunker where Hitler committed suicide." Courtesy of Franklin D. Roosevelt Library.

■ Hopkins in Moscow, late June 1941. Photograph by Margaret Bourke-White. Courtesy of Time & Life Pictures, licensed by Getty Images.

■ Hopkins at home in Georgetown, 1944. Photograph by Louise Dahl-Wolfe. Posthumous digital reproduction from original negative. Courtesy of Louise Dahl-Wolfe Archive, Center for Creative Photography. © Arizona Board of Regents.

With Roosevelt's blessing, Hopkins's candidate was Averell Harriman. During a break from the conference on August 20, Hopkins spent an afternoon fishing with Harriman on Lac de l'Épaule, not far from Quebec City. As they cast for small trout from a rowboat, the two old friends spoke of personal matters and batted around the pros and cons of Harriman's leaving London and taking on the Moscow ambassadorship. Harriman agreed with Hopkins that establishing a relationship of friendship and trust was vitally important not only for stability in postwar Europe but also because it would hasten the entry of the Soviet Union into the war against Japan. Several days later, after Harriman had returned to Washington and conferred with the president, he agreed to become the new ambassador to the Soviet Union. He and his daughter Kathleen would arrive in Moscow on October 18.[49]

Emboldened by the victory at Kursk, Stalin began to exploit his leverage over his Western allies, which he had started to do after Stalingrad. From Quadrant, Roosevelt and Churchill had sent a message to Stalin proposing that he meet with the two of them in Alaska.[50] In response Stalin belittled the Anglo-American military strategy, claiming—falsely—that Hitler had not "withdrawn a single division" but instead has continued to "transport fresh divisions" to the eastern front. Consequently, wrote Stalin, he could not "leave the front for so distant a point as Fairbanks." As an interim step that would lead to a Big Three summit late that year, he suggested that the foreign ministers of the three nations meet.[51] Roosevelt and Churchill promptly acquiesced.[52]

On the last day of the conference, Stalin sent a particularly harsh cable to the president and the prime minister. Suspecting that the British and Americans were deliberately keeping the Soviets out of the loop on the surrender terms being discussed with the new Italian government, thus treating his government as a mere "passive third [party] observer," Stalin warned, "I have to tell you that it is impossible to tolerate such [a] situation any longer."[53] Since Roosevelt and Churchill had sought to keep Stalin apprised of the surrender talks with the Italians, they were surprised and offended by the tone of his message. Roosevelt made a point of saying "We are both mad" as he entered the dining room to join Churchill and their guests for dinner on August 24. Hopkins's reaction is not recorded, but according to

Harriman's notes, the president's "anger took the form of making him gayer than usual, both before and after dinner," while the prime minister "arrived with a scowl and never really got out of his ill humor all evening—up to 3 a.m." Earlier that evening, after Roosevelt and Hopkins had departed the Citadel to return by train to Washington, Churchill told Harriman that he expected "bloody consequences" from the Soviets. "Stalin is an unnatural man," he growled. "There will be grave troubles."[54]

Hopkins arrived back in Washington in a state of complete exhaustion. Instead of returning to the White House, he checked into the new Bethesda Naval Hospital (opened in 1942) for the usual treatment: blood transfusions, vitamin injections, and rest. He later joked that the combination of Churchill and Quebec was "too much for him," but it was more than that. He was again brought down by his body's inability to absorb nutrients. This was no doubt aggravated by consecutive days and nights at Quadrant involving the consumption of far too much alcohol, coffee, and rich food and the smoking of countless cartons of cigarettes. While in the hospital Hopkins was annoyed to read a malicious feature article about himself in the *Chicago Daily Tribune*. Written by Walter Trohan—the same journalist who would later break the news on FDR's declining health—the piece analogized Hopkins to Grigori Rasputin and suggested that Hopkins, the spender "of other people's money," had cast a spell over Roosevelt and his family, just as Rasputin had captured the mind of Czar Nicholas and his family and "went on to sway Russia by the power of his eye." Accompanied by a large cartoon showing a leering Hopkins with a wild-haired Rasputin at his shoulder, the article implied that Hopkins was using the war to impose upon America a tax-and-spend government.[55] "Can't you dig up some bright young men in your [law] office who will tell me that these bastards can be sued for libel?" Hopkins wrote to Joe Davies.[56] He knew the answer before he wrote the letter. As a public figure he would find it difficult and very costly to win a libel suit. He dropped the idea.[57]

The doctors treating Hopkins recommended three months' rest; in less than two weeks he would be back on the job, claiming, "All those boys at the front are fighting & getting hurt & dying. I have a job to do here, & I'm going to do it."[58] Churchill, along with Clementine, had returned from Quebec and was again living in the White House. According to Alexander Cadogan of the British Foreign Office, Churchill spent "a large part of the day hurling himself violently in and out of bed, bathing at unsuitable moments and rushing up and down corridors in his dressing gown."[59] The president, dead tired and needing a break from the prime minister, departed to recuperate at Hyde Park, leaving Hopkins to fill in for him. Two days later, on the morning of September 11, Hopkins rose from his bed in the naval hospital to participate in a meeting of the CCS that Churchill convened in the state dining room of the White House. The meeting consisted of a review of the strategic situation in light of the Italian surrender and a plea by Churchill for a more rapid buildup of forces in Italy, even if it meant borrowing from resources dedicated to Overlord. Marshall assured the prime minister that everything possible was being done but made no suggestion that assets earmarked for Overlord would be diverted.[60]

As Hopkins was preparing to move from the hospital back into the White House, Winston and Clementine Churchill were celebrating their thirty-fifth wedding anniversary with the Roosevelts at Hyde Park. After supper the president drove them in his blue Ford Phaeton down the hill to the railroad siding, where they would depart for Quebec and the transatlantic crossing. "God bless you," said Churchill to FDR as he mounted the steps to his special rail coach. "I'll be over with you, next spring," called Roosevelt. He was referring to his plan to join Churchill in England around the time of Overlord.[61]

Recalling Hopkins's doubts about Churchill's conversion, Roosevelt knew it was going to be difficult in the coming months to hold the prime minister and his military chiefs to their apparent commitment to launch Overlord by "next spring." However, Churchill's agreement that Marshall would command Overlord was FDR's best assurance that the cross-Channel invasion would proceed as scheduled. Backed by Hopkins and Stimson, Roosevelt was convinced that Marshall was the only American general who could stand up to the arguments of Churchill and his cohorts that Overlord should be delayed in order to save lives and exploit opportunities in the Adriatic, the Aegean, and the Balkans.

As a result of rumors and leaks that were further distorted by the anti-Roosevelt press, the plan to announce the appointment of Marshall as commander of Overlord and to recall Eisenhower to Washington to become acting chief of staff was derailed. In September items appeared in two armed forces journals, reporting darkly that "powerful influences" would like to remove Marshall as chief of staff and kick him "upstairs" and that the command of forces in Europe would not be a promotion but simply a way to remove him from Washington. The views of General Arnold and Admiral King, who believed it was imperative that Marshall remain in Washington as chief of staff, may have prompted these stories. One editorial laid the blame at Hopkins's feet, claiming, "It is understood that Harry Hopkins prefers Lt. General Brehon B. Somervell [over Marshall as chief of staff]." Somervell was a controversial general whose effort to reorganize the Army's supply and administrative services was opposed by several officers who were probably among the leakers. He had been promoted to lieutenant general before many more senior officers, and this hadn't gone over well with a number of them. Reporters were quick to point out that before the war Somervell had worked for Hopkins as head of the WPA in New York City.

Once the name of Hopkins, the White House Rasputin, was thrown into the mix, a firestorm of conspiracy theories and anti-Semitism erupted. On the House floor, Republican Paul Shafer of Michigan, among others, charged that the Russian-loving Hopkins, backed by a "'sinister' clique" consisting of three Jews—Felix Frankfurter, Sam Rosenman, and David Niles (by then a White House political advisor)—was engineering a "New Deal plot" to get rid of Marshall and "use the war emergency as a means of communizing America."[62] Headlines and editorials stoked the fires. Marshall, whose wife was moving furniture out of the chief of staff's residence at Fort Myer in anticipation of what she thought would be her husband's assignment to command Overlord, said nothing until he heard about a Nazi propaganda broadcast in early October, announcing that he had been dismissed as chief of staff and that the president himself had taken over his command. Knowing Hopkins would appreciate one of his rare attempts at humor, Marshall sent a transcript of the broadcast along with a handwritten note to Hopkins, saying, "Dear Harry: Are you responsible for pulling this fast one on me? G.C.M." Hopkins showed the note to Roosevelt, who wrote in pencil at the bottom: "Dear George:—Only true in part. I am Chief of Staff *but* you are President. FDR."[63]

The attacks on Hopkins blew over. However, the criticism that command of Overlord would amount to a demotion for Marshall needed to be addressed. In an October 4, 1943, memorandum to Roosevelt, Hopkins laid out a case for appointing Marshall as commander "of all the allied forces, other than the Russian, attacking the Fortress of Germany." To "satisfy the British," he argued, "someone like Montgomery" could be placed in command of Operation Overlord, but sound military principles dictated that "a single commander"—that is, Marshall—have "command over the whole business." Hopkins concluded by telling the president, "There is a good chance of getting Churchill to agree to this."[64]

Hopkins was wrong. When Churchill was informed by Roosevelt of the plan to appoint Marshall as overall commander in Europe, he flatly refused.[65] Churchill's reason, according to Sherwood, was "his indefatigable determination to play his own strategic hand in the Eastern Mediterranean, the area that was now dearer to his heart than ever."[66] Roosevelt and Hopkins were stymied. The decision concerning who would command Overlord was put on hold.

In light of the Red Army's decisive victories at Stalingrad and Kursk, Stalin's stature as a world figure was immeasurably strengthened. He was finally ready to parley with Roosevelt and Churchill at a meeting of what would be called "the Big Three." On September 8 Stalin cabled that he could meet with the two of them, preferably in Tehran, in late November.[67] Over the next two months, Roosevelt and Churchill skirmished with Stalin over the place of the meeting, suggesting Cairo, Beirut, Asmara, Basra, Baghdad, or ships in the eastern Mediterranean.[68] Roosevelt argued that the distance between Tehran and Washington would present constitutional problems for him because bills passed by Congress automatically become law unless vetoed and returned within ten days. Stalin countered that he needed to be in constant communication with his commanders at the front; he claimed that more than five hundred divisions were fighting. He neglected to mention, however, that he was terrified of flying. And he ignored the fact that long-distance travel was much more difficult for the disabled president. At last, after Stalin said he would send Molotov in his place if Roosevelt insisted on meeting somewhere other than Tehran, FDR gave in.[69] The Army and Navy would have to figure out a way for him to meet the ten-day requirement.

Stalin's main goals at Tehran would be to get an ironclad assurance that U.S. and British forces would actually invade western France in the spring of 1944 and that the planning and buildup for the invasion were moving forward under a designated commander. He was convinced, however, that Churchill would again try to delay the invasion. He therefore made a point of letting Roosevelt know in advance of the conference that he and his colleagues had lost confidence in Churchill. In early October Ambassador Oumansky told Joe Davies (who Stalin and Oumansky knew was very close to FDR) that the Soviet leaders believed Churchill "was not concerned with beating Hitler in the most direct way, so much as he was in directing a political offensive which would enable Britain to dominate the Balkans and all of Europe in British interest."[70]

Hopkins too was losing confidence in Churchill's commitment to the cross-Channel invasion. His suspicions about the prime minister's motives were greatly intensified during the month of October. The first episode involved what Brooke called the "Rhodes madness."[71] In an operation conceived by Churchill to take advantage of the Italian surrender, a limited number of British troops were poised to take control of Italian garrisons on the Dodecanese islands in the Aegean Sea, including the island of Rhodes. However, the Germans beat them to the punch and occupied the islands. On October 7, when Roosevelt was out of town, Hopkins was on the receiving end of a cable followed by telephone calls from Churchill, frantically requesting the diversion of troops and landing craft otherwise committed to the Overlord buildup in order to dislodge the Germans from Rhodes. Hopkins told Churchill that his request would be rejected by Roosevelt and Marshall, which it promptly was.[72] Marshall later recalled telling Churchill, "God forbid if I should try to dictate, but not one American soldier is going to die on that goddamned island."[73] "The whole thing is sheer madness," wrote Brooke in his diary of Churchill's obsession with Rhodes. "The Americans are already desperately suspicious of him [Churchill], and this will make matters far worse."[74]

Later in October, when it seemed clear that the Big Three meeting would take place somewhere in the Middle East, Churchill confirmed the Americans' suspicions. On October 23 he cabled Roosevelt, begging him to meet with him—out of the presence of the Soviets and before they went on to meet Stalin—in order to arrive at an agreed position on "future Anglo-American operations." The cable was extraordinarily revealing. In it the prime minister stated that the decisions made at Quadrant in August "were open to very grave defects" and he essentially argued for a complete reexamination of whether Overlord should go forward as planned in May 1944. With the agreed date (November 1) for withdrawing seven divisions from Italy and sending them to Britain for Overlord only a week away, the British wanted to renege.[75] Hopkins, Stimson, and Marshall certainly did not desire the president to be exposed to another conference where Churchill and his British chiefs would reopen decisions concerning Overlord and the Italian campaign. And they did not want to give Stalin the impression that Roosevelt and Churchill were meeting in advance to conspire against him and the Soviets. It was decided, therefore, that Roosevelt would convene a conference in Cairo with Churchill and the combined chiefs before they went on to Tehran to meet with Stalin, but that invitations would also be extended to Molotov and General Chiang Kai-shek. (China had just signed the Four-Power Declaration of Moscow, thus conferring on China recognition as a major power.)

Churchill, of course, did not want Molotov—or any Russian—to be present while he was trying to persuade Roosevelt and the combined chiefs to delay Overlord, so he came up with a devious solution. He took it upon himself to invite Stalin to Cairo, making sure in his cable that Stalin knew that a Chinese military delegation, headed by Chiang, would also be there.[76] Churchill's ploy worked. Stalin refused to let Molotov attend. Unlike China, the Soviet Union was not at war with Japan. Stalin could not risk giving Japan a pretext to declare war on the USSR.

While Churchill was able to clear away one obstacle to his desire to get at Roosevelt one-on-one in Cairo, he did not anticipate another large roadblock that Roosevelt and Hopkins had thrown in his path: the presence of Chiang Kai-shek. By inviting Chiang, his glamorous and influential wife, and several Chinese generals, Roosevelt would be able to eat up much of the time at Cairo on issues involving China and the Far East, leaving little time for Churchill to practice his prodigious powers of persuasion on the president before leaving to meet Stalin.[77]

A few days before departing on the battleship *Iowa* for Cairo (to be followed by a flight to Tehran), Roosevelt, Hopkins, and the joint chiefs of staff met at Shangri-La for a final briefing. The president assured them that he would firmly resist attempts by Churchill and Brooke to delay Overlord. In response to a joint chiefs memo opposing involvement in the Balkans, FDR simply said, "Amen." Regarding his meetings with Chiang, the president said he wanted those meetings to "precede" any meetings with the British, presumably so he could stretch out sessions with Chiang and limit his time alone with Churchill.[78]

Reflecting on this last meeting stateside and expressing his concern about Roosevelt's tendency to depart from the script, Stimson wrote Hopkins a bon voyage letter of support and advice: "So the one prayer I make for the Commander-in-Chief is steadfastness—a very difficult virtue but one more needed than any other in this particular problem." He also told Hopkins that in his view, "Marshall's command of Overlord is imperative for its success."[79]

As Hopkins prepared to board the sparkling new 58,000-ton *Iowa* at Hampton Roads on Friday morning, November 12, he felt confident that this time the British would not succeed in postponing the assault on Fortress Europe. Since the summer of 1942 the balance of power had shifted decisively to the Soviet Union and the United States. By almost every measure—industrial production, troop strength, armaments, aircraft—both separately and together the Soviets and Americans dwarfed the power and political clout of not just the United Kingdom but the entire British Commonwealth. As long as the president fulfilled Stimson's wish and remained steadfast at Cairo, U.S.

strategy would prevail. Beyond Cairo, Hopkins was particularly keen about meeting Stalin again. Based on his constant dealings with Russians in Washington, Moscow, and elsewhere on lend-lease matters and his sessions with Davies, he was convinced that in order to forestall future conflict the Soviets needed to be respectfully treated as equal partners in winning the war and making the peace.[80] Hopkins believed that Roosevelt would try to follow that line in his talks with Stalin—he had exerted great effort in making sure such was the case—but that there would be trouble when it came to Stalin's aim to control territory in Eastern Europe as a buffer against the West, an objective that Hopkins felt could not realistically be denied.

"The whole world is watching for this meeting between the three of us," wrote Roosevelt to Stalin.[81] Demanding and difficult as it would be on his constitution, Hopkins couldn't wait to get there. He knew he had to guard against hubris, but he felt empowered by the opening of a slight separation in his relationship with the president. The new distance enabled him to view FDR more objectively, giving him space to function as more than an alter ego. In addition he was energized by his conviction that he more than anyone understood the shifting personal and strategic dynamics among the Big Three. With enhanced perspective and renewed vitality, Hopkins believed he was ready to step into his own and make a real contribution to the preservation of the shaky three-part coalition. He was convinced that this would be the most decisive and consequential of all the war meetings and that to be a part of it was to be a part of history itself. They were deciding not simply on the conduct of the war, but on the shape of the postwar world.

The president delayed the start of the transatlantic trip, invoking the old sailor's superstition about beginning a voyage on a Friday. The *Iowa* weighed anchor at six minutes after midnight on Saturday, November 13, and stood out to sea.

Tilting toward the Russians

Protected by two escort carriers (known as "baby flattops") and a screen of destroyers, the *Iowa*, bristling with 157 guns of her own, plowed eastward across the Atlantic at a cruising speed of twenty-five knots. Her human cargo, bound for the conferences at Cairo and Tehran, consisted of the president and his entourage. In addition to Hopkins, this included Pa Watson, Doc McIntire, George Fox (masseur), and Arthur Prettyman (valet); the U.S. Joint Chiefs of Staff, Marshall, King, Arnold, and Leahy; and more than one hundred military planners, strategists, commanders, and logistics experts. Notably not a single senior official from the State Department was aboard.

On the first evening at sea, Saturday, November 13, Roosevelt, Hopkins, Watson, and Leahy dined in the flag mess with the *Iowa*'s skipper, Captain John McCrea, the close friend of both Hopkins and the president and the man who had set up and managed the White House map room. With a mischievous glint in his eye Hopkins cajoled genial Pa Watson into betting five dollars that he, Hopkins, couldn't catch a fish from the deck of the massive battleship. Later that night, while FDR's party was watching a movie, Hopkins appeared with four fish and a mess boy who testified to his prowess with rod and reel. The president threw back his head and roared with laughter.[1]

On Sunday afternoon, just after lunch, Hopkins was with Roosevelt when he was wheeled outside his quarters to observe anti-aircraft exercises. As Lieutenant William Rigdon, the president's log keeper, explained, "Live ammunition was fired from a number of units of the ship's anti-aircraft battery (5-inch, 40 mm. and 20 mm. guns) to demonstrate for the Commander-in-Chief what a veritable curtain of fire a ship of this type can offer as a 'greeting' for enemy planes bent on attacking." Suddenly the great battleship swerved into the first of several zigzags and a sailor shouted over the ship's loudspeaker, "Torpedo defense! This is not a drill."[2] An officer on the bridge two decks above Hopkins and Roosevelt leaned over and shouted down, "It's the real thing! It's the real thing!" A torpedo had been fired at the *Iowa* and was streaking toward the dreadnought at forty-six knots. According to his notes, Hopkins asked FDR whether he wanted to go inside. "No—where is it?" asked the president, who called for Arthur Prettyman to take him to the starboard rail. Hopkins and the president watched as "everything fired at once at the wake of a torpedo six hundred yards away—the firing lasted about thirty seconds. The wake went well astern."[3] Shock waves from an underwater explosion hammered the *Iowa*'s hull.

All of the *Iowa*'s guns were immediately trained on the source of the torpedo; it turned out not to be a German U-boat but the U.S. destroyer *William D. Porter*, which was supposed to be protecting the big battleship. As part of a simulated attack, two crew members below decks on the star-crossed destroyer—thereafter nicknamed the *Willie Dee*—had accidentally fired an armed torpedo directly at the *Iowa*. Had officers on the *Willie Dee* not broken radio silence and warned the *Iowa* in time for it to take evasive action, the battleship, with the entire wartime leadership of the United States aboard, would have taken a direct hit. "Can you imagine," wrote Hopkins, "our own escort torpedoing an American battleship—the newest and biggest—with the President of the United States aboard—along with the Chief of Staff of the Army and the Chief of Naval Operations[?]" Relishing the interservice ribbing that would likely take place for years, Hopkins wrote, "In view of the fact that there were twenty Army officers aboard, I doubt if the Navy will ever hear the last of it."[4] Later he remarked that whoever launched the torpedo "must have been some damned Republican."[5] Admiral King, furious, placed the captain and entire crew of the *Willie Dee* under arrest, the first time in Navy history that this had happened. Following an inquiry in Bermuda, the captain and several officers were sentenced to shore duty and one of the torpedomen was sentenced to hard labor, although Roosevelt intervened and commuted his sentence. The *Willie Dee* resurrected herself in several Pacific battles, finally falling victim to a fatal kamikaze attack off Okinawa in June 1945.

The remainder of the week-long Atlantic crossing passed without incident, giving the president, Hopkins, and the joint chiefs plenty of time to plan for their meetings with Chiang and Churchill in Cairo and the Big Three conference with Stalin in Tehran. During these planning sessions, which took place in the admiral's cabin, Roosevelt, always with Hopkins at his elbow, provided for the first time a glimpse of his vision of the significance of China to the United States in the postwar world. "Fifty years hence," he predicted, China would serve as a counterweight to the British and other European powers in Asia, a check against Soviet ambitions in the region, and a bulwark against a resurgent Japan. In FDR's view, China should be admitted as an equal participant with the three other powers in postwar decision making.[6] He stressed, therefore, the importance of courting the generalissimo, his wife, and his entourage in Cairo not for China's military contributions to the war in the Pacific but to align China's interests with those of the United States for years to come.[7] With the objective of keeping China on his side, Roosevelt was already thinking about how to handle its postwar demands for Japanese and USSR territories and the desire of the United States for permanent military bases in the Pacific (e.g., Taiwan).[8]

Anticipating victory over Germany after Overlord, and possibly even an early collapse of the Third Reich, the president envisioned an occupation force of one million U.S. troops that would stay "for at least one year, maybe two."[9] Handed a map of Germany, he penciled in three proposed "occupation zones": an American in northwestern Germany as far east as the

Berlin-Stettin line; a Soviet east of that line; and a British to the south and west of the American zone.[10] "There would definitely be a race for Berlin," said the president, although it was not clear whether it would be against the Russians, the British, or both. Hopkins, in one of his rare comments for the record, suggested that the United States "be ready to put an airborne division into Berlin two hours after the collapse of Germany."[11]

Regarding postwar relations with the USSR, the president told Doc McIntire, "[Stalin] must be tired of sitting on bayonets, just as he must realize that the war is bound to break down his iron curtain, letting his millions see the higher living standards of other peoples." (Assuming McIntire's recall is accurate, this would be the first time since World War I that anyone used the term *iron curtain* in this way.)[12] Supremely confident that he could handle anyone, even Stalin, the president added, "If I can convince him that our offer of cooperation is on the square, and that we want to be comrades rather than enemies, I'm betting that he'll come in."[13]

Hopkins was skeptical but said nothing. He was of the view that Stalin responded to actions, not words; an "offer of cooperation" or a desire "to be comrades" would mean nothing to him.[14] Stalin could be moved only when U.S. troops waded ashore in western France and when the supply convoys arrived at Murmansk on schedule.

While Hopkins, aboard the *Iowa*, was approaching the straits of Gibraltar, his son Robert was in Italy, where American and British fighters under the overall command of General Eisenhower were stalled in the rain, mud, and mid-November cold just south of the sixth-century abbey fortress of Monte Cassino. Robert was filming a meeting between Major General Lucien Truscott of the U.S. 3rd Division and Major General G. W. R. Templer of the British 56th Division.[15] "We mustn't kid ourselves," said Truscott, scanning the German positions commanding the mountains to the north. "There's still a lot of fight left in the old son of a bitch."[16] On November 17 Robert crossed over to the American sector east of Roccamonfina to have his exposed film sent to the War Department. At Fifth Army headquarters in Caserta, he was informed by his commanding officer that he was to proceed immediately to Naples, where he would be given priority air passage across the Mediterranean to Tunis. He was issued new cameras and told to take enough film to last for a month. No one explained why he was being sent to Tunis, but Robert knew: "Dad was coming with the President."[17] Robert had again been summoned to serve as official photographer. He was waiting in Eisenhower's villa in Carthage (near Tunis), aptly named "Casa Blanca," when his father, "looking exhausted and not at all well," arrived with Eisenhower and the presidential party on the afternoon of November 20.[18] Joined by his two sons, Franklin Jr. and Elliott, the president and Hopkins had flown to Tunis from Oran, Algeria, on the Barbary Coast, where the *Iowa* was anchored in the great harbor.

The main purpose of the stopover in Carthage was to give Roosevelt an opportunity to size up Eisenhower. At the time, the president was inclined to appoint Marshall as commander of Overlord and to ask Eisenhower to return to Washington to succeed him as chief of staff. However, if Roosevelt was persuaded by the joint chiefs or others to keep Marshall in Washington, he would hand Overlord to Eisenhower. Either way, Roosevelt, who had met Eisenhower only briefly on two prior occasions, needed to take a close look at the man. As it turned out, the president's departure to Cairo was postponed until the following evening, so there was ample time for both FDR and Hopkins to get to know Eisenhower. Acting as tour guide, Eisenhower, with his luminous grin, sunny personality, and obvious intelligence, impressed Roosevelt. The two of them spent hours together in the back seat of a Cadillac while his driver, Kay Summersby (FDR put on the charm, calling her "Child"), led a squadron of jeeps containing Hopkins, his son, and others across battlefields both recent and ancient. The group stopped for a lunch of chicken sandwiches and deviled eggs among eucalyptus trees on the north bank of the Medjerda River, in the same valley where Robert and his unit had been overrun and driven back by the Germans in January. By this time Roosevelt and Eisenhower were hitting it off, Roosevelt calling him "Ike" and putting his hand on his arm, and Eisenhower, accustomed to dealing with military superiors and important politicians, instinctively knowing how to put his commander in chief at ease. When Telek, the male Scottie that Eisenhower shared with Summersby, jumped onto Roosevelt's lap, Eisenhower said, "I guess I think as much of him, Mr. President, as you do of Fala."[19]

Throughout the day, Eisenhower captivated Roosevelt, Hopkins, and everyone else within hearing distance with his command of military strategy and battlefield tactics; he was equally adept at lucidly summarizing the maneuvers of Hannibal in the Second Punic War and the recent winter battles at Medjez-el-Bab and Tébourba.[20] The question that hung in the air, however, was whether Eisenhower would be sent back to Washington to replace Marshall. At one point, Eisenhower's friend and aide Captain Harry Butcher lobbied Hopkins, arguing that Marshall was needed in Washington because of his "remarkable acumen and diplomacy" in dealing with Congress. He also told Hopkins that it would take Marshall six months to get the "feel" of commanding a mix of American and British ground, air, and sea forces, whereas Eisenhower had already learned through trial and error.[21]

In the back seat of the Cadillac, when he could see that Eisenhower was comfortable, the president leaned over and, according to Sherwood, addressed the issue. "Ike, you and I know who was the Chief of Staff during the last years of the Civil War but practically no one else knows. . . . I hate to think that 50 years from now practically nobody will know who George Marshall was. That is one of the reasons why I want George to have the big Command—he is entitled to establish his place in history as a great General."[22] This quote indicates that the president was inclined to give the Overlord command to Marshall, whereas Eisenhower came away with the opposite impression. In *Crusade in Europe*, published in 1948, the same year Sherwood's book was published, Eisenhower wrote that FDR told him it "was dangerous to monkey with a winning team," meaning he was leaning toward giving him the Overlord command and keeping Marshall in Washington as chief of staff.[23] From this distance, it is likely that Eisenhower's account is more authoritative because he was there; Sherwood, who must have based his account on what Hopkins or possibly someone else told him, was not. Or perhaps Eisenhower heard what he wanted to hear, a phenomenon experienced by countless others in the presence of Roosevelt.

After an all-night flight from Tunis, the Sacred Cow landed at Cairo West Airport on the morning of November 22. The president, Hopkins, Admiral Leahy, and Major John Boettiger, FDR's son-in-law, were driven to the

Kirk Villa, a spacious residence owned by Alexander Kirk, the American ambassador to Egypt, where they would stay for the duration of the Cairo conference. Situated in Giza, about seven miles west of Cairo and on the grounds of the Mena House Hotel, the villa had an unobstructed view of the pyramids and the Sphinx. Robert Hopkins, who had flown in another C-54 with the Secret Service detail, settled into a small house near the Kirk Villa.[24] The British delegation, including Churchill and his daughter Sarah, was distributed in villas along the road to Cairo. The accommodations were luxurious and the food and drink abundant. However, the stench of burning camel dung fouled the air. Flying and crawling insects were everywhere.[25]

According to Roosevelt's plan, the relatively brief Cairo conference was to be dominated by military and political matters involving China and the Far East, leaving little time for Churchill to meet with the president alone. It was the Chinese, mainly the blood of Chiang's Nationalists, who were holding down half of Japan's fighting strength, sustaining casualties second only to those of the Soviets. It was vitally important, therefore, to keep China fighting, although, as Churchill lamented in his memoirs, the talks at Cairo with the Chinese were "lengthy, complicated and minor."[26] The prime minister was perhaps correct that little was accomplished militarily, but he was wrong concerning political matters. As the historian Keith Sainsbury observed, "The political discussions at Cairo had profound implications for the future."[27]

The most significant of these discussions occurred during a three-hour dinner at Kirk Villa for Madame and Generalissimo Chiang on the evening of November 23. Churchill was not invited. Other than the president, Hopkins was the only American present. It was at this dinner that the president, though he found Chiang to be "grasping, weak and indecisive,"[28] made expansive postwar promises designed to keep Chiang's troops in the war and to ensure a long-term friendship between China and the United States, promises that had obviously been carefully shaped beforehand with Hopkins. According to notes of the meeting translated from Chinese into English (there is no official U.S. record), Roosevelt assured Chiang that China would be a permanent member of the Big Four in what was destined to become the United Nations after the war. China's territories in the north—Manchuria, Taiwan, and the Pescadores islands—which had been taken by the Japanese, would be restored, and the Ryukyu islands south of the Japanese mainland would be placed under a U.S.-China trusteeship. U.S. economic aid to China after the war would be given "close and practical consideration."[29]

Based on advice expressed in a paper prepared by Hopkins, the president flattered Chiang by telling him that the Soviets regarded him as the best person to lead China to stability.[30] He also told him that the Americans would support China at the talks in Tehran against Soviet territorial claims, particularly in Manchuria, provided Chiang promulgated democratic reforms that would allow the Communists a voice in governance. For his part, Chiang backed off his earlier agreement to a joint Soviet-Chinese-American trusteeship of Korea because he feared a Soviet foothold in the peninsula. Instead he advocated independence for Korea. Roosevelt agreed.[31]

Churchill's desire to get at Roosevelt one-on-one in Cairo was for the most part stymied. However, at a meeting of the Combined Chiefs of Staff with Roosevelt and Churchill on November 24, Hopkins looked on with deepening alarm and then anger as the prime minister dominated the discussion with depressing observations about the stalemate in Italy, missed opportunities in the Aegean, and what he regarded as harmful diversions of troops and landing craft from the Mediterranean to Great Britain (needed for the Overlord buildup). As always Churchill gave lip service to Overlord as a priority but was once again weaving an elaborate argument for postponement.[32]

Hopkins was ever mindful of the need to preserve Allied unity, and he still had a deep reservoir of affection for the prime minister. His patience, however, was wearing thin. Later that day he made a point of stopping by to see Lord Moran, who he knew would pass on what he said to Churchill. As Moran wrote in his diary, Hopkins was "full of sneers and jibes," complaining that "Winston hardly stopped talking and most of it was about his 'bloody Italian war.'" "Harry made it clear," continued Moran, "that if the P.M. takes this line at Teheran and tries again to postpone Overlord the Americans will support the Russians." Moran quoted Hopkins's exact words, which he said were delivered in a fierce and threatening tone: "Sure, we are preparing for a battle at Teheran. You will find us lining up with the Russians."[33]

The highlight of the Cairo conference was Thanksgiving dinner on November 25. "Let us make it a family affair," decreed the president.[34] And so it was. The fifteen guests included Roosevelt's son Elliott and son-in-law John Boettiger; Churchill and his daughter Sarah; Hopkins and his son Robert; and Pa Watson, a loveable uncle to all of them. "We had several cocktails before dinner, then went in and there was champagne," wrote Boettiger to his wife, Anna. "Harry had arranged an army band to play in the balcony of the drawing room."[35] The president wore a dinner jacket with black tie, and the prime minister arrived in his blue zippered siren suit.[36] Hopkins's wrinkled dark suit and oversized collar hung from his gaunt frame, but his eyes were alive, taking in the splendor of the occasion. "Two enormous turkeys were brought in with all ceremony," recalled Churchill. "The President, propped up high in his chair, carved for all with masterful, indefatigable skill."[37] In a toast to Churchill, Roosevelt told of the history of Thanksgiving and added, "Our American soldiers are now spreading the custom all over the world."[38] Responding with a toast that Robert Hopkins described as a "masterpiece of eloquence and drama," the prime minster thanked the president for his "warm and intimate friendship" and concluded by saying, "In these crucial times, you, Sir, are President of the United States and a great defender of the right."[39]

"It was Dad," wrote Robert, "who broke the dinner up when he found that some of the members of the party were talking business."[40] They retired to the drawing room for singing and dancing. Robert and most of the other men danced with Sarah Churchill Oliver, the only woman in the party. "She had her work cut out," said Churchill, "and so I danced with 'Pa' Watson, Roosevelt's trusted old friend and aide, to the delight of his chief who watched us from the sofa."[41] One of the guests, Bill Rigdon, said Roosevelt's laughter "was enough to wake the Pharaohs."[42]

Two days later the Sacred Cow winged east toward Iran, crossing the Suez and circling low over Jerusalem so that the president and Hopkins could spot some of the landmarks in the ancient city. After flying over the Syrian desert and the green valleys of the Tigris and Euphrates, the pilot followed the highway that ran north from Abadan to Tehran. Hopkins was pleased to see truck convoys on the highway and trains on the Trans-Iranian Railroad (sometimes running parallel to the highway) full of lend-lease supplies bound from Basra and other ports on the Persian Gulf into the USSR.[43] Harriman, seated beside Hopkins on the six-and-a-half-hour flight, had earlier orchestrated an American takeover of the railroad. (Harriman Brothers & Company, which he cofounded with his brother, owned the Union-Pacific Railroad, which their father had run.) He spent a good deal of time bending Hopkins's ear about providing economic assistance to the Soviet Union after the war to help restore its economy.

Because of security concerns, the Sacred Cow was not met by a welcoming party when it landed at Gale Morghe Airport outside Tehran. The president and his party, including Hopkins, were immediately taken in Army limousines to the American Legation, which was a considerable distance from the Soviet Embassy and British Legation. (Only two walls and a narrow road separated the Soviets from the British.) The president had earlier politely declined an invitation from the young shah of Iran to stay in one of his palaces.[44]

Stalin had arrived the day before. Escorted by twenty-seven fighter aircraft, the Soviet leader had flown in from Baku in an SI-47 with Lavrenti Beria, head of the NKVD, and one of the most feared men in the USSR. It was the first time Stalin had ever flown. Throughout the flight he had been terrified, especially when the plane hit air pockets. Compared with Roosevelt and Churchill, Stalin came to Tehran with a tiny delegation. Marshal Kliment Voroshilov, a vain, fun-loving former cavalryman, was the only ranking military officer in his party. The others in his group included Foreign Minister Molotov; Beria and his son Sergio, responsible for security and bugging Roosevelt's quarters; Stalin's physician; and a personal bodyguard of twelve Georgians.[45]

Late Saturday night, after finishing an intimate dinner with Roosevelt and Hopkins at the American Legation, Harriman was summoned to the Soviet Embassy. There he was met by Molotov, who told him that Nazi intelligence agents were aware that Roosevelt, Churchill, and Stalin were in Tehran and that assassination attempts were being planned. To thwart any such attempts, Molotov urged Roosevelt and his party to move into buildings in the Soviet Embassy compound. Harriman was skeptical but alerted Mike Reilly, head of the Secret Service, and General Donald Connolly, commander of the Persian Gulf Service Command. After midnight the three of them were given a tour of the rooms in a building on Soviet Embassy grounds set aside for the president. "The next morning we went up to the [American] Legation," recalled Harriman, "and talked to Hopkins." Hopkins and Roosevelt's other aides were suspicious concerning the motives of the Russians and the truth of their claims. There was also disagreement as to whether the American delegation should move into the Soviet Embassy and possibly alienate Churchill and the British.

Notwithstanding the reservations of Hopkins and others, the president welcomed the excuse to move into the Soviet compound—according to Harriman he was "delighted with the prospect"[46]—because his strategy all along had been to build a personal relationship with Stalin. He wanted to engage Stalin without Churchill in order to convince him that he had not conspired with Churchill to gang up on him at the conference table. As Hopkins confided to Lord Moran, "[Roosevelt] has come to Teheran determined ... to come to terms with Stalin, and he is not going to allow anything to interfere with that purpose. . . . After all, [he] had spent his life managing men."[47] On Sunday afternoon Beria was at the gates of the Soviet Embassy when Roosevelt and Hopkins arrived with Reilly and his Secret Service men riding on the running boards of the president's limousine, brandishing tommy guns. Jeeps loaded with American soldiers and the president's Filipino mess boys were also admitted into the walled compound.[48] The guards around the American Legation remained in place throughout the conference to maintain the illusion that FDR was still there.[49]

It has since been learned that Heinrich Himmler's SS, having discovered that the Big Three planned to meet in Tehran, did in fact organize an assassination attempt. Called "Operation Long Pounce," it involved SS officer Otto Skorzeny, who was already a Nazi hero for having snatched Mussolini from his Allied captors. Skorzeny had selected and trained an assassination team in German-occupied Ukraine. After Himmler received the go-ahead from Hitler, a group of Skorzeny's commandos landed by parachute near the city of Qom and made their way to Tehran. From a secret flat on the outskirts of Tehran, their radio signals were intercepted and decrypted by Soviet intelligence agents. All but six of the commandos were captured, and the assassination plot was called off by handlers in Berlin. The remaining six fled and hid among Bedouins in the mountains but were eventually tracked down and executed by Soviet troops.[50]

It was "a beautiful Iranian Sunday afternoon, gold and blue, mild and sunny," wrote Charles "Chip" Bohlen, the young Russian-speaking State Department officer who would serve as interpreter for the Americans.[51] To the dismay of Churchill, the first meeting between Roosevelt and Stalin was about to take place and he was not invited. All morning Churchill had pressed Roosevelt for a meeting so that the two of them could agree beforehand on the military strategy they would present to Stalin at the first plenary session of the conference. Roosevelt refused. He wanted to see Stalin before the plenary session and he wanted to see him alone, except, of course for the two interpreters, Bohlen and V. N. Pavlov.[52]

At a little after 3 p.m. Stalin, clad in his simple mustard-colored tunic and red striped trousers, with the Order of Lenin on his chest, strode "clumsily, like a small bear," across the compound to Roosevelt's white-columned villa. He was ushered into a sitting room decorated with "Tsarist gilt and Communist red stars," where he found the president seated in his wheelchair wearing a blue business suit. Hopkins and Harriman hovered outside in the hall as the doors to the sitting room were closed.[53] Inside, the two leaders shook hands, Roosevelt saying through the interpreters, "I am glad to see you. I have tried for a long time to bring this about." His pockmarked face registering pleasure, Stalin accepted blame for the delay, explaining that he was overly "occupied with military matters."[54] At first they engaged in small talk, taking the measure of one another. Roosevelt pointed to a framed photograph of Stalin on the wall and said he desired to have a photograph of the three leaders together. Stalin inquired whether the president was comfortable in his quarters and if he could be of service. FDR offered Stalin an American cigarette. They spoke of how doctors were telling them to cut back on smoking and "the benefits of fresh air."[55]

The president then turned to substance. "How was the situation on the Soviet battlefront?" he inquired. "Not too good," replied Stalin through his interpreter. Taking an implicit shot at the Anglo-American strategy in the Mediterranean and the failure to open a second front in France, Stalin said the Germans had "moved a new group of divisions" into Ukraine. Picking up on his point, Roosevelt said that drawing away "30 or 40 German divisions from the Eastern Front" was one of the main subjects to be discussed at the forthcoming conference.[56] Neither Roosevelt nor Stalin knew it at the time, but Hitler had already decided to move divisions from east to west. On November 3 he issued Führer Directive No. 51, which ordered a reinforcement of defenses in Western Europe because, he said, "all signs point[ed] to an offensive against the Western Front of Europe no later than spring, and perhaps earlier." Pursuant to Directive No. 51, Hitler sent General Rommel, a master of mobile warfare, to strengthen the Atlantic Wall. "To the snug staffs of the coastal sectors," wrote his biographer Desmond Young, Rommel "blew in like an icy and unwelcome wind off the North Sea."[57]

During the remaining half hour of their get-acquainted session, Roosevelt sought to ingratiate himself with Stalin and to distance himself from the British. He broached the subject of independence for India, suggesting that the two of them discuss a solution—"reform from the bottom, somewhat along the Soviet line"—at a later time after the war and recommending that the matter not be brought up at the conference in the presence of Churchill. He offered the possibility that after the war some portion of the "American-British merchant fleet" could be made available to the Soviet Union (although there is no evidence that he discussed this beforehand with the British). And he told Stalin that he disagreed with Churchill's opinion that France must be "quickly reconstructed as a strong nation."[58]

At a few minutes before 4 p.m. the Big Three and their aides began to assemble in a spacious hall in the Soviet Embassy. The first plenary session was about to begin. When Stalin entered, he spotted Hopkins in the crowd across the room. Instead of waiting for Hopkins to approach him, which was his habit, Stalin took the initiative and "walked over to greet him warmly." As Harriman, a keen observer of Stalin, recalled, "Stalin showed Hopkins a degree of personal consideration which I had never seen him show anyone else except Roosevelt and Churchill." Stalin "had not forgotten," said Harriman, that Hopkins, despite his ill health, had made the "exhausting and hazardous journey" to Moscow in the summer of 1941 to help the besieged Russian people. "It was an example of courage and determination that impressed Stalin deeply."[59]

Hopkins took his place to the left of Bohlen (who, as interpreter, was at FDR's immediate left) at the round conference table with a green baize cover. They were seated in large striped silk armchairs. The windows were curtained and the walls were covered with heavy tapestries. Soviet secret police stood guard around the room. Churchill's bodyguard of Sikhs and Roosevelt's Secret Service men were outside in the courtyard. The president opened on a light note, saying that "as the youngest of the three (he was sixty-one), he ventured to welcome his elders." With a nod to Stalin (age sixty-four) and his aides, Roosevelt welcomed the "new members of the family circle." Churchill (age sixty-eight) eloquently pointed out that this was the "greatest concentration of power the world ha[d] ever seen" and that the three of them "held in their hands the happy future of mankind."[60] Stalin, the host, made a few introductory remarks to his guests. "Now let us get down to business," he declared.[61]

Roosevelt began with a general survey of the war, concentrating first on the Pacific. Early on, Stalin gave FDR and the other Americans what they most wanted. Once Germany was defeated, he told them, the Soviets would be able to send troops to Siberia: "Then we shall by our common front be able to beat Japan."[62] This highly important concession by Stalin, which Hopkins reported was "made in a casual way and without raising his voice,"[63] may have been a negotiating ploy, designed to put the Americans in his debt from the very outset of the conference.

Turning to the war effort in the west, both Roosevelt and Churchill stressed the overall importance of Overlord. However, Churchill held forth at length on proposed operations into northern Italy and the eastern Mediterranean, noting that for these operations to successfully draw German troops away from the eastern front it might be necessary to delay Overlord by two or three months. The prime minister asked for Stalin's views. Before Stalin could answer, Roosevelt interjected, saying he was thinking about an operation in the northeast Adriatic, leading to a drive into Romania and a junction with the Red Army.[64] It is entirely possible that he did this for effect—to show some sympathy for Churchill before Stalin, with the president's acquiescence, slammed the door on any delay of Overlord. However, if it was for effect, Hopkins either did not pick it up or he played Roosevelt's game. Looking around the table he could see that the other Americans were flabbergasted by Roosevelt's remark, which sounded like a fundamental departure from his solemn commitment to Overlord. Hopkins scribbled a note to Admiral King: "Who's promoting that Adriatic business that the president continually returns to?" King replied, "As far as I know it is his own idea."[65] The notes were carefully preserved.

Predictably Stalin threw cold water on the diversionary schemes of Churchill and the Adriatic venture suggested by Roosevelt. In a barely audible voice, his eyes downcast, he insisted that Overlord, which in his view was the best way of assaulting Germany, should be "the basis for all 1944 operations." Any operations that did not directly support Overlord should not be undertaken. In this vein, he argued that after Rome was captured, troops in Italy should be sent to southern France to support the Overlord invasion that would be landing in northwestern France. It was not wise strategy, he said, to scatter forces all over the Mediterranean. As he waited for the interpreter to translate, Stalin calmly smoked and doodled on a notepad. His strategic pronouncements should have been music to General Marshall's ears, a vindication of everything he had been advocating since Pearl Harbor. Ironically, however, Marshall was not present. Having been told that there would be no plenary session that afternoon, he and General Arnold were touring the city of Tehran and could not be reached when the president changed his mind and summoned the joint chiefs to the four o'clock meeting.[66]

That evening the president hosted a steak and baked potato dinner for Stalin, Churchill, and their foreign ministers. Before dinner Hopkins watched intently for a reaction as Stalin sipped one of FDR's famous martinis—heavy on the vermouth, light on the gin, stirred in a pitcher of ice. "Well, it's all right," he pronounced, wincing, "but cold on the stomach."[67] The talk at dinner ranged over the future of France, the treatment of Germany after the war, and the wisdom of the unconditional surrender policy. Roosevelt was about to respond to a point involving access to the Baltic Sea, "when suddenly, in the flick of an eye," recorded Bohlen, "he turned green and great drops of sweat began to bead off his face." Hopkins, gravely concerned and suspecting the president might have been poisoned, stepped forward and accompanied Roosevelt as he was wheeled to his room. To everyone's relief, Hopkins returned later and said the president merely suffered an attack of mild indigestion and had decided to retire for the night.[68]

While Hopkins and the others remained, Churchill raised the question of Poland's postwar boundaries, stressing that Britain had gone to war over Poland and wanted it to be restored as a strong, independent state. Using matches to illustrate, the prime minister said he "would like to see Poland moved westward in the same manner as soldiers at drill execute the drill 'left close.'" In essence he was suggesting that much of new Poland be carved out of Germany and that the Soviet Union could annex all of the Polish lands up to the World War I-era Curzon Line, roughly the same territory that the Red Army seized in 1939. Stalin favored moving Poland's western boundary to the River Oder but was otherwise noncommittal, saying it would be "a good idea to reach an understanding" but that he needed "to look into the matter further."[69]

Monday, November 29, was to be an important day for Stalin, and it got off to a good start. At the marshal's daily 8 a.m. briefing by Sergio Beria, who had eavesdropped on the previous day's conversations of Roosevelt, Hopkins, and the other Americans living in the Soviet compound, he learned that in private "Roosevelt always expressed a high opinion" of him.[70] Stalin was pleased, although he must have realized that Roosevelt and his people were aware that they were being bugged. After lunch the president, having rebuffed Churchill's second request for a private meeting, welcomed Stalin's visit to his quarters. According to the notes of the visit, FDR explained to the Russian leader that he wished to "talk over informally" an important matter "relating to the future of the world." He then produced a rough handwritten sketch of a world peacekeeping organization, the forerunner to today's United Nations. As outlined in his sketch, Roosevelt envisioned a general assembly, a security council, and a third entity, "The Four Policemen"—consisting of the United States, the USSR, Great Britain, and China—that would be empowered to "deal immediately with any threat to the peace." Stalin was dubious, particularly with regard to the inclusion of China as one of the policemen, but he seemed intensely interested and did not reject the president's proposals out of hand.[71] There is no conclusive evidence that Hopkins influenced Roosevelt's thinking on how the UN would be structured. It is likely, however, that the two of them discussed this matter sometime during the morning before the president met with Stalin, when the president had nothing on his schedule.[72] Virtually every important observer commented that Hopkins was at the pinnacle of his influence at Tehran and that, with Roosevelt's approval, he functioned as de facto secretary of state.

At about three o'clock on Monday afternoon, Robert Hopkins was admitted into the ballroom of the Soviet Embassy to set up his cameras. During the next half hour, the Soviet, British, and American delegations assembled. Through the crowd Robert could see his father. Honor guards representing the three powers marched in, the British infantry with fixed bayonets, the Soviet troops in blue uniforms with slung tommy guns. A Russian military band played the three national anthems as Churchill, Stalin, and Roosevelt entered the great hall. Robert began taking motion pictures and still photos.[73] A British officer handed Churchill a crusader sword with a thirty-six-inch blade in a scarlet and gold scabbard. Turning to address Stalin, Churchill, in full voice, said he had been commanded by the king to present this sword of honor, the blade bearing the inscription: "To the steel-hearted citizens of Stalingrad, a gift from King George VI as a token of the homage of the British people."

Stalin accepted the "Sword of Stalingrad," held it for a moment with reverence, and then raised it to his lips. In a husky voice and with tears in his eyes, he expressed his appreciation on behalf of the citizens of Stalingrad. He walked over to Roosevelt, seated in his wheelchair, and invited him to inspect the sword. Then he clumsily handed the sheathed sword to Voroshilov, who accidentally let the scabbard slip off and crash to the floor. Stalin shot a grim-looking smile at his hapless general. The sword was the inspiration for Evelyn Waugh's *Sword of Honour* trilogy and is displayed today in the Museum of the Defense of Stalingrad.[74]

In his diary Robert recorded his first impressions of Stalin, noting that when he entered the crowded hall, "everyone in the room was immediately aware of his presence. It was almost as if someone had switched on a light as he entered." Robert was "amazed" at Stalin's "extremely short" stature (no "taller than 5'5") and completely gray hair and mustache. "There could be no doubt that this little man was a veritable leader of men."[75] Along with about twenty photographers, Robert went outside to take still photos of the three leaders, with Roosevelt seated in the middle. To his mother, Robert wrote that he "got the only 'straight' picture of the three. That is, the only picture in which they are all serious."[76] His father stood behind the three, almost out of the frame.

Stalin was the commanding figure at the second plenary session that convened a few minutes later in the large conference room. Again Hopkins was seated to the left of Bohlen. The meeting had hardly begun when Stalin asked, "Who will command Overlord?" Roosevelt replied that it had not yet been decided. Then, as if he was instructing one of his generals in the principles of warfare, Stalin noted gruffly that "nothing" would come of Overlord unless "one man was made responsible" for both its preparation and execution. Roosevelt leaned toward Admiral Leahy and whispered, as Leahy recalled, "That old Bolshevik is trying to force me to give him the name of our Supreme Commander. I just can't tell him because I have not yet made up my mind."[77]

Stalin pressed for a firm date to launch Overlord sometime during the month of May 1944; he "did not care whether it was the 1st, 15th or 20th, but that a definite date was important." Churchill resisted committing to a firm date, speaking at length of "great possibilities in the Mediterranean" that would warrant a delay in Overlord. Stalin, doodling wolf heads with a red pencil, looked up. "I would like to ask Mr. Churchill an indiscreet question," he said. "Do the British really believe in Overlord or are they only saying so to reassure the Russians?" Offended, Churchill refused to give him a straight answer. He replied that *if* the "conditions" were right, "it was the duty of the British Government to hurl every scrap of strength across the channel."[78] Later Hopkins scoffed at Churchill's prevarication, telling Lord Moran, "Sure, there was no God-damn alternative left."[79]

That evening Stalin hosted a banquet in the typical Russian style, with "an unbelievable amount of food" and "rivers of vodka and wine."[80] Throughout the evening he "overlooked no opportunity to needle Churchill," Bohlen noted at the time.[81] Hopkins felt sympathy for his old friend when Stalin suggested that the prime minister was "nursing some secret affection for the Germans" and "desired to see a soft peace."[82] Coming from a man who had cynically cut a deal with Hitler only four years before, when England stood alone, these were tough words to swallow. The president made no effort to relieve Churchill's evident discomfort at being the object of Stalin's sarcasm. "I did not like the attitude of the President, who not only backed Stalin but seemed to enjoy the Churchill-Stalin exchanges," wrote Bohlen, who later served as ambassador to the Soviet Union during the Eisenhower administration.[83]

With a view to shifting the focus away from Churchill, Hopkins rose and offered a toast to the Red Army. Stalin responded by recounting how the Red Army "had become steadily better" since its pathetic performance in the winter war against Finland. However, instead of staying on that subject, he threw out a proposal for the postwar treatment of Germany that he must have known would incense Churchill. "At least 50,000 and perhaps 100,000" German officers must be shot, he said, "with a sardonic smile and a wave of his hand."[84]

If this was meant to be a joke, Churchill was not amused. He was furious, declaring, "Such an attitude is contrary to the British sense of justice. The British Parliament and people will never tolerate mass executions. . . . The Soviets must be under no delusion on this point."[85] The president sensed that Stalin was not serious and tried to defuse the tension with a lame effort at humor. Saying it was his "function to mediate" disputes at the conference, Roosevelt proposed a compromise: only 49,000 German officers should be shot.[86] The moment might have passed had not Elliott Roosevelt, deep into the vodka and champagne, stood up and asked whether the 50,000 wouldn't "fall in battle anyway?" He then announced his agreement with Stalin's plan and said he was sure the "United States Army would support it." Stalin responded, "To your health, Elliott," and clinked his glass against his.[87]

Churchill had had enough. He rose from the table and stalked into an adjoining room. Within seconds, recalled Churchill, "hands were clapped upon [his] shoulders from behind and there was Stalin, with Molotov at his side, both grinning broadly and eagerly declaring that they were only playing": "Stalin has a very captivating manner when he chooses to use it, and I never saw him do so to such an extent as at this moment."[88] Assuaged, Churchill returned to the dinner, which ended on an ominous note. Responding to the prime minister's attempt to draw him out on the Soviet Union's postwar territorial aims, Stalin, who drank sparingly and rarely let down his guard, said, "There is no need to speak at the present time about any Soviet desires, but when the time comes, we will speak."[89]

After midnight Hopkins walked over to the British Legation to visit with Churchill alone. It was time to deliver a tough message, a message that only Hopkins could effectively deliver, given his close friendship with the prime minister. He could see that Churchill was tired and depressed. Gently and with utmost tact, he explained that the Americans and Soviets were adamant about launching Overlord in May and that the prime minister was "fighting a losing battle" in trying to postpone the inevitable. "Yield with grace," he urged.[90] The late-night visit might have been instigated by Roosevelt, but there is no evidence that such was the case. In any event, it apparently did the trick. Before falling asleep that night, Churchill indicated to Lord Moran that he had given up the fight. As Moran wrote in his diary, quoting Churchill's words to him that night, "Stupendous issues are unfolding before our eyes, and we are only specks of dust, that have settled in the night on the map of the world. . . . I fancy sometimes that I am nearly spent."[91]

The following morning, November 30, Churchill officially agreed to an unconditional recommendation by the CCS that Overlord be launched "during May," along with a supporting operation in southern France. Just before lunch Stalin was informed that Churchill and Roosevelt were in agreement. The long argument over strategy to defeat Nazi Germany had ended. At lunch with Roosevelt and Churchill, Stalin, who had been pushing for an invasion of western France for two years, "expressed his great satisfaction." To forestall a shift of several German divisions to the west, he pledged that the Red Army would initiate a series of offensives in the east in coordination with Overlord.[92]

While the Big Three were having lunch, Hopkins, filling in for the absent secretary of state, was over at the British Legation with Foreign Secretary Eden and Foreign Minister Molotov. At this luncheon meeting, the purpose of which was to discuss the political implications of the entry of Turkey into the war on the side of the Allies, Hopkins made a point that he would stress later at the final meeting of the Big Three at Tehran. Should Turkey come into the war, it might very well require "large" military commitments by the British and Americans in the Aegean, which would delay Overlord. Before meeting with the Turkish president, he cautioned, they should have a clear understanding concerning the limit of military assistance they could offer.[93] Hopkins's advice, which he wrote out in longhand for insertion in the minutes, was intended for Churchill. He wanted to make absolutely sure that in discussions with the Turks Churchill not make promises that would delay Overlord by a single day. As Sherwood noted, this was another instance when Hopkins earned the title "Lord Root of the Matter."[94]

"The table was set with British elegance," wrote Bohlen. He was recalling the evening of November 30, a celebration of Churchill's sixty-ninth birthday at the British Legation, the "high-water mark of Anglo-American-Soviet collaboration during the war."[95] Dressed in black tie, Hopkins sat with Eden and Molotov directly across the candlelit table from Churchill, Roosevelt, and Stalin. The dining room resembled "a Persian temple," recalled Brooke, with "Persian waiters in blue and red livery." Turbaned Sikhs guarded the doors.[96] Hopkins introduced his son to Stalin. "His face lit up with a smile," wrote Robert in his diary. Looking down at Robert's "leggins'" (which he had to wear because his pants were too long), Stalin said, "I am glad to see that you are a fighting man."[97]

For the most part the toasts were warm and witty, although Stalin could not "resist a jab at Churchill," recalled Bohlen. After referring to the president and the prime minister as "my fighting friends," he added with a smile and a twinkle in his eye, "If it is possible for me to consider Mr. Churchill as my friend."[98] Unlike the previous evening, Churchill did not take the bait. He proclaimed that the Soviet leader "was worthy to stand with the great figures of Russian history and merited the title, 'Stalin the Great.'" With a nod to the growth of Communism, Churchill remarked that the "complexions" of the British people were "becoming a trifle pinker," to which Stalin quickly responded, "That is a sign of good health!"[99] Carrying on the theme, Churchill, in good humor, lifted his glass to Stalin: "I drink to the proletarian masses." Stalin shot back, "I drink to the Conservative Party." Still standing, Churchill invoked the Almighty, declaring, "I believe God is on our side. At least I have done my best to make him a faithful ally." "And the devil is on my side," countered Stalin. "Everyone knows the devil is a Communist—and God, no doubt, is a good Conservative."[100]

According to Harriman, Hopkins made one of the wittiest after-dinner speeches he had ever heard, "in tribute to Churchill." The speech was never transcribed and was recalled only in part. Hopkins rose and announced that after making "a long and thorough study of the British Constitution, which is unwritten, and of the War Cabinet, whose authority and composition are not specifically defined, he had made a great discovery. The provisions of the British Constitution and the powers of the War Cabinet are just whatever Winston Churchill wants them to be at any given moment."[101] With just a few words Hopkins captured the greatness of the man and at the same time gently poked fun at him. Churchill took the barbed point with grace and laughed heartily along with everyone else.

The dessert, a massive tower of ice cream over a bed of ice, was held aloft on a salver by a Persian waiter who advanced toward Stalin in the midst of one of his toasts. For dramatic effect in the darkened room, a light had been inserted in the middle of the creation. As Stalin was speaking, the waiter moved behind him. Brooke looked on in horror as the tower of ice cream began tilting precariously, having been melted by the lamp, and yelled "Duck!" as the "whole wonderful construction" slid off and immersed Stalin's interpreter "from his head to his feet."[102] In a loud whisper, Air Marshal Sir Charles Portal, head of the Royal Air Force, quipped, "Missed the target."[103] The interpreter "carried on manfully," while Brooke sent for towels "to mop him down."[104]

Churchill raised his glass for the concluding toast, but Stalin asked for the privilege of making one more. It was a stirring tribute to the productivity of American industry and it was also an implied expression of gratitude for Hopkins's efforts. "The United States . . . is a country of machines," said Stalin. "Without the use of those machines, through Lend-Lease, we would lose this war."[105] It was perhaps at this point that Roosevelt caught Hopkins's eye across the table and paid him a rare personal compliment, recalled by Bohlen: "Dear Harry, what would we do without you?"[106]

The president ended the evening on a lofty note. "We have proved here at Teheran that . . . our nations can come together . . . for the common good of ourselves and of the world. So as we leave this historic gathering, we can see in the sky, for the first time, that traditional symbol of hope, the rainbow."[107]

After dinner Hopkins and Robert talked until 2 a.m.; it was their first opportunity to spend more than a few minutes together. "Dad told me about what he had done to contribute to the war effort," wrote Robert in his diary. His father was especially proud that "his 'baby,' the Lend-Lease, had done its bit toward winning the war."[108] When Robert rather naïvely questioned why the United States, a democracy, was helping the Soviet dictatorship, his father replied, "We're helping them because they are holding down 95 Nazi divisions."[109]

During the last day of the Tehran conference, Hopkins, for no apparent reason, was not there when Roosevelt, in the presence of Harriman and Molotov, in effect gave the green light to Stalin to install Soviet puppet governments in Poland and the Baltic states. In this tête-à-tête the president told Stalin that he personally agreed with his views on the governance of the Polish state and the movement of its borders to the west. However, because he might run for a fourth term in 1944 and did not want to lose the Polish vote, he did not intend to participate in open discussions on this subject. As to the Baltic states, Roosevelt, with a smile, told the marshal that that he did not intend to go to war with the Soviets when they annexed those three republics, but he asked Stalin, again because of his own electoral concerns, to make a statement concerning future elections in the Baltics. Stalin demurred, replying vaguely, "There will be plenty of opportunities for such an expression of the will of the people."[110]

The final plenary session at Tehran involving the Big Three was held at 6 p.m. on December 1. Hopkins was there, along with the foreign ministers of Great Britain and the Soviet Union. Roosevelt brought up Poland—not its boundaries but the "reestablishment" of relations with the Polish government-in-exile in London. Expressing doubt that the London Poles were capable of leading the Polish people, Stalin said he "was prepared to negotiate with them" but only if they "would go along with the partisans" (i.e., the Communists) and sever connections with German agents in Poland. Stalin's doubts and conditions were a portent of widening disagreements that would bedevil Hopkins during his final weeks in government and would lead to the cold war. On the question of Poland's boundaries, Roosevelt and Hopkins sat passively as Churchill opened the discussion, declaring that the "British Government wished to see a Poland strong and friendly to Russia."[111] Then, using a map supplied by Bohlen, Churchill and Stalin "virtually agreed on the future borders of Poland."[112] By remaining silent, Roosevelt and Hopkins effectively conveyed the acquiescence of the United States. As Eden later pointed out, their silence "was hardly calculated to restrain the Russians."[113]

The next morning, as they prepared to depart Tehran for Cairo, Hopkins, Leahy, and Bohlen were sitting in a jeep at the airport waiting for the president. Bohlen, who felt Roosevelt and Hopkins should have taken a more aggressive stance with Stalin and Molotov on Poland and the Baltic states, was expressing pessimism about future relations with the Soviets. As Bohlen recalled, "Admiral Leahy, who was in the front seat, turned his head and said to Hopkins with a sardonic smile, 'Well, Harry, all I can say is, nice friends we have now.'"[114]

Hopkins and the president returned to the Kirk Villa outside Cairo for what became known as "the Second Cairo Conference." For three hectic days Hopkins was thrown into wall-to-wall meetings with Ismet Inönü, the president of Turkey, and Numan Menemencioğlu, the Turkish foreign minister, over whether Turkey would immediately enter the war (it would not) and with the CCS on whether to cancel planned amphibious landings in Burma because of resource constraints (they were cancelled and Hopkins drafted the letter informing Chiang).[115]

But the big question—who would command Overlord?—needed to be resolved. The president had promised Stalin at Tehran that he would make the decision and let him know in a few days. Sometime on Saturday, December 4, Roosevelt called Hopkins to his villa to reveal his thinking. Having weighed the pros and cons of appointing Marshall to the command and having sized up Eisenhower, the president had changed his mind. Now he was inclined to keep Marshall in Washington to help him direct the war and to appoint Eisenhower to command Overlord. Hopkins made an impassioned case for giving the command to Marshall. Roosevelt was sympathetic. Both Hopkins and the president knew that Marshall desperately wanted the command. However, as the president explained to Hopkins, he was convinced by the advice of the joint chiefs, members of Congress, and General John Pershing, commander of American troops in Europe during World War I and senior statesman of the American military, that Marshall was indispensable in Washington and that the Overlord command would be seen as a demotion to a single theater of the war. He had tried to address this perception by having Marshall assume command of all forces in Europe, as proposed by Hopkins, but Churchill and the British chiefs vehemently objected.[116]

That evening, just before dinner, Hopkins arrived at Marshall's quarters. As Marshall later recalled, Hopkins told him "that the president was in some concern of mind over [his] appointment as Supreme Commander." Marshall, who had every reason to assume he would get the command, must have been crestfallen. He knew that if Roosevelt had decided to give him the nod, he would have come himself. By sending Hopkins, Marshall suspected, FDR had decided not to give him the command and was trying to find out how he would react. Or perhaps the president was hoping Marshall himself would rescue him from the unpleasant task of telling him that it was going to be Ike.

Hopkins was embarrassed to be put in this position. A great admirer of Marshall, he believed the chief of staff both deserved the command and was the right man for the job. Yet he also knew, as did Roosevelt, that Marshall would never come right out and ask for it. Rather than have a frank exchange, Hopkins had been instructed by Roosevelt not to reveal his probable decision but only to ascertain Marshall's state of mind so that

Roosevelt could calibrate his next move. In his conversation with Marshall, Hopkins probably adhered to the letter of these instructions while elaborating on the considerations that the president was weighing. Marshall refused to take Roosevelt off the hook. "I merely endeavored to make it clear that I would go along wholeheartedly with whatever decision the President made," recalled Marshall "He need have no fears regarding my personal reaction."[117]

The next day around lunchtime the president summoned Marshall to his villa. "After a great deal of beating about the bush," wrote Marshall, "he asked me . . . just what I wanted to do. Evidently it was left up to me." Marshall responded that in light of "all this business that had occurred in Washington and what Hopkins had told me," the president should "feel free" to act "in the best interest of the country" and not to "consider my feelings." In his oblique way, the president, acting as if Marshall had said he did *not* want the Overlord command, completed the conversation by saying, "Well, I didn't feel I could sleep at ease if you were out of Washington." He paused. Marshall said nothing. "Then it will be Eisenhower," said the president.[118]

On the morning of December 7, two years after the United States entered the war, Roosevelt and Hopkins flew to Tunis, where they were met by Eisenhower. As soon as the general climbed into the president's car, FDR said, "Well, Ike, you are going to command Overlord."[119] In conferring the big command on Eisenhower, Roosevelt must have known that if Overlord succeeded, Eisenhower, like Grant, would become a national hero and would have a clear pathway to political power.

The night before leaving for Dakar to board the *Iowa* for the trip back to the States, Hopkins and his son spent an evening alone at the Tunisian Palace, a French restaurant in Tunis. "Dad told me everything that was going on at home," wrote Robert to his mother, "and promised me he would send me pictures of Stephen and David." Stephen was in the Marine Corps, headed for combat in the Pacific. David was serving in the Pacific as a naval officer aboard the aircraft carrier *Essex* (commanded by Donald Duncan, brother of Hopkins's second wife, Barbara). When Robert and Harry said goodbye that night, they promised to meet again in Berlin.[120]

On the voyage home Hopkins and Roosevelt were cautiously optimistic. With a firm agreement to invade western France in the spring of 1944 and a commitment by Stalin to launch offensives in the east, they were convinced that Germany would be defeated in 1945, if not before. Roosevelt believed he had gotten through to Stalin, establishing a foundation for world peace and friendly relations with the Soviets, whereas Hopkins tended to regard their efforts as more akin to a realistic accommodation with the Soviet leader. Looking back on the Tehran conference, FDR told Elliott, "The biggest thing . . . was in making clear to Stalin that the United States and Great Britain were not allied in one common bloc against the Soviet Union. I think we've got rid of that idea once and for all. I hope so. The one thing that could upset the apple-cart, after the war, is if the world is divided again, Russia against England and us."[121]

Albeit a cliché, in truth Tehran was a turning point. For the wartime alliance with Great Britain, it was the moment when the balance of military power shifted, Churchill's resistance to Overlord was finally overcome, and the United States turned its attention from Britain to the Soviet Union. For Eastern Europe, it was the point when the option of effectively resisting Soviet political domination was likely foreclosed. And for Hopkins, wrote Bohlen, it was the time when his "influence was paramount."

The *Iowa* arrived off Chesapeake Bay on December 16. Hopkins radioed Louise, "Arrived well and ever so anxious to see you my darling. . . . Get out my heavy underwear and light the fire."[122]

A Soldier's Debt

When Hopkins stepped through the front door of his snug town-house at 3340 N Street in Georgetown, the fireplace was ablaze and the living room decorated with evergreen and holly. "It was the first time I have had Christmas in my own house for years," he wrote his son Stephen, "and Louie made it the pleasantest that I think I ever had in my life."[1]

On New Year's Day 1944 Harry and Louise hosted a group of friends for a housewarming party. "Suddenly," wrote Sherwood, Hopkins "seemed to droop and said he had a cold coming on and had better go upstairs to bed."[2] Three days later he checked into the Bethesda Naval Hospital, convinced that his cold had turned into the flu. But it was more than the flu. His weight was down to 126 pounds. The doctors concluded that his intestinal ailment—his inability to absorb nutrients—had returned with a vengeance, and they treated him, as they had many times before, with blood and plasma transfusions, vitamin injections, and a diet rich in protein and leafy vegetables.[3] Believing he was afflicted with nothing more than a mild case of the flu, Roosevelt cabled Churchill, "Harry is temporarily on the sick list."[4] When Churchill expressed concern, asking "for more news of Harry," FDR replied that Hopkins was getting better and "should be ready for full activity in a month's time."[5]

Hopkins was not the only one felled by the exhausting trip to Tehran. Stalin, returning to Moscow with a stop to survey the ruins of Stalingrad, endured a two-week ear infection. Churchill suffered another bout of pneumonia and was convalescing with Clementine at La Saadia, the villa on the outskirts of Marrakech, where he and the president had watched the sunset over the Atlas Mountains in January 1943. "I passed eighteen out of the twenty four supine," complained the prime minister. "I never remember such extreme fatigue and weakness in body."[6]

Roosevelt was likewise "feeling a *little* miserably" over the Christmas and New Year holidays at Hyde Park, recalled Cousin Daisy.[7] As usual, he dismissed his ailments as simply "the grippe," but in fact it was evident to those close to him that his health was deteriorating. Showing darker circles under his eyes, he had developed a persistent cough while sweating profusely and running low-grade fevers. His hands shook more than ever. He slept late, tired easily, and sometimes nodded off. His blood pressure was rising.[8]

In his last press conference of 1943, Roosevelt used ill health as a folksy vehicle for explaining the transformation of his administration and positioning himself to run for a fourth term. "Old Doctor New Deal," he told the reporters, had helped the nation recover from the ills of the depression. But when the United States suffered "a very bad accident"—meaning Pearl Harbor—"Doctor Win-the-War" was brought in as a replacement. The "patient"—that is, the nation—"is back on his feet," explained the president, but "he isn't wholly well yet, and he won't be until he wins the war." The reporters got the drift. One of them asked, "Does all that add up to a fourth term declaration?" Over their laughter, FDR responded, "Oh now—we are not talking about things like that now."[9]

While Hopkins was flat on his back in the hospital, his political enemies and the press did not let up. In his regular nationwide radio broadcast on January 14, 1944, the popular commentator Fulton Lewis Jr. claimed that Hopkins, as a civilian, was not legally eligible to occupy a bed at the naval hospital and then gratuitously revived the old allegations that Hopkins had lied when he denied telling a friend at the racetrack in 1938, "We will tax and tax and spend and spend and elect and elect" and that he had lied again when he testified at his confirmation hearing to be commerce secretary that he never registered to vote as a Socialist.[10]

During the third week of January, Hopkins's credibility was again questioned when he was summoned from the hospital to testify before a federal grand jury in one of those "only in Washington" political brouhahas that quickly recede from public memory. Simply put, Hopkins, the "White House Rasputin," had been accused by conservative Republicans of writing and signing a letter suggesting that he and, by implication, Roosevelt were cooperating in an effort to engineer the nomination of the liberal Republican Wendell Willkie to run for president again in 1944. In his ten-minute testimony to the grand jurors, Hopkins swore that the signature on the letter was not his, and he denied writing or dictating the letter. The grand jury apparently believed him, eventually indicting another man, George Briggs, for having forged Hopkins's signature. Briggs, who died of a stroke before going to trial, was an assistant to Secretary of Interior Harold Ickes, Hopkins's chief administration critic and rival.[11] Robert Hopkins believed the "Briggs affair" and the possible involvement of Harold Ickes "bothered his father more than almost any other attack on him."[12]

Since Hopkins was not bouncing back, doctors at the naval hospital recommended that he return to the Mayo Clinic for another operation aimed at both ruling out a recurrence of his stomach cancer and enlarging the absorptive surfaces in his small intestine.[13] To build up his strength for the surgery, Hopkins decided to accept the standing invitation of his wealthy friends John and Fannie Hertz to spend a few weeks at their home in Miami Beach resting in the sun. Writing to Mrs. Hertz in advance of the trip, he explained that at the insistence of his doctors he would be traveling with a nurse who would be giving him "two injections a day, plus an ungodly amount of medication."[14]

A few days before boarding the *Silver Meteor* for the trip south, Hopkins wrote a brief note to his eighteen-year-old son Stephen, who he knew would be with his fellow Marines in their amphibious attack on the Kwajalein Atoll in the Marshall Islands. "I presume you will be pretty busy during the next few weeks so I do not expect to hear from you," he wrote. "At any rate you know that I wish you the best of luck."[15] On February 12 Hopkins's nurse handed him a telegram from the president that had been put aboard the train at Jacksonville. "I am terribly distressed to have to tell you that Stephen was killed in action at Kwajalein. . . . I am confident that when we get details we will all be even prouder of him than ever. I am thinking of you much. F.D.R."[16]

A few weeks later, the letter Hopkins had written to Stephen was returned, undelivered. Private First Class Stephen Hopkins was killed by a Japanese bullet through the forehead while digging a foxhole with his hands. He had just finished running ammunition to a machine-gun emplacement in the jungle. Stephen never regained consciousness and died aboard a hospital ship. He was buried at sea.[17] Letters and telegrams of condolence to Hopkins poured in from all corners of the globe. The most memorable contained lines from *Macbeth* in fine calligraphy on a parchment scroll:

Stephen Peter Hopkins
Age 18

"Your son, my lord, has paid a soldier's debt;
He only liv'd but till he was a man;
The which no sooner had his prowess confirm'd
In the unshrinking station where he fought,
But like a man he died."

Shakespeare.
To Harry Hopkins from Winston S. Churchill
13 February, 1944[18]

Stephen's mother, Ethel Gross Hopkins, received no letters of sympathy from world leaders. In fact the blizzard of news reports about Stephen's death rarely even mentioned that she was his mother. In a hastily written letter to the *New York World Telegram* that was picked up by *Time* magazine, Ethel complained that she had been literally erased from the public image of Harry Hopkins and "his" three sons.[19] Yet to Harry she was tender and extraordinarily forgiving, composing perhaps the most poignant letter of all those that were written to him in the wake of Stephen's death:

> I wouldn't hurt you for anything in the world, but after the heart breaking news came about Stephen I wanted to shout from the housetops, over and over again—my son Stephen was killed. . . . I could not bear to be further removed from him by not being identified with him. It's terribly important to me to be his Mother at this time, just as important as when he was born.
>
> Do you remember when he was three weeks old and we so nearly lost him after his operation? His being saved then has always seemed to me to be a miracle. . . . Thanks to you and the security your earning have always given me, I was able to give him a normal, happy and regular existence. . . . He was always beautiful to look at and everyone loved him. Through your great achievements you were able to enrich his life with friendships and experiences with great—I want to say—all the great and important people who belong to this era. . . . He wanted so much to have you love him. After his appendix operation when you visited him, he said he felt closer to you than he ever had before. . . . All this is the way I wanted it to be.

Her concluding sentences expressed a generosity that must have touched Hopkins to the core:

> And there is one more thing I have wanted to say to you for a long long time. As the years go by and I become more aware of the kind of person I really am, I see more clearly why it was difficult for you many times; and I blame you less for leaving me. You know how and with whom you wanted to live your life and you have gone a long way.
>
> It does me good to say these things to you, and I hope you won't mind.
>
> Ethel[20]

How Hopkins bore his grief over the loss of Stephen is not known. There is no evidence that he turned to religion or some higher power. Nor are there any letters, written by him or others, that describe his feelings. Stephen's death must have affected him deeply, but in the parlance of those war years, when so many were experiencing the suffering and death of loved ones, he would characterize his loss and others' as "a very bad break" or a "terrible bit of luck."[21] To Marshall, Hopkins simply described his loss as "hard and biting."[22] Facing his own mortality as he prepared for life-threatening surgery, his choice was to force himself to put Stephen's death behind him and get on with the business of living. Advising Ethel to do the same, he quoted Shakespeare, like Churchill, and probably inspired by him, choosing the last scene of *Macbeth*, when Ross comforts Siward for the supposed death of his son, Macduff, who has confronted Macbeth: "Your cause of sorrow must not be measured by his worth for then it hath no end."[23]

To Roosevelt, Churchill expressed his concern about Hopkins's impending operation: "He is an indomitable spirit. I cannot help feeling anxious about his frail body and another operation. I shall always be glad for news about him for I rate him high among the Paladins."[24] At roughly the same time, March 29, the Paladin was being wheeled toward the operating room at Mayo Clinic. Louise recalled that Hopkins was upbeat, joking to the attendants, "O.K. boys, move right along. Open me up. Maybe you'll find the answer to the Fourth Term. Maybe not."[25] Marshall did not take the operation lightly. That day he cabled Hopkins, praying for his "early and complete recovery" and saying, "I know you have one great reserve in your favor and that is cold nerve and great courage."[26] Hopkins's entrails provided no clue as to whether FDR would run again. However, the surgeons reported that in their judgment the cancer had not recurred. They had performed "a reconstructive type of operation" in an effort to increase Hopkins's ability to absorb nutrients. "Time alone will tell its value," wrote one of them.[27]

Louise worked at the Mayo Clinic as a nurse's aide while Hopkins slowly healed. On May 7 an Army plane dispatched by Marshall flew her and Hopkins to the Greenbrier in White Sulphur Springs, West Virginia. The pre–Civil War resort—people had been taking the waters there since 1778—had been taken over by the Army in 1942, converted into a convalescent center, and renamed "Ashford General Hospital."[28] Hopkins was cared for by the medical staff in one of the luxurious cottages on the immaculately groomed grounds. His convalescence was nonetheless rocky. In late May he developed jaundice and had to be admitted to the hospital. Louise, who had returned to Washington, where she worked and cared for Diana, came down on the C&O Railroad for weekend visits.[29]

It didn't take long for congressional critics of Hopkins and Roosevelt to find out where Hopkins was recuperating. In the third week of May Republican Congressman Homer Ramey of Ohio questioned the authority of the War Department to permit Hopkins to be treated in an Army hospital. "The responsibility for Hopkins' presence at White Sulphur is wholly mine," responded Marshall.[30] The congressman backed off; he was not about to take on the imperious chief of staff of the U.S. Army.

As the date for the commencement of Overlord approached, Hopkins knew that Robert, stationed in England, was eager to go into France with the invasion forces as early as possible. Hopkins had already turned down Marshall's offer, in the wake of Stephen's death, to have Robert "pulled back . . . to safer ground."[31] He and Robert planned to honor their vow to meet again in Berlin.[32] On May 3, 1944, Hopkins wrote Eisenhower ("Dear Ike"), expressing his concern that Robert might not be allowed by his commanding officer to participate in the invasion because "one of [his] other boys had some bad luck in the Pacific." To the supreme Allied commander, Hopkins continued, "I hope you will allow Robert to go on the invasion whenever it comes off. . . . The war is 'for keeps' and I want so much to have all of my boys where the going is rough."[33] Taking time away from the crushing responsibilities of commanding the largest amphibious invasion in the history of warfare, Eisenhower responded with a three-page handwritten letter. Recognizing the emotional "cost" to Hopkins of putting another son's life on the line, Eisenhower wrote, "At the risk of appearing a bit sentimental, I simply must say that I admire and salute your attitude. . . . [Robert] will be treated as a soldier, on a strictly official basis. Nothing more; nothing less."[34]

While Hopkins gained strength at White Sulphur Springs, Roosevelt rested an entire month at Bernard Baruch's South Carolina plantation, recovering from what Doc McIntire told the press was "influenza plus respiratory complications."[35] In fact he was being treated for congestive heart failure, a diagnosis rendered by Dr. Howard Bruenn, a cardiologist who had examined FDR at Bethesda Naval Hospital on March 28, the day before Hopkins's operation at Mayo.[36] Were it not for the insistence of Anna, the president's daughter, McIntire would never have taken his patient to see a heart specialist. As it was, McIntire refused to believe that the president had a serious heart condition.

After Roosevelt returned to the White House, "brown as a berry, radiant and happy,"[37] he dispensed advice on the keys to healthy living in a letter to Hopkins:

> You have got to lead not the life of an invalid but the life of common or garden sense.
>
> I too, over one hundred years older than you are, have come to the same realization and I have cut my drinks down to one and a half cocktails per evening and nothing else. . . . Also, I have cut my cigarettes down from twenty or thirty a day to five or six a day. . . .
>
> The main gist of this is to plead with you to stay away until the middle of June at the earliest. I don't want you to come back until then. If you do come back before then you will be extremely unpopular in Washington, with exception of [*Washington Times Herald* publisher] Cissy Patterson who wants to kill you off as soon as possible—just as she does me.
>
> I had a really grand time down at Bernie's—slept twelve hours out of the twenty-four, sat in the sun, never lost my temper, and decided to let the world go hang. The interesting thing is the world didn't hang. I have a terrific pile in my basket but most of the stuff has answered itself anyway.
>
> Lots of love to you both. Tell Louise to use the old-fashioned hatpin if you don't behave.[38]

In his cottage at the Greenbrier during the first few days of June, Hopkins anxiously awaited news of the great invasion of Western Europe, which was supposed to take place by the end of May. On Monday night, June 5, he tuned in to Roosevelt's radio address trumpeting the fall of Rome. "The first of the Axis capitals is now in our hands," announced the president. "One up and two to go!" No mention was made of the cross-Channel invasion.[39] The same evening, at his dacha outside Moscow, Stalin sarcastically belittled the courage of his allies, predicting that the invasion would be called off if there was fog in the English Channel. "Maybe they'll meet with some Germans," he mocked.[40]

Just after midnight in Britain the throb of engines could be heard as hundreds upon hundreds of British and American warplanes and gliders sortied and flew west toward the Channel. Churchill was in his map room, memories of the senseless slaughter during World War I at the Somme and Passchendaele still graven in his mind. Clementine came in to say good night. "Do you realize," he said, "that by the time you wake up in the morning twenty thousand men may have been killed?"[41] The throb grew in volume to become a constant thunder that lasted for most of the day, "like a factory in the sky," remarked Ed Murrow.[42] By dawn on June 6 virtually everyone in the United Kingdom knew the invasion was on.

Hitler was not woken at his redoubt in Berchtesgaden. There were reports of landings in Normandy, but his generals were not sure whether or not this was the main invasion force. Besides, Hitler had been up until 3 a.m. reminiscing with Goebbels, and no one dared disturb his sleep.[43]

At 4 a.m. in the White House, Roosevelt, who had just been told by Marshall that the assault troops were on the beaches of Normandy, calmly instructed the switchboard operator to call all members of the White House staff and tell them to report for work at once. For the first time since May 1940, Hopkins was not on the list.

By mid-morning on June 6 news of the invasion reached Hopkins at his cottage. Nurses and doctors dropped by with bits and pieces. Church bells tolled in the little town. Hopkins kept his ear to the radio all day. That evening he listened as the president led the nation in prayer. He could only imagine what was going on in the White House. He later told Sherwood that during his months at the Mayo Clinic and at the Greenbrier, he had "thought endlessly" about the desperate struggle to put the American economy on a war footing and the bureaucratic battles to break production "bottlenecks." He also spent hours "trying to figure out" the answer to one of the great debates of World War II: whether it was a mistake to invade North Africa in 1942 instead of concentrating all forces for an invasion of France in 1942, or more likely 1943.[44] Probably because he played such a critical role in the decision to opt for North Africa, he wrestled with the question of whether in the long run lives would have been saved and the war against Germany would have ended sooner had he and Roosevelt heeded Marshall's advice and insisted on France. The debate continued for some years after Hopkins's death. Today most—by no means all—historians have concluded that North Africa and the Mediterranean, not France, made the best strategic sense for Anglo-American forces in 1942 and 1943.[45]

Hopkins returned to Washington on July 4 and resumed his convalescence at home, although he continued to have his office and secretary in the White House. He was "able to work only two or three hours a day,"[46] and he seldom left the house. The White House installed a direct telephone line, but the president rarely called. Having been out of the arena for more than six months, Hopkins lost touch with people and events. Marshall was worried that he would ignore doctor's orders and revert to his old habits. In a birthday letter, written as if he were the strict father Hopkins never had, Marshall wrote, "[I advise you] to be more careful, to conserve your energies and not to overdo and I am also prepared to damn you for your cigarettes, your drinks and your late hours. Confine your excesses to gin rummy."[47]

During Hopkins's long absence, the president understandably came to rely on other advisors and to seek companionship elsewhere. He leaned heavily on Admiral Leahy, his conservative, affable chief of staff, and his old friend from Hyde Park, Treasury Secretary Henry Morgenthau, for the kind of counsel Hopkins used to provide. For companionship Roosevelt turned to Anna; he enlisted her to arrange clandestine dinners and outings with the recently widowed Lucy Mercer Rutherfurd when Eleanor was out of town.[48] Consequently the temperature of the relationship between Hopkins and the president had cooled by several degrees.

Even had Hopkins returned in perfect health, he would have had little opportunity to restore his relationship with the president. Less than two weeks after he arrived back in Washington, Roosevelt boarded the *Ferdinand Magellan* for a month-long trip to the West Coast and then by cruiser to Pearl Harbor for meetings on Pacific strategy with Admiral Chester Nimitz and General Douglas MacArthur. While the president's train rolled slowly north and west, with a stop at Tranquility, Lucy's estate in Allamuchy, New Jersey, the Democratic convention was convening in Chicago.[49] When Roosevelt's train reached Chicago, Bob Hannegan, the convention chairman, came aboard. The delegates were pleased to know that the president had agreed to run again but were in turmoil over the vitally important vice-presidential selection. (Many suspected that FDR would not survive a fourth term.) Roosevelt's popularity had declined, and the political bosses were worried that if Henry Wallace, the left-leaning, pro-Soviet vice president, were to be renominated, it would weaken the ticket. The bosses needed a signal from the president as to his preference.

As usual, Roosevelt did not give them a straight answer. At first he told Hannegan that he favored Jimmy Byrnes. Then he dictated a letter that said he would be happy to run with Harry Truman or Bill Douglas.[50] From his train on Monday, July 17, he finally instructed convention leaders to go "all out" for Truman. It was a close call, but on the second ballot Truman was selected.[51]

Hopkins, of course, could not attend the Democratic convention that summer. However, there are indications that despite his poor health he had a hand in some of the political maneuvering that led up to the convention. According to a respected reporter, Hopkins asked one of his close associates, David Niles, to travel to New York City and warn Earl Browder, head of the American Communist Party, that under no circumstances should the party endorse Roosevelt. Such an endorsement, particularly if Wallace was to be on the ticket, would be exploited by Tom Dewey, the Republican nominee, and endanger Roosevelt's reelection.[52] In his diary Wallace himself set forth reasons supporting his belief that Hopkins was behind the efforts to replace him as vice-presidential nominee in favor of Truman.[53] Although Wallace did not provide hard evidence, it is entirely plausible that during the days before the convention, while recovering at the Greenbrier or at his home in Georgetown, Hopkins worked the phones with the politicos he had come to know so well during the 1940 convention.

Now that Hopkins was back in Washington, Churchill assumed that he still had the ear of the president. "I was not then aware," wrote Churchill, "of the change in the character of [Hopkins's] relationship with the President."[54] Since February Churchill had been arguing against the long-planned Anglo-American amphibious invasion of southern France, code-named Anvil, that was designed to support the right flank of Overlord, but Roosevelt had stood solidly behind Marshall and Eisenhower, instructing them to tell Churchill and the British chiefs that cancelling Anvil was not an option. In early August, with the hope that Hopkins could change FDR's mind, Churchill sent a long cable to Hopkins, again urging that Anvil be cancelled. This time he argued not that the Allied divisions scheduled for Anvil be diverted to Italy or to a venture into the Balkans but that they land in northwestern France and join the Overlord forces. Hopkins was astonished that Churchill would press for such a dramatic change in strategy, particularly since the Anvil operation was scheduled to begin in less than a week. He responded that he felt sure that the president would not budge and offered his own opinion that "it would be a great mistake to change strategy now; it would delay the sure liberation of France rather than aid it."[55]

By mid-August Hopkins was eager to get back to the center of action. The day the president returned from the Pacific, Hopkins "hurried" over to the White House to welcome him home. According to George Elsey, who witnessed the reunion, Roosevelt greeted Hopkins warmly, saying, "Hello, Harry. How are you doing? Are you going to come up with me and have some coffee?"[56] Hopkins went upstairs with the president, preparing to make himself once again indispensable. During the previous few weeks, he had inserted himself into the middle of what he thought was an important policy issue: whether the United States should continue to provide lend-lease supplies to the British after the defeat of Germany and, if so, for how long. The War Department was resistant to any extension, but Churchill and his diplomats in Washington had been pressing Hopkins to get the president to order a one-year extension.[57] Over coffee Hopkins advised Roosevelt to postpone a decision until the mid-September conference with Churchill and the British in Quebec (the second Quebec conference), when the British role in fighting the Japanese would be clarified. In the meantime, suggested Hopkins, the British should continue to be supplied. The president agreed.[58] Hopkins had known for weeks about the conference in Quebec and told Churchill he "hope[d] to be there," although Roosevelt had not yet invited him.[59] He believed his involvement in the lend-lease issue would guarantee him a place in the delegation.

It was not to be. The next day Henry Morgenthau, who had effectively replaced Hopkins as FDR's closest advisor, met privately with Roosevelt. Morgenthau had had a very successful summer. He was the leading figure at the Bretton Woods Conference in New Hampshire in July that established an international monetary system, including the International Monetary Fund and the International Bank for Reconstruction and Development (forerunner of the World Bank). Morgenthau had just returned from London, where Churchill, at Hopkins's suggestion, lobbied him hard for the lend-lease extension, confiding to Morgenthau that Britain was completely bankrupt.

The president was most interested in what Morgenthau had to say about Germany. When he was in London, explained Morgenthau, Anthony Eden briefed him on discussions that had taken place in Tehran concerning the postwar dismemberment and partition of Germany. Now that he knew that those issues lay unresolved, it was obvious to him that the United States must take the lead. "Nobody has been studying how to treat Germany roughly—along the lines you wanted," Morgenthau told FDR. He and his Treasury Department, he implied, were best suited to develop a comprehensive plan for harsh treatment of Germany.[60] Roosevelt's idea, expressed in a meeting at Tehran, involved a division of Germany into at least five states, with the industrialized regions of the Ruhr and Saar, along with Hamburg and the Kiel Canal, subject to international control. At one point during the meeting in Tehran, Roosevelt appeared to side with Stalin, who was pressing for total dismemberment and deindustrialization, saying, "Germany was less dangerous to civilization when it was in 107 provinces."[61] Although FDR

preferred to handle the issue of dismemberment himself, he gave Morgenthau the impression that he was free to prepare a plan for presentation at
the forthcoming conference with Churchill in Quebec.

In his own mind, Roosevelt perceived linkages between rough treatment
of postwar Germany, Great Britain's economic plight, and an earlier end to
lend-lease. If Germany was to be completely deindustrialized, he mused,
Britain could supplant the Ruhr and the Saar as Europe's economic engine.
This would spur Britain's economic recovery and at the same time lessen
her dependence on U.S. financial assistance. Hopkins's expertise on the
lend-lease issue, therefore, would be a small part of the much larger financial issues to be brought up by the British at Quebec; it was not enough to
get him a ticket on FDR's train. "If they [the British] bring up the financial
question," Roosevelt later said, "I will want Henry [Morgenthau] to come
to Quebec."[62]

There were other reasons why Roosevelt decided he did not need Hopkins in Quebec. With less than two months to go before the election, there
was no point in triggering the usual criticism from the Republicans and the
press whenever Hopkins, instead of Secretary of State Hull, accompanied
the president to an important conference. In addition Roosevelt knew that
Hopkins often sympathized with British positions, and he felt Morgenthau
would take a harder line with them at Quebec. At Tehran Churchill had
warned that a weak German state would lead to the domination of Europe
by the USSR; the president believed that Morgenthau was better suited to
counter this argument. Finally, the president might have been genuinely
concerned that Hopkins had not sufficiently recovered to withstand the
physical demands and stress of another conference.

There is no record of when or how Roosevelt let Hopkins know that he
would not be making the trip, the first and only wartime conference involving Roosevelt that he would not attend. The only clue is an August 28
cable by Hopkins to Churchill: "I am feeling ever so much better, [but] I
am inclined to think that I will not risk the dangers of a setback by fighting
the Battle of Quebec. Better men than I have been killed there."[63] Churchill
knew it was an excuse. Ill health had never before stopped Hopkins. He
would be "sorely missed" in Quebec, wrote Churchill.[64]

He might have been missed, but it was probably fortunate for Hopkins that he did not make the trip. On September 15 at the Citadel, moments after Roosevelt, with Morgenthau at his side, agreed to an extension of lend-lease aid to Britain, the prime minister and the president initialed an extraordinary document that soon became known to the world as the "Morgenthau Plan."[65] Originally entitled "Program to Prevent Germany from Starting World War III," the plan, drafted by Morgenthau and his team at Treasury, called for the complete deindustrialization of Germany after the war, including in particular the dismantling of all of the factories in the Ruhr and the Saar and a number of other harsh measures.[66] The document initialed at the Citadel was a much shorter, watered-down version. Nevertheless that plan envisioned postwar Germany as a pastoral nation in perpetuity, its economy largely limited to agriculture.

The night before, Churchill had violently objected to the Morgenthau Plan, saying it was "unnatural, un-Christian and unnecessary."[67] In the morning, however, he changed his mind after conferring with Frederick Lindemann, 1st Viscount Cherwell (not an economist, but a German-born, Oxford-trained science advisor), who stressed the advantages to the British economy of the elimination of Germany as a competitor.[68] No one would admit to a quid pro quo, but it appears that there was a tacit understanding with the Americans that Churchill would get the lend-lease extension if he signed on to the Morgenthau Plan. For his part, Roosevelt was intent on having Churchill agree not only because he thought it would help Britain's economy but also in order to satisfy Stalin's demands that the Western Allies match the Soviets in being tough on Germany. Within a few days after Morgenthau returned to Washington, the press got wind of the Morgenthau Plan, most likely through deliberate leaks, and began reporting that the plan was bitterly opposed by Stimson and Hull (correct); that the plan called for feeding the Germans no more than "three bowls of soup a day" (false); that it would cause the Germans to fight even harder (speculative); and that Roosevelt and Morgenthau "bribed" Churchill to accept the plan by promising an extension of lend-lease (closer to the truth).[69] For once Hopkins was not implicated, though he had approved the plan before Morgenthau went to Quebec.[70] The election was only six weeks away, and

Roosevelt was not pleased that voters were being told about a rift in his cabinet, particularly when the war effort demanded firm leadership and a united front. Republicans pounced on the issue.

While the heat was being turned up on Morgenthau in Washington, Hopkins was invited to Hyde Park to say farewell to Churchill, who was headed back to England. "He was obviously invited to please me," wrote Churchill. Describing a "curious incident at luncheon," Churchill recalled that Hopkins "arrived a few minutes late and the president didn't even greet him." Later that day Hopkins explained to Churchill his "altered position," meaning that his relationship with the president was not as close as it had been at Tehran. Referring to his poor health, Hopkins confided, "You must know I am not what I was." Yet during the next day or two, Churchill wrote, "Our affairs moved quicker as Hopkins appeared to regain his influence."[71]

Churchill's perception was accurate. In the weeks after the second Quebec conference, the president began to rely more and more on Hopkins. At the same time FDR distanced himself from the Morgenthau Plan, as well as from Morgenthau himself. He refused to see his treasury secretary or accept calls from him. In a lunch with Stimson in early October, Roosevelt, using popular slang of the day, grinned and said, "Henry Morgenthau pulled a boner!" as if he had nothing to do with the Morgenthau Plan. When Stimson read him the document he had initialed in Quebec, Roosevelt responded, "I have not the faintest recollection of this at all."[72]

Hopkins sought to take a step closer to the president by taking advantage of the vacuum created by the absence of Morgenthau. As a modest alternative to Morgenthau's plan, Hopkins brokered an interim directive, called JCS 1067, providing for a military government of Germany; it received the blessing of the War, Treasury, and State Departments.[73] Roosevelt was delighted to approve the directive because it put an end to the intracabinet squabbling that was hurting his campaign for a fourth term.

During the first week of October, Hopkins vastly improved his standing with the president by preventing him from making a major diplomatic blunder. It involved a seemingly innocuous cable, drafted by Admiral Leahy and signed by Roosevelt, which was ready to be wired from the White House map room to Churchill in London. The cable simply wished Churchill "good luck" on the trip he was about to take to meet with Stalin in Moscow to discuss the political structures the Soviets intended to establish as the Red Army moved into Eastern Europe. Churchill had urged Roosevelt to join him, but the president had to refuse because of the election.[74] Somehow Hopkins became aware of the cable. Without consulting anyone, he rushed from his second-floor office down to the map room and ordered the officers on duty to stop the transmission.[75]

As Hopkins instantly perceived, Churchill would regard the "good luck" message as a license to speak to the Soviets not only on behalf of Great Britain but on behalf of the United States as well. Also, unless Stalin was alerted, he would get the idea that Roosevelt had given Churchill authority to speak for him. Hopkins picked up the phone and called Charles Bohlen at the State Department. "Chip, get the hell over here in a hurry," he barked. When Bohlen arrived he "found Hopkins sitting in his White House office, one leg draped over the arm of a chair." Both agreed that the cable was dangerous because, as drafted, it could foreclose the role of the United States in peace talks concerning the fate of Eastern Europe. Hopkins asked Bohlen to begin drafting two substitute cables, one to Churchill and one to Stalin, while he went off to see the president.

Hopkins found the president in his bedroom, shaving. Not daring to tell him that he had already acted to stop its transmission, Hopkins explained the danger that he and Bohlen had seen in the "good luck" cable. "Realizing his mistake," Bohlen later wrote, "Roosevelt became somewhat agitated and instructed Hopkins to stop the message." The president "was relieved when Hopkins told him that he had taken the liberty of holding it."[76] Hopkins must have been equally relieved; he had taken an enormous risk in acting without authority to stop the transmission of a presidential cable.

The revised message wired to Churchill cautioned him not to make any commitments in the name of the president and, further, asked that Averell Harriman be permitted to attend all sessions with Stalin. The cable sent to Stalin, perhaps the more important of the two, read:

> You, naturally, understand that in this global war there is literally
> no question, political or military, in which the United States is not

interested. I am firmly convinced that the three of us, and only the three of us, can find the solution to the still unresolved questions. In this sense, while appreciating the Prime Minister's desire for a meeting, I prefer to regard your forthcoming talks as preliminary to a meeting of all three of us.

Stalin's reply made it apparent that Hopkins's judgment was unerring. "I had supposed that Mr. Churchill was going to Moscow in accordance with the agreement reached with you at Quebec," he wrote. "It happened, however, that this supposition of mine does not seem to correspond to reality."[77]

Hopkins's intervention was fortunate for Roosevelt, especially on the eve of the election, when scrutiny of foreign policy decisions was at its most intense. At what became known as the second Moscow conference (code-named "Tolstoy"), Churchill and Stalin secretly agreed to what Churchill himself later termed a "naughty document" that allocated spheres of influence on a percentage basis between the Soviets and the British in the Balkans. (For example, the document assigned the British a 90 percent interest in Greece and the Soviets a 75 percent interest in Bulgaria.)[78] Stalin signified his agreement by scrawling a large blue check mark across the document. Were it not for Hopkins, Roosevelt's name would have been associated with this cynical exercise in raw power politics at the expense of small nations.[79]

Hopkins was well on the way to completing a remarkable comeback. Marquis Childs, a fellow Iowan and one of Washington's most well-informed columnists, wrote, "Those of his enemies who took satisfaction in counting Hopkins out at the time of his illness after the Teheran Conference will have to guess again. His influence in the Administration is perhaps greater than it ever was."[80]

Nowhere was Hopkins more influential than in the area of foreign affairs. At a private dinner hosted by Joe Davies at Tregaron in mid-October, he told Davies that the proposed United Nations organization would not be effective unless the U.S. representative on its Security Council had "the power to commit our armed forces immediately when the occasion required."

He said the president should announce before the election that he intended to ask Congress to delegate that power, subject to guidelines specified by Congress. He knew many Republicans and isolationists would never agree to this proposal, but he believed it would appeal to the larger numbers of war-weary voters who yearned for a postwar peacekeeping organization with real teeth. And he predicted to Davies that once Roosevelt was elected, "that would settle the matter and give strength to the World Organization for Peace."[81]

A few days later Hopkins helped FDR and his other speechwriters prepare a major radio address to the Foreign Policy Association that was to be delivered by the president on October 21 at the Waldorf-Astoria in New York City.[82] The president added folksy touches, but the speech incorporated the very same proposals that Hopkins had conveyed earlier to Davies.[83] Although subject to congressional guidelines, the idea of authorizing a presidentially appointed UN representative to commit American troops to a foreign war was a bold, radical, and possibly unconstitutional departure from prior policy. American support for the League of Nations foundered over the covenant by members to use force against aggression. Nevertheless Hopkins and Roosevelt believed that without such a delegation of power, the UN would never become an effective world peacekeeping organization. The speech was a critical success. After sampling American opinion, Isaiah Berlin, the Russian-born political philosopher and historian then working at the British Embassy, reported to the British Foreign Office that the president's address "was fairly widely acknowledged as being an authoritative, courageous and masterly performance for which the public had been waiting."[84]

Elated by his reception in New York, the president's thirteen-car campaign train rolled through Ohio and Indiana to Chicago's Soldier Field and then, on the last weekend before the election, into the New England states. Hopkins did not make these trips. He needed to stay in Washington, close to Louise, who was described as being "ill" that fall. On November 1 she was hospitalized for a surgical procedure, likely a dilation and curettage in the aftermath of a miscarriage.[85]

Roosevelt's popularity surged in the final days, buoyed by startling news from the Pacific. General MacArthur had landed in the Philippines, thus making good on his famous "I shall return" vow. And the U.S. Navy had sunk or crippled much of what remained of the vaunted Japanese fleet in the Battle of Leyte Gulf. The day before the election, Hopkins wired Lord Beaverbrook, predicting, "Roosevelt will win by a landslide." If not, he promised, he would "underwrite the British national debt, join the Presbyterian Church and subscribe to the Chicago Tribune."[86] On election night Hopkins wired Churchill, "It's in the bag."[87] It wasn't quite a landslide, at least by Roosevelt's standards, but it was a decisive victory for the president over the Republican Tom Dewey. Roosevelt carried thirty-six states to Dewey's twelve and garnered 53.5 percent of the popular vote.

Soon after the election, Hopkins seized an opportunity to solidify his position as principal foreign affairs advisor. Roosevelt needed to appoint a successor to Cordell Hull, who had served since 1933 as secretary of state. Hull was critically ill, suffering from tuberculosis and diabetes, and had delayed his resignation announcement until after the election. He and several members of Congress pressed Roosevelt to appoint Jimmy Byrnes, who FDR had considered briefly for vice president and who was the popular and politically connected head of the Office of War Mobilization. Never forgetting that Byrnes had once told him, "Keep the hell out of my business," Hopkins opposed Byrnes, arguing that he was excessively strong-willed and would interfere with Roosevelt's practice of operating as his own secretary of state. Roosevelt agreed with Hopkins and rejected Byrnes as "too independent."[88] As Bohlen observed, "Hopkins intended to be a power in postwar foreign policy." His candidate to succeed Hull was Edward Stettinius Jr., the amiable former General Motors executive and chairman of U.S. Steel. Stettinius was Hopkins's protégé, having been recruited by him to head lend-lease and then to serve as undersecretary of state. "He was a decent man of considerable innocence," recalled Bohlen of Stettinius, unlikely to "cause much trouble" or to "disagree with anything Roosevelt and Hopkins wanted to do."[89] Hopkins persuaded Roosevelt that Stettinius would be a good choice to succeed Hull, politically acceptable, and content to reorganize the State Department while the two of them would manage foreign affairs.

Among New Dealers Stettinius was not a popular choice. Morgenthau complained that he was a "lifelong Republican" who was chosen because he would be a "good clerk."[90] Ickes wrote in his journal that Stettinius was nothing more than a "backslapper" and spread rumors that Hopkins engineered the appointment because Stettinius was giving him money on the side.[91]

Once Stettinius was in place, the way was cleared for Hopkins to arrange for the appointment of Bohlen to report to him as the State Department liaison with the White House. After a rocky beginning in Cairo, when Hopkins tried to provoke Bohlen by referring to his colleagues at the State Department (and presumably him) as "cookie pushers, pansies—and usually isolationists to boot," the two became close friends and mutual admirers.[92] Bohlen helped Hopkins understand that State Department professionals could add to the quality of decision making, particularly as the administration faced daunting issues in the coming days involving the future of Germany, Eastern Europe, and the structure of the United Nations. In addition Bohlen spoke Russian and was an expert on Soviet diplomacy, having spent years in Moscow at the U.S. Embassy before his service as assistant chief of the Russian section in Washington with the State Department's Division of European Affairs. Hopkins had strong ties with the British, but he needed Bohlen to help him with the Soviets for he knew that they would be presenting him with his most difficult challenges in the months ahead.

The days leading up to Christmas 1944 were particularly stressful. With the president at the "little White House" in Warm Springs, Georgia, Hopkins was on the receiving end of a hopelessly garbled phone call from Churchill. Hopkins could tell that the prime minister was "very angry" and that his call had something to do with "Greece." He knew that the British had landed troops in Greece to support the monarchy against attempts by Greek Communists to seize power. (By then, German troops had withdrawn.) However, he could not understand why Churchill was so exorcised. The next morning, Sunday, December 10, Hopkins figured out the problem. In the map room he discovered that Admiral King had ordered U.S. Navy LSTs not to transport supplies to the embattled British troops and their Greek sympathizers. Hopkins met with Leahy and told him that depriving the British of supplies "was like walking out on a member of your family who is in trouble." On his own initiative, Hopkins convinced Leahy to get King to countermand his order, which he promptly did. He also talked Churchill out of sending an intemperate protest to Roosevelt.[93]

A week later reports began streaming into the map room that the Germans had launched a surprise counteroffensive in the snowy forests of the Ardennes. Hitler had quietly amassed 2,500 tanks and 250,000 troops in a desperate bid to regain momentum, split the Allied armies, and drive to Antwerp on the North Sea. For the next ten days, with the help of overcast skies that crippled Allied air power, the Germans pushed the outnumbered American troops back into Belgium. Roosevelt returned to the White House, but there was nothing either he or anyone there could do except monitor battlefield reports and wait it out. The worsening news of what became known as the Battle of the Bulge cast a pall over wartime Washington, dashing hopes that victory in Europe was imminent.

In Georgetown something very odd was going on in the Hopkins household, the rationale for which remains a perplexing mystery. On December 6, 1944, the morning after Hopkins met in the White House with J. Edgar Hoover, head of the FBI, Louise was placed under "physical and technical surveillance," which meant that her daily movements were surreptitiously followed and described in reports by FBI agents. Six days later Hoover again conferred with Hopkins in the White House. The following day a tap on Hopkins's home telephone was installed and transcripts of all of Louise's conversations were made by eavesdropping agents. On December 23 Hopkins wrote a note to Helen Gandy, administrative assistant to Hoover, instructing her to *"shut the whole business off* at 3:30 this afternoon" and to deliver to Hopkins "the final findings at 5 at my office—east gate—this afternoon" (emphasis in the original).[94] Hundreds of pages of these FBI surveillance reports and transcripts of telephone conversations are now available in the Library of Congress.

Without citing any authority, two writers aware of this bizarre incident suggest that Roosevelt was upset about leaks of verbatim White House conversations to the *Washington-Times Herald* and that Louise was suspected because she was a friend of its right-wing publisher, Cissy Patterson, the first woman to run a major metropolitan newspaper, whom Roosevelt (and Hopkins) despised.[95] It is true that Roosevelt, like most presidents, was angered by leaks to the press from time to time—and there is plenty of documentation of his outbursts. But there is no evidence that he was particularly concerned about leaks in the weeks before Christmas.[96] Moreover, there were no items in the *Washington Times-Herald* during those weeks recounting the substance of private White House conversations. Nor is there any evidence in the reports and transcripts (or anywhere else) that Louise was a friend of Patterson. Louise was very social and knew a lot of people in Washington. It is unlikely, however, that she would befriend, much less have any substantive conversations with, an arch enemy of both the president and her own husband.

Given Hopkins's power and influence, it is also possible that he could have brought in the FBI because he suspected Louise was having an affair, a theory endorsed by two other writers, one of whom speculated that Hopkins thought she was having an affair with a woman.[97] Hopkins's absence during the first six months of 1944 supports this theory, and the circumstances surrounding Louise's illness and possible miscarriage during the fall buttress the argument that she had an affair with a man. But if sexual indiscretion was the motive, the FBI investigation yielded only a few words of potentially incriminating evidence; in a telephone conversation about the tendency of the nurse who cared for Louise in the hospital to reveal secrets when she had a "couple of drinks under her belt," Louise was ominously warned by a friend, "Put the quietus on it or you're headed for the river."[98]

Knowing, as Hopkins surely did, that Hoover kept dossiers on scandals within the presidential family to use to his advantage and to protect himself against attack, it is difficult to believe that Hopkins would enlist him to investigate whether his own wife was having an affair. If he actually suspected her—and there is no evidence that he did—it would have been more logical and discreet for him to have hired a private investigator. Hopkins had enough insight into Hoover and the ways of Washington to be wary of the powerful FBI director.

Based on interviews with those who knew Louise and the FBI reports, the more likely explanation for the investigation is that gossip and rumors had gotten to FDR or his family suggesting that Louise, by that time a heavy drinker, was apt to inadvertently reveal secrets or embarrassing information about the president when spirits loosened her lips.[99] The circumstances suggest that someone, possibly Roosevelt himself, made an offhand remark to Hopkins implying that Louise might be a security risk. She was certainly in a position to know and leak classified information, and she drank almost every day at cocktail and dinner parties with those at the top of wartime Washington who had a thirst for inside information. For example, those around Roosevelt knew that Louise's closest friend and fellow drinking partner was Betty Howe, wife of Army Air Force Lieutenant Colonel W. Deering Howe (wealthy heir of one of the founders of International Harvester). Deering Howe worked directly under Hap Arnold and was well aware of the top-secret Manhattan Project.

If, as seems likely, Hopkins authorized the investigation because his wife was regarded by someone—Roosevelt, the military, the FBI, or Hopkins himself—as a potential national security risk, there are no clues in the FBI reports and transcripts suggesting that she actually leaked secrets or other information that would embarrass the White House. But the fact that Hopkins participated in the initiation of a surreptitious FBI investigation of Louise, a woman who by all accounts he loved deeply, reveals the limits of his loyalty to her. At the same time, it shows how ambitious Hopkins was to protect and defend his position with the president. Whether Hopkins saw anything in the FBI reports that caused him to take further action or to confront Louise is unknown. What is known is that the couple spent Christmas Eve at home with Diana, and in the morning they drove up to Ardmore, Pennsylvania, to celebrate Christmas dinner with Louise's sister Mary Lloyd Macy Ludington (everyone called her Min).[100]

As 1944 drew to a close, Hopkins sought to soothe the bruised feelings of Churchill, who was still fuming over the reluctance of the Americans to come to the aid of British forces in Greece. Churchill was leaving for Athens to try to stabilize Greece by brokering a coalition government when he received Christmas greetings from Hopkins. "The raging battle and the overhanging clouds are the prelude to a sure and glorious victory for us,"

Hopkins wrote. "What a gallant role you play in the greatest drama in the world's history, no one knows better than I."[101]

In the Ardennes the skies cleared, allowing Allied air power to blunt the German offensive. General Patton's Third Army was rapidly marching north to hit the German flank. On the eastern front, the Red Army was poised to take Warsaw and envelop Budapest. In Hopkins's words, "the final assault on the German citadel" was about to begin.[102] The next act in "the greatest drama" would take place at Yalta on the Black Sea. In body and spirit, Hopkins had paid a "soldier's debt" in 1944. Nothing, however, could keep him from being at the Big Three conference in Yalta.

The Best They Could Do

I t was Hopkins's idea for the Big Three to meet on the Crimean peninsula, where Yalta, a small, moldering resort city, is located. "If we had
spent ten years on research," complained Churchill to Hopkins, "we could
not have found a worse place in the world than [Yalta]." "[Churchill] feels
he can survive it," wrote Hopkins to Roosevelt, "by bringing an adequate
supply of whiskey. He claims it is good for typhus and deadly on lice which
thrive in these parts."[1]

Beginning as far back as mid-September 1944, Roosevelt discussed with
Hopkins his desire to schedule a postelection conference with Stalin and
Churchill to plan the final assault on Germany, clarify the commitment
of the Soviets to join the war against Japan, organize the United Nations,
and address issues relating to the anticipated defeat of Germany. "I told the
president," recalled Hopkins, "that there was not a chance of getting Stalin
out of Russia . . . in the light of the military situation on Germany's eastern
front . . . and that we might as well make up our minds . . . to go to some
convenient point in Russia—preferably in the Crimea."[2]

With FDR's blessing, Hopkins met quietly in Washington with Andrei Gromyko, the new Soviet ambassador, to sound him out on whether there was a suitable place on the Crimean peninsula for a Big Three conference. Stalin soon cabled Roosevelt that he would "extremely welcome" a meeting in the Crimea on the USSR's Black Sea coast.[3] Hopkins knew that Roosevelt's other close advisors would urge the president not to risk his life by traveling thousands of miles within range of U-boats and enemy aircraft to meet Stalin. However, he believed that once the election was over, Roosevelt's adventurous spirit and his desire to have another opportunity to cultivate Stalin in a remote part of the world he had never visited would overcome all objections.

He was right. After many "cables back and forth getting exactly nowhere," Roosevelt finally agreed near the end of 1944 to meet Stalin in the Crimea at Yalta.[4] And once Churchill learned that the president would meet him alone in British-controlled Malta before flying to the Crimea, Churchill's objections dissipated. "I shall be waiting on the quay," cabled Churchill. "No more let us falter! From Malta to Yalta! Let nobody alter!"[5]

Hopkins too would be waiting for the president on the quay at Malta, but only after an exhausting marathon of fence-mending meetings in London, Paris, and Rome. On Sunday, January 21, 1945, the day after Roosevelt's low-key inauguration ceremony in the White House, Hopkins and Bohlen departed for Europe in the president's plane, the Sacred Cow. Hopkins had convinced Roosevelt that the trip was necessary in order to ease tensions with Churchill and de Gaulle and to get a firmer grip on the issues that the president would be facing at Yalta. In effect Hopkins would once again be functioning as secretary of state, in this case in place of Edward Stettinius. Stettinius later wrote that he thought the trip was "a great mistake" because "Hopkins had neither the strength nor the vitality to undertake the strain of both this trip and the Yalta Conference."[6]

Hopkins himself was worried that he might not survive. In a letter to twelve-year-old Diana written two days before he flew to Europe, he told her that in case "anything happened to [him]," Mrs. Roosevelt "would see that you got a good education and have a little money when you were through with schooling." Notably he did not indicate that Louise would have any obligation, financial or otherwise. With the letter Hopkins enclosed a copy of his will, although he had virtually no assets to pass on to Diana.[7] After refueling stops in Bermuda and the Azores, he and Bohlen landed in London, which was then being terrorized by German V-2 missile attacks launched from Antwerp. Churchill, still smarting from Stettinius's criticism of British interference in Italian politics and Admiral King's withholding of ships and supplies for British forces in Greece, was, according to Hopkins, in a "volcanic" frame of mind.[8] However, after some long nights with the prime minister, "Hopkins succeeded," wrote Bohlen, "in soothing Churchill's wounded feelings."[9]

Hopkins also succeeded in getting a foretaste of two of the important issues the Americans would face at Yalta. From Sir Alexander Cadogan, permanent undersecretary for foreign affairs, Hopkins learned that the Americans would have to take the lead at Yalta in opposing Stalin's attempt to get extra votes in the proposed UN General Assembly, one for each of the socialist republics. Britain would be of no help because it would be trying to get an extra vote for India, which it still controlled. After Bohlen briefed him on his meetings with leaders of the Polish government-in-exile (the so-called London Poles), Hopkins concluded that even though the United States would have the solid support of the British, it was going to be extremely difficult to negotiate an agreement at Yalta that would guarantee the inclusion of non-Communists in a Polish coalition government to be followed by free elections.[10]

Between meetings with Churchill, Cadogan, and Anthony Eden, Hopkins found time to invite Robert Hopkins's new English bride, Brenda Stephenson, to his suite at Claridge's for a lunch of Whitstable oysters. "My doctors have forbidden me to eat these, but I can't resist them," he remarked.[11] Later he complimented Robert on his choice of Stephenson, confessing that "he fell in love with her immediately."[12]

When Hopkins and Bohlen landed in liberated Paris, they were met by Robert, who had been recalled after three bitterly cold weeks photographing the fierce fighting of the 94th Infantry, called "Patton's Golden Nugget," in and around Tattingen, a heavily defended village on the German frontier.

It was at Tattingen that Master Sergeant Nicholas Oresko won the Medal of Honor for singlehandedly taking out two machine-gun bunkers and killing twelve German soldiers. Robert had been embedded with the GIs as they patrolled in foot-deep snow, cleared pillboxes under fire, and shivered in foxholes and chow lines. He was immensely relieved to have received orders to return to Paris and join his father to photograph the Yalta conference just as he had filmed the conferences at Casablanca and Tehran.[13]

Hopkins's objective in Paris was to improve relations with the French, which "were at a pretty low ebb." Before meeting with General de Gaulle, symbol of French resistance to the Nazis and by then acknowledged leader of France, he was warned by Foreign Minister Georges Bidault that it would be difficult. De Gaulle, he warned, "makes no effort to please."[14]

Bidault's admonition was dead on. Hopkins thought he could get through to de Gaulle, as he had with others, by being candid and forthright, recognizing past differences, admitting fault, and conveying a sincere desire to work toward solutions. The general responded with contempt, however, lecturing Hopkins on France's proper role in the world and complaining that he should have been invited to attend the forthcoming conference at Yalta. Even the prospect of a French zone of occupation in postwar Germany and a permanent seat on the Security Council did nothing to thaw Hopkins's chilly reception.[15] The next day, during a lunch with Bidault and the other cabinet ministers, Hopkins, acting on his own initiative, suggested that arrangements could be made for de Gaulle to attend the Yalta conference for the political discussions. He also extended an invitation to de Gaulle to meet with Roosevelt after the conference. As he explained to the ministers, he was confident that the president would agree to one or both of these proposals.[16] However, when Bidault conveyed Hopkins's proposals to de Gaulle, he "scorned both notions out of hand," wrote Jim Bishop, an American journalist and author. "He refused to consider them and waved Bidault away."[17]

While in Paris, Hopkins and Bohlen visited with Eisenhower, who was living on the outskirts of the city in the Brown House, the mansion of an Englishman who festooned the rooms with all manner of Napoleonic artifacts, including a replica of Napoleon's desert headquarters tent.[18] During a discussion of military strategy and the postwar occupation of Germany, Hopkins made a thinly veiled bid to be named high commissioner of Germany, a post that had not yet been filled. Cautioning Eisenhower that some right-leaning candidates might seek a robust revival of the German economy, he suggested that someone "of the liberal school"—meaning himself—should be appointed.[19] On the eve of Yalta, Roosevelt and Hopkins had distanced themselves from the pastoralization of Germany advocated in the Morgenthau Plan, but they still favored some form of dismemberment, notwithstanding the recommendation of the State Department that the administration support decentralization but not partition.

In Rome Hopkins, his son, and Bohlen spent the night in the Barberini Palace, the official residence of the U.S. ambassador to Italy. The next morning, Myron Taylor, FDR's Vatican envoy, accompanied them to the papal suite, where they were greeted by Pope Pius XII. Hopkins was invited into the library for a twenty-minute private meeting with the Holy Father and Monsignor Montini (who would become Pope Paul VI in 1963).[20] Whether anything of substance was discussed is not known. Taylor, probably not the best judge of Hopkins's emotions, later reported that when Hopkins emerged, "he was in a glow of exaltation, revealing a surprisingly deep religious feeling."[21] During his stay in Rome, Hopkins met with the Italian foreign minister and held press briefings in which he risked reigniting Churchill's ire by criticizing British interference in Italian politics. He felt that the Italian people should have a much greater say in governing the country and that the State Department should take a leadership role in helping the Italians achieve this goal.[22]

While Hopkins and Bohlen hopscotched their way across liberated Europe into southern Italy, the president and his party entered the Mediterranean on the recently commissioned heavy cruiser *Quincy* and were steaming toward Malta. According to Anna, who had been invited along because she could best manage her father and protect his health, Roosevelt had been getting daily reports on Hopkins and was none too pleased about all of the press conferences he was giving on matters of foreign policy and the forthcoming conference. "FDR and his immediate entourage are laying for

Harry," she wrote, "because of all the interviews he has given out concerning the Conf."[23]

After a day briefing Stettinius and his State Department delegation, which rendezvoused with the Hopkins party in Caserta, Italy, the strain of the late nights and back-to-back meetings fortified by coffee, cigarettes, and whiskey caught up with Hopkins. Of the three-hour flight to Malta Stettinius wrote, "Hopkins was so sick that we put him to bed on the plane."[24] He was suffering from abdominal pains and severe diarrhea, though he joked that he had been fine "until he saw the Pope."[25] Churchill too was ill on his flight from London to Malta. He was running a temperature, wrote Lord Moran, his physician, "a good beginning to a winter journey of three thousand miles."[26] Like Roosevelt, he was accompanied not by his wife but by his daughter, Sarah Oliver. Writing to Clementine about Churchill's fever during the flight to Malta in an unheated converted bomber, Sarah said that he looked "like a poor hot pink baby about to cry."[27]

Notwithstanding their ailments, both Hopkins and Churchill were up and figuratively "waiting on the quay" as the *Quincy* sailed slowly into the Grand Harbor at Valetta, Malta, on the morning of February 2, 1945. "A half dozen Spitfires darted back and forth" above the cloudless harbor, recalled Stettinius.[28] "Roosevelt sat on deck, his dark navy cape around his shoulders, acknowledging salutes from the British men-of-war and the rolling cheers of spectators crowding the quays," wrote Bohlen.[29] Hopkins watched the spectacle from the British light cruiser *Sirius*, while Churchill could be seen across the way at the rail of the *Orion* waving at the president with cigar in hand.[30]

When Bohlen approached the president after boarding the *Quincy* with Hopkins, he was "shocked" by the dramatic deterioration in Roosevelt's appearance in the two weeks since he had last seen him up close. "He was not only frail and desperately tired," he later recalled, "[but] he looked ill. I never saw Roosevelt look as bad as he did then, despite a week's leisurely voyage at sea, where he could rest."[31] Almost everyone in the American and British delegations who recorded their impressions of the president that day expressed alarm at the poor state of his health.

Churchill was the exception. That night he wrote Clementine, "My friend has arrived in the best of health and spirits."[32] His eagerness to spend the day with the president and plan a unified strategy for the meetings with Stalin at Yalta apparently blinded his powers of observation. He and his delegation were expecting to engage the president for hours on matters of military strategy and the future of postwar Europe. However, they were in for a major disappointment because Roosevelt chose to spend the afternoon of February 2 with Anna and Sarah on a leisurely motor tour of Valetta and the ancient capital, Medina. While the president was gone, Eden, speaking for Churchill as well as himself, complained to Hopkins, "We are going into a decisive conference and had so far neither agreed what we would discuss nor how we would handle matters with a Bear [meaning Stalin] who would certainly know his mind."[33]

Hopkins agreed. Under his direction and that of his White House team, the State Department had prepared several briefing notebooks (called "black books") for Roosevelt on key issues to be discussed and resolved with the British and Soviets. FDR was supposed to have studied these black books on the voyage to Malta. Unlike previous wartime conferences, Hopkins aimed to have the president fully prepared and staffed.[34] Now it appeared that the president intended to go to Yalta without taking the time to listen to Churchill's latest views. Hopkins feared that Roosevelt might not have even read the black books.

According to her notes, Anna did her best that evening to ward off Hopkins, Eden, Stettinius, and others who wanted time with her father. Since everyone needed to be at the airport by midnight to board planes for Yalta, she wanted to make sure the president got some rest before departing the *Quincy* for the all-night flight. While she was packing, Hopkins and Robert arrived at her cabin. "Harry demanded a drink," Anna wrote in her diary, "so I gave him my one bottle. A few minutes after they had left I went to get the bottle and it was gone."[35] It was obvious that Anna had lost her taste for Hopkins. While it is unlikely that FDR shared her caustic attitude, some of his daughter's aversion must have rubbed off on him.

The Sacred Cow, escorted by six twin-tail P-38 fighter planes, landed at Saki Airfield in the Crimea a few minutes after noon on February 3, 1945.

Churchill's Skymaster touched down twenty minutes later. All morning, transports bearing the seven hundred American and British delegates to the Yalta conference had been landing at ten-minute intervals.

Molotov and a group of Soviet officials were on the slushy tarmac under tented tables laden with caviar and vodka as Hopkins, along with Roosevelt's personal entourage (Anna, Stettinius, Harriman, Pa Watson), stepped cautiously down the stairway that had been rolled out to the Sacred Cow. After Churchill arrived and joined the group, the president emerged and was lowered to the ground in a small elevator cage. Mike Reilly quickly picked him up and deposited him into an open jeep. Hatless but wearing a heavy black overcoat, Hopkins stepped forward to greet the president, who leaned toward him with a wide smile. Robert Hopkins captured the moment, which he called his "favorite photograph of President Roosevelt and my father together."[36] FDR appeared surprisingly robust next to Hopkins, whose pale yellowish skin, wrote Churchill's physician, was "stretched tight over the bones" of his weary face.[37]

After Roosevelt and Churchill reviewed an honor guard, the delegations were packed into lend-lease Packards for a jarring eighty-mile drive over the mountains to Yalta. The entire route was lined with troops of at least two Soviet divisions, many of them women.[38] Through the wet snow and spitting rain Hopkins glimpsed the wreckage of warfare strewn across the barren landscape.

The autos bearing the president, Hopkins, and the other members of their party began arriving after dark at the Livadia Palace, a fifty-room, marble and limestone summer home built for Czar Nicholas II that was situated high above the tideless Black Sea, four miles outside of Yalta. They were greeted by Averell Harriman's daughter, Kathleen, who had been advising the Soviets on the renovation of the palace in preparation for the conference. From the fall of 1941 until April 1944, it had been occupied by German troops. When the Red Army forced them to flee, they stripped the palace of everything of value, damaging rooms and chopping down trees in the garden.[39] "Harry arrived not very well & went straight to bed with dia (can't spell it anyway)," wrote Kathleen to her friend Pamela Churchill. "The doctors ordered him to eat nothing but cereal & the fool had 2 large helpings of caviar, cabbage soup and sour cream & then his cereal. . . . That brought his pains back."[40] Hopkins was fortunate to be assigned a room of his own on the first floor, not too far from a bathroom. The president, of course, had his own bedroom plus a private bathroom and the czar's study for small meetings. Marshall occupied the imperial bedroom on the second floor. To the amusement of many, Admiral King, a notorious lecher, was assigned the czarina's feminine boudoir. Robert Hopkins found a tiny room with a cot under the eaves. In all, more than two hundred Americans were squeezed into the palace, and for the next eight days they would share six bathrooms.

Sometime after dinner Anna stopped by Hopkins's room and, according to her notes, "found him in a stew." He was again worried that the president was not sufficiently prepared for the conference and that he needed to meet with Churchill before confronting Stalin. "He made a few insulting remarks to the effect that . . . FDR had asked for this job and that now, whether he liked it or not, he had to do the work, and that it was imperative that FDR and Churchill have some prearrangements before the big Conf. . . . I had never quite realized how pro-British Harry is."[41] Hopkins was aware, of course, that his sarcasm irritated Anna and that she had come to dislike if not despise him. But he was in no mood that evening to coddle her. As far as he was concerned, Anna was being overly possessive, arbitrarily blocking his accustomed access to the president and interfering with matters of the highest importance. For the remainder of the president's life, Anna would position herself as his primary shield. Jonathan Daniels, the son of Josephus Daniels (Roosevelt's old boss at the Navy Department during World War I), who would become FDR's press secretary near the end of the war, believed Anna and her husband aspired to a kind of "regency"—similar to that of Edith Bolling Wilson—in which they would assume executive responsibilities in order to relieve the ailing president.[42]

Stalin would not arrive in the Crimea until the next morning. His eleven-car armored train was sweeping south through ruined cities and snow-blanketed countryside that had been ravaged by the recent fighting. Advance elements of his armies, led by Marshals Zhukov and Ivan Koniev, were already establishing bridgeheads on the Oder River, well inside Germany and less than fifty miles from Berlin. On January 27 Koniev's forces liberated Auschwitz, although the Russians did not broadcast the scope of the slaughter that had taken place there until May 7. Even then, no mention was made of the fact that the victims were overwhelmingly Jews.[43] Poland and southeastern Europe—Romania, the Balkans, and much of Hungary—were in Stalin's hands. At Yalta he would push to establish a new border for Poland on the Oder and the Western Niesse, thus transferring a swath of German territory to Poland in exchange for twice the amount of land he would seize from Poland in the east. Once inside the old German border, Red Army soldiers were encouraged to seek vengeance. Mass raping of German women and girls and wholesale theft and destruction of property began and would not cease until they overran Berlin and reached the River Elbe.

On Sunday morning, February 4, Stalin and his bodyguards settled into the Yusupov Palace, situated midway between the British and the Americans. Yusupov was once the home of the wealthy prince of the same name who had assassinated Rasputin in 1916. Stalin immediately summoned Molotov, Beria, and Beria's son, Sergio, for an intelligence briefing on the plans of the Western leaders and arrangements for electronic eavesdropping. This time they would not only bug the bedrooms but would also deploy directional microphones to pick up conversations of Roosevelt and others when they were in hallways and outdoors.[44]

Stalin would be prepared to meet his so-called allies. Likening them to a couple of pickpockets, Stalin, himself a former bank robber and extortionist, had confided a few months earlier to the Yugoslav Communist leader Milovan Djilas, "There's nothing they like better than to trick their allies.... [Churchill] is the kind of man who will pick your pocket of a kopeck, [but Roosevelt] is not like that. He dips in his hand only for bigger coins."[45] Stalin thus accorded Roosevelt a much greater degree of respect and regarded him as his most formidable adversary.

During the first dinner of the Big Three at Yalta, a lavish affair with sturgeon and five kinds of wine, Roosevelt committed a bit of a diplomatic faux pas when he jovially confided to Stalin that he and Churchill often referred to him as "Uncle Joe," a nickname that had entered their private vocabulary in 1942. Once translated, Stalin took umbrage, regarding it as patronizing and an affront to his dignity.[46] He was also not at all pleased when Churchill, making a pointed reference to Stalin's disdain for the rights of small nations, famously—and, in light of his "naughty document," hypocritically—commented after dinner, "The eagle shall permit the small birds to sing and care not wherefore they sang."[47]

Each afternoon for the next week, the Big Three and their key advisors would bring to the table in the grand ballroom of the Livadia Palace a set of differing objectives, priorities, and assumptions. A few of their differences were actually resolved; some, in loose language that can only be described as a deliberate fudge, appeared to be settled but would quickly unravel; and several others were tabled for future discussion. The negotiations were multifaceted and the issues were interlocking, with parties prevailing when they had the most leverage and compelled to give in when they did not.

The enduring myth of the conference is that a dying Roosevelt sold out Eastern Europe to Stalin and the Communists. For years politicians in France portrayed Yalta as the place where Roosevelt, with Churchill's acquiescence, carved up Europe into two blocs. Republicans in the United States claimed throughout the cold war that Yalta, like Munich in 1938, was one of the worst instances of craven appeasement to a tyrant. As late as 2005 President George W. Bush, in a speech in Latvia, said that Yalta was an "attempt to sacrifice freedom for the sake of stability, which left a continent divided and unstable. The captivity of millions in Central and Eastern Europe will be remembered as one of the greatest wrongs of history."[48]

In fact Eastern Europe was forfeited by the West not at Yalta but much earlier, in July 1942. As recounted earlier, it was during that month that Roosevelt and Hopkins, at the behest of Churchill and his military advisors, orchestrated the most important strategic decision of the war: to invade French North Africa instead of northwestern France. Militarily it was almost certainly the correct decision. The leaders were not fully aware of its consequences, but that decision, coupled with Eisenhower's slow progress in Tunisia, delayed the opening of the second front in France until June 1944. This enabled the Red Army, through battlefield successes, to occupy most of Eastern Europe by the time of the Yalta conference. At Tehran in late

1943 Stalin signaled his resistance to a non-Communist government in Po-land, and both Roosevelt and Hopkins sat passively as Stalin and Churchill discussed its future boundaries. Thus in February 1945 the Soviets had maximum leverage over the fate of Poland and the rest of Eastern Europe. They could be forced out only by another war, an option that was unthinkable when Germany had yet to be conquered and the war in the Pacific was far from over.[49]

Except on one issue—the inclusion of France on the commission that would control postwar Germany—it is difficult to assess with certainty the influence of Hopkins on the decisions made at Yalta. Throughout the conference, he was so sick that he spent most of the time in bed, leaving his room to attend the late afternoon plenary sessions, where he would sit behind Roosevelt and pass him notes of advice.[50] Doris Kearns Goodwin wrote that Hopkins "was in the best position to know what was really going on" at Yalta, his room being "a center of activity, with members of all three delegations stopping by to seek his advice."[51] Little is known, however, about the substance of these bedroom conversations.

Roosevelt's primary objectives at Yalta were twofold: a firm commitment by Stalin to enter the war against Japan; and resolution of remaining differences over the UN so that an organizing conference could be scheduled and the world would know that the Soviets were ready to cooperate in maintaining world peace. As to the first objective, Stalin needed no persuading, and it appears that Hopkins had no involvement. Nor did Hopkins have any role at Yalta in packaging the territorial concessions in the Far East that Stalin demanded as his price for declaring war on Japan, although Hopkins had been involved when most of these issues were discussed and largely settled at Tehran. In a meeting on February 8, from which Hopkins and Churchill were absent, Roosevelt and Stalin sealed the deal on Japan and the Far East territorial concessions.[52] In exchange for dominion over islands, ports, and railroads that would come largely at China's expense (Chiang would be informed later), Stalin agreed to enter the war against Japan two or three months after Germany was defeated. Two days later Churchill, "seeing no particular harm in the presence of Russia as a Pacific Power," agreed to the territorial settlement.[53]

It appears that Hopkins did have a hand in helping Roosevelt achieve his other main objective—an agreement leading to formation of the UN—which Hopkins regarded as "more important than anything else."[54] The three parties were divided over the scope of the veto power that could be exercised in the Security Council and whether and to what extent Great Britain and the Soviet Union should have extra votes in the General Assembly for countries under their control (e.g., India, Ukraine). Hopkins knew from his earlier meetings in London how strongly the British felt about an extra vote for India. He also sensed from the Soviet delegation that they were not really serious about pressing for a total of sixteen votes, one for each of their so-called autonomous republics. If Hopkins could get Churchill and Roosevelt to play their cards right, he saw the makings of a deal.

The deal began to play out at the plenary session on February 6. Based on a tutorial by Hopkins, Stettinius presented the American position on the scope of the veto: it should be used to block only actions and decisions but not mere discussion of an issue. The Soviets, as predicted, were suspicious and asked for time to study the proposal. Churchill, possibly because of bedroom lobbying by Hopkins, chimed in, saying he strongly supported the American position and was satisfied that it would protect the interests of the Soviets and the other powers on the Security Council. It was two against one on the veto issue.[55]

The next day Stalin compromised. Speaking through Molotov, he gave in on the veto and offered to narrow his remaining difference with the Americans by reducing his demand for votes in the General Assembly from sixteen to three.[56] By giving in on these issues early, Stalin hoped to earn credits that he could use later on issues of much greater importance to him, such as Polish boundaries and governance and German reparations. He was not overly concerned about the USSR becoming part of the UN because he believed that military strength and control of Eastern Europe would in the end be sufficient to protect Soviet interests.

It was up to Roosevelt to respond to Stalin's offer, but now the shoe was on the other foot. The Soviets and the British were aligned against the Americans, who had always believed that each nation should have only one vote in the General Assembly. (No one realized it at the time, but whether a nation had extra votes in the UN General Assembly would have little if any importance.) To preserve Allied unity Roosevelt could have been forced to play a compromise card. Instead he tried to dodge the issue, launching into a rambling, largely irrelevant monologue. From his seat behind the president, Hopkins sensed that Stalin was getting impatient and that the opportunity for a deal was slipping away. He "scribbled" a note and passed it up to Roosevelt: "Mr. President—I think you should try to get this referred to Foreign ministers before there is trouble."[57]

Roosevelt followed Hopkins's advice. At the foreign ministers meeting on February 8, the British continued to support Stalin's extra vote proposal, just as they said they would when Hopkins met with them in London. At the same meeting, the State Department, fearful of criticism back home, tried to avoid taking a position.[58]

Notwithstanding the stance of his own diplomats, Roosevelt changed his mind that day and privately dealt the compromise card, no doubt due to the advice of Hopkins and pressure from Churchill. The Soviets would get two extra votes in the General Assembly, one for Ukraine and one for Belorussia. Britain would get extra votes for India and her Commonwealth members.[59] In his diary Lord Moran wrote that Hopkins told him that Churchill was the one mainly responsible for convincing FDR to support Stalin's voting proposal. If this is an accurate report, it is likely that Hopkins was deliberately downplaying his own influence.[60]

Two days later Hopkins and Jimmy Byrnes, head of the Office of War Mobilization who would be responsible for putting a favorable spin on the Yalta accords to Congress and the public, persuaded Roosevelt that he should counterbalance the Soviet Union's two extra votes by asking that the United States be given two additional seats in the General Assembly.[61] Stalin promptly granted the president's request, but the extra vote provisions were kept secret until late March, when they were leaked to the *New York Herald Tribune*. A storm of criticism erupted not so much because the Soviets were given extra votes but because it was regarded as shameful and absurd for the United States to ask for a quid pro quo over such an inconsequential matter and then to keep it secret. Because of this and other details that leaked out in the spring of 1945, the word *Yalta* came to connote devious, secret concessions to Stalin in the minds of a large segment of the American people.[62]

———————————

For Churchill, the future balance of power in Europe was more important than the UN. Anxious to restore strong buffer states between the USSR and the British Isles, he wanted France rehabilitated as a major power, opposed saddling Germany with punitive reparations, and sought to avoid commitments regarding the dismemberment of Germany.[63] Fresh from his talks in London and Paris, Hopkins tended to side with Churchill and de Gaulle on the importance of restoring France. At the second plenary meeting on February 5, after Stalin and Roosevelt disagreed with Churchill's proposal to restore some of France's stature by giving it a seat on the Allied Control Commission that would run occupied Germany, Hopkins began a campaign to change Roosevelt's mind. He passed a note to Roosevelt, asking him to postpone further discussion of "French participation on Control Commission" until later. Roosevelt followed Hopkins's advice.[64]

Over the next few days Hopkins, aided by Freeman Matthews of the State Department, met with Roosevelt privately and convinced him to change his mind on giving France a place on the Control Commission. Just before the plenary session on February 10, Roosevelt told Stalin he had reversed his position and agreed with Churchill. Since this was a matter of secondary importance to him, Stalin yielded to the majority. Later that day at the plenary session, the Big Three granted France a seat on the Allied Control Commission.[65]

Stalin was also outmaneuvered on two other matters involving the future of Western Europe, although, again, there is little evidence that Hopkins had a direct role in influencing the outcome. Throughout the conference Stalin pressed for a commitment on how Germany would be dismembered and a final decision on the amount of reparations that would be extracted. He got neither. While it was agreed that the surrender terms would include a provision that Germany be dismembered, the issue of *how* it would be dismembered was consigned to a commission of the foreign ministers that never could agree. The reparations issue was referred to another commission.[66] Hopkins's only involvement was a note to Roosevelt during the seventh plenary session, when Stalin became uncharacteristically emotional due to British intransigence over the principles that would guide the proposed Reparations Commission. "Mr. President," he wrote, "the Russians have given in so much at this conference that I don't think we should let them down. Let the British . . . continue their disagreement. . . . Simply say it is all referred to the Reparations Commission." Roosevelt again took Hopkins's advice, which meant that the British and the Americans would be able to "grant or withhold reparations as they pleased" because, as the historian David Kennedy writes, through their postwar occupation zones they would control the "industrial heartland" of western Germany.[67]

Stalin could afford to be stymied on dismemberment, reparations, and the restoration of French stature, but territorial security, particularly Polish territory, was a "fundamental, even visceral, issue for Stalin."[68] It was critical to his regime that Poland, the historic gateway to aggression from the West, be maintained as a Soviet client state. Although not quite critical, it was nevertheless important to Churchill, and less so to Roosevelt, that Poland emerge from the Yalta conference with a promise of some vestige of independence. After all, the British had guaranteed Poland its independence in 1939, declared war when it was invaded, and were hosting its government-in-exile. Stalin, however, held most of the winning cards. His troops occupied much of the country; he had liquidated the cream of the Polish officer corps in the Katyn Forest; and to the further dismay of the West, he had already installed a puppet government temporarily seated in the eastern Polish city of Lublin that became known as the "Lublin Poles." Even before they departed for Yalta, Churchill and Roosevelt knew that they had been dealt a weak hand on Poland. Churchill confided to his private secretary, Jock Colville, "There is nothing I can do for poor Poland."[69] To a group of senators Roosevelt said, "The Russians have the power in Eastern Europe . . . and the only practicable course was to use what influence we had to ameliorate the situation."[70]

At Yalta Stalin played his cards skillfully, waiting for his counterparts to raise the issue of Poland and offering carefully timed concessions on the UN with a view to extracting something in return. Beginning on February 6 and for the next three days, Churchill, with support from Roosevelt and

Hopkins, took the lead in arguing that the Lublin Poles should be replaced by a *new* government that would include non-Communists within Poland and others drawn from leaders of the London Poles. The new government, they said, should then hold free and open elections.

Hopkins was deeply involved in supporting these arguments, at one point drafting a letter from Roosevelt to Stalin proposing that they invite representatives of the Lublin Poles and the London Poles to Yalta to work out a settlement.[71] Stalin and Molotov adroitly rejected this proposal and many others. Gradually the British and Americans backed down. Instead of establishing a new Polish government, the parties finally agreed that the existing Communist government would be "reorganized on a broader democratic basis." In addition, while the final agreement called for "free and unfettered elections," the provision for having the elections monitored and validated by the U.S. and British ambassadors was dropped from the final agreement. Their role was reduced to informing their governments "about the situation in Poland."[72]

Recognizing at once that the language of the final agreement on Poland was vague and subject to differing interpretations, Admiral Leahy remarked, "Mr. President, this is so elastic that the Russians can stretch it all the way from Yalta to Washington without ever technically breaking it." "I know, Bill—I know it," said Roosevelt. "But it's the best I can do for Poland at this time."[73]

Many have speculated as to whether it was the best he could do. Why, for example, didn't he and Hopkins use the promise of postwar financial incentives, such as low-interest loans and continued lend-lease aid, as leverage to extract airtight language on Poland and other concessions? Indeed a proposal for a $6 billion reconstruction loan had been made by Molotov to Harriman in January, but apparently it was never discussed at Yalta.[74] Perhaps, as the historian David Reynolds has plausibly suggested, financial incentives were not deployed as bargaining chips because Roosevelt feared that after the war America would be facing a recession and it would be extremely difficult, if not impossible, to get a Russian aid package through Congress.[75] Still, in retrospect it remains odd that the Americans never put some form of financial aid to the USSR on the table at Yalta.

Had Roosevelt and Hopkins been healthy at Yalta, would the fate of Eastern Europe, particularly Poland, have been any different? It seems unlikely. By all accounts, Hopkins's mental faculties and prodigious analytical powers were entirely intact both in the bedroom meetings and at the plenary sessions. Similarly, Roosevelt, having achieved his main objectives, reportedly played his weak hand on Poland "with his usual skill and perception."[76]

FDR was probably right—it was the best he could do. As mentioned earlier, the 1942 decision to delay the second front, engineered with Hopkins's "invaluable aid," had led to Soviet domination of Eastern Europe, although there is no evidence that Roosevelt and Hopkins foresaw that result. Short of war or a decision to abandon all efforts to achieve postwar cooperation by denying the Soviet Union moral and political recognition, the president had to give in. And even if he had held out for tighter language, in the end it wouldn't have made much difference. According to Harriman, Stalin "was bound to bend or break the agreements even if they had been sewn up more tightly."[77]

When the final plenary session broke up early on the afternoon of February 11, an exhausted Hopkins returned to his room while the Big Three, their advisors, and the military brass were escorted outside to the courtyard of the Livadia Palace. Once Roosevelt, Churchill, and Stalin were seated in the courtyard's center well, Robert Hopkins, who had been placed in charge of the photo shoot, set up his cameras along with the other official photographers. "I sensed a kind of euphoria among the principals and members of all three delegations for what had been accomplished," wrote Robert. "Their faces reflected relief from the strain of negotiations and there was a good deal of laughter and good-natured banter among them."[78]

For the next forty-five minutes Robert and the others took dozens of photographs, some showing Roosevelt slack-mouthed, weary, and drawn, a cigarette dangling from his fingers, others catching him when he was animated and fully engaged. At one point Stalin motioned Robert over and offered him an opportunity to accompany the Red Army and become "the first American to film the fall of Berlin." After the photo op Robert raced to his father's room and asked whether he could arrange for him to accept Stalin's offer. "You can't go," said Hopkins. According to Robert, his father told him the Soviets would never let him near the front, that if he somehow got to the front they wouldn't let him take photos, and that even if he could sneak a few photos, they would never let them leave the country.[79] In this Hopkins revealed an extraordinary degree of cynicism and distrust toward the Soviets. Perhaps he was already beginning to doubt whether they would honor the promises they made at Yalta.

The Yalta conference adjourned at 3:45 p.m., after Churchill, Roosevelt, and Stalin, in that order, signed the communiqué.[80] "Stalin, like some genie, just disappeared," recalled Sarah Oliver.[81] Churchill, who would soon pay a heavy price for the Polish settlement, felt lonely as he returned to his villa. The president, along with Harriman and Bohlen, departed by automobile for Sevastopol to view the battle damage and spend the night aboard the communications ship *Catoctin*. "Dad was too sick to make that trip," recalled Robert, so Stalin arranged for a car and driver to take the two of them to Simferopol, where a train with old wooden carriages that had once belonged to the Romanovs would take them back to the airfield at Saki.

In the dark and bitter cold, Hopkins and his son waited for what seemed like hours outside the locked train until someone arrived with a key. They were taken through the empty carriage to a compartment, where Hopkins undressed, put on pajamas, and climbed into a Pullman bed. Robert snapped a photo of his father in bed with a mug of tea, flashing a wan smile but looking positively cadaverous. An open pack of Lucky Strikes and a plate of untouched bread were on the night table next to him.[82] He would say of that experience, wrote Stettinius, "If I ever see a foreigner on a station platform in America again I'll show him the washroom and buy him a drink."[83]

When they awoke the next morning, the train was on a siding near the airfield at Saki. Within a few hours Hopkins joined Roosevelt and his party for the return flight to Egypt in the Sacred Cow. By late afternoon Hopkins and his son were back aboard the *Quincy*, which had been lying at anchor in the Great Bitter Lake, the saltwater lake that connects the northern and southern parts of the Suez Canal. Hopkins dashed off a wire to Louise: "Have finished conference and have arrived on second leg of journey where heavy underwear is not needed. Miss you terribly, and send you my dearest love. Call Avis [Bohlen's wife] up and tell her that Chip [Bohlen] is well but difficult to keep in nights."[84]

The mood of Roosevelt and others on the *Quincy* was that of "supreme exultation," as congratulatory messages flooded in from around the world. Commenting on the published portions of the Yalta communiqué, Herbert Hoover said the decisions at Yalta "offer a great hope to the world." William Shirer, the journalist who had watched the rise of the Third Reich from within, termed the Yalta accords "a landmark in human history." Even Hopkins, normally skeptical and harboring a more realistic view of how Stalin actually operated, was caught up in the euphoria. Recalling the mood on the *Quincy*, he later told Sherwood, "We really believed in our hearts that this was the dawn of a new day we had all been praying for and talking about for so many years. . . . We felt sure we could count on [Stalin] to be reasonable and sensible and understanding—but we never could be sure who or what might be back of him there in the Kremlin."[85]

For Hopkins and Roosevelt the euphoria would be short-lived. Once the effect of the laudatory telegrams, positive press reports and self-ongratulations subsided, they would eventually come to understand that at his core Stalin was, in the words of David Reynolds, "deeply xenophobic," viscerally suspicious of the "capitalist West."[86] Notwithstanding his words and understated manner, he would never abandon his insatiable craving for territorial security nor his dream of international revolution. Hopkins's notion that Stalin could be counted on to cooperate was a fleeting delusion. And Roosevelt's conviction that he could "personally handle Stalin" would be buried with him in a few months.[87]

Aboard the *Quincy* in the Great Bitter Lake, Hopkins and his son witnessed a historic meeting between the president and King Ibn Saud of Saudi Arabia, who had never been outside his country. Hopkins described the king as "a man of austere dignity, great power and a born soldier."[88] By contrast, in a letter to Cousin Daisy, FDR poked fun at the Arab leader, who arrived with an exotic entourage consisting of "his whole court, slaves (black), taster, astrologer and 8 live sheep. Whole party was a scream!"[89]

The meeting began amicably, as the king, a massive man whose legs had been severely wounded in battle, established rapport by pointing out that the two of them were "twins," since they were both the same age, rulers of their countries, and physically handicapped.[90] Following an exchange of gifts during which FDR promised to give the king a C-47 airplane similar to the Sacred Cow, the president turned the conversation to the resettlement of European Jews in Palestine, suggesting that the king should admit another ten thousand.[91] Roosevelt "was greatly shocked," wrote Hopkins, "when Ibn Saud, without a smile, simply said, 'No.'" According to Hopkins, FDR "brought the question up two or three times more," and each time the king firmly replied in the negative, making plain that the "Arab world" would never permit additional Jewish settlements in Palestine and inferring that the Arabs would "take up arms" over the issue.[92] In words that have resonated over the decades since 1945, the Saudi Arabian king warned the American president, as Bohlen recalled, that "Arabs would choose to die rather than yield their land to Jews."[93]

Churchill was "greatly disturbed" when Roosevelt told him at Yalta that he would be meeting in the Suez Canal with Ibn Saud as well as King Farouk of Egypt and Emperor Haile Selassie of Ethiopia. "[He] thought we had some deep laid plot to undermine the British Empire in these areas," wrote Hopkins.[94] Consequently the day after the *Quincy* emerged from the Suez following the meetings with the three rulers, Churchill arranged through Hopkins to meet with FDR in the harbor at Alexandria. For an hour or so Roosevelt, Churchill, and Hopkins sat in the sun on the *Quincy*. The president shrugged off his talks with Ibn Saud and the other potentates as uneventful. Instead they concentrated on Churchill's proposal that Britain have a role in the postwar research and development of atomic bombs. According to Churchill, Roosevelt "made no objection of any kind."[95]

The three of them "gathered afterwards in [FDR's] cabin for an informal family luncheon," wrote Churchill. They were joined by Churchill's daughter Sarah, his son Randolph, and Roosevelt's daughter Anna. Hopkins was there, although feeling none too well. A few minutes before four, Roosevelt and Churchill "bade affectionate farewells." "I thought he had a slender contact with life," wrote Churchill a few years later of his impression when he clasped the president's hand. "I was not to see him again."[96]

When the *Quincy* was about to depart Alexandria, a telegram from General de Gaulle arrived. At Yalta Hopkins had received word that de Gaulle had changed his mind and would be happy to meet with Roosevelt in Algiers, which was French territory. Now he was changing his mind again, reneging on his agreement. The president was angry. He dictated a petulant reply that Steve Early showed to Hopkins before it went out. Hopkins, bedridden in his stateroom, told Early to warn Roosevelt to tone down the message because it would alienate the French people. The president refused to back down— Early said the Boss's "Dutch" was up—so Hopkins insisted that Bohlen try to change Roosevelt's mind. According to Bohlen, he was getting nowhere with the president when he blurted out, "We can all admit that de Gaulle is being one of the biggest sons of bitches that ever straddled a pot." This got through to Roosevelt. His eyes "twinkled," he flashed "his famous smile" and "threw back his head" in laughter. "Oh, go ahead," he said to Bohlen, "you and Harry try your hand at a draft." Bohlen and Hopkins worked out a diplomatic reply, one "that avoided vituperation," and simply expressed regret that de Gaulle was unable to meet.[97] The president approved.

Claiming to be desperately ill, Hopkins emerged from his cabin on the afternoon of February 17 to join Roosevelt and Anna on deck as the *Quincy* cruised in the Mediterranean toward Algiers. He had something to tell the president, and he needed to do it face-to-face. Based on Anna's recollection, Hopkins said, "Chip and I are getting off at Algiers. . . . I'm sick. I mean really sick. I want to stop off and go to Marrakech and rest."[98]

FDR was annoyed and disappointed, muttering later that Hopkins had always rallied before and that he simply wanted to escape the boredom of a long trip at sea.[99] The president had already decided that he would address a joint session of Congress about the Yalta conference as soon as he returned to Washington. He was depending on Hopkins, and to a lesser extent on Bohlen, to help him write the speech during the homeward voyage. Later Anna went to Hopkins's stateroom to beg him to stay. "Truly, Anna," said Hopkins, "I am too sick to work. I mean it. . . . Tell your father to call Sam Rosenman in. He's in London and can fly down to Algiers."[100]

A recently discovered letter from Hopkins to Louise casts some doubt on whether Hopkins was as sick as he claimed. Dated February 15, the letter provides no indication that he was not feeling well, saying only that he was taking all meals in his room and only one "highball a day." In his lighthearted way, he told Louise that because of a forecast of "heavy weather" that would cause the cruiser "to roll admirably," he was "still undecided" but might depart the *Quincy* at Algiers and "loaf" for a few days in the sun in Marrakech before taking a "leisurely air trip home."[101] While it is possible to conclude from this that Hopkins was more bored than sick, it seems more reasonable to believe that he was downplaying his physical condition to his wife, preferring not to give her reason to worry. In addition the letter was written two days before he decided to leave the ship, and he could have gotten much worse during that time.

Anna rejoined her father on deck; he was wrapped in his navy cape against the wind. "Hopkins won't budge," she said. Roosevelt wearily replied, "Let him go."[102] The president must have felt that yet another of the few intimates he depended on over the years was leaving him. First it was Louis Howe, his campaign manager from his earliest days in politics, who had died in 1936; next it was Missy LeHand, who suffered debilitating strokes in 1941 and eventually died at the end of July 1944; and then it was his mother, Sara Delano. In the sick bay below decks, his beloved companion Pa Watson was in a coma, having suffered a stroke that would lead to his death two days hence. Gloom settled over the *Quincy*.

The next day after lunch, as Hopkins was about to go ashore at Algiers, he stopped by the president's stateroom. Roosevelt looked up, extended his hand, and coldly said, "Goodbye." His gaze immediately returned to the papers spread before him. Without looking back, Hopkins quietly slipped out the door. He would never see the president again.[103]

Hopkins regretted for the rest of his life that they parted in this way, but he had reached the limit of his endurance. Over the previous three weeks he had lost eighteen pounds. He was barely surviving on plasma and liver extract. He knew he could not get any real rest during the nine-day transatlantic crossing in rough seas while working on draft after draft of the president's speech. He had given his life to this man. Notwithstanding Roosevelt's evident anger, he believed he had earned a break. He would take a few days to regain some of his strength, and then he would fly home.

18

A Leave of Absence from Death

This time Hopkins did not rally. He landed in Washington on February 24, 1945, but was home for only two days before flying on to the Mayo Clinic in Minnesota. It was clearly no overstatement when Hopkins told FDR and Anna on the *Quincy* that he was sick, "I mean really sick."

Some physicians at Mayo diagnosed Hopkins as suffering from nontropical sprue (or celiac disease), an immune reaction triggered by gluten that prevents the villi and microvilli in the small intestine from absorbing nutrients. From hospital records it is not clear whether this was the controlling diagnosis, nor whether Hopkins was placed on a strict gluten-free diet.[1] Nevertheless with the aid of blood transfusions and some kind of a dietary regimen, he was starting to feel "much better" by the end of the first week of April, although he had regained almost none of the weight he lost at Yalta.[2]

While Hopkins recuperated in the hospital, Roosevelt and Churchill, in speeches and interviews about Yalta, oversold their interpretations of the agreements made there and papered over the compromises. At a joint session of Congress, FDR predicted that Yalta spelled an end to "spheres of influence" and gave birth to an organization that would ensure postwar peace. He touted the elastic agreement on Poland as "one outstanding example of joint action by the three major Allied powers," and then made a major public relations and political mistake by failing to disclose that the USSR and the United States were given extra votes to cast in the UN General Assembly.[3] In the House of Commons, Churchill professed his trust in Stalin and his Soviet colleagues, proclaiming, "Their word is their bond."[4] But in Moscow and Warsaw, the Yalta accords had already begun to fray. The Lublin government of Poland resisted "reorganization" by vetoing non-Communist candidates, excluding Western observers, and shipping rivals off to prison camps. The king of Romania was compelled by the Soviets to appoint a government dominated by Communists. Stalin announced that Molotov was too busy to join the other foreign ministers at the UN organizing conference in San Francisco. At the Mayo Clinic, Hopkins kept up with the news and corresponded with his colleagues and friends in Washington. He might well have spoken with the president by phone, but there is no evidence that he did and no extant written communications between the two of them after he left the *Quincy* at Algiers.

Throughout March Churchill peppered Roosevelt with cables, urging him to take a hard line with the Soviets on adherence to the letter of the Yalta agreements. With one notable exception (when Stalin accused the Americans of cutting a surrender deal with the Germans behind his back), Roosevelt resisted confrontation, striving to keep the alliance intact and preferring to let things work out over time. In his last message to Churchill, one of the very few he wrote himself during the final days of his life, he said, "I would minimize the Soviet problem as much as possible because these problems, in one form or another, seem to arise every day and most straighten themselves out. . . . We must be firm, however, and our course thus far is correct."[5]

That evening, April 11, Henry Morgenthau joined Roosevelt, Lucy Mercer, Cousin Daisy, and a couple of others for dinner in the little White House in Warm Springs, Georgia. "I was terribly shocked when I saw him," wrote Morgenthau in his diary. "I found he had aged terrifically and looked very haggard. His hands shook so that he started to knock over the glasses. . . . I was in agony watching him."[6] At about one o'clock the next day, while sitting for portrait artist Elizabeth Shoumatoff in the living room, papers spread before him on a card table, Roosevelt slumped forward. As Daisy later recalled, the president "put his hand up to the back of his head and said, 'I have a terrific pain in the back of my head.' And then he collapsed."[7] He died of a massive cerebral hemorrhage just before 3:30 p.m.

The telephone rang in Hopkins's room at the Mayo Clinic on the afternoon of April 12. It was Chip Bohlen calling from the White House. When he told Hopkins of the president's death, "there was a long silence at the other end of the phone," recalled Bohlen. "Then Hopkins said, 'I better be going to Washington.'"[8]

One of Hopkins's first thoughts was to reach out to Churchill, who at the time of Roosevelt's death was dining with Bernard Baruch at the Savoy in London. "I cannot tell you what goes through my mind and heart," Hopkins wrote from the hospital. "All I know is that we have lost one of our greatest friends and the world its most outstanding champion of freedom and justice."[9] The prime minister would receive Hopkins's wire in the morning. "I felt as if I had been struck a physical blow," recalled Churchill.[10]

Isidore Lubin, Hopkins's friend and colleague, arrived at the Mayo Clinic at 10 p.m. on April 12 to accompany Hopkins on the trip back to Washington for Roosevelt's funeral. Before boarding their flight the next morning, Hopkins called Robert Sherwood. According to Sherwood, Hopkins talked "with a kind of exultation," saying, "You and I have got something great we can take with us all the rest of our lives . . . because we know it's *true* what so many people believed about [FDR] and what made them love him. The President never let them down. That's what you and I can remember. Oh, we all know he could be exasperating . . . in the little things. . . . But in the big things—all of the things that were of real, permanent importance—he never let the people down."[11]

It was bedlam at Hopkins's home in Georgetown when he returned after a six-week absence on Friday afternoon, April 13. The telephone was constantly ringing as friends, government officials, and diplomats called to find out how he was and whether he could spare a moment to see them. Even President Truman, who had been chief executive for less than twenty-four hours, called and made an appointment to meet with Hopkins on Saturday morning prior to the funeral.

Each of the dozens of calls in and out of Hopkins's house during the next several days was duly transcribed by eavesdropping FBI agents. Inexplicably the electronic surveillance had been reinstituted on April 9, while Hopkins was still at the Mayo Clinic and would continue on and off until July 25, 1945. Based on notes by J. Edgar Hoover's secretaries, Hopkins knew his home phone was being tapped—indeed he almost certainly authorized it—but the reason why Louise was again under investigation remains unknown. In the dozens of pages of transcripts released after Hoover's death, the only tantalizing clue is that shortly before April 9 Hopkins was very angry with her because of something she did or said regarding Shangri-La, the presidential retreat.[12]

An enormous crowd stood in Lafayette Park as Hopkins was driven through the gates of the White House at about 11:30 a.m. on April 14. Roosevelt's casket had already been placed on a bier in the East Room near the Stuart portrait of George Washington. Truman greeted Hopkins in the Oval Office on the first floor, which by then had been emptied of FDR's papers and effects.[13] The two Harrys were old acquaintances. They first met in the fall of 1933, when Truman, as Missouri director of the federal re-employment service and presiding judge in Jackson County, worked with Hopkins in directing unemployed laborers to jobs on federal public works projects. Over the years, as Truman served as a Missouri senator and then as vice president, Hopkins had always been accessible and helpful to him, traits that he would never forget.[14] In his memoirs Truman praised Hopkins as a "man whom Roosevelt trusted implicitly . . . a dedicated man who never sought credit or the limelight, yet willingly bore the brunt of criticism, just or unjust. He was a rare figure in Washington officialdom." Truman confessed that like Roosevelt, "I, too, trusted [Hopkins] implicitly, and unless his health had been seriously impaired I hoped that he would continue with me in the same role he had played with my predecessor."[15]

As vice president, Truman was kept out of the loop, rarely even speaking with Roosevelt, much less brought into his confidence. Now that he was president, he needed to get up to speed on foreign affairs. He wanted "firsthand information about the heads of state" he would have to deal with, "particularly Stalin." He also wished to review with Hopkins "the whole situation in regard to Russia and Poland and the United Nations."[16] More than anyone else in or out of government, Hopkins was in the best position to tutor the new president. Besides, as Truman knew from prior experience, Hopkins "always told the truth. Never tried to fool you."[17]

In the barren Oval Office, picking at sandwiches on trays ordered from the White House kitchen, Truman asked questions but mostly listened as Hopkins described and characterized the world leaders he had met and explained the policies advocated and deals made by Roosevelt at Casablanca, Cairo, Tehran, and Yalta. Truman found Hopkins to be an invaluable source of information, with an eye for telling details and keen insights into personalities. "Stalin," he told Truman, "is a forthright, rough, tough Russian. He is a Russian partisan through and through, thinking always first of Russia. But he can be talked to frankly." These remarks, recorded by Truman in his memoirs, suggest that some of the optimism Hopkins had expressed in the immediate aftermath of Yalta regarding future dealings with Stalin had faded. Expressing confidence that Truman would "continue to carry out the policies of Franklin Roosevelt," Hopkins said he would offer Truman "all the assistance [he could]." As the two-hour meeting came to a close, Hopkins, perhaps fishing for an offer, told Truman that he "planned to retire from the government on May 12." Truman, of course, took the bait and said he would like Hopkins to stay on, health permitting. Hopkins was noncommittal but "promised [to] give the matter serious thought."[18]

At a few minutes before four, guests were being guided to their chairs in the East Room by White House ushers. Sherwood, already seated, felt a hand on his shoulder. It was Hopkins, "who looked like death, the skin of his face a dreadful cold white with apparently no flesh left under it."[19] Truman, with his wife, Bess, and daughter, Margaret, entered and approached the front row. No one rose to acknowledge the president of the United States. Two minutes later Eleanor Roosevelt entered. Everyone stood until she was seated by her son Elliott in the front row on the aisle. The funeral service began with the singing of "Eternal Father, Strong to Save," the Navy hymn. It was the hymn Roosevelt loved more than any other, the hymn that he and Churchill, with Hopkins just behind them, had sung four years earlier on the fantail of the *Prince of Wales*. At this moment Hopkins, standing next to Louise's chair, "looked angry," wrote the journalist Jim Bishop. Then "he burst into sobs and bent forward, clutching the chair."[20] The service was poignant but brief, lasting about twenty minutes.

As the guests queued to pay their last respects before the closed bronze casket, Hopkins invited Sherwood and his wife to stop by his house in Georgetown. Late that afternoon, Sherwood sat next to Hopkins's bed in his small upstairs room. Hopkins was in his pajamas but was sitting up in his bed, arms clutched around his knees. "He didn't seem like death now," wrote Sherwood. "Fire was shooting out of his sharp eyes in sunken sockets." "God damn it," Hopkins began, "now we've got to get to work on our own. . . . We've had it too easy all this time, because we knew he was there. . . . Whatever we thought was the matter with the world . . . we could take our ideas to him. . . . Well—he isn't there now, and we've got to find a way to do things by ourselves." It was almost as if Hopkins was assuming that he and the other Roosevelt loyalists would continue to work in the White House and run things. But that is not what he meant. His words and the passion behind them were meant to express both the depth of the national loss and confidence that America and its leaders would find "a way." Hopkins hoped that the brand of personal diplomacy that he learned from Roosevelt would be practiced by the new administration, but as a political realist he knew that he would be an unlikely bearer of the torch.

A moment later Hopkins touched on Truman's strengths and on why Roosevelt chose him as his potential successor over other contenders. Without referring to his own precarious health, he told Sherwood that he intended to resign and that the cabinet should do the same, except for Stimson and Forrestal, who should stay until the war was over. "Truman has got to have his own people around him, not Roosevelt's."[21]

In the Kremlin, Stalin, who appeared "deeply distressed" over Roosevelt's death, greeted Ambassador Harriman "in silence . . . holding his hand for perhaps thirty seconds before asking him to sit down." Harriman assured Stalin that Truman was likely to follow Roosevelt's foreign policy. "President

Roosevelt has died but his cause must live on," agreed Stalin. Harriman then remarked that the most effective way to honor Roosevelt and support Truman would be to reverse his decision and send Molotov to the UN organizing conference in San Francisco. Stalin promptly agreed.[22]

A week later Molotov stopped in Washington on his way to the San Francisco conference, which was to open on April 25. By this time Truman had decided to adopt a "get tough" attitude toward the Soviets on Poland and other matters subject to the Yalta accords. Truman's blunt way of speaking was, of course, his own, but his views toward the Soviets had been shaped not by Hopkins, who remained bedridden at home, but by those of Churchill, Stettinius, and Harriman, who had returned to Washington on April 20.[23] Meeting with Molotov in the Oval Office at 5:30 p.m. on April 23, Truman glossed over diplomatic niceties, repeatedly and sharply telling the Soviet foreign minister that the United States expected Marshal Stalin to carry out the Yalta agreements on Poland "in accordance with his word." No longer will relations between the United States and the USSR be conducted on "the basis of a one-way street," lectured the president. "I have never been talked to like that in my life," replied a visibly shaken Molotov. "Carry out your agreements and you won't be talked to like that," Truman shot back.[24] He concluded the interview with a curt "That will be all, Mr. Molotov."[25]

Truman's "straight one-two to the jaw,"[26] as Joe Davies described the meeting in his diary on April 30, signaled a departure from the seemingly more accommodating attitude of Roosevelt toward Soviet domination of Eastern Europe. It was "hardly the cause of the Cold War," writes the historian Daniel Yergin, but "it did symbolize the beginning of the postwar divergence that led to confrontation."[27] Had Hopkins not been sidelined by illness, he probably would have counseled a less confrontational approach, an approach that recognized the overriding importance of territorial security to Stalin and the difficulty of imposing Western-style notions of democracy on societies lacking a liberal tradition. The Soviets had sacrificed far too much in blood and treasure to risk another invasion across a neutral or unfriendly Poland, Hopkins would argue. Pointing to Roosevelt, he would likely contend that it is often better to defer decisions or slide around or over problems than risk stalemate or pushback through confrontation. Citing his own experiences, Hopkins would stress that the Soviet leadership could sometimes be moved by personal diplomacy.

However, even if Hopkins did provide the president such advice—and there's no proof that he did—it is unlikely that Truman, who had to show he was tough and decisive in his first encounter with the Soviets, would have softened his stance. Ever mindful of the failure at Munich in 1938, the new president likely thought his tough line would cause the Russians to back down. He was wrong. As soon as Molotov arrived at the UN organizing conference in San Francisco he insisted that the conferees admit the Communist-controlled government of Poland—the Lublin Poles—as a charter member. On May 5 he revealed that sixteen Polish underground leaders who were designated to go to Moscow to discuss the "reorganization" of the government pursuant to the Yalta agreements had been arrested. To make matters worse, he reopened an issue that had been settled at Yalta—the scope of the veto power in the Security Council—claiming that any permanent member should be able to veto the mere discussion of an issue.

Harriman and Bohlen, delegates at the San Francisco conference, were discouraged. On the flight back to Washington the two of them discussed "what could be done to restore amity in Soviet-American relations."[28] Bohlen suggested that were Roosevelt alive he would have sent Hopkins to meet with Stalin. Harriman agreed. Shortly after arriving in Washington, Harriman and Bohlen visited Hopkins in the bedroom of his Georgetown house to present the idea. "Hopkins's response," wrote Sherwood, "was wonderful to behold. Although he appeared too ill to get out of bed and walk across 'N' Street, the mere intimation of a flight to Moscow converted him into the traditional old fire horse at the sound of the alarm."[29]

The idea of sending Hopkins, who fairly or not had gained a reputation for understanding, if not sympathizing with, the Soviet point of view, was at odds with the president's "get tough" policy. However, by this time Truman was having second thoughts about its efficacy. During meetings with Davies, Truman had gained a better appreciation of why the Soviets were suspicious of America's motives, the corrosive effect of State Department hostility toward the Soviets and the need for personal contact with Stalin, which had been the essence of Roosevelt's and Hopkins's method of airing and resolving differences with the Soviets.[30] Eventually he settled on Hopkins as the logical choice to go to Moscow. By sending Hopkins, whom Stalin liked and respected, Truman would signal the Soviets that he intended to continue the Roosevelt policies of goodwill and cooperation. At the same time, Truman had been persuaded by Harriman that Hopkins, based on his relationship with Stalin, stood the best chance of convincing him to keep his word and adhere to the Yalta agreements.

On May 19 Truman cabled Stalin that he was sending Hopkins to Moscow to meet with him on "complicated and important questions."[31] The same day, he summoned Hopkins to the White House for final instructions on what would be his last mission. His principal objectives, he told Hopkins, were to reach a "fair understanding" with the Soviets on the reorganization of the Polish government and to arrange a Big Three meeting, preferably in the United States. Hopkins was to tell Stalin that the Americans "never made commitments that [they] did not expect to carry out to the letter and that [they] expected Stalin to carry out his agreements." Hopkins "was free," said Truman, "to use diplomatic language or a baseball bat if he thought that was the right approach."[32]

As he prepared for his mission to Moscow, Hopkins felt a surge of energy and optimism. Hitler was dead, having committed suicide on April 30, when the Red Army overran the center of Berlin. In the Pacific the Americans were closing in on the Japanese homeland, staging massive B-29 firebombing raids on Japanese cities from bases in the Marianas. Hopkins knew that the first "atomic fission" bomb was scheduled to be ready by August. "Surely if the soldiers of the United States, Great Britain, France and the Soviet Union can fight together and win a glorious military victory," he told an NBC radio audience on VE Day, "then, indeed, in spite of every difficulty, the Allied statesmen in San Francisco will create the basis for a just and lasting peace."[33]

Hopkins and his party—consisting of Louise, who was responsible for holding Hopkins to his diet and making sure he took his medications, and Chip Bohlen, their interpreter—departed Washington National Airport on May

23. (Louise and Hopkins nicknamed the plane "The Flying Boudoir.")[34] In Paris they were joined by Harriman. At lunch in Paris, Hopkins and Harriman were briefed by Eisenhower on the problems he was encountering with the Soviets mainly their failure to name a representative to the Allied Control Council for Germany. Flying across Germany toward Moscow on May 25, Hopkins peered down at the ruins of Berlin and remarked, "It's another Carthage."[35]

Shortly after arriving in Moscow, Hopkins arranged an interview at Spaso House, the U.S. Embassy, with George Kennan, who had developed a reputation as a brilliant young diplomat. Kennan would later author the famous "Long Telegram" that analyzed Soviet foreign policy as driven from within by "historic insecurities and Marxist ideology."[36] And he would be credited with conceptualizing what became known in foreign policy circles during the cold war as the doctrine of containment. Anticipating that the "Polish problem" would be the most difficult issue he would face in his talks with Stalin, Hopkins asked Kennan for his views. Kennan said there was nothing to be gained by engaging in negotiations with Stalin concerning the structure and composition of the Polish government. The United States should back off, he advised, and not take any responsibility for what Stalin proposed to do in Poland. "Then you think it's just sin . . . and we should be agin it?" asked Hopkins. "That's just about right," replied Kennan. "I respect your opinion," said Hopkins. "But I am not at liberty to accept it."[37]

When Hopkins entered the Kremlin on the evening of May 26 for the first of six separate sessions with Stalin he must have thought back to July 1941, when he took the initial steps to establish the collaborative relationship with the USSR that hastened the defeat of Germany. Now, almost four years later, his mission was to do everything in his power to prevent the relationship from dissolving. Stalin "certainly went out of his way to be extremely courteous to Hopkins," wrote Bohlen, "not only because of his regard for the advisor to Roosevelt but also because he wanted to make a slight bow in the direction of the new President."[38] During their first talk around the green baize table in Stalin's office, Hopkins explained that there were a number of issues to discuss, but his real reason for coming concerned "the fundamental relationship between the United States and the Soviet

Union." Citing a "deterioration" of American public opinion toward the USSR, Hopkins said that he and the "friends of Roosevelt's policy" were "alarmed and worried" that "the entire structure of world cooperation and relations with the Soviet Union" that Roosevelt and Stalin "had labored so hard to build would be destroyed."[39]

Stalin responded that those in "Soviet government circles," which presumably included him, were likewise alarmed. "It was their impression that the American attitude towards the Soviet Union had perceptibly cooled once it became obvious that Germany was defeated, and it was as though the Americans were saying that the Russians were no longer needed." He proceeded to calmly tick off several specific complaints, including the "unfortunate and even brutal" manner in which the U.S. government had curtailed lend-lease shipments. If this was done to pressure his government, he admonished, "then it was a fundamental mistake." Much can be accomplished if the Soviets are dealt with on a frank and friendly basis, he said, "but reprisals in any form would bring about the exact opposite effect."[40] Stalin's tone was measured but carried menace.

Hopkins wasn't rattled. He understood that it was more about treating the Soviet Union as one of the two most powerful nations in the postwar world than it was about the continuance of lend-lease. He assured Stalin that Truman, like Roosevelt, believed that the two great powers each shared worldwide interests and "could work out together any political or economic considerations at issue between them." The lend-lease "incident," reassured Hopkins, was caused by bureaucratic "confusion" and had no policy significance.[41]

Whether or not Hopkins's assurances had any effect on Stalin, the fact is that a number of the issues on his list were quickly settled. Stalin promised that as long as the Yalta agreements concerning territorial concessions in the Far East were honored, the Red Army would be prepared to enter the war against Japan by August 8, 1945. He supported the unification of China under the leadership of Chiang Kai-shek ("the best of the lot") and said he did not believe the Chinese Communist leaders could do the job. Told by Hopkins that the Russians had not yet appointed a member of the Allied Control Council for Germany, Stalin appointed Marshal Zhukov on the spot. He said he "fully agreed with the desirability of a four-power trust-eeship for Korea." And he told Hopkins that he had already consented to a Big Three meeting with Truman and Churchill "in the vicinity of Berlin."[42]

The presence of Louise Hopkins at the many cocktail receptions and dinners that accompanied the negotiating sessions "had an extraordinary effect on the Soviet marshals," wrote Bohlen. "She was not beautiful, but chic, with a great deal of wit and charm." The generals and Politburo members clustered around her, snickering like adolescent boys at her every remark. One evening she expressed an interest in taking home "something Russian." The next morning a truck arrived at Spaso House bearing a variety of furs, fabrics, and Ural stones. Louise was invited to select any or all items as gifts. When Hopkins learned of this, he told her she could select only one inexpensive item as a token of her appreciation. He did not want a repeat of the criticism that erupted in the fall of 1942 after it was claimed that she accepted expensive jewelry as a wedding present from Lord Beaverbrook.[43] Of course, Louise did not attend the substantive meetings. However, her warmth, gaiety, and sex appeal broke down social and cultural barriers, which in turn enhanced Hopkins's effectiveness at the bargaining table. As each day went by, Stalin and his colleagues became more and more relaxed and open with their American counterparts. The Russians held Hopkins in high regard for his ability to attract and hold such a spirited and attractive woman.

As expected, the most difficult and contentious issues involved Poland: the makeup of the reorganized government and the Red Army's arrest of sixteen Polish underground leaders. Even though Hopkins assured Stalin that America wanted a Poland friendly to the Soviet Union and told him at dinner that Churchill had misled the Americans regarding events inside Poland, the marshal gave little ground. After hours of discussion, Stalin finally agreed to permit four or five non-Lublin Poles, selected by Stalin and Hopkins and approved by both Truman and Churchill, to "consult" with a commission in Moscow about becoming a minority voice in the Polish government.[44] A few days later Churchill told Truman that he did not regard this as a long-term solution to the Polish problem and predicted trouble ahead. With regard to the arrest of the underground leaders, Stalin declined to release any of them, claiming they were all involved in "diversionist activities" and that they must stand trial, although he would see that they were treated "leniently."[45] Convinced that Stalin would move no further, Hopkins concluded that it was the best he could do.

The Polish people would pay a heavy price, but Hopkins's compromises yielded an important dividend. During their last session Hopkins asked Stalin to resolve the impasse that Molotov had created in San Francisco by again insisting on the power to veto the mere discussion of a matter in the UN Security Council. He reminded Stalin that he had agreed at Yalta that the veto should only apply to actions and decisions, not free discussion. Stalin turned to Molotov for an explanation and debated him in front of Hopkins. "Molotov, that's nonsense," he concluded and accepted the American position.[46] In doing so he repeated the pattern he followed at Yalta, conceding on the UN, which was not that important to him, in exchange for preservation of a virtually free hand in Poland, which he regarded as vital.

Despite the concessions Hopkins made on Poland, Truman, Churchill, and the Polish exiles in London felt they had little choice but to approve the deal he brokered. Harriman wrote Truman that Stalin would never understand America's "interest in a free Poland," but he added, "Harry's visit has been even more successful that I had hoped."[47] Even Kennan, who had counseled Hopkins not to even try to reach an agreement with Stalin on Poland, "admitted that Hopkins had managed to get the best deal possible."[48]

A few days before they departed, Foreign Minister Molotov and his wife hosted an elaborate "Victory" dinner for Hopkins and Louise at a huge ballroom in the Kremlin named for Catherine the Great. Among the some five hundred guests were the members of the Politburo and their wives, numerous generals, various commissars, representatives of all of the embassies in Moscow, and of course Harriman and Kennan. Harriman's daughter Kathleen was the only American woman other than Louise to attend.[49] Since there were women present and an orchestra for dancing, wine was substituted for vodka after dinner to curb the usual drunkenness.[50] Ivan Maisky, the former ambassador to Great Britain who later would be arrested for espionage and personally tortured by Beria, looked on as men vied for dances with the two American women. To the delight of the Russians, Hopkins took a turn with his wife. When the set ended, Hopkins, "emaciated, exhausted from dancing, with sweat glistening on his forehead," sidled over to Maisky and said, "You know I've got a leave of absence from death."[51]

Near the end of his final meeting with Stalin, Hopkins spoke of his plans to leave in the morning with stops in Berlin, Frankfurt, and Paris. He joked that while in Berlin "he might even be able to find Hitler's body." In all seriousness, Stalin replied that he was "sure that Hitler was still alive" and hiding somewhere. Taking his leave, Hopkins said the meetings had given him "renewed assurances" that "[the] two countries had so much in common that they could find a way to work out their problems." Stalin replied that he was in full agreement.[52]

Hopkins was still savoring the promise of a new era of cooperation when he landed the next day with Louise and Bohlen at Tempelhof Airdrome in Berlin, his plane being the first since VE Day to land there with civilians. Three years later Tempelhof would be ground zero of the cold war, the place where American pilots landed around the clock at ten-minute intervals to bring provisions for the citizens of West Berlin who were threatened with starvation by Stalin's blockade of ground transportation into the city. Although the era of cooperation would be short-lived, on the afternoon of June 7, when Hopkins and his party arrived, the Red Army brass turned out in force to greet them warmly. A photographer captured Louise flanked by a group of grinning Soviet officers as she and Hopkins toured the streets of the ruined city. They "smelled the odor of death," wrote Bohlen, and "inspected the bunker where Hitler committed suicide."[53] The officers allowed Hopkins to take a few books from Hitler's personal library, which he later gave to friends. At a light (except for vodka) buffet lunch with Marshal Zhukov and Andrei Vyshinsky, deputy foreign minister and director of political affairs in Berlin, Vyshinsky commented about the atmosphere of friendship and cooperation between the United States and the Soviet Union. Hopkins paused and responded, "It's a pity President Roosevelt didn't live to see these days. It was easier with him."[54]

For Louise and Hopkins, the highlight of their trip home was their long weekend in Paris, where they stayed in Eisenhower's suite at the Hotel

with Truman his growing doubts concerning the prospects for a coopera-
tive long-term relationship with the Soviet Union, though there is no such
indication in the contemporary records of the meeting.[60]

The press accounts of Hopkins's mission to Moscow were uniformly optimistic, the most commendatory coverage he had ever received. The *Washington Post* praised him for producing "what diplomats call a *détente* in our
relations with Russia."[61] The *Times* of London wrote that his mission "had
contributed to the easing of the situation [regarding the UN] and to the
better prospects of a Polish settlement."[62] In a radio broadcast, Raymond
Gram Swing, one of the nation's most influential and highest-paid radio
news commentators, said that many thought of Hopkins as "only a friend
of President Roosevelt," but his success in Moscow came "from him and his
own stature": "It is dawning on the public that he was a friend of President
Roosevelt because he had great abilities to contribute as well as devotion
and affection."[63] Thus for a few days in mid-June 1945 Hopkins was regarded as "something of a national hero," wrote Sherwood.[64]

In the years since, following the depths of cold war politics and rhetoric, a number of historians have commented favorably on Hopkins's mission. Geoffrey Roberts opined that Hopkins's efforts led to a "resolution
of the Polish dispute," and David Reynolds credited him with making "a
successful effort to settle the Polish question," although quite obviously
he settled no such thing.[65] John Charmley wrote that Hopkins produced
what "months of telegraphing and co-operation with the British had failed
to—some movement on Stalin's part."[66] Perhaps closer to the truth, Daniel
Yergin characterized Hopkins's meetings with Stalin as a "success" not for
ending the deadlock on Poland but because, at least for a time, he "reduced
both tension and suspicion" and improved Soviet-American relations.[67] In
a similar vein, Robert Dallek lauded Hopkins for temporarily easing "difficulties" with the Soviet Union and facilitating "compromises that gave
birth to the United Nations."[68]

If success is to be gauged by the adoption of American democratic
values in the governance of postwar Poland, Hopkins's mission was a failure. On the other hand, if evaluated on the basis of the perceived need to
preserve the relationship with the Soviet Union in order to defeat Japan

and launch the UN, his trip to Moscow was a success. As Hopkins foresaw when he confided his doubts to Bohlen on the flight home, there are moments in diplomacy when American principles of governance must give way to the maintenance of a relationship regarded as essential to national security. Otherwise, to borrow the words of Henry Kissinger, "deadlock is inevitable."[69]

The importance of the relationship Hopkins had established with Stalin since their first meeting in the summer of 1941 cannot be overstated. Stalin had spoken to Hopkins and to both Roosevelt and Hopkins thereafter more directly and honestly than he had conversed with any Westerner. The relationship was hardheaded and unsentimental; neither side was under any illusion. Yet it was a kind of friendship, a personal relationship launched by Hopkins that enabled the leaders of the two great powers to see and accept the limits of what was possible, not what was ideal.

19

The Root of the Matter

"I am getting ready to go see Stalin & Churchill," wrote Truman to his mother and sister on July 3, 1945. He was referring to the Potsdam conference, named for a suburb outside Berlin, the final wartime meeting of the Big Three. "I have to take my tuxedo tails. . . . preacher coat, high hat, low hat and hard hat . . . I have a briefcase all filled up with . . . suggestions on what I'm to do and say," he complained. "Wish I didn't have to go."[1]

Hopkins would not be going. He had just delivered his letter of resignation from the government, telling the new president that he would "not be able to accompany him" to Potsdam. "The time has come when I must take a rest," he wrote.[2] He had decided to resign not because of ill health—actually, he had gained some weight and his health was tolerable—but because he genuinely believed that Truman should surround himself with his own hand-picked advisors. Indeed by late June Truman had already named Jimmy Byrnes as his new secretary of state. It would be unseemly and possibly embarrassing for Hopkins to show up at Potsdam along with Byrnes because Stalin and Churchill had gotten used to dealing with Hopkins as de facto secretary of state. Besides, Hopkins knew from previous dealings that Byrnes would do everything in his power to diminish Hopkins's role as an advisor to Truman on foreign affairs. This was the man, after all, who had told him to keep the hell out of his business, and it was doubtful that anything had changed.

Hopkins had other plans. Through Sam Rosenman he had been offered a job in New York City as "impartial chairman" of the Coat and Suit Industry, a post involving labor-management mediation that would pay an annual salary of $25,000—enough to have qualified him for Roosevelt's proposed 100 percent tax—but would engage him only about one day a week. In addition he had offers from several New York book publishers to write about his career in government. He was eager to explore the details of these offers and to find a suitable place to work and live in Manhattan. Therefore at the beginning of the week of July 12, while Louise began packing their things in Georgetown and the Big Three—Truman, Churchill, and Stalin—were converging on Potsdam, Hopkins checked into the St. Regis Hotel on East Fifty-fifth Street.[3] During the next several days he negotiated a deal with Harper & Brothers that involved a hefty $50,000 advance and the editorial assistance of Cass Canfield, one of the founders of *Foreign Affairs*.[4] He planned to write at least two books, one on the war and the other on "Roosevelt as I knew him."[5] He also met with David Dubinsky, head of the International Ladies Garment Workers Union, and finalized his part-time job with the Coat and Suit Industry.

Louise came up from Washington to help on the search for a place to live. They finally settled on a house at 1046 Fifth Avenue. "Actually," wrote Diana much later, the "house" was a "mansion with an iron-gated courtyard facing the street—and the Metropolitan Museum across the way." It had six floors joined by "a sweeping staircase throughout" and an elevator.[6] In a letter to Diana, who was at camp in Maine that summer, Hopkins wrote, "[Your] room is overlooking Central Park, big enough for you to rattle around in, with a bathroom of your own."[7] How he planned to pay the rent is unknown. Neither he nor Louise had any savings. Even with the salary from his new job and the book advance (only part of which would actually be paid before delivery of a manuscript), he could not afford on his own to pay the rent on a six-story Manhattan mansion and at the same time support his family, live-in domestic help, and lavish lifestyle. "I would bet my bottom dollar," wrote Diana, "that the rent was paid by Averell Harriman."[8]

Meanwhile in Potsdam the cold war was about to begin in earnest with the disclosure by Truman to Stalin that the United States possessed a bomb "of unusual destructive force." The Soviets had learned about the supposedly secret Manhattan Project in March 1942, and their agents had been scouring the world since then to obtain uranium oxide and other components needed to build their own atomic bomb. When Truman casually informed Stalin on July 24 that the United States had won the race, Stalin knew the game had changed—the bomb gave the Americans enormous leverage. He also knew that they had already shared their secret with the British. Until the Russians caught up and built their own bomb, the Anglo-Americans "will force us to accept their plans," said Stalin to Molotov and Gromyko later that evening.[9]

Within a few years Hopkins's name would be dragged into a sensational investigation of whether he personally helped the Soviets catch up to the Americans. In 1949, after the Soviets had succeeded in developing their own bomb, George Racey Jordan, who had served as an Army Air Force major, claimed he had personally seen documents bearing Hopkins's signature and participated in telephone conversations proving that he personally expedited shipments of uranium oxide and top secret atomic bomb designs on lend-lease planes to the Soviets. "It is now apparent," he charged, "that Harry Hopkins gave Russia the A-bomb on a platter."[10]

With the aid of nationwide radio broadcasts by Fulton Lewis Jr. and the aggressive support of an aspiring California congressman, Richard Nixon, nine days of widely publicized hearings before the House Un-American Activities Committee were held in late 1949 and early 1950.[11] Virtually every newspaper and magazine in the country repeated the charges against Hopkins as they reported on the testimony presented during the hearings. In 1952, when Nixon was the Republican nominee for vice president, Major Jordan self-published a book entitled *From Major Jordan's Diaries* in which he elaborated on his claim that Hopkins knowingly helped the Soviets become a nuclear power. By that time Hopkins was not alive to defend himself. However, careful analysis of the testimony and documentary evidence presented by Jordan and others at the House hearings, together with the absence of any corroboration from millions of documents released from Soviet and U.S. archives in the decades since the 1940s, leads to the conclusion that Jordan either lied for publicity and profit or was delusional. Jordan's own testimony before the House was fraught with contradictions, the most blatant of which was his statement that in the spring of 1944 Hopkins called him from Washington and ordered him to expedite shipments of uranium to the Russians. When Jordan was subsequently informed that this was highly unlikely because Hopkins was flat on his back at the Mayo Clinic in Minnesota, he changed his testimony and said the conversation with Hopkins took place a year earlier, in 1943. Jordan's credibility was further undermined in the 1960s when he publicly "condemned fluoridation as a secret Russian revolutionary technique to deaden" the minds of Americans.[12] In the words of Eduard Mark, an Air Force historian, "The truth bears no resemblance at all to the allegations of the psychopathic Mr. Jordan."[13]

The charges that Hopkins aided the Soviet Union in developing the atomic bomb have been repeated so many times over the years that they have become embedded in the musings of conspiracy buffs and right-wing bloggers. Regarding Jordan's allegations against Hopkins, *Life* magazine warned that "once an event or allegation has taken on the compelling quality of 'news,' the system allows no pause for reflection and examination" before the press repeats it "like a mindless automaton."[14]

Hopkins and Louise spent their last vacation together at the summer home of Louise's sister Min and her husband, Nicholas Ludington, on Mount Desert Island, Maine. Chip Bohlen, having just returned from the meetings at Potsdam, and his wife, Ava, who were also friends of the Ludingtons, joined them for several days in August. "Harry was feeble," wrote Bohlen, "but eager to hear about the Potsdam Conference." Hopkins wanted to know how Truman had acquitted himself ("Well," said Bohlen) and about Stalin's reaction when he learned that Churchill, having lost his parliamentary majority, was replaced during the last days of the conference as British prime minister by Clement Atlee (Stalin was bewildered, unable to comprehend English politics).

Bohlen told Hopkins of the unraveling of the wartime alliance and his "growing apprehensions" about relations with the Russians. He was convinced that rather than embracing the idea of collective security, Stalin's main goal was to ensure his own country's security while at the same time encouraging revolution against capitalist societies in Western Europe and elsewhere. "Harry was inclined to dismiss ideology," wrote Bohlen, preferring to believe that Stalin was extending his reach into Central Europe because he was obsessed with territorial security. Hopkins had doubts about achieving peaceful coexistence, but he nevertheless counseled that "patient, careful dealings with Moscow were the proper answer to the problem." He clung to the hope that the relationship might be restored through personal contact at the highest level.

As the two friends talked "in the afternoon sun with a drink," the nuclear age was under way.[15] Atomic bombs had completely destroyed Hiroshima and Nagasaki, killing tens of thousands. A few days later, during a canoeing and hiking trip near her camp, Diana Hopkins woke up on a mountain "to the sound of church bells ringing" from villages below. "We knew at once that the war had ended," she recalled.

At summer's end, Diana, her father, and her stepmother moved into the Fifth Avenue mansion. They were accompanied by Mt. Vernon Lewis ("Mount"), who would serve as Hopkins's caregiver and driver; Mount's wife, Van Lou ("Fannie"), who had a dual role as housekeeper and Diana's nanny; Louise's brown poodle, Suzy; and Suzy's puppy, Lilli Marlene. Diana was enrolled in the eighth grade at the Brearley School, a girls' school overlooking the East River. Louise began working as a nurse's aide at Memorial Hospital.[16]

The extended family was shortly joined by Sidney Hyman, a reporter for the *Chicago Tribune* and former army officer who had been hired by Hopkins to organize his papers and help him write his books. Hyman, a graduate of the University of Chicago, had been introduced to Hopkins by his son David and Katherine Graham, later the publisher of the *Washington Post*. Both were friends of Hyman and fellow University of Chicago graduates. Hyman lived in the mansion and worked in an office on the first floor.[17] Hopkins cautioned him not to destroy any papers, saying, "The whole story of Roosevelt—and my story is part of it—is going to come out anyway in the next fifty years. And I don't see any point in trying to edit my past by destroying papers which showed precisely what I did and how I did it." According to both Hyman and Sherwood, Hopkins did not have either the discipline or the temperament to develop a theme and then sit down and grind out a book. Although Hyman put the voluminous papers into rough order, Hopkins would only "make quick samplings of their contents," and he adopted a "random, scattered approach" to the project. The paragraphs that he did commit to paper were "hastily dictated . . . rambling and repetitious," observed Sherwood.[18]

Hopkins's need to stay relevant and connected was at odds with the hours of reflective isolation required to write history. He kept up a lively correspondence, commiserating with Churchill, congratulating de Gaulle on the elections in France, joking with Beaverbrook, and dashing off occasional bits of advice to Truman. His Washington pals, plus Bernard Baruch, who lived nearby, would drop by for bridge games and gossip in the third-floor library, where Diana learned to "pour scotch and soda to their liking."[19] Every new visitor who passed through the large entry hall of the mansion paused to chuckle at Hopkins's collection of original cartoons of himself, colorful reminders of his prominence in government. In the White House Rose Garden, during Hopkins's last trip to Washington, Truman presented him with the Distinguished Service Medal, the capstone of his career. Incorporating the sentiments of Roosevelt, Churchill, and Stalin, the citation recognized Hopkins for his "selfless, courageous and objective contribution to the war effort" and his "piercing understanding of the tremendous problems incident to the vast military operations throughout the world."[20] After the ceremony Hopkins wrote a thank-you letter to Marshall, saying, "You instigated the . . . Medal for me and I want to hasten to tell you how greatly I appreciate it. Anyone would be less than human not to be altogether flattered."[21]

In early October Hopkins's health began to deteriorate again, although he told Sherwood and other friends that it was nothing more than "a touch of the flu."[22] In fact he was experiencing more and more bouts of vomiting and diarrhea. Reluctantly he had to renege on a planned trip to England to receive an honorary degree at Oxford and asked that it be postponed until the following June.[23] By mid-month "Hopkins was unable to do any real work of any kind," recalled Sherwood.[24] He was confined to the house, spending much of his time in his bedroom. Mount rigged up a stand in his room from which to hang intravenous bags of blood plasma, but the relief that such transfusions once afforded began to fade and then vanished.

The only elixir that gave Hopkins "new life," wrote Hyman, was the prospect that he would once again be sent on an important mission, empowered to intervene in a crisis. Thus when Hopkins learned that he might be called upon to arbitrate "crippling strikes" involving New York elevator operators and tugboat crews, he "got dressed [and] came downstairs" on at least two occasions and began "barking out orders and directions" on the telephone. Unfortunately for him, the strikes were settled without his help, and he returned to his bed on the third floor. "I may be wrong about this," said Hyman, "but I felt that he wanted very badly to be back on active duty again."[25]

"By November," wrote Diana, "[he] was confined to his bed. When I came home from school, Harry would call out from his bed, 'come and show me your homework, Diana.'" The teenager would reply, "Done it all, Daddy," and run upstairs to her room without stopping to chat. Later she "bitterly regretted" all her "blithe dismissals" of her father's efforts to reach out to her, locking herself in bathroom stalls at school and sobbing for hours.[26]

On November 9 Hopkins entered Memorial Hospital, telling his editor Cass Canfield that there was "nothing alarming about it" and his friend Ed Stettinius that it was nothing more than "an awful bore."[27] There was some initial improvement in his condition, but then he began a long, slow decline. Perhaps because he downplayed his illness or possibly because he had been hospitalized so many times before, he had surprisingly few visitors. In his diary Stettinius noted the "rather cold reaction of Churchill, Harriman and Bohlen" to Hopkins's confinement.[28] "It killed" Louise, wrote her friend Liz Gibbons, "that people were not visiting Harry as often as he deserved."[29] Louise arranged for the art patron Barbara Westcott to lend Hopkins a small Renoir to hang in his hospital room. Jock Whitney and Monroe Wheeler, director of the Museum of Modern Art, tutored Hopkins in modern art and arranged for paintings by Picasso, Utrillo, and others to be sent over to the hospital. The painting that Hopkins liked the most, by Serge Ferat, hung in his room until the end and then was gifted by Whitney to Louise.[30]

Robert Hopkins, who had returned from Europe and was temporarily living in New York with Brenda, his English bride, made almost daily visits to the hospital in December and January. "I could see his strength waning," wrote Robert of his father, but "nothing the doctors could do seemed to help." Robert was desperate. Believing that his father would rally if he was sent on another presidential mission, as he had rallied before, Robert called President Truman from a hall phone in the hospital. According to Robert, Truman was "sympathetic" to his request that his father be summoned for another mission, but he said he would need to talk to Hopkins's doctors. Later the president called back and said the doctors would not let Hopkins leave the hospital, much less travel.[31]

In Washington, Congress began its investigation into who was to blame for the Pearl Harbor attack. Monitoring the investigation from the hospital, Hopkins was worried that Admiral Stark and others would attempt to shift the blame to Roosevelt and even to himself. According to Sherwood, Hopkins asked his doctors for permission to go to Washington and testify, but the doctors refused. He was even more worried about his precarious financial situation as the prospect of ever completing his books or returning to work dimmed. To pay his mounting hospital and other expenses, he resorted to borrowing heavily from friends like Baruch.

Hopkins became weaker and weaker with each passing day, yet he continued to smoke incessantly. Fluid was building up in his abdomen and legs. He was increasingly jaundiced. The doctors told him that he had liver damage, though they added that it was not due to excessive consumption of alcohol (nor did they suggest it was caused by hepatitis contracted as a result of his frequent blood transfusions).[32] His body, held together by transfusions and sheer will, was simply starting to fail him. His contact with life, as Churchill had said about Roosevelt, was growing slender.

His last letter was dictated on January 22, 1946. It was a short but affectionate note to Churchill, who had passed through New York on his way to Florida without stopping to visit. "All I can say about myself," Hopkins joked, "is that I am getting excellent care, while the doctors are struggling over a very bad case of cirrhosis of the liver—not due, I regret to say, from taking too much alcohol." He closed by giving his "love to Clemmie and Sarah" and saying, "[I look forward to a] good talk with you over the state of world affairs, to say nothing of our private lives."[33]

For the next few days he remained "bright and alert," recalled Mount, although he had lost his appetite and his body was little more than skin stretched tightly over bones. Then he became more and more detached, staring blankly at visitors, saying nothing as he lay in his bed. Before lapsing into a coma, he spoke his last words to Mount: "You can't beat destiny."[34]

For Harry Hopkins, the end came on the morning of January 29, 1946. Louise was in the room when he died. He was fifty-five years old.

The next day Churchill, who had not responded to Hopkins's last letter, wired his farewell to Hopkins to the New York Times. "Few know better than I the service he rendered to the world cause," he wrote. "In Harry Hopkins [Roosevelt] found a man not only of wide ranging vision but of piercing eye. He always went to the root of the matter. . . . We do well to salute his memory. We shall not see his like again."[35]

The funeral was on Friday afternoon, February 1, at St. Bartholomew's Episcopal Church on Park Avenue. "Its edifice looks like it was plucked right out of Byzantium," remembered Diana.[36] In addition to Diana, other family members in attendance included David and his wife, Cherry, Hopkins's brother Lewis, and his sister Adah. Robert Hopkins, who had just traveled to the West Coast to start a new job, did not attend, nor did Ethel Gross Hopkins. Hundreds of the prominent and wealthy filled the pews, and a crowd of more than a thousand stood outside. Reverend Russell Clinchy helped conduct the service, just as he had done at Barbara Duncan's funeral in 1937 and at the White House wedding of Hopkins and Louise in 1942.[37] "Louie bore up well during the service," recalled Diana. "But I had to hold her tightly to keep her from collapsing as we slowly followed the casket out of the church to the mighty strains of 'The Battle Hymn of the Republic.'"[38]

Louise moved to a two-bedroom apartment on East Eighty-eighth Street with Diana, Mount, Fannie, and the two dogs. Hopkins had left her with some life insurance proceeds but little else. His estate listed assets of $33,775, consisting mostly of securities and cash, and debts of almost

$24,000, including $10,000 owed to Ethel.[39] Louise went back to work in the fashion industry, and by 1947 she was fashion coordinator for Bergdorf Goodman.[40] In September of that year she married Geoffrey Gates, director of Parsons School of Design. In later life, recalled Diana, Louise was "*very* anti-FDR," lashing out after downing a drink or two, "How can you like that man? He killed your father." She was bitter, feeling that Roosevelt's demands on Hopkins "drove" him to his grave.[41] Eighteen months after Gates died of brain cancer, Louise took her own life.

Some have written that Hopkins was nothing more than "Roosevelt's emissary," a mere fixer. Hopkins himself diminished his role in the Allied wartime coalition by saying he was only a "catalyst" that brought the prima donnas together. But he was far more than that. His genius—the invaluable service he rendered—was that he grasped from the beginning of America's involvement in what would become World War II that the key to victory was the creation and maintenance of an Anglo-American-Soviet coalition of military power sustained by economic cooperation. In the face of sharply conflicting ideologies and economic systems, interminable disagreements over strategy, perpetual fear and mistrust of one another, monumental egos, and a president who preferred to improvise on the spot rather than plan, Hopkins kept his focus on sustaining that coalition. Capturing this defining quality and playing on Hopkins's Anglophilia, Churchill joked that Hopkins was a member of the peerage, addressing him often as "Lord Root of the Matter."

In London in July 1942, when the coalition was about to fracture over the issue of invading North Africa instead of a direct assault on Western Europe, Hopkins played an indispensable behind-the-scenes role in nudging and steering the political and military players toward the most significant strategic decision of World War II without any messy resignations or public dissonance (with the possible exception of Lord Beaverbrook). At Tehran in 1943 it was Hopkins who persuaded Churchill to "yield with grace" on his opposition to a cross-Channel invasion. And throughout the war he pressed harder than anyone in the U.S. government to supply the USSR with everything they asked for as the Red Army and Soviet civilians spilled rivers of blood fighting more than two hundred German divisions on the eastern front.

In part because of Hopkins's single-minded powers of concentration, the Allied tripartite coalition hung together until Fascist Italy, Nazi Germany, and Hirohito's Japan were defeated. Hopkins is a counterfactualists' dream. Take him out of the picture, and the alliance might not have coalesced and held. To borrow Churchill's words, without the combined efforts of Great Britain, the USSR, and the United States, the whole world might have been plunged "into the abyss of a new Dark Age, made more sinister, and perhaps more protracted, by the lights of perverted science."[42]

Of course, aside from Hopkins, there were others—many others—who made significant contributions, and in the final analysis the success of the coalition was due to its overwhelming economic and military power. However, there can be no doubt that Hopkins was among the most significant contributors to the creation and maintenance of the coalition that won the war. He was the pectin and the glue of the Alliance, and while that claim can be overstated, there was, as FDR himself knew, no one else. Mistrusted by many, Hopkins had the trust of those whose actions and decisions would, for better or worse, carry the most weight at that moment in history. If this is Great Man history, Hopkins problematizes it as much as promulgates it, for he is not remembered himself as a great man, and that is as much by his own choice as by the inherent limits of Great Man history. George Marshall, not one to exaggerate, said of Hopkins, "The country will never even vaguely appreciate the service he rendered. He was one of the most courageous and self-sacrificing figures of the war."[43]

What was it about Hopkins? Of all the smart, talented, witty, and ambitious individuals that surrounded the Roosevelt presidency, why did an Iowa-born social worker and bureaucrat achieve such success in government and foreign affairs during the war? What was it that enabled him to become virtually indispensable in helping the president establish and preserve the winning coalition?

Fundamentally important to Hopkins's success was the experience he brought to the Roosevelt administration: twenty years of manipulating bureaucracies, cutting red tape, and dealing with local politicians to deliver relief, disaster assistance, and health care to the needy in New York and the Deep South. When the Great Depression crippled America in the early 1930s, he had already developed the organizational and leadership skills that were instantly valuable and much in demand. Those skills brought him to Washington and eventually into Roosevelt's inner circle. As the world changed and the war approached, Roosevelt recognized that Hopkins was uniquely qualified to organize and lead the delivery of war matériel to Great Britain and the Soviet Union. "Harry is the perfect Ambassador for my purposes," Roosevelt boasted. "He doesn't even know the meaning of 'protocol.' When he sees a piece of red tape he just pulls out those old garden shears and snips it. And when he's talking to some foreign dignitary, he knows how to slump back in his chair and put his feet up on the conference table and say, 'Oh *yeah*?'"[44]

At a deeper level, Hopkins's success was due to social savvy, what psychologists call "practical intelligence" or "emotional intelligence." He knew how to read people and situations and how to use that natural talent to influence decisions and actions. He had the "ability to sense another's feelings, convictions, intentions," wrote Marquis Childs.[45] He usually knew when to speak and to whom and when to remain silent. Whether it was at a wartime conference, alone with Roosevelt, or a private meeting with Stalin, when Hopkins chose to speak his words were measured to achieve effect.

But in the end the word that comes closest to capturing the quality that enabled Harry Hopkins to succeed is *touch*—"a little touch of Harry in the night." Shakespeare had this in mind in *Henry V* when he wrote about the disguised king moving among his troops the night before the battle of Agincourt. Like Hopkins, the king moved not as their superior but as "Harry," covering his fatigue with a "cheerful semblance" as he enlisted their trust and built a community of fighters amid fear and doubt. The two of them— Shakespeare's King Harry becoming one with the troops in the night and Hopkins bonding with the leaders of the United States, Britain, and the Soviet Union—shared a gift for connecting. They sensed that by deftly portraying that their lives were at risk (the king telling the troops "he would not be ransomed" and Hopkins's wasting body a testament to his courage), their brothers in arms would reciprocate, risking themselves for them: "For he today that sheds his blood with me Shall be my brother."

For Stalin it was *po dushe:* Hopkins spoke "from the soul." Churchill saw him "as a crumbling lighthouse from which there shone the beams that led great fleets to harbor." To Roosevelt he gave his life, asking "for nothing except to serve." They were the "happy few." And Hopkins had made himself one of them.

In the fog and drizzle, Hopkins's adult children, David, Robert, and Diana, along with three grandchildren and two great-grandchildren, crossed the flat Iowa landscape in a rental van, every field solidly planted with ripened corn and soybeans, the occasional maples flaming with the colors of autumn. A small wooden box containing Hopkins's ashes lay in Diana's lap. They were headed from the Des Moines airport to Grinnell, where the ashes would be interred in the city cemetery. It was September 27, 1973.

After a tour of the college campus, they "walked to see the house where Daddy grew up," wrote Diana. The small white frame house on Elm Street was marked by a sign that said, "Overnight Guests—Boyhood Home of Harry L. Hopkins." Inside the tiny living room they inspected the Victorian period pieces and talked of how it must have been for Al and Anna to have raised Harry and their other four children in that place.[46]

The next day, under a canopy that held off the rain, the Hopkins family and a cluster of guests gathered for the service. Glenn Leggett, president of Grinnell College, described Hopkins as "tough, knowledgeable, resourceful and tenacious—yes, all of these, but also possessed of the vision and sense of humanity that made his toughness and tenacity vehicles for a better state of mankind." Noting that Hopkins was "shaped and realized" by the landscape, schools, and college of Grinnell, Leggett said the city deserved to "make a final claim" on him because it "lies close to the heart of all America, whose needs he served with an enduring humanity."[47]

ACKNOWLEDGMENTS

In photographs of the World War II conferences, Harry Hopkins can sometimes be spotted in the background, surrounded by a crowd of admirals and generals. At the Atlantic conference in 1941, a photo shows him standing hatless some distance behind Roosevelt and Churchill, barely recognizable. At Yalta, the camera—perhaps his son's—caught him leaning forward from the shadows to whisper in Roosevelt's ear as Stalin was speaking at the far end of the table.

"He's spectral and fascinating," admitted one publisher when presented with the opportunity to take on this book. However, the problem at this "perilous moment" in the publishing business was that Hopkins "is not generally recognizable."

Thank you, Oxford University Press, for allowing me the chance to try to make Hopkins more recognizable—to show how he emerged from social work to walk with kings and touched them all.

Hopkins piqued my curiosity when I was working on a book I coauthored, *Arming of America*, which was about Louis Johnson, assistant secretary of war during FDR's administration and secretary of defense under Truman. Johnson was critical to the rearmament effort during World War II and a controversial public figure. During my research on Johnson, Hopkins kept coming up. He seemed everywhere and yet nowhere, despite the book to which this project owes its greatest debt: Robert Sherwood's *Roosevelt and Hopkins: An Intimate History*. However, it was his daughter, Diana, who brought him into sharper focus. Over drinks in our Georgetown house in 2006 with Diana and her daughter, I began to recognize Harry Hopkins in the tilt of Diana's head, her acerbic wit, her lack of pretense, and her conspicuous intelligence. Like Harry, Diana has led a fascinating life, much of it in the shadows. Fluent in Arabic and Farsi, she is rumored to have been a CIA agent, although her lips remain sealed.

Diana and many others, principally my book club friend Ann Charnley Meleney, whose father worked in the White House, encouraged me to dig deeper. Joe Goulden, a lifelong author and neighborhood pal, sent me numerous emails saying "Write on" and left dozens of World War II books on my doorstep. John Earl Haynes helped me put to rest the allegations that Hopkins was a Soviet spy, and Ed Miller patiently explained how the actions of three subcabinet political appointees led to the Pearl Harbor attack. Granddaughters June Hopkins and Audrey Young and a niece by marriage, Merloyd Ludington Lawrence, hunted down family letters and photos. John Fox, the FBI historian, helped me try to find out why J. Edgar Hoover, with Hopkins's approval, investigated Louise Macy, Hopkins's third wife. With the help of Richard Deering Howe and Johnny Russell, some light was shed on why the FBI investigation might have been conducted. The noted editor of the Joseph P. Kennedy papers and author of a biography of Cissy Patterson, Amanda Smith Hood, patiently responded to my queries about connections Hopkins might have had to the Kennedys, Drew Pearson, and Patterson. Thank you all.

Frequent trips up the I-95 corridor and into the Hudson Valley to Hyde Park were a joy. Periodically reprimanded by archivists Virginia Lewick, Matt Hanson, and Kirstin Carter (especially Virginia, my favorite nag), I tried to navigate the arcane rules governing those who paw through boxes and squint at microfilm in the research rooms of the Franklin D. Roosevelt Library. Bob Clark, a senior archivist and supersleuth, helped me track down and locate documents in the various collections. During breaks I would violate Park Service rules by letting Thatcher, my retriever, off the leash to romp across the spacious grounds, taking him down below Springwood, FDR's home on the bluff, to swim in the creek and the ice pond in the woods.

Special thanks go to Ted Jackson, the archivist in Special Collections at Georgetown University, who let me have an early peak at the documents and photos donated by Hopkins's son Robert. Also at Georgetown I want to thank Nick Sheetz, manuscripts librarian, and Scott Taylor, who patiently guided me through the papers of Harry and Robert and helped me select and copy photographs. At Harvard's Houghton Library, Kuo-Kai-Chin located a copy of the original "touch of Harry" account of Hopkins's talk in London in 1941 to a gathering of newspaper editors, and Emilie Hardman provided copies of other needed documents. Kristin LaFollette, Charis Emily Shafer, and Brittany Patch at Columbia's Center for Oral History helped me obtain transcripts of and accurate quotes from various oral histories.

The librarians and professional staff at Steptoe & Johnson, the law firm based in Washington, D.C., where I have practiced since 1975, were spectacularly generous and helpful. Particular kudos go to Constance Patriarca and Steven Shearer, research librarians who hunted for hundreds of books and source materials, and their boss, Ellen Brondfield, who allowed them to do it, and to Dianne Crump (especially you, Dianne with the two n's), Deirdre Drummond, Jennifer Matthey, and Emily Brown Clark, who formatted the final manuscript, scanned the photos, and burned the CDs.

This project never would have gotten off the ground if it were not for the patience and professionalism of Ellen Woodward, who introduced me to Kirsten Neuhaus, my agent. To say I am grateful to Kirsten is an understatement because it was she who had confidence in me and my slant on Harry, and it was she who shaped my proposal.

My largest debt is owed to Tim Bent, my editor at Oxford University Press. Like Hopkins, Tim prefers to see himself as little more than a mild catalyst, working in obscurity to occasionally identify a dangling participle or to scold me for using an exclamation point, noting Scott Fitzgerald's admonition that using an exclamation point is like laughing at your own joke. In reality he has been a force, pressing me relentlessly to drill deeper in order to help the reader understand—really understand—why he or she should read another book about Hopkins. "Forget your day job," Tim would say when my law practice interfered, and then he would instruct me on "controlled melancholy" and "opening the speculative spigot," concepts I never encountered in law school. It has been a privilege to be associated with a writer and editor of Tim's caliber. I will be ever grateful to him for guiding me and this book to publication.

To lead me through the final production process, Tim handed me off to a superb team of professionals at Oxford led by veteran Joellyn Ausanka. Joellyn, editorial assistant Keely Latcham, and copy editor Judith Hoover thoughtfully and promptly answered my questions and corrected my errors throughout production. Ellen McNamara, my extraordinarily intelligent and capable partner at Steptoe & Johnson, trained a final set of eyes on the manuscript, correcting numerous mistakes and providing insightful comments. I am immensely appreciative of all of their efforts and dedication.

Finally, profound thanks to my lifetime love and best friend, Nancy, who allowed me the space, time, and silence to devote to this six-year happy effort.

NOTES

Abbreviations

DHH   Diana Hopkins Halsted
FDR   Franklin Delano Roosevelt
FDRL   Franklin D. Roosevelt Library, Hyde Park, New York
FRUS   *Foreign Relations of the United States* (Washington, D.C.: Government Printing Office, 1958–1969)
GU   Georgetown University Library Special Collections Research Center, Washington, D.C.
HH   Harry Lloyd Hopkins
NYT   *New York Times*
PPA   *Public Papers and Addresses of Franklin D. Roosevelt*, Samuel I. Rosenman, ed. (13 vols., 1938–1950); cited by year covered by volume, i.e., *PPA*, 1933, etc.
RH   Robert Hopkins
WSC   Winston Spencer Churchill

Prologue: Moving In

1. Lord Moran (formerly, Sir Charles Wilson), *Churchill*, 241.
2. Childs, "The President's Best Friend," 9.
3. According to the biographer of Steve Early, FDR's press secretary, Roosevelt initiated this ritual and its name "two days after he became president," and it "continued well into the war." Levin, *The Making of FDR*, 318. Most likely FDR borrowed the name from the title of the Lillian Hellman play.
4. DHH, interview by Emily Williams, 28–29.
5. Churchill, *The Second World War*, 3:24.
6. Percy Cudlipp, editor of the *London Daily Herald*, Series B: "Research Notes on Roosevelt and Hopkins," i. (1940), Sherwood Papers (quotation from *Henry V*, Act IV, prologue).

Chapter 1: Ambitious Reformer

1. HH, speech at Grinnell College Chapel, February 22, 1939, HH Papers, Box 12, FDRL.
2. June Hopkins, *Sudden Hero*, 10–14.
3. Sherwood, *Roosevelt and Hopkins*, 16.

4. June Hopkins, *Sudden Hero*, 16–21; Beinart, *The Icarus Syndrome*, 17–21.

5. June Hopkins, *Sudden Hero*, 213n39.

6. Adams, *Harry Hopkins*, 32; McJimsey, *Ally of the Poor*, 8.

7. DHH interview, July 11, 1977, quoted in Tuttle, *Anglo-American-Soviet Relations*, 21.

8. Sherwood, *Roosevelt and Hopkins*, 15.

9. McJimsey, *Ally of the Poor*, 3–4, 6.

10. June Hopkins, *Sudden Hero*, 21, 25.

11. Charles Roberts, interview with Florence Kerr, July 29, 1974, 3, Grinnell College Archives.

12. Sherwood, *Roosevelt and Hopkins*, 17.

13. June Hopkins, *Sudden Hero*, 29, 22n47; Hopkins Academic Transcript, Grinnell College Archives.

14. McJimsey, *Ally of the Poor*, 12.

15. June Hopkins, *Sudden Hero*, 30; *The Scarlet and Black*, February 23, 1911, Grinnell College Archives.

16. June Hopkins, *Sudden Hero*, 31–32n88.

17. Richard Hofstadter, *The Age of Reform: From Bryan to F.D.R.*; Beinert, *The Icarus Syndrome*, 18, 24–25.

18. June Hopkins, *Sudden Hero*, 31n85.

19. Ibid., 33; Sherwood, *Roosevelt and Hopkins*, 22; McJimsey, *Ally of the Poor*, 34.

20. June Hopkins, *Sudden Hero*, 34–38.

21. Ibid., 37–39; Giffen and Hopkins, *Jewish First Wife*, 6.

22. Quoting Conant interview, in June Hopkins, *Sudden Hero*, 42n46.

23. Ibid., 42; Harry Hopkins, "Capital Punishment and Boys," *Survey Graphic*, April 25, 1914, 89.

24. Giffen and Hopkins, *Jewish First Wife*, 31. Accounts differ as to the place where they first met, some indicating they met in the hall of Christadora House, where they both had desks.

25. HH to Ethel Gross, February 13, 1913, letter no. 1 in Giffen and Hopkins, *Jewish First Wife*, 33.

26. HH to Ethel Gross, February 24, 1913, letter no. 2 in Giffen and Hopkins, *Jewish First Wife*, 34.

27. June Hopkins, *Sudden Hero*, 45–48; Giffen and Hopkins, *Jewish First Wife*, 3–6.

28. June Hopkins, *Sudden Hero*, 47–48.

29. Ibid., 48; Giffen and Hopkins, *Jewish First Wife*, 5–6.

30. HH to Ethel Gross, February 24, 1913, letter no. 2 in Giffen and Hopkins, *Jewish First Wife*, 34.

31. Ethel Gross to HH, March 17, 1913, letter no. 18, in Giffen and Hopkins, *Jewish First Wife*, 48.

32. Ethel Gross to HH, March 14, 1913, letter no. 12, in Giffen and Hopkins, *Jewish First Wife*, 43.

33. Ethel Gross Conant interview, quoted in June Hopkins, *Sudden Hero*, 51n74.

34. McJimsey, *Ally of the Poor*, 19; June Hopkins, *Sudden Hero*, 60; Sherwood, *Roosevelt and Hopkins*, 23.

35. William H. Matthews, *Adventures in Giving*, 108–9.

36. June Hopkins, *Sudden Hero*, 50, 61–65, 67–69, 127–30.
37. HH to Mrs. Hopkins, August 9, 1918 (telegram), letter no. 119, in Giffen and Hopkins, *Jewish First Wife*, 141.
38. Giffen and Hopkins, *Jewish First Wife*, 11–15.
39. June Hopkins, *Sudden Hero*, 130, 138, 140–43; McJimsey, *Ally of the Poor*, 30–34.
40. William Matthews to HH, February 7, 1919, part III, box 1, folder 5, HH Papers, GU.
41. Quote in Sherwood, *Roosevelt and Hopkins*, 29.
42. June Hopkins, *Sudden Hero*, 44.
43. Geoffrey T. Hellman, "House Guest," part 1, *New Yorker*, August 7, 1943, 25.
44. McJimsey, *Ally of the Poor*, 36–39.
45. Hellman, "House Guest," part 1, 25.
46. Lewis Hopkins to HH and Ethel Gross Hopkins, May 7, 1915, part 2, box 2, folder 11, HH Papers, GU; McJimsey, *Ally of the Poor*, 37.
47. McJimsey, *Ally of the Poor*, 40; June Hopkins, *Sudden Hero*, 145.
48. HH to Ethel Gross Hopkins, November 1, 1927, and Ethel Gross Hopkins to HH, November 8, 1927, letters nos. 180 and 182, Giffen and Hopkins, *Jewish First Wife*, 200–202.
49. McJimsey, *Ally of the Poor*, 40.
50. John Kingsbury, "Autobiographical Notes," Box 84, Kingsbury Papers; June Hopkins, *Sudden Hero*, 146. Kingsbury's notes indicate that Ethel had told him months before of Hopkins's affair.
51. HH to Ethel Gross Hopkins, July 18, 1928, letter no. 189, Giffen and Hopkins, *Jewish First Wife*, 209–10.
52. HH to Ethel Gross Hopkins, undated telegram, letter no. 195, Giffen and Hopkins, *Jewish First Wife*, 215; McJimsey, *Ally of the Poor*, 42n10.
53. HH to Ethel Gross Hopkins, April 1929, letter no. 199, Giffen and Hopkins, *Jewish First Wife*, 219–20.
54. June Hopkins, *Sudden Hero*, 146.

Chapter 2: Asks for Nothing Except to Serve

1. Kennedy, *Freedom from Fear*, 9.
2. HH, "I lived in New York in October of 1929," 1–2, part 1, box 54, folder 11, HH Papers, GU; Smith, *FDR*, 250.
3. FDR, Message to the Legislature, August 28, 1931, *1931 Public Papers of Governor Roosevelt*, 173.
4. Sherwood, *Roosevelt and Hopkins*, 32.
5. McJimsey, *Ally of the Poor*, 45–49; June Hopkins, *Sudden Hero*, 149–58.
6. FDR, Radio Address, April 7, 1932, *1932 Public Papers of Governor Roosevelt*, 572–73.
7. Letter, HH to Lewis Hopkins, September 8, 1932, quoted in Sherwood, *Roosevelt and Hopkins*, 33.
8. *Proceedings of the 1932 Democratic Convention*, 372–83.
9. FDR, Campaign Address, November 5, 1932, *PPA*, 1932, 860–65.

10. Schwarz, *The Interregnum of Despair*, 74.
11. *PPA*, 1933, 11–16.
12. Sherwood, *Roosevelt and Hopkins*, 40.
13. Perkins, *The Roosevelt I Knew*, 183–85.
14. Reminiscences of Frances Perkins (1961), vol. 4, pt. 3, p. 473, in the Oral History Collection of Columbia University.
15. Perkins, *The Roosevelt I Knew*, 183–85; Cohen, *Nothing to Fear*, 206–7.
16. Reminiscences of Frances Perkins (1961), vol. 4, pt. 3, p. 474, in the Oral History Collection of Columbia University.
17. HH to FDR, quoted in Schlesinger, *The Age of Roosevelt*, 2:264; McJimsey, *Ally of the Poor*, 61; Taylor, *American-Made*, 99–100.
18. Joanna C. Colcord, Russell Sage Foundation, to FDR, April 28, 1933, and Allen T. Burns to Henry Morgenthau Jr., Henry Morgenthau Correspondence Files, box 123, FDRL.
19. "Biographical Sketch of Harry L. Hopkins," June 1, 1938, Works Progress Administration Division of Information, National Archives RG 69, quoted in Taylor, *American-Made*, 102.
20. Sherwood, *Roosevelt and Hopkins*, 62; Taylor, *American-Made*, 103.
21. Taylor, *American-Made*, 103; McJimsey, *Ally of the Poor*, 52.
22. "Money Flies," *Washington Post*, May 23, 1933.
23. Sherwood, *Roosevelt and Hopkins*, 49; Taylor, *American-Made*, 103.
24. Quoted in Sherwood, *Roosevelt and Hopkins*, 52.
25. Kennedy, *Freedom from Fear*, 171.
26. Sherwood, *Roosevelt and Hopkins*, 45.
27. Taylor, *American-Made*, 113–18; McJimsey, *Ally of the Poor*, 58–59.
28. Quoted in Anderson, *The Presidents' Men*, 68.
29. "Professional Giver," *Time*, February 19, 1934; McJimsey, *Ally of the Poor*, 59–62; Taylor, *American-Made*, 119–22.
30. Sherwood, *Roosevelt and Hopkins*, 56.
31. McJimsey, *Ally of the Poor*, 67–69.
32. Quoted in Charles, *Minister of Relief*, 24.
33. Quoted in Sherwood, *Roosevelt and Hopkins*, 80.
34. Ernie Pyle, "Hopkins and Ickes Are Quite a Couple of Fellows in Real Life," *Washington Daily News*, October 26, 1935, 5.
35. Perkins, *The Roosevelt I Knew*, 191.
36. Kurtzman, *Hopkins and the New Deal*, 124–27. One of Hopkins's ideas that did not make it into the Social Security Act was compulsory national health insurance.
37. FDR to HH, June 29, 1934, HH Papers, box 96, FDRL; Taylor, *American-Made*, 154; June Hopkins, *Sudden Hero*, 176.
38. Dallek, *Roosevelt and American Foreign Policy*, 10, 12.
39. Freidel, *Launching the New Deal*, 377; Black, *Franklin Delano Roosevelt*, 290. In early April 1933, FDR was quoted as saying to Paul Claudel, the French ambassador, "Hitler is a madman and his counselors, some of whom I personally know, are even madder than he is."
40. Roberts, *The Storm of War*, 1–2; Shirer, *The Rise and Fall of the Third Reich*, 213–30; McJimsey, *Ally of the Poor*, 70; Taylor, *American-Made*, 154–55.

41. Adams, *Harry Hopkins*, 64–66; McJimsey, *Ally of the Poor*, 70–71; Taylor, *American-Made*, 154–55.

42. Lash, *Eleanor and Franklin*, 571.

43. McJimsey, *Ally of the Poor*, 76. Quote is from FDR's fireside chat, September 30, 1934, *PPA*, 1934, 420.

44. Quoted in Sherwood, *Roosevelt and Hopkins*, 65.

45. State of the Union text, *NYT*, January 5, 1935, 2.

46. Taylor, *American-Made*, 169.

47. Richberg, *My Hero*, 241.

48. Executive Order 7034, May 6, 1935, *PPA*, 1935, 163–68; Smith, *FDR*, 354.

49. Smith, *FDR*, 354–56.

50. Address by HH at WPA luncheon, Los Angeles, September 19, 1936, HH Papers, box 9, FDRL.

51. Childs, *I Write from Washington*, 22–23.

52. Sherwood, *Roosevelt and Hopkins*, 80, quoting Hugh Johnson. In the complete quote, Johnson said of Hopkins, "He has a mind like a razor, a tongue like a skinning knife, a temper like a Tartar and a sufficient vocabulary of parlor profanity—words kosher enough to get by the censor but acid enough to make a mule-skinner jealous. . . . He's just a high-minded Holy Roller in a semi-religious frenzy."

53. Charles, *Minister of Relief*, 207.

54. Address by HH at WPA luncheon, Los Angeles, September 19, 1936, HH Papers, box 9, FDRL.

55. Quoted in Charles, *Minister of Relief*, 208.

56. Sherwood, *Roosevelt and Hopkins*, 87, quoting from letter by Dorothy Thompson to Sherwood.

57. Helen Essary, "'Victory Train' Scenario Just a Joke," *Washington Times*, November 8, 1936.

58. *PPA*, 1937, 1–6.

59. Interview of Aubrey Williams, March 18, 1947, box 411, Sherwood Papers.

60. This letter, dated Wednesday, November 3, 1937, was discovered in 1999 among the effects of William Hauck, Hopkins's deceased government driver. Hauck's daughter, Bernie Light, delivered the letter to Diana Hopkins Halsted, Hopkins's daughter, who on October 13, 1999, turned it over to Hopkins's son Robert. In 2006 Robert Hopkins, now deceased, gave the letter and other documents written by or concerning his father to GU. This letter was not publicly available until 2010.

61. James A. Halsted, "Severe Malnutrition in a Public Servant of the World War II Era: The Medical History of Harry Hopkins," *Transactions of the American Clinical and Climatological Association* 86 (1974): 24; McJimsey, *Ally of the Poor*, 118–19; Sherwood, *Roosevelt and Hopkins*, 93.

62. Smith, *Hostage to Fortune*.

63. Smith, *FDR*, 397–98; McJimsey, *Ally of the Poor*, 119.

64. Tugwell, *The Democratic Roosevelt*, 449.

65. Kennedy, *Freedom from Fear*, 350–61.

66. HH, handwritten notes, n.d., HH Papers, box 298, FDRL.

67. Raymond Moley, *27 Masters of Politics* (New York: Funk and Wagnalls, 1949), 41.

68. Dunn, *Roosevelt's Purge*, 26, 114–16; McJimsey, *Ally of the Poor*, 121–22.

69. Taylor, *American-Made*, 415; Sherwood, *Roosevelt and Hopkins*, 102–4. The historian David Kennedy writes, "Hopkins almost certainly never said anything of the kind, but the phrase struck a responsive chord among those disposed to believe it and was still cited as biblical writ by anti–New Deal critics many decades later" (*Freedom from Fear*, 349).

70. Harriman and Hopkins had become friends on the Long Island croquet-playing circuit hosted by such luminaries as Herbert Bayard Swope. Parrish, *To Keep the British Afloat*, 24.

71. Taylor, *American-Made*, 419. Hopkins was confirmed as secretary of commerce by the Senate on January 23, 1939, with twenty-seven senators voting against him.

72. Quoted in Sherwood, *Roosevelt and Hopkins*, 111.

73. McJimsey, *Ally of the Poor*, 124. Regarding the farm, Hopkins disingenuously told the press that it would give his daughter a permanent home. "Diana of Iowa," *Time*, April 17, 1939.

74. Sherwood, *Roosevelt and Hopkins*, 92.

75. McFarland and Roll, *Louis Johnson*, 58; Joseph Davies to Marvin McIntyre, September 20, November 3, 1938, "A Post Factum Survey of Czechoslovak Crisis," September 21, 1938, Davies Papers; Maclean, *Joseph E. Davies*, 64.

76. Shirer, *Berlin Diary*, 126.

77. McFarland and Roll, *Louis Johnson*, 58–59; Sherwood, *Roosevelt and Hopkins*, 99–100; Taylor, *American-Made*, 452–53 (however, Taylor mistakenly stated that the West Coast trip was taken in March 1938).

78. McFarland and Roll, *Louis Johnson*, 57–65; Tuttle, *Anglo-American-Soviet Relations*, 38–39; Sherwood, *Roosevelt and Hopkins*, 100.

79. Black, *Franklin Delano Roosevelt*, 498.

80. McFarland and Roll, *Louis Johnson*, 42; Sherwood, *Roosevelt and Hopkins*, 101; Black, *Franklin Delano Roosevelt*, 498–99.

81. Quote from Hitler's January 30, 1939, speech in Reynolds, *From Munich to Pearl Harbor*, 53.

82. McJimsey, *Ally of the Poor*, 126; Sherwood, *Roosevelt and Hopkins*, 113–15.

83. DHH memo to author, April 19, 2011; Sherwood, *Roosevelt and Hopkins*, 117–18.

84. RH to Sherwood, quoted in Sherwood, *Roosevelt and Hopkins*, 118–19.

85. Joseph Davies to FDR, June 8, 1939, President's Secretary's File 24, folder "Belgium, 1938–1941," FDRL.

86. FDR to HH, August 22, 1939, quoted in Sherwood, *Roosevelt and Hopkins*, 119.

87. Alsop and Kintner, *American White Paper*, 1.

88. HH to brother Lewis Hopkins, September 13, 1939, Dr. George Fusterman to HH, September 13, 1939, box 61, folder 3, GU; McJimsey, *Ally of the Poor*, 127.

89. McJimsey, *Ally of the Poor*, 128; Sherwood, *Roosevelt and Hopkins*, 112.

90. Sherwood, *Roosevelt and Hopkins*, 112: McJimsey, *Ally of the Poor*, 127–28n26. When Hopkins was at the Mayo Clinic in the spring of 1945, at least one physician "with long experience in nutritional problems" noted in Hopkins's chart, "As far as I am concerned this is non-tropical sprue." James A. Halsted, "Severe Malnutrition in a Public Servant of the World War II Era: The Medical History of Harry Hopkins," box 1, folder 5, RH Papers, GU.

91. Sumner Welles to FDR, March 2, 1940, quoted in Brands, *Traitor to His Class*, 541.

92. Because Roosevelt perhaps hid his intentions by engaging in talks with Hopkins and others about retiring after the end of his second term, historians disagree about when he decided to seek a third term. In his biography of FDR, Conrad Black argues convincingly that after Roosevelt concluded in the early months of 1939 that "Hitler was a compulsive aggressor," he decided that he had to enter the race in 1940 and lead the country (*Franklin Delano Roosevelt*, 563–65).

93. Hellman, "House Guest," part 1, 27.

94. Quoted in Sherwood, *Roosevelt and Hopkins*, 17.

95. James Roosevelt, "My Father F.D.R.: His Lonely Last Days," *Saturday Evening Post*, November 7, 1959, 112.

96. James and Diana Halsted, interview with Franklin D. Roosevelt Jr., regarding Harry Hopkins, January 11, 1979, Oral History Interviews, FDRL.

97. McJimsey, *Ally of the Poor*, 108.

98. Quoted in Rader, "Harry L. Hopkins," 14.

99. McJimsey, *Ally of the Poor*, 102.

100. Paul Appleby (1952–53), p. 156, in the Oral History Collection of Columbia University.

101. Quoted in McKean, *Tommy the Cork*, 121.

102. Sherwood, *Roosevelt and Hopkins*, 2–3. The quote by Roosevelt to Willkie after the 1940 election was repeated by Willkie many times; Sherwood verified the quote with Mrs. Willkie (937n).

103. Sherwood, *Roosevelt and Hopkins*, 3.

Chapter 3: He Suddenly Came Out with It—The Whole Program

1. Florence Kerr (August 15, 1974), p. 75, in the Oral History Collection of Columbia University.

2. Quoted in Persico, *Franklin and Lucy*, 225.

3. Schlesinger, *The Age of Roosevelt*, 2:516–17.

4. Goodwin, *No Ordinary Time*, 20, 34–35.

5. Sherwood, *Roosevelt and Hopkins*, 206; Goodwin, *No Ordinary Time*, 15, 17.

6. Goodwin, *No Ordinary Time*, 88, quoting from interview of Elliott Roosevelt

7. Ibid., 88–89.

8. Part 1, series II, box 40, folders 1–6, HH Papers, GU.

9. Part 1, series II, box 40, folder 6, HH Papers, GU; Sherwood, *Roosevelt and Hopkins*, 106–7.

10. Tommy Thompson to Anna Boettiger, June 17, 1940, box 75, Halsted Papers, FDRL.

11. Tully, *FDR: My Boss*, 116.

12. Goodwin, *No Ordinary Time*, 198–99; Laura Shapiro, "The First Kitchen: Eleanor Roosevelt's Austerity Drive," *New Yorker*, November 22, 2010, 74–80.

13. Robert Sherwood wrote that Pa Watson was "described by everyone as 'loveable' and by a few as somewhat simple minded" (*Roosevelt and Hopkins*, 207).

14. Ibid., 9.

15. Lowenheim, Langley, and Jones, *Roosevelt and Churchill*, 94–95.

16. Olson, *Citizens of London*, 10.

17. Smith, *Hostage to Fortune*, 411; Beschloss, *Kennedy and Roosevelt*, 200.

18. Dimbley and Reynolds, *An Ocean Apart*, 136.
19. "Appropriations for National Defense," May 16, 1940, and "Additional Appropriations for National Defense," May 31, 1940, *PPA*, 1940, 198–205, 250–53.
20. 677th Press Conference, September 3, 1940, *PPA*, 1940, 375–90. According to the historian David Reynolds, the destroyers-for-bases deal was significant not because either side gained much from the deal but because it had "vast implications" on the ability of future presidents to conduct foreign affairs without seeking congressional approval (*From Munich to Pearl Harbor*, 85–87).
21. Sherwood, *Roosevelt and Hopkins*, 157–58; McFarland and Roll, *Louis Johnson*, 94–95.
22. Sherwood, *Roosevelt and Hopkins*, 154–55; Freidel, *Franklin D. Roosevelt*, 348–49.
23. Ickes, *The Secret Diaries*, 3:240.
24. Sherwood, *Roosevelt and Hopkins*, 172.
25. Smith, *FDR*, 449–51; McFarland and Roll, *Louis Johnson*, 98–99; Sherwood, *Roosevelt and Hopkins*, 164.
26. Sherwood, *Roosevelt and Hopkins*, 173.
27. Gilbert, *The Churchill War Papers*, 2:368.
28. Sherwood, *Roosevelt and Hopkins*, 173.
29. Smith, *FDR*, 458.
30. Peters, *Five Days in Philadelphia*, 136; Smith, *FDR*, 457.
31. Levin, *The Making of FDR*, 216–17; Sherwood, *Roosevelt and Hopkins*, 177–78.
32. Fleming, *Operation Sea Lion*, 53.
33. "War of the Unknown Warriors," radio speech by Winston Churchill, July 14, 1940, BBC broadcast London, The Churchill Centre, www.winstonchurchill.org/learn/speeches/speeches-of-winston-churchill/126-war-of-the-unknown-warriors.
34. Brands, *Traitor to His Class*, 555–56.
35. Quoted in Lash, *Eleanor and Franklin*, 619.
36. Edwin Lahey, "Delegates Mark Time; Wait for Fireworks at 8," *Chicago Daily News*, July 17, 1940; "By Acclamation" and "The Voice of the Convention," *Time*, July 29, 1940; Smith, *FDR*, 460–61.
37. Brands, *Traitor to His Class*, 556–57; Smith, *FDR*, 461.
38. Smith, *FDR*, 462–63.
39. Goodwin, *No Ordinary Time* 133; *Proceedings of the 1940 Democratic National Convention*, 238–39.
40. "F.D.R. Delays Speech Until V.P. is Named," *New York Daily News*, July 19, 1940; Smith, *FDR*, 463.
41. HH to FDR, President's Secretary's File, box 138, FDRL. "Mac" is Marvin McIntyre, "Felix" is Felix Frankfurter, and "Ben" is Ben Cohen. "Steve," "Tommy," "Sam," and "Missy" are Steve Early, Malvina Thompson, Sam Rosenman, and Missy LeHand.
42. DHH memo to author, April 19, 2011.
43. Quote in Felix Blair, "Harry L. Hopkins: Lender and Spender," *Life*, September 22, 1941, 88.
44. Sherwood, *Roosevelt and Hopkins*, 183.
45. Part 1, series II, box 40, folders 1, 5, HH Papers, GU; DHH memo to author, April 19, 2011.
46. Schlesinger, *White House Ghosts*, 33.

47. Sherwood, *Roosevelt and Hopkins*, 183.
48. Moss, *Nineteen Weeks*, 295–96.
49. Feis, *The Road to Pearl Harbor*, 76–87; Smith, *FDR*, 509.
50. Smith, *FDR*, 510; Langer and Gleason, *The Undeclared War*, 20–21.
51. Prange, *At Dawn We Slept*, 38, 39.
52. *Documents on American Foreign Relations*, 304–5. Explaining the purpose of the pact, Japan's foreign minister, Yosuke Matsuoka, wrote to the cabinet, "It is the United States that is encouraging the Chungking government. Should a solid coalition come to exist between Japan, Germany and Italy, it will become the most effective expedient to restrain the United States" (*Tokyo War Crimes Documents*, no. 1259).
53. Ickes, *Secret Diaries*, 3:352.
54. Barnes, *Willkie*, 226.
55. Brands, *Traitor to His Class*, 573–74; Burns, *Roosevelt*, 445.
56. Lash, *Roosevelt and Churchill*, 235.
57. Sherwood, *Roosevelt and Hopkins*, 190; Taylor, *American-Made*, 506.
58. Sherwood, *Roosevelt and Hopkins*, 191.
59. Address at Boston, October 30, 1940, *PPA*, 1940, 514–24.
60. Sherwood, *Roosevelt and Hopkins*, 199–200.
61. Lubell, *The Future of American Politics*, 51–57.
62. WSC to FDR, November 6, 1940, quoted in Lowenheim et al., *Roosevelt and Churchill*, 119–20.
63. McJimsey, *Ally of the Poor*, 132; Ogden, *Life of the Party*, 114–15.
64. Smith, *FDR*, 482.
65. Quoted in Davis, *War President*, 63; Kimball, *Churchill and Roosevelt*, 1:83.
66. Davis, *War President*, 64, 67.
67. Sherwood, *Roosevelt and Hopkins*, 224.
68. Winterbotham, *The Ultra Secret*, 58–59.
69. Kimball, *Churchill and* Roosevelt, 1:102–9; Churchill, *The Second World War*, 2:558–67.
70. Ibid., 2:567.
71. Quote in Sherwood, *Roosevelt and Hopkins*, 224, 942n (based on Sherwood's personal recollection).
72. Kimball, *The Most Unsordid Act*, 119.
73. Davis, *War President*, 59–62, 70.
74. Davis and Lindley, *How War Came*, 116–17.
75. McJimsey, *Ally of the Poor*, 134.
76. Sherwood, *Roosevelt and Hopkins*, 225.
77. FDR, press conference, December 17, 1940, *Complete Presidential Press Conferences*, 16:350–55; *PPA*, 1940, 604–9; Frank L. Kluckhorn, "Aid Plan Outlined; President Wants to Take Dollar Sign Out of Assistance," *NYT*, December 18, 1940.
78. Davis, *War President*, 81; *PPA*, 1940, 633–44.
79. Gallup, *The Gallup Poll*, 262 (interviewing dates January 11–16, 1941).
80. Smith, *FDR*, 486n; Sherwood, *Roosevelt and Hopkins*, 226 (Hopkins "provided the key phrase," but Sherwood was told it was originated by William S. Knudsen and Jean Monnet); Davis, *War President*, 84n55 (suggests phrase might also have been originated by Knudsen).

81. McJimsey, *Ally of the Poor*, 134.
82. "Guildhouse Housed Many Treasures," *NYT*, December 31, 1940.
83. Probert, *Bomber Harris*, 110.
84. Gilbert, *Churchill War Papers*, 2:1309.

Chapter 4: The Right Man

1. *PPA*, 1940, 663–72.
2. Sherwood, *Roosevelt and Hopkins*, 231. Based on an interview of Hopkins, Marquis Childs recounted this conversation using self-serving and somewhat implausible dialogue supplied by Hopkins, but the substance was the same as Sherwood's version. Childs, "The President's Best Friend," 9.
3. *PPA*, 1940, 645–49.
4. Adams, *Harry Hopkins*, 199.
5. Abramson, *Spanning the Century*, 276.
6. McJimsey, *Ally of the Poor*, 135; Sherwood, *Roosevelt and Hopkins*, 232; Sherwood, interview of Felix Frankfurter, May 25, 1946, box 411, Sherwood Papers, FDRL.
7. Nevile Butler to Foreign Office (Great Britain), January 4, 1941, FO 371/26179, British National Archives, Kew; McJimsey, *Ally of the Poor*, 135–36.
8. Adams, *Harry Hopkins*, 200; Baker, *Roosevelt and Pearl Harbor*, 50.
9. Beschloss, *Kennedy and Roosevelt*, 24; Davis, *War President*, 109.
10. Smith, *Hostage to Fortune*, 528.
11. Sherwood, *Roosevelt and Hopkins*, 234–35; McJimsey, *Ally of the Poor*, 136.
12. Parrish, *To Keep the British Afloat*, 132.
13. Davis, *War President*, 120.
14. Sherwood, *Roosevelt and Hopkins*, 235–36.
15. Leutze, *The London Journal*, 201, 216–17.
16. HH memo to FDR, January 10, 1941, FDRL, quoted in Sherwood, *Roosevelt and Hopkins*, 237.
17. HH handwritten, January 10, 1941, HH Papers, microfilm reel 19, FDRL; Davis, *War President*, 122.
18. Churchill, *The Second World War*, 3:23.
19. HH to FDR, January 10, 1941, HH Papers, microfilm, reel 19, FDRL.
20. Ibid. Hopkins probably put this in his report because he knew Roosevelt disliked Kennedy and would be pleased to hear that Churchill shared that feeling.
21. Brands, *Traitor to His Class*, 586.
22. HH to FDR, January 10, 1941, HH Papers, microfilm, reel 19, FDRL.
23. Leutze, *The London Journal*, 218–19.
24. Churchill, *The Second World War*, 3:23.
25. Leutze, *The London Journal*, 220.
26. Lash, *Roosevelt and Churchill*, 282.
27. Sherwood, *Roosevelt and Hopkins*, 236; Davis, *War President*, 121–22; Parrish, *To Keep the British Afloat*, 143.
28. Sherwood, *Roosevelt and Hopkins*, 240.
29. Lyttleton, *Memoirs*, 165–66.
30. Colville, *The Fringes of Power*, 333–34.

31. Churchill, *The Second World War*, 3:24.

32. Jenkins, *Churchill*, 648.

33. Leutze, *The London Journal*, 224–25.

34. HH to FDR, n.d., HH Papers, Box 298, FDRL.

35. Memo from James Brown to HH, reciting bills for purchases of warm clothing, January 16, 1941, box 60, folder 12, HH Papers, GU.

36. Sherwood, *Roosevelt and Hopkins*, 246; Wills, *Wartime Missions*, 5; Adams, *Harry Hopkins*, 206–7.

37. Charmley, *Churchill*, 402–7, 423–24, 433–34, 439.

38. Wills, *Wartime Missions*, 8–9; Adams, *Harry Hopkins*, 207.

39. Davis, *War President*, 128.

40. Moran, *Churchill*, 5–6 (Sir Charles Wilson, Churchill's physician, became Lord Moran in 1943).

41. Ibid.

42. Meachem, *Franklin and Winston*, 92; Stafford, *Roosevelt and Churchill*, 51–54.

43. Copy of FDR's penciled message to HH, January 1941, box 304, book 3: Hopkins in London, folder A, Sherwood Collection, FDRL.

44. Cloud and Olson, *The Murrow Boys*, 197.

45. Smith, *In All His Glory*, 217.

46. Parrish, *To Keep the British Afloat*, 172.

47. Percy Cudlipp, editor of the *London Daily Herald*, Series B: Research Notes on "Roosevelt and Hopkins," i. (1840), Sherwood Papers.

48. J. Edgar Hoover to Major General Edwin M. Watson, February 12, 1941, Hopkins MSS, box 304, file "Hopkins in London," folder A, FDRL.

49. Stafford, *Roosevelt and Churchill*, 54–55.

50. Lady Soames interview, Newton Collection, FDRL.

51. Pamela Churchill Harriman interview, Newton Collection.

52. Lady Soames interview, Newton Collection.

53. Parrish, *To Keep the British Afloat*, 150.

54. "Lindbergh's Formal Statement Before the House Committee," *NYT*, January 24, 1941; Kimball, *The Most Unsordid Act*, 189–90.

55. McJimsey, *Ally of the Poor*, 145–46.

56. Sherwood, *Roosevelt and Hopkins*, 257.

57. Colville, *The Fringes of Power*, 341.

58. "We Shall Come Through," *Times* (London), February 1, 1941.

59. Eric Seal, letter, February 2, 1941, quoted in Gilbert, *Winston S. Churchill*, 6:999–1000; Parrish, *To Keep the British Afloat*, 175.

60. Herschel Johnson to Sir Alan Lascelles, January 14, 1941, Buckingham Palace, box 304, book 3: Hopkins in London, folder A, Sherwood Collection, FDRL; Adams, *Harry Hopkins*, 205.

61. HH memo titled "Diary," January 30, 1941, box 304, book 3: Hopkins in London, folder A, Sherwood Collection, FDRL.

62. Eden, *Memoirs*, 357

63. Sherwood, *Roosevelt and Hopkins*, 260–61; Davis, *War President*, 130; McJimsey, *Ally of the Poor*, 146; Adams, *Harry Hopkins*, 211; Wills, *Wartime Missions*, 16.

64. Gilbert, *The Churchill War Papers*, 3:196–200.
65. HH to WSC, n.d., 4 25/3, Prime Minister's Office Records.
66. "There'll Always Be an England," *London Daily Express*, February 17, 1941, box 398, file "Clippings in London April, 1942," Sherwood Collection, FDRL; Adams, *Harry Hopkins*, 211.
67. "There'll Always Be an England."
68. Telegram, WSC to FDR, January 28, 1941, box 304, book 3: Hopkins in London, folder A, Sherwood Collection, FDRL.
69. Remarks by Pamela Churchill Harriman at the opening of the private papers of Harry L. Hopkins at Georgetown University, January 26, 1986, RH Papers, box 2, folder 30, GU.
70. Pamela Churchill Harriman interview, Newton Collection.
71. James and Diana Halsted, interview with Franklin D. Roosevelt Jr., regarding Harry Hopkins, January 11, 1979, Oral History Interviews, FDRL.
72. *Henry V*, Act IV, prologue.

Chapter 5: First Glimpse of Dawn?

1. "Wheeler Asserts Bill Means War," *NYT*, January 13, 1941. Frank L. Kluckhorn, "'Rotten', 'Dasterdly', Roosevelt Says of War Charge Made by Wheeler," *NYT*, January 15, 1941. "Filibuster Threat Renewed," *NYT*, February 25, 1941. Hedley Donovan, "Senate Tempers Rise," *Washington* Post, February 23, 1941.
2. Sherwood, *Roosevelt and Hopkins*, 264.
3. Davis, *War President*, 135–36.
4. Lend-Lease Act, March 11, 1941, chap. 11, 55 Stat. 31, codified as amended at 22 USC §§411–19.
5. Address, March 15, 1941, *PPA*, 1941,
6. "U.S. Rolls Sleeves to Rush Guns and Butter to British," *Newsweek*, March 24, 1941.
7. Davis, *War President*, 158.
8. Alsop and Kintner, Capital Parade column, "Roosevelt, Hopkins and Churchill," *Washington Post*, March 17, 1941; Childs, "The President's Best Friend," 73.
9. Sherwood, *Roosevelt and Hopkins*, 268.
10. Stimson diary, February 27, 1941.
11. Blum, *Roosevelt and Morgenthau*, 357.
12. Harriman and Abel, *Special Envoy*, 3, 17.
13. Davis, *War President*, 160; McJimsey, *Ally of the Poor*, 154; FDR to HH, March 27, 1941, Official File 4117, FDRL.
14. Jackson, *That Man*, 148.
15. Davis, *War President*, 161.
16. Quoted in Sherwood, *Roosevelt and Hopkins*, 268.
17. McJimsey, *Ally of the Poor*, 156.
18. Davis, *War President*, 162–63.
19. Sherwood, *Roosevelt and Hopkins*, 280.
20. Davis, *War President*, 139–42, 296; Sherwood, *Roosevelt and Hopkins*, 273.
21. McJimsey, *Ally of the Poor*, 161.
22. Blum, *From the Morgenthau Diaries*, 2:254.

23. McJimsey, *Ally of the Poor*, 161–62; Admiral Richmond K. Turner to Director of War Plans Division and Chief of Naval Operations, April 29, 1941, reel 39, item 1587, George C. Marshall Library, Lexington, Virginia.

24. Sherwood, *Roosevelt and Hopkins*, 296.

25. Adolf Berle, diary, May 26, 1941, FDRL.

26. Sherwood, *Roosevelt and Hopkins*, 297.

27. "Roosevelt Proclaims Unlimited Emergency, Will Resist Any Hitler Effort to Rule Seas," *NYT*, May 28, 1941.

28. "Moves are Secret," *NYT*, May 29, 1941. The historian Kenneth Davis points out that the transcript of this press conference does not appear in *PPA* 1941 and suggests that Sam Rosenman, knowing that FDR was not proud of his performance at this press conference, deleted it from the 1941 volume, which was published five years after Roosevelt died (*War President*, 771n57).

29. Davis, *War President*, 189.

30. Memo, HH to FDR, June 14, 1941, Hopkins MSS, box 308, file "Shoot on Site [*sic*]," FDRL; Sherwood, *Roosevelt and Hopkins*, 299.

31. *PPA*, 1941, 156.

32. Goodwin, *No Ordinary Time*, 243; Persico, *Franklin and Lucy*, 253–54; Davis, *War President*, 209–11.

33. Parks, *The Roosevelts*, 170, 177.

34. Bernard Asbell, "Missy: The Tragic Story of the Secretary Who Loved President Roosevelt," *Ladies' Home Journal*, June 1973, 121.

35. Quoted in Goodwin, *No Ordinary Time*, 245 (based on author's interview).

36. Willis, *FDR and Lucy*, 97; Persico, *Franklin and Lucy*, 254.

37. Reminiscences of Florence Kerr (August 15, 1974), p. 75, in the Oral History Collection of Columbia University.

38. Goodwin, *No Ordinary Time*, 244.

39. Roberts, *The Storm of War*, 156.

40. Sherwood, *Roosevelt and Hopkins*, 303.

41. Hitler to Mussolini, June 21, 1941, *Nazi-Soviet Relations* (files of the German Foreign Office), 349–53, quoted in Shirer, *The Rise and Fall of the Third Reich*, 849–51.

42. Colville, *The Fringes of Power*, 404.

43. Churchill, *The Second World War*, 3:371–72.

44. Welles, *The Time for Decision*, 170–71.

45. Churchill, *The Second World War*, 3:356–61.

46. Keegan, *The Second World War*, 179.

47. Langer and Gleason, *The Undeclared War*, 342, quoting Soviet Embassy, *Information Bulletin*, December 15, 1941.

48. Roberts, *The Storm of War*, 156–57; Davis, *War President*, 214.

49. Langer and Gleason, *Undeclared War*, 535–36; Davis, *War President*, 218–19.

50. Turner Catledge, "Our Policy Stated," *NYT*, June 24, 1941.

51. Ibid.

52. "Against Both Sides," *Time*, July 7, 1941, 11.

53. Sherwood, *Roosevelt and Hopkins*, 303–5.

54. Tuttle, *Anglo-American-Soviet Relations*, 84; Davis, *War President*, 223.

55. Interview by author of former senator Joseph Davies Tydings, grandson of Joe Davies, April 5, 2010.

56. Davis, *War President*, 224.

57. Davies, *Mission to Moscow*, 433.

58. Quoted in Maclean, *Joseph E. Davies*, 71.

59. Davis, *War President*, 225.

60. Joe Davies to Diary, July 8, 1941, box I:11 chrono files, Davies Papers; Davies, *Mission to Moscow*, 489.

61. Joseph E. Davies to HH, July 8, 1941, Hopkins MSS, Box 298, file "Footnotes: January–August 1941," FDRL.

62. Dunn, *Caught between Roosevelt and Stalin*, 128. In his dispatch to Foreign Minister Molotov dated July 12, 1941, Oumansky reported that "without naming Berle," he "complained [to Hopkins] that there were several circles" of anti-Soviet sentiment in the U.S. government and that Hopkins assured him that this would change. Ministerstvo inostrannyk del SSR [Foreign Ministry of the USSR], *Sovetsko-Amerikanskie otnosheniia vo vremia velikoi otechestvennoi voiny* [Soviet-American Relations During the Period of the Great Fatherland War, 1941–1945], vol. 1 (1941–1943), 65–66. Moscow: Izdatel'stvo politicheskoi literatury, 1984.

63. Sherwood, *Roosevelt and Hopkins*, 308–10; Davis, *War President*, 229.

64. Memorandum of Trip to Meet Winston Churchill, August 23, 1941, President's Secretary's File, Safe, Atlantic Charter, FDRL.

65. Joe Davies to Diary, June 23, 1941, Davies Papers.

Chapter 6: Vodka Has Authority

1. Elliott Roosevelt, *As He Saw It*, 27.

2. Davis, *War President*, 230.

3. Churchill, *The Second World War*, 3:427.

4. Davis, *War President*, 232.

5. Sherwood, *Roosevelt and Hopkins*, 311.

6. W[ar] M[inutes] (42), 71st conclusion, July 17, 1941, Cabinet Office Records 65, Public Records Office, London; Lash, *Roosevelt and Churchill*, 383.

7. Kimball, *Forged in War*, 90.

8. Leutze, *The London Observer*, 341–43, 353.

9. Quentin Reynolds, quoted in Sherwood, *Roosevelt and Hopkins*, 320.

10. Churchill, *The Second World War*, 3:385.

11. Adams, *Harry Hopkins*, 232.

12. Maisky quoted in Fenby, *Alliance*, 42; Davis, *War President*, 233.

13. Maisky, *Memoirs*, 179; Adams, *Harry Hopkins*, 232.

14. McJimsey, *Ally of the Poor*, 181, referring to contradictory views of Forrest Davis and Ernest Lindley; John Winant; John Daniel Langer; and Robert Sherwood.

15. HH to FDR, July 25, 1941, Hopkins MSS, box 298, file "Footnotes: January–August 1941," FDRL, quoted in Sherwood, *Roosevelt and Hopkins*, 318.

16. Memorandum by Acting Secretary of State (Welles), July 24, 1941, in *FRUS, Japan*, 2:529.

17. Executive Order No. 8832, July 26, 1941, 6 Fed. Reg. 3715 (July 29, 1941). The executive order was announced on Friday, July 25, 1941, after the close of financial markets. As explained in Miller, *Bankrupting the Enemy*, 191, the "order subjected to license all movements of Japanese assets in the United States." It was not an embargo.
18. Blum, *From the Morgenthau Diaries*, 3:378–79; Ickes, *The Secret Diaries*, 3:588.
19. Quentin Reynolds quoted in Sherwood, *Roosevelt and Hopkins*, 320.
20. FDR to HH, July 26, 1941, Hopkins MSS, box 306, file "Hopkins in Moscow," FDRL.
21. Davis, *War President*, 236–37.
22. HH Personal Letters, reel 19, FDRL, quoted in Adams, *Harry Hopkins*, 235.
23. Sherwood, *Roosevelt and Hopkins*, 321.
24. Sumner Welles to HH, July 27, 1941, HH Papers, box 298, FDRL.
25. Three-page memo by David McKinley entitled "Flight to Archangel with Mr. Harry Hopkins—July/August 1941," box 60, folder 9, HH Papers, GU (hereafter "McKinley memo"); draft of twenty-page article by HH concerning trip to see Stalin in July–August 1941, box 61, folder 2, HH Papers, GU (hereafter "Hopkins memo on Moscow trip—summer 1941").
26. McKinley memo.
27. Wills, *Wartime Missions*, 25; McKinley memo.
28. Wills, *Wartime Missions*, 25.
29. McKinley memo.
30. Hopkins memo on Moscow trip—summer, 1941, 12–13.
31. Ibid., 11–15.
32. Braithwaite, *Moscow 1941*, map 2: "The Invasion Route to Moscow."
33. Roberts, *The Storm of War*, 166–70; Bellamy, *Absolute War*, 239–46; Braithwaite, *Moscow 1941*, 163–65.
34. Shirer, *The Rise and Fall of the Third Reich*, 964, quoting *Nazi Conspiracy and Aggression*, 3:525–26, which is one of the Nuremberg documents (order dated July 31, 1941, emphasis added).
35. Hopkins memo on Moscow trip—summer, 1941, 15.
36. Davis, *War President*, 239.
37. Hopkins memo on Moscow trip—summer, 1941, 17.
38. Joe Davies diary entry, September 8, 1941, entitled "Hopkins' First Mission to Moscow," reporting comments made by HH at dinner (hereinafter "Davies diary on Hopkins in Moscow"), box I:11 chrono files, Davies Papers.
39. Hopkins memo on Moscow trip—summer, 1941, 1.
40. Ibid., 18.
41. Memo by HH of conference at the Kremlin on July 30, 1941, with Joseph Stalin, in *FRUS, 1941*, 1:803.
42. Hopkins memo on Moscow trip—summer, 1941, 1.
43. *FRUS, 1941*, 1:803.
44. Hopkins memo on Moscow trip—summer, 1941, 1.
45. Memorandum by Mr. Harry L. Hopkins, *FRUS, 1941*, 1:804.
46. Ibid., 1:805.

47. Sherwood, *Roosevelt and Hopkins*, 330.
48. Ibid.
49. Yeaton, *Memoirs*, 38, and appended review of Sherwood's *Roosevelt and Hopkins* by Walter Trohan that describes the argument between Yeaton and Hopkins.
50. Bourke-White, *Shooting the Russian War*, 207–8; McJimsey, *Ally of the Poor*, 185.
51. Memo by HH of conference with Vyacheslav Molotov, July 31, 1941, Hopkins MSS, box 306, file "Hopkins in Moscow," FDRL; Sherwood, *Roosevelt and Hopkins*, 332. Steinhardt's memo of the same conversation says that HH gave Molotov an assurance that if Japan attacked Russia, the United States would respond. Memo by Laurence A. Steinhardt of meeting between Harry L. Hopkins and Vyacheslav Molotov, July 31, 1941, Hopkins MSS, box 306, file "Hopkins in Moscow," FDRL.
52. Harriman and Abel, *Special Envoy*, 93.
53. Montefiore, *Stalin*, 269.
54. Shirer, *The Rise and Fall of the Third Reich*, 480.
55. Sherwood, *Roosevelt and Hopkins*, 333.
56. Memo by HH of conference at the Kremlin on July 31, 1941 with Joseph Stalin, in *FRUS, 1941*, 1:805–12.
57. HH to FDR, Cordell Hull, and Sumner Welles, August 1, 1941, in *FRUS, 1941*, 1:814.
58. *FRUS, 1941*, 1:808.
59. Roberts, *The Storm of War*, 156.
60. Ibid., 181; Sherwood, *Roosevelt and Hopkins*, 336–37; *FRUS, 1941*, 1:807–11.
61. Roberts, *The Storm of War*, 158.
62. Joe Davies, September 8, 1941, six-page journal report of Hopkins's account of his trip to Moscow given at stag dinner at Tregaron, box I:11, correspondence folder, Davies Papers.
63. *FRUS, 1941*, 1:812–13.
64. Bourke-White, *Shooting the Russian War*, 217; Tzouliadis, *The Forsaken*, 205.
65. Weinstein and Vassiliev, *The Haunted Wood*, 159, citing files in the KGB archives.
66. *FRUS, 1941*, 1:814, Sherwood, *Roosevelt and Hopkins*, 333–43.
67. McKinley memo.
68. Hopkins memo on Moscow trip—summer, 1941, 20.
69. McKinley memo.
70. Ibid.
71. Adams, *Harry Hopkins*, 241.
72. Bohlen, *Witness to History*, 22.
73. Reynolds, *Only the Stars Are Neutral*, 7–8.
74. Hopkins memo on Moscow trip—summer, 1941, 2.
75. Elliott Roosevelt, *As He Saw It*, 22.

Chapter 7: At Last We Have Gotten Together

1. Fenby, *Alliance*, 48; Morton, *Atlantic Meeting*, 28–29.
2. Kimball, *Churchill and Roosevelt*, 1:226.
3. Quoted in Fenby, *Alliance*, 48. For details of the voyage on *The Prince of Wales*, see Wilson, *The First Summit*, 72–81.

4. Sherwood, *Roosevelt and Hopkins*, 351.

5. Blum, *From the Morgenthau Diaries*, 2:264.

6. Persico, *Franklin and Lucy*, 256.

7. Bercuson and Herwig, *One Christmas in Washington*, 23.

8. Davis, *War President*, 257. The *Prince of Wales* exchanged fire with the *Bismarck* on May 24, 1941, three days before Hitler's pride was crippled by the guns of the *Rodney* and the *George V* and then sunk by torpedoes from the cruiser *Dorsetshire*.

9. Wilson, *First Summit*, 83.

10. Wilson, *First Summit*, 83; Davis, *War President*, 257–58.

11. Reilly, *Reilly of the White House*, 120; H. V. Morton, *An Account of Mr. Churchill's Voyage in H.M.S.* Prince of Wales, *in August 1941, and the Conference with President Roosevelt Which Resulted in the Atlantic Charter* (New York: Dodd Mead, 1943), 98.

12. Sherwood, *Roosevelt and Hopkins*, 363–64.

13. Ward, *Closest Companion*, 141.

14. Elliott Roosevelt, *As He Saw It*, 25.

15. Lyttelton, *Memoirs*, 164.

16. Davis, *War President*, 259.

17. Elliott Roosevelt, *As He Saw It*, 28.

18. Ward, *Closest Companion*, 141.

19. Martin, *Downing Street*, 58.

20. Churchill, *The Second World War*, 3:432.

21. Meachem, *Franklin and Winston*, 113–16.

22. Davis, *War President*, 351.

23. Churchill, *The Second World War*, 3:432.

24. Elliott Roosevelt, *As He Saw It*, 33.

25. Davis, *War President*, 264–65.

26. Tuttle, *Anglo-American-Soviet Relations*, 110.

27. Smith, *FDR*, 502.

28. Tuttle, *Anglo-American-Soviet Relations*, 121.

29. Brands, *Traitor to His Class*, 609, quoting FDR's press conference and Churchill's report to his cabinet.

30. Preamble to the Atlantic Charter. For complete text of the Atlantic Charter, see *FRUS, 1941*, 1:367–69.

31. Hastings, *Winston's War*, 198.

32. Sherwood, *Roosevelt and Hopkins*, 360.

33. Sumner Welles memo, August 11, 1941, in *FRUS, 1941*, 1:361–62; Welles, *Where Are We Heading?*, 13.

34. Davis, *War President*, 269–71; McJimsey, *Ally of the Poor*, 177.

35. Davis, *War President*, 273.

36. HH draft article, HH Papers, box 306, FDRL.

37. Ward, *Closest Companion*, 142.

38. W. P. Crozier, *Off the Record: Political Interviews, 1933–1945*, ed. A. J. P. Taylor (London: Hutchinson, 1973), 231.

39. HH to WSC, n.d. (1941), Hopkins microfilm, reel 11, FDRL.

40. Sherwood, *Roosevelt and Hopkins*, 363.

41. Adams, *Harry Hopkins*, 251.
42. WSC to HH, August 28, 1941, 3 224/2, Prime Minister's Office Records.
43. Davis, *War President*, 277–78.
44. Sherwood, *Roosevelt and Hopkins*, 385.
45. James Roosevelt and Shalett, *My Parents*, 113.
46. Davis, *War President*, 281.
47. Kathleen McLaughlin, "President Shuts Self from World," *NYT*, September 9, 1941.
48. Tully, *FDR: My Boss*, 105.
49. Levin, *The Making of FDR*, 247; Black, *Franklin Delano Roosevelt*, 607.
50. *PPA*, 1941, 439–40.
51. McJimsey, *Ally of the Poor*, 179.
52. Davis, *War President*, 285; "'Shoot First,' Navy Ordered in F.D.R's Blunt Warning," *Atlanta Constitution*, September 12, 1941; "First Day of Shooting War," Knoxville *Journal*, September 12, 1941; "F.D.R. Gives Shooting Order," *Chicago Daily Tribune*, September 12, 1941; "U.S. Navy Reading for 'Shooting War' in the Atlantic," *Washington Post*, September 14, 1941; "Lucas Defends F.D.R. Order to Shoot on Sight," *Chicago Daily Tribune*, September 18, 1941; "Majority Backs 'Shoot at Sight' Plan of Roosevelt," *The Sun*, September 26, 1941.
53. Speech by Charles Lindbergh delivered in Des Moines, Iowa, September 11, 1941, www.pbs.org/wgbh/amex/lindbergh/filmmore/reference/primary/desmoiness-peech.html.
54. Davis, *War President*, 285–87.
55. *PPA*, 1941, 438, 440–41.
56. Andrew, "Anglo-American-Soviet Intelligence Relations," 113; Brands, *Traitor to His Class*, 615.
57. Davis, *War President*, 325.
58. *PPA*, 1941, 481.
59. Tuttle, *Anglo-American-Soviet Relations*, 119–20.
60. McJimsey, *Ally of the Poor*, 189.
61. Dunn, *Caught between Roosevelt and Stalin*, 132.
62. "The Influence of Brigadier General Philip R. Faymonville on Soviet-American Military Relations," Intelligence file, box 29, Edwin M. Watson Papers, University of Virginia; Langer, "'The Red General,'" 208–21.
63. Quoted in McJimsey, *Ally of the Poor*, 189.
64. Davis, *War President*, 291–92.
65. Quoted in McJimsey, *Ally of the Poor*, 190.
66. Davis, *War President*, 293.
67. McJimsey, *Ally of the Poor*, 190.
68. Reynolds, Kimball, and Chubarian, *Allies at War*, 208.
69. Dunn, *Caught between Roosevelt and Stalin*, 132–33.
70. Yeaton, *Memoirs*, 44.
71. Braithwaite, *Moscow 1941*, 264–66, 269. This conversation has been repeated in several sources, although one historian has questioned whether the conversation actually took place.
72. Ibid., 274–75.

73. Davis, *War President*, 289–91; McJimsey, *Ally of the Poor*, 198–99.
74. Stettinius, *Lend-Lease*, 98.
75. Sherwood, *Roosevelt and Hopkins*, 377–79
76. Smith, *FDR*, 515–16.
77. Miller, *Bankrupting the Enemy*, 200. The other members of the committee were Edward Foley, general counsel of the Treasury Department, and Assistant Attorney General Francis Shea.
78. Smith, *FDR*, 518; Acheson, *Present at the Creation*, 26. Langer and Gleason, *The Undeclared War*, put it this way: "When it gradually became apparent what had happened, Hull and Roosevelt elected to leave the situation as it was, and in effect ratified the unplanned embargo" (655).
79. Prange, *At Dawn We Slept*, 169–71.
80. Ibid., 158–59.
81. Gordon W. Prange, interview with Captain Watanabe, February 12, 1949, cited in ibid., 13.
82. Davis, *War President*, 314–15.
83. Prange, *At Dawn We Slept*, 36, quoting Stimson diary, October 16, 1981.
84. Davis, *War President*, 315.
85. Ibid., 318.
86. Ibid., 321.
87. Hull, *Memoirs*, 2:1058.
88. Stimson diary (MS), November 7, 1941, Yale University, quoted in Freidel, *Franklin D. Roosevelt*, 397.
89. Quoted in Prange, *At Dawn We Slept*, 387.
90. "Asiatics Get Call; Japanese Asserts East Must End Exploitation 'With Vengeance,' " *NYT*, November 30, 1941.
91. Davis, *War President*, 333–34.
92. McJimsey, *Ally of the Poor*, 205; letter, HH to Mrs. Betsey Cushing Roosevelt, November 10, 1941, HH Papers, box 307, FDRL.
93. Quoted in McJimsey, *Ally of the Poor*, 206.
94. Baruch, *The Public Years*, 289–90.

Chapter 8: We Are All in the Same Boat Now

1. James Roosevelt and Shalett, *Affectionately, FDR*, 646.
2. *PPA*, 1941, 512–13.
3. Davis, *War President*, 336.
4. *PPA*, 1941, 512–13.
5. Sherwood, *Roosevelt and Hopkins*, 426–27; Davis, *War President*, 261, 338.
6. *Report of the Joint Committee on the Investigation of the Pearl Harbor Attack*, 79th Cong., 2nd sess., document 244, appendix D, "The Last Hours" (Washington, D.C.: U.S. Government Printing Office, 1946), 434–35.
7. Testimony of Commander Schulz, Hearings before the Joint Committee on the Investigation of the Pearl Harbor Attack, 79th Congress, 1st Sess., part 39, pp. 1005–6.
8. Langer and Gleason, *The Undeclared War*, 933–34.
9. Prange, *At Dawn We Slept*, 490–92; Smith, *FDR*, 534.

10. Brinkley, *Washington at War*, 85; Persico, *Roosevelt's Secret War*, 266.
11. Baker, *Human Smoke*, 441.
12. Brinkley, *Washington at War*, 86.
13. Persico, *Roosevelt's Secret War*, 266–67.
14. "Memorandum: December 7, 1941," HH Papers, box 6, folder 19, GU.
15. Davis, *War President*, 339.
16. "Memorandum: December 7, 1941," HH Papers, box 6, folder 19, GU.
17. Ibid.
18. Eleanor Roosevelt interview, Graff Papers, FDRL, quoted in Goodwin, *No Ordinary Time*, 289.
19. Davis, *War President*, 340; Brinkley, *Washington at War*, 87.
20. Harriman and Abel, *Special Envoy*, 111–12.
21. Churchill, *The Second World War*, 3:605.
22. Harriman and Abel, *Special Envoy*, 111.
23. Churchill, *The Second World War*, 3:606, 608.
24. "Memorandum: December 7, 1941," HH Papers, box 6, folder, 19, GU.
25. Tully, *FDR: My Boss*, 256.
26. Bercuson and Herwig, *One Christmas in Washington*, 90.
27. "Memorandum: December 7, 1941," HH Papers, box 6, folder 19, GU.
28. Ickes, *The Secret Diaries*, 3:662.
29. Reminiscences of Frances Perkins (1955), vol. 8, pt. 1, p. 69, in the Oral History Collection of Columbia University.
30. "Memorandum: December 7, 1941," HH Papers, box 6, folder 19, GU.
31. Persico, *Roosevelt's Secret War*, 235.
32. Stimson diary, December 7, 1941.
33. Richard Ketchum, "'Yesterday, December 7, 1941 . . .'" *American Heritage*, November 1989, 68.
34. Kendrick, *Prime Time*, 239–40.
35. Robert Sherwood, interview with Edward R. Murrow, September 16, 1946, Sherwood Papers, box 411, FDRL.
36. "FDR's 'Day of Infamy' Speech: Crafting a Call to Arms," *Prologue* 33, no. 4 (2001), www.archives.gov/publications/prologue/2001/winter/crafting a call to arms.
37. HH memo to self, December 8, 1941, Hopkins Papers, FDRL; Bercuson and Herwig, *One Christmas in Washington*, 92, say Hopkins suggested the second to the last sentence and Roosevelt approved. Sherwood, *Roosevelt and Hopkins*, 436, says the next to the last sentence, written mostly by Hopkins, was "the most platitudinous line in the speech." FDR to Congress, December 8, 1941, *PPA*, 1941, 514–15. All drafts are in the FDRL, except that which FDR read on December 8, 1941. It is in the Center for Legislative Archives at the National Archives Building, Washington, D.C.
38. *Parliamentary Debates: House of Commons*, ser. 5, vol. 376, col. 1358–61.
39. Sherwood, *Roosevelt and Hopkins*, 441.
40. Davis, *War President*, 352; Smith, *FDR*, 541.
41. *PPA*, 1941, 523–31.
42. Atkinson, *An Army at Dawn*, 208; Gilbert, *The Second World War*, 277.

43. Shirer, *The Rise and Fall of the Third Reich*, 897–900.

44. *PPA*, 1941, 532–33; Davis, *War President*, 352.

45. Frank L. Kluckhorn, "War Opened on US; Congress Acts Quickly as President Meets Hitler Challenge," *NYT*, December 12, 1941.

46. Telephone transcription quoted in Sherwood, *Roosevelt and Hopkins*, 440–41.

47. Davis, *War President*, 341.

48. Roberts, *The Storm of War*, 208.

49. Bellamy, *Absolute War*, 9–10, 473–76.

50. Braithwaite, *Moscow 1941*, 2, 277.

51. Maclean, *Joseph E. Davies*, 78–79; Sudoplatov et al., *Special Tasks*, 227.

52. Kimball, *Churchill and Roosevelt*, 1:283–84, 286–87.

53. Roberts, *Masters and Commanders*, 68–69.

54. Bercuson and Herwig, *One Christmas in Washington*, 120; FRUS, *The Conferences at Washington and Casablanca*, 50–52, 56.

55. "Great Decisions," *Time*, January 5, 1942.

56. Goodwin, *No Ordinary Time*, 302; Davis, *War President*, 306.

57. McJimsey, *Ally of the Poor*, 212; Moran, *Churchill*, 12.

58. WSC to War Cabinet, December 23, 1941, in Churchill, *The Second World War*, 3:665.

59. Interview of Alonzo Fields, in Goodwin, *No Ordinary Time*, 302.

60. *PPA*, 1941, 585–91; Goodwin, *No Ordinary Time*, 303.

61. DHH memo to author, April 19, 2011.

62. Quote from official minutes in Sherwood, *Roosevelt and Hopkins*, 455, 457; Pogue, *George C. Marshall*, 2:276.

63. Minutes by Major Sexton of meeting of FDR and WSC with advisors, including HH, December 26, 1941, 4:30 p.m., the White House, in FRUS, *The Conferences at Washington and Casablanca*, 101.

64. Sherwood, *Roosevelt and Hopkins*, 457.

65. Churchill, *The Second World War*, 3:673–74.

66. Davis, *War President*, 388–89; Parrish, *Roosevelt and Marshall*, 224–28.

67. Churchill, *The Second World War*, 3:670.

68. Bercuson and Herwig, *One Christmas in Washington*, 155; Goodwin, *No Ordinary Time*, 305.

69. Bercuson and Herwig, *One Christmas in Washington*, 115.

70. Churchill, *The Second World War*, 3:670.

71. Secretary of the British Chiefs of Staff (Leslie Hollis) to the Secretary War Department General Staff (Walter Bedell Smith), December 24, 1941, in FRUS, *The Conferences at Washington and Casablanca*, 267–68; Bercuson and Herwig, *One Christmas in Washington*, 157.

72. Bercuson and Herwig, *One Christmas in Washington*, 159–60.

73. Stimson diaries, December 25, 1941; Henry L. Stimson Papers, reel 7, vol. 36, Library of Congress.

74. DHH memo to author, April 19, 2010.

75. Bercuson and Herwig, *One Christmas in Washington*, 161–62.

76. Stimson diaries, December 25, 1941.
77. Bercuson and Herwig, *One Christmas in Washington*, 160; McJimsey, *Ally of the Poor*, 213.
78. Brands, *Traitor to His Class*, 644.
79. Stimson diaries, December 25, 1941.
80. Tuttle, *Anglo-American-Soviet Relations*, 129.
81. Sherwood, *Roosevelt and Hopkins*, 448.
82. Rosenman, *Working with Roosevelt*, 316; memo by Adolph Berle, January 6, 1942, Adolph A. Berle Papers, diary box 213, FDRL.
83. Sherwood, *Roosevelt and Hopkins*, 442–43. See a similar version of the story in Bercuson and Herwig, *One Christmas in Washington*, 217.
84. Lash, *Roosevelt and Churchill*, 16–17; quote from Byron's "Childe Harold" is from canto III, verse xxxv, *The Complete Poetical Works of Lord Byron* (Boston: Houghton Mifflin, 1905), 40.
85. Declaration by United Nations, January 1, 1942, *PPA*, 1942, 3–4.
86. Lash, *Roosevelt and Churchill*, 19–20.
87. Bercuson and Herwig, *One Christmas in Washington*, 219; Sherwood, *Roosevelt and Hopkins*, 448.
88. Memo of January 1, 1942, Adolph Berle Papers, diary box 213, FDRL.
89. Steve Early press conference, January 3, 1942, in Levin, *The Making of FDR*, 271.
90. FDR, Address on the State of the Union, January 6, 1942, *PPA*, 1942, 32–42.
91. Quoted in Sherwood, *Roosevelt and Hopkins*, 273–74.
92. Memo, Beaverbrook to FDR, December 29, 1941, box 314, book 5: Beaverbrook Raising the Sights, HH Papers, Sherwood Collection, FDRL.
93. HH memo, January 6, 1942, box 298, folder: Footnotes: January–April 1942, HH Papers, Sherwood Collection, FDRL.
94. Memo by HH of luncheon meeting with Ambassador Litvinov, January 6, 1942, Soviet Embassy, in *FRUS, The Conference at Washington and Casablanca*, 170–71.
95. Moran, *Churchill*, 13.
96. Sherwood, *Roosevelt and Hopkins*, 471–72; see also Davis, *War President*, 391–93.
97. HH memo, January 15, 1942, in *FRUS, The Conferences at Washington and Casablanca*, 209. See also HH Papers, box 3008, book 5, FDRL.
98. HH to Clementine Churchill, January 14, 1942, HH Papers, microfilm reel 11, FDRL.
99. Gilbert, *Winston S. Churchill*, 7:43.
100. McJimsey, *Ally of the Poor*, 221.
101. Hellman, "House Guest," part 1, 27.
102. Quoted in Buell, *Master of Sea Power*, 172.
103. HH to Jean Monnet, January 15, 1942, Hopkins microfilm, reel 12, HH Papers, FDRL.

Chapter 9: Some Sort of a Front This Summer

1. Sherwood, *Roosevelt and Hopkins*, 478, 491, 494.
2. Quoted in ibid., 495.
3. Rees, *Behind Closed Doors*, 123; Evans, *The Third Reich at War*, 403, 405; Braithwaite, *Moscow 1941*, 292–95.

4. Davis, *War President*, 403–9; Roberts, *Masters and Commanders*, 127.

5. Davis, *War President*, 412; Sherwood, *Roosevelt and Hopkins*, 498.

6. *PPA*, 1942, 105–16.

7. "Address is Called Inspiration to All," *NYT*, February 24, 1942, 5.

8. Brands, *Traitor to His Class*, 652. The only other attacks by the Japanese on the U.S. mainland during World War II involved the shelling of the Oregon coast near Fort Stevens in June 1942 by a submarine deck gun, which damaged a baseball diamond backstop; a few incendiary bombs that were dropped harmlessly into Oregon forests in September 1942 by a single-engine float plane launched from a submarine; and a small fraction of the thousands of rice-paper balloon bombs launched from Japan that actually reached the Pacific Coast during the winter and spring of 1945. Kennedy, *Freedom from Fear*, 746–47, 750n5.

9. Parrish, *Roosevelt and Marshall*, 233–38.

10. Kimball, *Churchill and Roosevelt*, 1:392–93, 398–99.

11. Pogue, *George C. Marshall*, 2:304; 306; Davis, *War President*, 485.

12. HH to FDR, March 14, 1942, HH Papers, box 298, FDRL.

13. Stimson and Bundy, *On Active Service*, 214.

14. Sherwood, *Roosevelt and Hopkins*, 520.

15. Stimson and Bundy, *On Active Service*, 416–17.

16. Parrish, *Roosevelt and Marshall*, 256.

17. Tully, *FDR: My Boss*, 263.

18. McJimsey, *Ally of the Poor*, 242.

19. Kimball, *Churchill and Roosevelt*, 1:437, 441.

20. Roberts, *Masters and Commanders*, 130.

21. Cable, HH to WSC, HH Papers, box 136, FDRL; HH to WSC, April 2, 1942, Map Room Papers, box 13, FDRL.

22. Parrish, *Roosevelt and Marshall*, 264–65, 269.

23. HH to FDR, April 9, 1942, HH Papers, box 298, FDRL.

24. Roberts, *Masters and Commanders*, 132–33.

25. Pogue, *George C. Marshall*, 2:306.

26. HH to FDR, April 9, 1942, HH Papers, box 298, FDRL; Sherwood, *Roosevelt and Hopkins*, 523.

27. Danchev and Todman, *War Diaries*, 246; Roberts, *Masters and Commanders*, 143–44.

28. Quoted in Sherwood, *Roosevelt and Hopkins*, 527, 529.

29. Ibid., 530–31; McFarland and Roll, *Louis Johnson*, 123–24.

30. FDR to George Marshall, April 13, 1942, HH Papers, box 298, FDRL.

31. Parrish, *Roosevelt and Marshall*, 269.

32. Kimball, *Churchill and Roosevelt*, 1:449.

33. Roberts, *Masters and Commanders*, 154, citing Cabinet Papers at the British National Archives, Kew, 69/4/59.

34. Parrish, *Roosevelt and Marshall*, 270.

35. Quoted in Roberts, *Masters and Commanders*, 155.

36. Sherwood, *Roosevelt and Hopkins*, 536.

37. Minutes of the Chiefs of Staff Meeting, April 14, 1942, Marshall MSS, folder "Trip to England, April, 1942," George C. Marshall Library, Lexington, Virginia; Minutes of War Cabinet Defence Committee, box 308, book 5: Hopkins in London, April 1942, Sherwood Collection, HH Papers, FDRL. See also Roberts, *Masters and Commanders*, 156, citing Cabinet Papers at the British National Archives, Kew, 69/4/61–62.

38. Roberts, *Masters and Commanders*, 156, citing Cabinet Papers at the British National Archives, Kew, 69/4, Defence Committee no. 10 (1942), 14/4 1942.

39. Roberts, *Masters and Commanders*, 157.

40. Pogue, *George C. Marshall*, 2:319–20.

41. Moran, *Churchill*, 35.

42. Quoted in Pogue, *George C. Marshall*, 2:319–20.

43. Hopkins received a copy of the cable FDR sent to Stalin inviting Molotov to Washington on April 11, 1942. Sherwood, *Roosevelt and Hopkins*, 527–28.

44. FDR to HH, April 11, 1942, Map Room file, box 13, FDRL.

45. Sherwood, *Roosevelt and Hopkins*, 541.

46. Hassett, *Off the Record*, 41.

47. Mrs. Laurence Lowman to HH, January 21, 1942, box 41, folder 5, HH Papers, GU.

48. HH to Barry Lowman, January 22, 1942, box 41, folder 5, HH Papers, GU.

49. DHH memo to author, April 19, 2011.

50. Geoffrey T. Hellman, "House Guest," part 2, *New Yorker*, August 14, 1943, 30; chapter 12 of draft manuscript by Halsted, box 6, folder 13, "James Halsted MS bio of HH 1979," RH Papers, GU.

51. Memoir by Liz Gibbons-Hanson, n.d., private collection of Merloyd Ludington Lawrence, Louise Macy's niece.

52. Goodwin, *No Ordinary Time*, 349.

53. Chapter 12 of draft manuscript by Halsted, box 6, folder 13, "James Halsted MS bio of HH 1979," RH Papers, GU; Dorothy Hale obituary, *NYT*, October 22, 1938, 34; Morris, *Rage for Fame*, 326–28; Herrera, *Frida*, 289–94.

54. Hellman, "House Guest," part 2, 30, 32.

55. President's Secretary's File, box 83, FDRL.

56. Roberts, *Masters and Commanders*, 172.

57. Kimball, *Churchill and Roosevelt*, 1:494 (first telegram) and 1:495–500 (second telegram).

58. Parrish, *Roosevelt and Marshall*, 276.

59. Montefiore, *Stalin*, 34, 39–41, 273–77.

60. Bellamy, *Absolute War*, 453, 456–57.

61. Eleanor Roosevelt, *This I Remember*, 250–51.

62. Rees, *Behind Closed Doors*, 131–32, citing O. A. Rzheshevskii, *Voina i Diplomatica* (Moscow: Nauka, 1997), 170; Sherwood, *Roosevelt and Hopkins*, 560.

63. Professor Cross's record of meeting with Molotov, May 29, 1942, HH Papers, box 311, FDRL; *FRUS, 1942*, 3:572–74; Brands, *Traitor to His Class*, 674.

64. This is the exact language of the key sentence in the Roosevelt-Molotov statement eventually released on June 11, 1942. See Kimball, *Churchill and Roosevelt*, 1:494; *FRUS, 1942*, 3:594.

65. Davis, *War President*, 500.

66. Sherwood, *Roosevelt and Hopkins*, 577.
67. Churchill, *The Second World War*, 4:341–42.
68. Roberts, *Masters and Commanders*, 176.
69. Interview of George C. Marshall by Forrest C. Pogue, 1956–57, George C. Marshall Library and Research Center, Lexington, Virginia, quoted in Parrish, *Roosevelt and Marshall*, 297. See similar statement in Pogue, *George C. Marshall*, 2:330.

Chapter 10: The Hopkins Touch
1. HH to WSC, June 6, 1942, HH Papers, box 298, FDRL.
2. Symonds, *The Battle of Midway*; Davis, *War President*, 474–81.
3. HH to WSC, June 6, 1942, box 298, FDRL.
4. Wedemeyer, *Wedemeyer Reports!*, 136; Parrish, *Roosevelt and Marshall*, 281–82.
5. Ziegler, *Mountbatten*, 183–85.
6. WSC to FDR, June 13, 1942, in *FRUS, Conferences at Washington and Casablanca*, 419–20.
7. Davis, *War President*, 506.
8. Danchev and Todman, *War Diaries*, 266–68.
9. Gilbert, *Winston S. Churchill*, 7:86.
10. Churchill, *The Second World War*, 4:380–81. Reynolds, *In Command of History*, 333–34, contends that Churchill apparently "conflated" his visit to Hyde Park in 1942 with that in September 1944. Nevertheless "what exactly happened at Hyde Park in 1942 will probably never be known, but we may presume that Churchill and Hopkins had a cursory discussion about the need for atomic cooperation, putting nothing on paper. The U.S. military was kept in the dark and cold-shouldered the British—hence the need for formal agreements in 1943 and 1944."
11. Davis, *War President*, 510.
12. Memo by WSC to FDR, June 20, 1942, in *FRUS, The Conferences at Washington and Casablanca*, 461–62.
13. Davis, *War President*, 522.
14. Churchill, *The Second World War*, 4:383; Davis, *War President*, 523–24.
15. Danchev and Todman, *War Diaries*, 269.
16. Churchill, *The Second World War*, 4:383.
17. Davis, *War President*, 524.
18. General Ismay's notes quoted in Churchill, *The Second World War*, 4:384.
19. Churchill, *The Second World War*, 4:384; Stimson and Bundy, *On Active Service*, 424.
20. Danchev and Todman, *War Diaries*, 269.
21. Kimball, *Churchill and Roosevelt*, 1:503.
22. Hellman, "House Guest," part 2, 33.
23. Chapter 12 of draft manuscript by Halsted, box 6, folder 13, "James Halsted MS bio of HH 1979, RH Papers, GU.
24. Hellman, "House Guest," part 2, 33; Goodwin, *No Ordinary Time*, 350.
25. Davis, *War President*, 542.
26. Sherwood, *Roosevelt and Hopkins*, 593–94.
27. George C. Marshall note, July 3, 1942, George C. Marshall Library and Research Center, Lexington, Virginia.

28. "Hopkins Wedding in the White House," *NYT*, July 5, 1942.

29. WSC to FDR, July 8, 1942, in Kimball, *Churchill and Roosevelt*, 1:520–21.

30. Davis, *War President*, 537.

31. Matloff and Snell, *Strategic Planning*, 268–69.

32. Hassett, *Off the Record*, 91.

33. Davis, *War President*, 540–42.

34. Hassett, *Off the Record*, 93.

35. Telegram, FDR to Marshall, July 14, 1942, War Department Chief of Staff Army, *Bolero*, 1942–43, referenced in Pogue, *George C. Marshall*, 2:340n61, and Matloff and Snell, *Strategic Planning*, 272n19.

36. Stimson and Bundy, *On Active Service*, 425; Pogue, *George C. Marshall*, 2:342.

37. Memo, FDR to HH, July 16, 1942, Marshall and King, book 5, folder "Hopkins to London, July 1942," box 308, Sherwood Collection, FDRL; HH's notes are referenced in Sherwood, *Roosevelt and Hopkins*, 603–5.

38. Memo, FDR to HH, July 16, 1942, box 308, Sherwood Collection, FDRL.

39. Parrish, *Roosevelt and Marshall*, 278.

40. HH to FDR, July 20, 1942, HH Papers, box 298, FDRL.

41. Ibid.

42. Parrish, *Roosevelt and Marshal*, 294.

43. Moran, *Churchill*, 44.

44. Bryant, *The Turn of the Tide*, 1:451; Roberts, *Masters and Commanders*, 248–49.

45. Danchev and Todman, *War Diaries*, 282.

46. Ibid., 282–83.

47. Gilbert, *Winston S. Churchill*, 7:151.

48. Butcher, *My Three Years with Eisenhower*, 29.

49. HH note, n.d., HH Papers, box 298, FDRL; Sherwood, *Roosevelt and Hopkins*, 609.

50. Papers of Sir John Kennedy, 4/2/4, Liddell Hart Centre for Military Archives, Kings College, London, 186.

51. Minutes of Combined Staff Conference, July 22, 1942, book 5, folder "Hopkins to London, July 1942," box 308, Sherwood Collection, FDRL.

52. Chapter 15 of draft manuscript by Halsted, box 6, folder 13, "James Halsted, MS bio of HH 1979, RH Papers, GU.

53. Memo FDR to HH, Marshall and King listing priorities, no date but probably July 23, 1942, book 5, Folder "Hopkins to London, July 1942," box 308, Sherwood Collection, FDRL.

54. Matloff and Snell, *Strategic Planning*, 280–81.

55. Danchev and Todman, *War Diaries*, 285.

56. King and Whitehill, *Fleet Admiral King*, 197.

57. Gilbert, *Winston S. Churchill*, 7:152.

58. The version quoted in Sherwood, *Roosevelt and Hopkins*, 611, differs slightly from the original, Hopkins to Roosevelt, July 25, 1942, Hopkins MSS box 308, file "July 1942, Hopkins in London," FDRL.

59. Danchev, *Very Special Relationship*, 68.

60. Memo, FDR to HH, Marshall and King, no date but it is a reply to July 25, book 5, Folder "Hopkins to London, July 1942," box 308, Sherwood Collection, FDRL. See also McJimsey, *Ally of the Poor*, 254–55n35.

61. Memo, FDR to HH, book 5, folder "Hopkins to London, July 1942," box 308, Sherwood Collection, FDRL.
62. Matloff and Snell, *Strategic Planning*, 282.
63. Danchev and Todman, *War Diaries*, 286.
64. Louise Macy to HH, July 23, 1942, series V, box 60, folder 5, HH Papers, GU.
65. Churchill, *The Second World War*, 4:448; Kimball, *Churchill and Roosevelt*, 1:541.
66. Kimball, *Churchill and Roosevelt*, 1:543–44.
67. "U.S. at War: Song of Happiness, *Time*, August 10, 1942; Hassett, *Off the Record*, 95–96; DHH memo to author, April 19, 2011.
68. Matloff and Snell, *Strategic Planning*, 282–83; Atkinson, *An Army at Dawn*, 16.
69. Keegan, *The Second World War*, 316.
70. Bland, *George C. Marshall*, 433.
71. Davis, *War President*, 550–51.
72. Kennedy, *Freedom from Fear*, 430.
73. Interview of George C. Marshall by Forest C. Pogue, 1956–57, George C. Marshall Library and Research Center, Lexington, Virginia, quoted in Parrish, *Roosevelt and Marshall*, 297. See similar statement by Marshall in Pogue, *George C. Marshall*, 2:330.

Chapter 11: Lighting the Torch

1. DHH memo to author, April 19, 2011.
2. Joseph P. Lash, *Love, Eleanor*, 400.
3. Lash, *A World of Love*, xxiv, xxxi.
4. Eleanor Roosevelt, *This I Remember*, 256.
5. Lash, *Eleanor and Franklin*, 506.
6. HH memo to self, July 1, 1942, box 57, folder 2, HH Papers, GU; Goodwin, *No Ordinary Time*, 351–54.
7. Hellman, "House Guest," part 1, 25; DHH memo to author, April 19, 2011.
8. Interview with DHH, quoted in Goodwin, *No Ordinary Time*, 351; DHH memo to author, April 19, 2011.
9. Elliott Roosevelt and Brough, *A Rendezvous with Destiny*, 318; Adams, *Harry Hopkins*, 289–90; Hellman, "House Guest," part 1, 25–26.
10. In his unpublished biography of Hopkins, James Halsted, husband of Diana, claimed that FDR's daughter, Anna Boettiger, leaked the details to Pearson. Chapter 12 of draft manuscript by Halsted, box 6, folder 13, "James Halsted, MS bio of HH 1979," RH papers, GU.
11. Ibid; Sherwood, *Roosevelt and Hopkins*, 612–14; DHH memo to author, April 19, 2011.
12. Churchill, *The Second World War*, 4:475.
13. Harriman and Abel, *Special Envoy*, 146–47; Kimball, *Churchill and Roosevelt*, 1:553.
14. In *Winston's War*, 259–60, Hastings says Stalin was "fully briefed," relying on an August 4, 1942, memo by Lavrenti Beria, Stalin's chief of intelligence, in *Ocherki Istorii Rossiikoi Veneshney Razvedki*. Hastings further wrote, without citing a source, that "Harry Hopkins talked with surprising freedom, though surely not ill intent, to an NKVD agent in the United States" (259).
15. Harriman and Abel, *Special Envoy*, 152.
16. Moran, *Churchill*, 138; Harriman and Abel, *Special Envoy*, 161; Davis, *War President*, 568–69.

17. Churchill, *The Second World War*, 4:502.

18. Harriman and Abel, *Special Envoy*, 160.

19. Matloff and Snell, *Strategic Planning*, 291.

20. Kimball, *Churchill and Roosevelt*, 1:577–79.

21. Davis, *War President*, 591–92.

22. Interviews of General Marshall by Forrest C. Pogue, 1956–57, 563, George C. Marshall Library and Research Center, Lexington, Virginia, quoted in Parrish, *Roosevelt and Marshall*, 297; Pogue, *George C. Marshall*, 2:402. Apparently Marshall did not specify the date when the quoted statement was made by President Roosevelt.

23. Davis, *War President*, 592; Adams, *Harry Hopkins*, 290–91.

24. Kimball, *Churchill and Roosevelt*, 1:583–84, 586–87, 589, 591–92.

25. *PPA*, 1942, 216–24.

26. Davis, *War President*, 600–601; Brands, *Traitor to His Class*, 688–89.

27. Sherwood, *Roosevelt and Hopkins*, 631; Davis, *War President*, 601.

28. FDR's September 7, 1942, message to Congress on stabilization, *PPA*, 1942, 356–67; fireside chat on cost of living, *PPA*, 1942, 368–77.

29. HH to Beaverbrook, September 26, 1942, Hopkins Personal Letters and Papers, reel 20, FDRL.

30. Elsey, *An Unplanned Life*, 25, 104.

31. Joseph Davies, Report to HH on Soviet press on Stalin-Churchill row, October 3, 1942, box I-12, chrono files, Davies Papers; McJimsey, *Ally of the Poor*, 261.

32. McJimsey, *Ally of the Poor*, 262–63; Roosevelt, memo for Lend-Lease Administrator, October 30, 1942, box 316, HH Papers, FDRL; Dunn, *Caught between Roosevelt and Stalin*, 154–55, 170–71.

33. Quoted in McJimsey, *Ally of the Poor*, 259–60

34. HH telegram to FDR, September 24, 1942, Map Room file, box 15, FDRL.

35. Davis, *War President*, 623–24 (includes partial quote of Executive Order 9250); Kennedy, *Freedom from Fear*, 629–30.

36. Robertson, *Sly and Able*, 323.

37. Sherwood, *Roosevelt and Hopkins*, 634.

38. Brands, *Traitor to His Class*, 690.

39. Hassett, *Off the Record*, 132.

40. Davis, *War President*, 647, 649–50.

41. Kimball, *Churchill and Roosevelt*, 1:660.

42. Tully, *F.D.R.: My Boss*, 263–64.

43. *PPA*, 1942, 451–52, 457.

44. Hastings, *Winston's War*, 280.

45. Davis, *War President*, 680–81.

46. Perry, *Partners in Command*, 139.

47. Eisenhower, *Crusade in Europe*, 122–27.

48. Brands, *Traitor to His Class*, 693.

49. Kimball, *Churchill and Roosevelt*, 2:4.

50. Telegram quoted in Eisenhower, *Crusade in Europe*, 133–34.

51. Statement of the President, November 17, 1942, HH Papers, box 298, FDRL.

52. Draft telegram, FDR to Eisenhower, November 15, 1942, HH Papers, book 8, footnote folder, FDRL; Sherwood, *Roosevelt and Hopkins*, 654.

53. Davis, *War President*, 700–701; Kimball, *Churchill and Roosevelt*, 2:5.

54. Davis, *War President*, 701, 709.

55. De Gaulle, *War Memoirs*, 2:379.

56. Clark, *Calculated Risk*, 130.

57. Reynolds, *In Command of History*, 329.

58. Kimball, *Churchill and Roosevelt*, 2:4.

59. De Gaulle, *War Memoirs*, 2:379.

60. Davis, *War President*, 706.

61. FDR to HH, November 13, 1942, box 214, Hopkins Papers, FDRL.

62. Sherwood, *Roosevelt and Hopkins*, 660–61.

63. Tuchman, *Stilwell*, 347, 350–51, 358–61.

64. Davis, *War President*, 638.

65. Goodwin, *No Ordinary Time*, 394; HH, "You and Your Family Will Be Mobilized," *American Magazine*, December 1942, 14.

66. Adams, *Harry Hopkins*, 302–3.

67. McJimsey, *Ally of the Poor*, 266–67; Blum, *The Price of Vision*, 147–49.

68. DHH, interview by Emily Williams.

69. Rhodes, *The Making of the Atomic Bomb*, 439–42; Speer, *Inside the Third Reich*, 225–29.

70. Gilbert, *Winston S. Churchill*, 7:254.

71. FDR's Address to *Herald Tribune* Forum, November 17, 1942, *PPA*, 1942, 485.

72. Rosenman, *Working with Roosevelt*, 364–65; Sherwood, *Roosevelt and Hopkins*, 665.

73. Original *Casablanca* screenplay by Julius J. Epstein, Philip G. Epstein, and Howard Koch is at www.weeklyscript.com/Casablanca.txt.

Chapter 12: The View from Marrakech

1. HH, memo to self, January 11, 1943, HH Papers, microfilm reel 20, FDRL. Sherwood quotes from this and other memoranda written by Hopkins during the trip, but his transcriptions are not always verbatim (*Roosevelt and Hopkins*, 669–74).

2. Parrish, *Roosevelt and Marshall*, 321.

3. HH, memo to self, January 11, 1943, HH Papers, box 330, FDRL.

4. Goodwin, *No Ordinary Time*, 402; Atkinson, *An Army at Dawn*, 265.

5. HH, memo to self, January 11, 1943, reel 20, HH Papers, FDRL.

6. FDR to WSC, December 11, 1942, FDR to WSC, December 2, 1942, in *FRUS, The Conferences at Washington and Casablanca*, 498–500, 494–95.

7. Parrish, *Roosevelt and Marshall*, 322–24.

8. Atkinson, *An Army at Dawn*, 269; Parrish, *Roosevelt and Marshall*, 325.

9. Atkinson, *An Army at Dawn*, 266.

10. HH, memos to self, January 1943, reel 20, Hopkins Papers, FDRL.

11. Danchev and Todman, *War Diaries*, 359–60.

12. Atkinson, *An Army at Dawn*, 217–62.

13. Stalin reminded Roosevelt and Churchill of their "promises" that a second front would be opened in the "spring of 1943." Telegram from Premier Stalin, November 28, 1942, in *FRUS, Conferences at Washington and Casablanca,* 494. Similar telegrams were sent to WSC on December 6, 1942, and to FDR on December 14, 1942. See Dallek, *The Lost Peace,* 36–37.

14. Robert Hopkins, *Witness to History,* 32–40.

15. RH memo, "Atmosphere of the Casablanca Conference," box 1, folder 39, RH Papers, GU.

16. RH manuscript, box 5, folder 5, RH Papers, GU.

17. Robert Hopkins, *Witness to History,* 3–4.

18. RH memo, "Atmosphere of the Casablanca Conference," box 1, folder 39, RH Papers, GU.

19. Fenby, *Alliance,* 166.

20. Eleanor Roosevelt, *This I Remember,* 282.

21. Meeting of the Combined Chiefs of Staff with FDR and WSC, January 18, 1943, 5:00 p.m., President's Villa, in *FRUS, Conferences at Washington and Casablanca,* 628.

22. Notes dictated by HH to Chief Ship's Clerk Terry, Saturday morning, January 23, 1943, HH Personal Letters, reel 20, FDRL, also quoted in Sherwood, *Roosevelt and Hopkins,* 688.

23. HH, note to "Jack," n.d., HH Papers, box 330, FDRL.

24. Wedemeyer, *Wedemeyer Reports!,* 181.

25. Leasor, *War at the Top,* 241.

26. *FRUS, Conferences at Washington and Casablanca,* 708–11.

27. Robert Hopkins, *Witness to History,* 49; Atkinson, *An Army at Dawn,* 290.

28. Sherwood, *Roosevelt and Hopkins,* 285

29. Robert Hopkins, *Witness to History,* 33, 34–37, 45.

30. Notes dictated by HH to Chief Ship's Clerk Terry, Saturday morning, January 23, 1943, HH Personal Letters, reel 20, FDRL.

31. WSC to HH, January 21, 1943, HH Papers, box 330, FDRL.

32. Robert Hopkins, *Witness to History,* 50.

33. Notes dictated by HH to Chief Ship's Clerk Terry, Saturday morning, January 23, 1943, HH Personal Letters, reel 20, FDRL, also quoted in Sherwood, *Roosevelt and Hopkins,* 690.

34. The plan envisioned that de Gaulle and Giraud would join forces and that Monnet would be brought in to keep them united. The main effort would be to create a French national army. Secretary of State Hull vetoed the idea of Monnet's involvement because he thought he was too closely aligned with de Gaulle and the British.

35. Elliott Roosevelt and Brough, *A Rendezvous with Destiny,* 330.

36. HH, Notes of Roosevelt-Giraud conversation, noon, President's Villa, January 19, 1943, in *FRUS, Conferences at Washington and Casablanca,* 646–47.

37. FDR to Hull, January 18, 1943, in *FRUS, Conferences at Washington and Casablanca,* 816.

38. Elliott Roosevelt, *As He Saw It,* 69.

39. FDR to Hull, January 18, 1943, in *FRUS, Conferences at Washington and Casablanca,* 816.

40. Ward, *Closest Companion,* 199.

41. Interview of RH, July 27, 1977, in Tuttle, *Anglo-American-Soviet Relations,* 182.

42. MacMillan, *The Blast of War*, 202; McJimsey, *Ally of the Poor*, 274–75; John Eisenhower, *Allies*, 241–47.

43. Notes by HH, January 24, 1943, in *FRUS, Conferences at Washington and Casablanca*, 840.

44. In his memoir Harold MacMillan says that he, Robert Murphy, and "Admiral Q." were responsible for getting Giraud and de Gaulle into the room with Churchill and Roosevelt (*Blast of War*, 203).

45. Events and exchanges on the morning of January 24, 1943, between Americans, British, and French are derived from de Gaulle, *War Memoirs*, 2:94–99; Sherwood, *Roosevelt and Hopkins*, 691, 693; John Eisenhower, *Allies*, 247; Fenby, *Alliance*, 174–76.

46. Robert Hopkins, *Witness to History*, 53.

47. January 26, 1943, communiqué quoted in de Gaulle, *War Memoirs* 2:95. See also reference in *FRUS, Conferences at Washington and Casablanca*, 725.

48. Murphy, *Diplomat among Warriors*, 204–6.

49. Memorandum presented to FDR, January 24, 1943, in *FRUS, Conferences at Washington and Casablanca*, 825–26. See also Funk, "The 'Anfa Memorandum,'" 246–53.

50. *FRUS, 1943*, 2:48–51. See also McJimsey, *Ally of the Poor*, 276.

51. Transcript of press conference, January 24, 1943, in *FRUS, Conferences at Washington and Casablanca*, 726–31.

52. Sherwood, *Roosevelt and Hopkins*, 697.

53. Transcript of press conference, January 24, 1943, in *FRUS, Conferences at Washington and Casablanca*, 729.

54. Meeting of the Combined Chiefs of Staff with Roosevelt and Churchill, January 18, 1943, 5:00 p.m., President's Villa, in *FRUS, Conferences at Washington and Casablanca*, 635.

55. Joint Chief of Staff Minutes of a Meeting at the White House, January 7, 1943, in *FRUS, Conferences at Washington and Casablanca*, 506.

56. HH-El Mokhri Conversation, January 23, 1943, Casablanca, in *FRUS, Conferences at Washington and Casablanca*, 703.

57. Stoler, *The Politics of the Second Front*, 77.

58. Churchill, *The Second World War*, 4:621.

59. Atkinson, *An Army at Dawn*, 295, 296; HH, memo to self, January 24, 1943, HH Papers, box 330, FDRL; Meachem, *Franklin and Winston*, 210; Goodwin, *No Ordinary Time*, 408.

60. Sherwood, *Roosevelt and Hopkins*, 694; Robert Hopkins, *Witness to War*, 56–57; Meachem, *Franklin and Winston*, 210; Moran, *Churchill*, 90.

61. Moran, *Churchill*, 90.

62. HH, memo to self, January 24, 1943, HH Papers, box 330, FDRL.

63. Pendar, *Adventure in Diplomacy*, 148.

64. FDR and WSC to Generalissimo Chiang, January 25, 1943, in *FRUS, Conferences at Washington and Casablanca*, 807–8, prepared by HH, quoted in Sherwood, *Roosevelt and Hopkins*, 694.

65. FDR and WSC to Premier Stalin, January 25, 1943, in *FRUS, Conferences at Washington and Casablanca*, 805–7, rewritten by HH and Harriman, quoted in Sherwood, *Roosevelt and Hopkins*, 694.

66. Jacob diary, 1/19, Papers of Sir Ian Jacob, Churchill Archive Centre, Cambridge.
67. HH, memo to self, January 24, 1943, HH Papers, box 330, FDRL.
68. Pendar, *Adventure in Diplomacy*, 150.
69. Robert Hopkins, *Witness to War*, 57, 59.
70. HH, memo to self, January 25, 1943, HH Papers, reel 20, FDRL.
71. Pendar, *Adventure in Diplomacy*, 151.
72. HH, memo to self, January 25, 1943, HH Papers, reel 20, FDRL, quoted in Sherwood, *Roosevelt and Hopkins*, 694.
73. Pendar, *Adventure in Diplomacy*, 151–52.
74. HH, memo to self, January 26, 1943, HH Papers, reel 20, FDRL.
75. Pendar, *Adventure in Diplomacy*, 151–52.
76. HH, memo to self, January 26, 1943, HH Papers, reel 20, FDRL.
77. Roberts, *The Storm of War*, 343; Roberts, *Masters and Commanders*, 349.
78. Roberts, *The Storm of War*, 343.
79. Keegan, *The Second World War*, 591. Total U.S. military deaths in battle and from other causes were 417,000. According to the Commonwealth War Graves Commission, total military deaths of the UK and its colonies were 384,000.
80. FDR and WSC to Premier Stalin, January 25, 1943, in *FRUS, Conferences at Washington and Casablanca*, 806.
81. Zhukov, *Vospominaniya i Razmyshleniya*, 2:314.
82. FDR and WSC to Premier Stalin, January 25, 1943, in *FRUS, Conferences at Washington and Casablanca*, 806.
83. The Soviet Union "lost at least 7 million men in battle and a further 7 million civilians" (Keegan, *Second World War*, 590).

Chapter 13: Fault Lines
1. Stalin to FDR, March 16, 1943. Similar cables from Stalin to FDR and/or WSC were sent on January 30, 1943, and February 16, 1943. All are cited in Butler, *My Dear Mr. Stalin*, 121–22, 113–14, 117–18.
2. FDR to Stalin, February 22, 1943, and WSC and FDR to Stalin, February 9, 1943, in Butler, *My Dear Mr. Stalin*, 119, 116–17. FDR watered down WSC's original draft, which said they were "aiming for August for a heavy operation."
3. WSC to HH and FDR, February 13, 1943, box 136, folder Winston S. Churchill (folder 2), HH Papers, FDRL.
4. Roberts, *Masters and Commanders*, 352.
5. Butcher, *My Three Years with Eisenhower*, 368.
6. Quoted in Hastings, *Winston's War*, 299.
7. Reynolds quoted in MacLean, *Joseph E. Davies*, 95.
8. Quoted in Dunn, *Caught between Roosevelt and Stalin*, 180.
9. *FRUS, 1943*, 3:683, 686–87, 695–96; Rees, *Behind Closed Doors*, 200. With his access to the White House map room, intelligence flowing into the State Department, and information from Bill Donovan's OSS agents, Hopkins must have known about the German peace feelers in Stockholm that started in early 1943 after the Stalingrad defeat.
10. MacLean, *Joseph E. Davies*, 96–101.

11. Diary entries of Joseph Davies, March 12–14, 1943, box I:12 chrono files, folders 10–14, March 1943, Davies Papers.
12. Joseph Davies to HH, March 23, 1943, box I:12 chrono files, folders 15–25, March 1943, Davies Papers.
13. Diary entry of Joseph Davies, March 14, 1943, box I:12 chrono files, folders 13–14, March 1943, Davies Papers.
14. Stalin to FDR, March 16, 1943, in Butler, *My Dear Mr. Stalin*, 121–22.
15. Memo by HH to FDR, March 16, 1943, in *FRUS, 1943*, 3:25.
16. Diary entry of Joseph Davies, March 12, 1943, box I:12 chrono files, folders 10–12, March 1943, Davies Papers.
17. Diary entry of Joseph Davies entitled "Roosevelt on Churchill and Stalin," April 12, 1943, box I:13 chrono files, folders 1–12, April 1943, Davies Papers.
18. FDR to Stalin, May 4, 1943, in Butler, *My Dear Mr. Stalin*, 129–30.
19. See Snyder, *Bloodlands*, and Davis, *No Simple Victory* for details on the Katyn-related massacres of Polish officers and enlisted men who were Soviet prisoners of war. According to Davis, the Germans discovered 4,500 bodies in the Katyn Forest, but approximately 25,000 Polish POWs were missing and never found.
20. Dunn, *Caught between Roosevelt and Stalin*, 184; McJimsey, *Ally of the Poor*, 293.
21. Sherwood, *Roosevelt and Hopkins*, 727.
22. Chiefs of Staff Committee (Trident) 10th meeting, 5:30 p.m., May 10, 1943, Cabinet papers, British National Archives, Kew.
23. National Archive, Kew, United Kingdom (formerly Public Records Office), PREM, 3/44/2, quoted in Atkinson, *The Day of Battle*, 7.
24. Atkinson, *The Day of Battle*, 1–4; Sherwood, *Roosevelt and Hopkins*, 728.
25. Adams, *Harry Hopkins*, 323.
26. Meeting of the Combined Chiefs of Staff with FDR and WSC, May 12, 1943, 2:30 p.m., White House, in *FRUS, The Conferences at Washington and Quebec*, 24–33.
27. Coakley and Leighton, *Global Logistics*, 61.
28. Editorial note, in *FRUS, Conferences at Washington and Quebec*, 19.
29. Meeting of the Combined Chiefs of Staff with FDR and WSC, May 12, 1943, 2:30 p.m., White House, in *FRUS, Conferences at Washington and Quebec*, 30.
30. Coakley and Leighton, *Global Logistics*, 64.
31. Danchev and Todman, *War Diaries*, 407.
32. Resolutions by the Combined Chiefs of Staff, May 20, 1943, in *FRUS, Conferences at Washington and Quebec*, 281–82.
33. Meeting of the Combined Chiefs of Staff with FDR and WSC, May 19, 1943, 6 p.m., White House, in *FRUS, Conferences at Washington and Quebec*, 119–22.
34. Moran, *Churchill*, 104.
35. Combined Chiefs of Staff Minutes, May 24, 1943, in *FRUS, Conferences at Washington and Quebec*, 189–97.
36. Quoted in Churchill, *The Second World War*, 4:810; Bryant, *The Turn of the Tide*, 514.
37. Churchill, *The Second World War*, 4:800.
38. Danchev and Todman, *War Diaries*, 411.
39. Moran, *Churchill*, 35.

40. Pogue, *George C. Marshall*, 3:202–3; Atkinson, *The Day of Battle*, 16–17.

41. In Churchill, *The Second World War*, 4:795, WSC wrote that it was HH who recited the first two lines. Parrish, in *Roosevelt and Marshall*, 350–51 agreed. Sherwood, *Roosevelt and Hopkins*, 729, and Goodwin, *No Ordinary Time*, 438, write that it was FDR who quoted those lines.

42. Moran, *Churchill*, 101.

43. Quoted in Sherwood, *Roosevelt and Hopkins*, 729.

44. Ibid., 728–29.

45. Taylor, *Beaverbrook*, 544; see memo by Beaverbrook to HH quoted in Sherwood, *Roosevelt and Hopkins*, 735–37.

46. Diary entry of Joseph E. Davies, May 20, 1943, box I:13, chrono files, folders 16–20, May 1943, Davies Papers.

47. Ibid.; diary entry of Joseph E. Davies entitled "Conference with Stalin," May 26, 1943, box I:13, chrono file, May 1943, Davies Papers.

48. Message no. 812, NKGB New York to NKGB Moscow, May 29, 1943, Second "Venona" Release, in Benson and Warner, *Venona*, 225.

49. See, e.g., "Soviet Aide Called an Unwitting Spy," *NYT*, October 15, 1990; Bill Gertz, "KGB Wanted Eleanor as Spy," *Washington Times*, October 13, 1995; Mark, "Venona's Source 19," 1–31.

50. Haynes and Klehr, "Alexander Vassiliev's Notebooks," Black Notebook, 88; "The Man in the Window," *Time*, January 3, 1949; emails from John Earl Haynes to author, August 25, 2010.

51. FDR to Marshal Stalin, June 2, 1943, in *FRUS, Conferences at Washington and Quebec*, 387, 383–85; see also Butler, *My Dear Mr. Stalin*, 135–38.

52. Identical letters from Stalin to FDR and WSC, June 11, 1943, in USSR Ministry of Foreign Affairs, *Correspondence*, 2:68; see also Butler, *My Dear Mr. Stalin*, 138–39 (message to FDR only).

53. Diary entry of Joseph E. Davies entitled "Hopkins' Anxiety," June 7, 1943, box I:13, chrono file, folders 16–20, May 1943–July 1943, Davies Papers.

54. Ibid.; diary entry of Joseph E. Davies entitled "Washington Conference Second Front Postponed," June 7, 1943, box I:13, chrono file, folders 16–20, May 1943–July 1943, Davies Papers.

55. Sherwood, *Roosevelt and Hopkins*, 737.

56. WSC to FDR, June 25, 1943, C-328, in Kimball, *Churchill and Roosevelt*, 2:278–79.

57. FDR to WSC, June 28, 1943, R-297, in Kimball, *Churchill and Roosevelt*, 2:283.

58. Jon Meacham's interview with Lady Soames, in *Franklin and Winston*, 226, n.

59. Memo of conversation between FDR and Morgenthau, May 15, 1942, Presidential diary, 1093, Henry Morgenthau Jr. Papers, FDRL.

60. Oscar Cox to HH, July 6, 1943, Cox Papers, FDRL.

61. Hitler Speeches, January 31, 1939, in *Trials of War*, and January 30, 1942, in Gilbert, *The Holocaust*, 285.

62. *FRUS, The Conferences at Washington, 1941–1942, and at Casablanca, 1943*, 455, n1; 455, n1; *FRUS, 1942*, 1:56–57 (text of memorandum for the president prepared by Hopkins).

63. *FRUS, Second Washington Conference*, 455, n1.

64. Howland, "Ambassador John Gilbert Winant,", 229–33.

65. Ibid., 235.

66. Wyman, *The Abandonment of the Jews*, 72–73, 74–75; Davis, *War President*, 735, 740.

67. Laqueur, *The Terrible Secret*, 223–28; Davis, *War President*, 740.

68. Beschloss, *The Conquerors*, 38–43.

69. HH, memo to self, March 27, 1943, HH Papers, box 329, FDRL. This memo is quoted and discussed in Breitman, *Official Secrets*, 182, 296n26.

70. Wood and Jankowski, *Karski*, 206.

71. "Why Didn't We Bomb Auschwitz? Can John McCloy's Memories Be Correct?" *Washington Post*, April 17, 1983. See also Edward T. Chase, "Why We Didn't Bomb Auschwitz," *Washington Post*, May 21, 1983.

72. Churchill, *The Second World War*, 3:24.

73. See, e.g., Wyman, *The Abandonment of the Jews*, 337.

74. Breitman and Kraut, *American Refugee Policy*, 246. See also Ciechanowski, *Defeat in Victory*, 182; Laqueur, *The Terrible Secret*, 232.

Chapter 14: The Alliance Shifts

1. Chapter 12 of draft manuscript by Halsted, box 6, folder 13, "James Halsted MS bio of HH 1979," RH Papers, GU.

2. DHH, interview by Emily Williams.

3. Ibid.

4. Quoted in Persico, *Franklin and Lucy*, 292, from interview of Anna Roosevelt Halsted by Bernard Asbell.

5. Quoted in Goodwin, *No Ordinary Time*, 271–72, from interview of Trude Lash by Goodwin.

6. Dr. James Halsted, Eleanor Roosevelt Oral History Project, FDRL, quoted in Persico, *Franklin and Lucy*, 292.

7. Ward, *Closest Companion*, 224–25.

8. Rosenman, interview with Joseph Lash, December 3, 1969, box 44, Lash Papers, FDRL.

9. Chapter 12 of draft manuscript by Halsted, box 6, folder 13, "James Halsted MS bio of HH 1979," RH papers, GU.

10. Quoted in Sherwood, *Roosevelt and Hopkins*, 752.

11. Adams, *Harry Hopkins*, 331.

12. Lash, *A World of Love*, 54.

13. Adams, *Harry Hopkins*, 331.

14. HH to Donald Duncan, September 10, 1943, Hopkins microfilm, reel 19, HH Papers, FDRL.

15. Remarks by Representative Alvin F. Weichel (Republican, Ohio), *Congressional Record*, December 15, 1943.

16. Goodwin, *No Ordinary Time*, 459.

17. Diary entry of Joseph Davies, July 5, 1943, box I:13, chrono files, folders 16–20, July 1943, Davies Papers.

18. Churchill, *The Second World War*, 5:82.

19. Log of the President's visit to Canada prepared by Chief Ship's Clerk William Rigdon for Tuesday, August 17, 1943, in FRUS, The Conferences at Washington and Quebec, 837.

20. Levin, The Making of FDR, 342 (the date of the trip is erroneous; it was August 17, not 18).

21. Log of the President's visit to Canada prepared by Chief Ship's Clerk William Rigdon for Tuesday August 17, 1943, in FRUS, Conferences at Washington and Quebec, 838.

22. HH to Geoffrey T. Hellman, n.d., HH Papers, box 329, FDRL.

23. Danchev and Todman, War Diaries, 441.

24. Log of the President's visit to Canada for August 17, 1983, in FRUS, Conferences at Washington and Quebec, 838.

25. Elsey, An Unplanned Life, 38–39.

26. Quoted in Meacham, Franklin and Winston, 235, from interview of George Elsey by Meachem.

27. Stimson to HH, August 4, 1943 with enclosed memorandum by Stimson, in FRUS, Conferences at Washington and Quebec, 448. See also Stimson and Bundy, On Active Service, 228.

28. Stimson to FDR, August 10, 1943, in FRUS, Conferences at Washington and Quebec, 496.

29. Meeting of the Combined Chiefs of Staff with FDR and WSC, August 19, 1943, 5:30 p.m.–7:45 p.m., The Citadel, in FRUS, Conferences at Washington and Quebec, 896.

30. Moran, Churchill, 117–18.

31. Dilks, The Diaries of Sir Alexander Cadogan, 554–55.

32. Sainsbury, Churchill and Roosevelt at War, 35.

33. Sherwood, Roosevelt and Hopkins, 747.

34. Frederick E. Morgan, transcript n.d., cited in Forrest E. Pogue, background material for The Supreme Commander, U.S. Military History Institute, Carlisle, Pennsylvania.

35. George C. Marshall, Oral History, Forrest C. Pogue, October 5, 1956, George C. Marshall Library, Lexington, Virginia.

36. Danchev and Todman, War Diaries, 445–46.

37. Leahy, I Was There, 213; Colonel Charles H. Donnelly autobiography, 633–34, U.S. Military History Institute, Carlisle, Pennsylvania.

38. Churchill to HH, February 27, 1943, in FRUS, Conferences at Washington and Quebec, 4; see also Persico, Roosevelt's Secret War, 223.

39. Cables from WSC to HH, February 16, 27 and March 20, 1943, in FRUS, Conferences at Washington and Quebec, 1–5.

40. Memorandum of Conference With the President, Vannevar Bush, June 24, 1943, in FRUS, Conferences at Washington and Quebec, 631–32.

41. FDR to HH, July 14, 1943, HH to FDR, July 20, 1943, FDR to Vannevar Bush, July 20, 1943, in FRUS, Conferences at Washington and Quebec, 633.

42. Draft Heads of Agreement, in FRUS, Conferences at Washington and Quebec, 637–38.

43. Agreement Relating to Atomic Energy, August 19, 1943, in FRUS, Conferences at Washington and Quebec, 1117–18.

44. FDR-WSC Meeting, August 19, 1943, afternoon, The Citadel, editorial note, in FRUS, Conferences at Washington and Quebec, 894. For an introduction to the tangled history of subsequent Anglo-American nuclear sharing agreements, see Edmonds, The Big Three, 399–402.

45. Memorandum of Meeting at 10 Downing Street on July 22, 1943, Harvey H. Bundy, in *FRUS, Conferences at Washington and Quebec*, 634.

46. Stimson to FDR, August 10, 1943, in *FRUS, Conferences at Washington and Quebec*, 496. With Hopkins's help, Churchill may have thought he came away with a win on nuclear sharing, but as events played out the United States never treated Great Britain as an equal partner.

47. Roberts, *Masters and Commanders*, 382–83; Keegan, *The Second World War*, 458–82; Bellamy, *Absolute War*, 554–81.

48. Memorandum for Mr. Hopkins, August 10, 1943, in *FRUS, Conferences at Washington and Quebec*, 624–27.

49. Harriman and Abel, *Special Envoy*, 224, 234.

50. FDR and WSC to Marshal Stalin, August 18, 1943, in *FRUS, Conferences at Washington and Quebec*, 1095–96.

51. Marshall Stalin to FDR and WSC, August 24, 1943, in *FRUS, Conferences at Washington and Quebec*, 1174–75.

52. FDR to Marshal Stalin, September 4, 1943, in *FRUS, Conferences at Washington and Quebec*, 1306–8.

53. Marshal Stalin to FDR and WSC, in *FRUS, Conferences at Washington and Quebec*, 1086–88.

54. Quoted in Harriman and Abel, *Special Envoy*, 225–26.

55. Walter Trohan, "'White House Harry' Hopkins—A Modern Rasputin," *Chicago Daily Tribune*, August 29, 1943.

56. HH to Joseph Davies, September 17, 1943, HH Papers, box 137, FDRL.

57. Sherwood, *Roosevelt and Hopkins*, 751.

58. Quoted in Ward, *Closest Companion*, 233.

59. Dilks, *The Diaries of Sir Alexander Cadogan*, 559.

60. Meeting of the Combined Chiefs of Staff with WSC, September 11, 1943, 11 a.m., State Dining Room, White House, in *FRUS, Conferences at Washington and Quebec*, 1229–36.

61. Ward, *Closest Companion*, 238–39.

62. Quoted in Sherwood, *Roosevelt and Hopkins*, 759–60.

63. George Marshall to HH with note by FDR, n.d., HH Papers, microfilm reel 21, FDRL.

64. HH Memorandum to the President, October 4, 1943, box 332, book 8, Sherwood Collection, FDRL.

65. Churchill, *The Second World War*, 5:304–6.

66. Sherwood, *Roosevelt and Hopkins*, 765.

67. Marshal Stalin to FDR, September 8, 1943, in *FRUS, Conferences at Washington and Quebec*, 1308–9.

68. *FRUS, The Conferences at Cairo and Teheran*, 23–72. The English spelling of the capital of Iran can be either "Teheran" or "Tehran." "Tehran" is used throughout the text.

69. FDR to Marshal Stalin, November 8, 1943, in *FRUS, Conferences at Cairo and Teheran*, 71; Parrish, *Roosevelt and Marshall*, 372–73.

70. Diary entry of Joseph Davies, October 2, 1943, Mexico City, box: I-14, chrono files, Davies Papers.

71. Danchev and Todman, *War Diaries*, 458.

72. HH, memos of telephone conversations with WSC, October 7, 9, 1943, HH Papers, box 299, FDRL; McJimsey, *Ally of the Poor*, 299.

73. Morison, *American Contributions*, 32; Bland, *George C. Marshall*, 622.

74. Danchev and Todman, *War Diaries*, 459.

75. WSC to FDR October 23, 1943, in *FRUS, Conferences at Cairo and Teheran*, 38–39, 110–12.

76. WSC to Stalin, November 12, 1943, in USSR Ministry of Foreign Affairs, *Correspondence*, 1:175.

77. FDR to WSC, October 25, 1943, and FDR to Generalissimo Chiang, October 27, 1943, in *FRUS, Conferences at Cairo and Teheran*, 39–40, 47.

78. Sidney Matthews, box 3, November 15, 1943, U.S. Military History Institute, Carlisle, Pennsylvania.

79. Stimson to HH, November 10, 1943, in *FRUS, Conferences at Cairo and Teheran*, 175–76; see also Sherwood Collection, book 8, FDRL.

80. Raymond Clapper, interview of HH, September 20 and October 28, 1943, Clapper Papers, box 23, Library of Congress.

81. FDR to Marshal Stalin, November 8, 1943, in *FRUS, Conferences at Cairo and Teheran*, 72.

Chapter 15: Tilting toward the Russians

1. Henry Arnold, notes, November 13, 1943, Arnold Papers, box 272, Library of Congress.

2. Log of President's trip, November 12–19, 1943, in *FRUS, The Conferences at Cairo and Tehran*, 279–80.

3. HH memo to self, undated, HH Papers, reel 20, FDRL.

4. Ibid.

5. Arnold, *Global Mission*, 455.

6. Elliott Roosevelt, *F.D.R.: His Personal Letters*, 2:1468.

7. Freidel, *Franklin D. Roosevelt*, 478.

8. Matloff, *Strategic Planning*, 343.

9. *FRUS, Conferences at Cairo and Tehran*, 256.

10. Matloff, *Strategic Planning*, 341 and map facing 341; *FRUS, Conferences at Cairo and Tehran*, 261.

11. *FRUS, Conferences at Cairo and Tehran*, 255.

12. The term, of course, was popularized by Churchill in his Fulton, Missouri, speech in March 1946, but according to the historian David Reynolds, "the term dates back at least to the First World War." And as Reynolds points out, it was used by Nazi propagandists in 1945 and by Churchill on occasion in 1945 (*In Command of History*, 43).

13. McIntire, *White House Physician*, 170–71.

14. Tuttle, *American-Anglo-Soviet Relations*, 213, 216–17.

15. Robert Hopkins, *Witness to History*, 70.

16. Tregaskis, *Invasion Diary*, 195.

17. Extracts from diary of RH, November 17–19, 1943, box 2, folder 18, Papers of RH, GU.

18. Robert Hopkins, *Witness to History*, 75.

19. Summersby, *Eisenhower Was My Boss*, 93.
20. Atkinson, *The Day of Battle*, 269; extracts from diary of RH, November 21, 1943, box 2, folder 18, Papers of RH, GU; Robert Hopkins, *Witness to History*, 75–76.
21. Butcher, *My Three Years with Eisenhower*, 449.
22. Quoted in Sherwood, *Roosevelt and Hopkins*, 770.
23. Eisenhower, *Crusade in Europe*, 197.
24. Extracts from diary of RH, November 22, 1943, box 2, folder 18, Papers of RH, GU; Roberts, *Masters and Commanders*, 435.
25. Parrish, *Roosevelt and Marshall*, 384.
26. Churchill, *The Second World War*, 5:328.
27. Sainsbury, *The Turning Point*, 216.
28. Kennedy, *Freedom from Fear*, 673.
29. Roosevelt-Chiang dinner meeting, November 23, 1943, 8 p.m., Roosevelt's Villa, in *FRUS, Conferences at Cairo and Tehran*, 322–23.
30. U.S. delegation memorandum (presumably written by Hopkins), November 23, 1943, in *FRUS, Conferences at Cairo and Tehran*, 376.
31. Sainsbury, *The Turning Point*, 191, 189; see final text of the Cairo communiqué, in *FRUS, Conferences at Cairo and Tehran*, 448–49.
32. Meeting of the Combined Chiefs of Staff with FDR and WSC, November 24, 1943, 11 a.m., Roosevelt's Villa, in *FRUS, Conferences at Cairo and Tehran*, 329–34.
33. Moran, *Churchill*, 140–42.
34. Churchill, *The Second World War*, 5:340.
35. John Boettiger Diary of Cairo and Teheran, November 25, 1943, 89, FDRL.
36. Elliott Roosevelt, *As He Saw It*, 159.
37. Churchill, *The Second World War*, 5:341.
38. *FRUS, Conferences at Cairo and Tehran*, 299.
39. Extracts from diary of RH, November 25, 1943, box 2, folder 18, RH Papers, GU; John Boettiger Diary of Cairo and Teheran, November 25, 1943, 89, FDRL.
40. Extracts from diary of RH, November 25, 1943, box 2, folder 18, RH Papers, GU.
41. Churchill, *The Second World War*, 5:341.
42. Rigdon and Derieux, *White House Sailor*, 75.
43. The President's Log at Teheran, November 27–December 2, 1943, in *FRUS, Conferences at Cairo and Teheran*, 460; Brands, *Traitor to His Class*, 731–32.
44. Harriman and Abel, *Special Envoy*, 262.
45. Montefiore, *Stalin*, 410–11.
46. Harriman and Abel, *Special Envoy*, 262–63.
47. Moran, *Churchill*, 143.
48. Montefiore, *Stalin*, 412.
49. Harriman and Abel, *Special Envoy*, 264.
50. Havas, *Hitler's Plot*, 159–60, 204, 218–22; Sudoplatov et al., *Special Tasks*, 130; Breuer, *Hoodwinking Hitler*, 4–8; Reilly, *Reilly of the White House*, 175–82. An account of the assassination attempt by Vadim Kirpichenko and Gevork Vartanyan was recounted at a book launch and is reported in an article by Vyacheslav Lashkul, RIA Novosti analyst, "How the Light Cavalry Foiled the Tehran Assassination Plot," http://forum.teamxbox.com/archive/index.php/t-238569.html.

51. Bohlen, *Witness to History*, 139.
52. Harriman and Abel, *Special Envoy*, 265.
53. Fenby, *Alliance*, 226–27.
54. FDR-Stalin Meeting, November 28, 1943, 3 p.m., Roosevelt's Quarters, Soviet Embassy, in *FRUS, Conferences at Cairo and Teheran*, 483.
55. Fenby, *Alliance*, 227.
56. Roosevelt-Stalin Meeting, November 28, 1943, 3 p.m., Roosevelt's Quarters, Soviet Embassy, in *FRUS, Conferences at Cairo and Teheran*, 482–86.
57. Keegan, *The Second World War*, 370–72; Harrison, *Cross-Channel Attack*; Young, *Rommel*, 169.
58. *FRUS, Conferences at Cairo and Teheran*, 48–86.
59. Harriman and Abel, *Special Envoy*, 268.
60. First Plenary Meeting, November 28, 1943, 4 p.m., Conference Room, Soviet Embassy, in *FRUS, Conferences at Cairo and Teheran*, 487.
61. Bohlen, *Witness to History*, 142.
62. *FRUS, Conferences at Cairo and Teheran*, 489.
63. Moran, *Churchill*, 135.
64. *FRUS, Conferences at Cairo and Teheran*, 493.
65. HH to Admiral King, n.d., HH Papers, box 332, FDRL.
66. *FRUS, Conferences at Cairo and Teheran*, 494–95, 464; Parrish, *Roosevelt and Marshall*, 401.
67. Bohlen, *Witness to History*, 143.
68. Ibid., 143–44.
69. *FRUS, Conferences at Cairo and Teheran*, 512.
70. Montefiore, *Stalin*, 414.
71. FDR-Stalin Meeting, November 29, 1943, 2:45 p.m., Roosevelt's Quarters, Soviet Embassy, in *FRUS, Conferences at Cairo and Teheran*, 529–33, 622 (sketch).
72. The President's Log at Teheran, in *FRUS, Conferences at Cairo and Teheran*, 465–66.
73. Excerpt from diary of RH, November 29, 1943, box 5, folder 4, RH Papers, GU.
74. Danchev and Todman, *War Diaries*, 485.
75. Excerpt from diary of RH, November 29, 1943, box 5, folder 4, RH Papers, GU.
76. Letter from RH to Ethel Gross, December 7, 1943, box 2, folder 3, RH Papers, GU.
77. Leahy, *I Was There*, 208.
78. Second plenary meeting, November 39, 1943, Conference Room, Soviet Embassy, 4 p.m., in *FRUS, Conferences at Cairo and Teheran*, 535, 538, 539.
79. Moran, *Churchill*, 147.
80. Bohlen, *Witness to History*, 147; Meachem, *Franklin and Winston*, 259.
81. Bohlen, *Witness to History*, 146.
82. Harriman and Abel, *Special Envoy*, 273.
83. Bohlen, *Witness to History*, 146.
84. Tripartite dinner meeting, November 29, 1943, 8:30 p.m., Soviet Embassy, in *FRUS, Conferences at Cairo and Teheran*, 554; Bohlen, *Witness to History*, 147.
85. Churchill, *The Second World War*, 5:374.
86. Elliott Roosevelt, *As He Saw It*, 189; Churchill, *The Second World War*, 5:374.
87. Montefiore, *Stalin*, 416.

88. Churchill, *The Second World War*, 5:374.

89. *FRUS, Conferences at Cairo and Teheran*, 555.

90. Bohlen, *Witness to History*, 148.

91. Moran, *Churchill*, 151.

92. The original recommendation of the combined chiefs said "by June 1st," but that was crossed out by Roosevelt. In his own handwriting, he substituted "during the month of May." *FRUS, Conferences at Cairo and Teheran*, 564, 563–68.

93. HH-Eden-Molotov Luncheon Meeting, November 30, 1943, 1:30 p.m., British Legation, in *FRUS, Conferences at Cairo and Teheran*, 571–75; Tripartite Luncheon Meeting, December 1, 1943, 1 p.m., Roosevelt's Quarters, Soviet Embassy, in *FRUS, Conferences at Cairo and Teheran*, 585–87.

94. HH memo, n.d., HH Papers, box 298, FDRL; Sherwood, *Roosevelt and Hopkins*, 796.

95. Bohlen, *Witness to History*, 149.

96. Danchev and Todman, *War Diaries*, 486, 488.

97. Extracts from diary of RH, November 30, 1943, box 2, folder 18, RH Papers, GU.

98. Bohlen, *Witness to History*, 149.

99. Tripartite dinner meeting, November 30, 1943, 8:30 p.m., British Legation, in *FRUS, Conferences at Cairo and Teheran*, 583–84.

100. Eden, *Memoirs*, 427.

101. Harriman and Abel, *Special Envoy*, 277; Sherwood, *Roosevelt and Hopkins*, 793.

102. Danchev and Todman, *War Diaries*, entry of November 30, 1943, 488–89.

103. Hugh Lunghi, quoted in Rees, *Behind Closed Doors*, 234.

104. Danchev and Todman, *War Diaries*, entry of November 30, 1943, 489.

105. Harriman and Abel, *Special Envoy*, 277.

106. Bohlen, *Witness to History*, 244.

107. *FRUS, Conferences at Cairo and Teheran*, 585.

108. Extract from diary of RH, November 30, 1943, box 2, folder 18, RH Papers, GU.

109. Robert Hopkins, *Witness to History*, 88.

110. FDR-Stalin Meeting, December 1, 1943, 3:20 p.m., Roosevelt's Quarters, Soviet Embassy, Bohlen's Minutes, in *FRUS, Conferences at Cairo and Teheran*, 594–96; Harriman and Abel, *Special Envoy*, 278–79.

111. Tripartite political meeting, December 1, 1943, 6 p.m., Conference Room, Soviet Embassy, in *FRUS, Conferences at Cairo and Tehran*, 596–604, 599.

112. Bohlen, *Witness to History*, 152.

113. Eden, *Memoirs*, 428.

114. Bohlen, *Witness to History*, 152.

115. Adams, *Harry Hopkins*, 349–50.

116. Stoler, *George C. Marshall*, 107–8; Parrish, *Roosevelt and Marshall*, 414–15.

117. Quotes from letter written by Marshall to Sherwood in Sherwood, *Roosevelt and Hopkins*, 803.

118. "An interview with George C. Marshall," Forrest C. Pogue, October 5, 1956, Marshall Files, George C. Marshall Research Library, Virginia Military Institute, Lexington, Virginia.

119. Larrabee, *Commander in Chief*, 438.

120. Handwritten letter from RH to Ethel Gross Hopkins, December 7, 1943, 14–15, box 2, folder 6, RH Papers, GU.

121. Elliott Roosevelt, *As He Saw It*, 206–7.

122. Wireless, HH to Louise Hopkins, December 16, 1943, Map Room file, box 17, folder 4 Sextant Conference, FDRL.

Chapter 16: A Soldier's Debt

1. HH to Stephen Hopkins, December 28, 1943, reel 16, Hopkins Papers, FDRL.

2. Sherwood, *Roosevelt and Hopkins*, 804.

3. McJimsey, *Ally of the Poor*, 313.

4. Cable, FDR to WSC, January 4, 1944, Messages, reel 3, FDRL.

5. Cable, FDR to WSC, January 25, 1944, Map Room file, box 18, FDRL.

6. Churchill, *The Second World War*, 5:430.

7. Ward, *Closest Companion*, 264.

8. Meachem, *Franklin and Winston*, 274; Goodwin, *No Ordinary Time*, 491–93.

9. FDR, press conference, December 28, 1943, *Complete Presidential Press Conferences*, 22:246–52.

10. Transcript of broadcast, January 14, 1944, box 60, folder 9, RH Papers, GU.

11. Adams, *Harry Hopkins*, 352–54.

12. Ibid., 353, based on interview of RH by Adams, May 15, 1976.

13. McJimsey, *Ally of the Poor*, 313; Dr. James A. Halsted, "Severe Malnutrition in a Public Servant of the World War II Era: The Medical History of Harry Hopkins," box 1, folder 5, RH Papers, GU.

14. HH to Mrs. John Hertz, February 2, 1944, HH Papers, reel 11, FDRL.

15. HH to Stephen Hopkins, February 2, 1944, HH Papers, microfilm reel 20, FDRL.

16. Telegram, FDR to Station Master, Jacksonville, Florida, February 12, 1944, HH Papers, reel 20, FDRL.

17. Chapter 13 of draft manuscript by Halsted, box 6, folder 13, "James Halsted MS bio of HH 1979, RH Papers, GU; McJimsey, *Ally of the Poor*, 341; Adams, *Harry Hopkins*, 355.

18. HH Papers, microfilm reel 20, FDRL; quote is from Act V, Scene 9 of *Macbeth*.

19. "Parents," *Time*, February 28, 1944, 46.

20. Giffen and Hopkins, *Jewish First Wife*, letter no. 266, February 15, 1944, 262–63.

21. McJimsey, *Ally of the Poor*, 340.

22. Pogue, *George C. Marshall*, 3:102.

23. Giffen and Hopkins, *Jewish First Wife*, letter no. 268, March 27, 1944, 264.

24. February 13, 1944, CHAR 20/156, Churchill Archives Centre, Churchill College, Cambridge, quoted in Fenby, *Alliance*, 274.

25. Chapter 13 of draft manuscript by Halsted, box 6, folder 13, "James Halsted, MS bio of Harry Hopkins 1979," RH Papers, GU; Lord Halifax to WSC, May 1, 1944, 3 27/9, Prime Minister's Office Records.

26. Telegram, George Marshall to HH, March 29, 1944, box 6, folder: Personal Health, 1942–1944, HH Papers, FDRL.

27. Letter from Dr. Paul A. O'Leary to Howard Hunter, April 1, 1944, box 6, folder 3, RH Papers, GU.

28. Adams, *Harry Hopkins*, 358; RH Papers, box 6, folder "James Halsted MS bio of Harry Hopkins 1979," GU.

29. Adams, *Harry Hopkins*, 358.

30. Handwritten by Marshall at bottom of memo by Persons to Chief of Staff, May 22, 1944, Marshall Papers, George C. Marshall Library and Research Center, Lexington, Virginia.

31. Marshall to HH, February 13, 1944, reel 19, HH Papers, FDRL.

32. Pogue, *George C. Marshall*, 3:102.

33. HH to Dwight Eisenhower, box 58, Eisenhower Presidential Papers, Eisenhower Library, Abilene, Kansas.

34. Dwight Eisenhower to HH, May 20, 1944, RH Papers, box 3, folder 9, GU.

35. McIntire, *White House Physician*, 184.

36. Ferrell, *The Dying President*, 35–41.

37. Hassett, *Off the Record*, 241.

38. FDR to HH, May 18, 1944, President's Secretary's File, Executive Office of the President, box 133, FDRL.

39. *PPA*, 1944, 147.

40. Quoted in Roberts, *Masters and Commanders*, 486.

41. Soames, *Clementine Churchill*, 468.

42. Bliss, *In Search of Light*, 81.

43. Roberts, *The Storm of War*, 472–73.

44. Sherwood, *Roosevelt and Hopkins*, 807.

45. Kimball, *Forged in War*, 153; Howard, *The Mediterranean Strategy*, 47; Keegan, *The Second World War*, 316; Reynolds, *From World War to Cold War*, 55–58.

46. Cable, HH to WSC, July 20, 1944, Map Room file, box 13, file 1944 (Outgoing), FDRL.

47. Marshall to HH, August 18, 1944, George C. Marshall Library and Research Center, Lexington, Virginia.

48. Goodwin, *No Ordinary Time*, 517–18.

49. Freidel, *Franklin D. Roosevelt*, 535–36.

50. Goodwin, *No Ordinary Time*, 527–28.

51. Ferrell, *The Dying President*, 78.

52. Beichman, "In a Smoke-Filled Room," 8–9.

53. Blum, *The Price of Vision*, 365, 371. In his biography of Hopkins, Adams asserts without explanation that Wallace's belief about Hopkins's involvement was mistaken. Adams, *Harry Hopkins*, 360.

54. Churchill, *The Second World War*, 6:149.

55. HH to WSC, August 7, 1944, Map Room file, box 13, FDRL.

56. Elsey, *An Unplanned Life*, 62.

57. Cable, WSC to HH, August 10, 1944, in *FRUS, The Conference at Quebec*, 16; McJimsey, *Ally of the Poor*, 342.

58. Memorandum by HH, August 18, 1944, in *FRUS, Conference at Quebec*, 160–61.

59. Cable, HH to WSC, July 20, 1944, Map Room file, box 13, file 1944 (Outgoing), FDRL; quoted in Sherwood, *Roosevelt and Hopkins*.

60. Morgenthau Diaries, August 19, 1944, FDRL. See also Blum, *From the Morgenthau Diaries*, 3:342.

61. Bohlen Minutes, December 1, 1943, in *FRUS, Conferences at Cairo and Teheran*, 596–604.
62. Quoted in Beschloss, *The Conquerors*, 118.
63. Cable from HH to WSC, August 28, 1944, in *FRUS, Conference at Quebec*, 20.
64. Churchill, *The Second World War*, 6:149.
65. Roosevelt-Churchill meeting, September 15, 1944, noon, The Citadel, in *FRUS, Conference at Quebec*, 360–61; Memorandum initialed by President Roosevelt and Prime Minister Churchill, September 15, 1944, in *FRUS, Conference at Quebec*, 466–67.
66. Briefing book prepared in the Treasury Department, September 9, 1944, in *FRUS, Conference at Quebec*, 128–44.
67. Roosevelt-Churchill dinner meeting, September 13, 1944, 8 p.m., the Citadel, memorandum by Harry Dexter White, in *FRUS, Conference at Quebec*, 326–28.
68. Beschloss, *Conquerors*, 129; Fenby, *Alliance*, 312.
69. Beschloss, *Conquerors*, 138–41; Fenby, *Alliance*, 318–19.
70. HH to Secretary of State, September 5, 1944, in *FRUS, Conference at Quebec*, 98.
71. Churchill, *The Second World War*, 6:161.
72. Henry Stimson diary, October 3, 1944.
73. McJimsey, *Ally of the Poor*, 346 and notes. JCS 1067 is reprinted as Document No. 26 in Kimball, *Swords or Ploughshares*, 130–33. See also letter expressing agreement by Secretary of State Hull to JCS 1067, subject to interpretation of economic directive allowing military commander to exercise discretion to assure health and safety of occupying forces. Document No. 27, 134.
74. Bohlen, *Witness to History*, 162.
75. Sherwood, *Roosevelt and Hopkins*, 833.
76. Bohlen, *Witness to History*, 162–63.
77. Cables to Stalin (via Harriman), October 4, 1944, and WSC, October 4, 1944, and Stalin's reply, October 8, 1944, in *FRUS, The Conferences at Malta and Yalta*, 6–8.
78. According to the historian David Reynolds, "naughty document" was the term Churchill actually used to characterize the percentages agreement with Stalin. Reynolds says that the cabinet offices excised the term from the translator's notes of the meeting because it "would give the impression to historians that these very important discussions were conducted in a most unfitting manner" (*In Command of History*, 462, n61). The translator was Major Birse.
79. Charmley, *Churchill*, 387.
80. Marquis Childs, "Hopkins' Influence Reaches Peak," *Washington Post*, December 4, 1944.
81. Box I:15, folders 7–11, October 1944–December 31, 1944, Davies Papers.
82. Ward, *Closest Companion*, 335–36.
83. Franklin D. Roosevelt, Address, October 21, 1944, *PPA*, 1944, 350.
84. Freidel, *Franklin D. Roosevelt*, 564–65; Nicholas, *Washington Despatches*, 441.
85. This supposition is based on numerous telephone conversations between Louise Hopkins and her friends, reports and verbatim transcripts of which are in the J. Edgar Hoover Official and Confidential File, reel 13, no. 87, Library of Congress.
86. HH to Lord Beaverbrook, November 6, 1944, Map Room file, box 13, FDRL.

87. HH to WSC, November 7, 1944, Map Room file, box 13, FDRL.

88. Quoted in McJimsey, *Ally of the Poor*, 347.

89. Bohlen, *Witness to History*, 166.

90. Morgenthau to sons, January 28, 1945, Henry Morgenthau III Private Archives, Cambridge, Massachusetts; Morgenthau, *Mostly Morgenthaus*, 398–99.

91. Ickes journal, box 20, folder 1944 November 14–December 31, Ickes Papers, Library of Congress.

92. Bohlen, *Witness to History*, 135.

93. HH memo, December 12, 1944, quoted in Sherwood, *Roosevelt and Hopkins*, 840, 841.

94. J. Edgar Hoover, Official and Confidential File, reel 13, no. 87, Library of Congress; HH Appointment Diary 1944, entries for December 5, 11, 16, 1944, HH Papers, GU.

95. Gentry, *J. Edgar Hoover*, 310–11; Persico, *Roosevelt's Secret War*, 358–59.

96. It is conceivable that there was concern about the leak of a cable from Churchill to General Ronald Scobie, his commander in Greece, urging Scobie to adopt a "ruthless policy" toward the Communists, which Drew Pearson published in the *Washington Post* on December 11, 1944. Hastings, *Winston's War*, 428. However, the FBI surveillance of Louise began on December 6, five days before the leak was published. In addition, while Louise was no doubt acquainted with Drew Pearson and his wife, she and Hopkins disliked him intensely because he had previously published unflattering stories about the two of them. There is no evidence that Louise socialized with Pearson or his wife and no reason why she would want to embarrass Churchill and the British, much less her own husband.

97. Theoharis, *From the Secret Files*, 325n (suggesting that Hopkins suspected his wife of having an affair or, quite implausibly, that he wanted to ensure that she followed doctor's orders and stayed home); Costigliola, *Roosevelt's Lost Alliances*, 317 (claiming Hopkins suspected Louise of having an affair with a woman, a theory both unlikely because of Louise's stable of male friends when she was single and unsupported by anything other than gossip about the mentally unbalanced nurse who cared for Louise during her surgery and who drove by the Hopkins residence at night).

98. Transcript of telephone conversation between Louise Hopkins and Ada Johnson, December 13, 1944, J. Edgar Hoover, Official and Confidential File, reel 13, no. 87, Library of Congress.

99. Author's interview of John Russell, half-brother of Betty Howe, friend of Louise, March 22, 2012; author's interview of Richard Deering Howe, son of W. Deering and Betty Howe, March 13, April 2, 2012; author's interview of Geoffrey McNair Gates Jr., stepson of Louise, January 2012; author's interview of John Fox, FBI historian, April 3, 2012; DHH, interview by Emily Williams; J. Edgar Hoover, Official and Confidential File, reel 13, no. 87, Library of Congress.

100. Based on comments made in various telephone conversations, J. Edgar Hoover, Official Confidential File, reel 13, no. 87, Library of Congress.

101. Cable, HH to WSC, December 21, 1944, HH Papers, reel 20, FDRL.

102. HH Papers, reel 20, FDRL. This was written in October 1945. It is also quoted in Sherwood, *Roosevelt and Hopkins*, 843.

Chapter 17: The Best They Could Do

1. HH to the President, January 24, 1945, in *FRUS, The Conferences at Malta and Yalta*, 39–40.
2. HH Papers, Reel 20, FDRL. The same memo, written by HH in October 1945, is quoted in Sherwood, *Roosevelt and Hopkins*, 843–45.
3. Marshal Stalin to President Roosevelt, October 19, 1944, in *FRUS, Conferences at Malta and Yalta*, 9.
4. HH Papers, reel 20, FDRL, quoted in Sherwood, *Roosevelt and Hopkins*, 844; Ambassador in the Soviet Union (Harriman) to the President, December 27, 1944, in *FRUS, Conferences at Malta and Yalta*, 22–23.
5. WSC to FDR, January 1, 1945, in *FRUS, Conferences at Malta and Yalta*, 26.
6. Stettinius, *Roosevelt and the Russians*, 48.
7. HH to DHH, January 19, 1945, box 40, folder 6, HH Papers, GU.
8. Quoted in Sherwood, *Roosevelt and Hopkins*, 847.
9. Bohlen, *Witness to History*, 168.
10. Ibid., 168–69; McJimsey, *Ally of the Poor*, 362–63.
11. Robert Hopkins, *Witness to History*, 129.
12. RH to Ethel Gross, March 5, 1945, box 4, folder 60, RH Papers, GU.
13. Robert Hopkins, *Witness to History*, 126–28.
14. Quoted in Sherwood, *Roosevelt and Hopkins*, 847.
15. Tuttle, *Anglo-American-Soviet Relations*, 244; McJimsey, *Ally of the Poor*, 361–62.
16. Bohlen, *Witness to History*, 170; Sherwood, *Roosevelt and Hopkins*, 847–48.
17. Bishop, *FDR's Last Year*, 278.
18. Bohlen, *Witness to History*, 170.
19. Butcher, *My Three Years with Eisenhower*, 748–51; Butcher, diary, January 27, 1945, folder 2, Butcher Papers, Eisenhower Library, Abilene, Kansas.
20. Robert Hopkins, *Witness to History*, 133–35.
21. Quoted in Sherwood, *Roosevelt and Hopkins*, 848.
22. Tuttle, *Anglo-American-Soviet Relations*, 244.
23. Anna Roosevelt Halsted Diary, February 3, 1945, Halsted MSS, box 21, file "Yalta Notes," Anna Roosevelt Halsted Papers, FDRL.
24. Stettinius, *Roosevelt and the Russians*, 57.
25. Dilks, *The Diaries of Sir Alexander Cadogan*, 705.
26. Moran, *Churchill*, 232.
27. Gilbert, *Winston S. Churchill*, 7:1163.
28. Stettinius, *Roosevelt and the Russians*, 68.
29. Bohlen, *Witness to History*, 171.
30. Stettinius, *Roosevelt and the Russians*, 68.
31. Bohlen, *Witness to History*, 171.
32. Gilbert, *Winston S. Churchill*, 7:1167.
33. Eden, *Memoirs*, 592.
34. McJimsey, *Ally of the Poor*, 360; Stettinius, *Roosevelt and the Russians*, 171.
35. Anna Roosevelt Boettiger notes on Yalta, February 2, 1945, box 84, Yalta Conference: U.S.S. Quincy, Halsted Papers, FDRL.
36. Robert Hopkins, *Witness to History*, 139.

37. Moran, *Churchill*, 243. Lord Moran, Churchill's physician, described Hopkins on February 7 as looking "ghastly—his skin was a yellow-white membrane stretched tight over the bones."

38. Bohlen, *Witness to History*, 17.

39. Plokhy, *Yalta*, 43–47.

40. Kathleen Harriman to Pamela Churchill, February 7, 1945, Pamela Harriman Papers, Library of Congress.

41. Anna Roosevelt Boettiger, notes on Yalta, February 3, 1945, box 84, Yalta Conference: U.S.S. Quincy, Halsted Papers, FDRL.

42. Jonathan Daniels, oral history, Harry S Truman Library, Independence, Missouri; Daniels, *White House Witness*, 266.

43. Bellamy, *Absolute War*, 636, 641–46.

44. Montefiore, *Stalin*, 425.

45. Djilas, *Conversations with Stalin*, 73.

46. Moran, *Churchill*, 223.

47. Sherwood, *Roosevelt and Hopkins*, 852.

48. Address in Riga, May 7, 2005, text from White House website, http://www.whitehouse.gov/news/releases/2005/05/20050507-8.html.

49. Reynolds, *Summits*, 108, 160, 161.

50. McJimsey, *Ally of the Poor*, 363; Byrnes, *Speaking Frankly*, 23; Moran, *Churchill*, 243.

51. Goodwin, *No Ordinary Time*, 579–80.

52. Roosevelt-Stalin meeting, February 8, 1945, 3:30 p.m., Livadia Palace, in *FRUS, Conferences at Malta and Yalta*, 766–71.

53. Churchill to Eden, January 28, 1945, Chartwell Papers, pre-1945, 20/209 (CAC), quote in Reynolds, *Summits*, 128.

54. Edward R. Stettinius, February 6, 1945, box 278, Stettinius Papers, University of Virginia Library, Charlottesville.

55. Third plenary meeting, February 6, 1945, 4 p.m., Livadia Palace, in *FRUS, Conferences at Malta and Yalta*, 660–71; McJimsey, *Ally of the Poor*, 364.

56. Fourth plenary meeting, February 7, 1945, 4 p.m., Livadia Palace, in *FRUS, Conferences at Malta and Yalta*, 708–18.

57. HH to the President, February 7, 1945, in *FRUS, Conferences at Malta and Yalta*, 729; facsimile reproduced in Sherwood, *Roosevelt and Hopkins*, 856.

58. Meeting of the Foreign Ministers, February 8, 1945, noon, Vorontsov Villa, in *FRUS, Conferences at Malta and Yalta*, 734–47.

59. Negotiations at Yalta concerning the UN veto in the Security Council and votes in the General Assembly based on McJimsey, *Ally of the Poor*, 364–65; Reynolds, *Summits*, 123, 125–27; and Sherwood, *Roosevelt and Hopkins*, 855–57.

60. Moran, *Churchill*, 243.

61. Plokhy, *Yalta*, 290.

62. Sherwood, *Roosevelt and Hopkins*, 876–77. See also exchange of letters between FDR, Stalin, and WSC in *FRUS, Conferences at Malta and Yalta*, 966–68, in which FDR asked that Stalin give the United States two extra votes if needed to mollify Congress and the American public and Stalin agreed to do so.

63. Reynolds, *Summits*, 124, 129–31.

64. Second plenary meeting, February 5, 1943, 4 p.m., Livadia Palace, in *FRUS, Conferences at Malta and Yalta*, 629, 634; facsimile of Hopkins's note is reproduced in Sherwood, *Roosevelt and Hopkins*, 859.

65. Reynolds, *Summits*, 132; Sherwood, *Roosevelt and Hopkins*, 858–59; Goodwin, *No Ordinary Time*, 580; Stettinius, *Roosevelt and the Russians*, 262; Harriman and Abel, *Special Envoy*, 402; FRUS, *Conferences at Malta and Yalta*, 573, 616–19, 710–11, 899–900.

66. Reynolds, *Summits*, 130–31.

67. Seventh plenary meeting, February 10, 1945, 4 p.m., Livadia Palace, in *FRUS, Conferences at Malta and Yalta*, 897, 902, 920; Reynolds, *Summits*, 131; HH to FDR, n.d., HH Papers, box 298, FDRL; Kennedy, *Freedom from Fear*, 804.

68. Reynolds, *Summits*, 160.

69. Colville, *The Fringes of Power*, 155, entry for January 23, 1945.

70. Campbell and Herring, *The Diaries of Edward R. Stettinius*, 214, entry for January 11, 1945.

71. Draft of letter from FDR to Marshal Stalin, and final letter, February 6, 1945, in *FRUS, Conferences at Malta and Yalta*, 726, 727. For other instances in which Hopkins assisted FDR on Poland, see Tuttle, *Anglo-American-Soviet Relations*, 260–64, and Stettinius, *Roosevelt and the Russians*, 260–61, 269–73.

72. Communiqué issued at the end of the conference, released February 12, 1945, in *FRUS, Conferences at Malta and Yalta*, 973–74.

73. Leahy, *I Was There*, 315–16.

74. Harriman and Abel, *Special Envoy*, 384–87; Freidel, *Franklin D. Roosevelt*, 592.

75. Reynolds, *Summits*, 141–42. Max Hastings maintains that financial incentives would not have softened Stalin's position on Poland (*Finest Years*, 353).

76. Harriman and Abel, *Special Envoy*, 389, quoting from Harriman's statement to the Joint Senate Committee on Armed Services and Foreign Relations in 1951.

77. Ibid., 390. George Kennan, counselor to the U.S. Embassy in Moscow, dispatched a long letter to Bohlen at Yalta advising that the United States abandon efforts to achieve postwar cooperation with the Soviets through negotiation and face up to the fact that Europe was already divided into spheres of influence. He recommended that plans for the UN be abandoned "as quickly and quietly as possible." Bohlen, *Witness to History*, 175. Bohlen disagreed with Kennan, believing that "the United States must try to get along with the Soviets." *Witness to History*, 177.

78. Robert Hopkins, *Witness to History*, 153.

79. Ibid., 154–55. See similar version entitled "Conversation with Stalin," box 4, folder 63, RH Papers, GU.

80. Plokhy, *Yalta*, 320.

81. Sarah Churchill and Medlicott, *Keep on Dancing*, 77–78.

82. Robert Hopkins, *Witness to History*, 156–57.

83. Stettinius, *Roosevelt and the Russians*, 285.

84. Wireless, HH to Louise Hopkins, in memo from Ogden Kniffen to Dorothea Krauss, February 13, 1945, Map Room file, box 131, FDRL.

85. Quoted in Sherwood, *Roosevelt and Hopkins*, 869–70.

86. Reynolds, *Summits*, 115.

87. FDR to WSC, March 18, 1942, in Kimball, *Churchill and Roosevelt*, 1:421.

88. HH memo to self, n.d., HH Papers, box 337, FDRL.

89. Ward, *Closest Companion*, 396.

90. Robert Hopkins, *Witness to History*, 166.

91. Bohlen, *Witness to History*, 203; Freidel, *Franklin D. Roosevelt*, 594.

92. HH memo to self, n.d., HH Papers, box 337, FDRL.

93. Bohlen, *Witness to History*, 203.

94. HH memo to self, n.d., HH Papers, box 337, FDRL.

95. Gilbert, *Winston S. Churchill*, 7:1222–23.

96. Churchill, *The Second World War*, 6:397.

97. Bohlen, *Witness to History*, 204–5.

98. Based on interview of Anna Roosevelt Boettiger, quoted in Bishop, *FDR's Last Year*, 450.

99. Rosenman, *Working with Roosevelt*, 521–22.

100. Based on interview of Anna Roosevelt Boettiger, quoted in Bishop, *FDR's Last Year*, 451.

101. HH to Louise Hopkins, February 15, 1945, private collection of Merloyd Ludington Lawrence, Louise's niece.

102. Bishop, *FDR's Last Year*, 451.

103. Ibid., 453; Sherwood, *Roosevelt and Hopkins*, 874. Frank Costigliola, in *Lost Alliances*, 490n282, maintains that Hopkins met with Roosevelt one more time in the White House, on March 2, 1945. As explained in an email dated December 12, 2011, from Robert Clark, an archivist at the FDRL, to the author, this assertion is erroneous. Several letters in Harry Hopkins Personal Papers microfilm and documents from the President's Secretary's Files provide virtually conclusive evidence that Hopkins was at the Mayo Clinic in Rochester, Minnesota, or March 2, 1945. Furthermore, as Clark points out, the basis for Professor Costigliola's contention—the entry "HH" in the White House usher book for March 2, 1945—most likely meant "Household," not "Harry Hopkins."

Chapter 18: A Leave of Absence from Death

1. James A. Halsted, M.D., "Severe Malnutrition in a Public Servant of the World War II Era: The Medical History of Harry Hopkins," box 1, folder 5, RH Papers, GU.

2. J. Edgar Hoover Official and Confidential File, microfilm, April 9, 1945, reel 13, Library of Congress.

3. McJimsey, *Documentary History*, doc. 144, especially 631–33, 648–49 (contains ad libs as well as text).

4. *Hansard's Parliamentary Debates*, 408:1267–95, February 27, 1945, quoting from column 1294.

5. Kimball, *Churchill and Roosevelt*, 3:630, R-742, April 11, 1945. See also Kimball, *The Juggler*, 179–80.

6. Blum, *From the Morgenthau Diaries*, 3:416.

7. Margaret Suckley, oral history.

8. Bohlen, *Witness to History*, 209.

9. Cable, HH to Churchill, April 12, 1945, HH Papers, reel 20, FDRL.

10. Churchill, *The Second World War*, 6:471.

11. Quoted in Sherwood, *Roosevelt and Hopkins*, 880–81.

12. J. Edgar Hoover Official and Confidential File, reel 13, no. 87, Library of Congress. According to *The Boss: J. Edgar Hoover and the Great American Inquisition* (Philadelphia: Temple University Press, 1988) by Athan G. Theoharis and John Stuart Cox, an FBI wiretap investigation of unnamed "White House aides" was commenced on August 21, 1945, at the request of Truman because Hopkins's reports of his meetings with Stalin in late May and early June 1945 had been leaked to Drew Pearson. Even if this investigation covered Hopkins and his wife, it does not explain why wiretaps were installed in Hopkins's home as early as April 6, 1945.

13. Bishop, *FDR's Last Year*, 650–51.

14. McCullough, *Truman*, 203, 213.

15. Truman, *Memoirs*, 30.

16. Ibid., 31.

17. Miller, *Plain Speaking*, 224.

18. Truman, *Memoirs*, 31–32.

19. Sherwood, *Roosevelt and Hopkins*, 881.

20. Bishop, *FDR's Last Year*, 655.

21. Sherwood, *Roosevelt and Hopkins*, 881–82.

22. Harriman and Abel, *Special Envoy*, 441–43.

23. Yergin, *Shattered Peace*, 79.

24. Truman, *Memoirs*, 79–82; Bohlen, *Witness to History*, 213.

25. Bohlen, *Witness to History*, 213.

26. Journal of Joseph Davies, April 30, 1945, box I:16 chrono file, folder 30, April 1945, Davies Papers.

27. Yergin, *Shattered Peace*, 83.

28. Bohlen, *Witness to History*, 215.

29. Sherwood, *Roosevelt and Hopkins*, 887.

30. Journal and diary of Joseph Davies, April 30, May 13, and May 21, 1945, box I:16 chrono file, folders 5–6, April 1945–May 1945, Davies Papers.

31. President Truman to Marshal Stalin, May 19, 1945, in *FRUS, The Conference of Berlin*, 1:21–22.

32. Truman, *Memoirs*, 258–59.

33. HH VE-Day Broadcast over NBC, May 8, 1945, HH Papers, reel 20, FDRL.

34. Louise Macy Hopkins, "We Flew across Europe," *Harper's Bazaar*, September 1945, 110.

35. Quoted in Sherwood, *Roosevelt and Hopkins*, 887.

36. Telegram of February 22, 1946, in Etzold and Gaddis, *Containment*, 53.

37. Kennan, *Memoirs*, 212–13.

38. Bohlen, *Witness to History*, 218.

39. *FRUS, The Conference of Berlin*, 1:26–27.

40. Ibid., 32–33.

41. Ibid., 27, 35.

42. Ibid., 29, 42, 46, 47, 85.

43. Bohlen, *Witness to History*, 221. See also, Adams, *Harry Hopkins*, 392.

44. HH, memo of private dinner meeting with Stalin, May 31, 1945, HH Papers, box 338, FDRL.
45. *FRUS, The Conference of Berlin*, 1:58–59.
46. Bohlen, *Witness to History*, 220.
47. *FRUS, The Conference of Berlin*, 1:61–62.
48. Plokhy, *Yalta*, 384.
49. Louise Hopkins, "We Flew across Europe," 160.
50. Harriman and Abel, *Special Envoy*, 469; Sherwood, *Roosevelt and Hopkins*, 908.
51. Quoted in Yergin, *Shattered Peace*, 105 and based on Maisky, *Memoirs*, 183.
52. HH, memos, June 1, 1945 and June 6, 1945, HH Papers, box 338, FDRL; see also *FRUS, The Conference of Berlin*, 1:29–30.
53. Bohlen, *Witness to History*, 222.
54. Zhukov, *Memoirs*, 667.
55. Snow and Aswell, *The World of Carmel Snow*, 117, 128–33, 137–38. Carmel Snow was for many years the editor of *Harper's Bazaar* and hired Louise Macy away from Hattie Carnegie in 1935.
56. Churchill, *The Second World War*, 6:582.
57. HH memo to self, July 13, 1945, HH Papers, reel 20, FDRL.
58. HH to Truman, n.d., Hopkins Papers, box 38, FDRL; Beschloss, *The Conquerors*, 241.
59. Bohlen, *Witness to History*, 222.
60. Joseph E. Davies, journal entries, June 13, 1945, box I:17 chrono files, folder June 1945, Davies Papers.
61. "Hopkins Returns," *Washington Post*, June 13, 1945.
62. "Success of Moscow Mission," *Times* (London), June 13, 1945.
63. Raymond Gram Swing, broadcast script, June 13, 1945, HH Papers, box 224, FDRL.
64. Sherwood, *Roosevelt and Hopkins*, 916.
65. Roberts, *Stalin's Wars*, 270–71; Reynolds, *From World War to Cold War*, 272.
66. Charmley, *Churchill*, 642.
67. Yergin, *Shattered Peace*, 104.
68. Dallek, *The Lost Peace*, 104.
69. Kissinger, *On China*, 453.

Chapter 19: The Root of the Matter

1. Truman to Mattie Truman (mother) and Mary Jane Truman (sister), July 3, 1945, Truman, *Memoirs*, 331.
2. HH to Truman, July 2, 1945, box 214, HH Papers, FDRL.
3. Rosenman to HH, June 5, 1945, HH Papers, reel 19, FRDL; transcript of telephone conversation, July 11, 1945, J. Edgar Hoover Official and Confidential File, reel 13, no. 87, Library of Congress.
4. Adams, *Harry Hopkins*, 396; Chapter 15 of draft manuscript by Halsted, box 6, folder 13, "James Halsted, MS bio of Hopkins 1979," RH Papers, GU.
5. HH to Lord Beaverbrook, July 6, 1945, box 60, folder 13, HH Papers, GU.
6. DHH to author, April 19, 2011.
7. HH to DHH, July 28, 1945, HH Papers, reel 21, FDRL.

8. DHH to author, April 19, 2011.
9. Quoted in Montefiore, *Stalin*, 442, 443.
10. "Investigations: Dark Doings," *Time*, December 12, 1949.
11. *Hearings Regarding Shipment of Atomic Material to the Soviet Union During World War II, Committee on Un-American Activities, House of Representatives, Eighty-first Congress* (Washington, D.C.: U.S. Government Printing Office, 1950).
12. FBI report, October 9, 1963, concluding that Major Jordan's allegations could not be substantiated, www.ernie1241.googlepages.com/documents, document 018 George Racey Jordan.
13. Eduard Mark, posted Sunday, February 15, 1997, 17:37:33–0500 re: George Racey Jordan, H-DIPLO, hdiplo@ouvaxa.cats.ohiou.edu.
14. "Speaking of News," *Life*, December 12, 1949, 24.
15. Bohlen, *Witness to History*, 243–44.
16. DHH to author, April 19, 2011.
17. Chapter 15 of draft manuscript by Halsted, box 6, folder 13, "James Halsted, MS bio of HH 1979," RH Papers, GU.
18. Quotes from Hyman's memo in Sherwood, *Roosevelt and Hopkins*, 920–21.
19. DHH to author, April 19, 2011.
20. The full text of the citation accompanying Hopkins's Distinguished Service Medal is in Sherwood, *Roosevelt and Hopkins*, 962.
21. HH to George Marshall, September 10, 1945, Marshall Papers, box 71, George C. Marshall Library, Lexington, Virginia.
22. Sherwood, *Roosevelt and Hopkins*, 927.
23. Adams, *Harry Hopkins*, 399.
24. Sherwood, *Roosevelt and Hopkins*, 927.
25. Quotes from Hyman memo in ibid., 928.
26. DHH to author, April 19, 2011.
27. HH to Cass Canfield, November 9, 1945, HH Papers, box 60, file 14, GU; HH to Edward Stettinius, November 9, 1945, HH Papers, reel 16, FDRL.
28. Campbell and Herring, *The Diaries of Edward R. Stettinius*, 445.
29. Memoir by Liz Gibbons-Hanson to DHH and James Halsted, n.d., private collection of Merloyd Ludington Lawrence.
30. Sherwood, *Roosevelt and Hopkins*, 929; DHH to author, April 19, 2011.
31. Robert Hopkins, *Witness to History*, 189–90.
32. The nature of the liver failure that was the immediate cause of Hopkins's death is open to question. The autopsy indicated that his liver failed because of hemochromatosis, an inability to metabolize iron. However, according to Dr. James Halsted, a later examination of the slides did not support this diagnosis. Halsted believed it "more plausible" that Hopkins's cirrhosis was caused by serum hepatitis contracted through numerous blood and pooled plasma transfusions. He discounts the most obvious cause—alcoholic cirrhosis—speculating with little firsthand knowledge that Hopkins was merely a "social drinker." Halsted, "Severe Malnutrition in a Public Servant of the World War II Era: The Medical History of Harry Hopkins," Clinical Nutrition Program, Division of Gastroenterology, Department of Medicine, Albany Medical College, Albany, New York, box 1, folder 5, RH Papers, GU.

33. Quoted in Sherwood, *Roosevelt and Hopkins*, 930–31; HH to Churchill, January 22, 1946, HH Papers, reel 11, FDRL.
34. McJimsey, *Ally of the Poor*, 397, based on interview by James Halsted of Mount Vernon and Fanny Lewis, February 3, 1977; see also Chapter 15 of draft manuscript by Halsted, box 6, folder 13, "James Halsted, MS bio of HH 1979," RH Papers, GU.
35. "Churchill Lauds Hopkins' Wisdom," *NYT*, January 30, 1946.
36. DHH to author, April 19, 2011.
37. Adams, *Harry Hopkins*, 401.
38. DHH to author, April 19, 2011.
39. "War Papers Listed in Hopkins Estate," *NYT*, May 14, 1947.
40. DHH to author, April 19, 2011.
41. DHH, interview by Emily Williams.
42. "Finest Hour," speech by Winston Churchill to House of Commons, June 18, 1940, The Churchill Centre, www.winstonchurchill.org/learn/speeches/speeches-of-winston-churchill/1940-finest-hour/126-war-of-the-unknown warriors.
43. "Good and Faithful Servant," *Time*, February 11, 1946.
44. Quoted in Sherwood, *Roosevelt and Hopkins*, 4.
45. Marquis W. Childs, "The President's Best Friend," *Saturday Evening Post*, April 26, 1941, 10.
46. DHH to "David and Dee," n.d. but written in the fall of 1947, lent to author by DHH.
47. Remarks of Dr. Glenn Leggett, president of Grinnell College, on the occasion of the burial of the ashes of Harry Lloyd Hopkins, Hazelwood Cemetery, Grinnell, Iowa, September 28, 1973, copy lent to author by DHH.

BIBLIOGRAPHY

Manuscripts, Personal Papers, Interviews and Oral Histories
Paul Appleby, Oral History Collection, Columbia University
Winston S. Churchill, Prime Minister's Office Records, Public Records Office, London.
Joseph E. Davies Papers, Manuscript Division, Library of Congress
Charles H. Donnelly Papers, U.S. Military Institute, Carlisle, Pennsylvania
Diana Hopkins Halsted, Eleanor Roosevelt Oral History Transcripts, Franklin D.
    Roosevelt Library, Hyde Park, New York
Diana Hopkins Halsted, interview by Emily Williams, oral historian, May 15, 1979,
    Franklin Roosevelt Library, Hyde Park, New York
James Halsted, biography of Harry Hopkins, draft manuscript, Robert Hopkins Papers,
    Special Collections, Georgetown University
Pamela Churchill Harriman interview, Newton Collection, Franklin D. Roosevelt
    Library, Hyde Park, New York
Pamela Churchill Harriman Papers, Manuscript Division, Library of Congress
Harry L. Hopkins Papers, Special Collections, Georgetown University
Harry L. Hopkins Papers, Franklin D. Roosevelt Library, Hyde Park, New York
Robert Hopkins Papers, Special Collections, Georgetown University
Harold L. Ickes Papers, Manuscript Division, Library of Congress
Florence Kerr, Oral History Collection, Columbia University
John Adams Kingsbury Papers, Manuscript Division, Library of Congress
Frances Perkins, Oral History Collection, Columbia University
Franklin D. Roosevelt Papers, Franklin D. Roosevelt Library, Hyde Park, New York
Robert E. Sherwood Papers, Houghton Library, Harvard University
Lady Soames interview, Newton Collection, Franklin D. Roosevelt Library, Hyde Park,
    New York
Diary of Henry L. Stimson, Manuscript Room, Sterling Memorial Library, Yale University
Margaret Suckley, oral history, Franklin D. Roosevelt Library, Hyde Park, New York

Books and Articles
Abramson, Rudy. *Spanning the Century: The Life of W. Averell Harriman.* New York:
    William Morrow, 1992.
Acheson, Dean. *Present at the Creation: My Years in the State Department.* New York:
    Norton, 1969.

Adams, Henry H. *Harry Hopkins: A Biography*. New York: G. P. Putnam's Sons, 1977.

Alsop, Joseph, and Robert Kintner. *American White Paper: The Story of American Diplomacy and the Second World War*. New York: Simon and Schuster, 1940.

Anderson, Patrick. *The President's Men*. Garden City, N.Y.: Doubleday, 1968.

Andrew, Christopher, "Anglo-American-Soviet Intelligence Relations." In *The Rise and Fall of the Grand Alliance, 1941–45*, ed. Ann J. Lane and Howard Temperly. Basingstoke, U.K.: Macmillan, 1995.

Arnold, Henry H. *Global Mission*. New York: Harper and Brothers, 1949.

Atkinson, Rick. *An Army at Dawn*. New York: Henry Holt, 2002.

Atkinson, Rick. *The Day of Battle*. New York: Henry Holt, 2007.

Baker, Leonard. *Roosevelt and Pearl Harbor*. New York: Macmillan, 1970.

Baker, Nicholson. *Human Smoke*. New York: Simon and Schuster, 2008.

Barnes, Joseph. *Willkie: The Events He Was Part of, the Ideas He Fought For*. New York: Simon and Schuster, 1952.

Baruch, Bernard. *The Public Years*. New York: Holt, Rinehart and Winston, 1960.

Beichman, Arnold. "In a Smoke-filled Room . . . Stalin's Defeat in 1944: A Look Back at Henry Wallace's Ouster as Vice-President." Working Papers in International Studies, Hoover Institution, Stanford University, I-94–10.

Beinert, Peter. *The Icarus Syndrome: A History of American Hubris*. New York: Harper, 2010.

Bellamy, Chris. *Absolute War*. New York: Knopf, 2007.

Benson, Robert Louis, and Michael Warner, eds. *Venona: Soviet Espionage and the American Response, 1939–1957*. Washington, D.C.: National Security Agency, Central Intelligence Agency, 1996.

Bercuson, David, and Holger Herwig. *One Christmas in Washington*. New York: Overlook Press, 2005.

Bernstein, Irving. *The Lean Years*. Boston: Houghton Mifflin, 1960.

Beschloss, Michael R. *The Conquerors: Roosevelt, Truman and the Destruction of Hitler's Germany, 1941–1945*. New York: Simon and Schuster, 2002.

Beschloss, Michael R. *Kennedy and Roosevelt: An Uneasy Alliance*. New York: Norton, 1980.

Bishop, Jim. *FDR's Last Year*. New York: William Morrow, 1974.

Black, Conrad. *Franklin Delano Roosevelt: Champion of Freedom*. New York: Public Affairs, 2003.

Bland, Larry I., ed. *George C. Marshall: Interviews and Reminiscences for Forrest C. Pogue*. Lexington, Va.: George C. Marshall Research Foundation, 1996.

Bliss, Edward, Jr. *In Search of Light: The Broadcasts of Edward R. Murrow, 1938–1961*. New York: Knopf, 1967.

Blum, John Morton, ed. *From the Morgenthau Diaries*. Vol. 2: *Years of Urgency, 1938–1941*. Boston: Houghton Mifflin, 1965.

Blum, John Morton, ed. *From the Morgenthau Diaries*. Vol. 3: *Years of War, 1941–1945*. Boston: Houghton Mifflin, 1967.

Blum, John Morton, ed., *The Price of Vision: The Diary of Henry A. Wallace, 1942–1946* (Boston: Houghton Mifflin, 1973).

Blum, John Morton. *Roosevelt and Morgenthau: A Revision and Condensation from the Morgenthau Diaries*. Boston: Houghton Mifflin, 1970.

Bohlen, Charles E. *Witness to History, 1929–1969*. New York: Norton, 1973.

Bourke-White, Margaret. *Shooting the Russian War*. New York: Simon and Schuster, 1942.

Braithwaite, Rodric. *Moscow, 1941*. New York: Knopf, 2006.

Brands, H. W. *Traitor to His Class*. Garden City, N.Y.: Doubleday, 2008.

Breitman, Richard. *Official Secrets: What the Nazis Planned, What the British and Americans Knew*. New York: Hill and Wang, 1998.

Breitman, Richard, and Alan Kraut. *American Refugee Policy and European Jewry, 1933–1945*. Bloomington: Indiana University Press, 1987.

Breuer, William B. *Hoodwinking Hitler: The Normandy Deception*. Westport, Conn.: Praeger, 1993.

Brinkley, David. *Washington at War*. New York: Knopf, 1988.

Bryant, Arthur. *The Turn of the Tide: A History of the War Years Based on the Diaries of Field Marshal Lord Alanbrooke, Chief of the Imperial General Staff*. Garden City, N.Y.: Doubleday, 1957.

Buell, Thomas B. *Master of Sea Power: A Biography of Fleet Admiral Ernest J. King*. Boston: Little, Brown, 1980.

Burns, James MacGregor. *Roosevelt: The Lion and the Fox, 1882–1940*. New York: Harcourt, Brace, 1956.

Burns, James MacGregor. *Roosevelt: The Soldier of Freedom*. New York: Harcourt Brace Jovanovich, 1970.

Butcher, Harry C. *My Three Years with Eisenhower*. New York: Simon and Schuster, 1946.

Butler, Susan, ed. *My Dear Mr. Stalin: The Complete Correspondence of Franklin D. Roosevelt and Joseph V. Stalin*. New Haven, Conn.: Yale University Press, 2005.

Byrnes, James F. *Speaking Frankly*. New York: Harper and Brothers, 1947.

Byron, George Gordon. *The Complete Poetical Works of Lord Byron*. Boston: Houghton, Mifflin, 1905.

Campbell, Thomas M., and George Herring, eds. *The Diaries of Edward R. Stettinius, Jr., 1943–1946*. New York: New Viewpoints, 1975.

Charles, Searle F. *Minister of Relief: Harry Hopkins and the Depression*. Syracuse, N.Y.: Syracuse University Press, 1963.

Charmley, John. *Churchill: The End of Glory*. New York: Harcourt Brace, 1993.

Childs, Marquis W. *I Write from Washington*. New York: Harper, 1942.

Churchill, Sarah, and Paul Medlicott. *Keep on Dancing*. New York: Coward, McCann & Geohagen, 1981.

Churchill, Winston S. *The Second World War*. Vol. 1: *The Gathering Storm*. Boston: Houghton Mifflin, 1948.

Churchill, Winston S. *The Second World War*. Vol. 2: *Their Finest Hour*. Boston: Houghton Mifflin, 1949.

Churchill, Winston S. *The Second World War*. Vol. 3: *The Grand Alliance*. Boston: Houghton Mifflin, 1950.

Churchill, Winston S. *The Second World War*. Vol. 4: *The Hinge of Fate*. Boston: Houghton Mifflin, 1950.

Churchill, Winston S. *The Second World War*. Vol. 5: *Closing the Ring*. Boston: Houghton Mifflin, 1951.

Churchill, Winston S. *The Second World War*. Vol. 6: *Triumph and Tragedy*. Boston: Houghton Mifflin, 1953.

Ciechanowski, Jan. *Defeat in Victory*. Garden City, N.Y.: Doubleday, 1947.

Clark, Mark W. *Calculated Risk*. New York: Harper & Brothers, 1950.

Cloud, Stanley, and Lynne Olson. *The Murrow Boys: Pioneers on the Frontline of Broadcast Journalism*. Boston: Houghton Mifflin, 1996.

Coakley, Robert W., and Richard M. Leighton. *Global Logistics and Strategy, 1943–1945*. Washington, D.C.: Office of the Chief of Military History, U.S. Army, 1968.

Cohen, Adam. *Nothing to Fear*. New York: Penguin Press, 2009.

Colville, John Rupert. *The Fringes of Power: 10 Downing Street Diaries, 1939–1955*. London: Hodder and Staughton, 1985.

Costigliola, Frank. *Roosevelt's Lost Alliances*. Princeton, N.J.: Princeton University Press, 2012.

Dallek, Robert. *Franklin D. Roosevelt and American Foreign Policy, 1932–1945*. New York: Oxford University Press, 1979.

Dallek, Robert. *The Lost Peace*. New York: HarperCollins, 2010.

Danchev, Alex. *Very Special Relationship: Field-Marshal Sir John Dill and the Anglo-American Alliance 1941–44*. London: Brassey's Defence Publishers, 1986.

Danchev, Alex, and Daniel Todman, eds. *War Diaries, 1939–1945: Field Marshal Lord Alanbrooke*. Berkeley: University of California Press, 2001.

Daniels, Jonathan. *White House Witness, 1942–1945*. Garden City, N.Y.: Doubleday, 1975.

Davies, Joseph E. *Mission to Moscow*. New York: Pocket Books, 1941.

Davis, Forrest, and Ernest K. Lindley. *How War Came*. New York: Simon and Schuster, 1942.

Davis, Kenneth S. *FDR: The War President, 1940–1943*. New York: Random House, 2000.

Davis, Norman. *No Simple Victory*. New York: Viking, 2007.

de Gaulle, Charles. *The Complete War Memoirs of Charles de Gaulle*. Vol. II: *Unity, 1942–1944*. New York: Simon and Schuster, 1964.

Dilks, David, ed. *The Diaries of Sir Alexander Cadogan, O.M., 1938–1945*. New York: G. P. Putnam's Sons, 1972.

Dimbley, David, and David Reynolds. *An Ocean Apart: The Relationship between Britain and America in the Twentieth Century*. New York: Random House, 1980.

Djilas, Milovan. *Conversations with Stalin*. New York: Harcourt, Brace & World, 1962.

Documents on American Foreign Relations. New York: World Peace Foundation, 1942.

Dunn, Dennis J. *Caught between Roosevelt and Stalin: America's Ambassadors to Moscow*. Lexington: University Press of Kentucky, 1998.

Dunn, Susan. *Roosevelt's Purge*. Cambridge, Mass.: Belknap Press of Harvard University Press, 2010.

Eden, Anthony. *The Memoirs of Anthony Eden, Earl of Avon: The Reckoning*. Boston: Houghton Mifflin, 1965.

Edmonds, Robin. *The Big Three: Churchill, Roosevelt and Stalin in Peace and War*. New York: Norton, 1991.

Eisenhower, Dwight D. *Crusade in Europe*. Garden City, N.Y.: Doubleday, 1948.

Eisenhower, John S. D. *Allies: Pearl Harbor to D-Day*. Garden City, N.Y.: Doubleday, 1982.

Elsey, George McKee. *An Unplanned Life*. Columbia: University of Missouri Press, 2005.

Etzold, Thomas H., and John L. Gaddis, eds. *Containment: Documents on American Policy and Strategy, 1945–1950*. New York: Columbia University Press, 1978.

Evans, Richard J. *The Third Reich at War*. New York: Penguin Press, 2009.

Feis, Herbert. *The Road to Pearl Harbor*. Princeton, N.J.: Princeton University Press, 1950.

Fenby, Jonathan. *Alliance: The Inside Story of How Roosevelt, Stalin and Churchill Won One War and Began Another*. San Francisco: MacAdam/Cage, 2006.

Ferrell, Robert H. *The Dying President: Franklin D. Roosevelt, 1944–1945*. Columbia: University of Missouri Press, 1998.

Fleming, Peter. *Operation Sea Lion*. New York: Simon and Schuster, 1957.

Foreign Relations of the United States: The Conference of Berlin (The Potsdam Conference), 1945. Washington, D.C.: U.S. Government Printing Office, 1960.

Foreign Relations of the United States: The Conferences at Cairo and Teheran, 1943. Washington, D.C.: U.S. Government Printing Office, 1961.

Foreign Relations of the United States: The Conferences at Malta and Yalta, 1945. Washington, D.C.: U.S. Government Printing Office, 1955.

Foreign Relations of the United States: The Conference at Quebec, 1944. Washington, D.C.: U.S. Government Printing Office, 1972.

Foreign Relations of the United States: The Conferences at Washington, 1941–42, and Casablanca, 1943. Washington, D.C.: U.S. Government Printing Office, 1968.

Foreign Relations of the United States: The Conferences at Washington and Quebec, 1943. Washington, D.C.: U.S. Government Printing Office, 1970.

Foreign Relations of the United States. Japan: 1931–1941. Washington, D.C.: U.S. Government Printing Office, 1943.

Foreign Relations of the United States, 1941. Vol. 1: *General, The Soviet Union*. Washington, D.C.: U.S. Government Printing Office, 1958.

Foreign Relations of the United States, 1942, Vol. 1: *General; The British Commonwealth; The Far East*. Washington, D.C.: U.S. Government Printing Office, 1960.

Foreign Relations of the United States, 1942, Vol. 3: *Europe*. Washington, D.C.: U.S Governement Printing Office, 1961.

Foreign Relations of the United States, 1943, Vol. 2: *Europe*. Washington, D.C.: U.S. Government Printing Office, 1958.

Foreign Relations of the United States, 1943. Vol. 3: *The British Commonwealth, Eastern Europe, the Far East*. Washington, D.C.: U.S. Government Printing Office, 1963.

Freidel, Frank. *Franklin D. Roosevelt: A Rendezvous with Destiny*. Boston: Little, Brown, 1990.

Freidel, Frank. *Launching the New Deal*. Boston: Little, Brown, 1973.

Funk, Arthur Layton. "The 'Anfa Memorandum': An Incident of the Casablanca Conference." *Journal of Modern History* 26 (1954), 246–54.

Gaddis, John Lewis. *George F. Kennan*. New York: Penguin Press, 2011.

Gallup, George A. *The Gallup Poll: Public Opinion, 1935–1971*. New York: Random House, 1971.

Gentry, Curt. *J. Edgar Hoover: The Man and His Secrets*. New York: Norton, 1991.

Giffen, Allison, and June Hopkins, eds. *Jewish First Wife, Divorced*. Lanham, Md.: Lexington Books, 2003.

Gilbert, Martin. *The Churchill War Papers*. 3 vols. New York: Norton, 1993–2000.

Gilbert, Martin. *The Holocaust: A History of the Jews of Europe During the Second World War*. New York: Holt, Rinehart and Winston, 1986.

Gilbert, Martin. *The Second World War*. New York: Henry Holt, 1989.

Gilbert, Martin. *Winston S. Churchill*. Vol. 6: *Finest Hour: 1939–1941*. Boston: Houghton, Mifflin, 1983.

Gilbert, Martin. *Winston S. Churchill*. Vol. 7: *Road to Victory, 1941–1945*. Boston: Houghton, Mifflin, 1986.

Goodwin, Doris Kearns. *No Ordinary Time: Franklin and Eleanor Roosevelt. The Home Front in World War II*. New York: Simon and Schuster, 1994.

Hansard's Parliamentary Debates. House of Commons, 5th series.

Harriman, W. Averell, and Elie Abel. *Special Envoy to Churchill and Stalin, 1941–1946*. New York: Random House, 1975.

Harrison, Gordon A. *Cross-Channel Attack*. Washington, D.C.: Department of the Army, 1951.

Hassett, William. *Off the Record with F.D.R., 1942–1945*. New Brunswick, N.J.: Rutgers University Press, 1958.

Hastings, Max. *Finest Years: Churchill as Warlord 1940–45*. London: HarperPress, 2009.

Hastings, Max. *Winston's War: Churchill, 1940–1945*. New York: Knopf, 2010.

Havas, Laslo. *Hitler's Plot to Kill the Big 3*. New York: Cowles, 1967.

Haynes, John Earl, and Harvey Klehr. "Alexander Vassiliev's Notebooks: Provenance and Documentation of Soviet Intelligence Activities in the United States." www.cwihp.org.

Herrera, Hayden. *Frida: A Biography of Frida Kahlo*. New York: Harper & Row, 1983.

Hofstadter, Richard. *The Age of Reform: From Bryan to F.D.R.* New York: Knopf, 1985.

Hopkins, Harry L. "You and Your Family Will be Mobilized," *The American Magazine*, December 1942.

Hopkins, June. *Harry Hopkins: Sudden Hero, Brash Reformer*. New York: St. Martin's Press, 1999.

Hopkins, Louise Macy. "We Flew Across Europe," *Harper's Bazaar*, vol. 79, part 2 (September 1945): 110–62.

Hopkins, Robert. *Witness to History. Recollections of a WW II Photographer*. Seattle: Castle Pacific, 2002.

Howard, Michael. *The Mediterranean Strategy in the Second World War*. New York: Praeger, 1968.

Howland, Nina Davis. "Ambassador John Gilbert Winant: Friend of Embattled Britain, 1941–1946." PhD dissertation, University of Maryland, 1983.

Hull, Cordell. *The Memoirs of Cordell Hull*. 2 vols. New York: Macmillan, 1948.

Ickes, Harold L. *The Secret Diaries of Harold L. Ickes*. Vol. 2: *The Inside Struggle, 1936–1939*. New York: Simon and Schuster, 1954.

Ickes, Harold L. *The Secret Diaries of Harold L. Ickes*. Vol. 3: *The Lowering Clouds, 1939–1941*. New York: Simon and Schuster, 1954.

Jackson, Robert H. *That Man: An Insider's Portrait of Franklin D. Roosevelt*, ed. John Q. Barrett. New York: Oxford University Press, 2003.

Jenkins, Roy. *Churchill*. New York: Farrar, Straus & Giroux, 2001.

Jordan, George Racey, with Richard L. Stokes. *From Major Jordan's Diaries*. New York: Bookmailer, 1958.

Keegan, John. *The Second World War*. New York: Penguin, 1990.

Kendrick, Alexander. *Prime Time: The Life of Edward R. Murrow*. New York: Random House, 2001.

Kennan, George F. *Memoirs 1925–1950*. Boston: Little, Brown, 1967.

Kennedy, David M. *Freedom from Fear: The American People in Depression and War, 1929–1945*. New York: Oxford University Press, 2005.

Kimball, Warren F., ed. *Churchill and Roosevelt: The Complete Correspondence*. 3 vols. Princeton, N.J.: Princeton University Press, 1984.

Kimball, Warren F. *Forged in War: Roosevelt, Churchill and the Second World War*. New York: Morrow, 1997.

Kimball, Warren F. *The Juggler: Franklin Roosevelt as Wartime Statesman*. Princeton, N.J.: Princeton University Press, 1991.

Kimball, Warren F. *The Most Unsordid Act: Lend-Lease, 1939–1941*. Baltimore: Johns Hopkins University Press, 1969.

Kimball, Warren F. *Swords or Ploughshares? The Morgenthau Plan for Defeated Nazi Germany, 1943–1946*. Philadelphia: J. P. Lippincott, 1976.

King, Ernest J., and Walter Muir Whitehill. *Fleet Admiral King: A Naval Record*. London: Eyre and Spottiswoode, 1953.

Kissinger, Henry. *On China*. New York: Penguin Press, 2011.

Kurtzman, Paul A. *Harry Hopkins and the New Deal*. Fairlawn, N.J.: R. E. Burdick, 1974.

Lane, Ann J., and Howard Temperly, *The Rise and Fall of the Grand Alliance*. Basingstoke, U.K.: Macmillan, 1995.

Langer, John Daniel. "'The Red General': Philip R. Faymonville and the Soviet Union, 1917–52." *Prologue*, Winter 1976.

Langer, William L., and S. Everett Gleason. *The Undeclared War, 1940–41*. New York: Harper and Brothers, 1953.

Laqueur, Walter. *The Terrible Secret: An Investigation into the Suppression of Information about Hitler's "Final Solution."* London: Weidenfeld and Nicolson, 1980.

Larrabee, Eric. *Commander in Chief: Franklin Delano Roosevelt, His Lieutenants, and Their War*. New York: Harper & Row, 1987.

Lash, Joseph P. *Eleanor and Franklin: The Story of Their Relationship, Based on Eleanor Roosevelt's Private Papers*. New York: Norton, 1971.

Lash, Joseph P. *Love, Eleanor: Eleanor Roosevelt and Her Friends*. Garden City, N.Y.: Doubleday, 1982.

Lash, Joseph P. *Roosevelt and Churchill, 1939–1941: The Partnership That Saved the West*. New York: Norton, 1976.

Lash, Joseph P. *A World of Love: Eleanor Roosevelt and Her Friends, 1943–1962*. Garden City, N.Y.: Doubleday, 1984.

Leahy, William D. *I Was There*. New York: Whittlesey House, 1950.

Leasor, James. *War at the Top: The Clock with Four Hands. Based on the Experiences of Sir Leslie Hollis*. London: Michael Joseph, 1959.

Leutze, James, ed. *The London Journal of General Raymond E. Lee, 1940–1941*. Boston: Little, Brown, 1971.

Leutze, James, ed. *The London Observer*. London: Hutchinson, 1971.

Levin, Linda Lothridge. *The Making of FDR: The Story of Steven T. Early, America's First Modern Press Secretary*. Amherst, N.Y.: Prometheus Books, 2008.

Lowenheim, Francis L., Harold D. Langley, and Manfred Jones, eds. *Roosevelt and Churchill: Their Secret Wartime Correspondence*. New York: E. P. Dutton, 1975.

Lubell, Samuel. *The Future of American Politics*. New York: Harper & Row, 1952.

Lyttleton, Oliver, Viscount Chandos. *The Memoirs of Lord Chandos*. London: Bodley Head, 1962.

Maclean, Elizabeth Kimball. *Joseph E. Davies: Envoy to the Soviets*. New York: Praeger, 1992.

MacMillan, Harold. *The Blast of War, 1939–1945*. New York: Harper & Row, 1967.

Maisky, Ivan. *Memoirs of a Soviet Ambassador: The War, 1939–43*. Trans. Andrew Rothstein. London: Hutchinson, 1967.

Martin, John. *Downing Street: The War Years*. London: Bloomsbury, 1991.

Mark, Eduard. "Venona's Source 19 and the 'Trident Conference' of May 1943: Diplomacy or Espionage?" *Intelligence and National Security* 13, no. 2 (1998), 131.

Matloff, Maurice. *Strategic Planning for Coalition Warfare, 1943–1944*. Washington, D.C.: Office of the Chief of Military History, 1959.

Matloff, Maurice, and Edwin M. Snell. *Strategic Planning for Coalition Warfare, 1941–1942*. Washington, D.C.: Office of the Chief of Military History, 1953.

Matthews, William H. *Adventures in Giving*. New York: Dodd, Mead, 1939.

McCullough, David. *Truman*. Simon and Schuster, 1992.

McFarland, Keith D., and David L. Roll. *Louis Johnson and the Arming of America: The Roosevelt and Truman Years*. Bloomington: Indiana University Press, 2005.

McIntire, Ross, in collaboration with George Creel. *White House Physician*. New York: G. P. Putnam's Sons, 1946.

McJimsey, George, ed. *Documentary History of the Franklin D. Roosevelt Presidency*. Vol. 14: *The Yalta Conference, October 1944–March 1945*. Bethesda, Md.: University Publications of America, 2000.

McJimsey, George. *Harry Hopkins: Ally of the Poor and Defender of Democracy*. Cambridge, Mass.: Harvard University Press, 1987.

McKean, David. *Tommy the Cork*. South Royalton, Vt.: Steerforth Press, 2004.

Meachem, Jon. *Franklin and Winston*. New York: Random House, 2003.

Miller, Edward S. *Bankrupting the Enemy: The U.S. Financial Siege of Japan before Pearl Harbor*. Annapolis, Md.: Naval Institute Press, 2007.

Miller, Merle. *Plain Speaking: An Oral Biography of Harry S. Truman*. New York: Berkley, 1974.

Moley, Raymond. *The First New Deal*. New York: Harcourt, Brace & World, 1966.

Montefiore, Simon Sebag. *Stalin: The Court of the Red Tsar*. London: Weidenfeld and Nicolson, 2003.

Moran, Lord. *Churchill: Taken from the Diaries of Lord Moran. The Struggle for Survival, 1940–1965*. Boston: Houghton Mifflin, 1966.

Morgenthau, Henry, III. *Mostly Morgenthau's: A Family History*. New York: Ticknor and Fields, 1991.

Morison, Samuel Eliot. *American Contributions to the Strategy of World War II*. London: Oxford University Press, 1958.

Morris, Sylvia Jukes. *Rage for Fame: The Ascent of Clare Booth Luce*. New York: Random House, 1997.

Morton, H. V. *Atlantic Meeting*. New York: Dodd, Mead, 1943.

Moss, Norman. *Nineteen Weeks: America, Britain and the Fateful Summer of 1940*. Boston: Houghton Mifflin, 2003.

Murphy, Robert D. *Diplomat among Warriors*. Garden City, N.Y.: Doubleday, 1964.

Nicholas, H. G., ed. *Washington Despatches, 1941–1945*. Chicago: University of Chicago Press, 1981.

Ogden, Christopher. *Life of the Party: The Biography of Pamela Digby Churchill Hayward Harriman*. Boston: Little, Brown, 1994.

Olson, Lynne. *Citizens of London: The Americans Who Stood with Britain in Its Darkest Finest Hour*. New York: Random House, 2010.

Parks, Lillian Rogers. *The Roosevelts: A Family in Turmoil*. Englewood, N.J.: Fleet, 1966.

Parrish, Thomas. *Roosevelt and Marshall: Partners in Politics and War*. New York: William Morrow, 1989.

Parrish, Thomas. *To Keep the British Afloat: FDR's Men in Churchill's London, 1941*. Washington, D.C.: Smithsonian Books, 2009.

Pendar, Kenneth. *Adventure in Diplomacy*. New York: Dodd, Mead, 1945.

Perkins, Frances. *The Roosevelt I Knew*. New York: Viking Press, 1946.

Perry, Mark. *Partners in Command*. New York: Penguin Press, 2007.

Persico, Joseph E. *Franklin and Lucy*. New York: Random House, 2008.

Persico, Joseph E. *Roosevelt's Secret War: FDR and World War II Espionage*. New York: Random House, 2001.

Peters, Charles. *Five Days in Philadelphia*. New York: Public Affairs, 2005.

Plokhy, S. M. *Yalta: The Price of Peace*. New York: Viking, 2010.

Pogue, Forrest C. *George C. Marshall*. Vol. 2: *Ordeal and Hope, 1939–1942*. New York: Viking, 1966.

Pogue, Forrest C. *George C. Marshall*. Vol. 3: *Organizer of Victory, 1943–1945*. New York: Viking, 1973.

Pownall, Henry. *Chief of Staff: The Diaries of Lieutenant-General Sir Henry Pownall*, ed. Brian Bond. London: Leo Cooper, 1972.

Prange, Gordon W. *At Dawn We Slept: The Untold Story of Pearl Harbor*. New York: McGraw-Hill, 1980.

Probert, Henry. *Bomber Harris: His Life and Times*. London: Greenhill, 2003.

Proceedings of the 1932 Democratic National Convention. Washington, D.C.: Democratic National Committee, 1932.

Proceedings of the 1940 Democratic National Convention. Washington, D.C.: Democratic National Committee, 1940.

Rader, Franklin J. "Harry L. Hopkins: The Works Progress Administration and National Defense, 1935–1940." PhD diss., University of Delaware, 1973.

Rees, Laurence. *Behind Closed Doors*. London: BBC Books, 2008.

Reilly, Michael, as told to William Slocum. *Reilly of the White House*. New York: Simon and Schuster, 1947.

Reynolds, David. *From Munich to Pearl Harbor*. Chicago: Ivan R. Dee, 2001.

Reynolds, David. *From World War to Cold War*. New York: Oxford University Press, 2006.

Reynolds, David. *In Command of History*. New York: Basic Books, 2005.

Reynolds, David. *Summits: Six Meetings That Shaped the Twentieth Century*. New York: Basic Books, 2007.

Reynolds, David, Warren F. Kimball, and A. Chubarian, eds. *Allies at War: The Soviet American and British Experience, 1939–1945*. New York: St. Martin's Press, 1994.

Reynolds, Quentin. *Only the Stars Are Neutral*. New York: Random House, 1942.

Rhodes, Richard. *The Making of the Atomic Bomb*. New York: Simon and Schuster, 1986.

Richberg, Donald. *My Hero*. New York: Putnam, 1954.

Rigdon, William, with James Derieux. *White House Sailor*. Garden City, N.Y.: Doubleday, 1962.

Roberts, Andrew. *Masters and Commanders*. London: Allen Lane, 2008.

Roberts, Andrew. *The Storm of War: A New History of the Second World War*. London: Allen Lane, 2009.

Roberts, Geoffrey. *Stalin's Wars*. New Haven, Conn.: Yale University Press, 2006.

Robertson, David. *Sly and Able: A Political Biography of James F. Byrnes*. New York: Norton, 1994.

Roosevelt, Eleanor. *This I Remember*. New York: Harper & Brothers, 1949.

Roosevelt, Elliott. *As He Saw It*. New York: Duell, Sloan and Pearce, 1946.

Roosevelt, Elliott, ed. *F.D.R.: His Personal Letters*. Vols. 1–4. New York: Duell, Sloane and Pearce, 1947–50.

Roosevelt, Elliott, and James Brough. *A Rendezvous with Destiny: The Roosevelts of the White House*. New York: G. P. Putnam's Sons, 1975.

Roosevelt, Franklin D. *Complete Presidential Press Conferences of Franklin D. Roosevelt*. 25 vols. New York: De Capo Press, 1972.

Roosevelt, Franklin D. *Public Papers and Addresses of Franklin D. Roosevelt*, comp. Samuel I. Rosenman. 13 vols. New York: Random House, 1938–50.

Roosevelt, Franklin D. *The Public Papers of Franklin D. Roosevelt, Forty-eighth Governor of the State of New York, 1929–1932*. 4 vols. Albany, N.Y.: J. B. Lyon, 1930–39.

Roosevelt, James, and Sidney Shalett. *Affectionately, FDR: A Son's Story of a Lonely Man*. New York: Harcourt, Brace, 1959.

Roosevelt, James, and Sidney Shalett. *My Parents: A Differing View*. Chicago: Playboy Press, 1976.

Rosenman, Samuel I. *Working with Roosevelt*. New York: Harper & Brothers, 1952.

Sainsbury, Keith. *Churchill and Roosevelt at War: The War They Fought and the Peace They Hoped to Make*. New York: New York University Press, 1994.

Sainsbury, Keith. *The Turning Point*. Oxford: Oxford University Press, 1985.

Schlesinger, Arthur M., Jr. *The Age of Roosevelt*. Vol. 2: *The Coming of the New Deal*. Boston: Houghton Mifflin, 1958.

Schlesinger, Robert. *White House Ghosts: Presidents and Their Speechwriters*. New York: Simon and Schuster, 2008.

Schwarz, Jordan A. *The Interregnum of Despair: Hoover, Congress and the Depression.* Urbana: University of Illinois Press, 1970.

Sherwood, Robert E. *Roosevelt and Hopkins: An Intimate History.* New York: Harper & Brothers, 1948.

Shirer, William L. *Berlin Diary: The Journal of a Foreign Correspondent, 1934–1941.* Baltimore: Johns Hopkins University Press, 1941.

Shirer, William L. *The Rise and Fall of the Third Reich: A History of Nazi Germany.* New York: Simon and Schuster, 1960.

Smith, Amanda, ed. *Hostage to Fortune: The Letters of Joseph P. Kennedy.* New York: Viking, 2001.

Smith, Jean Edward. *Eisenhower: In War and Peace.* New York: Random House, 2012.

Smith, Jean Edward. *FDR.* New York: Random House, 2007.

Smith, Sally Bedell. *In All His Glory: The Life of William S. Paley.* New York: Simon and Schuster, 1990.

Snow, Carmel, with Mary Louise Aswell. *The World of Carmel Snow.* New York: McGraw-Hill, 1962.

Snyder, Timothy. *Bloodlands.* New York: Basic Books, 2010.

Soames, Mary. *Clementine Churchill: The Biography of a Marriage.* Boston: Houghton Mifflin, 1979.

Speer, Albert. *Inside the Third Reich.* New York: Macmillan, 1970.

Stafford, David. *Roosevelt and Churchill: Men of Secrets.* Woodstock and New York: The Overlook Press, 2000.

Stettinius, Edward R. Jr. *Lend-Lease: Weapon of Victory.* New York: Macmillan, 1944.

Stettinius, Edward R. Jr. *Roosevelt and the Russians.* Garden City, N.Y.: Doubleday, 1949.

Stimson, Henry L., and McGeorge Bundy. *On Active Service in Peace and War.* New York: Harper & Brothers, 1948.

Stoler, Mark A. *George C. Marshall: Soldier Statesman of the American Century.* New York: Twayne, 1989.

Stoler, Mark A. *The Politics of the Second Front: American Military Planning and Diplomacy in Coalition Warfare, 1941–1943.* Westport, Conn.: Greenwood, 1977.

Sudoplatov, Pavel, and Anatoli Sudoplatov, with Jerrold L. Schecter and Leona P. Schecter. *Special Tasks: The Memoirs of an Unwanted Witness—A Soviet Spymaster.* Boston: Little, Brown, 1994.

Summersby, Kay. *Eisenhower Was My Boss.* New York: Prentice Hall, 1948.

Symonds, Craig L. *The Battle of Midway.* New York: Oxford University Press, 2011.

Taylor, A. J. P. *Beaverbrook.* London: Hamish Hamilton, 1972.

Taylor, Nick. *American-Made.* New York: Bantam Books, 2008.

Theoharis, Athan, ed. *From the Secret Files of J. Edgar Hoover.* Chicago: Ivan R. Dee, 1991.

Toll, Ian W. *Pacific Crucible.* New York: Norton, 2012.

Tregaskis, Richard. *Invasion Diary.* New York: Random House, 1944.

Trials of War: Criminals before the Nuremberg Military Tribunals. Washington, D.C.: U.S. Government Printing Office, 1949–53.

Truman, Harry S. *Memoirs by Harry S. Truman.* Vol. 1: *Year of Decisions.* Garden City, N.Y.: Doubleday, 1955.

Tuchman, Barbara W. *Stilwell and the American Experience in China, 1911–1945.* New York: Grove Press, 1971.

Tugwell, Rexford G. *The Democratic Roosevelt.* Garden City, N.Y.: Doubleday, 1957.

Tully, Grace. *F.D.R.: My Boss.* New York: Charles Scribner's Sons, 1949.

Tuttle, Dwight William. *Harry H. Hopkins and Anglo-American-Soviet Relations, 1941–1945.* New York: Garland, 1983.

Tzouliadis, Tim. *The Forsaken: An American Tragedy in Stalin's Russia.* New York: Penguin Press, 2008.

USSR Ministry of Foreign Affairs. *Correspondence between the Chairman of the Council of Ministers of the U.S.S.R. and the President of the U.S.A. and the Prime Ministers of Great Britain During the Great Patriotic War of 1941–1945.* New York: E. P. Dutton, 1958.

Ward, Geoffrey C., ed. *Closest Companion: The Unknown Story of the Intimate Friendship between Franklin Roosevelt and Margaret Suckley.* Boston: Houghton Mifflin, 1965.

Wedemeyer, Albert C. *Wedemeyer Reports!* New York: Henry Holt, 1958.

Weiner, Tim. *Enemies: A History of the FBI.* New York: Random House, 2012.

Weinstein, Allen, and Alexander Vassiliev. *The Haunted Wood: Soviet Espionage in America—The Stalin Era.* New York: Random House, 2009.

Welles, Sumner. *The Time for Decision.* New York: Harper and Brothers, 1944.

Welles, Sumner. *Where Are We Heading?* New York: Harper and Brothers, 1946.

Willis, Resa. *FDR and Lucy: Lovers and Friends.* New York: Rutledge, 2004.

Wills, Matthew B. *Wartime Missions of Harry L. Hopkins.* Bloomington, Ind.: Author House, 2004.

Wilson, Theodore. *The First Summit: Roosevelt and Churchill at Placentia Bay, 1941.* Boston: Houghton Mifflin, 1969.

Winterbotham, Frederick W. *The Ultra Secret.* New York: Harper & Row, 1974.

Wood, E. Thomas, and Stanislaw M. Jankowski. *Karski: How One Man Tried to Stop the Holocaust.* New York: Wiley, 1994.

Wyman, David. *The Abandonment of the Jews: America and the Holocaust, 1941–1945.* New York: Pantheon, 1984.

Yeaton, Ivan D. *The Memoirs of Ivan D. Yeaton, USA (Ret.), 1919–1953.* Stanford, Calif.: Hoover Institution on War, Revolution and Peace, 1976.

Yergin, Daniel. *Shattered Peace: The Origins of the Cold War.* New York: Penguin Books, 1990.

Young, Desmond. *Rommel, the Desert Fox.* New York: Harper & Brothers, 1950.

Zhukov, G. K. *The Memoirs of Marshal Zhukov.* New York: Delacorte Press, 1971.

Zhukov, G. K. *Vospominaniya i Razmyshleniya* (Memories and Reflections). Moscow, 1992.

Ziegler, Philip. *Mountbatten: The Official Biography.* London: Guild, 1985.

INDEX

Soviet Union (*continued*)
  human rights, 394
  iron curtain, 452n12
  Katyn massacre, 268
  Kennan's Long Telegram, 388
  Nazi-Soviet nonaggression pact, 50,
    127, 130, 196, 266
  North Africa invasion, 216
  Operation Barbarossa (attack on
    Soviets), 108–15, 118, 428n62
  Operation Overlord (cross-Channel
    invasion), 312
  Operation Typhoon (attack on
    Soviets), 151
  Pacific front, 301
  representation in the UN General
    Assembly, 358
  Russian War Relief rally, 205
  Soviet Protocol Committee, 232
  spheres of influence in postwar Europe,
    348
  unconditional surrender of Germany,
    259
  UN Security Council veto power,
    368–69
  voting rights in UN General Assembly,
    380
  war against Japan, 389
  war casualties, 262
  Winter War, 51–52
speechwriting
  Hopkins and, 68–69, 71–72, 76–77,
    147–48, 162, 164, 172–75, 181–82,
    349
  Rosenman and, 69, 105, 377
  Sherwood and, 6, 68–69, 71–72, 105
Stalin, Joseph. *See also photo section*
  Allied Control Commission, 370
  appeasement of Hitler, 47–48, 112,
    184, 266
  Battle for Stalingrad, 264
  Beaverbrook/Harriman mission,
    151–52
  Big Three (Tehran conference),
    299–301, 313–27, 367

Big Three (Yalta conference), 356,
    364–66, 369–70, 374
British election, 400
Casablanca conference, 245, 259–61,
    263
characterization of Allies, 365
and Churchill, 227, 295–96, 300,
    322–25
counterattacks Germans, 181
on death of Hitler, 392
Declaration by United Nations, 173
health issues, 332
and Hopkins, 5, 126–29, 131–33, 135,
    179, 316–17, 368–69, 383, 387,
    396, 408–9
invasion of North Africa, 226–27
lend-lease program, 307, 326
London Poles, 327
Manhattan Project, 399
Nazi-Soviet nonaggression pact,
    50–51, 130, 322
Operation Barbarossa (attack on
    Soviets), 110–11
Operation Overlord (cross-Channel
    invasion), 318, 321
Operation Typhoon (attack on
    Soviets), 151–52
Pearl Harbor attack, 167
postwar division of Eastern Europe,
    326–27
postwar Germany, 343–45
postwar Poland, 319, 371–73
postwar territorial issues, 267, 367
and Robert Hopkins, 321, 324, 373–74
and Roosevelt, 275, 315–16, 375,
    384–85
second front in Europe, 199
second Moscow conference (Tolstoy),
    346–48
Sword of Stalingrad, 320–21
territorial security, 385–86, 401
Trident conference, 275–76
as "Uncle Joe," 365–66
unification of China, 389
United Nations voting, 358